Phenomena Induced by Intermolecular Interactions

NATO ASI Series

Advanced Science Institutes Series

A series presenting the results of activities sponsored by the NATO Science Committee, which aims at the dissemination of advanced scientific and technological knowledge, with a view to strengthening links between scientific communities.

The series is published by an international board of publishers in conjunction with the NATO Scientific Affairs Division

A	**Life Sciences**	Plenum Publishing Corporation
B	**Physics**	New York and London
C	**Mathematical and Physical Sciences**	D. Reidel Publishing Company Dordrecht, Boston, and Lancaster
D	**Behavioral and Social Sciences**	Martinus Nijhoff Publishers
E	**Engineering and Materials Sciences**	The Hague, Boston, and Lancaster
F	**Computer and Systems Sciences**	Springer-Verlag
G	**Ecological Sciences**	Berlin, Heidelberg, New York, and Tokyo

Recent Volumes in this Series

Series B: Physics

Phenomena Induced by Intermolecular Interactions

Edited by
G. Birnbaum

U.S. Department of Commerce
National Bureau of Standards
Gaithersburg, Maryland

Plenum Press
New York and London
Published in cooperation with NATO Scientific Affairs Division

Proceedings of a NATO Advanced Research Workshop,
held September 5–9, 1983,
at the Château de Bonas, Castera-Verduzan, France

Library of Congress Cataloging in Publication Data

Main entry under title:

Phenomena induced by intermolecular interactions.

(NATO ASI series, Series B: Physics; vol. 127)
Includes bibliographies and indexes.
1. Infrared spectra—Congresses. 2. Absorption spectra—Congresses. 3. Intermolecular forces—Congresses. 4. Dipole moments—Congresses. 5. Polarization (Light)—Congresses. 6. Light— Scattering—Congresses. I. Birnbaum, George. II. Series: NATO ASI series. Series B, Physics; v. 127.
QC467.P54   1985   539′.6   85-12113
ISBN 0-306-42071-6

©1985 Plenum Press, New York
A Division of Plenum Publishing Corporation
233 Spring Street, New York, N.Y. 10013

Printed in the United States of America

PREFACE

This book is concerned with recent experimental and theoretical work dealing with phenomena created by the transient dipoles and polarizabilities produced by intermolecular interactions. The former produce absorption from the microwave to the optical regions of the spectrum and the latter produce Rayleigh and Raman scattering; such absorption and scattering would be absent without collisions. Static properties, such as dielectric constant, refractive index, and Kerr effect, also exhibit the effects of induced dipoles and polarizabilities.

The first observation of an infrared absorption spectrum produced by the collisions of molecules which ordinarily do not have an allowed dipole transition was reported in 1949 (Crawford, Welsh, and Locke). The first observation of depolarized Rayleigh spectra due to collisions in atomic gases appeared in 1968 (McTague and Birnbaum). However, it was not until 1977 that the first conference dealing with collision-induced phenomena was organized by J. D. Poll at the University of Guelph. This conference was mainly concerned with studies of collision-induced absorption in gases. Light scattering received more attention at the second meeting of the collision-induced community in 1978, at the E. Fermi Summer School on "Intermolecular Spectroscopy and Dynamical Properties of Dense Systems," organized by J. Van Kranendonk. However, the emphasis was still on collision-induced absorption in compressed gases, although some work on liquids, solid H_2, and related subjects such as rotational relaxation was included. The third induced phenomena conference, organized by F. Barocchi in Florence in 1980, dealt with the full scope of recent developments in induced phenomena in liquids and gases.

There have been a number of advances since the Florence conference, particularly in the use of molecular dynamics in the study of compressed fluids and in investigations of induced transitions accompanying allowed transitions. For these reasons and because the field as an entirety had not been subject to critical review, a NATO Advanced Research Workshop was held at the Château de Bonas, Castera-Verduzan, France, from September 5 to 9, 1983.

This workshop was attended by more than 50 scientists from various countries. Sessions were organized into broad categories including compressed gases and the effect of density in infrared absorption and light scattering; liquid state interactions in atomic and molecular systems; solid state, amorphous and ionic systems; and induced transitions in allowed spectra. A final category on related subjects included a wide variety of subjects in which collision-induced effects play an important role.

Most of the papers presented at the Advanced Research Workshop reviewed recent progress in a relatively small segment of the field, although some were of broad scope. In addition, there were a number of contributions dealing with recent research results. Following each of the sessions, which dealt with a major division of the subject, a workshop was held to discuss some of the important themes from a broad perspective, to assess the current status of research in the area, and to identify problems requiring future work.

A meeting of this scope would not have been possible without the capable guidance provided by an organizing committee. Its members included:

Prof. L. Frommhold, University of Texas at Austin, U.S.A.
Dr. P. Lallemand, Laboratoire de Spectroscopie Hertzienne, Paris, France
Dr. P. A. Madden, *Royal Signals and Radar Establishment Malvern, U.K.
Prof. J. D. Poll, University of Guelph, Canada
Prof. C. G. Gray, alternate, University of Guelph, Canada
Prof. G. A. Signorelli, University of Rome, Italy
Dr. F. Barocchi, alternate, Istituto di Elettronica Quantistica, Florence, Italy

Special thanks are due to Dr. P. Lallemand for his effective handling of the local arrangements in France and to Profs. L. Frommhold, J. D. Poll, J. C. Lewis, and G. Tabisz for their frequent advice and help. Prof. Frommhold's capable and generous help in preparing this book for publication is gratefully acknowledged. Finally, without the encouragement of Dr. H. T. Yolken and the support of the National Bureau of Standards, this enterprise would not have been possible.

This Advanced Research Workshop was sponsored and supported by the NATO Advanced Scientific Affairs Division. Additional financial support was provided by Centro Nationale de Ricerche (C.N.R.), Italy; Direction des Recherches Études et Techniques (D.R.E.T.), France; and the National Bureau of Standards, U.S.A.

G. Birnbaum
National Bureau of Standards
Gaithersburg, MD

----
*Now at Oxford University, U.K.

CONTENTS

SECTION 1: COMPRESSED GASES AND THE EFFECT OF DENSITY

A. Far Infrared and Infrared Absorption

B. Light Scattering

SECTION 2: LIQUIDS AND LIQUID STATE INTERACTIONS

A. Atomic Systems

B. Molecular Systems

SECTION 3: SOLID STATE, AMORPHOUS, AND IONIC SYSTEMS

SECTION 4: Induced Transitions in Allowed Spectra

SECTION 5: RELATED SUBJECTS

INTRODUCTION

This volume is a collection of reviews emphasizing recent advances in infrared absorption, Rayleigh and Raman scattering, and related phenomena that are produced by the dipole moments and the polarizabilities produced by intermolecular interactions. It is apparent that such spectra contain a great deal of information on atomic and molecular interactions and dynamics and that the possibility of extracting such information is an important reason for studying collision-induced spectra. Consequently, the Bonas workshop was organized into broad categories emphasizing the physical systems studied rather than the experimental or theoretical techniques employed. The topics chosen for review within each of the major categories were selected on the basis of the research interests of the invited experts. In addition to the reviews, there were contributions dealing with new developments, which, in most cases, were incorporated into the review papers prepared for this volume. These proceedings emphasize experimental and theoretical results and their interpretation, rather than experimental technique, theoretical derivations, or historical developments. Although the articles here are basically reviews, new material not published previously may be found in a number of them. Background and supplemental material may be found in the bibliography appended to this introduction.

At the end of each of the sections except the last, there is a discussion of the papers and topics presented therein. These summary or workshop reports represent the views of the authors rather than a consensus view of the participants of the workshop. Many critical assessments and suggestions for future research are to be found in these workshop reports, although such assessments also appear in many of the papers. In the following paragraphs, we present briefly a general view of the major subdivisions of this book.

The investigation of gas-phase induced spectra and the effect of density is the subject of Section 1. The identification and study of induction mechanisms are most readily accomplished in gases at low densities where bimolecular collisions predominate and complications arising from three and higher body interactions are minimized. Moreover, it is in gases that the most accurate measurements have been obtained and the most thorough analyses of the data have been made. Much of this analytical work has been based on the first few spectral moments, which can be calculated accurately since they are equilibrium properties of the system. However, more recently exact quantum mechanical calculations of collision-induced, two-body spectra have appeared. Such calculations with ab initio induced dipole moments and polarizabilities as input, give results in impressive agreement with experiment.

As the gas density is increased, pair interactions in three-body collisions become significant and cause profound changes in the spectra. The most widely encountered effect is a significant cancellation of the intensity. In addition, in certain cases, these three-body interactions cause a collisional interference which cancels a great deal of the spectrum at low frequencies, and a collisional narrowing of certain spectral features. These effects also occur in the liquid, where, however, higher-body interactions become significant.

The development of theories of liquid state spectra is greatly impeded by the difficulty of dealing with the dynamics of many-body (pairwise) interactions. Molecular dynamics computer simulations are therefore invaluable for studying collision-induced phenomena in liquids. Nevertheless, analytical shapes are indispensable for the analysis of spectra, and attempts have been made to derive spectral shapes at liquid densities, based on approximate treatments of the generalized Langevin equation. In the study of static properties related to collision-induced phenomena, continuum or local field models have been investigated. Section 2 and most of Section 4 discuss studies of collision-induced phenomena in liquids. Although there is about as much emphasis on liquids in this book as on gases, we suspect that the emphasis in future research may shift toward liquids, since the problems here are more complex and less understood.

As molecular motions in solids are generally very different from those in dense fluids, the induced spectra in these two phases can be drastically different. Collision-induced spectra in solids appear to be a fruitful field of study, as can be seen from the broad variety of subjects included in Section 3 on Solid State, Amorphous and Ionic Systems. Nevertheless, the work devoted to solids is still only a small fraction of that so far devoted to fluids.

In recent years, there has been a growing awareness that the contributions of induced effects to allowed spectra may be significant. For accurate analysis of allowed spectra, then, the induced contribution must be identified. However, the interplay of induced and allowed transitions offers a new challenge in collision-induced phenomena, and for both reasons, the role of allowed transitions in induced spectra must be studied. The progress in this relatively new area is reviewed in Section 4.

Although, in retrospect, it might have been possible to place the papers in Section 5, Related Subjects, in other sections, it is instructive to include them under a single heading and thus emphasize the many facets of collision-induced phenomena and the diversity of their applications. However, because of this diversity, a unified critique of this section was not feasible and a workshop report has, therefore, not been included. Several articles appear in Section 5 and elsewhere in this book which were not presented at the Workshop. These were included because it was deemed worthwhile to present a reasonably complete view of the field.

Finally, we note the emphasis on investigations of the collision-induced absorption (CIA) spectrum of the hydrogens, H_2, D_2, and HD. The study of these molecules has played an important role in developing both an understanding of CIA phenomena and in elucidating their many subtle properties in the gaseous, liquid and solid states. Although CIA in H_2 was observed as early as 1949, the study of CIA phenomena in the hydrogens in all states of matter has by no means been exhausted and continues to be an active field of research.

REFERENCES

Buckingham, A. D., 1959, Molecular Quadrupole Moments, in Quarterly Reviews (London), 13:183.

Colpa, J. P., 1965, Induced absorption in the infra-red, in: "Physics of High Pressures and the Condensed Phase," A. Van Itterbeck, ed., North-Holland Publishing Co., Amsterdam.

Moller, K. D., and Rothschild, W. G., 1971, Chap. 11, in: "Collision-Induced Spectra at Long wavelengths in Far-Infrared Spectroscopy," Wiley-Interscience, New York.

Sutter, H., 1972, Dielectric polzarization in gases, in: "Dielectric and Related Molecular Processes, Vol. 1, A Specialist Periodical Report," The Chemical Society, London.

Welsh, H. L., 1972, Pressure-induced absorption spectra of hydrogen, in: "MTP international Review of Science, Vol. 3, Spectroscopy," D. A. Ramsay, ed., Butterworths, London, University Park, Baltimore.

Gelbart, W. S., 1974, Depolarized Light Scattering by Simple Fluids, Adv. Chem. Phys., 26:1.

Van Kranendonk, J., 1974, Intermolecular spectroscopy, Physica, 73:156.

Rich, N. H., and McKellar, A. R. W., 1975, "A Bibliography on Collision-Induced Absorption," National Research Council of Canada, Herzberg Institute of Astrophysics, NRCC No. 15145.

Stuckert, R. A., Montrose, C. J., and Litovitz, T. A., 1977, Comparison of interaction induced light scattering and infrared absorption in liquids, in: "Faraday Symposia of the Chemical Society," No. 11.

Buckingham, A. D., 1978, Basic theory of intermolecular forces: Applications to small molecules, in: "Intermolecular Interactions From Diatomics to Biopolymers," B. Pullman, ed., John Wiley and Sons, New York.

Birnbaum, G., 1980, Collision-induced vibrational spectroscopy in liquids, in: "Vibrational Spectroscopy of Molecular Liquids and Solids," S. Bratos and R. M. Pick, eds., Plenum Press, New York and London.

Tabisz, G. C., 1980, Collision-induced Rayleigh and Raman scattering, in: "A Specialist Periodical Report, Molecular Spectroscopy," Vol. 6, The Chemical Society, London.

Intermolecular Spectroscopy and Dynamical Properties of Dense Systems, 1980, Scuola Internazionale di Fisica "Enrico Fermi," LXXV Corso, J. Van Kranendonk, ed., North-Holland Publishing Company, Amsterdam.

Frommhold, L., 1981, Collision-induced scattering of light and the diatom polarizabilities, Adv. Chem. Phys., 46:1.

Papers presented at the Conference on Collision Induced Phenomena: Absorption, Light Scattering, and Static Properties, 1981, Firenze, Italia, 2-5 September 1980, reprinted from Can. J. Phys., Vol. 59.

Birnbaum, G., Guillot, B., and Bratos, S., 1982, Theory of collision-induced line shapes - absorption and light scattering at low density, Adv. Chem. Phys., 51:49.

Birnbaum, G., 1982, The study of atomic and molecular interactions from collision-induced spectra, in: "Proceedings of the Eighth Symposium on Thermophysical Properties, Vol. 1: Thermophysical Properties of Fluids," J. V. Sengers, ed., The American Society of Mechanical Engineers, New York.

Keyes, T., and Ladanyi, B. M., 1984, The internal field problem in depolarized light scattering, Adv. Chem. Phys., in press.

Madden, P. A., 1984, Interaction induced phenomena in molecular liquids, in: "Molecular Liquids," A. J. Barnes, ed., D. Reidel Pub. Co., Dordrecht, The Netherlands.

Tipping, R. H., and Poll, J. D., 1985, Multipole moments of hydrogen and its isotopes, in: "Molecular Spectroscopy: Modern Research, Vol. III," K. N. Rao, ed., Academic Press, New York.

G. Birnbaum
National Bureau of Standards
Gaithersburg, MD

CLASSICAL MULTIPOLE MODELS: COMPARISON WITH *AB INITIO* AND

EXPERIMENTAL RESULTS

Katharine L. C. Hunt

Department of Chemistry
Michigan State University
East Lansing, MI 48824

ABSTRACT

Classical multipole models for collision-induced dipoles and polarizabilities often prove useful in analyzing interaction-induced light scattering and absorption spectra. In this review, the utility and limitations of the classical multipole model are illustrated by comparing results from the model with *ab initio* results for the dipole of Ne...HF, the polarizabilities of inert-gas atom pairs and the polarizability of $N_2...N_2$; predictions from the model are also compared with experimental results for collision-induced far IR absorption and rotational Raman scattering by CH_4, CD_4, CF_4, and SF_6. When single-center multipole models break down, estimates of collision-induced properties can be based on distributed multipole and distributed polarizability models, the electron-gas model and exchange-perturbation theories.

SPECTROSCOPIC APPLICATIONS OF CLASSICAL MULTIPOLE MODELS

Within the classical multipole model, collision-induced absorption in compressed gases and liquids is attributed to dipole moments induced in the molecules of the sample by the nonuniform multipolar fields of neighboring molecules. The model accounts for linear and nonlinear polarization of each sample molecule by the local field $\vec{F}$, the local field gradient $\overleftrightarrow{F}'$, and higher-order derivatives of the field. In spectroscopic applications the model has often been truncated at order R^{-5} or R^{-6} in the separation R between molecular centers. At this level the model incorporates the dipoles induced by the fields due to permanent moments of neighboring molecules (through the octupole or the hexadecapole),

1

dipoles induced in a molecule by the derivatives of the local field at its center (through $\overleftrightarrow{F}'''$, in general) and nonlinear response given to lowest order by the dipole hyperpolarizability β (Buckingham, 1967). An analogous model for the effective polarizabilities of sample molecules in the presence of others provides a classical explanation for observed collision-induced Rayleigh and Raman light scattering. Both induced dipoles and polarizabilities are modulated as the molecules vibrate, rotate, and undergo relative translational motion.

Because classical multipole models do not include overlap, exchange, or electron correlation effects, they cannot give accurate total dipoles or polarizabilities for molecules interacting at short range. Nevertheless, quite good agreement is often found between the predictions of classical models and experimental results for infrared (IR) and far IR absorption, as illustrated by recent studies of the far IR band of gaseous methane (Birnbaum and Cohen, 1975; Birnbaum, 1980; Birnbaum et al., 1983). Provided that the dipoles induced in sample molecules both by the octupoles Ω and by the hexadecapoles Φ of neighboring molecules are included in the classical model, the predicted stick spectrum modified by use of a semiempirical lineshape to account for translational broadening of the rotational lines reproduces the observed band contour well. Quantum mechanical lineshape calculations (Birnbaum et al., 1983) support the claim that the classical model yields a good fit of the spectrum--except in the high-frequency wing ($\omega > 500$ cm^{-1}), where the observed absorption intensities are significantly greater than the computed intensities. Multipole expansions carried beyond the first nonvanishing term in the classical model are also needed in analyzing pressure-induced spectra of N_2 and O_2. The observed intensities and band shapes for collision-induced far IR absorption by these species are not explained solely in terms of the dipole induced in one molecule by the field of the quadrupole of a second molecule (Birnbaum and Cohen, 1975, 1976a; Cohen and Birnbaum, 1977). The hexadecapole-induced dipole and the dipole induced by the second derivative of the quadrupolar field (Buckingham and Ladd, 1976) contribute to the measured absorption intensities. A detailed analysis of far IR absorption by N_2 (Poll and Hunt, 1981) includes anisotropic overlap induction as well as the dominant multipolar effects.

Similarly, classical multipole models have proven useful in analyzing collision-induced light scattering. For example, as shown by molecular dynamics simulations (Alder et al., 1973a,b, 1976, 1979; Berne et al., 1973) and quantum mechanical lineshape calculations (Frommhold et al., 1978a,b; Frommhold, 1981; Proffitt et al., 1981), the dipole-induced dipole (DID) model for the polarizability anisotropy of inert-gas atom pairs (Silberstein, 1917) yields roughly exponential lineshapes for collision-induced depolarized Rayleigh scattering, in good agreement with the experimental lineshapes (Barocchi and Zoppi, 1978; Frommhold, 1981; Proffitt et al., 1981) over a range of frequency shifts, temperatures, and pressures. The model fails only at large frequency shifts (e.g., $\omega > 200$ cm^{-1} for Ar) where short-range interactions are probed. Comparison of the DID values for the interaction-induced polarizability anisotropy and the interaction-induced change in mean polarizability suggests that two-body depolarized light scattering by the inert gases should be significantly more intense than *two-body* polarized light scattering (Frommhold and Proffitt, 1979a, 1980, 1981). Experimental results confirm this prediction about the integrated scattering intensities (Frommhold and Proffitt, 1979b, 1980; Proffitt and Frommhold, 1979, 1980; Proffitt et al., 1980), even though the change in mean polarizability is not given accurately by the DID model (Dacre and Frommhold, 1981, 1982). Further, classical models suffice to predict the presence of high-frequency wings in the depolarized Rayleigh spectra of CH_4, CD_4, CF_4, and SF_6 (Buckingham and Tabisz, 1977, 1978; Shelton and Tabisz, 1980a). For the tetrahedral species, the polarization induced by the local field gradient gives rise to rotational Raman scattering with ΔJ up to ± 3; while for octahedral molecules, scattering with ΔJ up to ± 4 results from the polarization induced by the second derivative of the local field.

A comprehensive study of nine independent interaction-induced spectra of liquid CS_2 (Cox and Madden, 1980, 1981; Madden and Cox, 1981) further shows the utility of classical multipole models in approximating collision-induced properties. Included in this study are six single-molecule forbidden spectra: the ν_1 near infrared absorption band (totally symmetric stretch), the isotropic and anisotropic ν_2 Raman bands (bending mode), the isotropic and anisotropic ν_3 Raman bands (asymmetric stretch), and the far infra-red band. The multipole model suggests that the lineshapes for these CS_2 spectra (collectively designated the "forbidden" spectra) should be similar, since to lowest order each is produced by induction mechanisms that vary as R^{-4} in the separation between molecular centers. The forbidden near and far IR spectra result in part from the dipoles induced in CS_2 molecules by the quadrupolar fields of neighboring molecules. In general, the forbidden Raman spectra reflect three different R^{-4} interaction contributions. One originates in the nonlinear polarization of a sample molecule by the laser field and the field due to the permanent quadrupoles of neighbors; therefore it depends on the molecular β hyperpolarizability. A second stems from polarization by the field due to the quadrupoles that are induced in neighboring molecules by the applied (laser) field. This contribution is governed by the dipole-quadrupole polarizability $\overleftrightarrow{A}$, as is the third contribution, which stems from the polarization of sample molecules by the local field gradient due to the dipoles induced in neighboring molecules by the applied field. Both the β hyperpolarizability and the A tensor vanish for a CS_2 molecule in its equilibrium configuration, but

$\overset{\leftrightarrow}{\beta}$ and $\overset{\leftrightarrow}{A}$ are nonvanishing when bending or asymmetric stretching removes the center of symmetry (Buckingham, 1967). In contrast to the forbidden spectra, the interaction-induced components of the single-molecule allowed spectra in the study (i.e., the wings of the isotropic and anisotropic Rayleigh spectra and the ν_1 aniso-tropic Raman wing) can be produced by an R^{-3} DID mechanism at lowest order. Based on the multipole analysis, it is expected that the forbidden spectra will have similar shapes, and that the for-bidden bands will be broader than the interaction-induced components of the allowed bands. Experimental results (Madden and Cox, 1981) accord with these predictions. At 295 K there is a striking difference between the line shape for the ν_2 anisotropic Raman spectrum and that for the ν_1 anisotropic Raman spectrum. The ν_3 polarized Raman band shows the same exponential drop-off at high frequency shifts from the band center as the ν_2 band, while the anisotropic Rayleigh band shows a more rapid decrease in intensity with increasing distance from the band center and resembles the ν_1 band. The differences between the forbidden spectra and the aniso-tropic Rayleigh spectrum are particularly clear on logarithmic plots of intensity vs. frequency at frequency shifts $\omega > 90$ cm^{-1} from the band center, where the shape of the full spectrum is largely determined by the shape of the two-particle spectrum (Ladd et al., 1979). Additionally, the spectra for CS_2 diluted in various solvents (OCS, CHBr$_3$, CBr$_4$, and C_5H_{10}) fit predictions based on the multipole model (Cox and Madden, 1981). More recent computer simulations of liquid CS_2 (Madden and Tildesley, 1983) support the experimental analysis by showing "excellent qualitative agreement with experiment on the existence and form of a common lineshape for the forbidden spectra at intermediate and high frequencies." There are small discrepancies between the experimental and calculated parameters characterizing the spectra, but Madden and Tildesley attribute these discrepancies to the limitations of the simulation routines, rather than to a breakdown of the multipole model for interpreting the spectra.

Detailed quantitative comparisons of classical multipole models with *ab initio* calculations and experimental results are clearly warranted, based on the work cited above and other studies showing the utility of multipole models (see, e.g., Buckingham and Fowler, 1983). In the next section, *ab initio* results for collision-induced properties are compared directly with results obtained from multipole expansions; calculations of the Ne...HF dipole (Fowler and Bucking-ham, 1983) and of inert-gas pair polarizabilities are taken as examples. In making the comparisons, *ab initio* values of the single-molecule charge moments and polarizabilities are generally used to evaluate terms in the multipole series.

Comparisons of a second type serve to test the validity of the multipole model in spectroscopic applications. For isolated molecules with ~ 20 electrons or fewer, it is possible to evaluate

permanent charge moments, linear and nonlinear dipole polarizabilities, higher-multipole response tensors, and the derivatives of
these properties with respect to normal vibrational coordinates by
ab initio calculation (Amos, 1979, 1980, 1984; Amos et al., 1980;
Williams and Amos, 1980). Values of these electrical properties
for isolated molecules can also be extracted by fitting experimental
lineshapes, if it is assumed that the classical multipole model
fixes the functional form of the collision-induced dipoles or polarizabilities (with the possible addition of short-range exponential
overlap corrections). The isolated-molecule moments and polarizabilities are then treated as adjustable parameters, to be determined by optimizing the fit to experimental spectra. Analyses of
the far IR absorption band of gaseous methane (Birnbaum et al.,
1983) and studies of its rotational Raman scattering spectrum
(Buckingham and Tabisz, 1977, 1978; Shelton and Tabisz, 1980a)
exemplify this approach; these analyses also permit comparisons of
ab initio and experimentally derived values for the octupole moment
and for the dipole-quadrupole polarizability of CH_4, as shown below.

An assessment of the multipole model follows the comparisons
with *ab initio* and experimental results. Methods of approximating
collision-induced properties for molecules interacting at short
range are reviewed in the concluding section. For reference,
symbols and abbreviations used in this paper are listed in the
appendix.

COMPARISON OF CLASSICAL MULTIPOLE MODELS AND *AB INITIO* RESULTS

A calculation of the total dipole of the van der Waals molecule
Ne...HF (Fowler and Buckingham, 1983) provides a test case for the
classical multipole model. Fowler and Buckingham determined the
total dipole of Ne...HF at self-consistent field (SCF) level, in a
calculation with 67 contracted Gaussian basis functions. For an
isolated HF molecule, 38 contracted functions were centered on the
H and F nuclei (a Gaussian (10s,6p,3d/5s,3p) basis contracted to
[5s,4p,2d/3s,2p]); this yields an SCF energy of -100.0532 a.u. at
the equilibrium internuclear separation of 1.7328 a.u. The SCF
energy compares well with the estimated Hartree-Fock limit for HF,
-100.071 a.u. (Cade and Huo, 1967). The neon basis of 29 contracted
Gaussian-type orbitals comprises the Dunning basis (Dunning, 1971)
augmented by two sets of d functions. The computed SCF energy for
neon is -128.54071 a.u., in comparison with the Hartree-Fock limit
of -128.547 a.u. (Roetti and Clementi, 1974). For the Ne...HF
supermolecule, a minimum with a well depth of $5.18 \cdot 10^{-5}$ a.u. is
found in the SCF potential surface for a linear configuration with
the Ne-F distance R ∿ 7.25 a.u. For pairs in the alternate Ne...FH
configuration, there is a shallow minimum at R ∿ 9 a.u., with a well
depth of $0.16 \cdot 10^{-5}$ a.u. Electron correlation effects are not
included in the calculations, and the restriction of the basis to

s, p, and d functions limits the accuracy of representation of higher-multipole polarization and hyperpolarization effects, but the work accounts for the predominant short-range exchange and induction effects. In general, the suitability of a basis for interaction-induced property calculations is indicated more reliably by the accuracy of single-molecule electric properties than by the energy. For the neon atom, the polarizability obtained in this work is 2.28646 a.u.; for comparison, Werner and Meyer (1976) have obtained α_{Ne} = 2.368 a.u. at SCF level, and the experimental value is 2.669 a.u. The SCF dipole of HF (0.7556 a.u.) compares favorably with the experimental result, μ = 0.7066 a.u. (Sileo and Cool, 1976); the calculated and experimental quadrupole moments are similarly in good agreement, Θ = 1.7655 a.u. from the SCF wave function vs. Θ = 1.75 ± 0.02 a.u. from the experimental work of DeLeeuw and Dymanus (1973). The calculated polarizability anisotropy for the HF molecule is 1.298 a.u., for comparison with Muenter's experimentally determined value (1972), $\alpha_{zz}-\alpha_{xx}$ = 1.48 ± 0.14 a.u.

Earlier calculations (Losonczy et al., 1974) had suggested that charge transfer makes a significant contribution to the energy at the SCF potential minimum, since the reported well depth exceeded the dipole-induced dipole interaction energy by a factor of $\sim$ 3. A smaller basis (40 contracted Gaussians) was used in this work, however, and corrections for basis-set superposition error were not made. Basis-set superposition error affects calculated inter-action energies for weakly bonded complexes in two ways. The principal source of error is an inequivalence between the quality of representation of the supermolecule in the full supermolecule basis and the quality of representation of the individual Ne and HF molecules by the single-molecule bases. In calculations on Ne...HF, the molecular subsystems are stabilized as they come together, since each can exploit the virtual orbitals of the other to lower its energy. Function counterpoise (or "ghost-orbital") methods remove much of the error from this source (Boys and Bernardi, 1970), though they tend to overestimate the correction needed (Fowler and Madden, 1983). In addition, an error in the interaction energy arises because the Ne atom develops a spurious polarity in the pair basis, leading to an apparent electrostatic interaction energy. The HF dipole is also altered in the pair basis, and superposition errors in the polarizability of neon result in errors in the computed induction energy. These latter errors are not removed by ghost-orbital corrections. Fowler and Buckingham found that standard ghost-orbital corrections changed the calculated Ne...HF well depth by more than a factor of four, even with the large basis used in their work. In contrast to the results of Losonczy et al., their results show no evidence of significant charge transfer at the SCF potential minimum. Taken as a crude measure of charge-transfer effects, Mulliken population analysis suggests that the net charge transfer is less than 10^{-4} e.

Fowler and Buckingham tested the convergence of the classical multipole series for the electrostatic potential, field, and field gradient of the HF molecule at points along the molecular axis. After comparing the multipole series with results obtained directly from the SCF wave function and classical expressions for the potential of a continuous charge distribution, they concluded that "the induction energy [of Ne...HF] is adequately represented by a 3-site multipole model in the region of the . . . minimum [in the SCF potential surface]". The 3-site model for HF includes moments through the hexadecapole at the bond center, and atomic charges, dipoles, and quadrupoles at the H and F nuclei. It gives the potential within 0.1% of the exact value and the field F_z within 0.5% for an Ne-F separation R of 6.0 a.u. Even in a single-site multipole model for HF with moments truncated at the hexadecapole, the error in F_z amounts only to 3% for R = 6 a.u.

In the classical multipole model, the principal contribution to the interaction-induced dipole comes from the linear polarization of the Ne atom by the field at its center due to the HF molecule. Subsidiary contributions arise from the back-induced dipole of HF (i.e., the dipole induced in the HF molecule by the field and field gradients due to the induced multipoles on the Ne atom), and from the polarization of the neon atom bilinear in the field from HF and the field-gradient from HF (B-tensor terms). The classical contribution from the γ hyperpolarizability of Ne is negligible. At the SCF minimum, the linear polarization of the Ne atom accounts for 91% of the total SCF dipole. Inclusion of back-induction and B-tensor terms further reduces the error: in the configuration Ne...HF, the error in the long-range form of the dipole is 5% for an Ne-F separation R = 7.5 a.u. and 12.5% for R = 6.0 a.u., the smallest R for which the dipole was calculated. The remaining discrepancy can be explained in part by considering basis-set superposition errors in the polarizability of Ne; these increase the effective Ne polarizability in the supermolecule and hence alter the SCF dipole by $\sim$ 4%.

At the SCF potential minimum, the long-range and SCF dipoles agree, when all significant contributions are retained in the long-range model. In contrast, if the multipole series for the field of the HF molecule is truncated at the quadrupole term and if back-induction and nonlinear response of the Ne atom are neglected, the resulting error in the Ne...HF dipole at the SCF minimum amounts to $\sim$ 20%. The error caused by neglect of exchange in calculating the Ne...HF dipole is estimated to be less than 5% at the potential minimum (Fowler and Buckingham, 1983).

The discrepancies between the SCF energies and the exact induction energies for Ne...HF are somewhat larger than the discrepancies between *ab initio* and long-range dipoles, even when the SCF energies have been corrected for basis-set superposition error

by the function counterpoise method. An additional correction of
the SCF results is needed to eliminate the spurious electrostatic
interaction energy of the HF dipole with the basis superposition
dipole of Ne. For the configuration Ne...HF, the induction energy
differs from the corrected SCF energy by about 10% when the Ne-F
distance is 12.0 a.u.; the difference rises to $\sim$ 25% at 9.0 a.u.,
drops to 10% at 7.5 a.u., and then rises sharply for separations
smaller than 7.25 a.u. For the configuration Ne...FH, the long-
range induction energy fits the SCF results for Ne-F distances
greater than 10 a.u.

Similarly detailed comparisons of *ab initio* pair polarizabilities
and pair polarizabilities from classical multipole models are
possible for the inert-gas diatoms, following the work of Dacre
(1978, 1981, 1982a-d) and Kress and Kozak (1977). The calculations
on helium and neon pairs employ large bases and incorporate correlation effects via single- and double-excitation configuration interaction; calculations on the heavier species are limited to the SCF
level. In each case the DID model (without higher-multipole terms)
represents the pair polarizability anisotropy well, for internuclear
separations exceeding the van der Waals minimum distance R_{min}. At
the van der Waals minimum for He...He, the total polarizability
anisotropy falls below the DID value by $\sim$ 10% if the DID value is
calculated using the experimental polarizability of an isolated
He atom. For Ne...Ne at the van der Waals minimum, the calculated
anisotropy falls below the DID value by $\sim$ 20%. At the van der
Waals minima for argon, krypton, and xenon pairs, the SCF anisotropies are approximately 5-15% smaller than the DID values obtained
using the SCF single-atom polarizabilities.

SCF calculations of pair polarizabilities for the diatomic
molecules H_2 (Bounds, 1979) and N_2 (Bounds et al., 1981) show the
same qualitative features. In their study of N_2 dimers in
collinear, T-shaped, cross-T and rectangular configurations, Bounds,
Hinchliffe and Spicer (1981) found that the DID model predicts the
interaction-induced polarizability of an N_2 dimer reasonably well
when the separation between molecular centers is greater than R $\sim$
8.0 a.u. Discrepancies between SCF results and DID predictions
appear to be greatest for the response of collinear molecules to
applied fields perpendicular to the internuclear axes.

On the other hand, the orientational average of the interaction-
induced polarizability $\Delta\bar{\alpha}$ for inert-gas pairs shows little resem-
blance to DID predictions (Dacre and Frommhold, 1982). In the DID
model, $\Delta\bar{\alpha}$ varies as R^{-6} in the separation R between the centers of
the interacting molecules, and it is positive. Configuration-
interaction (CI) calculations including single and double excitations
yield positive values of $\Delta\bar{\alpha}$ for He and Ne pairs at long range, but
at the van der Waals minima $\Delta\bar{\alpha}$ is negative and relatively large in
magnitude; in the range R < R_{min}, $\Delta\bar{\alpha}$ decreases monotonically with

decreasing R (Dacre, 1978, 1982a,b). The counterpoise-corrected SCF values of $\Delta\bar{\alpha}$ are also negative at the van der Waals minima for Ar, Kr, and Xe pairs (Dacre, 1982c,d). For the heavier inert gases, $\Delta\bar{\alpha}$ is negative and large in magnitude for $R < R_{min}$, except at very small R where the SCF value of $\Delta\bar{\alpha}$ rises sharply. It should be noted that the pair polarizability anisotropy for inert-gas atoms is non-zero at first order in the interatomic interaction (R^{-3}), while the orientational average $\Delta\bar{\alpha}$ vanishes at first order.

COMPARISON OF CLASSICAL MULTIPOLE MODELS AND EXPERIMENTAL RESULTS

Comparisons of calculated values of multipole moments and polarizabilities with values obtained by analyzing spectral invariants or lineshapes provide further tests of the validity of classical multipole models. In this section, studies of the far infrared spectra of CH_4 and SF_6 and studies of collision-induced depolarized light scattering by CH_4, CD_4, CF_4, and SF_6 are reviewed. These studies exemplify the quality of fit to experimental spectra obtained within the multipole model.

Birnbaum, Frommhold, Nencini, and Sutter have recently analyzed the far-infrared absorption band of gaseous methane at 195 K in the wavenumber region from 30-900 cm^{-1} (Birnbaum et al., 1983). Three classical mechanisms for interaction-induced polarization of methane molecules are included in this analysis. The first mechanism, polarization of one methane molecule by the field arising from the octupole moment of a neighbor, yields the lowest-order contribution to the long-range collision-induced dipole. The contribution varies as R^{-5} in the separation R between molecular centers. Radiative selection rules for transitions resulting from this induction mechanism are $\Delta J = 0, \pm1, \pm2,$ and ±3. A stick-spectrum representation shows, however, that this mechanism alone cannot produce sufficient absorption intensity at high frequency to fit the observed spectrum, indicating the need to include higher-order terms in the collision-induced dipole. At order R^{-6}, there are two additional induction mechanisms: both the hexadecapolar field and the octupolar field-gradient due to one methane molecule induce dipoles in its neighbors. For the first of these two R^{-6} mechanisms the radiative selection rules are $\Delta J = 0, \pm1, \pm2, \pm3,$ and ±4, while for the second the selection rules $\Delta J = 0, \pm1, \pm2,$ and ±3 govern simultaneous transitions in each of the interacting molecules. Band shapes for the two R^{-6} induction mechanisms are similar, with substantial high-frequency absorption, but the octupole-gradient contribution peaks $\sim$ 50 cm^{-1} higher than the hexadecapolar contribution. Birnbaum et al. (1983) determined the absolute values of the methane octupole moment Ω and hexadecapole moment Φ from an adjusted fit to the observed spectrum. Calculated spectra were obtained quantum mechanically using the isotropic Hanley-Klein intermolecular potential (Hanley and Klein, 1972). In the fitting procedure, the dipole-quadrupole polarizability A was fixed at 1.0 $\mathring{A}^4$ (Shelton and Tabisz, 1980a; see discussion below); A determines the CH_4 dipole induced by the first derivative of the field at the molecular origin, and thus it appears quadratically as a factor in the absorption intensity attributable to induction by the octupolar field gradient. The least-squares fit to the spectrum yields $|\Omega| = 2.01 \cdot 10^{-34}$ esu cm^3 and $|\Phi| = 5.0 \cdot 10^{-42}$ esu cm^4. For comparison, *ab initio* calculations including single and double excitations from a Hartree-Fock reference determinant give $\Omega = 1.85 \cdot 10^{-34}$ esu cm^3 and $\Phi = -3.088 \ 10^{-42}$ esu cm^4 (Amos, 1979). *Ab initio* values of high-order multipole moments and polarizabilities converge relatively slowly as the basis set size is increased (Schaefer, 1972), since the values depend on the charge distribution in regions (far from the atomic nuclei) that are not heavily weighted in variational calculations. Agreement between the *ab initio* value of the octupole moment and the experimentally derived value is good. The *ab initio* value of $|\Phi|$ is lower than that obtained from the spectral analysis. Use of the *ab initio* value to generate a spectrum would reduce the amplitude of the hexadecapole-induced dipole band by $\sim 60\%$; an increased value of the dipole-quadrupole polarizability A or an overlap dipole would then be needed to account for the observed absorption intensity in the range from 400 to 500 cm^{-1}. The values of Ω and Φ obtained by Birnbaum et al. give an excellent fit to the experimental spectrum in the full range from ~ 30 to 500 cm^{-1}. At high frequency (500-900 cm^{-1}) the absorption is considerably more intense than predicted with the three mechanisms listed above. The high-frequency wing must reflect higher-multipole effects, short-range exchange and overlap, and dispersion effects.

The collision-induced far infrared absorption band of SF_6 appearing in the range 0-180 cm^{-1} has been analyzed for molecules both in the gas phase and in the liquid phase (Birnbaum and Sutter, 1981). The analysis is of interest in the context of classical multipole theories, because the lowest-order contribution to the net dipole of an SF_6 pair interacting at long range comes from the polarization of each of the molecules by the field of the hexadecapole Φ of its neighbor. Vibrational difference bands overlap the high-frequency part of the collision-induced band and complicate the analysis, but two different spectral decompositions (used to remove absorption linear in the density) indicate that hexadecapolar induction does not provide sufficient absorption at high frequencies to account for the observed band shape. When effects of the second nonvanishing permanent multipole (with angular dependence $\ell = 6$) are included in the model, rotational transitions with $\Delta J = \pm 5$ or ± 6 are permitted in addition to the $\Delta J = 0, \pm 1, \pm 2, \pm 3, \pm 4$ transitions permitted with hexadecapolar induction alone. Inclusion of these effects does not cause a sufficient increase in the calculated absorption intensities at high frequencies to bring the experimental and theoretical spectra into agreement. High-frequency absorption might also be produced by double transitions with $\Delta J = 0, \pm 1, \pm 2,$

±3, ±4 for each molecule; these are allowed, because the second derivative of the field due to the hexadecapole of an SF_6 molecule may induce a dipole moment in a second molecule via the E-tensor of the second ($\overleftrightarrow{E}$ is the dipole-octupole polarizability tensor; Buckingham, 1967). If this polarization effect is included and the experimental spectra are fit with Φ and E taken as adjustable parameters, the E-tensor mechanism appears to dominate the lower-order induction by the hexadecapolar field. From this result and from the observation that the spectral invariant α_1 (the zeroth moment of the absorption coefficient, divided by the square of the density) for the far IR absorption band in SF_6 is less than half the value for He/Ar mixtures--where the absorption results entirely from overlap and dispersion effects--Birnbaum and Sutter have concluded that the high-frequency absorption by SF_6 reflects short-range anisotropic induction. Within the lineshape theory developed by Birnbaum and Cohen (1976b), extended to include anisotropic overlap effects with the same angular dependence as the leading multipole contribution (Birnbaum, 1980), a satisfactory fit has been obtained for the induced component of the SF_6 liquid spectra at 273 K and 233 K. The fit to the gas-phase spectrum is not good above 70 cm^{-1}, but uncertainties are associated with the removal of the 94 cm^{-1} difference band from the observed spectrum. The analysis by Birnbaum and Sutter gives an overlap contribution about three times larger than the hexadecapolar contribution in the gas phase and 7-10 times larger in the liquid phase.

An experimental value for the net dipole of a van der Waals complex in its equilibrium configuration can be obtained directly from Stark effect data for the complex. For example, the structure and the effective dipole of Ar...CO_2 have been determined by molecular beam electric resonance spectroscopy (Steed, Dixon, and Klemperer, 1979). Zero-field radiofrequency and microwave transitions were first analyzed and the magnitude of the dipole moment was then found from the second-order Stark effect on the frequency of a selected transition in applied electric fields up to 30 V/cm. The equilibrium structure of Ar...CO_2 is T-shaped with the Ar and C nuclei separated by R = 3.493 Å. For this structure, a classical multipole calculation of the dipole induced in the Ar atom by the quadrupole of the CO_2 molecule (Birnbaum, 1985),

$$\mu = -3\alpha_{Ar}\Theta_{CO_2}R^{-4}/2, \tag{1}$$

yields μ = 0.070 D, based on an argon atom polarizability of 11.08 a.u. and the measured quadrupole of CO_2, Θ = -4.2 esu (Buckingham and Disch, 1963). This result agrees surprisingly well with the experimentally determined dipole, μ = 0.06793 D.

A detailed test of the classical multipole model for collision-induced rotational Raman scattering (CIRS) has been made possible by accurate *ab initio* calculations of the higher-multipole polarizability tensors for CH_4 (Amos, 1979) and recent experimental studies of scattering by gaseous CH_4 and mixtures of CH_4 with argon and xenon (Penner et al., 1985). In the classical model (Buckingham and Tabisz, 1977, 1978) the net dipole moment of a molecule in a nonuniform electric field $\vec{F}$ is

$$\mu_\alpha = \mu_\alpha^{(o)} + \alpha_{\alpha\beta}^{(o)} F_\beta + \frac{1}{3} A_{\alpha,\beta\gamma} F'_{\beta\gamma} + \frac{1}{15} E_{\alpha,\beta\gamma\delta} F''_{\beta\gamma\delta} + \cdots$$

$$+ \frac{1}{2} \beta_{\alpha\beta\gamma} F_\beta F_\gamma + \frac{1}{6} \gamma_{\alpha\beta\gamma\delta} F_\beta F_\gamma F_\delta + \frac{1}{3} B_{\alpha\beta,\gamma\delta} F_\beta F'_{\gamma\delta} \qquad (2)$$

where $\vec{\mu}^{(o)}$ is the permanent dipole moment of the molecule, $\overleftrightarrow{\alpha}^{(o)}$ is the isolated-molecule polarizability, $\overleftrightarrow{A}$ and $\overleftrightarrow{E}$ are the dipole-quadrupole and dipole-octupole polarizabilities, and $\overleftrightarrow{\beta}$, $\overleftrightarrow{\gamma}$, and $\overleftrightarrow{B}$ are hyperpolarizabilities. The Greek subscripts designate Cartesian components of vectors or tensors and a repeated subscript implies summation over x, y, and z terms. The field $\vec{F}$ polarizing the molecule is the sum of an applied radiation field $\vec{E}_o$ and the field due to neighboring molecules. The effective polarizability $\overleftrightarrow{\alpha}$ that accounts for collision-induced scattering is obtained by differentiating $\vec{\mu}$ with respect to the applied field $\vec{E}_o$. A term in $\overleftrightarrow{\alpha}$ gives rise to rotational Raman scattering only if it involves an anisotropic molecular moment or an anisotropic response tensor (i.e., a tensor that reorients along with the molecular axes).

For CH_4 the isolated-molecule polarizability tensor $\overleftrightarrow{\alpha}^{(o)}$ is isotropic. Thus for a pair of CH_4 molecules, to lowest order in the inverse of the molecular separation (R^{-1}), CIRS originates in two A-tensor contributions to the oscillating dipole of one CH_4 molecule in the radiation field and the field of the second molecule (Buckingham and Tabisz, 1977, 1978; Shelton and Tabisz, 1980a). One contribution depends on the A tensor for the first molecule; it reflects the dipole polarization of that molecule by the field gradient due to the dipole that the external field induces in the second molecule. Another A-tensor contribution appears because the external field induces a quadrupole in the second molecule (via A_2) as well as a dipole, and the quadrupolar field polarizes the first molecule. The A-tensor terms in the collision-induced polarizability vary as R^{-4} in the separation between molecular centers. At order R^{-5}, there are additional contributions to the collision-induced polarizability. E-tensor terms represent the induction of a dipole in one molecule by the second derivative of the field due to its neighbor; these terms also represent direct induction of an octupole moment in the neighbor (by the applied field) and consequent polarization of the first by the octupolar field of its neighbor. $A_1 A_2$ terms also appear at order R^{-5} because the external field induces a quadrupole in one molecule (via A_1) and the field gradient of this induced quadrupole polarizes the second molecule (via A_2). Finally there is an R^{-5} contribution that depends on the hyperpolarizability β for one CH_4 molecule, which is polarized simultaneously by the external field and by the field due to the octupole moment of the neighboring molecule. The β hyperpolarizability of methane is small ($\sim -3 \cdot 10^{-52}$ $C^3m^3J^{-2}$, cf. Amos, 1979) and the scattering intensity associated with the β term is less than 1% of the scattering intensity from the dominant A-tensor mechanism. At 200 cm^{-1} the E-tensor contribution to the scattering intensity is roughly 5% of the dominant A-tensor contribution (based on estimates $|A| = 0.9$ $\mathring{A}^4$ and $|E| = 0.9$ $\mathring{A}^5$), and the A_1A_2 effects are somewhat smaller than the E-tensor contribution; at 600 cm^{-1}, all three contributions are similar in magnitude (Penner et al., 1985).

Comparison of the depolarized light scattering spectra of CH_4 and CD_4 supports the attribution of scattering with large frequency shifts to collision-induced rotational Raman scattering. Due to the difference in moments of inertia of the two species, the rotational transition frequencies in CD_4 are smaller than the frequencies for the corresponding transitions in CH_4 by a factor of two. In contrast, the translational component of the depolarized scattering spectrum (i.e., the component that originates in DID terms involving the isotropic single-molecule polarizabilities $\alpha^{(o)}$) should be only slightly less broad for CD_4 than for CH_4 (Shelton and Tabisz, 1980a). In fact, the observed spectra for CD_4 and CH_4 virtually superimpose at small frequency shifts, but the high-frequency tails differ markedly, showing "the clear signature of the contribution of CIRS to CH_4 and CD_4 spectra" (Shelton and Tabisz, 1980a).

Excellent agreement has been obtained between calculated two-body depolarized Rayleigh scattering spectra for $CH_4...CH_4$, $CH_4...Ar$ and $CH_4...Xe$ and the spectra obtained from experimental measurements over a range of densities (Penner et al., 1985). For inert gas atoms, $\overleftrightarrow{A}$, $\overleftrightarrow{E}$, and $\overleftrightarrow{\beta}$ vanish by symmetry. The depolarized scattering spectra for mixtures of methane and inert gases lack the A_1A_2 component, but still exhibit the components that depend on A and E for CH_4 and on $\alpha^{(o)}$ for the inert-gas atoms. Most critical as a test of the classical multipole model for CIRS in these cases is the comparison between *ab initio* values of A for CH_4 and the values deduced by fitting the experimental spectra for $CH_4...CH_4$, $CH_4...Ar$, and $CH_4...Xe$ in the frequency range from 200 to 400 cm^{-1}, where the translational component of the spectrum is weak and the rotational component is principally determined by the A-tensor effects (within the model). It should be noted that the experimentally derived values of A depend appreciably on the choice of intermolecular potentials. Penner et al. constructed an effective potential for $CH_4...CH_4$ by starting with the anisotropic RMK potential of Righini et al. (1981), adding the lowest-order anisotropic dispersion term, modifying the C-C repulsive interaction parameters (Meinander and Tabisz, 1983), and then selecting an isotropic potential to reproduce the angular average of the pair distribution function at 295 K (the temperature of the gases in the experimental studies). For CH_4...Ar the isotropic part of the potential derived by Buck et al. (1981) was used, while for CH_4...Xe the potential was approximated in terms of the Kr-Xe potential (Lee et al., 1975). From the depolarized scattering spectra of pure methane and methane-inert gas mixtures, with these assumed inter-molecular potentials, the values obtained for the methane dipole-quadrupole polarizability A are 0.90 ± 0.07 $\mathring{A}^4$ (from the CH_4...CH_4 spectrum), 0.84 ± 0.10 $\mathring{A}^4$ (from the CH_4...Ar spectrum) and 0.87 ± 0.10 $\mathring{A}^4$ (from the CH_4...Xe spectrum), yielding an expected value of $|A| = 0.88 \pm 0.05$ $\mathring{A}^4$. This agrees well with the *ab initio* value $A = 0.79$ $\mathring{A}^4$, obtained from a configuration-interaction calculation with a C/6s, 4p, 3d H/3s, 1p basis (Amos, 1979); the C-H bond distance used in the calculation is 1.108 $\mathring{A}$, the average bond distance in the ground vibrational state. Earlier calculations limited to the self-consistent field level have yielded $A = 0.81$ $\mathring{A}^4$ (John et al., 1980) and $A = 0.79$ $\mathring{A}^4$ (Rivail and Cartier, 1979), both for a C-H bond distance of 1.0935 $\mathring{A}$. Other experimental studies have given A values of 1.0 ± 0.1 $\mathring{A}^4$ (induced light scattering, Shelton and Tabisz, 1980a), 2.35 (virial coefficient data, Isnard et al., 1976, and infrared lineshape analysis, Gray, 1969), 2.67 (molecular beam scattering, Buck et al., 1981), and the group of values 2.71, 0.88, and 0.89 $\mathring{A}^4$ (NMR relaxation times, Rajan et al., 1974). To summarize, the multipole model correctly predicts the shape of the depolarized scattering spectra of gaseous methane and of mixtures of methane and inert gases, over the range of frequency shifts studied. Values of the A tensor deduced by analyzing the spectral intensity agree well with *ab initio* results; and agreement with the A values deduced from the anisotropic parts of intermolecular potentials is satisfactory.

For CF_4 as for CH_4, the classical multipole model accounts for the existence of a depolarized Rayleigh band with collision-induced rotational Raman scattering in the far wings. For CF_4, however, the observed intensity of scattering at large frequency shifts is greater than that calculated using a bond polarizability model (Buckingham, 1967; Buckingham and Tabisz, 1978) to estimate A and E. For SF_6 molecules the A tensor vanishes (as for all centrosymmetric species), and the E-tensor terms give rise to the lowest-order CIRS effect within the multipole model. Again in this case the observed intensity of scattering in the far wings is larger than that calculated from the model. It is interesting to note that double-E transitions (i.e., E_1E_2 terms analogous to the A_1A_2 terms discussed above) dominate the lowest-order E terms, if the bond-polarizability model value for E is assumed. To explain the observed intensities, it is necessary to include higher-multipole effects in the calculations, or to include short-range effects that result in transitions with the same rotational selection rules and a similar profile. The possibility of interaction-induced frame distortion has been raised (Bucaro and Litovitz, 1971; Ho and Tabisz, 1973; Howard-Lock and Taylor, 1974), but estimates by Shelton and Tabisz (1980b) show that its effect is negligible in CIRS by CH_4, CF_4, CCl_4, and SF_6.

ASSESSMENT OF THE CLASSICAL MULTIPOLE MODEL FOR COLLISION-INDUCED PROPERTIES

The classical multipole model necessarily breaks down for molecules interacting at short range, where overlap and exchange effects are significant--yet in a number of the cases discussed above, excellent agreement has been found between observed collision-induced spectra and predictions based on the model, with discrepancies found primarily in the high-frequency spectral wings. Thus, useful information on molecular moments and polarizabilities may be obtained from collision-induced spectra by expressing interaction-induced properties as sums of classical multipole terms and parametrized overlap corrections. Though further information on overlap effects is clearly needed, *ab initio* calculations of the Ne...HF dipole and of inert-gas polarizability anisotropies show an interesting feature: in these two cases, near the minima in the pair potential the long-range model provides more accurate results for the pair property than for the corresponding potential surface.

Direct, quantitative information on the appropriate truncation points of the multipole series for pair properties is limited. However, *ab initio* studies of the Ne...HF dipole (Fowler and Buckingham, 1983) show that truncating the series for μ at the quadrupole-induced dipole introduces substantial error not inherent in the long-range model itself. Rotational transitions with ΔJ ranging to ± 3 and ± 4 are evident in the interaction-induced depolarized scattering spectra of methane (Buckingham and Tabisz, 1977, 1978; Shelton and Tabisz, 1980a; Penner et al., 1985) and in the far-infrared absorption spectra (Birnbaum, 1975; Birnbaum et al., 1983); such transitions are associated with terms varying as R^{-4} to R^{-6} within the classical model. Similarly, spectral analyses make it clear that the lowest-order term in the multipole series for the $N_2...N_2$ and $O_2...O_2$ pair dipoles does not account for the far IR bandshapes.

To assess the importance of the classical R^{-4} to R^{-6} terms in interpreting observed spectra, accurate values of the higher multipoles, higher-multipole polarizabilities and hyperpolarizabilities are needed (Buckingham and Tabisz, 1977; Amos, 1979; Birnbaum et al., (1983). Order of magnitude estimates can be based on distributed-charge, distributed-dipole and bond-polarizability models. If the higher-multipole contributions to measured intensities are comparable to or larger than the overlap corrections, simple point-charge or point-dipole models that fit only the first nonvanishing molecular moment are not adequate for spectral analysis. Also, in such a case, distinct higher-multipole terms should appear explicitly in the expression for the pair dipole or polarizability used to fit the observed spectrum. Subject to these provisos, collision-induced properties can often be represented by addition of a short-range exponential overlap term to a truncated multipole series, particularly for small, weakly interacting molecules with nonvanishing multipoles of low order.

Multipole models are not well suited to approximate interaction-induced changes in dipoles or polarizabilities in two identifiable cases:

a) For highly symmetric species, effects of low order in R^{-1} typically vanish, and the relative importance of overlap, exchange, and dispersion is greater. Clear examples come from studies of inert-gas heterodiatom dipoles, which are entirely attributable to overlap, exchange, orbital distortion (Birnbaum et al., 1984) and dispersion (Buckingham, 1959). Studies of interaction-induced changes in mean polarizabilities of inert-gas atom pairs provide other examples. As noted above, $\Delta\bar{\alpha}$ vanishes at order R^{-3} in the DID model, while the R^{-6} term (second order in the atomic inter-action) is smaller than the exchange contribution at the van der Waals minimum. The classical R^{-6} term is comparable to the R^{-6} dispersion term in order of magnitude (Buckingham and Clarke, 1978). Similarly, difficulties in fitting the collision-induced absorption and CIRS spectra for SF_6 within the classical model are probably tied to the high symmetry of an isolated SF_6 molecule. Inclusion of a short-range overlap term in the collision-induced dipole makes it possible to reproduce the general shape of the far IR band in this case.

b) Slow convergence or divergence of the single-center multi-pole expansion in energetically accessible regions of configuration space restricts the applicability of the multipole model, particu-larly in studies of large molecules. The series diverges if the molecules are oriented so that the distance from the origin in one molecule to a charge element in the other is smaller than an intra-molecular distance—even when the molecular charge distributions do not overlap. As outlined in the next section, collision-induced properties can be evaluated for molecules in such orientations by use of distributed multipole models (cf., Stone, 1981) and distrib-uted polarizability models (Applequist, 1977; Hunt, 1984).

When charge transfer, hydrogen bonding or other specific inter-actions occur, the chemical nature of the interacting species must be considered. Although charge transfer is apparently negligible for the Ne...HF van der Waals complex, it is expected to be important in complexes of HF with species having larger polarizabilities and lower ionization potentials, such as Xe. Controversy about the role of electrostatic interactions in determining the structures and binding energies of noncovalent complexes (for a recent example, see Buckingham and Fowler, 1983, and Baiocchi et al., 1983) may be resolved by *ab initio* studies in which total interaction energies are split into electrostatic, polarization, charge transfer and exchange repulsion components (see, e.g., Morokuma, 1971; Lathan and Morokuma, 1975; Umeyama and Morokuma, 1976, 1977). The results hold interest in the present context because the validity of the multipole model for collision-induced properties should roughly parallel its validity for interaction energies. Kollman (1977) has performed component analyses on the SCF interaction energies of a wide variety of complexes involving first and second row elements. The 431G basis sets (Ditchfield et al., 1971) utilized in this work are relatively small, but the results suggest that electrostatic energy calculations permit "semiquantitative predictions of the energies and shapes" of the complexes. In fact, Kollman has concluded that "the electrostatic energy does an excellent job of predicting the directionality of many interactions, including Cl_2...Cl_2, HF...HF, HCl...HCl, F^-...HOH, and Cl^-...HOH." This by no means implies that the remaining components of the interaction energy are negligible. Obviously, exchange repulsion plays a critical role in determining the intermolecular-distance dependence of the interaction energy. For complexes with bond strengths greater than 1 kcal/mol, the other components are quite important; however, the electrostatic energy often correlates well with the total SCF energy both in relative magnitude and in directionality. When the equilibrium structure of a complex differs from the predictions of a simple electrostatic model, the difference may reflect the inaccuracy of the truncated model as an approximation to the full electrostatic energy (Kollman, 1977). For example, a point-quadrupole model incorrectly predicts a T-shaped structure for Cl_2...Cl_2. To cite a second example (also from Kollman, 1977), for H_3N...SO_2 the minimum in the SCF potential is found when the SO_2 axis is nearly perpendicular to the molecular axis of NH_3. This is close to the minimum found by considering the electrostatic energy alone, but far from the minimum predicted by a dipole-dipole model. Exceptions to the trends of Kollman's electrostatic model are found for Li— acting as an electrophile and for the proton affinities of methyl-substituted amines (Umeyama and Morokuma, 1976); and exceptions are expected for heavy, highly polarizable species (e.g., for charge transfer complexes involving I_2) and for complexes with "back-bonding" in the π electron system. Weakly interacting species of low polarity also fall outside the model. Similar component analyses of interaction-induced dipoles and polarizabilities are needed; these should yield useful insights, particularly if performed for a range of intermolecular distances and relative orientations.

BEYOND THE CLASSICAL MULTIPOLE MODEL

Definitive quantum mechanical results for collision-induced properties can only be obtained from large-scale *ab initio* calculations including correlation effects. To date, few calculations have been performed at this level; results are available for the He...H dipole (Ulrich et al., 1972, Meyer, 1985), the He...H_2, H_2...H_2, and He...Ar dipoles (Meyer, 1985), and the polarizabilities of He...He (Dacre, 1978, 1982a) and Ne...Ne (Dacre, 1982b). Calculations restricted to the self-consistent field level have been performed for the dipoles of the inert-gas pairs Ne...Ar, Ne...Kr, and Ar...Kr (Matcha and Nesbet, 1967, Birnbaum et al., 1984), the dipole of Ne...HF (Fowler and Buckingham, 1983), the polarizabilities of the inert-gas pairs Ar...Ar, Kr...Kr, and Xe...Xe (Dacre, 1982c,d), and the polarizabilities of H_2...H_2 (Bounds, 1979) and N_2...N_2 (Bounds et al., 1981). Factors affecting the accuracy of *ab initio* results have been identified in the discussion of *ab initio* pair polarizability calculations (Hunt, 1985). It should be noted that relatively large basis sets are required to obtain accurate pair properties, particularly when the basis consists of uncontracted Gaussian functions. As shown in the analysis of the Ne...HF dipole (Fowler and Buckingham, 1983), "ghost-orbital" corrections often modify the computed interaction energies and properties significantly (see also Ostlund and Merrifield, 1976). Further corrections are essential when "size-inconsistent" wavefunctions are generated by the *ab initio* method, as in a single- and double-excitation configuration interaction (CISD) calculation. The raw CISD result for a property of a pair of molecules at infinite separation is not equal to the sum of the isolated-molecule properties, also computed at CISD level, indicating size-inconsistency. Meyer (1971, 1973) and Davidson (1974) have proposed approximate methods of accounting for the most important higher excitations. The methods have been used by Diercksen, Kramer, and Sadlej (1981) and extended by Ahlrichs (1979; Zirz and Ahlrichs, 1984).

Although the *ab initio* method is clearly the method of choice when practicable, its extensive computational requirements prompt interest in approximate methods of representing overlap, exchange, and dispersion effects. Such methods should be useful in determining interaction-induced properties near the van der Waals minima of potential surfaces, where numerical precision may be difficult to attain in *ab initio* work.

For molecules interacting at long range, the only correction to the classical multipole model is associated with dispersion effects, the effects of correlations between the fluctuating charge distributions on the molecular centers. For the dipoles of inert-gas heterodiatoms (Byers Brown and Whisnant, 1973; Whisnant and Byers Brown, 1973) and the polarizabilities of H...H

(Buckingham et al., 1973) and He...He (Certain and Fortune, 1971), the dispersion contributions have been evaluated within the framework of perturbation theory. Simple integral expressions analagous to those for the van der Waals energy coefficients C_n (Dalgarno, 1967; Mavroyannis and Stephen, 1962) have also been derived for the long-range dispersion dipole coefficient D_7 (Galatry and Gharbi, 1980; Craig and Thirunamachandran, 1981; see also Hunt, (1980)) and for the polarizability coefficients $\overleftrightarrow{A}_6$ (Hunt et al., 1981). These expressions reflect the nonlinear polarization of each of the interacting molecules by the fields and field gradients of the fluctuating multipoles on the neighboring center (and simultaneously by an applied field, for the polarizability calculations). Additionally, field-induced correlations between the fluctuating multipoles on one center affect the other and thus contribute to dispersion dipoles and polarizabilities. Damping of the long-range contributions as a result of overlap between the interacting charge distributions has been treated by Giraud and Galatry (1980) and by Hunt (1984), but the effects of intramolecular correlation on intermolecular exchange and correlation remain outside the scope of these approximate methods.

At intermediate range, effects of the distribution of charge within the molecules are manifested in the interaction-induced properties. Distribution effects are represented implicitly by the higher-order terms in the multipole model; as noted in the previous section, however, the standard multipole series may diverge in regions of configuration space accessible to molecules with non-overlapping charge distributions. In contrast, by use of point-charge or distributed multipole models, it is possible to generate series that yield the electrostatic potential of a charge distribution and converge at all points outside the distribution itself. An accurate distributed multipole analysis of *ab initio* wave-functions has been developed recently by Stone (1981). As an extension of the Mulliken population analysis, the procedure assigns dipole, quadrupole, and higher multipole populations (as well as charge populations) to pairs of primitive basis functions and thus to atoms and interatomic bonds within a molecule. Typically the multipole expansion of the atomic contributions terminates at a relatively low order determined by the maximum angular momentum quantum number of the orbitals in the basis; also, the expansion of the potential due to the overlap density (or bond contribution) converges rapidly. The analysis requires relatively little computational effort (Stone, 1981); at the same time, it permits the evaluation of electrostatic interaction energies when the lowest-order multipole terms do not dominate (Buckingham and Fowler, 1983).

The distributed multipole analysis describes a fixed charge distribution. For calculations of collision-induced properties, information on the extent and direction of local charge shifts in response to an applied field is needed as well. In one simple

model accounting for the distribution of polarizable matter throughout a molecule, a point-polarizable dipole is located at each of
the atomic nuclei. The dipole induced at a given nucleus is determined by the effective field at the nucleus, taken as the sum of the
external field and the fields set up by the dipoles induced at each
of the other nuclei. Applequist, Carl, and Fung (1972; see also
Applequist, 1977) have parametrized the model to fit the polarizabilities of saturated compounds containing C, H, O, N, and F, with
each of the atomic dipoles assumed to be isotropically polarizable.
The model has been generalized by incorporating anisotropic response
to the local field at each center (Birge, 1980) and higher multipole
induction (Applequist, 1983). The model has found applications in
the theory of depolarized light scattering by liquids (Keyes and
Ladanyi, 1977) and in molecular dynamics simulations of light
scattering by CS_2 (Ladanyi, 1983) and by tetrahedral molecules
(Neumann, 1984; Posch, 1985). Calculations of the polarizability
anisotropy of two SF_6 molecules within this approximation (Buckingham and Hunt, 1981) yield a polarizability anisotropy that exceeds
the single-center DID estimate substantially for certain configurations, but differs little from the DID result after orientational
averaging. Posch (1985) has found that the point-atom polarizability approximation yields average pair anisotropies slightly
smaller than the single-center DID estimates for CCl_4.

A recently developed model (Hunt, 1984) accounts for the *continuous* distribution of polarizable matter in a molecule, using
nonlocal polarizability densities calculated quantum mechanically
in order to determine how charge shifts in response to applied
fields. In this model, the ω-frequency component of the polariza-
tion $\vec{P}_{ind}(\vec{r},\omega)$ induced at point $\vec{r}$ in a molecule by a field $\vec{F}(\vec{r}',\omega)$
due to charges not part of that molecule is given by

$$\vec{P}_{ind}(\vec{r},\omega) = \int d\vec{r}' \; \overleftrightarrow{\alpha}(\vec{r},\vec{r}';\omega) \cdot \vec{F}(\vec{r}',\omega)$$

$$+ \frac{1}{2}\int_{-\infty}^{\infty} d\omega' \int d\vec{r}' \int d\vec{r}'' \; \overleftrightarrow{\beta}(\vec{r},\vec{r}',\vec{r}'';\omega-\omega',\omega'):$$
$$\vec{F}(\vec{r}',\omega-\omega')\,\vec{F}(\vec{r}'',\omega')$$

$$+ \frac{1}{6}\int_{-\infty}^{\infty} d\omega' \int_{-\infty}^{\infty} d\omega'' \int d\vec{r}' \int d\vec{r}'' \int d\vec{r}''' \overleftrightarrow{\gamma}(\vec{r},\vec{r}',\vec{r}'',\vec{r}''';\omega-\omega'-\omega'',\omega',\omega''):$$
$$\vec{F}(\vec{r}',\omega-\omega'-\omega'')\,\vec{F}(\vec{r}'',\omega')\,\vec{F}(\vec{r}''',\omega'')$$

$$+ \cdots . \tag{3}$$

In this equation, $\overleftrightarrow{\alpha}(\vec{r},\vec{r}';\omega)$ represents the linear response to the
applied field, while nonlinear response is described in terms of
$\overleftrightarrow{\beta}$, $\overleftrightarrow{\gamma}$ and higher-order tensors. The response is modeled as nonlocal

because the field-induced shift in charge at one point depends upon the charge redistribution at all other points within the molecule, and because $\overleftrightarrow{\alpha}$, $\overleftrightarrow{\beta}$, and $\overleftrightarrow{\gamma}$ yield the polarization at $\vec{r}$ induced by the perturbing field (rather than by the local field, which includes contributions from charges on the same molecule). The nonlocal polarizability density was originally defined in quantum mechanical sum-over-states form (Maaskant and Oosterhoff, 1964), but numerical evaluation is based on a relationship (Hunt, 1983) between the longitudinal components of the spatial Fourier transforms of the polarizability densities and known or readily computed charge susceptibility densities (Krauss and Neumann, 1979; Krauss and Stevens, 1982; Krauss et al., 1979, 1980; another useful computational method is given by Linder et al., 1980, and Malinowski et al., 1981.)

In calculations of pair dipoles or polarizabilities within this model, the perturbing field $\vec{F}(\vec{r}')$ acting on one molecule is expressed as the sum of the applied field $\vec{E}(\vec{r}')$ and the field due to the polarization of the neighboring molecule. The polarization of the neighbor is then separated into three terms: the permanent polarization determined by the unperturbed charge distribution, the polarization induced by the external field and by interactions with the first molecule, and the purely quantum mechanical fluctuating polarization that gives rise to van der Waals forces. A self-consistent solution of the equations for the polarizations of each of the interacting molecules is obtained by iteration, and the total dipole and polarizability of the pair are evaluated by setting

$$\int d\vec{r} \ [\vec{P}_1(\vec{r}) + \vec{P}_2(\vec{r})] = \vec{\mu} + \overleftrightarrow{\alpha} \cdot \vec{E}_o + \ldots , \qquad (4)$$

where $\vec{P}_i(\vec{r})$ is the net polarization of molecule i in the presence of the other molecule and a uniform applied field $\vec{E}_o$. The resulting pair dipoles and polarizabilities include electrostatic, induction, and dispersion contributions, each corrected for overlap effects (Hunt, 1984). Exchange effects must be treated separately in the model. As a useful first approximation, an additive correction can be obtained by requiring that the full pair wavefunction be properly antisymmetrized (Lacey and Byers Brown, 1974; Oxtoby and Gelbart, 1975).

Short-range exchange effects are incorporated directly in the theoretical framework of the electron-gas model and exchange-perturbation methods. The electron gas model is rooted in the Hohenberg-Kohn theorem (1964), a proof of the existence of a functional that yields the energy of a molecule from the charge density. In calculations to date, the functional appropriate for a uniform electron gas has generally been employed (Harris et al., 1974; Heller et al., 1975), with corrections for nonuniformity via a

21

gradient expansion. Harris and Pratt (1985) have recently obtained
a form of the energy functional that is exact at Hartree-Fock level,
and they have developed a related method of calculating suscepti-
bilities. This advance in density functional theory, together with
a method of treating induction effects beyond first order (Harris,
1984) should soon be exploited in pair property calculations.

Additionally, two exchange-perturbation methods are currently
under investigation for use in pair property calculations: label-
free exchange perturbation theory and a Brillouin-Wigner type of
perturbation theory developed by Stone, Hayes, and Hurst (Stone and
Hayes, 1982; Hayes and Stone, 1984; Hayes, Hurst, and Stone, 1984).
Identification of an appropriate zeroth-order Hamiltonian often
poses a problem in perturbation treatments of intermolecular interactions because it is inconsistent with the Pauli principle to
assign a particular electron to a particular molecular center.
Both the label-free perturbation theory and the Brillouin-Wigner
type of perturbation theory circumvent this problem, though in
different ways.

The label-free formalism constitutes a direct Rayleigh-
Schrödinger perturbation theory with a fully antisymmetrized
zeroth-order wavefunction (Jansen, 1967; Ritchie, 1968a, 1968b).
A projection operator Λ_i is defined for each possible assignment i
of electrons to the interacting molecules. From the antisymmetrized
wavefunction for the pair, the operator Λ_i projects out only those
terms corresponding to the ith electron assignment. For a particular
assignment, the zeroth order Hamiltonian H_{oi} and the perturbation
term V_i are readily identified. The perturbation expansion is
based on the choice of unperturbed Hamiltonian

$$H_o = \sum_i H_{oi} \Lambda_i \qquad (5)$$

leaving the perturbation

$$V = \sum_i V_i \Lambda_i$$

With these definitions, both H_o and V are individually
invariant with respect to exchange of electrons between the interacting systems. Identical results for pair dipoles are obtained
from a direct evaluation at lowest order in the label-free perturbation theory and from application of the Lacey-Byers Brown
exchange-antisymmetrization method (1974). For He...H (Mahanty
and Majumdar, 1982) and for the inert gas heterodiatoms, the
resulting pair dipoles are too small in magnitude. A study of
He...H (Juanós i Timoneda and Hunt, 1985) shows that more accurate
results for the pair dipole (cf. Ulrich et al., 1972; Meyer, 1985)
can be obtained by calculating the energy of the pair in the
presence of an applied field, and differentiating with respect to
the field to find the dipole. The results are not equivalent

because the Hellmann-Feynman theorem is not satisfied for the approximate wavefunctions generated by the label-free theory.

In the Brillouin-Wigner type of perturbation theory, the complete Hamiltonian for the combined system is used without separation into a zeroth-order term and a perturbation term. Slater determinants constructed from the occupied orbitals on both molecules are used as the expansion functions. When carried through second order in the intermolecular interaction, this treatment includes the effects of electrostatic interactions, induction, charge transfer, exchange (both pairwise-additive and nonadditive contributions), and dispersion (Stone, 1984). Modifications of the intramolecular correlation by overlap are represented, as are simultaneous charge-transfer/correlation effects. Interaction energies in good agreement with *ab initio* results have been obtained in studies of He...He and Be...Be.

In conclusion, the classical multipole model for pair properties often provides a useful starting point for the analysis of inter-action-induced spectra. Lineshape and intensity data of high accuracy have recently become available for collision-induced pro-cesses in the gas phase. These data show limitations of the classical model, provide tests for *ab initio* calculations of single-molecule and pair properties, and provide impetus for the development of new approximate methods. The electron gas model with the energy functional determined by Harris and Pratt (1985) and the exchange-perturbation methods hold considerable promise for application in calculating collision-induced properties of molecules at short range. Linking results from these theories with the classical multipole model at long range should make it possible to account for interaction-induced scattering and absorption over an extended frequency range.

APPENDIX: LIST OF SYMBOLS AND ABBREVIATIONS

$\overleftrightarrow{A}$ Molecular dipole-quadrupole polarizability tensor; determines both the dipole induced by the local field gradient $\overleftrightarrow{F}'$ at the center of a molecule and the field-induced quadrupole

A   A single constant that suffices to fix the A tensor for tetrahedral species; for a tetrahedral molecule oriented with vertices at (1,1,1), (1,-1,-1), (-1,1,-1), and (-1,-1,1), $A = A_{xyz}$

$\overleftrightarrow{B}$ Lowest order dipole-quadrupole hyperpolarizability; determines the induced dipole bilinear in a perturbing field and a perturbing field gradient

CI   Configuration interaction

CIRS   Collision-induced rotational Raman scattering

CISD   Configuration-interaction calculations or wave functions with single and double excitations from Hartree-Fock reference determinants

DID   Dipole-induced dipole

$\vec{E}_o$ External field or applied (laser) field

$\overset{\leftrightarrow}{E}$ Molecular dipole-octupole polarizability; determines both the dipole induced in a molecule by the second derivative of the local field and the field-induced octupole

$\vec{F}$ Perturbing field; sum of the external field and the field produced by neighboring molecules

SCF   Self-consistent field

$\overset{\leftrightarrow}{\alpha}^{(o)}$ Polarizability tensor for an isolated molecule

$\overset{\leftrightarrow}{\beta}$ Lowest-order molecular hyperpolarizability; determines the contribution to the dipole moment quadratic in a perturbing field

$\overset{\leftrightarrow}{\gamma}$ Second molecular hyperpolarizability; determines the contribution to the dipole moment cubic in a perturbing field

$\Delta\bar{\alpha}$ Orientationally averaged change in polarizability due to molecular interactions

Θ Quadrupole moment

Φ Hexadecapole moment

Ω Octupole moment

REFERENCES

Ahlrichs, R., 1979, Comput. Phys. Commun., 17:31.
Alder, B. J., Strauss, H. L., and Weis, J. J., 1973a, J. Chem. Phys., 59:1002.
Alder, B. J., Weis, J. J., and Strauss, H. L., 1973b, Phys. Rev. A7:281.
Alder, B. J., Strauss, H. L., Weis, J. J., Hansen, J. P., and Klein, M. L., 1976, Physica (Utrecht), B83:249.
Alder, B. J., Beers, J. C., Strauss, H. L., and Weis, J. J., 1979, J. Chem. Phys., 70:4091.
Amos, R. D., 1979, Molec. Phys., 38:33.

Amos, R. D., 1980, Molec. Phys., 39:1.

Amos, R. D., 1984, Chem. Phys. Letters, 108:185.

Amos, R. D., Buckingham, A. D., and Williams, J. H., 1980, Molec. Phys., 39:1519.

Applequist, J., 1977, Acc. Chem. Res., 10:79.

Applequist, J., 1983, J. Math. Phys., 24:736.

Applequist, J., Carl, J. R., and Fung, K.-K., 1972, J. Amer. Chem. Soc., 94:2952.

Baiocchi, F. A., Reiher, W., and Klemperer, W., 1983, J. Chem. Phys., 79:6428.

Barocchi, F., and Zoppi, M., 1978, Phys. Lett., A66:99.

Berne, B., Bishop, M., and Rahman, A., 1973, J. Chem. Phys., 58:2696.

Birge, R. R., 1980, J. Chem. Phys., 72:5312.

Birnbaum. G., 1975, J. Chem. Phys., 62:59.

Birnbaum, G., 1980, in: "Intermolecular Spectroscopy and Dynamical Properties of Dense Systems, Proceedings of the International School of Physics 'Enrico Fermi,' Course LXXV," J. Van Kranendonk, ed., North-Holland, Amsterdam, 111.

Birnbaum, G., 1985, unpublished results.

Birnbaum, G., and Cohen, E. R., 1975, J. Chem. Phys., 62:3807.

Birnbaum, G., and Cohen, E. R., 1976a, Molec. Phys., 32:161.

Birnbaum, G., and Cohen, E. R., 1976b, Can. J. Phys., 54:475.

Birnbaum, G., and Sutter, H., 1981, Molec. Phys., 42:21.

Birnbaum, G., Frommhold, L., Nencini, L., and Sutter, H., 1983, Chem. Phys. Letters, 100:292.

Birnbaum, G., Krauss, M., and Frommhold, L., 1984, J. Chem. Phys., 80:2669.

Bounds, D. G., 1979, Molec. Phys., 38:2099.

Bounds, D. G., Hinchliffe, A., and Spicer, C. J., 1981, Molec. Phys., 42:73.

Boys, S. F., and Bernardi, F., 1970, Molec. Phys., 42:73.

Bucaro, J. A., and Litovitz, T. A., 1971, J. Chem. Phys., 54:3846.

Buck, U., Schleusener, J., Malik, D. J., and Secrest, D., 1981, J. Chem. Phys., 74:1707.

Buckingham, A. D., 1959, in: "Propriétés optiques et acoustiques des fluids comprimés et actions intermoléculaires, Centre National de la Recherche Scientifique, Paris, 57.

Buckingham, A. D., 1967, Advan. Chem. Phys., 12:107.

Buckingham, A. D., and Clarke, K. L., 1978, Chem. Phys. Letters, 57:321.

Buckingham, A. D., and Disch, R. L., 1963, Proc. Roy. Soc. London, A273:275.

Buckingham, A. D., and Fowler, P. W., 1983, J. Chem. Phys., 79:6426.

Buckingham, A. D., and Hunt, K. L. C., 1981, Molec. Phys., 40:643.

Buckingham, A. D., and Ladd, A. J. C., 1976, Can. J. Phys., 54:611.

Buckingham, A. D., and Tabisz, G. C., 1977, Optics Letters, 1:220.

Buckingham, A. D., and Tabisz, G. C., 1978, Molec. Phys., 36:583.

Buckingham, A. D., Martin, P. H., and Watts, R. S., 1973, Chem. Phys. Letters, 21:186.

Byers Brown, W., and Whisnant, D. M., 1973. Molec. Phys., 25:1385.

Cade, P. E., and Huo, W. H., 1967, J. Chem. Phys., 47:614.
Certain, P. R., and Fortune, P. J., 1971, J. Chem. Phys., 55:5818.
Cohen, E. R., and Birnbaum, G., 1977, J. Chem. Phys., 66:2443.
Cox, T. I., and Madden, P. A., 1980, Molec. Phys., 39:1487.
Cox, T. I., and Madden, P. A., 1981, Molec. Phys., 43:307.
Craig, D. P., and Thirunamachandran, T., 1981, Chem. Phys. Letters, 80:14.
Dacre, P. D., 1978, Molec. Phys., 36:541.
Dacre, P. D., 1981, Can. J. Phys., 59:1429.
Dacre, P. D., 1982a, Molec. Phys., 45:17.
Dacre, P. D., 1982b, Can. J. Phys., 60:963.
Dacre, P. D., 1982c, Molec. Phys., 45:1.
Dacre, P. D., 1982d, Molec. Phys., 47:193.
Dacre, P. D., and Frommhold, L., 1981, J. Chem. Phys., 75:4159.
Dacre, P. D., and Frommhold, L., 1982, J. Chem. Phys., 76:3447.
Dalgarno, A., 1967, Advan. Chem. Phys., 12:143.
Davidson, E. R., 1974, in: "The World of Quantum Chemistry", R. Daudel and B. Pullman, ed., D. Reidel Publishing Company, Boston, 17.
DeLeeuw, F. H., and Dymanus, A., 1973, J. Molec. Spectrosc., 48:427.
Diercksen, G. H. F., Kramer, W. P., and Sadlej, A. J., 1981, Chem. Phys. Letters, 82:117.
Ditchfield, R., Hehre, W. J., and Pople, J. A., 1971, J. Chem. Phys., 54:7241.
Dunning, T. H., 1971, J. Chem. Phys., 55:716.
Fowler, P. W., and Buckingham, A. D., 1983, Molec. Phys., 50:1349.
Fowler, P. W., and Madden, P. A., 1983, Molec. Phys., 49, 913.
Frommhold, L., 1981, Advan. Chem. Phys., 46:1.
Frommhold, L., and Proffitt, M. H., 1979a, Chem. Phys. Letters, 66: 210.
Frommhold, L., and Proffitt, M. H., 1979b, J. Chem. Phys., 70:4803.
Frommhold, L., and Proffitt, M. H., 1980, Phys. Rev., A21:1279.
Frommhold, L., and Proffitt, M. H., 1981, J. Chem. Phys., 74:1512.
Frommhold, L., Hong, K. H., and Proffitt, M. H., 1978a, Molec. Phys., 35:665.
Frommhold, L., Hong, K. H., and Proffitt, M. H., 1978b, Molec. Phys., 35:691.
Galatry, L., and Gharbi, T., 1980, Chem. Phys. Letters, 75:427.
Giraud, M., and Galatry, L., 1980, Chem. Phys. Letters, 75:18.
Gray, C. G., 1969, J. Chem. Phys., 50:549.
Hanley, H. J. M., and Klein, M., 1972, J. Phys. Chem., 76:1743.
Harris, R. A., 1984, J. Chem. Phys., 81:2403.
Harris, R. A., and Pratt, L. R., 1985, J. Chem. Phys., 82:856.
Harris, R. A., Heller, D. F., and Gelbart, W. M., 1974, J. Chem. Phys., 61:3854.
Hayes, I. C., and Stone, A. J., 1984, Molec. Phys., 53:83.
Hayes, I. C., Hurst, G. J. B., and Stone, A. J., 1984, Molec. Phys., 53:107.
Heller, D. F., Harris, R. A., and Gelbart, W. M., 1975, J. Chem. Phys., 62:1947.

Ho, J. H. K., and Tabisz, G. C., 1973, Can. J. Phys., 51:2025.

Hohenberg, P., and Kohn, W., 1964, Phys. Rev. B, 136:864.

Howard-Lock, H. E., and Taylor, R. S., 1974, Can. J. Phys., 52:2436.

Hunt, K. L. C., 1980, Chem. Phys. Letters, 70:336.

Hunt, K. L. C., 1983, J. Chem. Phys., 78:6149.

Hunt, K. L. C., 1984, J. Chem. Phys., 80:393.

Hunt, K. L. C., 1985, this volume.

Hunt, K. L. C., Zilles, B. A., and Bohr, J. E., 1981, J. Chem. Phys., 75:3079.

Isnard, P., Robert, D., and Galatry, L., 1976, Molec. Phys., 31: 1789.

Jansen, L., 1967, Phys. Rev., 162:63.

John, I. G., Backsay, G. B., and Hush, N. S., 1980, Chem. Phys., 51:49.

Juanós i Timoneda, J., and Hunt, K. L. C., 1985, to be published.

Keyes, T., and Ladanyi, B. M., 1977, Molec. Phys. 33:1271.

Kollman, P., 1977, J. Amer. Chem. Soc., 99:4875.

Krauss, M., and Neumann, D. B., 1979, J. Chem. Phys., 71:107.

Krauss, M., and Stevens, W. J., 1982, Chem. Phys. Letters, 85:423.

Krauss, M., Neumann, D. B., and Stevens, W. J., 1979, Chem. Phys. Letters, 66:29.

Krauss, M., Stevens, W. J., and Neumann, D. B., 1980, Chem. Phys. Letters, 85:423.

Kress, J. W., and Kozak, J. J., 1977, J. Chem. Phys., 66:4516.

Lacey, A. J., and Byers Brown, W., 1974, Molec. Phys., 27:1013.

Ladanyi, B. M., 1983, J. Chem. Phys., 78:2189.

Ladd, A. J. C., Litovitz, T. A., and Montrose, C. J., 1979, J. Chem. Phys., 68:4031.

Lathan, W. A., and Morokuma, K., 1975, J. Am. Chem. Soc., 97:3617.

Lee, J. K., Henderson, D., and Barker, J. A., 1975, Molec. Phys., 29:429.

Linder, B., Lee, K. F., Malinowski, P., and Tanner, A. C., 1980, Chem. Phys., 52:353.

Losonczy, M., Moskowitz, J. W., and Stillinger, F. H., 1974, J. Chem. Phys., 61:2438.

Maaskant, W. J. A., and Oosterhoff, L. J., 1964, Molec. Phys., 8:319.

Madden, P. A., and Cox, T. I., 1981, Molec. Phys., 43:287.

Madden, P. A., and Tildesley, D. J., 1983, Molec. Phys., 49:193.

Mahanty, J., and Majumdar, C. K., 1982, Phys. Rev. A, 26:2334.

Malinowski, P., Tanner, A. C., Lee, K. F., and Linder, B., 1981, Chem. Phys., 62:423.

Matcha, R. L., and Nesbet, R. K., 1967, Phys. Rev., 160:72.

Mavroyannis, C., and Stephen, M. J., 1962, Molec. Phys., 5:629.

Meinander, N., and Tabisz, G. C., 1983, J. Chem. Phys., 79:416.

Meyer, W., 1971, Int. J. Quantum Chem. Symp., 5:341.

Meyer, W., 1973, J. Chem. Phys., 58:1017.

Meyer, W., 1985, this volume.

Morokuma, K., 1971, J. Chem. Phys., 55:1236.

Muenter, J. S., 1972, J. Chem. Phys., 56:5409.

Neumann, M., 1984, Molec. Phys., 53:187.

Ostlund, N. S., and Merrifield, D. L., 1976, Chem. Phys. Letters, 39:612.

Oxtoby, D. W., and Gelbart, W. M., 1975, Molec. Phys., 30:535.

Penner, A. R., Meinander, N., and Tabisz, G. C., 1985, Molec. Phys., 54:479.

Poll, J. D., and Hunt, J. L., 1981, Can. J. Phys., 59:1448.

Posch, H., 1985, this volume.

Proffitt, M. H., and Frommhold, L., 1979, Phys. Rev. Lett., 42:1473.

Proffitt, M. H., and Frommhold, L., 1980, J. Chem. Phys., 72:1377.

Proffitt, M. H., Keto, J. W., and Frommhold, L., 1980, Phys. Rev. Lett., 45:1843.

Proffitt, M. H., Keto, J. W., and Frommhold, L., 1981, Can. J. Phys., 59:1459.

Rajan, S., Lalita, K., and Babu, S. V., 1974, J. Magn. Reson., 16:115.

Righini, R., Maki, K., and Klein, M. L., 1981, Chem. Phys. Letters, 80:301.

Ritchie, A. B., 1968a, Phys. Rev., 171:125.

Ritchie, A. B., 1968b, J. Chem. Phys., 49:2167.

Rivail, J. L., and Cartier, A., 1979, Chem. Phys. Letters, 61:469.

Roetti, C., and Clementi, E., 1974, J. Chem. Phys., 60:4725.

Schaefer, H. F., 1972, "The Electronic Structure of Atoms and Molecules," Addison-Wesley Publishing Company, Reading.

Shelton, D. P., and Tabisz, G. C., 1980a, Molec. Phys., 40:299.

Shelton, D. P., and Tabisz, G. C., 1980b, Chem. Phys. Letters, 69:125.

Silberstein, L., 1917, Phil. Mag., 33:92, 521.

Sileo, R. N., and Cool, T. A., 1976, J. Chem. Phys., 65:117.

Steed, J. M., Dixon, T. A., and Klemperer, W., 1979, J. Chem. Phys., 70:4095.

Stone, A. J., 1981, Chem. Phys. Letters, 83:233.

Stone, A. J., 1984, in: "Molecular Liquids--Dynamics and Interactions", A. J. Barnes, W. J. Orville-Thomas, and J. Yarwood, ed., D. Reidel Publishing Company, Boston, 1.

Stone, A. J., and Hayes, I. C., 1982, Faraday Disc. Chem. Soc., 73:19, 109, 113.

Ulrich, B. T., Ford, L., and Browne, J. C., 1972, J. Chem. Phys., 57:2906.

Umeyama, H., and Morokuma, K., 1976, J. Am. Chem. Soc., 98:4400.

Umeyama, H., and Morokuma, K., 1977, J. Am. Chem. Soc., 99:1316.

Werner, H.-J., and Meyer, W., 1976, Phys. Rev. A, 13:13.

Whisnant, D. M., and Byers Brown, W., Molec. Phys. 26:1105.

Williams, J. H., and Amos, R. D., 1980, Chem. Phys. Letters, 70:162.

Zirz, C., and Ahlrichs, R., 1984, Inorg. Chem., 23:26.

AB INITIO CALCULATIONS OF COLLISION INDUCED DIPOLE MOMENTS

Wilfried Meyer

Fachbereich Chemie
Universität Kaiserslautern
D-675 Kaiserslautern, Germany

ABSTRACT

    Theoretical attempts to obtain dipole moment functions of colli-
sion complexes are reviewed. The induced dipole moments represent
rather small distortions of the electron distribution. Therefore,
perturbation theory has been used to investigate contributions from
induction, exchange and dispersion interactions separately. In order
to include couplings between these effects, the collision complex is
best treated as a molecule in SCF and CI type calculations which can
be carried to high numerical significance. SCF plus approximate dispersion dipoles appear to yield good agreement with experiment for
most dissimilar rare gas systems, but this is due to fortuitous cancellation of the usually neglected intraatomic correlation and underestimated dispersion. As exemplified here for He-Ar, intraatomic
correlation raises the exchange dipole by as much as 30%, and the
dispersion dipole turns out three times larger than a perturbation
estimate of the leading term has indicated. The basis superposition
error, which may be large in CI calculations, is effectively avoided
by using nonorthogonal local orbital sets. For the complexes He-H_2
and H_2-H_2, orientation dependent dipole functions are presented with
an estimated accuracy of about 2%. It is shown that the adequate
treatment of induction contributions may require a multiconfiguration
reference CI. Based on an eight-term H_2-H_2 dipole function and an
anisotropic potential, low temperature emission spectra are obtained
from a purely quantum mechanical treatment.

INTRODUCTION

Translational and rotational collision induced absorption (CIA) spectra typically show rather broad line shapes due to the short lifetime of the collision complexes. The intensity depends sensitively on the dipole moment function and the interaction potential over only a relatively small region around the collision diameter (Birnbaum et al., 1981, 1982). While there are numerous sources of information on potentials, such as spectroscopic data, molecular beam experiments or bulk properties (for a review see, e.g., Maitland et al., 1981), the dipole moment function appears to be accessible only from inverting CIA spectra or from theoretical treatments. Theoretical dipole moment functions are important not only for the fundamental understanding of the CIA phenomenon, but in particular for predicting line shapes and intensities for temperatures not investigated, or not accessible in the laboratory. This is of considerable interest for systems like H_2-H_2, and H_2 with noble gas atoms, whose CIA spectra are essential for an understanding of the thermal emission of planetary atmospheres, an important source of information on these atmospheres (Trafton, 1966; Linsky, 1969; Tipping, 1985).

The mechanisms which generate the collision induced dipole moments have first been discussed by Buckingham (1959, 1967). They are, of course, closely related to the interaction terms known from van der Waals potentials. At long range, dispersion forces lead to a dipole moment function which can be expressed in form of an inverse odd power expansion starting with D_7R^{-7}, while a static multipole moment of order ℓ creates an induced moment proportional to $R^{-\ell-2}$. At short range, where the electron distributions overlap, exchange effects lead to an "overlap" dipole contribution with a basically exponential distance dependence, and to a damping of the dispersion moment as well. In cases with largely different electronegativities of the two colliding molecules, there may also be significant charge transfer contributions to the dipole moment. For systems with a non-vanishing static moment, the static-induced moment is usually dominant at the distances of interest. Otherwise, e.g. for dissimilar noble gas atoms, the overlap contribution dominates around the collision diameter, with dispersion dipoles contributing in the range from -10% to -40%.

A reliable determination of collision induced dipole moments raises problems similar to the well known ones encountered in calculations of van der Waals potentials. First of all, the dipole moments are rather small and represent only minor distortions of the charge distribution. E.g., for He-Ar, the dipole moment of 0.0075 a.u. (1 a.u. = 2.54 Debye) at the conventional collision diameter (5.65 Bohr) corresponds to a shift of the Ar outer-shell charge center by only 0.00075 Bohr, as compared to its "radius" of $\sqrt{<r^2>}/10$ ~ 1.3 Bohr, or to a charge transfer of only 0.001 e^-. A perturbational treatment, which seems natural for such small effects, runs at a shorter range into the problems notorious for the perturbational handling of exchange effects. The application of standard quantum chemical methods, i.e. variational SCF and CI, which can nowadays be performed with high numerical significance, faces the problem of the so-called basis set superposition error: Since a finite basis set of one-electron functions is necessarily incomplete, the electrons of collision partner A make some use of the basis functions of collision partner B, thus leading to artificial charge distortions. These distortions become more apparent in a calculation for A only, but using the full basis of the collision complex AB. A straight subtraction of the two dipole moments obtained in this way from that of the collision complex - the counterpoise method of Boys and Bernardi (1970) often used for interaction potentials - is justified only when the superposition errors are relatively small, because there is a tendency for overcorrection. It is clear, then, that the computation of collision induced dipole moments is rather demanding even for relatively small systems. And indeed, only a few calculations have been performed so far. In this contribution we briefly discuss the previous work, which concerns dissimilar rare gas atoms and the system He-H2, and present new results on the systems He-Ar, He-H2 and H2-H2 which for the first time account for electron correlation effects on the dispersion part as well as on the exchange part of the induced dipole moments. Finally, collision induced emission spectra are discussed for H2-H2 at very low temperatures, as calculated in a fully quantum mechanical treatment of the collision process, using for the first time in such work an anisotropic potential.

COLLISION SYSTEMS OF RARE GAS ATOMS

Dipole moments of dissimilar rare gas atom collision complexes originate from dispersion and exchange effects only. The overlap or exchange dipole moment has first been investigated by Matcha and Nesbet (1967) for He-Ne, He-Ar, and Ne-Ar. This SCF calculation used so-called "double zeta plus polarization" basis sets optimized at the very short distance of 2 Bohr. At distances around the collision diameter "severe numerical cancellations" occurred, i.e. basis set superposition errors probably enhanced by insufficient numerical precision of the integral evaluation. The calculations were, therefore, performed at relatively small separations and the results subsequently extrapolated on the basis of their apparent exponential R-dependence. A theoretical line shape for He-Ar, obtained by McQuarrie and Bernstein (1968) from Matcha and Nesbet's dipole moment function, indicated that this function was somewhat too small. This prompted Levine (1967) to estimate the leading D7 coefficient for the dispersion dipole moment by a semiclassical treatment based on the Drude model. Byers Brown and Whisnant (1973) reduced the perturbational expression for D7 to frequency dependent atomic properties (a reformulation has been given by Galatry and Gharbi in 1980). These properties involve dipole and quadrupole transition moments between excited states and are therefore hardly accessible from optical properties. The theoretical determination of such properties is very difficult, and accurate results are available only for H and He from a variation perturbation treatment by Whisnant and Byers Brown

(1973). However, these authors succeeded in relating the dominant term D_7 to the van der Waals coefficient C_6 and a ratio of atomic quantities which can be obtained following procedures used for calculating atomic polarizabilities. They determined D_7 values for rare gas atom pairs up to Ar-Kr. The approximation involved was shown to be in error by only about 10% for He-He but the accuracy for heavier systems is difficult to assess. The D_7 values derived in this way are the only ones available so far. At the collision diameter the D_7 dispersion dipole moments account for about -10% to -20% of the overlap dipole, except for He-Ne. It should be kept in mind, though, that significant contributions are to be expected from higher-order terms D_9, D_{11} etc., when judged from the contribution of the corresponding terms to the van der Waals interaction potential at collision diameter distances. These have never been estimated thus far.

The negative dispersion dipole, in combination with the Matcha and Nesbet SCF dipole, increased the discrepancy with experiment. Lacey and Byers Brown (1974) then derived a theory of the overlap contribution based on the assumption of pure exchange between otherwise undistorted Hartree-Fock wavefunctions of the colliding atoms, thus completely avoiding the source of superposition errors. As had already been discussed by Buckingham (1959) for He-H, the dominant contribution leads to the rule that the larger atom is negative. The exchange dipoles fall off nearly exponentially but they depend critically on the description of the orbital tails, as indicated by the inadequacy of a double zeta basis set for He-Ne and He-Ar. There was good agreement with Matcha and Nesbet's results for Ne-Ar, but the opposite sign for He-Ne and a difference of a factor of two for He-Ar were obtained. In the latter case, excellent agreement was reached with dipole curves deduced from experiment. For H-He, however, there is a disturbing discrepancy with the CI calculations of Ulrich et al. (1972), which has apparently not been resolved thus far. There are no experimental data for this system but it is potentially of astrophysical interest. As a convenient test for computational procedures which are discussed below we have performed exploratory calculations for H-He. The results are displayed in Fig. 1. We find good agreement with the dispersion dipole of Byers Brown at long range, but our exchange dipole is considerably larger than his, in fair agreement with Ulrich et al.'s results at short distances. On the other hand, the dispersion dipole of the latter is too large by one order of magnitude. The rather erratic shape of their long range potential indicates inconsistencies in their calculations.

Based on Smith's (1972) distortion model for exclusion principle controlled interactions, which implies additive and transferrable atomic dipole moments, Bentley (1979) analyzed molecular multipole moments for homonuclear diatomics from SCF wavefunctions and derived heteronuclear dipole moments in qualitative agreement with Matcha and Nesbet's values. Quantitatively reliable results can certainly not be expected from such a treatment. This remark also applies to the very recent treatment of exchange and dispersion dipoles on the basis of electron gas theory and Drude model shell displacements by Pearson

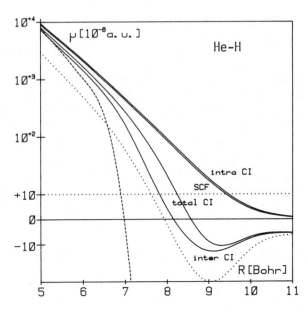

Fig. 1 Collision induced dipole moment for He-H. Full lines:
this work; intra: only He intraatomic correlation; inter:
only H-He interatomic correlation. Dotted lines: Lacey and
Byers Brown (1974); dashed line: Ulrich, Ford and Browne
(1972). Note the change to logarithmic scale at 10^{-5} a.u.

et al. (1984). Deviations from more accurate results are in the
order of a factor of two for both effects. For completeness, we
mention that pure exchange dipoles have also been calculated by
Shlyapnikov and Shmator (1980) with particular emphasis on the tails
of the wavefunction. Their results for He-Ne and Ar-Kr are in fair
agreement with those of Lacey and Byers Brown.

A careful comparison of theoretical line shapes with experiment
has been performed by Birnbaum, Brown and Frommhold (1981) for mixtures of Ar with He, Ne, and Kr. Using semiempirical potentials of
Hartree-Fock plus dispersion (HFD) type, empirical exponential-plus-
dispersion dipole functions were found to fit the experimental
profiles perfectly for Ar-Ne and Ar-Kr, but there remained a +4%
average deviation for He-Ar. While the theoretical dipoles of Lacey
and Byers Brown (1974) were in agreement with empirical ones to
within 5% and 15% for He-Ar and Ar-Kr, respectively, there were
rather large deviations of -45% and -30% for Ne-Ar and Ne-Kr, respectively. These findings prompted Birnbaum, Krauss and Frommhold
(1984) to recalculate the overlap dipole from Hartree-Fock wavefunctions. The STO basis set was again essentially of double zeta
quality, but augmented by single diffuse s and d functions optimized
for dipole polarizability. No systematic attempt was made to examine

larger basis sets, but saturation of the basis set was indicated by small effects from orbital exponent variation. Agreement with experiment was significantly improved in the case of Ne-Ar for which the theoretical dipole moment appears to be correct to within 5%. For Ar-Kr, however, it is now too large by about 20%. The surprisingly large differences between the pure exchange and the SCF dipole results should not be taken as evidence for a large distortion contribution in SCF since they are probably connected with some approximations made in the actual calculations of Lacey and Byers Brown.

Considering the accuracy of the experimental intensities which is in the order of 10% (Birnbaum et al., 1981), and the sensitivity of the theoretical intensities to the potential – a 1% variation in the collision diameter may cause a change of 10% in the intensities – the overall agreement between experiment and theory based on the Hartree-Fock plus dispersion dipole appears satisfactory. We point out, however, that to a certain extent the agreement is fortuitous. Electron correlation is included only in form of the leading D_7 dispersion term derived by Whisnant and Byers Brown (1973). No estimate exists for higher order terms. They may well add up to a contribution comparable to D_7 and therefore reduce the intensities by 20 to 30%. On the other hand, the inclusion of intraatomic correlation increases the "size" of the noble gas atoms, as the correlated $\langle r^2 \rangle$ expectation values indicate, which are larger than the corresponding HF values by 0.6% for He and Ar, and by a surprising 3% for Ne (Reinsch and Meyer, 1976). Therefore, the exchange interaction and thus the overlap dipole may be expected to increase. Indeed, intraatomic correlation enhances the exchange repulsion for He-He and He-H$_2$ by about +10% (Bertoncini and Wahl, 1973; Meyer et al., 1980), but for Ne-Ne by as much as 20% (Meyer and Reinsch, 1978). A similar increase in the exchange dipole is quite likely, and it may be expected to cancel to some extent the neglected higher order dispersion terms. The delicate balance between these two effects is probably responsible for the Hartree-Fock plus D_7 dipole being too small for He-Ar but too large for Ne-Kr.

A CI calculation of these two correlation effects seems very desirable but meets with severe problems. First of all, the basis set superposition errors are usually much larger for correlated wavefunctions since saturation of the correlation space is out of question. Secondly, the convergence of dispersion effects with increase of the basis set is known to be extremely slow. If the basis set is tailored to account especially well for dispersion terms – i.e. by adding mainly diffuse functions – there is an artificial enhancement of the effect of the intraatomic correlation because electron charge moves into the outer fringes of the wavefunction. A way out may be to calculate the two correlation effects separately using different basis sets, but there is a non-negligible coupling between the two, as well known from work concerning the dispersion potential (Maeder and Kutzelnigg, 1976; Meyer et al., 1980).

In view of these problems, we have undertaken to calculate correlated dipoles for He-Ar - the smallest system for which accurate measurements are available - using the following procedures (Meyer and Frommhold, 1985):

1) The Hartree-Fock wavefunction is transformed to localized orbitals in order to identify intraatomic and interatomic (dispersion) correlation terms.

2) Superposition errors are avoided at the CI level by restricting the intraatomic correlation to a "local" orbital basis which is made from the atoms "own" basis functions only by projecting out the occupied Hartree-Fock orbitals. This is easily implemented in the self-consistent electron pairs (SCEP) technique (Meyer, 1976a; Meyer et al., 1984), which allows use of different orbital sets for different electron pairs, or even non-orthogonal external orbitals.

3) The Hartree-Fock basis set of Gaussian type functions (GTOs) (14s, 10p contracted to 10s, 7p for Ar, 10s contracted to 6s for He) is first augmented by 2d, 1f sets for Ar and 2p, 1d sets for He, which are carefully optimized for intraatomic correlation. Single diffuse d and f sets for Ar as well as p and d sets for He are then added and optimized to account for dipole and quadrupole atom polarizabilities as well as the corresponding terms of the dispersion attraction.

4) The size-consistency coupled electron pair approximation (CEPA-1) (Meyer, 1973; Kutzelnigg, 1978) is used in order to account

Table 1. Interaction energies and dipole moments for He-Ar at R = 5.5 Bohr, in 10^{-6} a.u.

	E	μ
SCF	826	7618
SCF + intra-CI	1159	10090
SCF + inter-CI	-57	5132
SCF + intra- and inter-CI	391	7455
Experiment	240[b]	7240[a]
other calculations:		
Matcha and Nesbet (1967), SCF	900	4050
Whisnant and Byers Brown (1973), D7		-821
Lacey and Byers Brown (1974), exchange		7560
exchange + D7		6740
Birnbaum et al. (1984), SCF	810	7300
SCF + D7		6480
Ahlrichs et al. (1977), SCF	819	

[a]"best fit" from Birnbaum et al. (1981)
[b]HFD fit potential from Aziz et al. (1979)

for higher-order substitutions, since otherwise the intraatomic correlation reduces the dispersion terms unduly.

The various contributions to the dipole moment, as obtained at R = 5.5 Bohr, which is slightly below the collision diameter, are shown in Table 1. The SCF (exchange plus distortion) dipole is fairly close to the best previous value (Birnbaum et al., 1984), but the deviation of 4% is not insignificnat for the comparison with experiment. It is difficult to say which value is more reliable. STO functions have a certain advantage in describing the tail region of the wavefunction, but our 9p GTO set is more flexible than the 4p STO set. Intraatomic correlation is seen to increase the overlap dipole by surprising 30%. Interatom correlation adds a dispersion dipole which is about three times as large as the D7 term of Whisnant and Byers Brown (1973) and brings the total dipole back to a value which is only slightly smaller than the pure SCF value. It deviates by only +3% from the "best fit" empirical dipole of Birnbaum et al. (1981). This is a rather gratifying agreement, probably somewhat fortuitous again since we do not expect our intra- and interatomic correlation contributions to have individually converged to this margin. From a counterpoise calculation we find the basis superposition error to amount to only 0.5% at both levels, SCF and CI, well below the 5% accuracy we may claim for the final dipole moment. The dispersion dipole multiplied by R^7 shows a maximum at about 5.2 Bohr, indicating the range where short range damping effects begin to effectively reduce the dispersion terms. Because the damping functions are unknown, it is difficult to separate the individual dispersion terms from the total dispersion dipole. Figure 2 displays the He-Ar dipole functions from various sources. None of the theoretical curves show a curvature comparable to that of the "best fit" empirical dipole function. It is difficult to see which effect could cause this curvature. The empirical function has an unreasonably large D7 term, and the fit of the experimental intensities is not good. Thus, an experimental reinvesttigation of the He-Ar system would be desirable.

In order to further characterize our calculation, we note that our Hartree-Fock repulsion energy is in complete agreement with earlier calculations (Ahlrichs et al., 1977; Birnbaum et al., 1984), but intraatomic correlation increases this repulsion by as much as 40%. On the other hand, our dispersion attraction is considerable larger than that implied by the long-range coefficients C_6 to C_{10} and the HFD model damping (Aziz et al., 1979). The total potential shows a well depth of 22 K at 6.75 Bohr as compared to 29.5 K at 6.58 Bohr from the most recent semi-empirical potential (Aziz et al., 1979). This is reasonable for a calculation limited to f-functions and indicates that our dipole moment is probably slightly too large. That intraatomic correlation is really essential is underlined by the fact that its neglect leads to a well depth of 45 K.

The He-Ar calculations presented here demonstrate that exchange effects due to intraatomic correlation and higher order dispersion terms may contribute significantly to the induced dipole. Only by

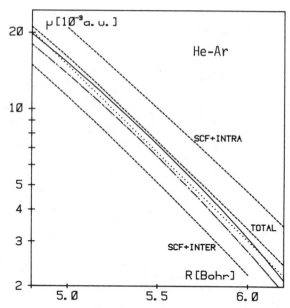

Fig. 2 Collision induced dipole moment for He-Ar. Dashed lines:
this work, SCF and CEPA calculations. Full line: "best fit"
dipole of Birnbaum et al. (1981). Dashed-dotted line:
exchange + D7 dipole of Lacey and Byers Brown (1974).
Dotted line: SCF + D7 dipole of Birnbaum et al. (1984).

chance do they cancel each other to a large extent, as in He-Ar.
Their combined contribution may well account for the differences
between theory and experiment remaining to this day for other rare
gas systems.

INDUCED DIPOLE MOMENTS FOR He-H$_2$ AND H$_2$-H$_2$

As already mentioned, collision induced absorption by He-H$_2$ and
H$_2$-H$_2$ is very important for the understanding of the thermal emission
from the atmospheres of the major planets. Laboratory measurements
have recently been performed for these two systems down to 77 K
(Birnbaum, 1978), but the astrophysical applications require extrapolations to even lower temperatures and thus call for reliable
dipole moment functions. The leading contributions to the dipole
moments is expected to be induced by the permanent quadrupole moment
of H$_2$. While the long range expansion coefficients are readily obtained from known quantities, the exchange effects, which are signif-

icant around the collision diameter, can only be obtained from quantum chemical calculations.

The first calculation on a molecular collision complex has been performed by Berns et al. (1978) for He-H_2. Using a valence bond approach based on orbitals as obtained from the noninteracting systems, they could avoid superposition errors as well as artifacts from the orthogonalization of the orbitals, but they had to accept severe limitations in the calculations due to the nonorthogonality of the orbitals. Selecting different sets of VB structures, various exchange and dispersion contributions to the dipole moments could be analyzed. The D_{23} induction term turned out to follow remarkably closely an R^{-4} dependence. It is dominated by the exponentially increasing exchange term D_{01} only from the collision diameter on inward. Dispersion contributions were found to be small everywhere ($D_7 = 61.8$) and even changed sign at shorter distances.

Wormer and van Dijk (1979) concluded from this result that an SCF wavefunction should account well for all important dipole contributions and performed such calculations for various angles and bond distances. Differences to the former results were in the range of 5-10%. These dipole moments have been used in a recent analysis of the experimental He-H_2 far infrared spectrum together with an empirical isotropic potential and have been shown to yield intensities which are lower than the observed ones by about 15-20% (Birnbaum et al., 1984). This discrepancy may originate from the neglect of electron correlation and vibrational averaging in the dipole moment, from defects in the isotropic potential used, or perhaps from neglecting the anisotropic components of the potential.

In particular in view of the important question whether or not line shape calculations for systems involving H_2 may indeed be reduced to considering only isotropic potentials, as always has been done so far, it seemed very desirable to obtain a reliable theoretical dipole moment function. We have, therefore, recalculated the He-H_2 dipole moment from highly correlated CI wavefunctions at the mean bond length of $\langle r_{HH} \rangle = 1.449$ Bohr. Using this bond length effectively accounts for vibrational averaging as suggested earlier (Meyer, 1976b). Guided by the experience from our work on the He-H_2 interaction potential (Meyer et al., 1980), a mixed two-center/ one-center basis set of GTOs has been used in order to avoid artificial enhancement of the anisotropies. Thus, 7s and 1p inner GTOs are attached to each proton, but more diffuse 2s, 2p and 2d GTO sets are placed at the center of the molecule. For He, a 10s, 4p, 2d GTO set is used. This basis set of 52 contracted functions accounts for about 95% of the intra- and intermolecular correlation energies. Table 2 displays the dipole polarizabilities and static moments obtained for He and H_2, respectively. At the CI level, all properties are in agreement with accurate values to within one percent, except for the small q_4 which deviates somewhat more. It should be noted that at the SCF level α(He) is too small by 5% whereas $q_2(H_2)$ is too large by 8% so that the induction dipole D_{23} overshoots by 3%. An

Table 2. Pertinent properties of He, H_2 and He-H_2
at long range, in atomic units.

		SCF	CI	accurate[a]
He	α	1.320	1.382	1.385
H_2	$\alpha_{\parallel}$	6.773	6.765	6.766
	$\alpha_{\perp}$	4.762	4.714	4.752
	q_2	0.525	0.480	0.485
	q_4	0.359	0.333	0.353
He-H_2	D_{23}[b]	1.20	1.17	1.163
H_2-H_2	D_{2023}[b]	4.94	4.62	4.552
	D_{2233}	0.77	0.72	0.712

[a]Kolos and Wolniewicz (1967); Karl et al. (1975);
Poll and Wolniewicz (1978).
[b]obtained by fitting the long range part of the
calculated dipole moment function.

unexpected complication arises from the fact that q_2 is still too
large by 4% for the principal natural orbital of a correlated H_2.
This implies that a standard type CI calculation including single and
double substitutions from the Hartree-Fock reference function would
yield the same error for the induction dipole. One has, therefore,
to include either triple substitutions or, as we have chosen here,
all single and double substitutions from a multiconfigurational reference function comprising the four most important H_2 double substitutions, in addition to the Hartree-Fock function. The SCEP technique, which has recently been extended to the multiconfiguration
reference case (Werner and Reinsch, 1982), has been used in our calculation with an internally contracted reference function (Meyer,
1978).

As usual, angular and distance dependence of the dipole moment
are separated by an expression in spherical harmonics (Poll and van
Kranendonk, 1961),

$$\mu_M(\vec{r},\vec{R}) = \frac{4\pi}{\sqrt{3}} D_{\lambda L}(r,R) \ Y_\lambda^m(\hat{r}) \ Y_L^{M-m}(\hat{R}) \ C(\lambda L1;m,M-m) \ . \tag{1}$$

Summation over indices appearing repeatedly is understood. $\vec{r}$ is the vector connecting the protons of H_2 and $\vec{R}$ connects He with the center of H_2; $\hat{r}$ and R are the corresponding unit vectors. In order to relate the expansion coefficients $D_{\lambda L}$ to the dipole moments calculated in a body-fixed frame, one may choose $\vec{R}$ as z-axis. This leads to M=m, $Y_L^{M-m}=(2L+1/4\pi)^{1/2}$, and

$$\mu_M(\vec{r},\vec{R}) = \left(\frac{4\pi(2L+1)}{3}\right)^{1/2} D_{\lambda L}(r,R) \; Y_\lambda^M(\hat{r}) \; C(\lambda L1;M0) \; . \tag{2}$$

With $\mu_z = \mu_0$ and $\mu_x = -\sqrt{2}\,Re\{\mu_1\}$, one gets explicitly

$$\mu_z = \left[\sqrt{\lambda+1}\; D_{\lambda,\lambda+1} - \sqrt{\lambda}\; D_{\lambda,\lambda-1}\right] P_\lambda^0(\hat{r}\cdot\hat{R}) \; , \tag{3}$$

$$\mu_x = -\left[\sqrt{\lambda}\; D_{\lambda,\lambda+1} + \sqrt{\lambda+1}\; D_{\lambda,\lambda-1}\right] P_\lambda^1(\hat{r}\cdot\hat{R}) \; \left(\frac{(\lambda-1)!}{(\lambda+1)!}\right)^{1/2} \; . \tag{4}$$

At long range, one finds (Poll and van Kranendonk, 1961)

$$D_{\lambda,\lambda+1} = \alpha \; q_\lambda \; \sqrt{\lambda+1} \; R^{-\lambda-2} \; ; \; D_{\lambda,\lambda-1} = 0 \; . \tag{5}$$

Dipole moments have been calculated for three orientations of the H_2, namely for the angles $(\hat{r},\vec{R})= 0^0$, 45^0 and 90^0, respectively. This allows to determine the four leading terms in the expansion (1). The calculated coefficients $D_{\lambda L}$ are displayed in Fig. 3. As shown in Table 3, fitting the calculated He-H_2 dipole moment to its asymptotic form yields a D_{23} in very good agreement with the accurate value. This demonstrates that the CI wavefunction used separates correctly for large internuclear distances. As in the case of He-Ar, intramolecular and intermolecular correlation, identified on the basis of the localized HF orbitals, are both by no means negligible. From Table 3 it can be seen that intramolecular correlation mainly affects D_{23} via the correction of $q_2(H_2)$ and $\alpha(He)$ as discussed above, while the dispersion reduces the isotropic exchange term. At 5 Bohr, where D_{01} is dominant, this reduction amounts to about 15%. A change in sign as predicted by Berns et al. (1978) is not observed. A long range fit of $D_{01}(R)$ yields $\simeq -0.7R^{-7}$. These calculations will be described in detail elsewhere (Meyer et al., 1985). As discussed by Borysow and Frommhold (1985), our dipole moments lead to theoretical line shapes in close agreement with experiment.

40

Table 3. Correlation effects on the leading terms D_{01} and D_{23}
for He-H_2 (in 10^{-6} a.u.).

R [Bohr]	5.0		7.0	
	D_{01}	D_{23}	D_{01}	D_{23}
SCF	809	263	30	54
SCF + intra-CI	786	258	30	51
SCF + intra- and inter-CI	676	255	16	51

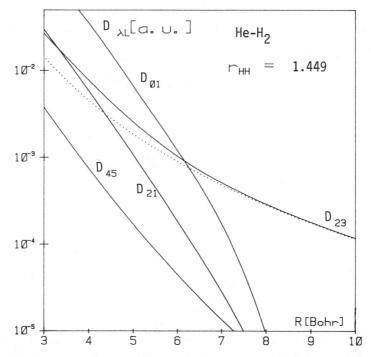

Fig. 3 Dipole moment expansion coefficients $D_{\lambda L}(R)$ for He-H_2, see
Eq. (4), in atomic units. Dotted line: asymptotic form, see
Eq. (5).

For H_2-H_2, the quadrupole induced anisotropic dipole is dominant
over all distances of interest. Due to the defect in q_2, this term
is off by 8% for a SCF calculation, and still by 4% for singles and
doubles CI. Thus we have again applied a multiconfiguration reference function comprised of the 9 leading configurations which account
for intramolecular correlation. The basis set used is the same as
just described. The dipole moment function is expanded as

$$\mu_M(\vec{r}1,\vec{r}2,\vec{R}) = \frac{(4\pi)^{3/2}}{\sqrt{3}} D_{\lambda_1\lambda_2\lambda L}(r1,r2,R) \ Y_{\lambda_1}^{m1}(\hat{r}1)Y_{\lambda_2}^{m2}(\hat{r}2)Y_L^{M-m}(\hat{R})$$

$$\times \ C(\lambda_1\lambda_2\lambda;m1m2m) \ C(\lambda L1;m,M-m) \ . \tag{6}$$

For two homonuclear diatomics, λ_1 and λ_2 are restricted to be even, L is odd due to the parity of the dipole moment, and exchange of the identical molecules requires $D_{\lambda_2\lambda_1\lambda L}= (-)^{\lambda+1} D_{\lambda_1\lambda_2\lambda L}$. Starting from a set of 18 geometries, it has been found that only the following 8 leading terms could be determined with sufficient numerical significance:

$$D_{2023}=-D_{0223}, \ D_{2021}=-D_{0221}, \ D_{2233}, \ D_{2211}, \ D_{4045}=-D_{0445} \ .$$

The latter two of these terms are already two orders of magnitude smaller than the leading term D_{2023}. The calculations were finally carried out for five different orientations of the H_2 with the following values for the angles $(\hat{r}_1,R),(\hat{r}_2,R)$, and the dehedral angle between the planes $\hat{r}1,\hat{R}$ and $\hat{r}2,\hat{R}$:

$$90^0,0^0,0^0; \ 90^0,135^0,0^0; \ 0^0,45^0,0^0; \ 45^0,135^0,0^0; \ 45^0,90^0,90^0.$$

Again, $r1$ and $r2$ are taken as $\langle r\rangle=1.449$ Bohr in order to account for vibrational averaging. The results are displayed in Fig. 4. As in the previous case, the fit of the calculated dipole moments to their long-range form results again in values for D_{2023} and D_{2233} which agree nicely with those derived from the long-range expressions,

$$D_{2023} \rightarrow 1/\sqrt{3}(\alpha_\parallel+2\alpha_\perp)q_2R^{-4} \ ; \ D_{2233} \rightarrow \sqrt{8/15}(\alpha_\parallel-\alpha_\perp)q_2R^{-4} \ . \tag{7}$$

In particular, D_{2023} is remarkably well described by a R^{-4} dependence over all distances investigated, i.e. down to 3 Bohr. The short range modifications reach only about 10% at the collision diameter (5.7 Bohr). The term D_{2021} is of purely short range origin and is larger than 20% of the leading D_{2023} only at distances shorter than the collision diameter. It is difficult to assess the reliability of the small terms D_{4045} and D_{2211}, but they appear to be of little significance for spectral calculations anyway. As to the correlation contributions, they affect D_{2023} to 8% due to the corresponding reduction of q_2, but dispersion contributions remain rather small because of their small anisotropy. As compared to He–H_2, the static induction term D_{2023} is larger than the corresponding D_{23} by a factor of 5, due to the ratio of the polarizabilities. On the other hand, the isotropic D_{01} of He–H_2 has no counterpart in H_2–H_2. Apart from this term, shape and relative size of the corresponding terms are quite similar in He–H_2 and H_2–H_2: if the He–H_2 terms D_{23}, D_{21}, and

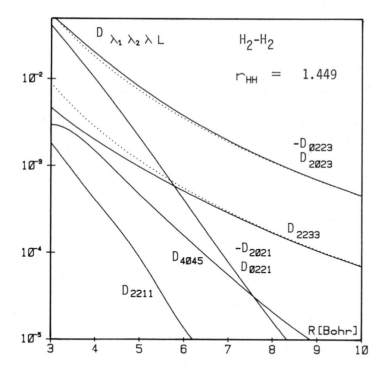

Fig. 4 Dipole moment expansion coefficients $D_{\lambda_1\lambda_2\lambda L}$ of H2-H2, Eq. (6) in a.u. Dotted lines: Asymptotic form according to Eq. (7).

D45 are scaled by a factor of 8 and R is changed by 0.6 Bohr, they approximate the D2023, D2021, and D4045 terms of H2-H2, respectively. Clearly, an orientation averaged H2 acts simply like a somewhat larger He. Like in the case of He-H2, we estimate the accuracy of our dipole moment function in the region around the collision dia- meter to about 2%. A full description of the calculations will be given by Meyer et al. (1985). Borysow and Frommhold (1985) show in this volume that the line shapes calculated from our dipole function and a semi-empirical isotropic potential give excellent agreement with the experimental data.

COLLISION INDUCED EMISSION OF NORMAL HYDROGEN GAS

Using the dipole data for H2-H2 discussed above, the spontaneous emission intensities for collision induced radiation have been calcu- lated for several temperatures below 40 K (Schaefer and Meyer, 1984). The purely quantum mechanical procedure folows the treatment of simpler systems by Doyle (1968) and Sando and Dalgarno (1971).

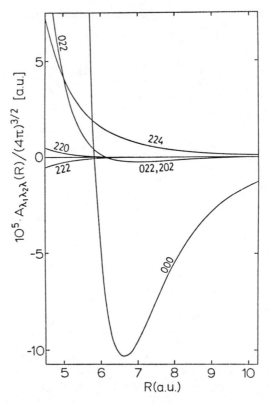

Fig. 5 Expansion coefficients $A_{\lambda_1\lambda_2\lambda L}(R)$ of the H_2–H_2 interaction potential, see Eq. (8).

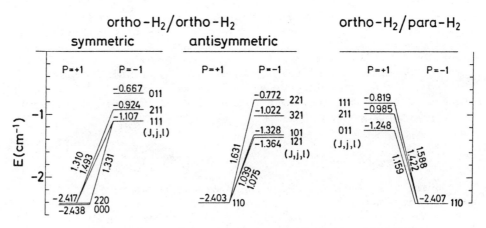

Fig. 6 Calculated bound state energy levels for H_2–H_2.

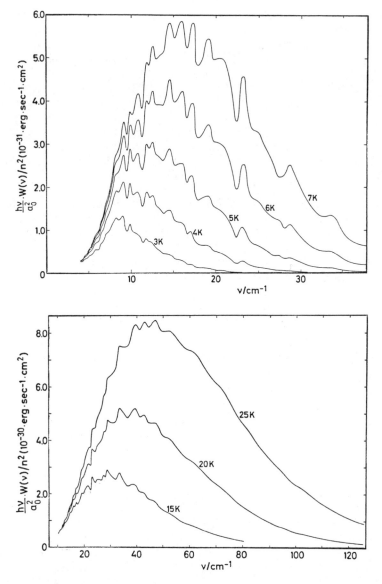

Fig. 7 Calculated collision induced emission spectra of normal hydrogen at low temperatures.

The interaction potential used has been expanded as

$$V(\vec{r}_1, \vec{r}_2, \vec{R}) = A_{\lambda_1\lambda_2\lambda}(r_1, r_2, R) \; Y_{\lambda_1}^{m_1}(\hat{r}_1) \; Y_{\lambda_2}^{m_2}(\hat{r}_2) \; Y_{\lambda}^{m}(\hat{R})$$

$$\times \; C(\lambda_1\lambda_2\lambda; m_1 m_2 m) \; . \tag{8}$$

The six leading terms accounted for in the calculations are shown in Fig. 5. This potential has been obtained from ab initio calculations (Meyer, 1980; Schaefer and Liu, 1981). Although it is not yet fully described in the literature, it has already been successfully tested against various experimental data (Monchik and Schaefer, 1980; Buck et al., 1983; Koehler and Schaefer, 1983). Agreement is very satisfactory, in particular for properties which probe the anisotropic components of the potential sensitively. The main defect of this potential, a somewhat too small isotropic dispersion attraction, can be traced to the limitations of the basis set functions up to f which account only for contributions up to C_{10}. Thus, the depth of the well is short of experimental estimates by about 10%, and the root of the potential is obtained as 5.82 Bohr, as compared to the experimental values ranging from 5.63 to 5.76 Bohr (see Buck et al., 1983). The dimer bound state energies obtained from this potential by iterative close coupling calculations agree with spectroscopic measurements (Watanabe and Welsh, 1964; McKellar and Welsh, 1974) also to about 10%. The calculated energy levels are shown in Fig. 6. For continuum-bound transitions, energy-normalized scattering wavefunctions are obtained from a close coupling procedure as described in detail previously (Schaefer and Meyer, 1979). Assuming a Maxwellian distribution, integration over initial and final states yields radiation intensities as displayed in Fig. 7. The structures observed at very low temperatures are due to continuum-bound transitions. At higher temperatures continuum-continuum transitions dominate. The structures above 30 cm^{-1} are mainly due to "coupled crossings" and orbiting resonances.

Unfortunately, the steep increase in the number of contributing rotational channels limits the calculations at present to temperatures below 40 K so that comparison with laboratory measurements is not yet possible. For the same reason, an absorption spectrum, which is easily generated from the emission data by accounting for stimulated emission, would be limited to wavenumbers below 200 cm^{-1}, i.e. to the pure translational part of the collision induced spectrum.

REFERENCES

Ahlrichs, R., Pluco, R., and Scoles, G., 1977, Chem. Phys. 19:119.
Aziz, R.A., Nain, V.P.S., and McConville, J.S., 1979, J. Chem. Phys. 70:4330.
Bentley, J., 1979, J. Chem. Phys. 70:3125.
Berns, R.M., Wormer, P.E.S., Mulder, F., and van der Avoird, A., 1978, J. Chem. Phys. 69:2102.
Bertoncini, P.J., and Wahl, A.C., 1973, J. Chem. Phys. 58:1259.
Birnbaum, G., 1978, JQSRT 19:51.
Birnbaum, G., Brown, M.S., and Frommhold, L., 1981, Canad. J. Phys. 59:1544.
Birnbaum, G., Guillot, B., and Bratos, S., 1982, Adv. Chem. Phys. 51:49.
Birnbaum, G., Krauss, M., and Frommhold, L., 1984, J. Chem. Phys. 80:2669.

Borysow, J., and Frommhold, L., 1985, this volume.
Boys, S.F., and Bernardi, F., 1970, Mol. Phys. 42:73.
Buck, U., Huisken, F., Kohlhase, A., Otten, D., Schaefer, J., 1983, J. Chem. Phys. 78:4439.
Buckingham, A.D., 1959, "Proprietes Optiques et Acoustiques de Fluids Comprimes et Actions Intermoleculaires", p. 57, Centre de la Recherche Scientifique, Paris.
Buckingham, A.D., 1967, Adv. Chem. Phys. 12:107.
Byers Brown, W., and Whisnant, D.M., 1973, Mol. Phys. 25:1385.
Doyle, R.O., 1968, JQSRT 8:1555.
Galatry, L., and Gharbi, T., 1980, Chem. Phys. Letters 75:433.
Karl, G., Poll, J.D., and Wolniewicz, L., 1975, Canad. J. Phys. 53:1781.
Koehler, W.E., and Schaefer, J., 1983, J. Chem. Phys. 78:4862.
Kolos, W., and Wolniewicz, L., 1967, J. Chem. Phys. 46:1426.
Kutzelnigg, W., 1978, in "Methods of Electronic Structure Theory", ed. Schaefer III, H.F., vol. IIIa, p. 129, Plenum, New York.
Lacey, A.J., and Byers Brown, W., 1974, Mol. Phys. 27:1013.
Levine, H.B., 1967, Phys. Rev. 160:159.
Linsky, J.L., 1969, Astrophys. J. 156:989.
Maeder, F., and Kutzelnigg, W., 1976, Chem. Phys. Letters 37:285.
Maitland, G.C., Rigby, M., Smith, E.B., and Wakeham, W.A., 1981, "Intermolecular Forces - Their Origin and Determination", Clarendon Press, Oxford.
Matcha, R.L., and Nesbet, R.K., 1967, Phys. Rev. 160:72.
McKellar, A.R.W., and Welsh, H.L., 1974, Canad. J. Phys. 52:1082.
McQuarrie, D.A., and Bernstein, R.B., 1968, J. Chem. Phys. 49:1958.
Meyer, W., 1973, J. Chem. Phys. 58:1017.
Meyer, W., 1976a, J. Chem. Phys. 64:2901.
Meyer, W., 1976b, Chem. Phys. 17:27.
Meyer, W., 1978, in "Methods of Electronic Structure Theory", ed. Schaefer III, H.F., vol. IIIa, p. 413. Plenum, New York.
Meyer, W., 1980, unpublished results.
Meyer, W., Ahlrichs, R., and Dykstra, C.E., 1984, in "Advanced Theories and Computational Approaches to the Electronic Structure of Molecules", D. Reidel Publ. Comp., Dortrecht, Holland.
Meyer, W., 1985, in preparation.
Meyer, W., and Frommhold, L., 1985, in preparation.
Meyer, W., Frommhold, L., and Birnbaum, G., 1985, in preparation.
Meyer, W., Hariharan, P.C., and Kutzelnigg, W., 1980, J. Chem. Phys. 73:1880.
Meyer, W., and Reinsch, E.A., 1978, unpublished results.
Monchik, L., and Schaefer, J., 1980, J. chem. Phys. 73:6153.
Pearson, E.W., Waldman, M., and Gordon, R.G., 1984, J. Chem. Phys. 80:1543.
Poll, J.D., and Wolniewicz, L., 1978, J. Chem. Phys. 68:3053.
Reinsch, E.A., and Meyer, W., 1976, Phys. Rev. A14:915.
Sando, K.M., and Dalgarno, A., 1971, Mol. Phys. 20:103.
Schaefer, J., and Liu, B., 1981, unpublished results.
Schaefer, J., and Meyer, W., 1979, J. Chem. Phys. 70:344.
Schaefer, J., and Meyer, W., 1984, in "Electronic and Atomic

    Collisions", Eichler, J., Hertel, I.V., Stolterfoht, N.,
    editors, p. 529, Elsevier Science Publishers.
Shlyapnikov, G.V., and Shmator, I.P., 1980, <u>Soviet Phys. JETP</u>
    52:1050.
Smith, F.T., 1972, <u>Phys. Rev.</u> A5:1708.
Tipping, R.E., 1985, this volume.
Trafton, L.M., 1966, <u>Astrophys. J.</u> 146:558.
Trafton, L.M., 1973, <u>Astrophys. J.</u> 179:971.
Ulrich, B.T., Ford, L., and Browne, J.C., 1972, <u>J. Chem. Phys.</u>
    57:2906.
Watanabe, A., and Welsh, H.L., 1964, <u>Phys. Rev. Letters</u> 13:810.
Werner, H.J., and Reinsch, E.A., 1982, <u>J. Chem. Phys.</u>76:3144.
Whisnant, D.M., and Byers Brown, W., 1973, <u>Mol. Phys.</u> 26:1105.
Wormer, P.E.S., and van Dijk, G., 1979, <u>J. Chem. Phys.</u> 70:5695.

A COMPARATIVE STUDY OF THE DIELECTRIC,

REFRACTIVE AND KERR VIRIAL COEFFICIENTS

T. K. Bose

Département de physique
Université du Québec à Trois-Rivières
Trois-Rivières, Québec G9A 5H7 Canada

ABSTRACT

It is shown that the dielectric second virial coefficient minus the refractive second virial coefficient is related to the integrated collision-induced absorption for binary interactions. The dielectric second virial coefficient of an atomic gas is compared to the collision-induced polarized scattered spectrum, being both related to the symmetric part of the interaction polarizability tensor. The Kerr second virial coefficient and the collision-induced depolarized scattered spectrum are also compared since they are related to the anisotropic part of the interaction polarizability tensor.

Experimental results are used to show resemblances as well as discrepancies between various methods.

INTRODUCTION

In this paper we emphasize the relation that exists between the dielectric virial coefficients and the refractive virial coefficients on the one hand, and collision-induced absorption on the other. Indeed, such comparison may sometimes lead to the recognition of some as yet unknown collision-induced band (Birnbaum and Bose, 1979; Birnbaum, 1980).

The knowledge of dielectric and refractive virial coefficients is important not only for comparison with collision-induced absorption, but also with collision-induced light scattering data. Much theoretical work (O'Brien et al., 1973; Fortune and Certain,

1974; Clarke et al., 1978) has been devoted to the understanding of diatomic polarizability of atomic gases (Dacre, 1978; Dacre and Frommhold, 1982). The diatomic polarizability is expressed through an excess polarizability which is defined as the polarizability of a system of two interacting atoms minus the sum of the polarizabilities of the isolated (non-interacting) atoms. The polarizability of an isolated atom is a scalar, but the diatomic polarizability is a tensor. The two invariants of the diatomic polarizability tensor are its trace and its anisotropy. The trace can be measured experimentally by the dielectric second virial coefficient and the collision-induced polarized scattered spectrum. The anisotropy is obtained by collision-induced depolarized light scattering as well as the Kerr second virial coefficient.

RELATION BETWEEN THE COLLISION-INDUCED ABSORPTION AND VIRIAL COEFFICIENTS

For a gas, one can always express the dielectric constant in the form of a virial expansion:

$$\frac{\varepsilon - 1}{\varepsilon + 2} V_m = A_\varepsilon + B_\varepsilon / V_m + C_\varepsilon / V_m^2 + \ldots \tag{1}$$

where ε is the static dielectric constant; V_m is the molar volume; and A_ε, B_ε and C_ε are, respectively, the first, second and third dielectric virial coefficients, representing contributions from individual molecules, pairs and triplets. For a multipolar gas, the dielectric second virial coefficient will include two terms (Buckingham and Pople, 1955; Bose and Cole, 1970; Sutter and Cole, 1970):

$$B_\varepsilon = B_{or} + B_{ind} \, ,$$

where B_{or} measures the contribution of the pair interaction of the induced dipole moments produced by the multipolar field (molecular field), and B_{ind} is the contribution of the pair interaction of the induced dipole moments produced by the applied external field.

For any reasonable interpretation of the experimental results, one must be able to separate B_{ind} and B_{or}. This is possible by measuring the refractive index of the gas. The optical analogue of the Claussius-Mossotti expression obtained by writing $n^2 = \varepsilon$, is given by

$$\frac{n^2 - 1}{n^2 + 2} V_m = A_R + B_R / V_m + C_R / V_m^2 + \ldots \tag{2}$$

where n is the refractive index and A_R, B_R and C_R are, respectively, the first, second and third refractivity virial coefficients. B_R corresponds to B_{ind} because B_{or}, being of molecular origin, does not contribute at optical frequencies. Therefore, in principle, measurements of B_ε and B_R would permit one to identify the interaction effect due to the molecular field as well as the external field.

Another way of determining B_{or} is to obtain the collision-induced spectrum in the far-infrared region (Ho et al., 1971). Combining Eqs. (1) and (2) one gets,

$$\frac{\varepsilon - 1}{\varepsilon + 2} - \frac{n^2 - 1}{n^2 + 2} = \frac{A_\varepsilon - A_R}{V_m} + \frac{B_\varepsilon - B_R}{V_m^2} + \frac{C_\varepsilon - C_R}{V_m^3} + \ldots \tag{3}$$

On approximating $\varepsilon + 2 \simeq 3$ and $n^2 + 2 \simeq 3$, we have

$$\frac{\varepsilon - n^2}{3} = \frac{A_\varepsilon - A_R}{V_m} + \frac{B_\varepsilon - B_R}{V_m^2} + \frac{C_\varepsilon - C_R}{V_m^3} + \ldots \tag{4}$$

It is possible to determine the virial coefficients associated with a given band denoted by the subscript λ from measurements of the absorption coefficient $\alpha_\lambda(\omega)$. Thus, by using the Krammers-Kronig relation

$$(\varepsilon - n^2)_\lambda = \frac{2c}{\pi} \int_0^\infty \frac{\alpha_\lambda(\omega)}{\omega^2} \, d\omega$$

and the virial expansion

$$\int_0^\infty \frac{\alpha_\lambda(\omega)}{\omega^2} \, d\omega = \frac{A_\lambda}{V_m} + \frac{B_\lambda}{V_m^2} + \frac{C_\lambda}{V_m^3} + \ldots \tag{5}$$

we obtain

$$3 B_{or} = 3(B_\varepsilon - B_R) = \frac{2c}{\pi} \sum_\lambda B_\lambda \tag{6}$$

where c is the velocity of light and ω is the angular frequency.

COMPARISON OF EXPERIMENTAL RESULTS OF COLLISION-INDUCED ABSORPTION
AND DIELECTRIC AND REFRACTIVE VIRIAL COEFFICIENTS

We shall use Eq. (6) to compare the experimental results taken from dielectric and refractive virial coefficients as well as integrated collision-induced absorption. We shall limit our comparison to CO_2, CH_4, SF_6 and N_2O, since the experimental data of dielectric and refractive virial coefficients, as well as collision-induced absorption, are generally available for these gases.

CO_2 is an ideal system for this kind of comparison. It has a large B_ϵ and a small B_R. The precision on the difference between $(B_\epsilon - B_R)$ is therefore rather high. Table 1 gives the experimental results obtained from different sources. B_{or} in the third column is derived as a difference between B_ϵ and B_R. In the fourth column, B_{FIR} gives the experimental value of the collision-induced absorption measured in the far infrared. One can easily see that the agreement between B_{or} and B_{FIR} values is very reasonable, within the limits of experimental errors.

The situation, however, is much worse if we have a case where B_ϵ and B_R are comparable in size. This happens to be true for CH_4. Although there is agreement within the experimental limits, it is clear that the precision of the measurement has to be improved before comparison in cases like CH_4 becomes reasonable.

Sometimes, however, there are surprises as in the case of SF_6. The discrepancy between $(B_\epsilon - B_R)$ and B_{FIR} has been attributed to a missing collision-induced absorption band in the infrared. Although this band has never been observed experimentally, it can be estimated quite easily by considering SF_6 as a vibrating dipole.

The vibrating dipole induces a dipole moment in the molecular pair which will appear in the same frequency region as the active vibrational bands. The contribution of this collision-induced band to the dielectric second virial coefficient may be estimated from

$$B_{IR} = 2 \ (A_\epsilon - A_R) \ N_A \alpha^2 \sigma^{-3} I_6 \tag{7}$$

where N_A is Avogadro's number, α is the isotropic polarizability, σ is the molecular diameter and

$$I_6 = \int_0^\infty x^{-6} \ \exp \ [-V(x) \ / \ kT] \ 4\pi x^2 \ dx \tag{8}$$

Here $x = r/\sigma$, r is the intermolecular distance, $V(x)$ is the interaction potential, T is the absolute temperature and k is Boltzmann's constant. One can easily see that this effect is only important in systems like SF_6, where the molecule possesses a large atomic polarizability and intense infrared bands. However, this effect is negligible for CO_2 and CH_4.

Another interesting example for this kind of comparison is N_2O, which differs from CO_2 in that although it has a large quadrupole moment, it also possesses a small dipole moment. Table 2 gives the experimental results from the dielectric as well as far-infrared measurements. The discrepancy in this case between B_{FIR} and $(B_\epsilon - B_R)$ is rather large.

Table 1

GAS	TEMP.	$B_\varepsilon \times 10^{12}$ EXPT	$B_R \times 10^{12}$ EXPT	$B_{or} \times 10^{12}$ ($= B_\varepsilon - B_R$)	$B_{FIR} \times 10^{12}$ EXPT	$B_{FIR} \times 10^{12}$ CALCULATED[c]	$(B_{FIR} + B_{IR}) \times 10^{12}$
	K	$m^6\ mole^{-2}$	$m^6\ mole^{-2}$	$m^6\ mole^{-2}$	$m^6\ mole^{-2}$	$m^6\ mole^{-2}$	$m^6\ mole^{-2}$
CO_2	322.5	50.7 ± 0.9[a]					
	302.5	57.6 ± 0.9[a]					
	296	60.0 (est.)		57	62 ± 6[b]	1.0	63
	298		3.2 ± 1.0[d]				
CH_4	302.7	7.68 ± 0.30[e]	6.6 ± 0.4[f]	1.08	1.66[g]	0.087	1.76
SF_6	326	63.3 ± 2.8[h]	36.0 ± 1.8[i]	27.3			
	298				0.53[j]	24.2	24.73

a: Bose and Cole, 1970; b: Ho et al., 1971; c: Values of the molecular constants used in the cal-culations of B_{IR} from Eq. (7) using the Lennard-Jones potential are given in the references asso-ciated with the values. For SF_6, the values $\sigma = 4.68$ Å and $(\varepsilon/k) = 439$ were used with the (7-28) potential. (J. C. McCoubrey and N. M. Singh, Trans. Faraday Soc. 55:1826 (1959)); d: A. D. Buckingham and C. Graham, Proc. R. Soc. London Ser. A, 336:275 (1974); e: T. K. Bose, J. S. Sochanski and R. H. Cole, J. Chem. Phys. 57:3592 (1972); f: St-Arnaud and Bose, 1976; g: G. Birnbaum and E. R. Cohen, J. Chem. Phys. 62:3807 (1975); h: C. Hosticka and T. K. Bose, J. Chem. Phys. 60:1318 (1974); i: J. M. St-Arnaud and T. K. Bose, J. Chem. Phys. 71:4951 (1979); j: A. Rosenberg and G. Birnbaum, J. Chem. Phys. 52:683 (1970).

53

Table 2. N_2O Gas

Temp	$B_\varepsilon \times 10^{12}$ (experimental)	$B_R \times 10^{12}$ (extrapolated)	$B_{or} \times 10^{12}$ $(= B_\varepsilon - B_R)$	$B_{FIR} \times 10^{12}$ calculated from quadrupole moment
K	m^6 mole^{-2}	m^6 mole^{-2}	m^6 mole^{-2}	m^6 mole^{-2}
303	$(32.3 \pm 1.3)^\ell$	$(0 \pm 2)^\ell$	32 ± 3	$(57)^{m,n}$

ℓ: (Kirouac and Bose, 1973);   m: (Baise, 1971)
n: (Copeland and Cole, 1973)

In fact, the quadrupole moment of N_2O derived from the dielectric second virial coefficient result (Kirouac and Bose, 1973) agrees rather well with that obtained by Buckingham et al. (1968) from induced birefringence. On the other hand, B_{FIR} calculated on the basis of the quadrupole moment as measured by Baise (Baise, 1971; Copeland and Cole, 1973) in N_2O is rather high compared to B_{or} obtained from dielectric measurements. Part of the anomaly could well be the difficulty of separating the allowed transition from the collision-induced band. It should be mentioned, however, that the value of B_{FIR} quoted in Table 2 is due to a correction pointed out by Copeland and Cole (1973), and is based on their corrected quadrupole moment of N_2O. The discrepancy between B_{or} and B_{FIR} would be much higher with the quadrupole moment of N_2O as deduced by Baise. The inclusion of B_{IR}, which could not be calculated due to the lack of experimental A_R values in the literature, would further enhance the discrepancy between the dielectric and spectroscopic measurements.

DIELECTRIC SECOND VIRIAL COEFFICIENT OF ATOMIC GASES AND ITS RELATION WITH POLARIZED SCATTERED SPECTRUM

In the case of atomic gases, the experimental values of the dielectric second virial coefficient and the refractive second virial coefficient are very similar. This indicates, that within the experimental errors, the difference between the polarizability at low frequency $\alpha^{stat}(r)$ and the polarizability at visible frequency $\alpha^{opt}(r)$ is negligible. The interest in atomic systems is of course due to their theoretical simplicity. In a collisional encounter the diatomic polarizability varies with the internuclear distance. The dielectric second virial coefficient is given by the expression

$$B_\varepsilon = (2\pi N_A^2 / 3\varepsilon_0) \int_0^\infty \alpha(r) \, \exp \, [-V(r) / kT] \, r^2 \, dr \qquad (9)$$

where the trace $\alpha(r)$ is $(\alpha_\| + 2\alpha_\perp) / 3$, $V(r)$ is the interaction potential and ε_0 is the dielectric constant of empty space.

Experimentally, it is difficult to determine accurately the dielectric second virial coefficient of monatomic gases, especially of helium and neon. One can achieve reasonable accuracy in the measurement of B_ε for these gases only by using differential techniques which were developed by Cole and co-workers (Sutter and Cole, 1970) and Buckingham et al. (1970). It is easy to show that any attempt to determine B_ε based on an absolute determination of the dielectric constant could lead to errors as large as 100%. The reasons are quite obvious if one looks at the results of the argon measurements. In the case of an absolute measurement, the density is converted to pressure through the use of the pressure second virial coefficient B_P, and the Clausius-Mossotti equation takes the form:

$$[(\varepsilon - 1) / (\varepsilon + 2)] \, (RT / P) = A_\varepsilon + (B_\varepsilon - A_\varepsilon B_P)(P / RT) + \ldots \qquad (10)$$

For argon at room temperature

$$A_\varepsilon = 4.140 \times 10^{-6} \, m^3 \, mole^{-1},$$

$$B_P = -11 \times 10^{-6} \, m^3 \, mole^{-1},$$

and $B_\varepsilon \simeq 1 \times 10^{-12} \, m^6 \, mole^{-2}$

We then have $A_\varepsilon B_P \simeq 45 \times 10^{-12} \, m^6 \, mole^{-2}$, which means that B_ε is about 2% of the total $(B_\varepsilon - A_\varepsilon B_P)$.

Thus if we make a 2% error in the value of B_P, a 100% error will be made in B_ε. It happens quite often that B_P values from different laboratories differ from each other by 2% to 3%. A precision of 5% or 10% in B_ε based on an absolute measurement would only mean that the experimental result has been deduced by assuming an absolute certainty on the value of B_P. Besides, any error in the experimental curve (Eq. (10)) would cause even larger errors in B_ε. It can therefore be concluded that absolute measurements cannot lead to any precise determination of B_ε.

Differential techniques in the case of the dielectric constant or the refractive index are very similar. In the following paragraph we shall illustrate the differential method developed by Buckingham et al. (1970). In the case of the refractive index (St-Arnaud and Bose, 1976), the method consists in measuring the sum of the path lengths of two similar cells (Fig. (1)), one of which is filled with gas at density d and the other evacuated. After opening the valve between the two cells, the density is nearly halved and one measures again the optical path lengths. Since the linear term in density remains the same before and after the expansion and only the quadratic and higher order terms change, we can determine the second refractivity virial coefficient, B_R, directly from the change of the optical path lengths.

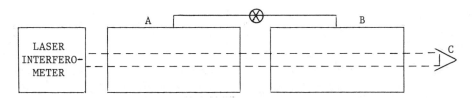

Fig. 1. Schematic diagram of the differential technique: A and B are two similar optical cells and C is a reflector.

If D_A is the change in the index of refraction when the gas is expanded from cell A to cell B, and D_B the change for expansion from B to A, we get

$$[D_A / (n_A - 1)] + [D_B / (n_B - 1)] =$$

$$-(B_n / 2A_n^2) [(n_A - 1) + (n_B - 1)] + \ldots \quad (11)$$

where n_A is the refractive index of the gas in cell A before expansion and n_B is the corresponding refractive index in B. One has

$$A_R = (2/3)A_n$$

$$B_R = (2/3)B_n - (1/9)A_n^2$$

and $(n - 1) d^{-1} = A_n + B_n d + C_n d^2 + \ldots$

In the case of the dielectric constant, the capacitances of cells A and B are connected in parallel and the expression corresponding to Eq. (11) is given by

$$[D_A / C(\varepsilon_A - 1)] + [D_B / C(\varepsilon_B - 1)] =$$

$$-(1/2) \ [B_\varepsilon' / (A_\varepsilon')^2] \ [(\varepsilon_A - 1) + (\varepsilon_B - 1)] \ \ldots \quad (12)$$

where C is the average geometric capacitance of the two cells, and where

$$A_\varepsilon' = 3A_\varepsilon; \quad \text{and} \quad B_\varepsilon' = 3 \ (B_\varepsilon + A_\varepsilon^2)$$

The experimental results of B_ε for atomic gases existing in the literature are either derived from absolute measurements of the dielectric constant (Vidal and Lallemand, 1976), or from differential measurements based on a modified Burnett expansion as developed by Cole and co-workers (Orcutt and Cole, 1967; Bose and Cole, 1970; Sutter and Cole, 1970). Whereas the absolute measurements of B_ε for atomic gases have to be discarded altogether, the B_ε values based on Cole's method are quite reasonable.

One of the drawbacks of the existing B_ε values for atomic gases is that they have all been measured at only one temperature. This makes it very difficult to make a serious comparison between any theoretical model and experimental results. With B_ε known at one temperature, we end up comparing two numbers: a computed B_ε and a measured B_ε. The measurement of B_ε as a function of temperature will enable us to test the functional form of the polarizability trace tensor $\alpha(r)$ in terms of r. Such a test can also be made if one can measure the spectral distribution of the collision-induced polarized spectrum along with the intensity. Unfortunately, the measurement of the collision-induced polarized spectrum is difficult. The signals obtainable are extremely weak, and may therefore produce large errors.

In his recent review article (Frommhold, 1981) on the theoretical and experimental studies of the collision-induced polarized spectrum, Frommhold compared the collision-induced results with the dielectric second virial coefficient of atomic gases at room temperature. The choice of the potential function was found to be particularly important for wave mechanical computations of the lineshape of the collision induced spectra. A difference of 12% was obtained in the spectra of neon by using a Lennard-Jones 6-12 potential instead of a more refined MSV potential.

The functional form of the polarizability trace tensor given by the DID model (Buckingham and Pople, 1955) is written as

$$\alpha(r) = (4\pi\varepsilon_0)^{-1}(4\alpha^3 / r^6) \quad (13)$$

B_ε calculated with the above expression of $\alpha(r)$ always leads to positive values. Since experimental values of B_ε of helium and neon are negative at room temperature, it is clear that the DID model does not represent the correct trace.

There have been several quantum mechanical approaches to properly investigate the helium-helium interaction. Buckingham and Watts (1973) used an uncorrelated Hartree-Fock scheme to properly define the wave function of the helium diatom. They took 16 and 18 function basis sets and their results showed some dependance on the basis set. O'Brien, et al., (1973), using a 30 function Gaussian basis set, obtained for the first time the negative B_ε of helium at room temperature. Based on this quantum mechanical result, the trace $\alpha(r)$ in Eq. (9) has been approximated by Frommhold by the relation

$$\alpha(r) = (A_6 / r^6) - \lambda_t \exp(-r/r_t) \tag{14}$$

where the first term refers to the long range DID interaction, and the second term is based on the quantum mechanical calculation for the short range interaction.

The coefficient A_6 differs from $4\alpha^3$ of the DID model because of a dispersion-type correction to the polarizability of one atom in the presence of the other. Buckingham (1956) has shown that the deviation of A_6 from the DID model is due to hyperpolarization. The corrected expression for A_6 is given by

$$A_6 = 4\alpha^3 + (5\gamma C_6 / 9\alpha) \tag{15}$$

where γ is the hyperpolarizability and C_6 is the coefficient of r^{-6} in the dispersion force.

Using Eq. (14) for $\alpha(r)$ Frommhold (1981), fitted both the dielectric second virial results as well as line shapes for the collision-induced polarized spectrum with the same set of parameters A_6, λ_t and r_t for each atomic gas.

We have recently determined the dielectric second virial coefficient of neon at two different temperatures using the differential technique developed by Buckingham et al. (1970). Using the constants A_6, λ_t and r_t given by Frommhold we calculated B_ε with Eq. (9). Table 3 gives the experimental as well as calculated B_ε values. The two calculated B_ε values based on different potential functions differ only slightly from each other. This seems to indicate that B_ε is not as sensitive to the potential function as the lineshape of the collision induced spectra (Frommhold, 1981). It is clear from the experimental measurement at only two temperatures that the best chance for obtaining the right functional form of $\alpha(r)$ is by measuring B_ε over a wide temperature range.

B_ε in Table 3 is calculated with the following constants given by Frommhold for neon:

$$A_6 = 224.2a_0^9, \quad \lambda_t = 65a_0^3, \quad r_t = 0.70a_0 \text{ and } 4.34a_0 < r < 5.67a_0$$

where $a_0 = 0.52917706 \times 10^{-10}$ m.

Table 3. Neon gas

Temp	$B_\varepsilon \times 10^{12}$ expt	$B_\varepsilon \times 10^{12}$ L-J potential[a]	$B_\varepsilon \times 10^{12}$ MSV potential[b]
K	m^6 mole^{-2}	m^6 mole^{-2}	m^6 mole^{-2}
300	-0.17 ± 0.01	-0.16	-0.17
77	-0.11 ± 0.01	-0.12	-0.13

a: Lennard-Jones (12,6) potential with $\varepsilon = 0.494 \times 10^{-14}$ erg and $\sigma = 3.09$ Å
b: MSV potential by Siska et al. J. Chem. Phys. 55: 5762 (1971).

The *ab initio* calculation of neon has recently been improved by Dacre (1982a). By a combination of configuration interaction (CI) and self-consistent field (SCF) calculations he obtained a B_ε equal to -0.15×10^{-12} m^6 mole^{-2} at 298 K. This value is much closer to our experimental result than previous theoretical values (Kress and Kozak, 1977; Dacre, 1981). In fact, Dacre's systematic *ab initio* calculation of all monatomic gases has contributed much to our understanding of the collision induced phenomena. Although his B_ε for helium agrees extremely well with the available experimental results (Orcutt and Cole, 1967; Kirouac and Bose, 1976), those for heavier atoms like argon (Dacre, 1982b) and krypton (Dacre, 1982c) are generally much smaller than the experimental values (Orcutt and Cole, 1967; Bose and Cole, 1970). This may well be due to the fact that accurate polarizability calculations generally require large basis sets, which become computationally more difficult and expensive as systems become larger.

In Table 4 are listed the recent theoretical and experimental values of B_ε for helium, neon and argon.

KERR SECOND VIRIAL COEFFICIENT OF GASES AND ITS RELATION WITH DEPOLARIZED SCATTERED SPECTRUM

As has been pointed out earlier, the anisotropy of the polarizability tensor is responsible for the Kerr virial coefficient as well as depolarized light scattering. A strong uniform electric field applied to a fluid induces a difference between the refractive indices of the fluid in directions parallel and perpendicular to the field. This phenomenon is known as the Kerr effect or electric birefringence. Both the theoretical as well as the experimental development of the Kerr effect in its present form is largely due to the works of Buckingham and co-workers (Buckingham, 1955, 1962, 1981; Buckingham and Pople, 1955; Buckingham and Dunmur, 1968). The molar Kerr constant is defined as

$$_mK = \lim_{E \to 0} \left[\frac{6n \, (n_{/\!/} - n_\perp) \, V_m}{(n^2 + 2)^2 \, (\varepsilon + 2)^2 \, E^2} \right] \tag{16}$$

where n and ε are the isotropic refractive index and dielectric constant of the gas, $n_{/\!/}$ and $n_\perp$ are the refractive indices for light polarized parallel and perpendicular to the electric field E and V_m is the molar volume. The molar Kerr constant can be expanded as a series in molar volume (Buckingham and Sutter, 1976)

$$_mK = A_K + B_K \, V_m^{-1} + C_K V_m^{-2} + \ldots \tag{17}$$

where A_K, B_K, C_K ... are the first, second and third Kerr virial coefficients. A_K is the «ideal gas» value of the molar Kerr constant and represents the contribution of isolated molecules to $_mK$. B_K represents the initial deviation of $_mK$ from ideality due to pair interaction. C_K and higher coefficients represent deviations due to triplet and higher-order interactions.

For nonpolar molecules A_K can be written as

$$A_K = \frac{N_A}{81\varepsilon_0} \left[\gamma + \frac{3}{5} \, (kT)^{-1} \, (\alpha_{\alpha\beta} \, a_{\alpha\beta} - 3\alpha a) \right] \tag{18}$$

where γ is the hyperpolarizability, $\alpha_{\alpha\beta}$ and $a_{\alpha\beta}$ are the static and the optical polarizability tensors. For axially symmetric molecules $(3/2) \, (\alpha_{\alpha\beta} \, a_{\alpha\beta} - 3\alpha a)$ reduces to the product of the static and optical polarizability anisotropies $(\alpha_{/\!/} - \alpha_\perp) \, (a_{/\!/} - a_\perp)$. The optical polarizability anisotropies have been determined from depolarization studies of scattered laser light. For atomic gases, however, the anisotropy for isolated molecules is zero and the first Kerr virial coefficient reduces to $A_K = (N_A\gamma \, / \, 81\varepsilon_0)$.

Table 4

GAS	AUTHOR	TEMP.	$B_\epsilon(SCF) \times 10^{12}$ m^6 mole^{-2}	$B_\epsilon(SCF + CI) \times 10^{12}$ m^6 mole^{-2}	$B_\epsilon(EXPT) \times 10^{12}$ m^6 mole^{-2}
Helium	Dacre (1982d)	294	-0.085	-0.062	
	Kress and Kozak (1977)	322	-0.093		
	Certain and Fortune (1974)	322	-0.094		
	Orcutt and Cole (1967)	322			-0.06 ± 0.04
	Kirouac and Bose (1976)	294			-0.059 ± 0.009
Neon	Dacre (1982a)	298	-0.14	-0.15	
	Kress and Kozak (1977)	322	-0.10		
	Orcutt and Cole (1967)	322			-0.30 ± 0.10
	Bose et al.[a]	300			-0.17 ± 0.01
	Bose et al.[a]	77			-0.11 ± 0.01
Argon	Dacre (1982b)	322	-.048		
	Bose and Cole (1970)	322			-0.72 ± 0.12

a: Bose, T. K., Huot, J., and St-Arnaud, J. M., (to be published).

61

The second Kerr virial coefficient may be related to the product of the optical and static pair polarizability anisotropies, $\beta(r)$ by

$$B_K = \frac{2\pi N_A^2}{405\epsilon_0 kT} \int_0^\infty \beta^{opt}(r) \, \beta^{stat}(r) \, \exp\left(-\frac{V(r)}{kT}\right) r^2 dr \qquad (19)$$

If we assume $\beta^{stat}(r) = \beta^{opt}(r)$, we get

$$B_K = \frac{2\pi N_A^2}{405\epsilon_0 kT} \int_0^\infty \left[\beta^{stat}(r)\right]^2 \exp\left(-\frac{V(r)}{kT}\right) r^2 dr \qquad (20)$$

The DID model for the polarizability anisotropy is given by:

$$\beta^{stat}(r) = (6\alpha^2 / 4\pi\epsilon_0 r^3) \left[1 + (\alpha / 4\pi\epsilon_0 r^3) + 0(r^{-6})\right] \qquad (21)$$

Effects of pressure on depolarized light scattering may also be analysed to give information on collision-induced polarizability anisotropies. From such studies one can obtain the two body depolarized intensity $I_{ZX}^{(2)}$, which is directly proportional to the Kerr second virial coefficient provided that dispersion is negligible.

Experimentally, the molar Kerr constant can be written as

$$\frac{2(n_{//} - n_\perp)}{27E^2} V_m = A_K + V_m^{-1} \left[B_K + A_K \left(\frac{2N_A\alpha}{3\epsilon_0} + \frac{N_A a}{6\epsilon_0}\right)\right] + 0(V_m^{-2}) + \ldots \qquad (22)$$

V_m is normally connected to pressure through the use of the pressure second virial coefficient, leading to

$$\frac{2(n_{//} - n_\perp)}{27E^2} \frac{RT}{P} = A_K + \frac{P}{RT} \left[B_K + A_K \left(\frac{2N_A\alpha}{3\epsilon_0} + \frac{N_A a}{6\epsilon_0}\right) - A_K B_P\right]$$
$$+ 0\left(\frac{P}{RT}\right)^2 + \ldots \qquad (23)$$

We have estimated that for argon at room temperature B_K is about five times as large as $A_K B_P$. This would mean that an error in the B_P value is not very serious for the absolute determination of the Kerr second virial coefficient.

Table 5 shows that there still exists serious discrepancies between the Kerr second virial coefficient and collision-induced depolarized light scattering data. There is however rather good agreement among several laboratories (Barocchi and Zoppi, 1978; Frommhold and Proffitt, 1978; Shelton and Tabisz, 1981) in the experimental determination of the two-body collision-induced depolarized light scattering data of argon. In view of the wide agreement of the data and recent developments of the experimental techniques (Zoppi et al., 1981) of the collision-induced depolarized light scattering, it seems to us that improvement is necessary in the experimental approach to the Kerr second virial coefficient. In this connection, the analysis proposed recently by Dunmur et al. (1983) to explain the discrepency between the two-body collision-induced depolarized light scattering and the Kerr second virial coefficient does not appear fully satisfactory.

Table 5

Gas	$\dfrac{B_K EXPT}{B_K DID}$	$\dfrac{I_{ZX}^{(2)} EXPT}{I_{ZX}^{(2)} DID}$
Ar	0.73^q 0.65^r	1.01^s
Kr	0.62^q 0.63^r	0.85^t
CH_4	1.40^r	1.03^s

q: Lennard-Jones potential (Buckingham and Dunmur, 1968);
r: Lennard-Jones potential (Dunmur et al., 1979);
s: Aziz potential (Shelton and Tabisz, 1981);
t: Lennard-Jones potential (Watson and Rowell, 1974).

ACKNOWLEDGEMENTS

It is a pleasure to thank Mr. J. Huot for computer calculations, Dr. J. M. St-Arnaud for stimulating discussions, Dr. G. Lefebvre and Dr. L. Marchildon for their suggestions concerning this manuscript. I would also like to thank the referee and the editor for many useful comments. This work was supported by the National Sciences and Engineering Research Council of Canada and by the Government of Quebec through the FCAC fund.

REFERENCES

Baise, A., 1971, Far infrared absorption in compressed nitrous oxide, Chem. Phys. Lett., 9:627.
Barocchi, F., and Zoppi, M., 1978, Collision-induced light-scattering spectra and pair polarizability of gaseous argon, Phys. Lett., A66:99.
Birnbaum, G., 1980, Determination of molecular constants from collision-induced far-infra-red spectra and related methods, in: «Intermolecular spectroscopy and dynamical properties of dense systems», Vol. 75, J. Van Kranendonk, ed., North Holland Publishing Co., Amsterdam.
Birnbaum, G., and Bose, T. K., 1979, Comparison of dielectric and refractive virial coefficients and collision induced absorption bands, J. Chem. Phys., 71:17.
Bose, T. K., and Cole, R. H., 1970, Dielectric and pressure virial coefficients of imperfect gases. II. CO_2-argon mixtures, J. Chem., Phys., 52:140.
Buckingham, A. D., 1955, Theoretical studies of the Kerr effect II: The influence of pressure, Proc. Phys. Soc., A68:910.
Buckingham, A. D., 1956, The polarizability of a pair of interacting atoms, Trans. Faraday Soc., 52:1035.
Buckingham, A. D., 1962, Frequency dependence of the Kerr constant, Proc. R. Soc., A267:271.
Buckingham, A. D., 1981, Small molecules in electric and optical fields, in: «Molecular electro-optics: electro-optic properties of macromolecules and colloids in solution», Sonja Krause, ed., NATO advanced study institutes series, Plenum Press, New York.
Buckingham, A. D., Cole, R. H., and Sutter, H., 1970, Direct determination of the imperfect gas contribution to dielectric polarization, J. Chem. Phys., 52:5960.
Buckingham, A. D., Disch, R. L., and Dunmur, D. A., 1968, The quadrupole moments of some simple molecules, J. Am. Chem. Soc., 90:3104.
Buckingham, A. D., and Dunmur, D. A., 1968, Kerr effect in inert gases and sulphur hexafluoride, Trans. Faraday Soc., 64:1776.
Buckingham, A. D., and Pople, J. A., 1955a, The dielectric constant of an imperfect nonpolar gas, Trans. Faraday Soc., 51:1029.
Buckingham, A. D., and Pople, J. A., 1955b, Theoretical studies of the Kerr effect I: Deviations from a linear polarization law, Proc. Phys. Soc., A68:905.
Buckingham, A. D., and Sutter, H., 1976, Gas phase measurement of the Kerr effect in some n-alkanes and cyclohexane, J. Chem. Phys., 64:364.

Buckingham, A. D., and Watts, R. S., 1973, The polarizability of a
    pair of helium atoms, Molec. Phys., 26:7.
Clarke, K. L., Madden, P. A., and Buckingham, A. D., 1978, Collision-
    induced polarizabilities of inert gas atoms, Molec. Phys.,
    36:301.
Copeland, T. G., and Cole, R. H., 1973, Far-infrared absorption and
    quadrupole moment of nitrous oxide, Chem. Phys. Lett., 21:
    289.
Dacre, P. D., 1978, A calculation of the helium pair polarizability
    including correlation effects, Molec. Phys., 36:541.
Dacre, P. D., 1981, A calculation of the neon pair polarizability
    including correlation effects, Can. J. Phys., 59:1439.
Dacre, P. D., 1982a, A calculation of the neon pair polarizability
    including correlation effects II. Inclusion of the confi-
    guration interaction basis extension corrections, Can. J.
    Phys., 60:963.
Dacre, P. D., 1982b, An SCF calculation of the pair polarizability
    of argon, Molec. Phys., 45:1.
Dacre, P. D., 1982c, Pair polarizabilities of the heavy inert gases
    II. SCF calculations of the pair polarizabilities of Krypton
    and Xenon, Molec. Phys., 47:193.
Dacre, P. D., 1982d, On the pair polarizability of helium, Molec.
    Phys., 45:17.
Dacre, P. D., and Frommhold, L., 1982, Rare gas diatom polariza-
    bilities, J. Chem. Phys., 76:3447.
Dunmur, D. A., Hunt, D. C., and Jessup, J. E., The influence of
    intermolecular interactions on the Kerr effect in gases II.
    Experimental results for spherical top molecules, Molec.
    Phys., 37:713.
Dunmur, D. A., Manterfield, M. R., and Robinson, D. J., 1983,
    Depolarized light scattering studies of the collision-
    induced polarizability anisotropy of atoms and spherical
    top molecules, Molec. Phys., 50:573.
Fortune, P. J., and Certain, P. R., 1974, Dielectric properties of
    helium: The polarizability of diatomic helium, J. Chem.
    Phys., 61:2620.
Frommhold, L., 1981, Collision-induced scattering of light and
    the diatom polarizabilities, Advan. Chem. Phys., 46:1.
Frommhold, L., and Proffitt, M. H., 1978, About the anisotropy of
    the polarizability of a pair of argon atoms, Molec. Phys.,
    35:681.
Ho, W., Birnbaum, G., and Rosenberg, A., 1971, Far-infrared
    collision-induced absorption in CO_2. I. Temperature
    dependence, J. Chem. Phys., 55:1028.
Kirouac, S., and Bose, T. K., 1973, Dielectric and pressure virial
    coefficients of imperfect gases. Pure N_2O, J. Chem. Phys.,
    59:3043.
Kirouac, S., and Bose, T. K., 1976, Polarizability and dielectric
    properties of helium, J. Chem. Phys., 64:1580.

Kress, J. W., and Kozak, J. J., 1977, Determination of the pair polarizability tensor for the Ne diatom, J. Chem. Phys., 66:4516.

O'Brien, E. F., Gutschick, V. P., McKoy, V., and McTague, J. P., 1973, Polarizability of interacting atoms: Relation to collision-induced light-scattering and dielectric models, Phys. Rev. A, 8:690.

Orcutt, R. H., and Cole, R. H., 1967, Dielectric constant of imperfect gases. III. Atomic gases, hydrogen, and nitrogen, J. Chem. Phys., 46:697.

Shelton, D. P., and Tabisz, G. C., 1981, A comparison of the collision-induced light scattering by argon and by isotropic molecular gases, Can. J. Phys., 59:1430.

Sutter, H., and Cole, R. H., 1970, Dielectric and pressure virial coefficients of imperfect gases. I. Polar halogenated methanes, J. Chem. Phys., 52:132.

Vidal, D., and Lallemand, M., 1976, Evolution of the Clausius-Mossotti function of noble gases and nitrogen at moderate and high density, near room temperature, J. Chem. Phys., 64:4293.

Watson, R. C., and Rowell, R. L., 1974, Depolarized light scattering from Ar, Kr, CH_4, SF_6 and $C(CH_3)_4$ at pressures around 1 atm, J. Chem. Phys., 61:2666.

Zoppi, M., Barocchi, F., Proffitt, M. H., and Frommhold, L., 1981, Determination of the collision-induced depolarized Raman light scattering cross section of the argon diatom, Can. J. Phys., 59:1418.

THE INFRARED AND RAMAN LINE SHAPES

OF PAIRS OF INTERACTING MOLECULES

Jacek Borysow and Lothar Frommhold

Physics Department
University of Texas at Austin
Austin, Tx 78712

ABSTRACT

   Existing line shape computations of collision-induced infrared
and Raman spectra are reviewed. The theory of free-free transitions
of binary molecular complexes is sketched. For line shape calculations, two extreme standpoints are of a special interest. One
attempts the most realistic modeling of the molecular interaction as
a basis for critical comparisons of the fundamental theory with measurements, for predicting unknown spectra from theory, for determining empirical induced dipole and polarizability models, and for
providing exact quantum profiles to test line shape models. Examples
of such computations have no adjustable parameters and agree closely
with measured profiles on an absolute intensity scale if spectra are
obtained at low densities where binary collisions prevail. The other
extreme aims for the generic features of collision-induced spectra
from minimal specific assumptions. Selected line shape functions
with three or more adjustable parameters are capable of approximating
certain spectral components closely, are inexpensive to compute and
can be used for temperature interpolation of computed or measured
spectra. Various previously proposed model functions differ strikingly with respect to the goodness of fit attainable.

INTRODUCTION

   Infrared and Raman spectra of ordinary molecules are well understood (Herzberg, 1945 and 1967). Here, we are concerned with the
shapes of spectra of "supermolecules" consisting of two non-reactive
monomers interacting via van der Waals or other forces. These may be
bound dimers, or short-lived collisional complexes in the free state.

67

We will emphasize "collision-induced" spectra arising from free-free transitions, but the bound-bound and bound-free spectral contributions involving dimers can usually not be separated from the former and most discussions of collisional induction must necessarily address the dimer contributions. We will assume that the gas densities are low so that three-, four- etc. body interactions are negligible; spectral profiles of liquids and solids are shaped by many-body interactions and will not be considered here. Recently, Birnbaum et al. (1982) have published an excellent review article on the subject of collision-induced spectral line shapes in the low-density limit. We can, therefore, restrict ourselves to the review of new developments, and material covered in that review will be included only to the extent desirable for a self-contained document. We note that the term monomer used above is meant to designate the basic constituents of a gas, which may be atoms or molecules, usually in the electronic ground state.

Principally, we are interested in the non-polar gases, pure or mixed, whose monomers are not infrared active; electronic transitions are discussed by Julienne (1985) and will only marginally concern us here. Four mechanisms are known which induce a dipole by collisional interaction (Buckingham, 1967; Meyer, 1985): i. polarization of an atom/ molecule in the electric multipole field of another molecule; ii. short-range electronic overlap forces arising from electron exchange; iii. long-range dispersion forces arising from electron intercorrelation; and iv. frame distortion if molecular symmetries are perturbed in the collision. We will also briefly discuss collision-induced Raman spectra which arise from variations of monomer polarizabilities during collisional interaction. These are caused by fluctuations of the local fields due to the presence of a collisional partner, and to some lesser extent by overlap forces. A unified line shape theory applicable to both infrared and Raman spectra is outlined below.

HISTORICAL SKETCH

Collision-induced infrared absorption was discovered by Welsh and associates in 1949, in an attempt to observe an infrared absorption band of oxygen dimers (Welsh 1972). In pure and mixed gases a great variety of collision-induced absorption spectra is now known, ranging from purely translational and rotational spectra in the far infrared to fundamental and overtone rotation-vibration spectra in the near infrared. Several reviews of experimental work have been published. We mention the work of Ketelaar (1959), Filimonov (1959), Vodar and Vu (1963), Colpa (1965), Tonkov (1970), Welsh (1972), a volume of lectures edited by Van Kranendonk (1980); see also the October issue (vol. 59, 1981) of the Canadian Journal of Physics which contains a special section on collisional induction. The spectra have usually broad features because of the short lifetime ($\sim 10^{-12}$ sec) of collisional complexes. At not too high pressures collision-induced intensities are independent of pressure if normalized by the square of density. At high enough densities, intercollisional interference (Van Kranendonk, 1968) and other many-body effects modify the appearance of binary spectra which must be avoided for our purpose. Especially at the lowest frequencies one may find density-dependent normalized absorption coefficients, $\alpha/n_A n_B$, due to many-body interactions (Poll, 1980).

The basic theory of collision-induced absorption (CIA) has been developed by Van Kranendonk and coworkers (1951, 1957, 1958, 1959; with Kiss, 1959; with Poll, 1961) and other authors (Mizushima, 1949 and 1950; Britton and Crawford, 1958; Colpa and Ketelaar, 1958). These authors emphasize spectral moments and sum formulae which can be computed at lesser expense than exact line shapes. However, one may expect that the shape of induced spectra, with its "differential" features like slopes and curvatures, and its fine structures related to dimers, will depend to a greater degree on the exact details of the molecular interactions than the spectral moments which are integrals, i.e. averages of the spectral function. Therefore, there have been many attempts to construct translational band shapes from more or less sophisticated dynamical models. In the short historical overview that follows, somewhat arbitrarily we suppress the extensive literature on theoretical band shapes of bound-free transitions, such as the ones arising from electronic transitions $^3\Sigma_g \rightarrow \, ^3\Sigma_u$ of H_2 (James and Coolidge, 1939), which may be considered the inverse of a collision-induced process. Work of this kind is of considerable interest and predates the discovery of CIA. The band shape of electronic CIA was considered by Erkovitch (1960) who in a wave mechanical framework obtains the coefficient of continous absorption of two hydrogen atoms in $^3\Sigma_u \rightarrow \, ^3\Sigma_g$ transitions. The work was repeated with a more realistic potential of the initial state, with significantly different results (Solomon, 1964). In the Born-Oppenheimer approximation, when dealing with electronic CIA (Julienne, 1985), one needs separate interaction potentials for initial and final states, but otherwise electronic CIA is formally similar as our main subject, supermolecular CIA. For the latter, Nikitin (1959) develops a line shape theory in quasi-classical approximation, applicable to induced rotational and vibrational absorption bands of nonpolar molecules undergoing binary collisions. Maryott and Birnbaum (1962) give a Fourier integral treatment of an induced dipole function consistent with a classical rotating multipole, assuming straight-line trajectories but taking into account the finite size of colliding CO_2 molecules. Tanimoto (1966) considered CIA band shapes of rare gas mixtures using wave mechanics. By assuming an exponential repulsive potential, the radial Schrödinger equation was solved analytically. The transition matrix elements of the dipole operator were obtained in closed form by choosing a range parameter solely for mathematical integrability. The spectral function is thus calculated by a single numerical integration. Trafton (1966) considered the H_2-H_2 system for its astrophysical interest and presented exact quantum calculations of the translational shape, based on a Lennard-Jones 6-12 potential and an empirical dipole moment; such calculations must of course be done by numerical procedures at all levels. These papers develop the line shape theory from the dynamics of molecular colli-

69

sions, with more or less realistic assumptions concerning the interactions. Alternatively, a more statistical language can be adopted
based on the dipole autocorrelation function (Tokuyama and Mori,
1975; Birnbaum et al., 1982). Still another valid approach has been
to consider the collisional pair as a kind of supermolecule and use
standard expressions formulated for ordinary molecules (Herzberg,
1945 and 1967) to compute its infrared or Raman spectra, replacing
the radial bound-state wavefunctions by properly normalized free-
state ones. In this case, additional summations over the various
transitions with identical energy differences must be made (Frommhold
et al., 1978a). The various descriptions lead to identical results.

Levine and Birnbaum (1967) developed a classical model line
shape on the basis of straight-line trajectories and a suitable dipole function. Levine (1967) gave a quantum model based on the same
assumptions. These concepts could also be applied to the case of
collision-induced scattering (CIS) of light (Levine and Birnbaum,
1968). Subsequent attempts based on classical mechanics and more or
less realistic potential and induction operator models are known both
for CIA and CIS.* According to Bohr's correspondence principle, classical mechanics provides a useful description of molecular collisions
if large numbers of partial waves are involved, $m\bar{v}b_{max}/\hbar \gg 1$, that
is for massive systems at high temperatures. Here, m designates the
reduced mass, $\bar{v}$ the thermal average of the relative speed, b_{max} the
range of the interaction and $\hbar$ Planck's constant. Under such conditions, theoretical profiles based on Newtonian mechanics may be expected to describe measured ones over a limited range of frequencies,
$|\hbar\omega| \ll kT$ (k= Boltzmann constant, T= temperature). This limitation
is related to the fact that classical profiles are symmetric, $g_c(\omega) = g_c(-\omega)$, while quantum profiles, as well as measurements, satisfy
detailed balance,

$$g(-\omega) = e^{-\hbar\omega/kT} g(\omega) \ . \tag{1}$$

Various symmetrizing factors have been proposed, such as $\exp(-\hbar\omega/2kT)$
and $(1 + \exp(-\hbar\omega/kT))/2$, which will generate a symmetric (and suppos-
edly nearly classical) spectral profile from the measurements or,
inversely, convert a classical line shape into one which satisfies
detailed balance (1). However, as far as we know, there is no rigorous basis for any one of these and a great many functions can be
invented that are equally effective in symmetrizing measured profiles
but are mutually inconsistent at high frequencies. A comparative
study of various symmetrization techniques shows that some of the

---

*We mention the works of McQuarrie and Bernstein (1968), Gersten and
Foley (1966 and 1968), Okada et al. (1968), Brenner and McQuarrie
(1971), Strauss and Weiss (1979) and Weiss and Strauss (1980) dealing
with CIA. For CIS, we have the works by Gersten (1971), Lallemand
(1971), Frommhold (1975) and Bafile et al. (1983).

common procedures lead to functions which differ widely from classical profiles (Borysow, Moraldi and Frommhold 1985). Furthermore, we mention that the effect of dimers (viz. bound-bound and bound-free spectral components), and of scattering resonances, can rarely be ignored in intermolecular spectroscopy but cannot be computed very well on the basis of classical mechanics. For all these reasons, a quantum mechanical theory of the spectral profile appears to be indispensable.

The early efforts in CIA line shapes were followed by a number of quantum computations based on more or less realistic potential and dipole models. Similar wave mechanical efforts are known for CIS. All of these will be considered below, in the section headed RESULTS. In an attempt to broadly summarize these efforts, we note that two extreme standpoints are of a special interest: the generic and the specific modeling of CIA/CIS spectra. On the one hand, it is possible to describe the general features of such spectra from minimal assumptions concerning the interactions. Drastically simplified molecular dynamics, etc., can be used to define simple model line shape functions which, under favorable conditions and after suitable adjustment of a few parameters, may approximate exact profiles quite well over a limited range of intensities. If such generic profiles are inexpensive to compute and approximate the spectra accurately over a significant portion of the profile, they are of great utility. Some such models will be considered in the last section below. On the other hand, it is clear that much is to be gained by modeling the specific details of induction operator and potential as realistically as possible, for example, for the comparison of spectroscopic measurements with the fundamental theory.

Computed line shapes depend strongly on the details of induction operator and potential model. Small variations (~1%) of such parameters as range and relative strength of the induction operator components, the collision diameter σ, the slope of the potential model near σ, etc., cause surprisingly large variations (~10%) of computed profiles. Inversely, since measured spectra of high quality may be thought of as defining accurately the induction operator (and, to a lesser extent, the potential) at separations of the spectroscopic interactions, $R \simeq \sigma$, a most discriminating analysis of measurements appears to be possible by fitting theoretical to measured line shapes. For accurate work, it would be a grave mistake to ignore the wealth of information available on intermolecular potentials. Enormous theoretical and experimental efforts are being undertaken in many laboratories to determine intermolecular forces on the broadest possible basis (Maitland et al., 1981). For most rare gas systems, and for a number of simple molecular systems, sophisticated semi-empirical potential models exist which are consistent with a broad selection of transport, equilibrium and beam scattering data, and with the fundamental theory at near and distant range. These were shown to be much superior, for example, to the Lennard-Jones model that once was popular. However, for other systems of current interest in astrophysics (viz. H_2-CH_4 etc.), no widely tested potential models seem to exist and CIA/CIS spectroscopy may be helpful in determining certain parameters of interaction potential models for such systems if accurate measurements at several temperatures exist.

For most CIA/CIS line shape computations of molecular systems, only isotropic interaction potentials have been considered to date. However, Schaefer and Meyer (1985) compute the collision-induced emission (CIE) spectra of H2-H2 at low temperatures (<40K), using their recent anisotropic ab initio interaction potential. Other recent work has investigated the effect of the anisotropy of the H2-He system on the translation/ rotational band (Moraldi et al., 1985). A guarded summary of the scarce work with anisotropic potentials would be that for the systems H2-H2 and H2-He the anisotropy does apparently not much affect the line shapes and intensities, but more work is required for a more critical assessment, even for these systems. Other molecular systems, of course, have greater anisotropies and it is not at all clear whether these can be neglected. A better understanding of the effect of the anisotropy of the potential on the CIA/CIS spectra is needed. For the computation of specific profiles numerical procedures must be used and computational expenses are not negligible even if the isotropic potential approximation is employed. Nevertheless, a significant advantage for the analysis of experimental data, for the testing and development of simple and dependable model line shape functions, and for the important astrophysical applications involving temperature interpolation of measured spectra etc., appear to justify such efforts to the fullest extent.

THEORY

In view of the extensive literature quoted, it is sufficient to compile here the basic equations needed for exact line shape computations. The absorption coefficient at the temperature T and angular frequency $\omega = 2\pi c \nu$, arising from collision-induced dipoles, can be written as

$$\alpha(\omega;T) = \frac{4\pi^2}{3\hbar c} n_A n_B \ \omega(1 - e^{-\hbar\omega/kT}) \ V \ g(\omega;T) \ , \tag{2}$$

where n_A, n_B are number densities of the dissimilar gases A,B; for like pairs, the product $n_A n_B$ must be replaced by $n^2/2$. V is the volume and $g(\omega;T)$ the spectral density, defined in terms of the matrix elements $\langle t|\vec{\mu}_{ss'}|t'\rangle$ of the induced electric dipole moment $\vec{\mu}$, by the "golden rule" of quantum mechanics,

$$V \ g(\omega;T) = \sum_{ss'} P_s \ \sum_{tt'} V \ P_t \ |\langle t|\vec{\mu}_{ss'}|t'\rangle|^2 \ \delta(\omega_{ss'} + \omega_{tt'} - \omega) \tag{3}$$

where the subscripts s = {j1,m1,v1,j2,m2,v2} and t= {ℓ,m_ℓ,E_t} denote molecular and translational states, respectively; a prime denotes final states and P_t and P_s are normalized Boltzmann factors (Birnbaum et al., 1982 and 1984b). Positive frequencies correspond to absorption, but the spectral function $g(\omega;T)$ is also defined for negative frequencies which correspond to emission. We note that the absorption coefficient $\alpha(\omega;T)$ differs from the spectral function $g(\omega;T)$ by a factor correcting for stimulated emission. In CIS, the spectral function $g(\omega;T)$ is directly related to the Raman scattering cross section and thus to measurement; in this case, we substitute for the dipole an induced polarizability and positive frequency shifts correspond to the Stokes wing (Frommhold et al., 1978).

If linear molecules are involved, we express the νth component of the induction operator in terms of vector coupled functions,

$$\mu_\nu^{(r)}(R,\Omega,\Omega_1,\Omega_2) = \frac{(4\pi)^{3/2}}{\sqrt{2r+1}} \sum_{\lambda_1\lambda_2\Lambda L} B_{\lambda_1\lambda_2\Lambda L}(R) \; Y_{L\lambda_1\lambda_2\Lambda}^{r\nu}(\Omega,\Omega_1,\Omega_2) \quad (4)$$

with $\nu = 0, \pm1, ..\pm r$, and $Y_{L\lambda_1\lambda_2\Lambda}^{r\nu}(\Omega,\Omega_1,\Omega_2) =$

$$\sum_{MM_1M_2M_\Lambda} C(\lambda_1\lambda_2\Lambda;M_1M_2M_\Lambda) \; C(L\Lambda r;MM_\Lambda\nu) \; Y_L^M(\Omega) \; Y_{\lambda_1}^{M_1}(\Omega_1) \; Y_{\lambda_2}^{M_2}(\Omega_2) \; . \quad (5)$$

The Ω,Ω_1,Ω_2 are the orientations of the vector joining the molecular centers of mass, and of the internuclear axes of molecules 1 and 2, respectively. If other than linear molecules are involved, the spherical harmonics $Y_L^M(\Omega)$ must be replaced by rotation matrices (Frost, 1973).

For CIA, the rank of the dipole induction operator is $r=1$. In this case, Eq. 4 is identical with similar expressions given previously (Poll and Hunt, 1976; Hunt and Poll, 1978; Nikitin, 1959). For depolarized CIS spectra, on the other hand, the induced polarizability is of the second rank, $r=2$, and for trace scattering we have $r=0$. Similar tensor notation was used in light scattering elsewhere (Berne and Pecora, 1976; Frenkel and McTague, 1980). We note that the induction operators in (4) depend on the vibrational coordinates R_1,R_2, and B is here understood as the vibrational average if purely rotational/ translational spectra are considered, or else as a vibrational transition element if the fundamental or overtone induced bands are considered. For symmetric molecules, only even λ_1 and λ_2 occur; if one (or both) of the collisional partners are nonrotating atoms, one (or both) of the λ_1,λ_2 are identically zero. After some algebra, it is seen that the spectral function can be written as a multiple sum of incoherent components labeled $\lambda_1\lambda_2\Lambda L$,

$$V g(\omega;T) = \sum_{\lambda_1\lambda_2\Lambda L} \sum_{j_1j_1'j_2j_2'} (2j_1+1)P_{j_1}C(j_1\lambda_1 j_1';000)^2 (2j_2+1)P_{j_2}$$

$$\times C(j_2\lambda_2 j_2';000)^2 \; V \; G_{\lambda_1\lambda_2\Lambda L}(\omega - \omega_{j_1j_1'} - \omega_{j_2j_2'};T) \; . \quad (6)$$

If vibrational induced bands are considered, in the argument of the spectral function the rotational transition frequencies $\omega_{jj'}$ must be

supplemented by the vibrational ones, $\omega_{vv'}$. In any case, in the isotropic potential approximation, only translational spectral functions
G are computed numerically and the complete spectrum can then be constructed by superposition of properly shifted translational components,

$$V\, G_{\lambda 1\lambda 2\Lambda L}(\omega;T) = \lambda_o^3 \hbar \sum_{\ell\ell'} (2\ell+1)\, C(\ell L\ell';000)^2\, w(\ell\ell'j1\mathring{j}1j2\mathring{j}2) \quad (7)$$

$$\times \int_0^\infty |\langle \ell,E_t|B_{\lambda 1\lambda 2\Lambda L}(R)|\ell',E_t+\hbar\omega\rangle|^2\, e^{-E_t/kT}\, dE_t\ .$$

For like pairs, the weight $w(..)$ accounts for molecular symmetry. At
high enough temperature, and for dissimilar pairs, we may assume a
constant $w=1$. The radial wave functions $|\ell,E_t\rangle$ or $\psi(R;\ell,E_t)/R$ are
solutions of the Schrödinger equation of relative motion of the collisional pair,

$$\frac{-\hbar^2}{2m}\frac{d^2\psi}{dR^2} + \left(V_o(R) + \frac{\hbar^2\ell(\ell+1)}{2mR^2} - E_t\right)\psi = 0\ . \tag{8}$$

For easy integration in (7), they are assumed to be energy normalized,

$$\int_0^\infty \psi^*(R;\ell,E_{t'})\,\psi(R;\ell,E_t)\,dR = \delta(E_{t'}-E_t). \tag{9}$$

If the system under consideration forms dimers, the integral (7) over
E_t must include a sum over bound states; in that case the normalization of ψ requires that the δ-function to the right of (9) is replaced by the Kroneker $\delta_{vv'}$ symbol as usual, where v is the vibrational quantum number of the dimer. Our treatment, which is described in somewhat greater detail elsewhere (Birnbaum et al., 1984b;
Meyer et al, 1985) assumes an isotropic interaction potential. Anisotropic potentials mean an enormous complication (Birnbaum et al;,
1984b; Schaefer and Meyer, 1985; Moraldi et al;, 1985); such work is
of considerable interest. The anisotropy of important molecules,
such as H2, is quite small and can often be neglected.

The formalism sketched can be considered a unified treatment of
CIA and CIS line shapes. It is important that the integration over
pre-dissociating states (7) must be done with care if scattering resonances are encountered. Extremely sharp resonances can be included
in the discrete sum over bound states, but the broader resonances require a carefully tailored energy grid for an exact integration. We
note that for the integration over energy in (7), even high-order (20
to 40 point) Gauss-Laguerre integration formulae were found inadequate. Third-order spline integration gave the necessary flexibility
to account for shape resonances, and satisfactory results were
obtained for a truncated integration interval from $E_t \simeq kT/100$ (instead of 0) to 15kT (instead of ∞). Similarly, the improper radial

integrals $\langle \ell E|B|\ell'E'\rangle$ can simply be truncated at an R_{max} of 12 – 20
Å; only for the treatment of the far wing, i.e. for ω with $G(0)/G(\omega)$
$> 10^3$, a proper estimate of the truncated part is needed. For a
given L and each ℓ value, the few allowed ℓ' are obtained from the
properties of the $C(\ell L\ell'; 000)$ and (7) can be rewritten as a single
sum over ℓ. This sum is truncated at a suitable ℓ_{max}, but substantial savings of computer time seem possible if the truncated part is
estimated by simple numerical techniques currently under study in our
laboratory.

The spectral function (6) consists of a number of lines at rotational transition frequencies of the monomers ($j_1 \neq j_1'$ and $j_2 = j_2'$; or
$j_2 \neq j_2'$ and $j_1 = j_1'$), lines at sums and differences of such rotation frequencies (simultaneous transitions; both $j_1 \neq j_1'$ and $j_2 \neq j_2'$), and a
translational component ($j_1 = j_1'$ and $j_2 = j_2'$; or $j_1 = j_2'$ and $j_2 = j_1'$).
Equation 6 shows how the λ_1, λ_2 impose selection rules on the molecular transitions, and Eq. 7 shows similarly how the expansion parameter L controls translational transitions through basic properties
of the Clebsch–Gordan coefficients; $C(j\lambda j'; 000) = 0$ unless the value
of the sum of j, λ and j' is an even integer and the triangular
inequalities are satisfied. We note that Eq. 7 describes the main
computational efforts of line shape calculations. Radial wavefunctions are obtained at thousands of grid points, usually with the
Numerov algorithm (Cooley, 1961; Cashion, 1963). For a numerical
precision of ~1% of the end result, five thousand radial matrix ele-
ments $\langle \ell E_t|B|\ell'E_{t'}\rangle$ are computed for H_2–H_2 at 50K, and more for the
more massive systems and higher temperatures. On a Cyber 170/750,
this amounts to thousands of seconds of central processor time. In
comparison with this, all other calculations needed for the line
shape are instantaneous. Among other things, this remark illustrates
the savings that are possible if the computation of Eq. 7 is avoided
by substituting for $VG(\omega;T)$ suitable generic functions of the type
discussed in the last section below. We note that the use of modern
array processors or class VI supercomputers reduces the computational
expense substantially.

RESULTS

CIA of Mixed Monatomic Gases

The existence of very careful measurements of He-Ar and Ne-Ar
CIA spectra, such as Bosomworth and Gush's (1965), has stimulated
theoretical research particularly on these systems. Ab initio computations of the induced dipole moment are known: Matcha and Nesbet
(1967); Whisnant and Byers Brown (1973); Lacey and Byers Brown
(1974); Bentley (1979); Shlyapnikov and Shmator (1980); Birnbaum et
al. (1984a); Meyer and Frommhold, 1985; see also Meyer, 1985).
Furthermore, several quantum line shape calculations are known based
on these, or alternatively on empirical induced dipole models, and on
more or less realistic potentials, see the works of Tanimoto (1966);
Levine (1967); Sears (1968); Marteau and Schuller (1972); Sharma and

Hart (1974 and 1975); Shlyapnikov and Shmator (1980); Birnbaum et al. (1981 and 1984a); Raczynski (1982, 1983 and 1984); and Meyer and Frommhold (1985). Our detailed line shape analyses of the rare gas systems has uncovered an error of the ab initio induced dipole data for the systems containing neon which has recently been corrected (Birnbaum et al., 1984a). We mention that it has, furthermore, demonstrated that the inclusion of the lowest-order dispersion term leads to profiles that are discernibly superior in reproducing the measurements; a moment analysis, on the other hand, could not demonstrate the improvement (Birnbaum et al., 1981). The use of obsolete potential models, such as the Lennard-Jones model, could be shown to lead to computed spectral profiles which approximate the measurements less closely than current potential models (Birnbaum et al., 1981). For accurate work, it is, therefore, of great importance to use an interaction potential which is consistent with the widest selection of empirical and theoretical data possible, especially those that define the region around the collision diameter σ. Modern reviews of the potential field, such as Maitland et al.'s (1981), are invaluable sources of the most useful information on interactions.

In Fig. 1, the theoretical Ne-Ar absorption coefficient, $\alpha(\omega;T)/n_A n_B$, and the spectral function, $g(\omega;T)$, are compared with a measurement (Bosomworth and Gush, 1964). These are based on an advanced interaction potential (Aziz, 1984) and on the recent ab initio dipole moment (Birnbaum et al., 1984a) supplemented by the lowest order dispersion part (Whisnant and Byers Brown, 1973). Except at the lowest frequencies < 50 cm^{-1} where the intercollisional effect may have affected the measurement, the agreement is within our rough

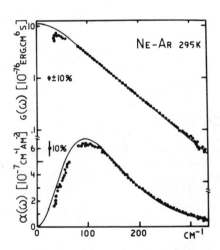

Fig. 1 Ne-Ar absorption coefficient (lower part) and spectral function at 295K.

estimate of the experimental uncertainty (±6%), in most places even better. Both theory and measurement are expressed in absolute intensity units and no adjustable parameters are employed. The ab initio induced dipole data used in these computations are among the most advanced data presently available, but we note that these are not necessarily the definitive ones; higher-order dispersion terms and, perhaps, dispersion damping functions as known from potential modeling, should be included but are at present not known (Meyer, 1985). From unpublished modeling attempts, it is believed that the inclusion of such refinements cannot remove the observed minor inconsistency at low frequencies. We mention that in the computations shown in Fig. 1, a summation over one hundred partial waves was undertaken; about 10,000 radial matrix elements were computed. The result was tested with the help of sum formulae for the 0th, 1st and 2nd moments of the spectra (Moraldi, 1983 and 1984). Agreement is within 1%; only the theoretical zeroth moment is ~3% smaller than its sum formula. This difference is due to the Ne-Ar dimer contribution, which was suppressed in the line shape computation as it appears at the experimentally unaccessible frequencies from 0-20 cm^{-1}; the sum formula, however, includes a dimer contribution of this magnitude.

Quantum line shapes for other monatomic systems are also known. For the most accurate work, agreement with measurements (when available) is typically at the 10% level. H-He was considered by Ulrich et al. (1972); Xe-Ar by Marteau and Schuller (1972); Li-He, Na-He, Li-Ne, Na-Ne by Bottcher et al. (1973); He-Ar, Ne-Ar, and Ar-Kr by Birnbaum et al. (1981); He-Xe by Raczynski (1982 and 1983); He-Ar, Ne-Ar, Ne-Kr, Ar-Kr by Birnbaum et al. (1984). For the first time, highly correlated wavefunctions were used in such work for He-Ar (Meyer and Frommhold, 1985). Inconsistencies relative to measurements at low frequencies (like in Fig. 1) are sometimes observed; small inconsistencies seen elsewhere probably reflect uncertainties of potential and induction operator models. For CIA dipole spectra of diatomic systems, the multiple sums in (6) consist of a single term with L=1 (and, of course, $\lambda_1 = \lambda_2 = \Lambda = j_1 = j_1' = j_2 = j_2' = 0$ and r=1). Line shape computations of electronic free-bound transitions of H-H were mentioned above (Solomon, 1964). The shapes of the similar free-bound and free-free electronic transitions $X^1\Sigma_g^+ \rightarrow A^1\Sigma_u^+$ of He-He have also been reported (Sando and Dalgarno, 1971; and Sando, 1971). Recent work of interest for the physics of lasers is described by Julienne (1985); we mention especially the studies of group VI - rare gas systems, and the gain profiles ("negative absorption") of such systems discussed in the article on collision-induced electronic spectral profiles. A spectral function which differs from (7) was used by Sharma and Hart (1974 and 1975) with little justification. The resulting He-Ne and He-Ar line shapes are inconsistent with computations based on (7), assuming identical input (Birnbaum et al., 1981). Spectral moments computed from these profiles are inconsistent with the values calculated with Hartye et al.'s (1975) widely used sum formulae.

CIS of Monatomic Gases

  Collision-induced light scattering was first investigated by
McTague and Birnbaum (1971). Recently, stimulated by the availability of consistent binary spectra, a theoretical effort was undertaken
to compute rare gas diatom polarizabilitities from first principles
(Dacre, 1978, 1981, 1982a-d). If these ab initio data are combined
with the most advanced interaction potentials currently available,
CIS spectra are computed which show a very satisfactory agreement
with the measurements (Dacre and Frommhold, 1982). In Figure 2a, we
compare the depolarized spectra of the isotopic pairs ^{4}He-^{4}He and
^{3}He-^{3}He with theoretical spectra based on the ab initio induced polarizability and an advanced interaction potential (Aziz et al.,
1979). Remarkably good agreement with ·the measurement is observed
over a range of intensities approximating 500:1; no adjustable parameters are used. For the other like-pair systems (Ne-Ne, Ar-Ar,
Kr-Kr, Xe-Xe), induced polarizabilities could, of course, not be
obtained from first principles with the rigor of the He-He work.
Whereas for the Ne-Ne system configuration interaction is accounted
for to some limited extent, for the heavier systems this is out of
question and empirical estimates of the effect of electron correla-

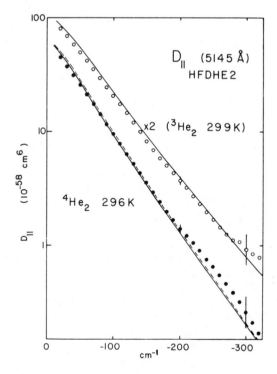

Fig. 2a Depolarized CIS spectra of the helium isotopes (Dacre and
    Frommhold, 1982).

tion, based on the He-He and Ne-Ne computations, had to be used. Depolarized line shapes computed from these show an amazing degree of
consistency with measurements, often over a range of intensities that
exceeds 10^5:1 (!), usually within the experimental errors of less
than 10% (Dacre and Frommhold, 1982). Empirical induced polarizability models derived from the depolarized spectra differ very little
from the ab initio results (Proffitt et al., 1981; Frommhold, 1981).
We note that for most of the like rare gas systems, very accurate
interaction potentials exist; the small remaining differences between
the best current potentials affect the computed CIA spectra relatively little (Dacre and Frommhold, 1982). For depolarized spectra, we
have L=2 (and $\lambda_1 = \lambda_2 = \Lambda = j_1 = j_1' = j_2 = j_2' = 0$ and r=2); again, the multiple sum in (6) consists of a single term.

It is clear that the main contribution to the depolarized CIS
spectra is due to the classical dipole-induced dipole (DID) anisotropy, but small overlap corrections, usually of opposite sign
relative to the leading DID term, must be applied at near range in
order to reproduce the spectroscopic measurements from theory. However, there seems to be some uncertainty about the form of this correction. One school uses a three-parameter induction operator
(Barocchi and Zoppi, 1981),

$$B(R) = 6\alpha^2/R^3 + B_6/R^6 - B_0 \exp(-R/R_0) \ , \tag{10}$$

to fit three moments of Ar-Ar and similar depolarized spectra (Bafile
et al., 1983; Barocchi and Zoppi, 1985); a classical line shape
theory is used to eliminate the unphysical solutions.* For argon at
room temperature and at not too high frequencies, a classical theory
is a reasonable approximation. However, the coefficient B_6 needed
for a fit is one to two orders of magnitude larger than the fundamental theory suggests (Buckingham and Clarke, 1978; Hunt et al., 1981;
Dacre, 1978 - 1982; Hunt, 1985). The other school uses a two parameter model, Eq. 10 with $B_6=0$, to fit the measurement accurately with
a quantum profile, over the full range of intensities of 10^5:1
(Proffitt et al., 1981). At separations near the collision diameter,
the second and third terms of (10) are small relative to the leading
term, and with the measurements available, we seem to have reached

---

*Moment analysis uses polarizability model functions like (10) and
determines the two or three parameters (B_0, R_0; B_6) by setting an
equal number of theoretical sum formulae equal to the corresponding
spectral integrals of the measurement. In this way, multiple solutions of the moment equations are often found which solve the mathematical problem equally well. We have looked at a number of such
cases and have found invariably that, if line shapes are computed,
only one solution of the moment equations is reasonably consistent
with the measured line shape. All other solutions show striking
disagreement with the measured profile despite the matched moments.

the limit of resolution of a very discriminating analysis. More measurements at other temperatures are needed for significant progress in this field. Although these differences of the anisotropy models (10) are perhaps not too important for the binary spectra, we know that they lead to significantly different theoretical many-body spectra of liquids and should, therefore, be understood well (Bafile et al., 1983).

Depolarized translational spectra of systems involving molecules, which are treated as non-rotating systems, can similarly be considered: for CH₄-CH₄ see Prengel and Gornall (1976), and Proffitt and Frommhold (1979). The translational spectra of anisotropic gases (H_2 and D_2) have been recently communicated (Bafile et al., 1985; Brown et al., 1985). Allowed rotational Raman lines show a broad collision-induced shoulder which was recently investigated for H_2-H_2 and D_2-D_2 (Proffitt et al., 1985). Envelopes of rotational dimer bands have been seen in CIS spectroscopy (Prengel and Gornall, 1976; Frommhold et al., 1978a and 1978b). There is no doubt that in many cases dimers contribute significantly to the observed spectra, even at room temperatures. Free-bound scattering cross sections of H-H as function of the wavelength of the incident light, from zero frequency to Lyman α, have been computed from first principles; a resonance Raman scattering treatment was used for the first time for collisional pairs (Federman and Frommhold, 1982).

For the case of induced <u>polarized</u> scattering, on the other hand, we have r=0 and L=0. Polarized CIS spectra cannot be measured very accurately because they are feeble and superimposed with the much

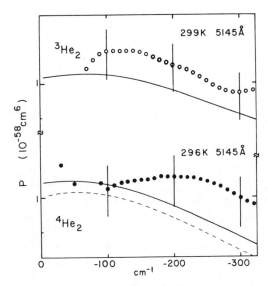

Fig. 2b Polarized CIS spectra of the helium isotopes (Dacre and Frommhold, 1982).

more intense depolarized component. The trace of the induced polarizability is very small and is, therefore, hard to compute accurately
from the fundamental theory. For the helium isotopes, Fig. 2b shows
a comparison of measurement and theory; under the circumstances the
agreement is satisfactory. Also, for most other like rare gas systems, reasonable agreement between theoretical and measured CIS spectra is observed (Dacre and Frommhold, 1982).

CIA of Linear Molecules: H_2-He

The absorption spectra of H_2-He are of great astrophysical
interest (Linsky, 1969; Trafton, 1973; Tipping, 1985). Translational
spectra were computed from quantum theory by Trafton (1973), while
the rotational S lines were added with the help of some model line
shape. Exact profiles of translational/ rotational spectra could recently be computed from the fundamental theory (Birnbaum et al.,
1984b). Available ab initio induced dipole moment computations
(Berns et al., 1978; Wormer and van Dijk, 1979; Meyer, 1985) suggest
that the first sum in (6) consists of only three significant terms:
the isotropic overlap, $L, \lambda_1 = 1, 0$; the anisotropic overlap 1,2; and
the quadrupole induced dipole 3,2; we have of course $\lambda_2 = 0$ and $\Lambda = 2$.
Rotational hydrogen lines appear for $j_1 \neq j_1'$. Figure 3 shows the three

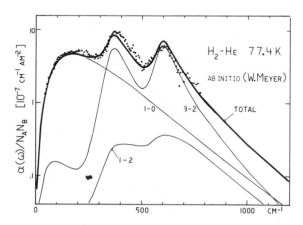

Fig. 3 CIA Rotational/Translational Spectrum of H_2-He, based on
Meyer's new ab initio dipole components.

components and their superposition; Birnbaum's (1978) measurement is also given for comparison. Agreement in the 10% range is observed at all temperatures. The Gengenbach-Hahn potential (1972) used in these computations supports no bound states or scattering resonances. Meyer's (1985) ab initio dipole data, obtained with highly correlated wavefunctions, allows to reproduce the spectroscopic measurements more closely than an earlier computation based on uncorrelated dipoles (Birnbaum et al., 1984b). We note that the ab initio trans-lational/ rotational CIA spectra can be modeled rather accurately over the temperature range from 50 to 300K in seconds from simple relations given by Borysow et al. (1984). Spectra computed on the basis of a recent ab initio potential are about 10% less intense relative to a computation based on the Gengenbach-Hahn potential (Birnbaum et al., 1984b). We note that the measurement of CIA spec-tra in the mixture must be corrected for the H_2-H_2 contribution, and Fig. 3 shows the "difference spectrum" due to the dissimilar pair. The accuracy of difference spectra is necessarily not as good as that of the spectra of unmixed gases.

Hydrogen

CIA spectra of H_2-H_2 are of great interest in astrophysics (Trafton, 1966; Tipping, 1985). Translational spectra were computed from quantum theory by Trafton and Linsky, while the rotational S-lines were added with the help of a model line shape. Recent ab initio work (Meyer et al., 1985) has shown that for this system mainly five induction components matter: the quadrupole induced parts, $\lambda_1\lambda_2\Lambda L= 0223$ and 2023 which are equal; the anisotropic overlap parts 0221 and 2021 (also equal); and the quadrupole-induced double transition part (2233). For line shape computations, we select a recent isotropic potential of the HFD type (McConville, 1981), which was extensively tested with virial and beam scattering data (Buck et al., 1983). On the basis of this model, we conclude that the hydro-gen dimer features two bound states ($v=0$; $\ell= 0$ and 1), a narrow ($\ell=2$) and a broad ($\ell=3$) scattering resonance, which must be considered carefully in the integration of (7) when line shapes are computed. Figure 4 shows the translational/ rotational profile for the tempera-ture of 77K, obtained from first principles. The computed spectrum is in close agreement with the measurement (Birnbaum, 1978). Similar excellent agreement is observed at the other temperatures for which measurements exist (Meyer et al., 1985), except, perhaps, at the highest frequencies where the measurements are somewhat uncertain. Earlier work by Trafton established the significance of the H_2-H_2 ab-sorption process in the atmospheres of the outer planets (1966). Calculations were extended to higher temperatures by Linsky (1969), who also considers shapes of the fundamental and overtone bands in some approximative framework. Recent ab initio calculations of the translational/ rotational CIA spectra over a wide range of tempera-tures and wavenumbers have been closely approximated by a set of very simple model functions so that these spectra can be computed in seconds on small computers, without the need of cumbersome compu-tations (J. Borysow et al., 1985).

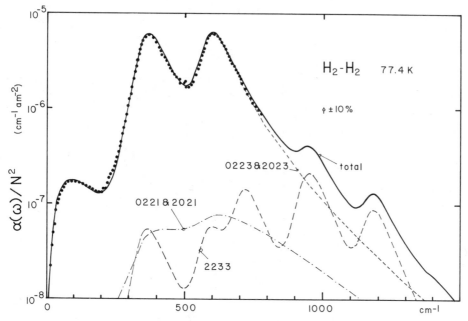

Fig. 4 CIA Translation/Rotational Spectrum of H_2-H_2.

In the Voyager infrared spectra of Jupiter and Saturn's upper atmosphere diminutive, unexplained structures were seen near the centers of the hydrogen $S_o(0)$ and $S_o(1)$ rotational lines (Hanel et al., 1979; Gautier et al., 1983). It is, therefore, interesting that our recent attempts to compute the hydrogen translational/ rotational CIA spectrum from first principles indicated narrow, surprisingly strong structures due to bound-free transitions involving the hydrogen dimer (Meyer et al., 1985); see the dotted lines in Fig. 5. These structures have not been seen in the laboratory measurements, presumably on account of the low resolution of $10 - 20cm^{-1}$ commonly employed in such work. However, if the theoretical structures are convoluted with a $4.3cm^{-1}$ slit function simulating the response of Voyager's monochromator, structures very similar to the ones seen in the Voyager spectra result (heavy curve, Fig. 5). In fact, if a detailed accounting of the temperature distribution arising from radiative transfer in Jupiter's atmosphere is made, the resulting theoretical structures match closely the measurement (Frommhold et al., 1984). We note that McKellar (1984) advanced independently an equivalent empirical explanation of these structures, on the basis of similar dimer structures seen at low temperatures (~20K) in laboratory recordings of the induced <u>vibrational</u> band (McKellar and Welsh, 1974).

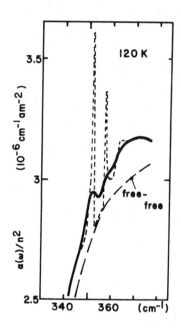

Fig. 5 Hydrogen dimer structures in the $S_0(0)$ rotational line.

Schaefer and Meyer (1985) have computed the collision-induced emission (CIE) spectrum of H_2-H_2 at low temperatures (<40K) using for the first time in such work an anisotropic potential. That spectrum can in principle be converted to an absorption spectrum by changing the sign of ω and accounting for stimulated emission, Eq. 1 and 2.

Other Linear Molecules

Quantum spectra of several other systems involving linear molecules (H_2-N_2, N_2-N_2, N_2-Ar, etc.) have been computed from isotropic potential models, known quadrupole moments, etc. at temperatures from 50-160K primarily for the purpose of modeling Titan's atmosphere (A. Borysow and Frommhold, 1985). Titan has an atmosphere consisting mainly of nitrogen and is the only object known with an atmosphere similar to the Earth's. Note the remark below concerning high dimer concentrations which may be equally applicable to some of these systems.

CIA with Tetrahedral Molecules

If molecules like CH_4 are involved, the line shape formulae (6,7) must be modified by replacing spherical harmonics by rotation matrices as pointed out elsewhere (Birnbaum et al., 1983). An isotropic interaction potential (Hanley and Klein, 1972) is assumed for the computations shown in Fig. 6. Pure octopole- and hexadecapole

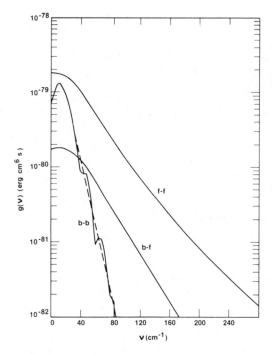

Fig. 6 Octopole-induced spectral function of CH4-CH4, shown are the free-free, bound-free and bound-bound contributions separately.

induced dipoles are assumed. The free-free (f-f), bound-free (b-f), and bound-bound (b-b) line shapes are shown for the pure octopole-induced part (L,Λ= 4,3); the small free-bound contribution is included in the curve marked b-f. These contributions are superimposed and combined with a similar three-part hexadecapole-induced profile (L,Λ= 5,4) for the fit of the measurement (which is not shown).

Typical methane potentials have well depths over Boltzmann constant, ε/k, of ≈186K, and substantial dimer concentrations are thus predicted at 195K, the temperature of the measurement (Birnbaum et al., 1983). This fact raises an interesting question to be addressed in the future. If dimer concentrations reach a critical level of perhaps a few percent, one cannot ignore monomer-dimer collisions and their induced spectra. Under such circumstances, one needs to develop a line shape theory based on ternary interactions; we have reached the limit of the binary theory. However, it may be possible to treat dimers (which would be relatively stable under these conditions) like an admixed species; separate accounting for monomer-monomer and monomer-dimer "binary" collisions may be sufficient to generate a reasonable approximation of CIA/CIS spectra. Present treatments do not consider the latter and may, therefore, be less useful the lower the temperatures, or the higher the pressures are of a measurement. Indeed show the fits of CH₄-CH₄ CIA spectra small deviations at high frequencies which are at present not understood. While we do not suggest that these must be due to ternary interactions, it is clear that the problem of high dimer concentrations has to be studied in more detail as it may have an effect even at the higher frequencies.

Work on other systems (H_2-CH_4, N_2-CH_4, etc.) is in progress (A. Borysow and Frommhold, 1985) but, unfortunately, the uncertainties in the interaction potentials are considerable and attempts are being made to model the interaction potentials along with the induction operator. Such work is motivated by the astrophysical interest in these systems (Tipping, 1985).

Quantum Profiles: Summary

We have seen that exact translational/ rotational CIA/CIS quantum line shapes of most binary molecular systems are now obtained routinely. Apart from molecular spectroscopic constants which are usually well known (Herzberg, 1945 and 1967), the computation requires an (isotropic) interaction potential and induced dipole function as input. Conversely, good measurements of CIA/CIS spectra can be considered to define these functions of the interaction in a region near the collision diameter σ. Discriminating line shape analyses of measured CIA/CIS spectra are possible. Less than two years prior to this writing the previous reviewers of the field of CIA/CIS line shapes (Birnbaum et al., 1982) pointed out that much recent progress was made with exact quantum calculations of translational band shapes in rare gases and rare gas mixtures, but relatively little had been accomplished with regard to the calculation of molecular band shapes; a regrettable lack of work with anisotropic potentials was also mentioned (Birnbaum et al., 1982). Above, we have shown exact molecular band shape computations which have evolved in the mean time; at present, the limitations appear to be due to insufficient CIA/CIS measurements and, sometimes, to the lack of accurate potential models, especially for some systems of astrophysical interest (H_2-N_2, H_2-CH_4, N_2-CH_4, etc.). Problems arising from dimer concentrations in excess of a few percent have been pointed out; all moment and line shape theories which neglect ternary interactions must be used with caution under such conditions. The first work with anisotropic potentials was also cited. Anisotropic potentials introduce an enormous complication to the numerical computations, but for the H_2-H_2 and H_2-He systems the final results apparently do not differ very much from the isotropic approximation. Clearly, more work is required to study the effect of anisotropic interactions, especially for the more anisotropic systems. No exact collision-induced vibrational quantum band shapes have been computed yet although, in principle, this is possible and should pose no special problems. The formalism (6,7) has also been applied to the computation of translational/ rotational CIS spectra of molecular hydrogen and deuterium which are superimposed with the allowed Raman S(0) and S(1) lines. For CIA of H_2-H_2 and H_2-He, the new ab initio induced dipole data now available have led to quantum profiles which are in a very close agreement with the existing measurements. There seems to be little need for empirical induced dipole models for these systems. For other systems, empirical dipole models have been obtained by modifying certain parameters (such as multipole moments and range parameters) until a good fit of the measurements is obtained. Although, in this report, we have emphasized the comparison of CIA/CIS measurements with new results of the fundamental theory, we do not want to suggest that this exhausts the usefulness of quantum line shape computations. In quantum line shape analysis, many characteristic features of measured spectra, such as amplitudes, widths, slopes, curvatures, dimer structures etc. can be utilized; it appears to be a remarkably discriminating tool.

MODEL LINE SHAPES

To the casual observer, the spectral functions $G(\omega;T)$ of various systems and temperatures look more or less alike: in a semi-logarithmic grid, one notices a concave, almost straight line, with more or less convex curvature near zero frequency. Such simple shape suggests that functions can be found that are inexpensive to compute and which approximate the exact profiles, Eq. 7, after adjustment of a few parameters. With the help of such model line shapes, complete translational/ rotational spectra can be constructed with efficiency even on small computers, according to Eq. 6. A great many expressions have been proposed that range from the simplest empirical model (a Lorentzian with exponential wings attached, Welsh and Hunt, 1963; Buontempo et al., 1975; Poll and Hunt, 1981) to elaborate quantum schemes (Weyland, 1978; Davies et al., 1982). We also mention recent work based on information theory (Joslin and Gray, 1984 and 1985; Dagg and Gray, 1985), and a caveat concerning the use of the information theoretical line shape in the collision-induced spectroscopies (Meinander and Tabisz, 1984). Birnbaum and Cohen's (BC) model (1976) is perhaps the most elegant of the proposed profiles, and one of the most successful ones in terms of modeling real quantum shapes (A. Borysow et al., 1984; J. Borysow et al., 1985). It is based on a minimum of specific assumptions and is known to approximate certain measurements closely (Birnbaum et al., 1982). From the above it is clear that exact quantum profiles are available for many systems and temperatures, and we find it interesting to study how well various model functions approximate these. Recent work has shown that least mean squares fits based on the BC model, especially of the quadrupole-induced components at high temperatures, are remarkably good, with rms deviations in the 1% range, even if the range of fitted intensities is as great as 500:1 (A. Borysow et al., 1984 and 1985; J. Borysow et al., 1985). We note that beyond that, a rapid deterioration of the far wing fit is observed which for most applications may be of no consequence. However, at temperatures of less than 80 K, especially with the overlap induced components, less satisfactory fits result, with rms deviations exceeding 10%, the more the lower the temperature. The BC model has three parameters which, for quantum systems, can be defined from the 0th, 1st and 2nd spectral moments; these in turn can be readily computed from potential and induction operators (Moraldi, 1983 and 1984). Spectra of H2-He can thus be generated rather inexpensively which approximate the exact quantum profiles closely (A. Borysow et al., 1984). This fact suggests an interesting, simple alternative to the full quantum line shape calculations which were seen to be rather involved. However, at the lowest temperatures (~50K) the quality of the fit deteriorates because certain components are not well approximated by the BC line shape at low temperature.

Recent work has shown that none of several existing alternative model line shapes give fits that are superior to the ones based on the BC model, but some are strikingly inferior. We mention that, for example, fits based on the Lorentzian model, at peak-to-wing intensity ratios of only 10:1, show rms deviations of ~10% or so, and maximal deviations in the 30% range, which make this model a rather inaccurate one that is best avoided. Profiles of the short-range operators ($L, \Lambda = 1, 0$ and $1, 2$) are not well approximated by a single BC model, but are fitted better by a similar profile called K_0 model (J. Borysow et al., 1985). Corrections obtained for these fits are about one-half the size of those for the BC model.

Significant improvements are possible by combining the BC and K_0 models,

$$S\Gamma(\omega) = \frac{S}{1+\epsilon} \left\{ \frac{\tau_1}{\pi} \exp\left(\frac{\tau_2}{\tau_1} + \tau_0 \omega \right) \frac{z K_1(z)}{1 + \omega^2 \tau_1^2} \right.$$

$$\left. + \epsilon \frac{\tau_3}{\pi} \exp\left(\frac{\tau_3}{\tau_4} + \tau_0 \omega \right) K_0(z') \right\} \quad , \qquad (11)$$

with $z = \left[(1 + \omega^2 \tau_1^2)(\tau_2^2 + \tau_0^2) \right]^{1/2} / \tau_1$

and $z' = \left[(1 + \omega^2 \tau_4^2)(\tau_3^2 + \tau_0^2) \right]^{1/2} / \tau_4$,

where τ_0 equals $\hbar / 2kT$. K_0 and K_1 are Bessel functions for which simple numerical approximations exist. The amplitude S, which equals the zeroth moment of the model function $S\Gamma(\omega)$, is found to be practically indistinguishable from the zeroth moment of the spectral function, $G(\omega)$, because of the high quality of the fits. The parameter ϵ determines how much of the K_0 model is to be mixed with the BC model. The four parameter model (11) represents the quantum mechanical calculations with full accuracy over a wide range of frequencies and intensities. The deviations from quantum profiles are small at all frequencies. As an example, in Fig. 7 we have plotted relative corrections as function of frequency (at T=77K),

$$C(\omega) = (G_{L\lambda}(\omega; T) - F(\omega; T)) / F(\omega, T) \quad , \qquad (12)$$

which must be applied to the model function $S\Gamma(\omega;T)$ to obtain the exact quantum profiles. A component of the hydrogen spectrum (L,Λ= 1,2) computed on the basis of recent potential (McConville, 1981) and ab initio induced dipole is considered (Meyer et al., 1985). The deterioration observed for the three parameter fits in the far wing is completetely avoided at low temperatures.

Summarizing, it can be said that generic functions exist which approximate exact quantum profiles quite closely over a range of peak-to-wing intensities of roughly 1000:1. Typical rms deviations of the fit amount to 1 or 2%, and maximal deviations from the exact profile are less than 5% for the induction operators and temperatures studied so far (A. Borysow et al. 1984; J. Borysow et al. 1985). However, in several instances, the existing model functions had to be generalized to a four parameter expression (11) for a sufficient accuracy.

For simplicity, we have limited our discussions above to systems which do not form dimers to any significant extent. However, if dimer contributions to the spectra cannot be ignored, two profiles instead of one have to be modeled: the free-free plus bound-free plus free-bound ones on the one hand, and the bound-bound one seen in Fig. 6 on the other; it seems unlikely that their superpositions can be represented accurately by a single three- or four-parameter expression (A. Borysow and Frommhold 1985). While for some applications this may be quite acceptable, it is a clear warning not to use

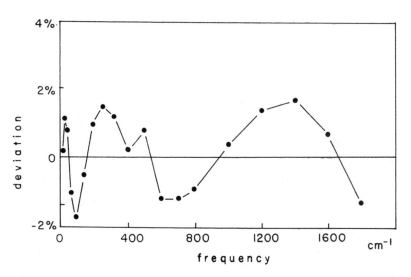

Fig. 7 Relative corrections for the four parameter model function (11) to reproduce the H_2-H_2 L,Λ= 1,2 profile at 77K.

model profiles indiscriminately. In important cases, one will have to carefully check the quality of the fit with exact quantum line shapes before analytical work with model profiles can be considered meaningful. Specific quantum profiles seem to be indispensable even for work with the most intriguing model profiles.

Acknowledgments. Our special thanks go to Aleksandra Borysow, Drs. M. Moraldi and P. Kielanowski for their help with the tensor notation we have used in Eqs. 4-7; CIA and CIS line shapes of molecular systems could thus be treated within the same formal theory by proper choice of the rank r of the induction operator. It is a pleasure to acknowledge invaluable conversations on the line shape problem with Dr. G. Birnbaum during the years of an ongoing collaboration. The support of the NSF-AST8310786 grant is acknowledged.

REFERENCES

Aziz, R.A., Nain, V.P.S., and McConville, J.S., 1979, J. Chem. Phys. 70:4330.
Aziz, R. A., 1984, J. Chem. Phys. 81:779.
Bafile, U., Magli, R., Barocchi, F., Zoppi, M., and Frommhold, L., 1983, Mol. Phys. 49:1149.
Bafile, U., Ulivi, L., Zoppi, M., and Barocchi, F., 1985, Chem. Phys., in press.
Bancewicz, T., 1983, Mol. Phys. 50:173.
Barocchi, F., and Zoppi, M., 1980, "Intermolecular Spectroscopy and Dynamical Properties of Dense Systems", J. Van Kranendonk, Editor, Soc. Italiana di Fisica, Bologna, p. 237.
Barocchi, F., Zoppi, M., Proffitt, M.H., and Frommhold, L., 1981, Canad. J. Phys. 59:1418.
Barocchi, F., and Zoppi, M., 1985, this volume.
Bentley, J., 1979, J. Chem. Phys. 70:3125.
Berne, B.J., and Pecora, R., 1976, "Dynamic Light Scattering", Wiley (New York).
Berns, R.M., Wormer, P.E.S., Mulder, F., and van der Avoird, A., 1978, J. Chem. Phys. 69:2102.
Birnbaum, G., and Cohen, E.R., 1976, Canad. J. Phys. 54:593.
Birnbaum, G., 1978, JQSRT 19:51.
Birnbaum, G., Brown, M.S., and Frommhold, L., 1981, Canad. J. Phys. 59:1544.
Birnbaum, G., Guillot, B., and Bratos, S., 1982, Adv. Chem. Phys. 51:49.
Birnbaum, G., Frommhold, L., Nencini, L., and Sutter, H., 1983, Chem. Phys. Letters 100:292.
Birnbaum, G., Krauss, M., and Frommhold, L., 1984a, J. Chem. Phys. 80:2669.
Birnbaum, G., Chu, S.I., Dalgarno, A., Frommhold, L. and Wright, E.L., 1984b, Phys. Rev. A29:595.
Borysow, A., Moraldi, M., and Frommhold, L., 1984, JQSRT 31:235.

Borysow, A., and Frommhold, L., 1985, in preparation.
Borysow, J., Moraldi, M., and Frommhold, L., 1985, in preparation.
Borysow, J., Trafton, L., Frommhold, L., and Birnbaum, G., 1985,
        Astrophys. J., to appear.
Bosomworth, D.R., and Gush, H.P., 1965, Canad. J. Phys. 43:751.
Bottcher, C., Dalgarno, A., and Wright, E.L., Phys. Rev. A 1:1606.
Brenner, S.L., and McQuarrie, D.A., 1971, Canad. J. Phys. 49:837.
Britton, F.R., and Crawford, M.F., 1958, Canad. J. Phys. 36:761.
Brown, M. S., Proffitt, M. H., and Frommhold, L., 1985, Chem. Phys.,
        in press.
Buck, U., Huisken, F., Kohlhase, A., Otten, D., and Schaefer, J.,
        1983, J. Chem. Phys. 78:4439.
Buckingham, A.D., 1967, Adv. Chem. Phys. 12:107.
Buckingham, A.D., and Clarke, K.L., 1978, Chem. Phys. Letters 57:231.
Bulanin, M.O., and Kouzov, A.P., 1982, Opt. Spectrosc. (USSR) 53:266.
Buontempo, U, Cunsolo, S., Jacucci, G., and Weiss, J. J., 1975,
        J. Chem. Phys. 63:2570.
Cashion, J.K., 1963, J. Chem. Phys. 39:1872.
Colpa, J.P., and Ketelaar, J.A.A., 1958, Mol. Phys. 1:343.
Colpa, J.P., 1965, "Physics of High Pressure and Condensed Phase",
        p. 490, North-Holland, Amsterdam.
Cooley, J.W., 1961, Math. Compt. 5:363.
Crawford, M.F., Welsh, H.L., and Locke, J.L., 1949, Phys. Rev.
        75:1067.
Dacre, P.D., 1978, Mol. Phys. 36:541.
Dacre, P.D., 1981, Canad. J. Phys. 59:1439.
Dacre, P.D., 1982a, Canad. J. Phys. 60:963.
Dacre, P.D., 1982b, Mol. Phys. 45:1.
Dacre, P.D., 1982c, Mol. Phys. 45:17.
Dacre, P.D., 1982d, Mol. Phys. 47:193.
Dacre, P.D., and Frommhold, L., 1982, J. Chem. Phys. 76:3447.
Dagg, I. R., and Gray, C. G., 1985, this volume.
Davies, R.W., Tipping, R.H., and Clough, S.A., 1982, Phys. Rev.
        A26:3378.
Doyle, R.O., 1968, JQSRT 8:1555.
Erkovitch, S.P., 1960, Opt. Spectrosc. 8:162.
Federman, S.R., and Frommhold, L., 1982, Phys. Rev. A 25:2012.
Filimonov, V.N., 1959, Usp. Fiz. Nauk 69:565.
Frenkel, D., and McTague, J.P., 1980, J. Chem. Phys. 72:2801.
Frommhold, L., 1975, J. Chem. Phys. 63:1687.
Frommhold, L., Hong, K.H., and Proffitt, M.H., 1978a, Mol. Phys.
        35:665.
Frommhold, L., Hong, K.H., and Proffitt, M.H., 1978b, Mol. Phys.
        35:691.
Frommhold, L., 1981, Adv. Chem. Phys. 46:1.
Frommhold, L., Samuelson, R.E., and Birnbaum, G., 1984,
        Astrophys. J., 283:L79.
Frost, B.S., 1973, J. Chem. Soc. Faraday Trans. II 69:1142.
Gengenbach, R., and Hahn, C., 1972, Chem. Phys. Letters 15:604.
Gersten, J., and Foley, H.M., 1966, J. Chem. Phys. 45:3885.
Gersten, J., and Foley, H.M., 1968, J. Chem. Phys. 49:5254.
Gersten, J.I., 1971, Phys. Rev. A 4:98.

Hanley, H.J.M., and Klein, M.K., 1972, J. Chem. Phys. 76:1743.

Hartye, R.W., Gray, C.G., Poll, J.D., and Miller, M.S., 1975, Canad. J. Phys. 29:825.

Herzberg, G., 1945, "Spectra of Diatomic Molecules", van Norstrand Reinhold Cy., New York.

Herzberg, G., 1967, "Infrared and Raman Spectra of Polyatomic Molecules", van Norstrand Cy., Inc., Princeton.

Hunt, J.L., and Poll, J.D., 1978, Canad. J. Phys. 56:950.

Hunt, K.L.C., Zilles, B.A., and Bohr, J.E., 1981, J. Chem. Phys. 75:3079.

Hunt, K.L.C., 1985, this volume.

James, H.M., and Coolidge, A.S., 1939, Phys. Rev. 55:184.

Joslin, C.G., and Gray, C.G., 1984, Chem. Phys. Letters 107:249.

Joslin, C.G., and Gray, C.G., 1985, this volume.

Julienne, P.S., 1985, this volume.

Ketelaar, J.A.A., 1959, Record Chem. Prog. 20:1.

Lacey, A.J., and Byers Brown, W., 1974, Mol. Phys. 27:1013.

Lallemand, P., 1971, J. Physique (Paris) 32:119.

Levine, H.B., 1967, Phys. Rev. 160:159.

Levine, H.B., and Birnbaum, G., 1967, Phys. Rev. 154:86.

Levine, H.B., and Birnbaum, G., 1968, Phys. Rev. Letters 20:439.

Linsky, J.L., 1969, Astrophys. J. 156:989.

Maitland, G.C., Rigby, M., Smith, E.B., and Wakeham, W.A., 1981, "Intermolecular Forces – Their Origin and Determination", Clarendon Press, Oxford.

Marteau, P., and Schuller, F., 1972, J. Physique (Paris) 33:645.

Maryott, A.A., and Birnbaum, G., 1962, J. Chem. Phys. 36:2026.

Matcha, R.L., and Nesbet, R.K., 1967, Phys. Rev. 160:72.

McConville, G.T., 1981, J. Chem. Phys. 74:2201.

McQuarrie, D.A., and Bernstein, R.B., 1968, J. Chem. Phys. 49:1958.

McKellar, A. R. W., 1984, Canad. J. Phys., 62:760.

McTague, J.P., and Birnbaum, G., 1971, Phys. Rev. A 3:1376.

Meinander, N., and Tabisz, G.C., 1984, Chem. Phys. Letters 110:388.

Meyer, W., Frommhold, L., and Birnbaum, G., Phys. Rev. A, to appear.

Meyer, W., 1985, this volume.

Meyer, W., and Frommhold, L., 1985, in preparation.

Mizushima, M., 1949, Phys. Rev. 76:1268.

Mizushima, M., 1950, Phys. Rev. 77:149 & 150.

Moraldi, M., 1983, Chem. Phys. 78:243.

Moraldi, M., Borysow, A., and Frommhold, L., 1984, Chem. Phys. 86:339.

Moraldi, M., Frommhold, L., and Meyer, W., 1985, in preparation.

Nikitin, E.E., 1959, Opt. Spectr. 7:441.

Okada, K., Kajikawa, T., and Yamamoto, T., 1968, Progr. Theoret. Phys. 39:863.

Poll, J.D., and Van Kranendonk, J., 1961, Canad. J. Phys. 39:189.

Poll, J.D., and Hunt, J.L., 1976, Canad. J. Phys. 54:461.

Poll, D.J., 1980a, in "Intermolecular Spectroscopy and Dynamical Properties of Dense Sysytems", J. Van Kranendonk, ed., Soc. Italiana di Fisica, Bolgna.

Poll, D.J., 1980b, presentation at the Conference on Collision-Induced Phenomena, Firenze, Italy, Sept. 2-5.

Poll, J.D., and Hunt, J.L., 1981, Canad. J. Phys. 59:1449.
Prengel, A.T., and Gornall, W.S., 1976, Phys. Rev. A 13:253.
Proffitt, M.H., and Frommhold, L., 1979, Chem. Phys. 36:197.
Proffitt, M.H., Keto, L.W., and Frommhold, L., 1981, Canad. J. Phys. 59:1459.
Proffitt, M.H., Brown, M.S., Hunt, K.L.C., and Frommhold, L., 1985, in prep.
Raczynski, A., 1982, Chem. Phys. 72:321.
Raczynski, A., 1983, Chem. Phys. Letters 96:9.
Raczynski, A., 1984, Chem. Phys. 88:129.
Sando, K.M., and Dalgarno, A., 1971, Mol. Phys. 20:103.
Sando, K.M., 1971, Mol. Phys. 21:439.
Schaefer, J., and Meyer, W., 1985, in prep.
Sears, V.F., 1968, Canad. J. Phys. 46:1163.
Sharma, R.D., and Hart, R.R., 1974, Chem. Phys. Letters 27:589.
Sharma, R.D., and Hart, R.R., 1975, Phys. Rev. A 12:85.
Shlyapnikov, G.V., and Shmator, I.P., 1980, Sov. Phys. JETP 52:1050.
Solomon, P.M., 1964, Astrophys. J. 139:999.
Strauss, H.L., and Weiss, Sh., 1979, J. Chem. Phys. 70:5788.
Tanimoto, O., 1966, Progr. Theor. Phys. (Kyoto) 33:585.
Tipping, R.E., 1985, this volume.
Tokuyama, M., and Mori, H., 1975, Prog. Theor. Phys. 54:918 and 55:411.
Tonkov, M.V., 1970, "Spectroscopy of Interacting Molecules" (in Russian), p. 5, Leningrad University Press.
Trafton, L.M., 1966, Astrophys. J. 146:558.
Trafton, L.M., 1973, Astrophys. J. 179:971.
Ulrich, B.T., Ford, L., and Browne, J.C., 1972, J. Chem. Phys. 57:2906.
Van Kranendonk, J., and Bird, R.B., 1951, Physica 17:953 & 986.
Van Kranendonk, J., 1957, Physica 23:825.
Van Kranendonk, J., 1958, Physica 24:347.
Van Kranendonk, J., 1959, Physica 25:337.
Van Kranendonk, J., and Kiss, Z.J., 1959, Canad. J. Phys. 37:1137.
Van Kranendonk, J., 1968, Canad. J. Phys. 46:1173.
Van Kranendonk, J., 1980, Editor, "Intermolecular Spectroscopy and Dynamical Properties of Dense Systems", Soc. Italiana di Fisica, Bologna.
Vodar, B., and Vu, H., 1963, JQSRT 3:397.
Welsh, H.L., and Hunt, J.L., 1963, JQSRT 3:385.
Welsh, H.L., 1972, MTP Int. Rev. Sci., "Spectroscopy", Phys. Chem., Series one, vol. 3, A.D. Buckingham and D.A. Ramsay, Editors, Butterworths, London.
Weiss, Sh., and Strauss, H.L., 1980, J. Chem. Phys. 72:1813.
Weyland, A., 1978, Physica 92A:295.
Whisnant, D.M., and Byers Brown, W., 1973, Mol. Phys. 26:1105.
Wormer, P.E.S., and van Dijk, G., 1979, J. Chem. Phys. 70:5695.

COLLISION-INDUCED ABSORPTION

IN THE MICROWAVE REGION

Ian R. Dagg

Physics Department
University of Waterloo
Waterloo, Ontario, Canada

ABSTRACT

A review of experimental microwave results is presented for collision-induced absorption in various nonpolar gases, gas mixtures and liquids in the frequency region from 0.3 to 4.6 cm^{-1}. It is pointed out that the data are needed for an accurate determination of the spectral invariant, γ, and may be related to two and three body relaxation times. Also discussed are the intercollisional interference effects in rare gas mixtures.

INTRODUCTION

Collision-induced microwave absorption in a nonpolar gas was first reported by Birnbaum et al. (1954) in compressed CO_2. Later Birnbaum and Maryott (1962) detected induced absorption in N_2 and C_2H_4. Since then microwave absorption has been reported in a number of nonpolar gases, namely CH_4 (Dagg et al., 1974; Urbaniak et al., 1976; Urbaniak et al., 1977), SF_6 (Urbaniak et al., 1977a), H_2 (Dagg et al., 1975), CF_4 (Urbaniak et al., 1976; Urbaniak et al., 1977) and C_2H_6 (Dagg et al., 1982). In addition CO_2 has been studied in more detail at various temperatures by Maryott and Birnbaum (1962) in the 0.3 and 0.8 cm^{-1} regions and by Ho et al. (1966) at 0.3 cm^{-1}. More recently, the measurements have been extended to the higher frequency regions of 1.1, 2.3 and 4.6 cm^{-1} where the absorption coefficient is larger and more accurate low density data may be obtained (Dagg et al., 1974; Dagg et al., 1975; Dagg et al., 1978). Nitrogen has also been further studied by Ho et al.(1968) at 0.3 cm^{-1} over a wide temperature range and later by Dagg et al. (1974) at the higher frequencies of 1.1 and 2.3 cm^{-1}. The measurements were further extended by Dagg et al. (1975) and Urbaniak et al. (1977) to include a wider temperature range and Dagg et al. (1978) have obtained results at 4.6 cm^{-1} at 295 K.

Collision induced microwave absorption in gaseous binary mixtures of nonpolar gases was first reported by Maryott and Kryder (1964) at 0.8 cm^{-1} for which CO_2 was mixed in turn with He, H_2, N_2, CH_4, C_2H_6 and SF_6. Later, Dagg et al. (1974a) working at 2.3 cm^{-1} measured the absorption of CO_2 mixed with Ar and with CH_4. Results have also been reported at 1.1 and 2.3 cm^{-1} for N_2 mixed with CH_4 and with Ar (Dagg et al., 1974).

Collision induced microwave absorption was first detected in a mixture of rare gases by Dagg et al. (1977) for the gases Ne and Kr. Results have now been reported for the rare gas mixtures Ne-Xe and Ar-Xe at 4.4 cm^{-1} by Dagg et al. (1978) and at 2.3 cm^{-1} (Dagg et al., 1978a: Dagg et al., 1980) as well as for the gaseous mixtures Ne-Kr, Ar-Kr and Kr-Xe (Dagg et al., 1980).

Microwave absorption in nonpolar liquids was first observed by Bleaney et al. (1947) and later by Whiffen (1950) who has reported measurements for CCl_4, CS_2, C_2Cl_4, C_6H_6, $C_{10}H_{18}$ and C_6H_{12}. Further results on a number of these compounds as well as for a series of alkanes have been obtained by Dagg and Reesor (1972), Dagg and Reesor (1974) and by Read et al. (1979). Certain other results on some of these compounds have been reported by Garg et al. (1965), Dasgupta and Smythe (1974) and by Stumpfer (1975). The above results are taken in the temperature range relatively close to room temperature. Lower temperature results for liquid N_2, CH_4, and CF_4 have been ontained by Urbaniak et al. (1977).

Theoretical interest and understanding in collision-induced absorption in the microwave region has (up to now) been largely related to low density compressed nonpolar glasses.

EXPERIMENTAL TECHNIQUES

As the absorption is extremely small in the microwave region, it has generally been necessary to use sensitive cavity techniques to measure absorption in nonpolar gases (Birnbaum et al., 1954; Dagg et al., 1974). The loss tangent, $\tan \delta = \varepsilon''/\varepsilon'$, where ε' and ε'' are the real and imaginary parts of the dielectric constant, is obtained from

$$\tan \delta = [1/Q_a - 1/Q_o] \qquad (1)$$

where Q_a and Q_o are respectively the measured Q of the cavity filled with the absorbing gas and with a reference (non-absorbing) gas at the same frequency. The plane wave absorption coefficient

$A(\upsilon)$ is related to tan δ by

$$A(\upsilon) = 2\pi\upsilon\sqrt{\varepsilon'(\upsilon)} \ \tan \ \delta \ = 2\pi\upsilon\varepsilon''(\upsilon)/\sqrt{\varepsilon'(\upsilon)} \qquad (2)$$

where υ is the frequency in cm^{-1}. The equivalent absorption path length would be of the order of $Q\lambda/2\pi$ where λ is the wave length. Normally a Q of the order of 40,000 or more is possible for a high pressure cavity which is also usable at low temperatures. As discussed below, tan δ is proportional to υ over most of the microwave region for the nonpolar compressed gases and so there is considerable advantage in working at the higher frequencies especially if the absorption is extremely small. However the many useful measurements made in the lower frequency regions from 0.3 to 0.8 cm^{-1} (referred to above) generally agree well within the limits of error with later higher frequency results in the 1.1, 2.3, and 4.6 cm^{-1} regions. In the case of the rare gas mixtures, it was necessary to work at 2.3 and 4.6 cm^{-1} because of a reduced absorption due to intercollisional interference effects. However an extension of microwave techniques to even higher frequencies (above 4.6 cm^{-1}) becomes very expensive and it is relatively difficult to apply the cavity technique.

For nonpolar liquids, cavity (Bleaney et al. 1947), wave guide (Dagg and Reesor, 1963) and interferometer (Garg et al., 1965; Read et al., 1979) methods have been used in the microwave frequency region.

THEORETICAL CONSIDERATIONS

The absorption coefficient $A(\omega)$ at frequency ω is given by the formula (Birnbaum et al., 1982),

$$A(\omega) = (2\pi\omega/3\hbar cV)(1 - \exp(- \ \beta \ \hbar\omega)) \ I(\omega) \qquad (3)$$

where $\omega = 2\pi c\upsilon$, c is the speed of light, V is the system volume, $\beta = 1/kT$ where k is Boltzmann's constant, $\hbar$ is Planck's constant and T is the absolute temperature. The intensity, $I(\omega)$, is the power spectrum of the total dipole moment autocorrelation function, $\phi(t)$, and is given by

$$I(\omega) = (2\pi)^{-1}\int_{-\infty}^{\infty} \exp \ (-i\omega t) \ \phi(t) \ dt \qquad (4)$$

The function $\phi(t)$ is defined by $\phi(t) = \langle\vec{M}(t)\cdot\vec{M}(o)\rangle$, where the brackets denotes the expectation value for an equilibrium ensemble of the unperturbed system and $\vec{M}$ is the total dipole moment in volume V. Then for bimolecular collisions we have for n similar molecules,

$$\langle\vec{M}(t)\cdot\vec{M}(o)\rangle = n^2/2 \ \langle\vec{\mu}(t)\cdot\vec{\mu}(o)\rangle \qquad (5)$$

where $\vec{\mu}$ is the dipole moment induced in a pair and $\langle\vec{\mu}(t)\cdot\vec{\mu}(o)\rangle$ is an average over all configurations of the pair (Birnbaum et al., 1982). At sufficiently low densities the absorption then depends on the square of the density. For a mixture containing n_a and n_b particles of type a and b respectively we have

$$\langle \vec{M}(t) \cdot \vec{M}(o) \rangle = n_a n_b \langle \vec{\mu}(t) \cdot \vec{\mu}(o) \rangle \tag{6}$$

In the low density limit the absorption is then proportional to the product of the densities, $n_a n_b$.

The spectral invariant γ is defined in terms of ω as

$$\gamma = \beta \, \hbar/2 \int_0^\infty A(\omega) \, \omega^{-1} \coth(\beta \, \hbar\omega/2) d\omega \tag{7}$$

and the integrated absorption α is given as

$$\alpha = \int_0^\infty A(\omega) \, d\omega \tag{8}$$

In the low frequency region where $\hbar\omega \ll kT$

$$A(\omega) = (4\pi^2 \beta/3cV) \, \omega^2 I(\omega) \tag{9}$$

and in terms of υ one obtains for the low frequencies

$$\gamma = (2\pi c)^{-1} \int_0^\infty d\upsilon A(\upsilon) \upsilon^{-2} \tag{10}$$

It has also been useful to define a relaxation time τ as

$$\tau = \int_0^\infty \phi(t) \, dt/\phi(o)$$

Over the very low frequency microwave region the function $I(\omega)$ is essentially constant so that one obtains

$$A(\upsilon)/\upsilon^2 = 2\pi\varepsilon''(\upsilon)/\upsilon = 8\pi c^2 \tau\gamma \tag{11}$$

In the microwave region the results have generally been quoted in terms of the complex dielectric constant. An equivalent classical expression to eq. (11), namely

$$\varepsilon''(\upsilon)/\upsilon = 2\pi c\tau[\varepsilon'(o) - \varepsilon'(\infty)] \tag{12}$$

is obtained by using the Kramers-Kronig relation and substituting for γ.

Generally the integrated absorption coefficient and the dielectric constant have been expressed as polynomial expansions in the density. Correspondingly, theoretical expressions for α and γ have been derived which are related to the expansion coefficients. The theory and the experimental results at low densities are then compared to yield values for the parameters associated with the dipole induction mechanism. The density expansion of $\phi(t)$ and τ are discussed below.

B. Microwave Results

Although the losses are small in the microwave region, it is evident from eq. (10) that microwave results for collision induced absorption in nonpolar gases and the gas mixtures are important as they define the low frequency value of $A(\upsilon)/\upsilon^2$ which makes a large contribution to γ. The far infrared results are generally uncertain below about 30 cm^{-1}. (More recently, laser results near 16 cm^{-1} have been useful in further defining the low frequency absorption profile.) As an example, the experimental data for low density nitrogen (Stone et al., 1984) at 228.3 K are shown in Fig. (1). It is seen that the microwave result agrees well with an extrapolation of the far infrared and laser results as well as with a theoretical line shape function $\hat{I}(\upsilon)$ due to Joslin and Gray (1984). This function is plotted as the solid line in the figure.

As discussed by Cohen and Birnbaum (1977) and by Gray and Gubbins (1981) the results at low density for the two quantities, α and γ, can be used in deriving values for the quadrupole and other

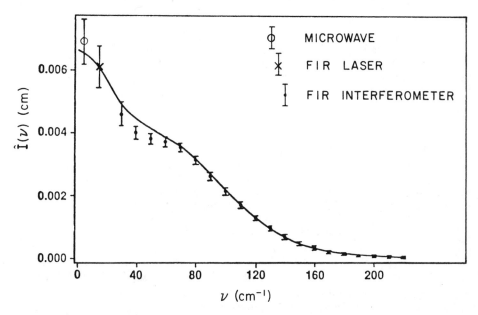

Fig. 1. The experimental data for low density N$_2$ at 228.3K. The solid curve is the normalized line shape function $\hat{I}(\upsilon)$ of Joslin and Gray (1984).

multipole moments of the molecular charge distribution. The microwave and infrared results have been used in determining values for γ for N_2 and CO_2 by Dagg et al. (1975) and for CH_4 and CF_4 by Urbaniak et al. (1976), for C_2H_4 by Dagg et al.(1981) and for SF_6 by Urbaniak et al. (1977). The microwave data for these gases are listed in Table 1. Here, as discussed below, the imaginary part of the dielectric constant, $\varepsilon''(\upsilon)$, is expressed as a power expansion of the density, ρ, where $\varepsilon_n''(\upsilon)$ is the coefficient of ρ_n with ρ in amagat units.

For the rare gas mixtures, the ratio of α to γ is related to the induced dipole strength and range parameters associated with overlap induction (Birnbaum et al., 1982). The microwave results for $(\varepsilon_2''(\upsilon)/\upsilon)_{ab}$ are listed in Table 2 for the rare gases (a and b). Both the infrared (Quazza et al., 1976) and the microwave results are used to determine γ_{ab} in the low density limit.

It may be mentioned that a linear dependence of $\varepsilon''(\upsilon)$ on density has been observed by Dagg et al. (1978) for CF_4 for which values of $\varepsilon_1''(\upsilon)/\upsilon$ are found to vary from 8.85 to 9.95 x 10^{-9} cm amagat^{-1} ($\pm$ 10%) in the temperature range 318 to 248 K. This linear dependence arises as a result of a small dipole moment created by centrifugal distortion (Ozier and Rosenberg, 1973).

RELAXATION TIMES

As discussed by Birnbaum et al. (1967) the microwave collision induced absorption results may be analyzed by making a density expansion of the induced dipole correlation function, $\phi(t)$. Then one obtains a power expansion in the imaginary part of the complex dielectric constant, $\varepsilon''(\upsilon)$, in the nth power of the density (ρ)

$$\varepsilon_n''(\upsilon) = [\varepsilon_n'(o) - \varepsilon_n'(\infty)] \, 2\pi c \upsilon \tau_n \qquad (13)$$

where $\tau_n = \int_o^\infty \phi_n(t)dt/\phi_n(o)$. Poll (1980) has discussed under what conditions such a density expansion is valid. The times τ_n may be termed n-body relaxation times although strictly speaking ρ_n relaxation times may be more appropriate. The quantities $[\varepsilon_n'(o) - \varepsilon_n'(\infty)]$ are directly related to the dielectric virial coefficients. According to Eq. (13) the far infrared results can be used along with the measured values of ε'' to obtain a value for τ_n. From this equation the factor $\varepsilon_n''(\upsilon)/\upsilon$ is expected to be constant for lower density compressed gases over the microwave region as has been verified, for example in N_2 (see for example Dagg et al. (1975)).However, it appears that $\varepsilon_2''(\upsilon)/\upsilon$ may have changed slightly in the case of CO_2(Dagg et al., 1978) at the relatively high frequency of 4.6 cm^{-1}.

Table 1. The experimental values of $\varepsilon_2''(\upsilon)/\upsilon$ and $\varepsilon_3''(\upsilon)/\upsilon$ at various temperatures for a number of nonpolar gases as determined in the 1.1 to 4.6 cm^{-1} region. The relaxation times τ_2 and τ_3 are defined by Eq. (13).

Gas	Ref.	T (K)	$\varepsilon_2''(\upsilon)/\upsilon$ x 10^{10} (cm amagat^{-2})	$-\varepsilon_3''(\upsilon)/\upsilon$ x 10^{13} (cm amagat^{-3})	τ_2 x 10^{13} (s)	τ_3/τ_2
N_2	(a)	333	1.52 + 0.10	1.62 + 0.70	3.90	1.21
		313	1.81 + 0.07	2.74 + 0.55	4.03	1.21
		295	1.91 + 0.11	2.72 + 0.92	4.12	1.21
		268	2.28 + 0.10	3.44 + 0.69	4.36	1.21
		253	2.47 + 0.10	3.72 + 0.65	4.50	1.21
		233	2.67 + 0.07	4.71 + 0.48	4.68	1.21
		208	3.20 + 0.15	6.00 + 0.90	4.96	1.22
	(b)	156	5.65 + 0.10	16.9 + 1.6	5.81	1.22
		133	7.59 + 0.21	23.2 + 4.2	6.34	1.22
		124	8.76 + 0.40	31.7 + 12.0	6.59	1.22
CO_2	(a)	363	73 + 2	132 + 32		
		333	94 + 2	253 + 55	7.90	
		295	139 + 3	496 + 63	8.22	1.10
		273	175 + 3	633 + 120	8.96	
CF_4	(c)	318	3.54 + 0.15			
		295	4.13 + 0.15			
		268	5.17 + 0.25			
		248	5.71 + 0.25			
CH_4	(c)	295	0.65 + .08			
		253	0.75 + 0.14			
		233	0.94 + 0.14			
		208	1.10 + 0.14			
C_2H_4	(d)	295	38.4 + 1.6	289 + 60	3.74	
C_2H_6	(e)	295	4.85 + 0.20	30.2 + 5		
H_2	(a)	295	0.086 + 0.015			
		77	0.237 + 0.024			
SF_6	(f)	295	2.2 + 0.6			

(a) Dagg et al. (1975); (b) Urbaniak et al. (1977); (c) Urbaniak et al. (1976); (d) Dagg et al. (1981); (e) Dagg et al. (1982); (f) Urbaniak et al. (1977a).

101

Table 2. The experimental microwave values for a number of
mixtures of nonpolar gases at 295 K for the dielectric
loss $(\varepsilon_2''(\upsilon)/\upsilon)_{ab}$ associated with the density product $\rho_a\rho_b$
and $(\varepsilon_3''(\upsilon)/\upsilon)_{ab}$ associated with a higher order density
product. The relaxation time τ_d for the rare gases is
calculated from the dielectric loss and Eq. (14).

Gas Mixture	Ref.	$(\varepsilon_2''(\upsilon)/\upsilon)_{ab} \times 10^{10}$ (cm amagat^{-2})	$\tau_d \times 10^{13}$ (s)	$-(\varepsilon_3''(\upsilon)/\upsilon)_{ab} \times 10^{11}$ (cm amagat^{-3})
Ne–Xe	(a)	2.39 ± 0.13	1.17	
Ne–Kr		0.94 ± 0.13	1.26	
Ar–Xe		2.59 ± 0.22	1.57	
Ar–Kr		0.84 ± 0.13	2.18	
Kr–Xe		3.88 ± 0.22	$(2.40)_{est.}$	
He–Xe		< 0.24		
He–Ar		$. \quad < 0.24$		
CH_4–Ar	(b)	0.54 ± 0.1		
CF_4–Ar		1.93 ± 0.2		
				$\rho_a^2\rho_b$
CO_2–Ar	(c)	40 ± 6		4.4 ± 1.6
CO_2–CH_4		75 ± 10		9.8 ± 3.0
CO_2–He	(d)	$5\text{–}9 \pm 4$		
CO_2–H_2		8 ± 4		
CO_2–N_2		26 ± 4		
CO_2–C_2H_6		120 ± 12		
CO_2–SF_6		312 ± 31		
				$\rho_a\rho_b(\rho_a+\rho_b)$
N_2–CH_4	(e)	4.90 ± 0.80		0.152 ± 0.05
N_2–Ar		3.66 ± 0.30		0.095 ± 0.015

(a) Dagg et al. (1980); (b) Urbaniak et al. (1976); (c) Dagg et al.
(1974a); (d) Maryott and Kryder (1964); (e) Dagg et al. (1974).

The microwave results for $\varepsilon_n''/(\upsilon)$ for CO_2 and N_2 at various
temperatures, T, are shown in Table 1 for the 1.1 to 4.6 cm^{-1}
region as well as the associated relaxation time τ_2 and also τ_3
where sufficient data exist. From the theoretical expressions
(Birnbaum et al., 1967) for $\varepsilon_2''(\upsilon)$ and $\varepsilon_3''(\upsilon)$ and the measured
temperature dependence for N_2 and CO_2 the relaxation times τ_2 and
τ_3 are found to vary approximately as $T^{-0.50}$ in agreement with
the theoretical expression derived by Maryott and Birnbaum (1962).
At each temperature the ratio of τ_3/τ_2 is approximately 1.22 for
N_2 and 1.1 for CO_2. Experimentally determined (approximate)
expressions for the temperature dependence of $\varepsilon_n''(\upsilon)$ have been
given for N_2,(Urbaniak et al., 1977) CO_2,(Dagg et al., 1975) and
for CH_4 and CF_4 (Urbaniak et al., 1976).

GAS MIXTURES

A. Rare Gases – Intercollisional Interference

For the rare gas mixtures, the microwave results have demonstrated experimentally the intercollision interference effects
treated theoretically by Van Kranendonk (1968), Lewis (1972) and
by Lewis and Van Kranendonk (1972). Some typical results are
shown in Fig. (2) in which the ratio $\varepsilon''(\upsilon)/\upsilon$ is plotted against
the product density, $\rho_a(Ne)\rho_b(Xe)$ for various ratios of the
densities of Ne and Xe (Dagg et al., 1978a). The three results at
4.4 cm^{-1} show the expected dependence of the absorption on the
ratio of the lighter to heavier atom with a very pronounced
intercollisional interference effect (or reduction in absorption
strength) for the ratio 0.59. Fig. (2) illustrates the point made
by Poll (1980) that if measurements are made at a fixed frequency,
the density can be made low enough so that an interpretation in
terms of a density expansion becomes possible. Thus at
sufficiently low densities, the absorption becomes proportional to
the product of the densities, irrespective of the mixture ratio.
As expected theoretically, the effect is even more pronounced at
2.3 cm^{-1} at a lower product density (Dagg et al., 1978b).

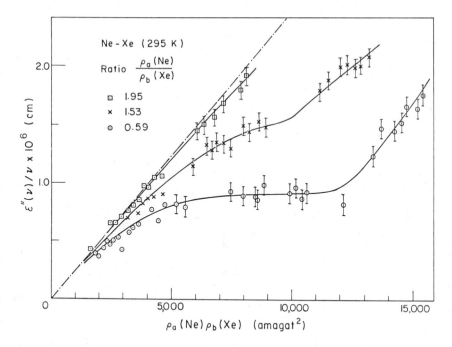

Fig. 2.   The experimental values of ε''/υ at 4.4 cm^{-1} as a
function of the density product of the gases Ne and Xe
at 295 K (Dagg et al., 1978a).

The binary or intracollisional absorption coefficient is extrapolated from the highest ratio of the density of neon to xenon and together with infrared results yields a value for the low density limit of γ_{ab} for the mixture. The value for the relaxation time τ_d is obtained from

$$(\varepsilon_2"(\upsilon)/\upsilon)_{ab} = 4c^2\gamma_{lab}\tau_d \qquad (14)$$

where τ_d is equivalent to τ_2. This classical expression is equivalent to Eq. (13) for pure translational absorption induced by overlap interaction and γ_{lab} is the coefficient for $\rho_a\rho_b$ in a density expansion of γ_{ab}. The values for $(\varepsilon_2"(\upsilon)/\upsilon)_{ab}$ are given for various rare gas mixtures in Table 2 as well as values for τ_d. Many-bodied effects are also evident in Fig. 2 at relatively high density products.

B. Other Gaseous Mixtures

The results for $(\varepsilon_2"(\upsilon)/\upsilon)_{ab}$ for a number of gaseous mixtures are given in Table 2. As in the case of the single component gas, the results have been related to the induction mechanism of one or other of the molecules of the colliding pair. There is some advantage in studying a mixture, CO_2-Ar, for example (as well as CO_2 alone) if the effect of the anisotropy of the potential function is large as for pure CO_2. The N_2-CH_4 mixture is of current astrophysical interest in studying radiant absorption in the atmosphere of Titan. (Courtin, 1982; Hunt et al., 1983)

LIQUIDS AND HIGH DENSITIES

Collision-induced absorption in the nonpolar molecules N_2, CH_4 and CF_4 has been studied in the 2.3 cm^{-1} region from room temperature and below. The results for $\varepsilon"(\upsilon)/\upsilon$ are shown in Table 3. It is of interest to note that for N_2, there has been observed (Urbaniak et al., 1977) a smooth transition in the factor $\varepsilon"(\upsilon)/\upsilon\rho^2$ from the gas to the liquid phase at densities of the order of 380 amagat. This factor (although much smaller here than in the low density gas) decreases only slightly with density, ρ, from 338 amagat at 125 K to 645 amagat at 77 K. For liquid CH_4 and CF_4 the factor $\varepsilon"(\upsilon)/\upsilon\rho^2$ was relatively close to the extrapolated low density, gaseous value in contrast to the case of N_2.

For the nonpolar liquids CCl_4 and CS_2, cyclohexane, benzene and trans-decalin at or near room temperature, tan δ is nearly linear with frequency from 0.3 to 1.1 cm^{-1} and possibly higher. (Whiffen, 1950; Dagg and Reesor, 1972; 1974). However, tan δ reaches a maximum value in the 1.0 to 3.0 cm^{-1} region for the molecules n-hexane, n-heptane, n-nonane and n-decane and possibly for other alkanes. The interpretation of these liquid and high density results awaits a fuller theoretical understanding of CIA in the condensed state.

Table 3. Microwave values for $\varepsilon''(\upsilon)/\upsilon$ for some nonpolar liquids at various temperatures. Results for the molecules benzene, cyclohexane, trans-decalin and a series of alkanes are listed elsewhere, (Whiffen, 1950; Dagg and Reesor 1972, 1974). For some alkanes, $\varepsilon''(\upsilon)/\upsilon$ shows a maximum in the microwave region.

Liquid	Ref.	T (K)	Density (amagat)	$\varepsilon''(\upsilon)/\upsilon \times 10^5$ (cm)
N_2	(a)	125	338	3.7 ± 0.4
		125	362	4.3 ± 0.4
		125	382	4.3 ± 0.4
		125	396	4.7 ± 0.4
		125	417	4.8 ± 0.4
		104	533	7.9 ± 1.0
		77	645	10.2 ± 1.0
CH_4	(a)	172	425	2.3 ± 0.6
		112	591	5.8 ± 0.5
CF_4	(a)	193	337	11 ± 2
		177	373	16 ± 2
		164	394	22 ± 3
		151	403	30 ± 5
		140	415	32 ± 5
CCl_4	(b)	295	235	174 ± 17
CS_2	(b)	295	381	154 ± 15

(a) Urbaniak et al. (1977); (b) Dagg and Reesor (1972).

REFERENCES

Birnbaum, G., Guillot, B. and Bratos, S., 1982,"Theory of Collision-Induced Line Shapes - Absorption and Light Scattering at Low Density"., ed. Prigogine, I. and Rice, S.A., Advances in Chemical Physics, John Wiley and Sons, Inc.
Birnbaum, G., Levine, H.B. and McQuarrie, D.A., 1967, J. Chem. Phys., 46:1557.
Birnbaum, G. and Maryott, A.A., 1962, J. Chem. Phys., 36:2032.
Birnbaum, G., Maryott, A.A. and Wacker, P.F., 1954, J. Chem. Phys., 22:1782.
Bleaney, B., Loubser, J.H.N. and Penrose, R.P., 1947, Proc. Phys. Soc. London, A59:185.
Cohen, E.R. and Birnbaum, G., 1977, J. Chem. Phys., 66:2443.

Courtin, R., 1982, Icarus, 51:466.

Dagg, I.R., Leckie, W.D. and Read, L.A.A., 1980, Can. J. Phys.,
58:633.

Dagg, I.R., Read, L.A.A. and Andrews, B., 1981, Can. J. Phys.,
59:57.

Dagg, I.R. and Reesor, G.E., 1963, Can. J. Phys. 41:1314.

Dagg, I.R. and Reesor, G.E., 1972, Can. J. Phys., 50:2397.

Dagg, I.R. and Reesor, G.E., 1974, Can. J. Phys., 52:29.

Dagg, I.R., Reesor, G.E. and Urbaniak, J.L., 1974, Can. J. Phys.,
52:821.

Dagg, I.R., Reesor, G.E., and Urbaniak, J.L., 1974a, Can. J.
Phys., 52:973.

Dagg, I.R., Reesor, G.E. and Urbaniak, J.L., 1975, Can. J. Phys.,
53:1764.

Dagg, I.R., Reesor, G.E. and Wong, M., 1977, Chem. Phys. Lett.,
51:90.

Dagg, I.R., Reesor, G.E., and Wong, M., 1978, Can. J. Phys.,
56:1037.

Dagg, I.R., Reesor, G.E., and Wong, M., 1978a, Can. J. Phys.,
56:1046.

Dagg, I.R., Reesor, G.E., and Wong, M., 1978b, Can. J. Phys.,
56:1559

Dagg, I.R., Smith, W., and Read, L.A.A., 1982, Can. J. Phys.
60:16.

Dasgupta, S., and Smyth, C.P., 1974, J. Chem. Phys., 60:1746.

Garg, S.K., Kilp, H. and Smyth, C.P., 1965, J. Chem. Phys.,
43:2341.

Gray, C.G. and Gubbins, K.E., 1981, Mol. Phys., 42:843.

Ho, W., Kaufman, I.A., and Thaddeus, P., 1966, J. Chem. Phys.,
45:877.

Ho, W., Kaufman, I.A. and Thaddeus, P., 1968, J. Chem. Phys.
49:3627.

Hunt, J.L., Poll, J.D., Goorvitch, D. and Tipping, R.H., 1983,
Icarus, 55:63.

Joslin, C.G. and Gray, C.G., 1984, Chem. Phys. Lett., 107:249.

Lewis, J.C., 1972, Can. J. Phys., 50:2881.

Lewis, J.C. and Van Kranendonk, J., 1972, Can. J. Phys., 50:352.

Maryott, A.A. and Birnbaum, G., 1962, J. Chem. Phys., 36:2026.

Maryott, A.A. and Kryder, S.J., 1964, J. Chem. Phys., 41:1580.

Ozier, J. and Rosenberg, A., 1973, Can. J. Phys., 51:1882.

Poll, J.D., 1980, "Intermolecular Spectroscopy and Dynamical
Properties of Dense Systems," ed. J. Van Kranendonk,
Proceedings of the International School of Physics,
p.45, North-Holland Publishing Co., Amsterdam.

Quazza, J., Marteau, Ph., Vu, H. and Vodar, B., 1976, J. Quant.
Spectrosc. Radiat. Transfer, 16:491.

Read, L.A.A., Dagg, I.R. and Reesor, G.E., 1979, Rev. Sci. Instr.,
50:1553.

Stone, N.W.B., Read, L.A.A., Anderson, A., Dagg, I.R. and
Smith W., 1984, Can. J. Phys., 62:338.

Stumper, U., 1975, Advan. Mol. Relaxation Processes, 7:189.

Urbaniak, J.L., Dagg, I.R., and Reesor, G.E., 1977, Can. J. Phys., 55:496.

Urbaniak, J.L., Reesor, G.E., and Dagg, I.R., 1976, Can. J. Phys., 54:1606.

Urbaniak, J.L., Reesor, G.E., and Dagg, I.R., 1977a, Can. J. Phys., 55:671.

Van Kranendonk, J., 1968, Can. J. Phys., 46:1173.

Whiffen, D.W., 1950, Trans. Faraday Soc., 46:124.

COLLISION-INDUCED ABSORPTION IN

N_2 AT VARIOUS TEMPERATURES

I.R. Dagg and C.G. Gray*

Physics Department
University of Waterloo
Waterloo, Ontario
Canada

*Physics Department
University of Guelph
Guelph, Ontario
Canada

ABSTRACT

Experimental results are given for collision-induced absorption spectra in N_2 in the spectral region below 360 cm^{-1} over a range of temperatures from 126 to 343 K. These results and the theoretical expressions for the two lowest spectral moments are used to determine values of the quadrupole moment of the N_2 molecules for various isotropic intermolecular potentials. The values so obtained are independent of temperature. Further the experimental line shapes are shown to be well represented by a classical theoretical calculation based on a combination of Mori and information theory.

INTRODUCTION

We report here some recent experimental results (Stone et al., 1984; Dagg et al., 1984) for collision-induced absorption in N_2 in the spectral region below 360 cm^{-1} over a range of temperatures from 126 to 343 K. For each temperature the absorption profile is determined for the low density limit for which the absorption is proportional to the square of the density.

The spectral moments have been analyzed according to the recent theory of Gray and Gubbins (1981) relating to quadrupole-induced absorption from which the quadrupole moment, Q, may be determined at each temperature.

Further, the experimental line shapes may be compared with recent theoretical calculations of Joslin et al. (1985). These authors have given a classical theoretical calculation of the line shape for N_2, based on quadrupolar induction, and using a combination of Mori and information theories.

PREVIOUS WORK

On the theoretical side, there have been many calculations of the spectral moments, both quantum and classical, including the work of Poll and Van Kranendonk (1961), Gray (1971) and Birnbaum and Cohen (1976). The most elaborate treatment is that of Cohen (1976) and Cohen and Birnbaum (1977) which includes a wide range of multipoles, polarizability and overlap induction mechanisms including corrections for anisotropy of the potential. Previous work on the line shape was based on line – shape engineering (a term coined by G. Birnbaum) (see Poll and Hunt 1981; Birnbaum and Cohen, 1976; Buontempo et al., 1975), in which the rotational stick spectrum is calculated quantum mechanically and translational broadening of each line is introduced via an empirical line shape function, which contains adjustable parameters. In contrast, the treatments of Joslin et al. (1984) contain no adjustable parameters.

We restrict attention in this paper to the gas spectrum. For theoretical discussion of the liquid spectrum see Guillot and Birnbaum (1983), and Joslin et al., (1985).

On the experimental side, the first collision-induced absorption spectrum of N_2 in the submillimetre region was reported by Heastie and Martin (1962). Since then, improved data have been obtained by Gebbie et al. (1963), Bosomworth and Gush (1965) and by Rastogi and Lowndes (1974). Most of the work has been done at or near room temperature but more recently Buontempo et al. (1975) have obtained the absorption spectrum at 124 K and in addition Harries (1979) has published some observations between 200 and 353 K. There also exist some results in the microwave region at various temperatures (Dagg et al., 1975; Urbaniak et al., 1977).

EXPERIMENTAL PROCEDURE

The experimental results were obtained by means of three different techniques. Between 40 and 360 cm^{-1}, Fourier transform infrared spectrometry was used, and at two fixed points, 15.1 and

84.2 cm^{-1}, the absorption was measured using an optically pumped far infrared laser. The results at 15.1 cm^{-1} contributed to the extrapolation of the absorption curves toward the microwave region, and the results at 84.2 cm^{-1} served to confirm the radiometric accuracy of the absorption profiles as determined from the interferometer measurements. The earlier results of Dagg et al. (1975) and Urbaniak et al. (1977) were used at the microwave end of the spectrum, nominally at 2.3 and 4.7 cm^{-1}.

RESULTS

The results obtained at six different temperatures are shown in Fig. (1) where $A(\omega)/\rho^2$ is plotted versus the frequency ν in cm^{-1}, where $\omega = 2\pi c\nu$ and ρ is the number density in cm^{-3}. The curves for each temperature represent smoothed averages of three or four different sets of data. The laser measurements (indicated by open symbols) are seen to agree well with the interferometer results.

From these data it is found that the half-width of the band increases linearly with temperature at 0.19 ($\pm$ .02) cm^{-1}K^{-1} and the frequency of maximum absorption increases linearly with temperature at 0.20 ($\pm$ .02) cm^{-1}K^{-1}.

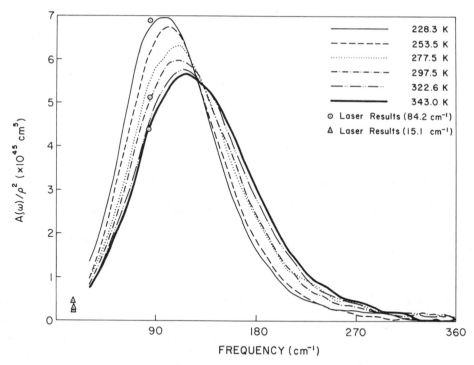

Fig. 1.   Plots of $A(\omega)/\rho^2$ vs. the frequency in cm^{-1} for various temperatures as labelled.

111

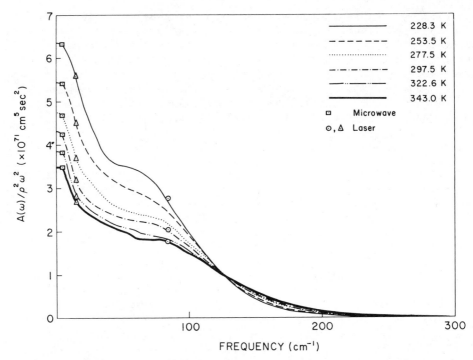

Fig. 2. Plots of $A(\omega)/\rho^2\omega^2$ vs. the frequency for various
temperatures as labelled. The curves represent a
reasonable fit to all the data but only the microwave
and laser results are shown explicitly.

In Fig. (2) the function $A(\omega)/\rho^2\omega^2$ is plotted against
the frequency υ in cm^{-1} for each temperature using the
interferometer, laser and microwave results. The curves drawn for
each temperature represent a reasonable fit to all of these data.

From the plots of the experimental data are determined
the spectral invariants α_1 and γ_1 defined by Gray and
Gubbins(1981). The resulting values for these quantities are
given in Table 1.

A COMPARISON WITH THE THEORETICAL LINE SHAPE

The present results at 228 K are compared in Fig. (3) and
Fig. (4) to the theoretical line shape calculations of Joslin et
al.(1984). These authors define a normalized reduced line-shape
function $I(\upsilon)$ (which is proportional to $A(\upsilon)/\upsilon^2$) which is shown as

Table 1. The spectral invariants α_1 and γ_1 determined from the experimental results. These quantities are defined according to Gray and Gubbins (1981).

Temperature (K)	α_1 ($\times 10^{31} \mathrm{cm}^{15} \mathrm{sec}^{-1}$)	γ_1 ($\times 10^{58} \mathrm{cm}^{15} \mathrm{sec}$)
343	1.38	5.51
322.6	1.37	5.66
297.5	1.36	6.12
277.5	1.42	6.69
253.5	1.37	7.41
228.3	1.43	8.64
212	1.34	9.15
179	1.40	11.02
149	1.54	14.76
126	1.58	17.72

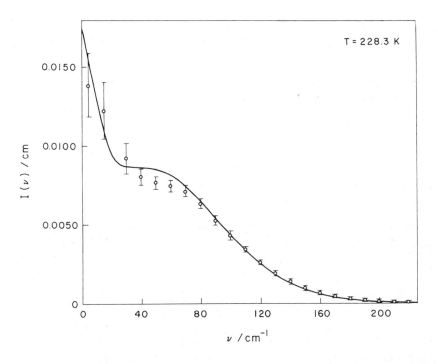

Fig. 3. A comparison of the theoretical spectrum of Joslin et al. (1984) shown as the solid line with the present experimental results shown as dots and estimated error bars. The $I(\upsilon)$ is normalized to unity from $-\infty$ to $+\infty$.

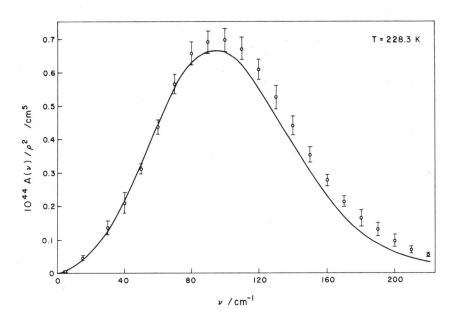

Fig. 4. A comparison of the computed absorption coefficient of
Joslin et al. (1984) with the experimental results.

the solid line in Fig. (3) and the corresponding computed
absorption coefficient is represented by the solid line in Fig.
(4). The present experimental points (with the estimated errors)
are seen in both these figures to be in good agreement with the
theory. In Fig. (5) is shown the theoretical variation of $I(\upsilon)$
with the temperature. Again the qualitative trends agree with
the experimental results as may be seen from a comparison with
the experimental curves of Fig. (2).

It must be emphasized that in this theory there are no
adjustable parameters in the calculation; the theoretically
calculated spectral moments (up to the fourth moment) are used as
input to the theories. The LJ potential used has the parameters
$\varepsilon/\kappa = 91.5$ K and $\sigma = 3.68$ Å and the value of Q was taken to be
-1.46 B as recommended by Buckingham (1981).

THE QUADRUPOLE MOMENT

The quadrupole moment Q of N_2 may be determined from the
experimental results for α_1 and γ_1 and the theory of Gray and
Gubbins (1981). For this determination, an isotropic
intermolecular potential function is required. In Table 2 are
listed the values obtained for Q using several different
potential functions. The values $Q(\alpha_1)$ and $Q(\gamma_1)$ refer
respectively to the values of Q determined from the data and from
the theory for the spectral invariants α_1 and γ_1.

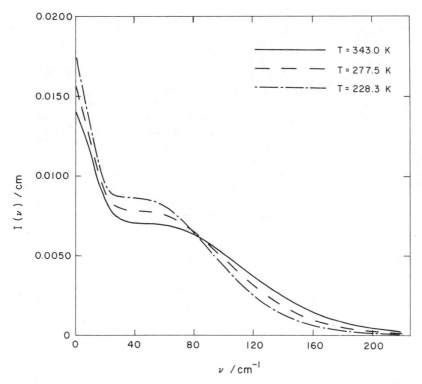

Fig. 5   The computed line shape function of Joslin et al. (1984) at
several temperatures.

It may be seen that the values of Q so obtained are independent
of temperature.   The average value of $Q(\gamma_1)$ is approximately 3% less
than that for $Q(\alpha_1)$ for each potential.   This difference may arise
from contributions from other induction mechanisms which give rise
to a relatively larger absorption in the higher frequency regions.
The contributions from other mechanisms has been estimated by Poll
and Hunt (1981) to amount to approximately 6% of the total
absorption.

The effect of including the hexadecapole term in determining a
value for Q may be estimated from the theoretical expressions for α_1
and γ_1 given by Cohen and Birnbaum (1977) and their analysis of
previous experimental results for collision–induced absorption in
N_2.   We then find that the values of $Q(\alpha_1)$ and $Q(\gamma_1)$ would be
reduced from those quoted in Table 2 by approximately 5.8% and 1.7%
respectively bringing these two values into close agreement.
However, Poll and Hunt (1981) have shown that overlap induction also
contributes significantly to the absorption and further that there
is an interference effect between the hexadecapolar and overlap

Table 2. Values of the quadrupole moment of nitrogen calculated for various potential functions using the theory of Gray and Gubbins (1981) for quadrupolar induction. The quadrupole values labelled $Q(\alpha_1)$ and $Q(\gamma_1)$ are determined using the theory and the experimental results for α_1 and γ_1 respectively. (B = 10^{-26} e.s.u.)

Potential ε/k(K) σ(Å)	Lennard-Jones 95.0 3.698		Lennard-Jones 91.5 3.681		Billing-Fisher[a] 85.0 3.686	
Temperature (K)	$Q(\alpha_1)$ (B)	$Q(\gamma_1)$	$Q(\alpha_1)$ (B)	$Q(\gamma_1)$	$Q(\alpha_1)$ (B)	$Q(\gamma_1)$
343.0	1.52	1.49	1.50	1.47	1.46	1.43
322.6	1.52	1.47	1.50	1.45	1.46	1.41
297.5	1.52	1.46	1.50	1.45	1.46	1.41
277.5	1.54	1.48	1.52	1.46	1.47	1.44
253.5	1.52	1.48	1.50	1.46	1.47	1.44
228.3	1.55	1.51	1.53	1.50	1.51	1.48
212	1.49	1.50	1.47	1.48	1.46	1.47
179	1.51	1.49	1.49	1.48	1.49	1.47
149	1.55	1.54	1.53	1.51	1.54	1.53
126	1.52	1.51	1.51	1.50	1.53	1.51
Q_{mean}	1.52	1.49	1.51	1.48	1.49	1.46

(a) See Poll and Hunt (1981).

induction mechanisms. As these additional contributions are small and their determination sensitive to small errors in α_1 and γ_1 we prefer to quote our values (in Table 2) obtained by considering only quadrupolar induction.

Comparison with Other Results for Q

It is generally agreed that the most accurate experimental method for determining the quadrupole moment, Q, is that used by Buckingham et al. (1968). Buckingham (1981) has obtained a value of Q equal to 1.46 B. As seen in Table 2, this suggests that the isotropic form of the Billing-Fisher potential as discussed by Poll and Hunt (1981) is the most suitable for our analysis. Indeed Poll and Hunt favour this potential in their treatment of collision-induced absorption in N_2. They also obtain a value of Q equal to 1.46 B.

Theoretical calculations using the SCF approximation usually provide values of Q somewhat lower than 1.40 B although the

accuracy depends on the size of the basis set used as is evident
in the work of Cade et al. (1966), Christiansen and McCullough
(1977), and Amos (1980). However, in a recent calculation
(Amos, 1980) are quoted values of Q equal to 1.46, 1.65 and
1.34B.

In summary, the present values of Q are in good agreement
with those values obtained by other workers.

References

Amos, R.D., 1980, Mol. Phys., 39:1.
Birnbaum, G. and E.R. Cohen, 1976, Can. J. Phys., 54:593.
Bosomworth, D.R. and Gush, H.P., 1965, Can. J. Phys., 43:751.
Buckingham, A.D., Disch, R.L. and Dunmur, D.A., 1968, J. Am.
    Chem., Soc. 90:3104.
Buckingham, A.D., 1981, private communication.
Buontempo, U., Cunsolo, S., Jacucci, G. and Weis, J.J., 1975,
    J. Chem. Phys. 63:2570.
Cade, P.E., Sales, K.D., and Wahl, A.C., 1966, J. Chem. Phys.,
    44:1973.
Christiansen, P.A. and McCullough, E.A., 1977, J. Chem. Phys.,
    67:1877.
Cohen, E.R., and Birnbaum, G., 1977, J. Chem. Phys., 66:2443.
Cohen, E.R., 1976, Can. J. Phys., 54:475.
Dagg, I.R., Anderson, A., Read, L.A.A., Yan, S. and Smith, W.,
    1984. (To be published and presented at annual meeting of
    C.A.P. Sherbrooke, Que. June 1984.)
Dagg, I.R., Reesor, G.E. and Urbaniak, J.L., 1975, Can., J.
    Phys., 53:1764.
Gebbie, H.A., Stone, N.W.B. and Williams, D., 1963, Mol. Phys.,
    6:215.
Guillot, B., and Birnbaum, G., 1983, J. Chem. Phys., 79:686.
Gray, C.G., and Gubbins, K.E., 1981, Mol. Phys., 42:843
    These authors derive expressions for the spectral
    invariants α_1 and γ_1 for molecules of general shape (not
    necessarily axial) for the case of quadrupolar induction.
    For linear molecules the expressions reduce to those found
    in Cohen and Birnbaum (1977) for quadrupolar induction when
    misprints in the polarizability anisotropy terms are
    corrected.
Gray, C.G., 1971, J. Phys., B4:1661.
Harries, J.E., 1979, J. Opt. Soc. Am., 69:386.
Heastie, R. and Martin, D.H., 1962, Can. J. Phys. 40:122.
Joslin, C.G., Gray, C.G., and Gburski, Z., 1984, Mol. Phys.
    (in press) For a pure information theory calculation, see
    Joslin, C.G. and Gray, C.G., 1984, Chem. Phys. Lett.
    107:249.

Joslin, C.G., Singh, S. and Gray, C.G., 1985, Can. J. Phys.,
    submitted for publication.
Poll, J.D. and Hunt, J.L., 1981, Can. J. Phys., 59:1448.
Poll, J.D. and Van Kranendonk, J., 1961, Can. J. Phys., 39:189.
Rastogi, A., and Lowndes, R.P., 1974, J. Phys. B., 10:495.
Stone, N.W.B., Read, L.A.A., Anderson, A., Dagg, I.R. and Smith,
    W., 1984, Can. J. Phys., 62:338.
Urbaniak, J.L., Dagg, I.R., and Reesor, G.E., 1977, J. Can.
    Phys., 55:496.

FAR INFRARED ABSORPTION SPECTRA IN GASEOUS METHANE

FROM 138 TO 296 K

Paolo Codastefano, Paolo Dore and Luca Nencini

Dipartimento di Fisica - Università di Roma "La Sapienza"
P.le Aldo Moro, 2 - 00185 Roma, Italy

ABSTRACT

The rototranslational collision-induced absorption spectrum of gaseous CH_4 has been measured from 40 to 600 cm^{-1} at five different temperatures, from 138 to 296 K. Assuming that octopolar and hexadecapolar induction mechanisms contribute to the absorption, we have derived the octopole and hexadecapole electric multipoles from the analysis of the spectral moments α and γ. We discuss the differences between our values and previous ones and we give an easy temperature interpolation of the moments of the collision-induced rototranslational methane spectra.

INTRODUCTION

The FIR collision-induced rototranslational absorption spectra of CH_4 is of great interest, because CH_4 is an important molecule and a model of the tetrahedral type. The CH_4 spectrum is unusual, in that the total absorption is mainly induced by two electrical multipoles, namely the octopole and hexadecapole. The permanent dipole, arising from the centrifugal effect of rotation on the molecule, gives a very small contribution which decreases with decreasing temperature (Ozier, 1971; Watson, 1971; Fox, 1971). It has already been proved that the FIR spectroscopy is an unique tool in the determination of molecular multipoles. Moreover, since methane is an important constituent of the atmospheres of the outer planets, information can be obtained on the properties of these atmospheres from a detailed knowledge of its spectrum.

The first CI rototranslational absorption spectra of gaseous CH_4 at room temperature were recorded by Birnbaum and Rosenberg

(1968) and by Weiss et al. (1969). Detailed spectra have then been measured at four different temperatures down to 163 K, in the frequency range 30-600 cm^{-1} (Birnbaum, 1975). Recently, the data were extended up to 900 cm^{-1} at 296 and 195 K (Birnbaum et al., 1983). From the analysis of the spectral moments it has been shown (Birnbaum and Cohen, 1975; Cohen and Birnbaum, 1977) that the absorption is mainly due to the dipoles induced in a collisional partner by the electric field associated with the octupole (Ω) and the hexadecapole (ϕ) moments of the CH$_4$ molecule. In the same analysis the effect of the anisotropic part of the intermolecular potential and of an anisotropic overlap induction mechanism have been studied, but, at the moment, the spectral shapes and the importance of these contributions are still not known.

In a recent work (Birnbaum et al., 1983) the absorption band shapes have been analyzed by considering the Ω- and ϕ- induction mechanism. Translational profiles, resulting from rigorous quantum mechanical computations, have been used to describe the single rotational lines. In the framework of these computations, the significance of bound and predissociating dimers in the spectrum was pointed out. It has been shown that it is possible to get a good description of the experimental band shapes considering the collision-induced rotational transitions in single molecules;   the double transition contribution is present but appears to be almost negligible. By using this fitting procedure, new values for Ω and ϕ were evaluated, which were in reasonable agreement with those previously obtained by means of the moment analysis.

It must be recalled that also higher multipoles (Birnbaum et al., 1983) and interference terms (Birnbaum and Cohen, 1975; Cohen and Birnbaum, 1977) (due to the anisotropic part of the intermolecular potential) between the different induction mechanisms, should in principle be taken into account.

For a further insight into the absorption processes, it is important to study the temperature dependence of the absorption spectra. We report here the results of new measurements at five different temperatures down to 138 K, in the frequency range 40-600 cm^{-1}. We present an analysis of the effects of temperature on the spectral moments. Our aim was also to parametrize the temperature dependence of the absorption intensities. Indeed, it is important to provide a reliable way of predicting the absorption of gaseous methane because of its importance in the study of planetary atmospheres (see, for example Fox and Ozier, 1971; Courtin, 1982).

EXPERIMENTAL RESULTS

The experimental apparatus and the procedure used to derive the absorption coefficient A(ν) are reported elsewhere (Dore et al., 1983). The absorption coefficient A(ν) is defined as

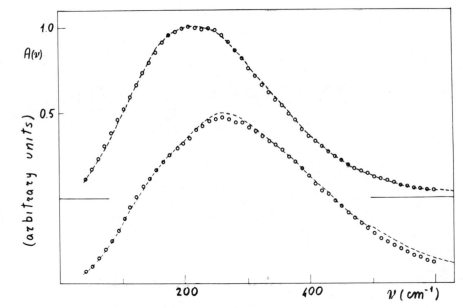

Fig. 1: Absorption coefficients A(ν) at 195 (upper) and 296 K (lower). ο ο ο ο ο present results; — — — — from Birnbaum (1975). A(ν) are plotted in arbitrary units. In our data the maximum value is $9.24 \cdot 10^{-6}$ cm^{-1} amagat^{-2} at 296 K and $1.22 \cdot 10^{-5}$ cm^{-1} amagat^{-2} at 195 K.

$$A(\nu) = \frac{1}{\ell \rho^2} \ln \frac{I_o(\nu)}{I(\nu)} \tag{1}$$

As the length ℓ of our cell is one meter, we needed a density of about 30 amagats in order to optimize the absorption. For any experimental condition, the density ρ was determined through accurate measurements of temperature and pressure by using the detailed data reported by Goodwin (1971). We have verified that, within the accuracy of the experimental data, the absorption is proportional to ρ^2, due to binary collisions, in the density range 10 ÷ 40 amagats. Only at the lowest temperature (138 K) was it necessary to work at a lower density ($\sim$ 10 amagats) to avoid the condensation of the gas. Therefore, at this temperature, the data are less accurate and we have not been able to verify if the absorption is proportional simply to ρ^2.

In Fig. 1 our experimental results at T=296 K and T=195 K are compared with previous ones (Birnbaum, 1975). The agreement between the spectral shapes is generally quite good. As concerning the absolute absorption intensities, our data are systematically higher ($\sim$10%) than the previous ones. It must be noted that in the figure the previous absorption profiles have been normalized to ours. As

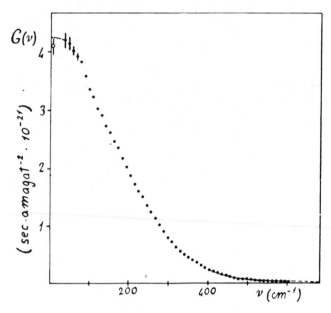

Fig. 2: Reduced line shape $G(\nu)$ at 195 K. The vertical bars indicate the uncertainty in the $A(\nu)$ values at low frequencies.
The microwave value (0) is from Urbianak et al., (1976).
The broken lines are the extrapolations used to evaluate
the spectral moments.

evident in Fig. 1, our room temperature data do not show the bump
at about 500 cm^{-1}, which had been observed in previous measurements.

In the analysis of the experimental results the two spectral
moments α are γ will be considered. α and γ are given by

$$\alpha = \int_0^\infty A(\omega)\,d\omega \tag{2}$$

$$\gamma = \int_0^\infty G(\omega)\,d\omega \tag{3}$$

where the reduced line shape $G(\nu)$ is defined by

$$G(\omega) = \frac{\hbar}{2kT}\,\frac{A(\omega)}{\omega\,tgh(\hbar\omega/2kT)} \cdot \tag{3-a}$$

In Fig. 2 we report, for example, $G(\nu)$ at 195 K. Because the spectral
shapes were measured at a density which optimized the absorption over

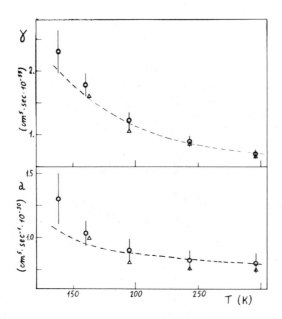

Fig. 3: Spectral moments α and γ versus temperature. ○ ○ ○ ○
present results; △ △ △ data from Birnbaum and Cohen (1975);
— — — — best fit of present data (excluding the 138 K data)
by using Eq. (4) and (5).

over the whole band, our data are less accurate in the low and high
frequency wings. Figure 2 shows how this low frequency uncertainty
affects G(ν). We also report, for comparison, the microwave result
(Urbianak et al., 1976) at 2.3 cm⁻¹. The agreement is quite
satisfactory, expecially at higher temperatures. In the figure we
show the extrapolation used for the evaluation of the spectral moments. We have verified that, within the experimental accuracy, the
high frequency wings can be well approximated by an exponential
function. The temperature variation of the spectral moments α and
γ is shown in Fig. 3. From an analysis of the absolute accuracy of
our data and of the employed extrapolations, we estimate a 10%
error of our values. Only at 138 K the error is higher, as previously
noted. In the figure, we also report for comparison the experimental
values of α and γ from Birnbaum and Cohen (1975).

ANALYSIS OF THE SPECTRAL MOMENTS

It has been shown that both spectral moments (Birnbaum and
Cohen, 1975; Cohen and Birnbaum, 1979) and the absorption profiles
(Birnbaum et al., 1983) can be accounted for by assuming that only
the Ω- and φ- induction mechanisms contribute to the absorption.
In particular, it has been shown that double transitions (Birnbaum
et al., 1983) contribute to the integral absorption less than 5%.
Since the absolute accuracy of our data is 10%, we shall neglect
this contribution. Under this hypothesis, the sum rules for the

spectral moments α and γ read (Gray, 1971; Birnbaum and Cohen, 1975):

$$\alpha = \alpha_\Omega + \alpha_\phi, \tag{4-a}$$

where the octopolar contribution α_Ω is given by

$$\alpha_\Omega = \frac{38\pi^2 \bar{\alpha}^2}{5 \, c \, I} \left(\frac{\Omega^2}{\sigma_o^7}\right) I_{10} + \frac{15}{4} \frac{I}{m\sigma_o^2} I_{12} , \tag{4-b}$$

and the hexadecapolar contribution α_ϕ is given by

$$\alpha_\phi = \frac{800\pi^2\bar{\alpha}^2}{7 \, c \, I} \left(\frac{\phi^2}{\sigma_o^9}\right) I_{12} + \frac{33}{10} \frac{I}{m\sigma_o^2} I_{14} . \tag{4-c}$$

In the same way, we have

$$\gamma = \gamma_\Omega + \gamma_\phi ; \tag{5-a}$$

with

$$\gamma_\Omega = \frac{32\pi^2\bar{\alpha}^2}{5c \, k \, T} \left(\frac{\Omega^2}{\sigma_o^7}\right) I_{10} ; \tag{5.-b}$$

and

$$\gamma_\phi = \frac{40\pi^2\bar{\alpha}^2}{7c \, k \, T} \left(\frac{\phi^2}{\sigma_o^9}\right) I_{12} . \tag{5-c}$$

In the above relations, $\bar{\alpha}$ is the isotropic polarizability, σ_o in the molecular diameter, I is the moment of inertia, and m is the reduced mass. The values of these constants are reported by Birnbaum and Cohen (1975). The dimensionless temperature dependent I_n integrals are defined as

$$I_n = 4\pi \int_o^\infty g(x) \, x^{-n} x^2 dx , \tag{6}$$

where $x = r/\sigma_o$. The low density radial distribution function in the classical limit is given by

$$g(x) = \exp\left(-V(x)/kT\right) \tag{6-a}$$

where $V(x)$ is the isotropic intermolecular potential.

Birnbaum and Cohen (1975) obtained the multipole moments Ω and

124

Values of octopole and hexadecapole electric multipoles.

	Ω $(10^{-34}x$ esu cm$^3)$	ϕ $(10^{-42}x$ esu cm$^3)$	Ω^2/σ_o^7 $(10^{-16}$erg)	ϕ^2/σ_o^9 $(10^{-16}$erg)
Cohen and Birnbaum (1975)(LJ)	2.22±.12	4.8±.5	4.67±.51	1.56±.31
Cohen and Birnbaum (1977)(HK) 195K	1.94	4.64	4.1	1.74
Present work (HK)	2.16±.04	5.0±.3	5.1±.2	1.9 ±.2
Birnbaum et al. (1983) (HK)	2.0±.1	5.0±.4	4.4±.4	2.0±.3

ϕ from the experimental values of α and γ on the basis of the above relations (4), (5) and (6). These values, obtained by using the Lennard–Jones potential, are reported in Table I. A more detailed analysis is reported by Cohen and Birnbaum (1977). Values for Ω and ϕ were obtained at two temperatures (296 and 195 K) for three different potential models: the Lennard Jones (LJ) potential ($\sigma_o = 3.758$ A), the Kihara (K) potential (Kihara, 1953) ($\sigma_o = 3.662$ A) and the more refined Hanley Klein (HK) potential (Hanley and Klein, 1972) ($\sigma_o = 3.68$ A). Table I gives the above values of Ω and ϕ obtained at 195 K by using the HK potential. Table I also gives the values of (Ω^2/σ_o^7) and (ϕ^2/σ_o^9), because they are somewhat invariant with respect to the different values of σ_o employed in the three potentials. The values of the multipole moments obtained at the other temperature, 296 K, are not significantly different.

In the present work we tried to obtain the multipole moments by fitting the temperature dependence of our experimental values of α and γ. We verified that the results are not appreciably dependent on the chosen potential model. Furthermore we verified that introducing quantum corrections in the evaluation of the I_n integrals (Hartye et al., 1975) does not significantly affect their values even at the lowest temperature. As concerning the temperature dependence of α and γ, the results we obtained were inconsistent with the observed high value of the spectral moments at the lowest temperature (Fig. 3). Indeed, in the vicinity of the condensation point, clusters of all sizes of molecules are likely present in the gas. Therefore, at T=138 K, three body or higher order interactions are probably responsible for the observed disagreement between the experimental data and theory based on binary interactions. We recall that at 138 K, we were unable to check the ρ^2-dependence of the absorption on account of the limited pressure range available. Therefore we performed the fitting neglecting the 138 K data and so obtained good consistency with the data at higher temperatures, as reported in Fig. 3. In addition to the results discussed above, table I reports our results for Ω, ϕ, Ω^2/σ_0^7, and Ω^2/σ_0^9, and also the values derived by Birnbaum et al. (1983) from the analysis of the spectral shapes. The general agreement is reasonable, considering the different analysis and measurements employed.

Finally, for the astrophysical applications, it is useful to parametrize the effect of the temperature on the absorption spectral moments in the temperature range 160-296 K. With this aim we have used the empirical power law (Dore et al., 1983).

$$X(T) = a \ (T/T_o)^b \qquad\qquad (7)$$

where T_o=273 K and X(T) represents α or γ. The best fit values of a and b are given in Table II. Therefore, in spite of the ambiguities discussed above in the results obtained, it is now possible to predict the intensity of the binary absorption spectrum of gaseous methane at any temperature in the range 160-296 K.

T A B L E II

Values of the coefficients a and b in
Eq. (7) which give the temperature dependence of α and γ, in the range 296-160 K.

	a	b
$\alpha \cdot 10^{32}$ (cm^5 sec^{-1}) $\gamma \cdot 10^{59}$ (cm^5 sec)	81.0 76.2	- 0.37 - 1.43

CONCLUSION

The analysis of the spectral moments indicates the presence of spectral contributions, appearing only at low temperatures, besides those due to binary octupole and hexadecapole induction. Considering the different induction mechanisms which may contribute to the absorption spectrum, the results obtained seem to indicate that multipole field gradient terms, higher multipoles, anisotropic overlap and anisotropic potential are not responsible for the excess absorption at low temperatures. Indeed, a sudden relative increase of these spectral contributions cannot be explained; on the contrary, our results indicate that the extra absorption is strongly temperature dependent. We believe that the observed inconsistencies might be attributed to molecular clusters which may be present near the condensation point. For this reason these data must be disregarded in an analysis based on the binary interaction hypothesis.

As concerning the results reported in Table I, we want to point out that they are in reasonable agreement, as already noted. However, it is important to note that our moment analysis and the line shape analysis (Birnbaum et al., 1983) give rather different relative weight to the octopolar and hexadecapolar contributions to the total absorption. Considering relations (4), we can introduce the ratio $R=\alpha_\Omega/\alpha_\phi$, and from our moment analysis we obtain $R=2.2$. The line shape analysis gives more relative weight to the ϕ-contribution ($R=1.8$), although the high frequency spectrum, where this contribution is more important, is nevertheless underestimated. These results lead us to suggest that in the high frequency part of the spectrum there are absorption mechanisms other than the binary Ω- and ϕ- induction. In addition, the effect of the anisotropy of the potential should be considered. In view of these small but unknown contributions to the spectrum, the values of Ω and ϕ obtained by the line shape and moment analysis should be considered as effective values. In order to get new information about this problem, as well as on the anomalous low temperature absorption, new measurements are now in progress.

ACKNOWLEDGEMENTS

The authors wish to thank Prof. L. Frommhold and Prof. G. Birnbaum for the helpful discussions.

REFERENCES

Birnbaum, G., 1975, J. Chem. Phys., 62:59
Birnbaum, G., and Cohen, E. R., 1975, J. Chem. Phys., 62:3807
Birnbaum, G., Frommhold, L., Nencini, L., Sutter, H., 1983, Chem. Phys. Lett., 100:292
Cohen, E. R., and Birnbaum, G., 1977, J. Chem. Phys., 66:2443
Courtin, R., 1982, Icarus, 51:446
Fox, K., 1972, Phys. Rev., A6:907
Fox, K., and Ozier, I., 1971, Astrophys. Jour., 166:L95
Goodwin, R. D., 1971, "Tables of provisional values of thermodynamic function for Methane", Nat. Bur. Stand. Rep., 10715
Gray, C. G., 1971, J. Phys., B4:1661
Hanley, H. J., and Klein, M., 1972, J. Chem. Phys., 76:1743

Hartye, R. W., Gray, C. G., Poll, J. D., Miller, M. S., 1975, Mol. Phys., 29:825

Kihara, T., 1953, Rev. Mod. Phys., 25:381

Ozier, I., 1971; Phys. Rev. Lett., 27:1329

Urbianak, J. L., Reesor, G. E., and Dagg, I. R., 1976, Can. J. Phys., 54:1606

Watson, J. K. G., 1971, J. Mol. Spectrosc., 40:536

INDUCED VIBRATIONAL ABSORPTION IN THE HYDROGENS

S. Paddi Reddy

Department of Physics
Memorial University of Newfoundland
St. John's, Newfoundland, A1B 3X7 Canada

ABSTRACT

A review of the collision-induced absorption spectra of H_2, D_2 and HD in their vibrational spectral regions with particular emphasis on most recent experimental results is presented. It includes the measurements and analyses of the induced vibrational spectra of the pure gases as well as those of their binary mixtures with inert and other simple gases, obtained under a variety of experimental conditions.

INTRODUCTION

In their ground electronic states, isolated homonuclear diatomic molecules such as H_2 and D_2 do not possess permanent static or vibrational electric dipole moments because they have a center of symmetry and consequently are inactive in vibrational and rotational electric dipole absorption. However, such molecules give rise to collision-induced absorption (CIA) because of the transient electric dipole moments induced in them by intermolecular interactions which are operative during binary and higher-order collisions. These induced dipoles depend on the intermolecular separation as well as on the orientation and internuclear separation of the individual molecules and are, consequently, modulated by the vibrational, rotational, and relative translational motions of the molecules. Pure translational absorption occurs in the microwave and far infrared regions, whereas rotational-translational absorption and vibrational-rotational-translational absorption occur in the infrared spectral regions at higher frequencies.

Collision-induced absorption, first observed by Crawford et al. (1949) in the fundamental bands of compressed O_2 and N_2, was soon identified in the fundamental band of hydrogen by Welsh et al. (1949). In the past thirty five years the CIA spectra of the fundamental and overtone bands of H_2 in the pure gas and its binary mixtures with inert and some simple gases have been studied over a wide range of temperatures and pressures in considerable detail. Further studies of CIA of the vibration-rotation spectra of HD, D_2, N_2, O_2 and $C\ell_2$ in the pure gases and some binary mixtures with inert and some simple gases have also been made.

Some earlier work on CIA has been reviewed by Ketelaar (1959), Filimonov (1959), Colpa (1965) and Tonkov (1970); in particular, a comprehensive review of the work done until 1971 on the translational, rotational and vibrational CIA spectra with the main emphasis on the experimental results has been given by Welsh (1972). Van Kranendonk (1974), Poll (1980) and Birnbaum et al. (1982) have reviewed several aspects of the theory of CIA. A comprehensive bibliography on CIA through 1975 has been compiled by Rich and McKellar (1976). The main emphasis of the present review will be directed to more recent work on the collision-induced vibrational absorption of H_2, HD and D_2 in the gas phase.

GENERAL CHARACTERISTICS AND ROTATIONAL SELECTION RULES IN CIA SPECTRA

In general collision-induced spectra have a characteristic broad and diffuse appearance because of their origin in the interaction of two or more molecules. In the CIA spectra, for gas densities up to a few hundred amagat, the line profile is affected by density only to a minor degree and the induced spectral line retains a nearly constant shape which is characteristic of binary collisions. Pressure-narrowing of the spectral lines of CIA, which will be discussed later, may occur at densities beyond several hundred amagat. The width of a CIA line depends basically on the short duration of the induced dipole moment. The collision duration is given by $\Delta t = \bar{R}/\bar{v}$ where $\bar{R}$ is the range of the induction mechanism and $\bar{v}$ is the mean relative speed of one molecule with respect to its collision partner; hence the resulting width of the line is of the order $\Delta \nu = 1/2\pi c\Delta t = \bar{v}/2\pi c\bar{R}$. Also the relative kinetic energy of the molecules is approximately $(1/2)m\bar{v}^2 \simeq (3/2)kT$ and thus the half-width shows a $T^{1/2}$ dependence. Exceptions to the diffuse nature of CIA are the fine structure lines due to Van der Waals complexes of the low pressure gases (to be discussed later) and the zero-phonon lines of the solid phases (see, for example, Prasad et al., 1978). In contrast to the behavior of the induced dipoles arising from collisions, the vibrating and rotating dipoles in isolated molecules are unperturbed between collisions, but collisions do disturb the free motions of these molecules and broaden the spectral lines associated with them.

The electric dipole moment μ induced in a pair of homonuclear molecules can be represented as the sum of (i) a short-range electron-overlap moment μ_{ov} which, to a first approximation, varies exponentially; (ii) a long-range quadrupole-induced and angle-dependent moment μ_q which varies asymptotically as $1/R^4$; and (iii) an intermediate range hexadecapole-induced and angle-dependent moment μ_h which varies as $1/R^6$, where R is the intermolecular separation. The first two mechanisms have been taken into account in the theoretical treatment of the phenomenon of CIA in the "exponential-4" model for the induced dipole moment (Van Kranendonk, 1958). The first part is mainly isotropic and gives rise to the $Q_{ov}(J)$ ($\Delta J = 0$) transitions where J is the rotational quantum number. The second part gives rise to the $O(\Delta J = -2)$, $Q_q(\Delta J = 0)$ and $S(\Delta J = +2)$ transitions. In this part, the isotropic component of the polarizability of a colliding molecule contributes to the intensity of the single transitions $O(J)$, $Q(J)$ ($J \neq 0$) and $S(J)$ and double transitions of the $Q(J) + Q(J)$ and $Q(J) + S(J)$; on the other hand, the anisotropic component of the polarizability contributes a small amount to the above transitions and also gives rise to the double transitions $S(J) + S(J)$. The term μ_h resulting from the polarization of a molecule by the hexadecapole field of its collision partner gives rise to much weaker transitions corresponding to the rotational selection rule $\Delta J = 0$, ± 2 and ± 4. The transitions corresponding to $\Delta J = 4$ are known as U transitions which are of some interest for the hydrogens. U branch transitions are expected to occur both as single $U(J)$ and double $Q(J) + U(J)$ transitions (and possibly $U(J) + S(J)$ transitions which have not yet been observed). We note that the "level mixing mechanism" (see Herman, 1970) in quadrupolar induction may also contribute a small amount to the $\Delta J = 4$ transitions on account of the anisotropy of the potential. We also note that the anisotropic part of μ_{ov} contributes a small amount to the transitions with $\Delta J = 0$, ± 2.

SUMMARY OF EXPERIMENTAL WORK

Since the discovery of CIA, the fundamental band of gaseous H_2 has been the subject of numerous investigations under a variety of experimental conditions. The band has been studied in pure H_2 and in binary mixtures with foreign gases such as He, Ne, Ar, Kr, Xe, N_2, CO, O_2 and HCℓ at pressures in the range of a hundred Torr to 5000 atm, and temperatures from 17 to 423 K with absorption path lengths from a fraction of a cm to 220 m. Considerable work was done on the fundamental bands of HD and D_2, but it was not as extensive as on the fundamental band of H_2. Some experimental work was done on the 2-0 and 3-0 bands of H_2 mainly in the pure gases with the exception of the 2-0 band in mixtures with Ar and N_2. The 2-0 band of D_2 was studied in the pure gas and in mixtures with Ar and N_2. In all, there have been about sixty published papers to date on the experimental work on the vibrational spectra of gaseous H_2, HD and D_2 in CIA. For references on the earlier work the reader is referred to the review article by Welsh (1972) and the bibliography compiled by Rich and McKellar (1976).

REPRESENTATIVE VIBRATIONAL SPECTRA IN CIA

Illustrative examples of CIA spectra of the H_2 fundamental band in the pure gas at 77, 196 and 298 K for gas densities 43.3, 39.4 and 38.5 amagat, respectively, are shown in Fig. 1. The positions of the single transitions $O_1(J)$[a], $Q_1(J)$ and $S_1(J)$ calculated from the constants of the free molecule (Foltz et al., 1966) are shown along the wavenumber axis (similarly in the following figures) and the extent of different groups of single and double transitions are marked over the absorption peaks. Almost all the molecules of H_2 are distributed among the rotational levels J = 0 and 1 at 77 K, and J = 0 to 3 at 196 and 298 K. It is evident from Fig. 1 that both the shape of the bands and the dip in the Q branch depend in a character-istic fashion on the temperature of the gas. A very interesting aspect of CIA spectra of the fundamental bands is the occurence of a characteristic dip in the Q branch with low- and high- frequency maxima denoted by Q_P and Q_R in Fig. 1. The separation between Q_P and Q_R is density and temperature dependent. Van Kranendonk (1968) explained these dips as an intercollisional interference arising from the negative correlations existing between the dipoles induced in successive collisions of a molecule with the other molecules of the gas. Lewis (1972, 1973, 1976) gave a detailed kinetic theory of this effect. For a detailed review the reader is referred to Lewis (1985).

Double transitions $S_1(J) + S_0(J)$ arising from the anisotropy of the polarizability in the quadrupolar induction mechanism are observed in the high frequency wing of the main transitions at suffi-ciently high densities. Figure 2 illustrates these double transi-tions in the fundamantal band of H_2 at 77 K for gas densities of 150, 227 and 321 amagat (Sen et al., 1980). U branch transitions arising from the weaker hexadecapolar induction mechanism occur at even higher frequencies in the band. Figure 3 shows the U-branch transi-tions in the fundamental band of H_2 at 77 K for gas densities of 437, 473 and 518 amagat in the spectral region 5400 - 6200 cm^{-1} (Reddy et al., 1980). The calculated positions of $U_1(1)$ and $Q_1(J = 0,1) + U_0(1)$ are shown along the wavenumber axis (see also Gibbs et al., 1974).

Illustrative examples of enhancement absorption profiles of the fundamantal band of H_2 in H_2-He, H_2-Ne, H_2-Ar, H_2-Kr and H_2-Xe ob-tained with a 1 m cell with base densities of H_2 in the range 5 to 20 amagat and partial densities of the inert gases in the range 67 to 117 amagat are shown in Fig. 4. For comparison, an absorption pro-file of the band in pure H_2 gas at 37 amagat is also shown in the same figure. The decrease in the width of the individual transitions

---

[a]The subscripts used for O, Q, S etc., indicate Δv values. Thus 1 indicates the vibrational transition v = 1 ← v = 0, and 0 indicates a pure rotational transition with no change in v.

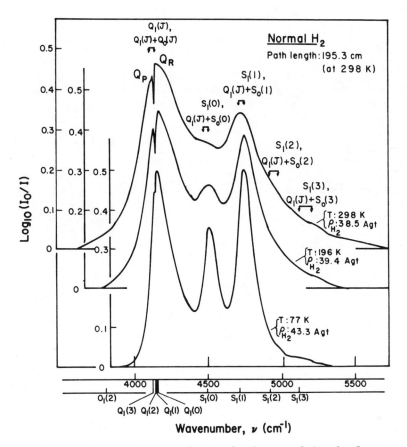

Fig. 1. Absorption profiles of the fundamental band of gaseous H_2 at 77, 196 and 298 K (Reddy et al., 1977).

with the increase in reduced mass and therefore a decrease in the relative velocities of the colliding pair is clearly evident. The characteristic dip with Q_P and Q_R components of the Q branch occurs at the $Q_1(1)$ position. In general, the Q_P component is less intense than Q_R. However, in the enhancement spectrum of H_2-Xe, the Q_P component has anomalous intensity distribution. This has now been interpreted as due to the asymmetry of the intercollisional dip (see Lewis, 1985). Stronger S lines in the spectra of H_2-Ar, H_2-Kr and H_2-Xe can be understood on the basis of larger polarizabilities of the perturbing gases Ar, Kr and Xe.

INTEGRATED ABSORPTION COEFFICIENTS AND BINARY AND TERNARY ABSORPTION COEFFICIENTS

The absorption coefficient $\alpha(\nu)$ at a given wavenumber ν (in cm^{-1}) of an absorbing gas is given by

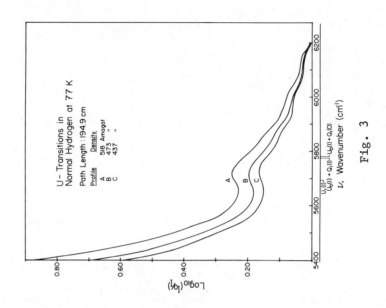

U - Transitions in
Normal Hydrogen at 77 K

Path Length : 194.9 cm

Profile	Density
A	518 Amagat
B	473 "
C	437 "

$U_0(1) + Q_1(1) - U_0(1) + Q_1(0)$

ν, Wavenumber (cm^{-1})

Log$_{10}$ (I_0/I)

Fig. 3

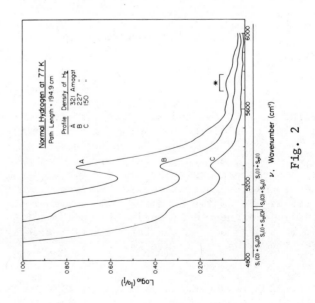

Normal Hydrogen at 77 K

Path Length = 194.9 cm

Profile	Density of H$_2$
A	321 Amagat
B	227 "
C	150 "

$S_1(0) + S_0(0)$ | $S_1(1) + S_0(0)$, $S_1(0) + S_0(1)$ | $S_1(0) + S_0(0)$

ν, Wavenumber (cm^{-1})

Log$_{10}$ (I_0/I)

Fig. 2

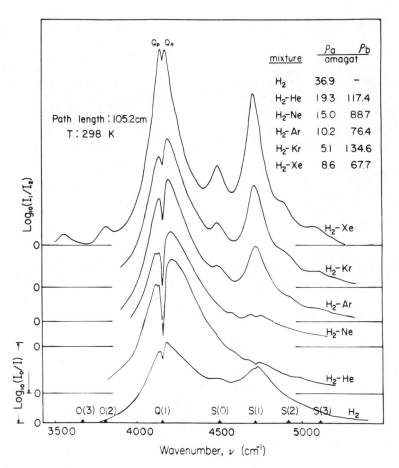

Fig. 4. Profiles of the enhancement of absorption of the fundamental band of H_2 by He, Ne, Ar, Kr and Xe at 298 K (Reddy
et al., 1977) for H_2; Reddy and Chang (1973) for H_2-He
and H_2-Ne; Prasad (1984) for H_2-Ar and H_2-Kr; Varghese and
Reddy (1969) for H_2-Xe.

$$\alpha(\nu) = (1/\ell) \, \ln[I_0(\nu)/I(\nu)] , \qquad (1)$$

where $I_0(\nu)$ and $I(\nu)$ are the intensities of radiation transmitted by
the evacuated cell of sample path length ℓ, and the cell when filled
with the absorbing gas at density ρ_a, respectively. For mixtures
(say, of species a at density ρ_a with species b at density ρ_b) it is
useful to define an enhancement absorption coefficient $\alpha_{en}(\nu)$ as

$$\alpha_{en}(\nu) = (1/\ell) \, \ln[I_1(\nu)/I_2(\nu)] , \qquad (2)$$

where $I_1(\nu)$ is the intensity transmitted by the species a alone at
density ρ_a, and $I_2(\nu)$ is the intensity transmitted by the mixture.

Related absorption coefficients $\bar{\alpha}(\nu) \equiv \alpha(\nu)/\nu$, and $\bar{\alpha}(\nu) \equiv \bar{\alpha}_{en}(\nu) \equiv \alpha_{en}(\nu)/\nu$, are also frequently used.

The integrated absorption coefficients $\int \alpha(\nu)\ d\nu$ etc., and higher moments are of great interest as they are time-independent equilibrium quantities and as such are much more theoretically tractable than the frequency-dependent absorption coefficients themselves. The integrated absorption coefficients can be conveniently expressed as power series in densitiies. Thus, for the pure gas,

$$\int \alpha(\nu)\ d\nu = \alpha_{1a}\ \rho_a^2 + \alpha_{2a}\ \rho_a^3 + \cdots, \tag{3}$$

and for a mixture

$$\int \alpha_{en}(\nu)\ d\nu = \alpha_{1b}\ \rho_a\ \rho_b + \alpha_{2b}\ \rho_a\ \rho_b^2 + \cdots \tag{4}$$

The temperature-dependent quantities α_{1a} and α_{1b} (in cm^{-2} $amagat^{-2}$) are the binary absorption coefficients and α_{2a} and α_{2b} (in cm^{-2} $amagat^{-3}$) are the ternary absorption coefficients. Analogous quantities $\bar{\alpha}_{1a}$ and $\bar{\alpha}_{1b}$ (in $cm^6\ s^{-1}$), and $\bar{\alpha}_{2a}$ and $\bar{\alpha}_{2b}$ (in $cm^9\ s^{-1}$) can be defined (see Reddy et al., 1977).

An important fact about the H_2 molecule is that it is nearly spherically symmetric so that in pure H_2 or H_2-foreign gas mixtures rotationally inelastic collisions are relatively infrequent. Consequently, it is physically meaningful to decompose an absorption profile into separate components or bands, each corresponding to a different rotational transition in a vibrational band. This procedure is described later in this paper. The decomposition yields absorption coefficients for each separate component or band and each of these absorption coefficients when integrated over frequency admits of a virial expansion analogous to Eqs. (3) and (4). Thus it is meaningful to speak of the binary absorption coefficient, for example, for the overlap components or for a particular S or U line.

Plots of $(1/\rho_a^2) \int \alpha(\nu)\ d\nu$ versus ρ_a (Eq. 3) and $(1/\rho_a\rho_b) \int \alpha_{en}(\nu)\ d\nu$ versus ρ_b (Eq. 4) have shown linear relations (see, for example, Reddy et al., 1977, and Prasad and Reddy, 1975). The values of the binary absorption coefficients α_{1a} and $\bar{\alpha}_{1a}$ and of the ternary absorption coefficients α_{2a} of the fundamental bands of H_2, HD and D_2 at 77, 196 and 298 K, obtained from the linear least squares fit of the experimental data (Reddy et al., 1977; Reddy and Prasad, 1977; Penny et al., 1982) are listed in Table 1. Up-to-date values of the binary absorption coefficients of the fundamental bands of H_2, HD and D_2 in their binary mixtures with foreign gases at 298 K and the corresponding references are given in Table 2.

THEORETICAL ASPECTS OF CIA PERTAINING TO VIBRATIONAL BANDS

The early theory of the integrated absorption coefficients for collision-induced vibration-rotation bands has been given by Van

Table 1. Absorption coefficients[a] of the fundamental bands of H_2, HD and D_2.

	T (K)	Binary absorption coefficient		Ternary absorption coefficient
		α_{1a} $(10^{-3}cm^{-2}amagat^{-2})$	$\tilde{\alpha}_{1a}$ $(10^{-35}cm^6s^{-1})$	α_{2a} $(10^{-6}cm^{-2}amagat^{-3})$
n H_2[b]	77	1.42 ± 0.05	1.32 ± 0.05	1.5 ± 1.5
	196	1.87 ± 0.05	1.74 ± 0.05	4.9 ± 1.3
	298	2.46 ± 0.03	2.30 ± 0.03	4.7 ± 0.7
HD[c]	77	1.07 ± 0.06	1.15 ± 0.06	3.8 ± 1.9
	196	1.58 ± 0.05	1.71 ± 0.07	4.2 ± 1.4
	298	2.14 ± 0.05	2.32 ± 0.05	3.7 ± 1.5
n D_2[d]	77	0.70 ± 0.03	0.92 ± 0.04	3.6 ± 0.7
	196	0.98 ± 0.05	1.29 ± 0.07	1.3 ± 1.2
	298	1.34 ± 0.02	1.76 ± 0.03	0.8 ± 0.5

[a]Ranges of error indicated are standard deviations. [b]Reddy et al. (1977). [c]Reddy and Prasad (1977). [d]Penney et al. (1982).

Kranendonk (1951 a,b; 1957, 1958, 1959). Some aspects of the theory were also given by Mizushima (1949, 1950), Britton and Crawford (1958) and Colpa and Ketelaar (1958). Later work is due to Poll (1971), Karl et al. (1975) and Poll and Hunt (1976). In this section a brief review of the theory is presented.

The electric dipole moment $\vec{\mu}$ induced by the intermolecular interaction in a pair of colliding molecules 1 and 2 is a function of the separation of the centres of mass of the molecules, $\vec{R} \equiv (R,\Omega)$, and the internuclear separations and orientations, $\vec{r}_1 \equiv (r_1,\omega_1)$ and $\vec{r}_2 \equiv (r_2,\omega_2)$, with respect to a space fixed coordinate system. A spherical component μ_ν of the induced dipole moment $\vec{\mu}$ can be expanded as a sum of components, each with a definite angular dependence (Poll and Van Kranendonk, 1961; Poll and Hunt, 1976),

$$\mu_\nu(\vec{r}_1 \vec{r}_2 \vec{R}) = \frac{(4\pi)^{3/2}}{\sqrt{3}} \sum_{\lambda_1\lambda_2\Lambda L} A_\Lambda(\lambda_1\lambda_2 L; r_1r_2R) \, \Psi_{1\nu}^{\lambda_1\lambda_2\Lambda L}(\omega_1\omega_2\Omega) \quad (5)$$

where

$$\Psi_{1\nu}^{\lambda_1\lambda_2\Lambda L} = \sum_{\mu M} C(\Lambda L1; \nu-M,M) \, C(\lambda_1\lambda_2\Lambda; \nu-M-\mu,\mu)$$
$$\times \, Y_{\lambda_1,\nu-M-\mu}(\omega_1) \, Y_{\lambda_2\mu}(\omega_2) \, Y_{LM}(\Omega) . \quad (6)$$

Table 2. Binary absorption coefficients[a] of the fundamental bands of nH_2, HD and nD_2 in binary mixtures with inert and other simple gases at 298 K.

Mixture	Binary absorption coefficient		Reference
	α_{1b} $(10^{-3}cm^{-2}amagat^{-2})$	$\tilde{\alpha}_{1b}$ $(10^{-35}cm^6s^{-1})$	
H_2-He	1.71 ± 0.02	1.63 ± 0.02	Prasad (1976)
H_2-Ne	2.51 ± 0.03	2.40 ± 0.03	Reddy and Chang (1973)
H_2-Ar	5.99 ± 0.06	5.55 ± 0.06	Prasad (1976)
H_2-Kr	8.02 ± 0.01	7.56 ± 0.01	Reddy and Lee (1968)
H_2-Xe	11.99 ± 0.05	11.34 ± 0.05	Varghese and Reddy (1969)
H_2-O_2	6.42 ± 0.04	6.12 ± 0.04	"
H_2-N_2	5.4	5.11	Hare and Welsh (1958)
HD-He	0.84 ± 0.02	0.94 ± 0.02	Prasad and Reddy (1975)
HD-Ne	1.84 ± 0.06	2.03 ± 0.06	Prasad and Reddy (1976)
HD-Ar	4.41 ± 0.06	4.84 ± 0.06	"
HD-Kr	5.81 ± 0.11	6.34 ± 0.11	Prasad and Reddy (1977)
HD-Xe	9.22 ± 0.29	10.05 ± 0.29	"
D_2-He	0.82 ± 0.01	1.08 ± 0.01	Russell et al. (1974)
D_2-Ne	1.24 ± 0.02	1.66 ± 0.02	"
D_2-Ar	2.71 ± 0.04	3.57 ± 0.04	Pai et al. (1966)
D_2-N_2	2.95 ± 0.05	3.90 ± 0.06	"

[a]Ranges of error indicated are standard deviations.

The functions $\Psi_{1\nu}^{\lambda 1\lambda 2\Lambda L}$ transform like vectors under rotation and involve spherical harmonics and Clebsch–Gordan coefficients. The expansion coefficients $A_\Lambda(\lambda_1\lambda_2L;r_1r_2R)$ characterize the contributions of a given symmetry under rotation that are possible. The isotropic overlap contribution to the dipole moment is described by the coefficient $A_0(001;r_1r_2R)$ and is usually represented by a model involving a short-range exponential dependence on R. The dipoles due to quadrupole induction are described by the coefficients $A_2(203)$ and $A_2(023)$. For homonuclear diatomic molecules the center of mass coincides with the center of symmetry of the charge distribution and the $A_\Lambda(\lambda_1\lambda_2L)$ are different from zero only for even values of λ_1 and λ_2. For molecules such as HD for which the center of mass does not coincide with the center of symmetry of the charge distribution this restriction does not apply.

The applications to the induced fundamental band, in which we are mainly interested in this paper, involve the matrix element of the dipole moment for the $v'' = 0 \to v' = 1$ transition. The vibrational matrix elements of $\vec{\mu}$ can be written in the same form as Eq. (5), provided the coefficients $A_\Lambda(\lambda_1\lambda_2 L; r_1 r_2 R)$ are replaced by the appropriate $0 - 1$ vibrational matrix elements $B_\Lambda(\lambda_1\lambda_2 L; R)$ where

$$B_\Lambda(\lambda_1\lambda_2 L; R) = \langle v_1''=0, \ v_2''=0 | A_\Lambda(\lambda_1\lambda_2 L; r_1 r_2 R) | v_1'=1, \ v_2'=0 \rangle . \qquad (7)$$

For other vibrational bands (e.g. the first overtone) there would be a different set of coefficients like the $B_\Lambda(\lambda_1\lambda_2 L; R)$. In Eq. (7) we have not indicated explicitly that, due to rotation-vibration interaction, the vibrational states depend also on the rotational quantum numbers.

The total overlap-induced dipole moment, when it is not too large, consists of an exchange term (Britton and Crawford, 1958) and a deformation term (Van Kranendonk and Bird, 1951 a,b). These two terms are approximately equal for H_2-H_2. The isotropic overlap moment is along the intermolecular axis and decreases exponentially with increasing R. The corresponding coefficient in the expansion of the dipole moment matrix element appropriate to the fundamental band is assumed to have the form

$$B_0(001;R) = \lambda e k_1 \, e^{-(R-\sigma)/\rho} , \qquad (8)$$

where e denotes the electronic charge, σ the molecular diameter corresponding to the intermolecular potential $V(\sigma) = 0$ and

$$k_1 = \langle v''=0 | r-r_0 | v'=1 \rangle \qquad (9)$$

is the $0 \to 1$ transition element of the internuclear displacement r with respect to its equilibrium value r_0. In the above equations, λ and ρ are parameters to be determined from experiment; the dimensionless parameter λ is a measure of the magnitude of the dipole transition moment and ρ denotes its range. The coefficient given by Eq. (8) describes the part of the dipole that is completely isotropic and the corresponding rotational selection rule is $\Delta J = 0$ (i.e., the Q branch in the vibrational bands). If there is any anisotropic overlap induction, described by coefficients of the form $B_2(201;R)$ or $B_2(021;R)$, the selection rules $\Delta J = 0, \pm 2$ are also possible (see Poll et al., 1975; Reddy and Chang, 1973).

The angle-dependent, long-range quadrupole-induced dipole moment varies as $1/R^4$ and the angle-dependent intermediate range hexadecapole-induced dipole moment varies as $1/R^6$. The observed spectra of H_2 indicate that the hexadecapole-induced dipole moment is very much weaker than the quadrupole-induced dipole moment. For the quadrupolar induction, the coefficients in Eq. (7) have the form

$$B_2(203;R) = \sqrt{3} \, \langle 0 | Q_{2_1} | 1 \rangle \, \langle 0 | \alpha_2 | 0 \rangle \, R^{-4} , \qquad (10)$$

$$B_2(023;R) = \sqrt{3} \langle 0|\alpha_1|1\rangle \langle 0|Q_{2_2}|0\rangle R^{-4} , \tag{11}$$

where α_i (i = 1,2) is the mean polarizability and Q_{2i} is the quadrupole moment of molecule i. The matrix elements in Eqs. (10) and (11)
refer to vibrational matrix elements (as before, the J dependence of
the vibrational states is not explicitly indicated but is implied).
The rotational selection rules can be obtained from Eqs. (5) and (7)
and are $\Delta J_1 = 0$, ± 2 combined with $\Delta J_2 = 0$, or $\Delta J_2 = 0$, ± 2 combined
with $\Delta J_1 = 0$. The quadrupolar induction thus gives the single Q, S
and O transitions as well as double transitions of the type
$Q_{\Delta v}(J_1) + O_{\Delta v}(J_2)$, $Q_{\Delta v}(J_1) + Q_{\Delta v}(J_2)$ and $Q_{\Delta v}(J_1) + S_{\Delta v}(J_2)$. The
anisotropy γ of the polarizability is taken into account by coeffi-
cients of the type (Poll and Hunt, 1976)

$$B_\Lambda(223;R) = \sqrt{2(2\Lambda+1)} \ W(2213;\Lambda 1) \ R^{-4}$$

$$\times \ \{\langle 0|\gamma_1|1\rangle \langle 0|Q_{2_2}|0\rangle - (-)^\Lambda \langle 0|Q_{2_1}|1\rangle \langle 0|\gamma_2|0\rangle \ \} . \tag{12}$$

In this case, double transitions $S_{\Delta v}(J_1) + S_{\Delta v}(J_2)$ corresponding to
$\Delta J_1 = 2$ and $\Delta J_2 = 2$ can take place. For the weaker hexadecapolar
induction (L = 4) similar expressions for the expansion coefficients
can be written. The rotational selection rules in this case are
$\Delta J_1 = 0$, ± 2, ± 4 combined with $\Delta J_2 = 0$, or $\Delta J_1 = 0$ combined with
$\Delta J_2 = 0$, ± 2, ± 4. The hexadecapolar induction gives Q, S, O, M and U
transitions. Of these, the U transitions ($\Delta J = +4$) are of some
significance. In CIA spectra of the fundamental bands the single
$U_1(J)$ and double $Q_1(J) + U_0(J)$ transitions occur with appreciable
intensity under suitable experimental conditions.

The Overlap Binary Absorption Coefficient

The overlap binary absorption coefficient of the fundamental
band can be expressed as

$$\tilde{\alpha}_{1,ov} = \frac{8\pi^3}{3h} \int B_0(001;R)^2 \ g_0(R) \ d^3R \tag{13}$$

where $g_0(R)$ is the low density limit of the pair distribution
function. On substitution of Eq. (8) in Eq. (13), we obtain

$$\tilde{\alpha}_{1,ov} = \frac{8\pi^3}{3h} (\lambda e)^2 \langle 0|r-r_0|1\rangle^2$$

$$\times \int \exp[-2(R-\sigma)/\rho] \ g_0(R) \ 4\pi R^2 \ dR , \tag{14}$$

$$= \lambda^2 I \ \tilde{\gamma} , \tag{15}$$

where

$$\tilde{\gamma} = \frac{8\pi^3}{3h} e^2 \sigma^3 |\langle 0|r-r_0|1\rangle|^2 , \tag{16}$$

140

and has the dimensions of the binary absorption coefficient (i.e., $cm^6 sec^{-1}$). The temperature-dependent dimensionless integral $I(T*)$ which represents the average R-dependence of $|B_o(001;R)|^2$ is given by

$$I(T*) = 4\pi \int_o^\infty \exp\left\{-2(x-1)\frac{\sigma}{\rho}\right\} g_o(x)x^2 \, dx \,, \tag{17}$$

where $x = R/\sigma$. The classical value of I, i.e., I_{cl}, can be obtained by calculating the integral given by Eq. (17), using the low density limit of the classical pair distribution function,

$$g_o(x) = \exp\left\{-V^*(x)/T^*\right\} \,, \tag{18}$$

where $V^*(x) = V(R/\sigma)/\varepsilon$ and $T^* = kT/\varepsilon$ are "reduced" quantities. Throughout this paper, we use the Lennard-Jones potential which is represented by

$$V(x) = 4\varepsilon\left[x^{-12} - x^{-6}\right] \,. \tag{19}$$

The quantity ε is the depth of the potential well. Classical statistical mechanics is applicable at high temperatures. At intermediate temperatures, where quantum effects should be included, the integral I can be expressed as (Van Kranendonk, 1958; see also Gibbs et al., 1979),

$$I = I_{cl} - \Lambda^{*2} I^{(2)} + \Lambda^{*4} I^{(4)} + .., \tag{20}$$

where $\Lambda^* = \{h^2/2m_r\varepsilon\sigma^2\}^{1/2}$ is the quantum mechanical wavelength introduced by Boer (1949), m_r being the reduced mass of the colliding pair of molecules. At low temperatures the pair correlation function must be calculated by completely quantum mechanical methods.

Lth Order Multipole-Induced Binary Absorption Coefficient

The expansion coefficients $B_\Lambda(\lambda_1\lambda_2L;R)$ for multipole-induced dipoles, which involve the theoretical matrix elements of the quadrupole moment and polarizability of the hydrogens, have been numerically calculated (see, for example, Hunt et al., 1984 and the references therein). Similarly, the theoretical matrix elements of the hexadecapole moment of H_2 and D_2 have also been evaluated by Karl et al. (1975). We present here expressions for the integrated absorption, Eqs. (21) to (28), in a form which has frequently appeared in the literature but different by a factor c (speed of light) from the definition used above. To write these equations in terms of the B- vibrational matrix elements, see Poll and Hunt (1976).

The integrated binary absorption coefficient of a specific Lth order multipole-induced transition, where m designates all the quantum number characterizing the transition, is given by Poll (1971) and Karl et al. (1975)

$$\tilde{\alpha}_{Lm} = \frac{1}{\rho^2} \int \frac{\alpha_m(\nu)}{\nu} \, d\nu \tag{21}$$

$$= \frac{4\pi^3 e^2}{3hc} n_o^2 a_o^5 \left(\frac{a_o}{\sigma}\right)^{2L+1} \tilde{J}_L \, X_{Lm} \, , \tag{22}$$

where

$$X_{Lm} = P_{J_1} P_{J_2} \left[C(J_1 L J_1'; 00)^2 \langle v_1 J_1 | Q_{L_1} | v_1' J_1' \rangle^2 \right.$$

$$\times C(J_2 0 J_2'; 00)^2 \langle v_2 J_2 | \alpha_2 | v_2' J_2' \rangle^2$$

$$+ C(J_2 L J_2'; 00)^2 \langle v_2 J_2 | Q_{L_2} | v_2' J_2' \rangle$$

$$\times C(J_1 0 J_1'; 00)^2 \langle v_1 J_1 | \alpha_1 | v_1' J_1' \rangle^2 \left. \right] + Y_{Lm} \tag{23}$$

and

$$\tilde{J}_L = 4\pi(L+1) \int_o^\infty x^{-2(L+2)} g_o(x) x^2 dx \, . \tag{24}$$

In Eqs. (21) to (28), L denotes the order of multipolar induction, i.e. L=2 for quadrupolar induction, and L=4 for hexadecapolar induction, etc., e is the electronic charge, n_o is Loschmidt's number, a_o is the first Bohr radius, σ the intermolecular separation corresponding to the intermolecular potential $V(\sigma) = 0$, the $\langle |Q_L| \rangle$ are the matrix elements for L-pole induction, the $\langle |\alpha| \rangle$ are the matrix elements of the isotropic polarizability, $g_o(x)$ is the pair correlation function for the gas and $x = R/\sigma$, where R is the intermolecular separation; the subscripts 1 and 2 refer to the two colliding molecules. To take into account quantum corrections at intermediate temperatures, $\tilde{J}_L$ can be expressed by an equation similar to Eq. (20). In Eq. (23), if one chooses the specific $v_1 = 0$ and $v_2 = 0$, the two terms within the square bracket will be identical, so that if one is omitted the constant 4 in Eq. (22) must be replaced by 8. The normalized Boltzmann factors P_J (i.e., $\underset{J}{\Sigma} = 1$) are given by

$$P_J = \frac{g_T(2J + 1)\exp(-E_J/kT)}{\underset{J}{\Sigma} g_T(2J + 1)\exp(-E_J/kT)} \, , \tag{25}$$

where g_T is the nuclear statistical weight of the molecule in a given rotational state and E_J is the rotational energy. g_T is 1 and 3 for the even and odd J, respectively, for H_2 and 6 and 3 for the even and odd J, respectively, for D_2. Equation (25) applies to equilibrium H_2, equilibrium D_2 or even other polar molecules. However, for normal H_2 or normal D_2 in which the conversion of the ortho to para species or vice versa is not allowed

$$\underset{\text{even } J}{\Sigma} P_J \, / \, \underset{\text{odd } J}{\Sigma} P_J = \frac{1}{3} \text{ for } H_2 \text{ and } 2 \text{ for } D_2. \tag{26}$$

The quantities $C(J\ L\ J';00)$ are Clebsch-Gordan coefficients and their squares are given by (Rose, 1957)

$$C(J\ 0\ J':00)^2 = \delta_{JJ'} \tag{27}$$

$$C(J\ 2\ J-2;00)^2 = \frac{3J(J-1)}{2(2J-1)(2J+1)} \qquad \text{(O transitions)}$$

$$C(J\ 2\ J;00)^2 = \frac{J(J+1)}{(2J-1)(2J+3)} \qquad \text{(Q transitions)}$$

$$C(J\ 2\ J+2;00)^2 = \frac{3(J+1)\ (J+2)}{2(2J+1)\ (2J+3)} \qquad \text{(S transitions)}$$

$$C(J\ 4\ J+4;00)^2 = \frac{35(J+1)\ (J+2)\ (J+3)\ (J+4)}{8(2J+1)\ (2J+3)\ (2J+5)\ (2J+7)} \qquad \text{(U transitions)}$$

The term Y_{Lm} in Eq. (26) is small compared to X_{Lm} and accounts for the contribution of the anisotropy of polarizability of the L-pole transitions. It is given by McKellar and Welsh (1971a), Sen et al. (1980)

$$
\begin{aligned}
Y_{Lm} = P_{J_1}\ P_{J_2}\ \Big\{ & C(J_1 L J_1';00)^2\ C(J_2 2 J_2';00)^2 \\
& \times \frac{2}{9}\ \langle v_1 J_1 | Q_{L_1} | v_1' J_1' \rangle^2\ \langle v_2 J_2 | \gamma_2 | v_2' J_2' \rangle^2 \\
+ & C(J_1 2 J_1';00)^2\ C(J_2 L J_2';00)^2 \\
& \times \frac{2}{9}\ \langle v_2 J_2 | Q_{L_2} | v_2' J_2' \rangle^2\ \langle v_1 J_1 | \gamma_1 | v_1' J_1' \rangle^2 \\
- & \frac{4}{15}\ C(J_1 2 J_1';00)^2\ C(J_2 2 J_2';00)^2 \\
& \times \langle v_1 J_1 | Q_{2_1} | v_1' J_1' \rangle\ \langle v_2 J_2 | \gamma_2 | v_2' J_2' \rangle \\
& \times \langle v_2 J_2 | Q_{2_2} | v_2' J_2' \rangle\ \langle v_1 J_1 | \gamma_1 | v_1' J_1' \rangle \Big\},
\end{aligned}
\tag{28}
$$

with the proviso that for $L \neq 2$ the negative cross term in Eq. (28) is to be omitted.

Since γ is small for H_2, this term contributes a small amount to the main transitions such as $Q_{\Delta V}(J)$, $Q_{\Delta V}(J_1) + Q_{\Delta V}(J_2)$, $S_{\Delta V}(J)$, $Q_{\Delta V}(J_1) + S_{\Delta V}(J_2)$, etc., but accounts completely for the transitions of the type $S_{\Delta V}(J_1) + S_{\Delta V}(J_2)$.

PROFILE ANALYSIS

Line shape functions used in the analysis of CIA spectra were discussed by Welsh (1972) in his review article. Recently Birnbaum et al. (1982) gave the theory of collision-induced lineshapes. The reader is referred to these two articles for the background information on line shapes (see also Borysow and Frommhold, 1985).

More recent analyses of the enhancement absorption profiles of the fundamental band of H_2 in H_2-X (X = He, Ar, Kr and Xe) were given by Mactaggart and Welsh (1973), Mactaggart et al. (1973) and McKellar et al. (1975). The intercollisional interference in the $S_1(1)$ line in H_2-He was analyzed by Poll et al. (1975). The absorption profiles of the fundamental and overtone bands of H_2, HD and D_2 in pure gases are more complex owing to the occurrence of many double transitions. The absorption profiles of the main transitions of the fundamental band of H_2 in the pure gas were analyzed by Reddy et al. (1977), those of the $S_1(J) + S_0(J)$ transitions by Sen et al. (1980) and those of the $U_1(J)$ and $Q_1(J) + U_0(J)$ transitions by Reddy et al. (1980). The absorption profiles of the induced fundamental band of HD in the pure gas were analyzed by Reddy and Prasad (1977) (see also McKellar, 1973). The enhancement absorption profiles of the fundamental band of HD in HD-X (X = He, Ne, Ar, Kr and Xe) were analyzed by Prasad and Reddy (1975, 1976, 1977). The main transitions of the fundamental band of D_2 in the pure gas were analyzed by Penney et al. (1982) and the $S_1(J) + S_0(J)$ transitions by Gillard et al. (1984). A summary and references of the earlier analyses of the fundamental band of H_2 in pure gas were given by Reddy et al. (1977). In the analyses all the researchers mentioned in this paragraph used the Levine-Birnbaum line shape (1967) and Van Kranendonk's dispersion-type line shpae (1968) for the intracollisional part and the intercollisional part, respectively, of the overlap-induced Q components and the dispersion type line shape or its modified version for the quadrupole-induced Q and S lines. In the following paragraphs we describe the line shape functions used in the profile analyses mentioned here.

The dimensionless absorption coefficient $\tilde{\alpha}(\nu)$ $(\equiv \alpha(\nu)/\nu)$ at a given wavenumber ν of a band is given by the relation (Van Kranendonk, 1968; Mactaggart and Welsh, 1973)

$$\tilde{\alpha}(\nu) = \sum_{m,n} \frac{\tilde{\alpha}^0_{nm} W_n(\Delta\nu)}{1 + \exp(-hc\,\Delta\nu/kT)}, \tag{29}$$

where n stands for the induction mechanism and n = ov, q, or h represents overlap, quadrupolar, or hexadecpolar induction, respectively, m represents a specific transition arising from a given mechanism, $\tilde{\alpha}_{nm}^0$ is a parameter indicating twice the maximum absorption coefficient at the molecular frequency $\nu_m(cm^{-1})$, $W_n(\Delta\nu)$ with $\Delta\nu = \nu - \nu_m$ represents the line shape function of the n type. The factor $[1 + \exp(-hc\,\Delta\nu/kT)]$ on the right side of Eq. (35) satisfies the detailed balance condition and converts the symmetrized line shape $\tilde{\alpha}_{nm}^0\,W_n(\Delta\nu)$ into the observed asymmetric line shape. The line shape function in Eq. (29) for the overlap transitions is represented by

$$W_{ov}(\Delta\nu) = W_{ov}^0(\Delta\nu)\,D(\Delta\nu). \tag{30}$$

Here, the intracollisional line shape function $W_{ov}^0(\Delta\nu)$ is represented by the Levine-Birnbaum (1967) expression as

$$W_{ov}^0(\Delta\nu) = (2\Delta\nu/\delta_d)^2\,K_2(2\Delta\nu/\delta_d), \tag{31}$$

where K_2 is the modified Bessel function of the second kind and δ_d is the intracollisional half-width at half-height. The function $D(\Delta\nu)$ is the intercollisional line form and is represented by Van Kranendonk (1968) as

$$D(\Delta\nu) = 1 - \gamma\,[1 + (\Delta\nu/\delta_c)^2]^{-1}, \tag{32}$$

where γ is a constant which is normally assumed to be unity to give zero absorption at the dip occurring at the molecular frequency ν_m and δ_c is the intercollisional half-width at half-height and equals to $1/2\pi c\tau_c$, where τ_c is the mean time between collisions. See the article by Lewis, this volume, for a discussion of asymmetries in W_{ov} owing to phase shifts. The line shape function for the quadrupolar transitions is represented by the dispersion-type function

$$W_q(\Delta\nu) = 1/[1 + (\Delta\nu/\delta_q)^2], \tag{33}$$

where δ_q is the quadrupolar half-width at half-height. A similar expression for the hexadecapolar transitions is written as

$$W_h(\Delta\nu) = 1/[1 + (\Delta\nu/\delta_h)^2] \tag{34}$$

with δ_h representing the corresponding characteristic half-width. In this discussion δ_d, δ_q or δ_h ($\delta(cm^{-1}) = 1/2\pi c\tau$) gives the collision duration τ in the corresponding induction mechanism. Lewis and Van Kranendonk (1972) have considered the correlations between all collisions in the collision sequence and have shown that in such a case

$$\delta_c = (1-\tilde{\Delta})/2\pi c\tau_c, \tag{35}$$

where $\tilde{\Delta}$ is the mean persistence-of-velocity and is 0.24 for H_2-He, 0.02 for H_2-Ar and is even smaller for the case of heavier perturbers.

Although the dispersion line shape seems to be reasonably adequate to represent the quadrupolar lines of CIA vibrational spectra at low and moderate gas densities, it is not entirely satisfactory as it gives more intensity in the high frequency wings of the spectra at high gas densities. Recently, Gillard et al. (1984) in the analysis of the CIA spectra of $S_1(J) + S_0(J)$ transitions of the fundamental band of D_2 at 77 K for gas densities 80 - 140 amagat represented the quadrupolar transitions with a modified dispersion line shape given by

$$W_q(\Delta\nu) = 1/[1 + (\Delta\nu/\delta_{q_2})^2 + (\Delta\nu/\delta_{q_4})^4], \tag{36}$$

where δ_{q_2} and δ_{q_4} are the parameters which characterize the line shape. Earlier, in the analysis of the U transitions in the fundamental band of H_2, Reddy et al. (1980) used a similar fourth power term in the line shape to represent the total high frequency wing of the quadrupolar transitions. We note here that Lewis and Tjon (1978) have shown that the $(\Delta\nu/\delta_{q_4})^4$ term is the dominant asymptotic term for a hard repulsive force. While the line shape with $(\Delta\nu/\delta_{q_4})^4$ term is not exact, it is considered to be a good approximation for the lines arising from the quadrupolar-induced dipole moment where the characteristic length scale for the induced dipole moment is greater than the length scale in which the radial motion of the colliding molecules reverses.

Methodology

The aim of the profile analysis is to obtain satisfactory fits between the experimental absorption profiles and the synthetic profiles, with appropriate line-shape functions for the overlap and quadrupolar (and hexadecapolar, if necessary) groups of transitions and thereby to separate the overlap and quadrupolar (and hexadecapolar, if necessary) contributions in the absorption intensity of the band and to derive certain characteristic molecular parameters of the collision process. In the analysis of the absorption profiles of the H_2, HD and D_2 fundamental bands, the required relative intensities of the overlap-induced components were calculated from the Boltzmann factors and those of the main quadrupolar-induced transitions were calculated from the theoretical matrix elements of the quadrupole moment (Birnbaum and Poll, 1969) and polarizability (Poll, 1977).

The relative maximum intensity factors $\tilde{\alpha}_{ovm}^0$ and $\tilde{\alpha}_{qm}^0$ (Eq. 35), the half-width parameters δ_d, δ_c and δ_q (Eqs. 37 – 39) were adjustable parameters in the computer program; a shift parameter for the molecular frequency ν_m was also introduced to account for any possible perturbations in the energy levels. Several trial values of the adjustable parameters were used for the computation of the synthetic profiles until the best nonlinear least-squares fits to the experimental profiles were obtained (see, for example, Reddy et al., 1977).

An illustrative example of computer analysis of an absorption profile of the fundamental band of H_2 at 77 K for a density of 43.3 amagat is shown in Fig. 5. The results of the profile analyses of

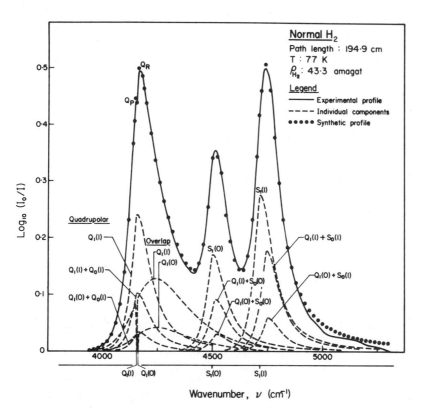

Fig. 5. Analysis of the fundamental band of H_2 in the normal gas at a density of 43.3 amagat at 77 K. The solid curve is the experimental profile. The dashed curves represent 2 overlap-induced and 9 quadrupole-induced computed components and the dots the summation of these (Reddy et al., 1977).

the fundamental bands of H_2, HD and D_2 in the pure gases are presented in Table 3. Within the range of densities used, δ_d and δ_q are found

Table 3. Results of profile analysis[a] of the fundamental bands of H_2, HD and D_2.
(δ_d: intracollisional half-width, δ_q: quadrupolar half-width, τ_d and τ_q: collision durations, Ov: overlap contribution, Quad: quadrupolar contribution).

	T (K)	δ_d (cm^{-1})	τ_d ($10^{-14}s$)	δ_q (cm^{-1})	τ_q ($10^{-14}s$)	Ov (%)	Quad (%)
n H_2^b	77	192 ± 5	2.8	53 ± 1	10.0	23	77
	196	211 ± 6	2.5	86 ± 1	6.2	31	69
	298	248 ± 3	2.1	107 ± 2	5.0	38	62
HD^c	77	145 ± 6	3.7	38 ± 1	14.0	27	73
	196	162 ± 2	3.3	66 ± 1	8.0	36	64
	298	199 ± 2	2.7	81 ± 2	6.6	46	54
n D_2^d	77	119 ± 10	4.5	37 ± 1	14.3	21	79
	196	158 ± 4	3.4	58 ± 2	9.2	38	62
	298	164 ± 6	3.2	80 ± 5	6.6	41	59

[a]Ranges of error indicated are standard deviations. [b]Reddy et al. (1977). [c]Reddy and Prasad (1977). [d]Penney et al. (1982).

to be independent of density at each temperature. Figure 6 gives plots of the average values of δ_d and δ_q versus $T^{\frac{1}{2}}$ for all the three gases. When extrapolated to T = 0, δ_d takes values 133, 88 and 70 cm^{-1} for H_2-H_2, HD-HD and D_2-D_2 collision pairs, respectively. Large value of δ_d at T = 0 implies that the duration of the collision is still small at absolute zero temperature because the overlap induction occurs mainly in the region of the strong repulsive forces between the molecules of the colliding pairs. As a matter of fact, at T = 0 where all substances exist in the solid phase, the translational energy spectrum manifests itself in the form of a broad phonon energy spectrum of the crystal lattice. The straight lines from the plots of δ_q versus $T^{\frac{1}{2}}$ gives $\delta_q = aT^{\frac{1}{2}}$, where a = 6.16, 4.65 and 4.30 $cm^{-1}/(degree)^{\frac{1}{2}}$ for H_2-H_2, HD-HD and D_2-D_2, respectively. As the densities used for the pure gases in the study of the main transitions of the fundamental bands were limited to 60 amagat only, it was not possible to derive a definite relation for the density dependence of δ_c. The values of δ_c for the maximum densities used vary between 0.9 cm^{-1} for D_2-D_2 at 77 K

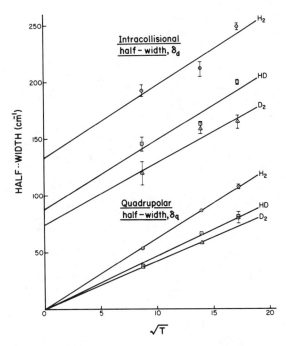

Fig. 6. Half width parameters δ_d and δ_q versus the square root of the absolute temperature T for H_2, HD and D_2 (adopted from Reddy, Varghese and Prasad (1977), Reddy and Prasad (1977) and Penney, Prasad and Reddy (1982), respectively).

to 3.5 cm^{-1} for H_2-H_2 at 298 K.

Overlap Parameters for H_2-H_2, HD-HD and D_2-D_2

The values of binary absorption coefficients $\alpha_{1a\ ov}$ and $\tilde{\alpha}_{1a\ ov}$ and of the ternary absorption coefficient $\alpha_{2a\ ov}$ for H_2, HD and D_2 (see the Section on Integrated Absorption Coefficients) are listed in Table 4. The theory of the overlap binary absorption coefficients as applied to the fundamental bands of CIA is given in an earlier section. The integral I_{c1} (Eq. 23) depends on σ/ρ. To obtain the most probable value of σ/ρ for the collision pair, the following procedure was used. The values of I_{c1} were calculated by a computer program for a series of values of σ/ρ in the range 0.070 to 0.140 at intervals of 0.002 for reduced temperatures T^* from 0.5 to 20.0 at intervals of 0.5. Quantum corrections $I^{(2)}$ and $I^{(4)}$ (see, for example, Gibbs et al., 1979) were used to obtain I (Eq. 20). λ^2 was assumed to be independent of temperature. $\tilde{\gamma}$'s were calculated from Eq. (16) using the matrix elements $<0|r-r_0|1>$ supplied by Poll (1977).

Table 4. Absorption coefficients[a] of the overlap part of the fundamental bands of H_2, HD and D_2.

	T (K)	Binary absorption coefficient		Ternary absorption coefficient
		α_{1a} ov (10^{-3}cm^{-2}amagat^{-2})	$\tilde{\alpha}_{1a}$ ov (10^{-35}cm^{6}s^{-1})	α_{2a} ov (10^{-6}cm^{-2}amagat^{-3})
n H_2^b	77	0.25 ± 0.02	0.24 ± 0.02	3.0 ± 0.5
	196	0.56 ± 0.02	0.54 ± 0.02	2.5 ± 0.5
	298	0.93 ± 0.04	0.90 ± 0.04	2.6 ± 0.8
HD^c	77	0.28 ± 0.03	0.31 ± 0.03	1.5 ± 0.8
	196	0.60 ± 0.03	0.67 ± 0.03	0.8 ± 0.8
	298	0.97 ± 0.06	1.08 ± 0.06	2.8 ± 1.7
n D_2^d	77	0.12 ± 0.01	0.16 ± 0.01	1.4 ± 0.2
	196	0.33 ± 0.01	0.45 ± 0.01	1.5 ± 0.3
	298	0.47 ± 0.02	0.64 ± 0.03	1.5 ± 0.6

[a]Ranges of error indicated are standard deviations. [b]Reddy et al. (1977). [c]Reddy and Prasad (1977). [d]Penney et al. (1982).

Finally, for a series of values of σ/ρ, I's were calculated and the corresponding calculated values of $\lambda^2 I$ as a function of T were fitted to the experimental values of $\lambda^2 I$ by using a least squares procedure. The values of σ/ρ and λ for H_2-H_2, HD-HD and D_2-D_2 obtained from similar fits are given in Table 5. Values of ρ, σ and λ (Eq. 8) for these collision pairs are also included in the same table.

Overlap Parameters for Other Collision Pairs

Prior to the study of the fundamental band of H_2, HD and D_2 in CIA, Reddy and Chang (1973) and Russell et al. (1974) studied the enhancement CIA spectra of the fundamental bands of H_2 and D_2, respectively, in the binary mixtures with He and Ne at several temperatures in the range 77 - 298 K. These authors determined the overlap parameters without performing profile analysis by the procedure described below. The binary absorption coefficient can be expressed as (Van Kranendonk, 1958)

$$\tilde{\alpha}_{1b} = \lambda^2 I\tilde{\gamma} + (Q'_{L_1} \alpha_2/e\sigma^4)^2 J\tilde{\gamma}, \tag{37}$$

Table 5. Overlap parameters for various collision pairs.

Collision pair	ρ/σ	λ (10^{-3})	σ $(\overset{\circ}{A})$	ρ $(\overset{\circ}{A})$	$\mu_{ov}(\sigma)$ $(10^{-2}ea_0)$[a]	Reference
H_2-H_2	0.071	3.7	2.928	0.21	2.0	Reddy et al. (1977) (see Penney et al., 1982)
HD-HD	0.074	4.7	2.928	0.22	2.6	Reddy and Prasad (1977) (see Penney et al., 1982)
D_2-D_2	0.073	4.0	2.928	0.21	2.2	Penney et al. (1982)
H_2-He	0.088	5.6	2.757	0.24	2.9	Reddy and Chang (1973)
H_2-He	0.087		2.75	0.24		Sears (1968a)
H_2-Ne	0.100	9.0	2.854	0.29	4.9	Reddy and Chang (1973)
D_2-He	0.086	4.7	2.742	0.24	2.6	Russell et al. (1974)
D_2-Ne	0.090	8.5	2.839	0.26	4.6	"
He-Ar	0.110		3.0	0.33	0.45	Sears (1968b)
Ne-Ar	0.092		3.1	0.29	0.59	"

[a] ea_0 = 2.54 Debye.

where the terms on the right represent $\tilde{\alpha}_{1b}$ ov and $\tilde{\alpha}_{1b}$ q, respectively. The values of λ^2I were obtained from the experimental values of $\tilde{\alpha}_{1b}$ and the calculated values of $\tilde{\alpha}_{1b}$ q. Then, by using a procedure similar to the one described above, various overlap parameters for H_2-He, H_2-Ne, D_2-He and D_2-Ne were obtained, which are also listed in Table 5. It will be interesting to separate the overlap and quadrupolar contributions to the intensity of the bands in these mixtures by the method of profile analysis and re-estimate the overlap parameters. Sears (1968a,b) estimated the overlap parameters of H_2-He, He-Ar and Ne-Ar by a different approach and these are also listed in the same table.

$S_1(J) + S_0(J)$, $U_1(J)$ and $Q_1(J) + U_0(J)$ Transitions

Absorption profiles of the fundamental band of H_2 obtained at
77 K for gas densities in the range 100 - 325 amagat show discrete
absorption peaks corresponding to $S_1(J) + S_0(J)$ transitions (cf.
Fig. 2). These profiles were analyzed by Sen et al. (1980) by
assuming line shapes given by Eqs. (36) - (39) and using the theoretical matrix elements of the quadrupole moment (Poll and Wolniewicz,
1978), isotropic polarizability (Poll, 1971) and anisotropy of polarizability (Poll, 1979), of the H_2 molecule. An example of the
analysis of such an absorption profile is presented in Fig. 7. The

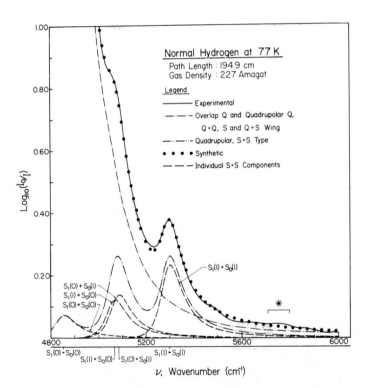

Fig. 7. Analysis of an absorption profile of the fundamental band of
n H_2 in the pure gas at 227 amagat and 77 K in the region 4800 -
6000 cm^{-1}. The solid curve is the experimental profile. The
dots represent the total synthetic profile which is the sum of
the dash-dot curve representing the wing of the overlap and main
quadrupolar transitions and the dash-double-dot curve representing the total contribution of the quadrupolar $S_1(J) + S_0(J)$
components arising from the anisotropy of polarizability. The
individual $S_1(J) + S_0(J)$ transitions are shown by dashed curves.
The asterisk represents $U_1(1)$ transition (see Fig. 8) (Sen et
al., 1980).

half-width δ_q of the $S_1(J) + S_0(J)$ transitions at 77 K obtained from the analysis is 54 ± 2 cm^{-1}, which is in agreement with the value obtained for the main quadrupole-induced transitions by Reddy et al. (1977). As mentioned earlier, Gillard et al. (1984) analyzed the $S_1(J) + S_0(J)$ transitions of D_2 at 77 K by assuming the modified dispersion line shape (Eq. 36) for all the quadrupole-induced lines.

Absorption profiles of the fundamental band of H_2 in the region 5400 – 6200 cm^{-1} obtained at 77 K for gas densities in the range 300 – 520 amagat show a distinct absorption peak corresponding to $U_1(1)$ transition (cf. Fig. 3). Reddy et al. (1980) analyzed these profiles by representing the total high frequency of the overlap- and quadrupole- induced transitions by a modified dispersion line shape similar to Eq. (36), and the U transitions by the dispersion line shape (Eq. 34) as well as by the Levine-Birnbaum line shape similar to Eq. (31). The reason for representing the total wing of the overlap and quadrupolar induced transitions by a modified dispersion line shape was the inadequacy of the simple dispersion line shape to represent the high frequency wing at high density. Relative intensities of the U branch transitions were calculated from the theoretical matrix elements of the hexadecapole moment (Karl et al., 1975) and of the isotropic polarizability (Poll, 1971) of H_2. Satisfactory fits for the experimental profiles were obtained by either the dispersion or the Levine-Birnbaum line shape for the U transitions, although the former was found slightly better. A sample analysis of an absorption profile for the U transitions, for which a dispersion line shape was used, is shown in Fig. 8. The half-width, δ_h, for the U transitions at 77 K obtained from the analysis is 118 ± 8 cm^{-1}. From the $\exp(-R)$, R^{-4} and R^{-6} dependency of the induced dipole moment in a colliding pair of molecules for the overlap, quadrupolar and hexadecapolar induction mechanism, respectively, it is expected that the half-width of the hexadecapolar transitions should have a value in between those of overlap and quadrupolar transitions. This is indeed the case, for example, for H_2 at 77 K $\delta_d = 192 \pm 5$ cm^{-1}, $\delta_q = 54 \pm 2$ cm^{-1} and $\delta_h = 118 \pm 8$ cm^{-1}. Finally the binary and ternary absorption coefficients of the $S_1(1) + S_0(1)$ and $U_1(1)$ transitions obtained from the profile analysis described here are presented in Table 6.

Enhancement Absorption Profiles of the H_2 and HD Fundamental Bands

---

From the analyses of the enhancement absorption profiles of the fundamental band of H_2 in H_2-X mixtures, several parameters for the collision pairs were obtained by Welsh and collaborators. Paremeters for the HD-X mixtures were also obtained by Prasad and Reddy in a similar manner. The values of δ_d and δ_q obtained from these analyses and the appropriate references are summarized in Table 7. We note that the values given in this table correspond to densities at which pressure-narrowing has not set in. The half-width δ_c of the

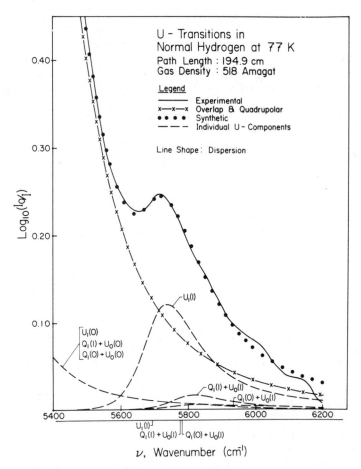

Fig. 8. Analysis of an absorption profile of the fundamental band of H_2 in the pure gas at 518 amagat and 77 K in the region 5400 – 6200 cm^{-1}. The solid curve is the experimental profile. The dots represent the total synthetic profile which is the sum of the dash-x curve representing the total wing of the overlap and the quadrupolar components and the dashed curves representing various single and double U transitions (Reddy et al., 1980).

intercollisional dip is highly density-dependent and satisfies the relation

$$\delta_c = a \, \rho_b + b \, \rho_b^2, \quad (a \gg b),$$ (44)

where ρ_b is the density of the perturbing gas. The quantity a is related to the collision parameter σ_{12} of the colliding molecules 1

154

Table 6. Absorption coefficients[a] of the transitions $S_1(1) + S_0(1)$ and $U_1(1)$ of n H_2 at 77 K.

Transition	Binary absorption coefficient		Ternary absorption coefficient
	α_{1a}	$\tilde{\alpha}_{1a}$	α_{2a}
	$(10^{-6} cm^{-2} amagat^{-2})$	$(10^{-38} cm^6 s^{-1})$	$(10^{-9} cm^{-2} amagat^{-3})$
$S_1(1) + S_0(1)$[b]	6.84 ± 0.21	5.26 ± 0.16	7.08 ± 0.98
$U_1(1)$[c]	1.38 ± 0.09	0.98 ± 0.06	0.17

[a]Ranges of error indicated are standard deviations. [b]Sen et al. (1980). [c]Reddy et al. (1980).

and 2 by the equation (Chapman and Cowling, 1952)

$$a = (1-\tilde{\Delta}) \, \sigma_{12}^2 \, n_0/c \, (\pi m_r/2kT)^{1/2}. \tag{45}$$

Here, $\tilde{\Delta}$ is the mean persistence of velocity ratio, n_0 is the Loschmidt's number and m_r is the reduced mass of the collision pair. $\tilde{\Delta}$ is given by

$$\tilde{\Delta} = (M_1/2) + (M_1^2/2M_2^{1/2}) \, \ln[(M_2^{1/2}+1)/M_1^{1/2}], \tag{40}$$

where $M_1 = m_1/(m_1+m_2)$ and $M_2 = m_2/(m_1+m_2)$, m_1 and m_2 being the individual masses of the colliding molecules. The values of a and b determined from the experimental data and the values of σ_{12} determined from Eq. (39) along with those of σ_{12}^{LJ} (Lennard-Jones diameter) are listed in Table 8. It is interesting to note that b is positive for the H_2-X mixtures and negative for the HD-X mixtures.

We also note that negative frequency shifts for the quadrupole-induced lines were observed in several cases of CIA. In particular, of all the systems studied, H_2-Xe (Varghese et al., 1972, Mactaggart, 1971) and HD-Xe (Prasad and Reddy, 1977) systems showed frequency shifts up to 15 cm^{-1} and 6 cm^{-1} respectively at 298 K and these shifts varied with the density of the perturbing gas. May et al. (1964) expressed the frequency shifts $\Delta\nu$ of the Raman lines of the H_2 fundamental band at gas densities of 800 amagat by the relation $\Delta\nu = a'\rho + b'\rho^2$, where

$$a' = K_{rep} I_1 - K_{att} I_2. \tag{41}$$

Table 7. Results of profile analysis[a,b] of the fundamental bands of H_2 and HD in binary mixtures with inert gases.

Mixture	T (K)	Intracollisional half-width, δ_d (cm^{-1})	Quadrupolar half-width, δ_q (cm^{-1})	Reference
p H_2–He	77	150	85	Mactaggart and Welsh (1973)
n H_2–He	77	150[c]	–	"
n H_2–He	196	175[c]	–	"
n H_2–He	298	195[c]	–	"
n H_2–Ar	160	140	63	"
n H_2–Ar	196	160[c]	–	"
n H_2–Ar	298	185[c]	–	"
n H_2–Kr	196	140[c]	–	"
n H_2–Kr	298	160[c]	–	"
n H_2–Xe	298	138[c]	–	"
n H_2–Ar	152	–	55	Mactaggart et al. (1973)
p H_2–Ar	160	–	55	"
n H_2–Kr	212	–	63	"
n H_2–Xe	298	–	71	"
HD–He	298	177 ± 2	77 ± 3	Prasad and Reddy (1975)
HD–Ne	298	148 ± 3	86 ± 3	Prasad and Reddy (1976)
HD–Ar	298	148 ± 1	66 ± 2	"
HD–Kr	298	144 ± 3	60 ± 2	Prasad and Reddy (1977)
HD–Xe	298	135 ± 3	55 ± 2	"

[a]Ranges of error indicated are standard deviations. [b]The collision duration can be calculated from the relation $\tau = 1/2\pi c\delta$. [c]Value obtained from published graph.

156

Table 8. Coefficients a and b in the equation $\delta_c = a\rho_b + b\rho_b^2$ for H_2- and HD- mixtures with inert gases.

Mixture	T (K)	a (10^{-2} cm^{-1} amagat^{-1})	b (10^{-5} cm^{-1} amagat^{-2})	σ_{12}^a (Å)	LJ σ_{12} (Å)
H_2-He[b]	18	1.8	-	3.13	-
H_2-He[b]	62	2.6	-	2.78	-
H_2-He[c]	77	3.3	2.1	2.97	2.75[d]
H_2-He[c]	195	5.6	1.6	2.99	2.75[d]
H_2-He[c]	300	7.3	1.2	3.10	2.75[d]
H_2-Ar[c]	160	6.8	13.0	3.42	3.17[e]
H_2-Kr[c]	212	(10.0)	(16.0)	(3.90)	3.33[e]
H_2-Xe[c]	298	(14.0)	(15.0)	(4.18)	3.55[e]
HD-He[f]	298	4.86	-4.96	2.92	2.742[d]
HD-Ne[g]	298	5.66	-9.11	2.98	2.839[d]
HD-Ar[g]	298	5.15	-	2.83	3.167[d]
HD-Kr[h]	298	5.01	-1.26	2.78	3.26[d]
HD-Xe[h]	298	5.30	-36.7	2.86	3.514[d]

[a]Calculated from 'a' given in column 3. [b]McKellar et al. (1975).
[c]Mactaggart and Welsh (1973). [d]From the combining rule σ_{12} = (1/2)$(\sigma_1 + \sigma_2)$. [e]From the spectra of Van der Waals complexes (McKellar and Welsh, 1971a). [f]Prasad and Reddy (1975). [g]Prasad and Reddy (1976). [h]Prasad and Reddy (1977)).

Here, K_{rep} and K_{att} are positive constants representing repulsive and attractive intermolecular forces, respectively, and I_1 and I_2 are temperature-dependent integrals involving the pair distribution function and the intermolecular potential.

Lewis (1976, 1985) has incorporated phase shifts into the kinetic theory of intercollisional interference; while the resultant frequency shift in the dip is more complicated than the shift of Raman lines, a relation similar to Eq. (47) was obtained. For H_2-Xe, the negative a' indicates that the attractive forces predominate over the repulsive forces.

THE OVERTONE BANDS

The CIA spectrum of H_2 in the first overtone region observed by Welsh et al. (1951) was interpreted as the superposition of a 2-0 pure overtone band and a (1-0) + (1-0) double vibrational band. This interpretation was confirmed by the observation of Herzberg (1952) of the CIA spectrum of H_2 in the second overtone region which was composed of a 3-0 pure overtone band and a (2-0) + (1-0) double vibrational band. A collision-induced spectrum observed in the atmosphere of Uranus and Neptune at 8270 Å by Kuiper (1949) was identified by Herzberg (1952) as the $S_3(0)$ transition of H_2. Similar CIA spectra of these planets observed at 6420 Å by Spinrad (1963) is mainly due to $S_4(0)$ transition of H_2. For other details of the collision-induced effects of the H_2 overtone spectra in planetary atmospheres and relevant references, see Tipping (1985) and Welsh (1969).

Although CIA spectra of the fundamental bands of H_2, HD and D_2 have been widely studied and well understood, the properties of the spectra of H_2 and D_2 in the overtone regions have not been precisely delineated. After the first laboratory observation of CIA of H_2 in the first overtone region by Welsh et al. (1951), Hare and Welsh (1958) investigated this region at very high gas densities at room temperature and concluded that the absorption was mainly from quadrupolar induction. Watanabe et al. (1971) showed from the analysis of the observed absorption profiles at 24 K that the quadrupolar induction alone accounts for the absorption; however, discrepancies exist between the observed and the calculated profiles. Subsequently Watanabe (1971) interpreted the discrepancies in terms of different density dependence of the intensities of single and double transitions. McKellar and Welsh (1971b) obtained somewhat improved spectra in pure H_2 at 85 K and enhancement absorption profiles in H_2-Ar and H_2-N_2 in the temperature range 106 - 116 K and performed profile analysis. Even though there is somewhat overall agreement between the observed and calculated profiles, discrepancies still exist in the regions of the main peaks in pure H_2; the calculated intensities in H_2-Ar and H_2-N_2 are somewhat too high. Recently Silvaggio et al. (1981) observed very weak absorption (less than 10% even at peaks) at 122 and 273 K and analyzed the profiles with Birnbaum-Cohen line shape (1976) using Lennard-Jones potential.

McKellar and Welsh (1971b) made the first quantitative measurement of CIA spectrum of H_2 in the second overtone region. Their analysis of the absorption profiles showed several discrepancies between the experimental and calculated profiles. Reddy and Kuo (1971) first observed CIA of D_2 in the first overtone region in the pure gas and in D_2-Ar and D_2-N_2 mixtures at room temperature. Analysis of enhancement absorption profiles of D_2-Ar and D_2-N_2 showed no overlap contribution to the intensity of the Q branch. No overtone CIA spectrum has yet been observed for HD.

Recently a systematic study of the CIA overtone bands of H_2 and D_2 under wide ranges of temperatures and densities was begun in the present author's laboratory. The first overtone spectra of H_2 were obtained by van Nostrand (1983) and the second overtone band of H_2 and the first overtone band of D_2 were recorded by Gillard (1983). The profile analysis of these spectra is currently underway. Typical spectra of the 2-0 band of H_2 at 77 K for gas densities of 182, 272 and 365 amagat are presented in Fig. 9. In this figure the extent of various pure overtone as well as double vibrational transitions are marked over the absorption peaks. Figure 10 shows the first observation of the double transitions of the type $S_2(J) + S_0(J)$ and $S_1(J) + S_1(J)$ for gaseous H_2 which arise in the quadrupolar induction mechanism due to anisotropy of the polarizability. The spectra presented were obtained at 77 K for gas densities of 644, 794 and 914 amagat. Preliminary analysis of these absorption profiles shows a marked 'pressure-narrowing' for these transitions which will be discussed in the next section. The CIA spectra of the 3-0 band of H_2 at 77 K for gas densities of 647, 775 and 894 amagat are presented in Fig. 11; these show an intercollisional interferance dip in the Q branch. In this figure the peaks associated with the dip are marked as Q_P and Q_R. In addition to the main transitions, transitions of the type $S_2(J) + S_1(J)$ can also be seen in the same figure. The dip in Q branch and the S + S type of transitions in the 3-0 band are observed here for the first time.

PRESSURE NARROWING OF QUADRUPOLE-INDUCED TRANSITIONS

De Remigis et al. (1971) first observed that the half-width δ_q of the quadrupole-induced transitions in the fundamental band of H_2 in H_2-Ar mixtures remained constant for densities up to ~ 300 amagat and then decreased approximately linearly with the density of argon. Similar behavior was also observed for H_2-Kr and H_2-Xe mixtures by Mactaggart et al. (1973). To illustrate this pressure-narrowing effect at high density, two absorption profiles of the fundamental band of H_2 in H_2-Kr mixtures at 212 K, one obtained at a density of 545 amagat of krypton and the other obtained at 32 amagat of krypton are presented in Fig. 12. For the density ranges used in these studies δ_q decreased approximately by 50%. In a recent study of the S + S transitions of H_2 in the pure gas at 77 K in the first overtone region for high gas densities in our laboratory, van Nostrand (1983) observed that δ_q of these transitions decreased linearly from 43 to 30 cm^{-1} for the densities in the range 640 to 940 amagat (see Fig. 10).

At low and intermediate densities the constant values of δ_q and τ_q are characteristic of the quadrupolar induction. Zaidi and Van Kranendonk (1971) have interpreted the narrowing of the quadrupole-induced transitions at very high densities in terms of mutual diffusion of H_2 molecules in the foreign gas.

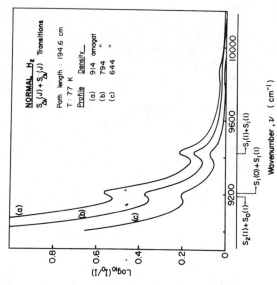

Fig. 10. S + S transitions of nH_2 in the first overtone region at 77 K (van Nostrand, 1983).

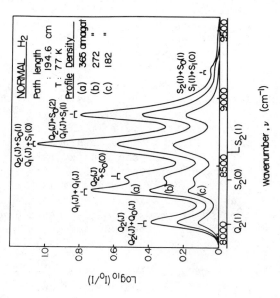

Fig. 9. Spectra of nH_2 in the first overtone region at 77 K (van Nostrand, 1983).

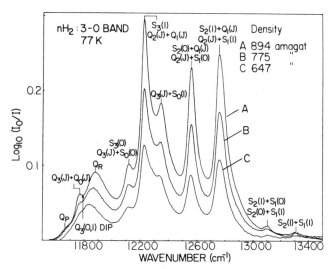

Fig. 11. Absorption profiles of normal H_2 in the second overtone region at gas densities of 894, 775 and 647 amagat at 77 K (Gillard, 1983).

The reader is referred to the original papers of Zaidi and Van Kranendonk (1971) and Desai and Yip (1968) for further insight into the phenomenon of pressure–narrowing. Barnabei et al. (1985) also deal with some aspects of pressure–narrowing in the rotational spectra of dense fluids.

INTERFERENCE EFFECTS IN THE SPECTRA OF HD

The HD molecule in the ground electronic state, unlike H_2, possesses a weak permanent electric dipole moment ($\mu^A \approx 10^{-3}$ Debye) which gives rise to the allowed R and P lines ($\Delta J = \pm 1$) in the vibrational-rotational spectra. "Allowed" vibrational-rotational transitions first observed by Herzberg (1950) have been studied extensively (see Rich and McKellar (1983) and the references therein). Like the H_2 molecule, HD also exhibits CIA which arises from the induced dipole moments (typically, $\mu^I \approx 10^{-2}$ Debye). It is possible for the allowed and induced dipoles to interfere either constructively or destructively and the effect is most noticeable when the allowed dipole is small and the density is sufficiently high. Such an inter-ference effect, termed as "intracollisional interference" was noticed

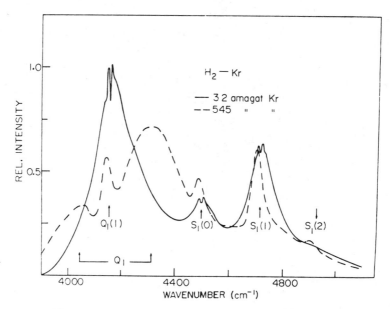

Fig. 12. Profiles of the enhancement of the fundamental band of H_2 by Kr at low (32 amagat) and high (545 amagat) densities (212 K). The profiles are normalized to give the same peak intensities for the $S_1(1)$ component. The pressure narrowing is clearly observed for the $S_1(1)$ as well as the $S_1(0)$ component. Also note the shift of the peaks of the $S_1(1)$ and $S_1(0)$ lines (Mactaggart et al., 1973).

in HD-Kr (Poll et al., 1976) and HD-Xe (Prasad and Reddy, 1977) by the observation of a relatively sharp $R_1(1)$ line in the enhancement spectra. Earlier McKellar (1973) interpreted the asymmetry of the $R_1(0)$ line of HD, studied at densities up to 60 amagat, as due to a 'resonant interference' between the continuum and a discrete level. Tipping et al. (1978) applied the theory developed by Poll et al. (1976) to McKellar's data on pure HD and showed that the net intensities of the allowed line in pure HD were subject to destructive interference.

A complete explanation of the interference effects in the HD spectra was given by Herman (1979) who showed that there is an additional contribution which arises from the interference between the induced dipoles in successive collisions with an intensity proportional to ρ_{HD}^3 in pure HD or $\rho_{HD} \rho_b^2$ in a mixture.

Herman et al. (1979), within the impact approximation used in the theory of pressure broadening, derived theoretical expressions for the line shape and intensity of R and P lines of the 1-0 band of gaseous HD which took into account the interplay between μ^A and μ^I induced during binary collisions. The interference between μ^A and μ^I on the one hand and that between μ^I's induced in successive collisions on the other gave a line shape which was the superposition of a Lorentzian and an anomalous profile which was found to be in reasonable agreement

162

with the experiment. Recent experiments on these interference effects in the $R_1(0)$ and $R_1(1)$ lines in pure HD by Rich and McKellar (1983) and in HD-He, HD-Ne and HD-Ar by McKellar and Rich (1984) agree well with the theory of Herman et al. (1979). A detailed account of the interference effects of HD is given by Poll (1985).

FINE STRUCTURE DUE TO VAN DER WAALS COMPLEXES

At densities of the order of 1 amagat or less and low temperatures a fine structure appears for each of the components in the fundamental bands of the hydrogens. This fine structure was first observed by Watanabe and Welsh (1964) in the fundamental band of H_2 and interpreted as arising from the transitions between the bound states of the $(H_2)_2$ complex. Subsequently several studies of the spectra of the H_2-X (X = Ne, Ar, Kr, Xe, H_2, D_2, N_2 and CO), $(HD)_2$, D_2-X (X = D_2, Ne, Ar, Kr and Xe) complexes have been made at pressures as low as 100 Torr using path lengths as high as 200 m and a spectral resolution of the order of 0.1 cm^{-1}. A review of the work done on some of these complexes was given by Welsh (1972). Altogether there are nine published papers to date on the experimental studies of these Van der Waals complexes. In a recent paper, McKellar (1982) obtained new spectra of the complexes H_2-Ar, HD-Ar and D_2-Ar at 77 K and H_2-Kr at 97 K. With improved experimental conditions in this work, the resulting spectral line width at half maximum was found to be as low as 0.1 cm^{-1} in some cases; predissociation was clearly observed as line broadening in the $S_1(0)$ structure of HD-Ar and H_2-Kr. For details of this work as well as for the references of the earlier work the reader is referred to the original paper of McKellar (1982). The overall structure of different components of the spectra of the Van der Waals complexes was interpreted on the basis of a non-rigid rotator model for the complex invoking the rotational quantum number l for it. The selection rule for l is $\Delta l = \pm 1$ for the Q components of the band, which gives R and P branches and $\Delta l = \pm 1, \pm 3$ for other branches which gives R, P, T and N branches. For theoretical work on the complexes the reader is referred to Le Roy and Van Kranendonk (1974) and the references therein.

CONCLUSION

The material presented here summarizes the results of the work done on the CIA vibrational bands of H_2, HD and D_2 in gas phase, mostly from the point of view of an experimentalist. Although the line shapes represented by Eqs. (39) and (40) for the quadrupole- and hexadecapole- induced lines appear satisfactory in analyzing the central region of an induced band, it is recognized that the line shapes are not satisfactory in the high frequency wing far from the band origin (see also Borysow et al., 1984). Recently we found that the quadrupole-induced lines when represented by a modified dispersion line shape with a fourth power term in the denominator (Eq. 42) gave better fits for the absorption profiles in the high frequency wings also (see, for example, Gillard, Prasad and Reddy, 1984).

We also suggest that the line shapes developed by quantum mechanical methods and applied to translational CIA spectra of rare gas mixtures and the rotational spectrum of H_2 (see, Borysow and Frommhold, 1985) may be also applicable to the vibrational bands of the hydrogens.

In the evaluation of the dimensionless integrals such as I and J, Lennard-Jones intermolecular potential has been used (see, for example, Gibbs et al., 1979). It is suggested that these integrals may now be evaluated using more accurate intermolecular potentials which are presently available.

ACKNOWLEDGMENTS

This work was supported by a grant from the Natural Sciences and Engineering Council of Canada. The author is grateful to several of his past graduate students who collaborated in the work presented here and in particular to Dr. R. D. G. Prasad for his fruitful collaboration in the past ten years. Sincere thanks are also extended to Dr. George Birnbaum for his helpful comments on the manuscript of this article and for his editorial patience.

REFERENCES

Barnabei, M., Buontempo, U., and Maselli, P., 1985, This Volume.

Birnbaum, A., and Poll, J. D., 1969, J. Atmos. Sci., 26:943.

Birnbaum, G., and Cohen, E. R., 1976, Can. J. Phys., 54:593.

Birnbaum, G., Guillot, B., and Bratos, S., 1982, Adv. Chem. Phys., 51:49.

Borysow, J., Moraldi, M., and Frommhold, L., 1984, J. Quant. Spectrosc. Radiat. Transfer, 31:235.

Borysow, J., and Frommhold, L., 1985, This Volume.

Britton, F. R., and Crawford, M. F., 1958, Can. J. Phys., 36:761.

Chapman, S., and Cowling, T. G., 1952, "The Mathematical Theory of Non-Uniform Gases", 2nd edition, Cambridge University Press, Cambridge, England.

Colpa, J. P., and Ketelaar, J. A. A., 1958, Mol. Phys., 1:343.

Colpa, J. P., 1965, "Physics of High Pressures and the Condensed Phase", Van Itterbeek, A., ed., North-Holland Publishing Company, Amsterdam.

Crawford, M. F., Welsh, H. L., and Locke, J. L., 1949, Phys. Rev., 75:1607.

de Boer, J., 1949, Repts. Prog. Phys., 12:305

De Remigis, J., Mactaggart, J. W., and Welsh, H. L., 1971, Can J. Phys., 49:381.

Desai, R. C., and Yip, S., 1968, Phys. Rev. 166:129.

Filimonov, V. N., 1959, Usp. Fiz. Nauk, 69:565, Sov. Phys.-Usp., 2:565.

Foltz, J. V., Rank, D. H., and Wiggins, T. A., 1966, J. Mol.
    Spectrosc., 21:203.
Gibbs, P. W., Gray, C. G., Hunt, J. L., Reddy, S. P., Tipping, R.
    H., and Chang, K. S., 1974, Phys. Rev. Lett., 33:256.
Gibbs, P. W., Hunt, J. L., and Poll, J. D., 1979, Can. J. Phys.,
    57:981.
Gillard, P., 1983, "Aspects of Collision-Induced Absorption of
    Hydrogen and Deuterium", Ph.D. Thesis, Memorial University of
    Newfoundland.
Gillard, P. G., Prasad, R. D. G., and Reddy, S. P., 1984, J. Chem.
    Phys., 81:3458.
Hare, W. F. J., and Welsh, H. L., 1958, Can. J. Phys., 36:88.
Herman, R. M., 1970, J. Chem. Phys., 52:2040.
Herman, R. M., 1979, Phys. Rev. Lett., 42:1206.
Herman, R. M., Tipping, R. H., and Poll, J. D., 1979, Phys. Rev. A.,
    20:2006.
Herzberg, G., 1950, Nature, 166:563.
Herzberg, G., 1952, Astrophysics J., 115:337.
Hunt, J. L., Poll, J. D., and Wolneiwicz, L., 1984, Can. J. Phys.,
    62:1719.
Karl, G., Poll, J. D., and Wolneiwicz, L., 1975, Can. J. Phys.,
    53:1781.
Ketelaar, J. A. A., 1959, Record of Chemical Progress, 20:1.
Kuiper, G. P., 1949, Astrophys. J., 109:540.
Le Roy, R. J., and   Kranendonk, J., 1974, J. Chem. Phys., 61:4750.
Levine, H. B., and Birnbaum, G., 1967, Phys. Rev., 154:72.
Lewis, J. C., 1972, Can. J. Phys., 50:2881.
Lewis, J. C., and Van Kranendonk. J., 1972, Can. J. Phys., 50:352.
Lewis, J. C., 1973, Can. J. Phys., 51:2455.
Lewis, J. C., 1976, Physica, 82A:500.
Lewis, J. C., and Tjon, J. A., 1978, Physica, 91A:161.
Lewis, J. C., 1985, This Volume.
Mactaggart, J. W., 1971, "Band Shapes in Pressure-Induced Infrared
    Absorption and Their Applications to the Molecular Dynamics of
    Dense Gases", Ph.D. Thesis, University of Toronto.
Mactaggart, J. W., and Welsh, H. L., 1973, Can. J. Phys., 51:158.
Mactaggart, J. W., De Remegis, J., and Welsh, H. L., 1973, Can. J.
    Phys., 51:1971.
May, A. D., Varghese, G., Stryland, J. C., and Welsh, H. L., 1964,
    Can. J. Phys., 42:1058.
McKellar, A. R. W., and Welsh, H. L., 1971a, J. Chem. Phys.,
    55:595.
McKellar, A. R. W., and Welsh, H. L., 1971b. Proc. Roy. Soc. London,
    A 322:421.
McKellar, A. R. W., 1973, Can. J. Phys., 51:389.
McKellar, A. R. W., Mactaggart, J. W., and Welsh, H. L., 1975, Can.
    J. Phys., 53:2060.
McKellar, A. R. W., 1982, Faraday Discuss. Chem. Soc., 73:89.
McKellar, A. R. W., and Rich, N. H., 1984, Can. J. Phys., 62:1665.

Mizushima, M., 1949, Phys. Rev., 76:1268.
Mizushima, M., 1950, Phys. Rev., 77:149; 150.
Pai, S. T., Reddy, S. P., and Cho, C. W., 1966, Can. J. Phys., 44:2893.
Penney, R. J., Prasad, R. D. G., and Reddy, S. P., 1982, J. Chem. Phys., 77:131.
Poll, J. D., and Hunt, J. L., 1976, Can. J. Phys. 54:461.
Poll, J. D., 1971, "Proceedings I.A.U. Symposium 40 on Planetary Atmospheres", Reidel, Dordrecht, Holland eds., p. 384.
Poll, J. D., Hunt, J. L., and Mactaggart, J. W., 1975, Can. J. Phys., 53:954.
Poll, J. D., and van Kranendonk, J., 1961, Can. J. Phys. 39:189.
Poll, J. D., Tipping, R. H., Prasad, R. D. G., and Reddy, S. P., 1976, Phys. Rev. Lett., 36:248.
Poll, J. D., 1977 and 1979, Private Communications.
Poll, J. D., and Wolneiwicz, L., 1978, J. Chem. Phys., 68:3053.
Poll, J. D., 1980, "Proceedings of the International School of Physics Enrico Fermi, Course LXXV, Intermolecular Spectroscopy and Dynamical Properties of Dense Systems", Van Kranendonk, J., ed., North-Holland Publishing Company, New York.
Poll, J. D., 1985, This Volume.
Prasad, R. D. G., and Reddy, S. P., 1975, J. Chem. Phys., 62:3582.
Prasad, R. D. G., 1976, "Collision-Induced Infrared Absorption Spectra of the Fundamental Bands of Hydrogen Deuteride and Hydrogen", Ph.D. Thesis, Memorial University of Newfoundland, p. 53.
Prasad, R. D. G., and Reddy, S. P., 1976, J. Chem. Phys. 65:83.
Prasad, R. D. G., and Reddy, S. P., 1977, J. Chem. Phys. 66:707.
Prasad, R. D. G., Clouter M. J., and Reddy, S. P., 1978, Phys. Rev., A17:1690.
Prasad, R. D. G., 1984, Private Communication.
Reddy, S. P., and Cho, C. W., 1965, Can. J. Phys., 43:793.
Reddy, S. P., and Lee, W. F., 1968, Can. J. Phys., 46:1373.
Reddy, S. P., and Kuo, C. Z., 1971, J. Mol. Spectrosc., 37:327.
Reddy, S. P., and Chang, K. S., 1973, J. Mol. Spectrosc., 47:22:
Reddy, S. P., and Prasad, R. D. G., 1977, J. Chem. Phys., 66:5259.
Reddy, S. P., Varghese, G., and Prasad, R. D. G., 1977, Phys. Rev., A15:975.
Reddy, S. P., Sen. A., and Prasad, R. D. G., 1980, J. Chem. Phys., 72:6102.
Rich, N. H., and McKellar, A. R. W., 1976, Can. J. Phys., 54:486.
Rich, N. H., and McKellar, A. R. W., 1983, Can. J. Phys., 61:1648.
Rose, M. E., 1957, "Elementary Theory of Angular Momentum", John Wiley & Sons, Inc., New York.
Russell, W. E., Reddy, S. P., and Cho, C. W., 1974, J. Mol. Spectrosc., 52:72.
Sears, V. F., 1968a, Can. J. Phys., 46:1163.
Sears, V. F., 1968b, Can. J. Phys., 46:2315.
Sen. A., Prasad, R. D. G., and Reddy, S. P., 1980, J. Chem. Phys., 72:1716.

Silvaggio, P. M., Goorvitch, D., and Boese, R. W., 1981, J. Quant. Spectrosc. Radiat. Transfer, 26:103.

Spinrad, H., 1963, Astrophys. J., 138:1242.

Tipping, R. H., Poll, J. D., and McKellar, A. R. W., 1978, Can. J. Phys., 56:75.

Tipping, R. H., 1985, This Volume.

Tonkov, M. V., 1970, "Spektroskopiya Vzaimodeistvuyushchikh Molekul (Spectroscopy of Interacting Molecules) Bulanin, M. O., ed., Leningrad University Press, Leningrad.

Van Kranendonk, J., and Bird, R. B., 1951a, Physica, 17:953.

Van Kranendonk, J., and Bird, R. B., 1951b, Physica, 17:968.

Van Kranendonk, J., 1957, Physica, 23:825.

Van Kranendonk, J., 1958, Physica, 24:347.

Van Kranendonk, J., 1959, Physica, 25:337.

Van Kranendonk, J., 1968, Can. J. Phys., 46:1173.

Van Kranendonk, J., 1974, Physica, 73:156.

van Nostrand, E., 1983, "Collision-Induced Spectra of Molecular Hydrogen in the First Overtone Region at 77,201 and 295 K", M.Sc. Thesis, Memorial University of Newfoundland.

Varghese, G., and Reddy, S. P., 1969, Can. J. Phys., 47:2745.

Varghese, G., Ghosh, S. N., and Reddy, S. P., 1972, J. Mol. Spectrosc., 41:291.

Watanabe, A., and Welsh, H. L., 1964, Phys. Rev. Lett., 13:810.

Watanabe, A., 1971, Can. J. Phys., 49:1320.

Watanabe, A., Hunt, J. L., and Welsh, H. L., 1971, Can. J. Phys., 49:860.

Welsh, H. L., Crawford, M. F., and Locke, J. L., 1949, Phys. Rev., 76:580.

Welsh, H. L. Crawford, M. F., MacDonald, J. C. F., and Chisholm, D. A., 1951, Phys. Rev., 83:1264.

Welsh, H. L., 1969, J. Atmospheric Sci., 26:835.

Welsh, H. L., 1972, "MTP International Review of Science, Physical Chemistry Vol. 3, Spectroscopy", Ramsay, D. A., ed., Butterworths, London.

Zaidi, H. R., and Van Kranendonk. J., 1971, Can. J. Phys., 49:385.

SIMULTANEOUS TRANSITIONS IN COMPRESSED GAS MIXTURES

C. Brodbeck and J.-P. Bouanich

Laboratoire d'Infrarouge
Associé au CNRS
Bât. 350, Université Paris-Sud
91405 Orsay Cédex, France

ABSTRACT

This paper reviews the simultaneous transitions that have
been observed in the liquid, solid and gaseous phases as well as
the different theories of integrated intensities for these transitions. The formulation of Colpa and Ketelaar for an infrared
active vibration in one molecule inducing a dipole moment in a
Raman active neighboring molecule is presented. An application of
this formulation for H_2+CF_4 and H_2+SF_6 mixtures has shown that the
Kihara potential used to determine the molecular pair distribution
function leads to a better agreement of the binary absorption
coefficients than the Lennard-Jones potential.

Some results obtained recently on the simultaneous transitions in N_2+SF_6 gas mixtures are presented. As the N_2 density
increases, the integrated intensities show a slight deviation from
linearity, the bands are markedly narrowed, and their absorption
maxima are shifted. A qualitative interpretation of these effects
is given.

New results on the bandshape of the simultaneous transition
in N_2 (fundamental band) + CO_2 (ν_3 band) gas mixtures are
analyzed. Under certain experimental conditions, this band shows
two maxima corresponding probably to the P- and R-branches of the
ν_3 band of CO_2. This profile is compared with that calculated from
the convolution of the infrared spectra of the ν_3 band of CO_2 and
the isotropic and anisotropic Raman spectra of N_2.

INTRODUCTION

A simultaneous transition (ST), also called a double transition, involves the simultaneous absorption of one quantum of energy by two colliding molecules and is caused by the distortion of the electronic charge distribution of one molecule as the result of the electric field produced by the other molecule. In general, an active vibrating dipole and/or quadrupole in one molecule induces during a collision a dipole in a neighboring molecule with a Raman active vibrating polarizability. The absorbed photon has a frequency which is theoretically the sum, or in favorable cases the difference, of frequencies of the transitions for the individual molecules. The possibility of the observation of simultaneous excitation in light scattering in liquid hydrogen was recently mentioned by Bulanin and Kouzov (1982).

Among collision—induced absorption phenomena, the STs have a particular place. If the intermolecular potential is approximately isotropic, and if the coupling between the internal (vibration-rotation) degrees of freedom of the interacting molecules is weak, the intensity of a spectral band associated with ST is additive over all molecular pairs. Then, contrary to single induced transitions, the cancellation effect occurring in the absorption due to clusters of three or more molecules does not exist in STs (Van Kranendonk, 1957, 1958, 1959).

Here, we review briefly the STs that have been observed in the solid, liquid and gaseous phases. Most of this work concerns the frequency of the bands and their integrated intensity. Although there exist the review papers of Ketelaar (1959), Filimonov (1960) and Colpa (1965), we believe it is helpful to summarize the papers published up to the time of writing.

Since the work of Welsh and coworkers (for instance Allin et al., 1967) concerning solid H_2, recent investigations by Souers et al. (1979, 1980) on liquid and solid mixtures of H_2 and its isotopic forms D_2, T_2, HT, HD and DT, mixtures of interest as hydrogen fusion fuel, have shown the presence of numerous separate lines identified as STs. Ron and Hornig (1963) have observed the double excitation from v=0 to v=1 in the HCl crystal. Avrillier et al. (1976) have studied HCl and HBr in the second and third overtone regions. Marteau et al. (1964) analyzed the ST involving the fundamental vibrations of CO and N_2 in the solid, liquid and gaseous phases.

In the liquid phase at room temperature, Ketelaar (1956) and coworkers (1955, 1956, 1957) have studied STs in mixtures of CS_2 or haloforms with various halogen—containing compounds.

Further investigations dealt with CS_2 with some haloforms, I_2 and CCl_4 (Badilescu, 1968, 1970, 1971). Bulanin and Orlova (1961, 1966) and Bulanin and Melnik (1968) have observed STs of H_2 dissolved in $C_2F_3Cl_3$, $C_2F_2Cl_4$, C_2Cl_4, PCl_3, SO_2 and in group IV tetrachlorides. In the course of a study of hydrogen-bonded molecules, Burneau and Corset (1972, 1973) have recorded STs in various liquid mixtures of biological interest consisting of two types of molecules which are proton donors and acceptors. Chesnoy et al. (1979) have shown that the absorption spectrum of liquid HCl in the first overtone region is mainly due to the ST of two HCl molecules from v=0 to v=1, (1-0).

In the spectra of H_2 in liquefied NF_3, CF_4, SF_6 and CCl_2F_2, several new absorption bands ascribed to STs have been obtained by Bulanin and Melnik (1967). For infrared active molecules such as CF_4, SF_6 or NF_3 dissolved in liquefied gases (N_2, O_2, H_2), STs have been observed by Bulanin (1973). In this paper, he has also reviewed the cryosystems prior to 1972. We have recently analyzed the ST of SF_6 (ν_3) dissolved in liquid oxygen (1-0) (Brodbeck et al., 1982).

In the gaseous phase, the two normal modes that are simultaneously excited may refer to electronic, vibrational, rovibrational or rotational transitions. STs in which at least one molecule undergoes an electronic transition have been observed in compressed oxygen only (McKellar et al., 1972).

The collision-induced absorption bands of gaseous H_2 arising from single or double transitions have been the subject of numerous experimental and theoretical studies (Reddy, 1984; Borysow and Frommhold, 1984). The analysis of collision-induced spectra of pure O_2 or N_2 (Shapiro and Gush, 1966) requires the consideration of STs that involve a rotational transition of one molecule associated with a vibrational transition of the other. In some favorable cases, the spectra of STs involving compressed mixtures of H_2 with other gases show a rotational structure due to the wide separation of the rotational levels of H_2. The double transitions arise from the Q-branch or S-transitions of H_2 associated with the vibrational transition of the second molecule. The following STs have been observed:
- H_2, in the ground vibrational state, mixed with CO (1-0) (Colpa and Ketelaar, 1958a) or CO_2 (ν_3) (Ketelaar and Rettschnick, 1961);
- H_2, undergoing the fundamental vibrational transition (1-0), mixed with N_2 (1-0) (Coulon, 1958), HCl (1-0) (Coulon et al., 1955), HBr (1-0) (Coulon and Vu, 1957), CO_2 (ν_3) (Fahrenfort and Ketelaar, 1954; Rinehart, 1959), N_2O (ν_1, ν_3, $2\nu_1$, $\nu_1+\nu_3$, $\nu_2+\nu_3$) (Coulon and Vu, 1959), SiF_4 (ν_3, ν_4) (Rinehart, 1959), CF_4 (ν_3) (Rinehart, 1959; Ketelaar and Rettschnick, 1961; Bouanich et

al., 1975; Bouanich and Brodbeck, 1977), SF_6 (ν_3) (Schacht-schneider, 1959; Ketelaar and Rettschnick, 1961; Bouanich and Brodbeck, 1977);
– H_2, undergoing the first overtone transition (2–0), mixed with CF_4 (ν_3) (Ketelaar and Rettschnick, 1963; Bouanich et al., 1975) or SF_6 (ν_3) (Ketelaar and Rettschnick, 1963).

With N_2 or O_2 as Raman active molecules, no rotational structure is apparent. Vibrational STs have been observed for N_2 associated with CO (1–0) (Marteau et al., 1964), CO_2 (ν_2, ν_3) (Fahrenfort and Ketelaar, 1954; Rinehart, 1959), CF_4 (ν_3) (Rinehart, 1959), SF_6 (ν_3, ν_4) (Schachtschneider, 1959; Akhmed-zhanov and Bulanin, 1974; Akhmedzhanov et al., 1976a,b; Brodbeck et al., 1981a,b), and for O_2 associated with CO_2 (ν_3) (Fahren-fort and Ketelaar, 1954) or SF_6 (ν_3) (Brodbeck et al., 1981a). To our knowledge, the only gas mixture that does not contain N_2, O_2 or H_2, for which STs have been observed, is CH_4 (ν_1) + CO_2 (ν_3) (Rinehart, 1959).

This paper concerns STs in compressed gas mixtures that involve an infrared active vibration of one molecule and a Raman active vibration of the other. The theory of integrated inten-sity for STs was first developed by Fahrenfort (1955) from the pioneering work of Van Kranendonk and Bird (1951) on collision-induced absorption. Then, Hooge and Ketelaar (1957) and Colpa and Ketelaar (1958b,c) established basic formulas that may be applied to STs associating an infrared active vibration and a Raman active one.

In the next section, we present the formulation obtained by Colpa and Ketelaar (1958b,c) in which the mechanism of STs is attributed to dipole–induced dipole coupling. We also review briefly the theoretical work published afterwards. Recent results of intensities are analyzed in relation to that theory. We then discuss the accuracy of intensity measurements and consequently the relevancy of using an improved theory. The third section deals with features recently observed in the ST spectra of SF_6+N_2 mixtures concerning variations of intensities, bandwidths and bandshifts with N_2 gas density. Finally, we present new results on the profiles of the STs arising from the ν_3 band of CO_2 associated with the fundamental transition of N_2 or H_2. These profiles are analyzed by applying a theory recently developed by Velsko and Oxtoby (1980).

INTENSITY OF SIMULTANEOUS TRANSITIONS IN GAS MIXTURES

Theoretical Intensity

Let us consider a pair of interacting molecules A and B. The total dipole induced in this pair by the action of molecular fields is

$$\vec{\mu}_{AB} = \vec{E}_B \overset{\leftrightarrow}{\alpha}_A + \vec{E}_A \overset{\leftrightarrow}{\alpha}_B \tag{1}$$

where $\vec{E}_B$ is the field due to molecule B at the position of molecule A, $\overset{\leftrightarrow}{\alpha}_A$ is the polarizability tensor of molecule A, and reciprocally. In most of the STs that have been observed, one molecule (A) has a vibration that is Raman active and the other (B) a vibration that is infrared active. Mukhtarov (1959) has shown that a ST occurs only if at least one mode of vibration is Raman active. Thus, the induced dipole $\vec{\mu}_{AB}$ arises primarily from the interaction of the vibrating dipolar electric field of B with the vibrating polarizability of A according to $\vec{\mu}_{AB} = \vec{E}_B \overset{\leftrightarrow}{\alpha}_A$. Although the permanent dipole of B may be equal to zero, its derivative with respect to a normal coordinate must be different from zero.

An electric field is also produced by the vibrating quadrupole moment, or higher order moments, of molecule A or B. The induction by a quadrupolar field is preponderant for STs in a mixture of homopolar molecules such as pure H_2 (Reddy, 1984) or $H_2 + N_2$ (Coulon, 1958). Finally, overlap forces may cause an induced dipole moment, but this induction has always been neglected in the analysis of STs.

The experimental integrated intensity is defined by

$$S' = \int_{band} K(\nu) \cdot \nu^{-1} \, d\nu \tag{2}$$

Here, $K(\nu)$ is the measured absorption coefficient at wavenumber ν, obtained from

$$K(\nu) = \ln[I_0(\nu)/I(\nu)] \, L^{-1} \tag{3}$$

where I_0 and I are respectively the background and gas spectral outputs, and L is the optical pathlength.

The theoretical integrated intensity for interacting pairs AB undergoing the transition i→f is given by

$$S' = \frac{8\pi^3}{3hc} \left\{ \frac{P_i}{d_i} - \frac{P_f}{d_f} \right\} n_A n_B < |\vec{\mu}_{if}(\vec{R})|^2 > \tag{4}$$

The degeneracy of the initial levels i is

$$d_i = (2J_i^A + 1)(2J_i^B + 1) \tag{5}$$

where J_i^A and J_i^B are the rotational quantum numbers of A and B, and P_i, the population density for the initial pair state, is assumed to be equal to the product $P_i^A \cdot P_i^B$. Analogous formulas may be applied for the final state f. If the final state refers to rovibrational levels, P_f is negligible because at room or low temperature practically all the molecules are in their ground vibrational state.

If an isotropic intermolecular pair potential $V(R)$ is assumed, the density of interacting molecular pairs in an elementary volume is $n_A n_B 4\pi R^2 g(R) dR$ where n_A and n_B are the number of molecules A and B per unit volume, R is the intermolecular distance, and $g(R)$ is the pair distribution function. In the classical treatment of the translation, at low densities and not too low temperatures, this function has the simple form

$$g(R) = \exp\{-V(R)/kT\} \tag{6}$$

$\langle |\vec{\mu}_{if}(\vec{R})|^2 \rangle$ is the average over the distance and orientation of the squared matrix elements of the induced dipole moment $\vec{\mu}_{AB}(R)$, i.e.

$$\langle |\vec{\mu}_{if}(\vec{R})|^2 \rangle = \int_0^\infty 4\pi R^2 g(R) \sum_{m_i, m_f} |\langle i\, m_i | \vec{\mu}_{AB}(R) | f\, m_f \rangle|^2 \, dR \tag{7}$$

Here $\langle i\, m_i |$ and $\langle f\, m_f |$ denote the vibration–rotation eigen-functions for the pair, with m_i and m_f as degenerate magnetic quantum numbers. Thus the total intensity of a vibrational ST can be expressed as

$$S' = \frac{8\pi^3}{3hc} n_A n_B \sum_{J_i, J_f} \frac{P_i^A \, P_i^B}{(2J_i^A + 1)(2J_i^B + 1)} \langle |\vec{\mu}_{if}(\vec{R})|^2 \rangle \tag{8}$$

where $\langle |\vec{\mu}_{if}(\vec{R})|^2 \rangle$ is given by Eq.(7).

Van Kranendonk (1957) has shown that the non–central forces have a very small influence on the total intensity if the angle-dependent part of V is small compared to kT.

If one assumes that the dipolar field of the infrared active molecule B plays the most important role in the induction of a dipole moment in the Raman active molecule A, induction by quadrupolar fields of A or B and by the weaker overlap forces may be neglected. The components of $\vec{\mu}_{AB}$ are then the sum of contributions from the products of the components of the polarizability tensor $\overleftrightarrow{\alpha}_A$ with the components of the electric field at molecule A due to molecule B. Although the molecules are interacting, the total nuclear wavefunction of the pair is supposed to be the product of the unperturbed rovibrational wavefunctions of the isolated molecules. This approximation may be justified by the general agreement between the observed wavenumbers of STs and the theoretical sum of the wavenumbers of the isolated molecule transitions. The summations of the matrix elements are performed by taking into account the selection rules for the rotational transitions $\Delta J_A=0,\pm2$ and $\Delta J_B=\pm1$ (for a linear molecule B); thus, the intensity S' becomes

$$S'= \frac{64\pi^4}{3hc} \, n_A n_B \langle\mu_B\rangle^2 \, \{x_A \langle\alpha_A\rangle^2 + \frac{2}{9} \, y_A \, \langle\gamma_A\rangle^2\} \, I_6 \tag{9}$$

Here, $\langle\mu_B\rangle$ is the matrix element of the vibrational transition of B and $\langle\alpha_A\rangle$ and $\langle\gamma_A\rangle$ are the vibrational matrix elements of the isotropic and anisotropic parts of the polarizability tensor $\overleftrightarrow{\alpha}_A$. The value of x_a is 1 for the Q-branch and 0 for the O- and S-branches. The y_A parameter is given by

$$y_A = \sum_{J_i^A} \, P_i^A \, C(J_i^A 200 | J_f^A \, 0)^2 \tag{10}$$

where C is a Clebsch-Gordan coefficient. I_6 is the integral

$$I_6 = \int_0^\infty R^2 \, \exp\{-V(R)/kT\} \, R^{-6} dR \tag{11}$$

Sophisticated intermolecular potentials have been developed for some specific gas mixtures but do not exist for the gas mixtures that we have studied. Moreover, our analysis is restricted to isotropic potentials. Then, to determine I_6, one generally uses the Lennard-Jones potential

$$V(R) = 4\epsilon \, [(\sigma/R)^{12} - (\sigma/R)^6] \tag{12}$$

Other isotropic potentials, the parameters of which can be roughly estimated for any gas mixtures from the usual combination rules, have been considered, such as the sphericalized Kihara potential

$$V(R\leqslant 2a) = \infty$$

$$V(R>2a) = 4\epsilon \left[(\frac{\sigma-2a}{R-2a})^{12} - (\frac{\sigma-2a}{R-2a})^6 \right] \tag{13}$$

or the modified (exp-6) Buckingham potential

$$V(R<m) = \infty$$

$$V(R \geqslant m) = \frac{\epsilon}{1 - 6/\gamma} \ \{\frac{6}{\gamma} \ \exp \ [(1 - \frac{R}{R_m})] - (\frac{R}{R_m})^{-6} \ \} \tag{14}$$

The meaning of the parameters for these potentials may be found in various papers (for instance Sherwood and Prausnitz, 1964).

If we introduce the infrared active band intensity S_B' (in cm^{-1} $Amagat^{-1}$) given by

$$S_B' = \frac{8\pi^3}{3hc} \ n_B^0 \ \langle\mu_B\rangle^2 \tag{15}$$

the expression for the intensity of a ST per unit density of each component of the mixture, the so-called binary absorption coefficient (in cm^{-1} $Amagat^{-2}$), becomes

$$S_{AB}' = S_B' \ 8\pi \ n_A^0 \{x_A \langle\alpha_A\rangle^2 + \frac{2}{9} \ y_A \ \langle\gamma_A\rangle^2\} \ I_6 \tag{16}$$

where n_B^0 and n_A^0 are the number of molecules B and A per unit volume at STP. This formula obtained by Colpa and Ketelaar (1958c) shows that the binary absorption coefficient S_{AB}' is proportional to the infrared active band intensity S_B'.

Other authors have developed theories dealing with the intensity of STs. From the previous work (Galatry and Vodar, 1955, 1956), Galatry (1959) obtained a comparable formula in which i) the anisotropic part of the polarizability tensor of the Raman active molecule is neglected, ii) the dipole induction by the vibrating quadrupole of each molecule of the pair is included, and iii) the anisotropic part of the dispersion intermolecular potential is introduced in the pair distribution function. Shinoda and Mitsuya (1976) have determined the contribution arising from the coupling between the electronic state of the infrared active molecule and the nuclear vibration of the Raman active molecule. They applied their formalism to the CO_2-N_2 and CO_2-H_2 systems.

Comparison with Experimental Results

The absorption of the bands associated with STs is very weak. The ratio of S_B' to $S_{AB}' \cdot \rho_{AB}$, where ρ_{ab} is the density of interacting pairs, is about 10^6 in the most favorable case. Thus, to observe ST bands in the gas phase, one needs long optical pathlengths and/or high pressures. However, these transitions are more easily detectable when a strong infrared active band such as the ν_3 fundamental of CF_4 or SF_6 is involved.

For intensity measurements, the main problem arises from the

determination of the baseline. This determination is quite impre-
cise because the ST bands are rather broad and, in any case, more
or less superimposed on infrared active bands of molecule B,
induced bands of molecule A, or ST bands arising from infrared or
Raman transitions near the active modes. The band intensities are
therefore difficult to measure accurately, i.e. with a relative
error less than 10%. Comparison among literature data for the same
binary absorption coefficient shows discrepancies that often exceed 20%. Another source of error is the evaluation of the partial
densities for the mixture components. If accurate PVT data are
available, we estimate that uncertainties in densities should not
exceed 2%, using an experimental technique described previously
(Brodbeck et al., 1981b).

Let us examine the results obtained for the STs in H_2 + CF_4
and H_2 + SF_6 gas mixtures that involve the ν_3 bands of CF_4 or SF_6
and the Q_1-branch and $S_1(1)$ transition of H_2 (Bouanich and
Brodbeck, 1977). The intensities are proportional to the density ρ
(in Amagat) of each component, Fig. 1, in agreement with Eq.(9).
Thus an experimental value for the binary absorption coefficient
S'_{AB} can be determined and compared with calculated values. The
calculations require knowledge of the infrared active band intensity, the matrix elements for the polarizability of H_2, and the
data for the intermolecular potential.

The intensities of the ν_3 bands of CF_4 and SF_6 have been
determined with a relative error estimated to be 5%, at best. The
vibration-rotation matrix elements for the polarizability tensor
of H_2 are accurately known, but this is not the case for any other
Raman active molecule as different values of vibrational matrix
elements are generally available. The evaluation of I_6, Eq.(11),
is most critical, as it strongly depends on the choice of the
intermolecular potential. We have used two isotropic potentials,
namely the Lennard-Jones and the Kihara potentials. The parameters
ϵ, σ and a for H_2, CF_4 and SF_6 have been determined by minimizing
the rms deviation δ between experimental and calculated values of
the second virial coefficient B(T) at different temperatures T
(Table 1). The rms deviations δ are smaller, especially for CF_4
and SF_6, for the Kihara potential than for the Lennard-Jones
potential simply because the Kihara potential includes three
adjustable parameters. Using the usual combination rules

$$a = \frac{a_A + a_B}{2} \qquad \sigma = \frac{\sigma_A + \sigma_B}{2} \qquad \epsilon = \sqrt{\epsilon_A \epsilon_B} \qquad (17)$$

to determine the potential parameters for the molecular pairs H_2-
CF_4 and H_2-SF_6, we have calculated I_6. A considerable difference
is obtained between the results of I_6 derived from the two
potentials. As shown in Table 2, the agreement between experimental and calculated binary absorption coefficients is generally
better for the Kihara potential than for the Lennard-Jones poten-

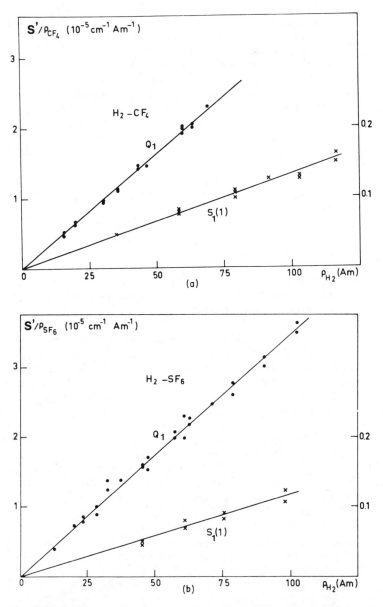

Fig. 1. STs in $H_2(1-0) + CF_4(\nu_3)$ and $H_2(1-0) + SF_6(\nu_3)$. Variation of the integrated absorption coefficient S' per unit density of CF_4 (a) or SF_6 (b) with the density of H_2. The left-hand scales refer to the Q_1-branch and the right-hand scales to the $S_1(1)$ transition (from Bouanich and Brodbeck, 1977).

Table 1. Potential parameters determined from second virial coefficient data (from Bouanich and Brodbeck, 1977).

gas	V(R)	a	σ	ϵ/k	δ
		(Å)	(Å)	(K)	$(cm^3\ mol^{-1})$
H_2	LJ(6–12)	–	2.944	32.0	0.06
(−175°C:150°C)	Kihara	0.142	2.874	38.6	0.05
CF_4	LJ(6–12)	–	4.744	151.5	0.82
(0°C:350°C)	Kihara	0.728	4.313	292.3	0.08
SF_6	LJ(6–12)	–	5.843	190.2	6.3
(0°C:280°C)	Kihara	1.061	4.463	553.4	1.0

Table 2. Calculated results and experimentally determined binary absorption coefficients S'_{AB} (from Bouanich and Brodbeck, 1977).

transition	t	V(R)	$I_6 \times 10^{-21}$	$S'_{AB} \times 10^7$	
	$(°C)$		(cm^{-3})	$(cm^{-1}\ Am^{-2})$	
				calc.	exp.
Q_1	28	LJ(6–12)	8.10	2.53	3.26
(H_2-CF_4)	–	Kihara	9.54	2.98	
$S_1(1)$	28	LJ(6–12)	8.10	0.115	0.134
(H_2-CF_4)	–	Kihara	9.54	0.136	
Q_1	75	LJ(6–12)	5.43	2.35	3.47
(H_2-SF_6)	–	Kihara	8.96	3.88	
$S_1(1)$	75	LJ(6–12)	5.43	0.100	0.12
(H_2-SF_6)	–	Kihara	8.96	0.166	

tial. This superiority of the Kihara potential is corroborated by the results obtained by Akhmedzhanov et al. (1976a,b) on the gas mixtures of N_2 with SF_6 or CO_2. Akhmedzhanov et al. (1976b) have also shown that for N_2+SF_6 the Kihara and the Buckingham potentials, Eqs.(13) and (14), lead to the same good results for S'_{AB}.

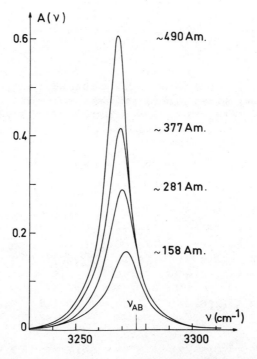

Fig. 2. ST in $N_2(1-0)$ + $SF_6(\nu_3)$. Band profiles $A(\nu) = K(\nu)L$ at various N_2 densities (from Brodbeck et al., 1981b).

It should be noted that the validity of the combination rules used for a, σ and ε may be questionable because of the huge differences between the potential parameters of SF_6 or CF_4 and those of H_2.

In spite of all the uncertainties, the overall agreement between experimental and calculated values may be considered as a confirmation that the induction by a vibrating dipolar field is essentially responsible for the observed absorption. Indeed, some improvements could be introduced in these calculations by considering the anisotropic part of the intermolecular potential or additional mechanisms for the induced dipole by quadrupolar field or overlap induction produced by exchange forces. However, we estimate that these improvements would be worth considering only if a better intermolecular potential and more accurate experimental intensities were available.

RECENT RESULTS IN SIMULTANEOUS TRANSITION SPECTRA

The ST of the ν_3 band of SF_6 associated with the fundamental vibration of N_2 has been extensively studied (Brodbeck et al., 1981a,b) for low pressures of SF_6 (up to 10 bar) and densities of N_2 up to 490 Amagat. The band profiles of this ST are shown in Fig. 2 for various N_2 densities. The recorded spectra exhibit a simple profile, contrary to the ν_3 band of SF_6 which is overlapped by several hot bands and isotopic bands, and has a complicated structure (Brodbeck et al., 1980). The observed bands are spread over about 100 cm^{-1} and are essentially due to the Q—branch of N_2. As the N_2 density increases, the infrared absorption of the double transition increases, but both the frequency of the absorption maximum and the bandwidth decrease. All these results are discussed below.

Nonlinear Effects in the Band Intensities

The intensities are proportional to the N_2 gas density only below 200 Amagat. For higher densities, slight deviations may be observed from linearity in Fig. 3. If one assumes that the vibrational coupling between interacting molecules is negligible, the intensity is additive over all molecular pairs. Hence these nonlinear effects arise mainly from the number of colliding pairs that is density dependent. The low density limit of the pair distribution function g(R), Eq.(6), is no longer valid at high densities and should be corrected by terms that depend on the density (Van Kranendonk, 1957).

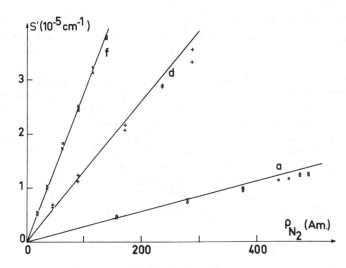

Fig. 3. ST in $N_2(1-0) + SF_6(\nu_3)$. Density dependence of the
integrated intensity; a, d and f correspond to experiments performed at P (SF_6) equal to 0.47, 2 and 4 bars,
respectively. Note the deviation from linearity at high
densities (from Brodbeck et al., 1981b).

Wavenumber of the Band Peak

Theoretical and experimental wavenumbers. The theoretical wavenumber ν_{AB} of a vibrational ST is the sum or difference of the
vibrational wavenumbers of the infrared and Raman single molecule
transitions (Hooge and Ketelaar, 1957; Ketelaar, 1959): $\nu_B + \nu_A$ and
$|\nu_B - \nu_A|$. Only sum absorption bands have been found in compressed
gas mixtures, because even at room temperature the vibrational
levels with v > 0 are not sufficiently populated to permit
observation of a ST in which one molecule is excited and the other
de-excited.

The theoretical wavenumber of the ST involving the ν_3 band of
SF_6 and the Q_1-branch of N_2 is equal to 3276 cm^{-1} and does not
coincide with the experimental value determined from the maximum
absorption extrapolated to zero N_2 density, i.e. 3274 cm^{-1}. We
estimate that more accurate wavenumber measurements should be
performed for this ST, particularly at low N_2 and SF_6 densities.
If this experimentally determined wavenumber should prove to be
different from the theoretical value, then the wavefunction of the
molecular pair could not strictly be expressed as the product of
unperturbed wavefunctions.

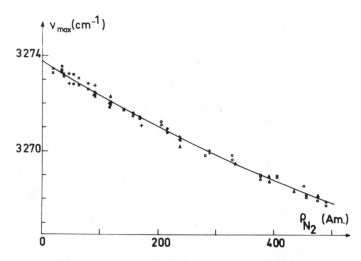

Fig. 4. ST in $N_2(1-0)$ + $SF_6(\nu_3)$. Wavenumbers for the maximum
absorption versus N_2 densities. The solid line is the
result of a fitting procedure (from Brodbeck et al.,
1981b).

Frequency shift. As the N_2 density increases from a low density to
500 Amagat, the maximum of the absorption of N_2+SF_6 exhibits, as
shown in Fig.4, a shift to lower wavenumbers of about 6 cm^{-1}. This
frequency shift, nearly proportional to the N_2 density, is probably related to the collisional displacement of the ν_3 band of SF_6
perturbed by N_2 and to the Raman shift of self-perturbed N_2.
Indeed, our experiments on SF_6 diluted in compressed N_2 have shown
that the ν_3 band center is shifted by -2.5 cm^{-1} in the N_2 density
range 0-150 Amagat.

Experimental Bandwith

For the ST in N_2+SF_6 mixtures, the experimental bandwidth $\Delta\nu$ (full
width at half height) is roughly constant for nitrogen densities
up to about 100 Amagat and decreases slightly for higher densities
(Fig.5). This narrowing is approximately proportional to the density, and the bandwidth $\Delta\nu$ decreases from about 20 cm^{-1} to 11 cm^{-1}
in the N_2 density range 100-500 Amagat. We have also observed this
pressure narrowing for the ST in O_2+SF_6 mixtures (Brodbeck et al.,
1981a), and for the ST involving the ν_3 band of CF_4 associated
with the fundamental band of H_2 for $\rho(H_2)\geqslant200$ Amagat. An attempt
to analyze these results is presented in next section.

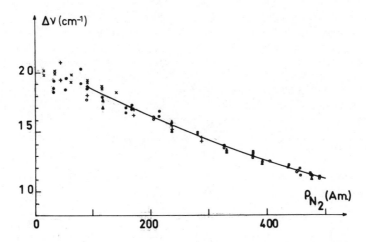

Fig. 5. ST in $N_2(1-0) + SF_6(\nu_3)$. Bandwidth $\Delta\nu$ as a function of N_2 gas densities. The solid curve is the result of a fitting procedure applied to data above 100 Amagat (from Brodbeck et al., 1981b).

BANDWIDTH AND BANDSHAPE ANALYSES

Theory

In a recent paper, Velsko and Oxtoby (1980) have derived an expression relating the bandshapes of STs to the bandshapes of the associated single molecule transitions. If one assumes long-range interactions between molecules A and B, and small overlap between the wavefunctions of their internal degrees of freedom, the pair dipole autocorrelation function (CF) for a ST, $\Phi_{AB}(t)$, is expressed as the product of the CF for the infrared active band $\Phi_B(t)$ of B perturbed by A, with the CFs for the isotropic $\Phi_{A,i}(t)$ and anisotropic $\Phi_{A,a}(t)$ Raman spectra of molecules A

$$\Phi_{AB}(t) \propto \langle R_{AB}^{-6} \rangle \; \Phi_B(t) \left[3\Phi_{A,i}(t) + \Phi_{A,a}(t) \right] \tag{18}$$

It is important to note that here $\langle R_{AB}^{-6} \rangle$ is considered to be the average over the static pair distribution function; i.e. the translational broadening has been neglected. This broadening is due to the finite duration of collisions that produce the induced dipoles. To account for this broadening Birnbaum (1983) expressed the total CF as the product of three CFs when the potential is isotropic : $\Phi_A(t)$, $\Phi_B(t)$ and $\Phi_t(t)$. The translational CF $\Phi_t(t)$ represents the collision induction that broadens the spectrum due to the convolution of $\Phi_A(t)$ and $\Phi_B(t)$. The considerable effect that $\Phi_t(t)$ has on the total spectrum when the bandwidth of the translational spectrum is a significant fraction of the rotational bandwidth is illustrated in the paper by Guillot and Birnbaum (1984). Of course, as the translational width decreases, its effect on the ST bandshape decreases.

Bandwidth

The translational bandwidth $\Delta\nu_t$ is inversely proportional to the lifetime τ of the colliding pair

$$\Delta\nu_t = (2\pi c\tau)^{-1} \tag{19}$$

The band narrowing that has been observed (Fig.5) arises probably from the decrease of $\Delta\nu_t$. At high densities, the collision duration τ is increased as the result of multiple collisions with nearby molecules and the band is consequently narrowed. This effect is similar to that observed in pressure induced spectra of H_2-Ar mixtures (De Remigis et al., 1971), and interpreted in terms of a density dependent diffusion coefficient (Zaidi and Van Kranendonk, 1971; Van Kranendonk and Gass, 1973; Van Kranendonk, 1980).

At sufficiently low pressures, we may assume binary collisions. Then the collision duration is given by (Birnbaum, 1980)

$$\tau = \overline{\Delta R}/\overline{v} \tag{20}$$

where $\overline{\Delta R}$ is the range of the square of the induced dipole moment and $\overline{v}$ is the average relative velocity proportional to $(T/m)^{1/2}$; m is the reduced mass of the interacting pair and T is the absolute temperature. At low densities, the spectrum arises from isolated binary collisions and the bandwidth $\Delta\nu_t$ is density independent, in agreement with experimental bandwidths $\Delta\nu$.

We have checked the proportionality of bandwidths with $m^{-1/2}$ in experiments performed at room temperature and low densities in i) $H_2(1-0) + SF_6(\nu_3)$ and $N_2(1-0) + SF_6(\nu_3)$ and ii) $H_2(1-0) + CO_2(\nu_3)$ and $N_2(1-0) + CO_2(\nu_3)$. The ratio between the bandwidths $\Delta\nu$ for H_2 (Q-branch) + SF_6, 63 cm^{-1}, and for N_2 (Q-branch, essentially) + SF_6, 20 cm^{-1}, is close to $[m(N_2-SF_6)/m(H_2-SF_6)]^{1/2}$: 3.15 versus 3.44. For the second set of experiments, the agreement is not satisfactory: the ratio between $\Delta\nu$ for H_2(Q-branch) + CO_2, 90 cm^{-1}, and for N_2(Q-branch, essentially) + CO_2, 65 cm^{-1}, is equal to 1.4, whereas the value of $[m(N_2-CO_2)/m(H_2-CO_2)]^{1/2}$ is 2.44.

With regard to the temperature dependence of the bandwidths, the variation of $\Delta\nu$ with $T^{1/2}$ is approximately verified for the ST of H_2(Q-branch) + SF_6(ν_3) (Bouanich and Brodbeck, 1977) measured at 75°C, $\Delta\nu$=68 cm^{-1}, and at 25°C, $\Delta\nu$=63 cm^{-1}. This result is not very significant owing to the small difference of the temperatures used, but, as far as we know, there are no other experimental data for bandwidths of a ST in a gas mixture at different temperatures.

All the above results indicate that the bandwidth is not determined by only the translational motion. Actually the bandshape of a ST also arises both from the rovibrational motion perturbed by the intermolecular interaction and from the vibration-rotational coupling of each molecule. Indeed, the profile of a ST may be theoretically represented by the convolution of three band profiles: the Raman, the infrared and the "translational" profiles. The latter band cannot be observed by itself and therefore must be computed.

Let us consider the influence of these effects on the bandwidths of the STs in SF_6(ν_3) or CO_2(ν_3) mixed with H_2(Q_1) or N_2(1-0). The bandwidth of the ν_3 band of SF_6 perturbed by H_2 or N_2, about 8 cm^{-1}, is small compared to the bandwidth of the ν_3 band of CO_2 perturbed by H_2 or N_2, estimated to be 48 cm^{-1}, and leads to a smaller contribution to the bandwidths of the STs. The Raman band arises mainly from the narrow isotropic Q-branch and has a weak influence on the ST bandwidth, especially for H_2 for which only the Q-branch is involved. The translational width, that is proportional to $m^{-1/2}$, is particularly great for mixtures containing H_2. We therefore estimate that the translational effect plays an important role in N_2+SF_6, and is dominant for H_2+SF_6 for which $\Delta\nu \approx \Delta\nu_t$. On the other hand this effect has a minor influence for N_2 + CO_2, and it is not surprising that the proportionality of $\Delta\nu$ with $m^{-1/2}$ is not verified for the second set of experiments.

Bandshape

The band profiles have been recently examined for two STs involving the ν_3 band of CO_2 associated with the fundamental transition of N_2 or H_2. Under certain experimental conditions, specifically a few bars of CO_2 and pressures of N_2 less than 200 bars, the ST spectra of N_2+CO_2 exhibit, Fig. 6, a shallow dip around the band centre. This structure with two maxima probably arises from the P- and R-branches of the ν_3 band of CO_2 perturbed by N_2. Under similar experimental conditions, the ST spectra of H_2+CO_2 show, Fig. 6, a broader band without any splitting.

Using the formalism of Velsko and Oxtoby, Eq.(18), we have

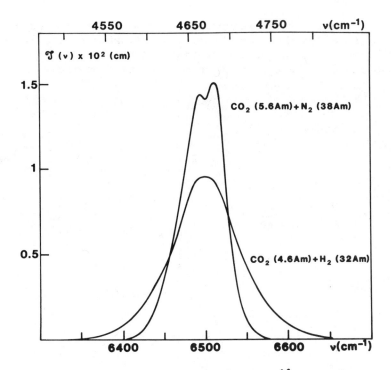

Fig. 6. Experimental normalized bandshapes $\mathfrak{J}(\nu) = K(\nu)/(\nu S')$ for the STs $H_2(Q_1) + CO_2(\nu_3)$ and $N_2(1-0) + CO_2(\nu_3)$. The bottom scale refers to $H_2 + CO_2$ and the top scale to $N_2 + CO_2$.

calculated a profile for the ST band in $N_2 + CO_2$ gas mixtures. $\Phi_{AB}(t)$ has been derived from the infrared spectrum of the ν_3 band of CO_2 perturbed by N_2, recorded in our laboratory, and from the synthetic isotropic and anisotropic Raman spectra calculated by Berens et al. (1981). The "theoretical" profile for the ST, which is the convolution of the infrared and Raman bands, observed under the same conditions as the double transition, has been obtained from the Fourier transform of $\Phi_{AB}(t)$. As may be seen in Fig. 7, this profile displays a P-R structure much more pronounced than that experimentally observed.

The discrepancy is probably caused by the neglect of the translational broadening in the formalism developed by Velsko and Oxtoby. As mentioned previously, this broadening is expected to be relatively small; therefore, except around the band center, the calculated profile is in reasonable agreement with the experimental profile. On the other hand, the influence of the translational effect in H_2+CO_2 gas mixtures yields a broader band, and conceals the split structure that originates from the ν_3 band of CO_2.

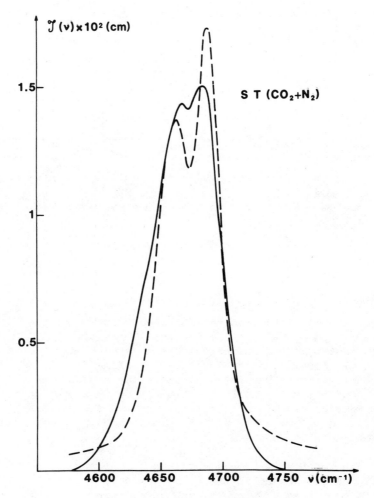

Fig. 7. ST in $N_2(1-0)$ + $CO_2(\nu_3)$. Experimental (———) and calculated (− − −) normalized bandshapes.

CONCLUSION

Simultaneous transitions were extensively studied during the decade 1955-1965. The measurements were aimed mostly at determining frequencies and integrated intensities of the ST bands, and were obtained with rather large uncertainties. The intensities have been calculated on the basis of dipoles induced by a vibrating dipolar field, with the neglect of the fields of higher order multipoles and of overlap induction. For spherical molecules with strong infrared active bands, in mixtures with H_2, N_2 or O_2, considering only such induction (theory of Colpa and Ketelaar) is a good approximation. By use of a Kihara potential in the pair distribution function, an overall agreement has been obtained between experimental and calculated binary absorption coefficients for the gas mixtures SF_6-H_2 and CF_4-H_2. However, the general lack of accurate data for the band intensities and for the intermolecular potentials does not allow one to test more deeply the validity of the theory. In any case, more accurate potentials are being developed and more accurate intensity measurements are being made.

Recent measurements of the spectra of N_2+SF_6 over a large pressure range of gas mixture have shown the following features:
 –the non-linearity of intensity with $\rho(N_2)$ for high N_2 densities;
 –the shift to low frequencies of the maximum absorption position with increasing N_2 density;
 –the probable non-coincidence, within experimental error, of the theoretical wavenumber with the experimental value extrapolated to zero density of each component of the mixture;
 –the pressure narrowing of the band for $\rho(N_2)$ above 100 Amagat.
A qualitative interpretation of these results has been proposed. Accurate experiments over a sufficiently large pressure range are needed to confirm these effects. Such measurements would be helpful in indicating the needed theoretical developments.

The bandshape analysis of a ST has been investigated for the first time. The band profile of the double transition involving the ν_3 band of CO_2 and the fundamental vibration of N_2 shows at low density a shallow dip arising from the P-R structure of the ν_3 band of CO_2 perturbed by N_2.

The only existing theory for the bandshapes of STs has not proved satisfactory and should be improved to take into account the translational effect. Indeed, the study of the bandshape is complicated, as it depends both on the perturbed rovibrational transitions of each colliding molecule and on the translational

motion. For a better understanding of STs, experimentally determined bandshapes, especially over a wide range of temperature and
density, are required.

REFERENCES

Akhmedzhanov, R., and Bulanin, M. O., 1974, Chem. Phys. Lett.,
    24:218.
Akhmedzhanov, R., Gransky, P. V., and Bulanin, M. O., 1976a,
    Can. J. Phys., 54:519.
Akhmedzhanov, R. , Bulanin, M. O., Granskii, P. V.,and
    Leshchinskii, A. S., 1976b, Opt. Spectrosc., 41:409.
Allin, E. J., May, A. D., Stoicheff, B. P., Stryland, J. C., and
    Welsh, H. L., 1967, Appl. Opt., 6:1597.
Avrillier, S., Mitra, S. S., and Vu, H., 1976, J. Chem. Phys.,
    64:2202.
Badilescu, S., 1968, Rev. Roum. Chim., 13:1297.
Badilescu, S., 1970, Rev. Roum. Chim., 15:1931.
Badilescu, S., 1971, Rev. Roum. Chim., 16:9.
Berens, P. H., White, S., R., and Wilson, K. R., 1981,
    J. Chem. Phys., 75:515.
Birnbaum, G., 1980, in: "Vibrational Spectroscopy of Molecular
    Liquids and Solids", S. Bratos and R. M. Pick, ed.,
    p.147, Plenum, New York.
Birnbaum, G., 1983, private communication.
Bouanich, J.-P., and Brodbeck, C., 1977, J. Quant. Spectrosc.
    Radiat. Transfer, 17:777.
Bouanich, J.-P., Roffey, B. J., and Welsh, H. L., 1975, in:
    "Molecular Spectroscopy of Dense Phases", M. Grosmann,
    S. G. Elkomoss and J. Ringeissen,ed.,p.563, Elsevier, Ams-
    terdam.
Borysow, A., and Frommhold, L., 1985, this volume.
Brodbeck, C., Bouanich, J.-P., and Jean-Louis, A., 1981a,
    Can. J. Phys., 59:1434.
Brodbeck, C., Bouanich, J.-P., Figuière, P., and Szwarc, H.,
    1981b, J. Chem. Phys., 74:77.
Brodbeck, C., Bouanich, J.-P., Nguyen-Van-Thanh, and Rossi, I.,
    1982, J. Mol. Structure, 80:261.
Brodbeck, C., Rossi, I., Strapélias, H., and Bouanich, J.-P.,
    1980, Chem. Phys., 54:1.
Bulanin, M. O., 1973, J. Mol. Structure, 19:59.
Bulanin, M. O., and Kouzov, A. P., 1982, Opt. Spectrosc., 53:266.
Bulanin, M. O., and Melnik, M. G., 1967, Opt. Spectrosc., 23:273.
Bulanin, M. O., and Melnik, M. G., 1968, Opt. Spectrosc., Suppl.3
    (Mol. Spectrosc.II):106.
Bulanin, M. O., and Orlova, N. D., 1961, Opt. Spectrosc., 11:298.
Bulanin, M. O., and Orlova, N. D., 1966, Opt. Spectrosc., Suppl.2
    (Mol.Spectrosc.I):135.

Burneau, A., and Corset, J., 1972, J. Chem. Phys., 56:662.
Burneau, A., and Corset, J., 1973, Can. J. Chem., 51:2059.
Chesnoy, J., Ricard, D., and Flytzanis, C., Chem. Phys., 42:337.
Colpa, J. P., 1965, in: "Physics of High Pressure and the
        Condensed Phase", A. Van Itterbeck, ed., p.490,
        North-Holland Publishing, Amsterdam.
Colpa, J. P., and Ketelaar, J. A. A., 1958a, Mol. Phys., 1:14.
Colpa, J. P., and Ketelaar, J. A. A., 1958b, Mol. Phys., 1:343.
Colpa, J. P., and Ketelaar, J. A. A., 1958c, Physica, 24:1035.
Coulon, R., 1958, Thesis, J. Rech. C.N.R.S., 9:305.
Coulon, R., and Vu, H., 1957, C. R. Acad. Sci. Paris, 245:2247.
Coulon, R., and Vu, H., 1959, in: "Colloques Internationaux du
        C.N.R.S., Propriétés optiques et acoustiques des
        fluides comprimés", p.99, C.N.R.S., Paris.
Coulon, R., Robin, J., and Vodar, B., 1955, C. R. Acad. Sci.
        Paris, 240:956.
De Remigis, J., McTaggart, J. W., and Welsh, H. L., 1971,
        Can. J. Phys., 49:381.
Fahrenfort, J., 1955, Thesis, University of Amsterdam.
Fahrenfort, J., and Ketelaar, J. A. A., 1954, J. Chem. Phys.,
        22:1631.
Filimonov, V. N., 1960, Soviet Phys. Usp., 2:894.
Galatry, L., 1959, Thesis, J. Rech. C.N.R.S., 10:43.
Galatry, L., and Vodar, B., 1955, C. R. Acad. Sci. Paris,
        240:1072.
Galatry, L., and Vodar, B., 1956, C. R. Acad. Sci. Paris,
        242:1871.
Guillot, B., and Birnbaum, G., 1985, this volume.
Hooge, F. N., and Ketelaar, J. A. A., 1957, Physica, 23:423.
Ketelaar, J. A. A., 1956, Rec. Trav. Chim., 75:857.
Ketelaar, J. A. A., 1959, Spectrochim. Acta, 14:237.
Ketelaar, J. A. A., and Hooge, F. N., 1955, J. Chem. Phys.,
        23:749.
Ketelaar, J. A. A., and Hooge, F. N., 1957, Rec. Trav. Chim.,
        76:529.
Ketelaar, J. A. A., and Rettschnick, R.P.H., 1961, J. Chem. Phys.,
        35:1909.
Ketelaar, J. A. A., and Rettschnick, R. P. H., 1963, Z. Physik,
        173:101.
Ketelaar, J. A. A., Hooge, F. N., and Blasse, G., 1956,
        Rec. Trav. Chim., 75:220.
McKellar, A. R. W., Rich, N. H., and Welsh, H. L., 1972,
        Can. J. Phys., 50:1.
Marteau, P., Scatena, G., and Vu, H., 1964, C. R. Acad.Sci. Paris,
        258:3453.
Mukhtarov, C. K., 1959, Opt. Spectrosc., 6:108.
Reddy, S. P., 1985, this volume.
Rinehart, R. W., 1959, Thesis, University of Minnesota.
Ron, A., and Hornig, D. F., 1963, J. Chem. Phys., 39:1129.
Schachtschneider, J. H., 1959, Thesis, University of Minnesota.

Shapiro, M. M., and Gush, H. P., 1966, Can. J. Phys., **44**:949.
Sherwood, A. E., and Prausnitz, J. M., 1964, J. Chem. Phys., 41:413.
Shinoda, H., and Mitsuya, M., 1976, Bull. Chem. Soc. Japan, **49**:410.
Souers, P. C., Fearon, D., Garza, R., Kelly, E. M., Roberts, P. E., Sanborn, R. H., Tsugawa, R. T., Hunt, J. L. and Poll, J. D., 1979, J. Chem. Phys., **70**:1581.
Souers, P. C., Fuentes, J., Fearon, E. M., Roberts, P. E., Tsugawa, R. T., Hunt, J. L., and Poll, J. D., 1980, J. Chem. Phys., **72**:1679.
Van Kranendonk, J., 1957, Physica, **23**:825.
Van Kranendonk, J., 1958, Physica, **24**:347.
Van Kranendonk, J., 1959, Physica, **25**:337.
Van Kranendonk, J., 1980, in: "Intermolecular Spectroscopy and Dynamical Properties of Dense Systems", J. Van Kranendonk, ed., p.228, North-Holland Publishing, Amsterdam.
Van Kranendonk, J., and Bird, R. B., 1951, Physica, **17**:953, 968.
Van Kranendonk, J., and Gass, D. M., 1973, Can. J. Phys., **51**:2428.
Velsko, S. P., and Oxtoby, D. W., 1980, J. Chem. Phys., **73**:4883.
Zaidi, H. R., and Van Kranendonk, J., 1971, Can. J. Phys., **49**:385.

MOLECULAR MOTIONS IN DENSE FLUIDS FROM INDUCED ROTATIONAL SPECTRA

M. Barnabei, U. Buontempo, and P. Maselli

Dipartimento di Fisica, Università degli Studi di Roma
"La Sapienza"
Piazzale Aldo Moro, 2 - 00185 Rome (Italy)

ABSTRACT

Induced rototranslational absorption spectra of systems of
simple molecules are analyzed in order to derive the pure translational profile. Our analysis shows that from the spectra it is possible to derive parameters suitable to describe the observed density
effects. The density dependence of these parameters is discussed
with the help of simple models.

INTRODUCTION

A very large effort has been devoted in recent years to the
study of molecular motions in dense fluids on a time scale of the
order of a picosecond, with the aim of clarifying the microscopic
processes which determine the value of macroscopic transport coefficients.

Induced spectra seem to be one of the most promising techniques
to reach this goal (Van Kranendonk, 1980). Indeed both the induced
dipole moment and the induced polarizability are strongly dependent
on the separation of the interacting molecules and thus the induced
spectrum reflects the intermolecular dynamics of the system.

Depolarized Rayleigh scattering from fluids of spherical molecules has been extensively studied for several years (Madden, 1980;
An et al., 1979). It is, however, difficult to extract from these
spectra information on the relative motion of pairs of molecules
because of the strong cancellation which occours between the two,
three and four body terms (Ladd et al., 1979). For this purpose
it may be more convenient to study the quadrupole induced absorption

spectra; in fact, due to the shorter range of this induction mechanism, as well as to the different symmetry, in dense gases the cancellation effects are less important than those of the induced Rayleigh scattering.

In spite of this advantage, no systematic efforts have been devoted to the analysis of the density effect on the induced rotational spectra, although the earliest observations of the density narrowing of the rotovibrational spectra of H_2 (De Remigis et al., 1971; MacTaggart et al., 1973) have clearly indicated the possibilities to obtain from such spectra information on molecular dynamics (Zaidi and Van Kranendonk, 1971; Van Kranendonk and Gass, 1973).

We will present here a brief review of the available experimental results on the induced rotational spectra of simple molecules and we will discuss how from such spectra it is possible to derive information on the elemental molecular processes.

In principle, similar information can be obtained also from the collision induced absorption spectra of noble gases mixtures (Buontempo et al., 1980), which arise mainly from the overlap induction mechanism. Since the overlap induction range is one order of magnitude smaller than the molecular dimensions, these spectra mainly reflect the dynamics of a pair of colliding particles at very short times and thus the observed density effects in the liquid are related to the rattling component of the particles motion (Buontempo et al., 1981; Guillot et al., 1982); a detailed discussion of such effects is given elsewhere (Lewis, 1985).

The analysis of the absorption spectra due to multipolar induction is generally very complex, because these spectra reflect the rotational and the translational dynamics, as well as the coupling between intermolecular and intramolecular degrees of freedom. For this reason we will limit our considerations to the induced rotational spectra of H_2, D_2 and N_2. In these systems the interaction potential is nearly isotropic and thus it is possible to separate the translational and the rotational motions (Buontempo et al., 1979; Buontempo et al., 1983). Thus, from the spectra of such systems we can derive a correlation function of variables which depend only on the intermolecular distances. For strongly anisotropic systems the separation is no longer possible, unless there is a large time scale difference between the rates of intermolecular and intramolecular processes (Madden and Cox, 1981; Madden and Tildesley, 1983).

SURVEY OF THE EXPERIMENTAL RESULTS

H_2-Ar and D_2-Ar mixtures

The induced dipole moment autocorrelation function can be generally expressed as

$$C(t) = \sum_{i \neq j; k \neq \ell} < \vec{\mu}_{ij}(0) \cdot \vec{\mu}_{k\ell}(t) >$$

where μ_{ab} is the dipole moment induced in molecule b by molecule a. In dilute mixtures the dipole moment induced in different pairs (i,j,k all different) are uncorrelated. Thus, in the dipole moment autocorrelation function, only the two and three body terms are present

$$C(t) = \sum_{i \neq j} < \vec{\mu}_{ij}(0) \cdot \vec{\mu}_{ij}(t) > + \sum_{i \neq j \neq k} < \vec{\mu}_{ij}(0) \cdot \vec{\mu}_{ik}(t) > \qquad (1)$$

The "allowed" Raman spectra of H_2-Ar mixtures show that the rotational motion is nearly free even at liquid densities (Keijser et al., 1974; Keijser et al., 1974a). Therefore, we assume an isotropic intermolecular potential. Moreover, it has been shown that the induction mechanism is mainly quadrupolar (Bachet et al., 1983). Thus the dipole moment can be expressed as

$$\mu_{ij} = -grad \left[\frac{Q\alpha}{8\pi\varepsilon_o} \cdot \frac{1}{r_{ij}^3} (1-3\cos^2\phi) \right]$$

where α is the argon polarizability, Q is the quadrupole moment and ϕ is the angle between the direction of the quadrupole axis and the vector $\vec{r}_{ij}$; $\vec{r}_{ij}$ is the distance between the particles i and j.

Performing the angular average we obtain for the classical correlation function $C(t)$ the following expression (Buontempo et al., 1979)

$$C(t) = \left(\frac{\alpha Q}{4\pi\varepsilon_o}\right)^2 \sum_{i \neq j; i \neq k} < \frac{15}{2} \frac{\left[\vec{r}_{ij}(0) \cdot \vec{r}_{ik}(t) \right]^3}{r_{ij}^7(0) \cdot r_{ik}^7(t)} - \frac{9}{2} \frac{\vec{r}_{ij}(0) \cdot \vec{r}_{ik}(t)}{r_{ij}^5(0) \cdot r_{ik}^5(t)} > \cdot$$

$$< P_2 \cos\theta(t) >$$

where $P_2(x)$ us the second order Legendre polynomial and $\theta(t)$ is the angle swept out by the molecular axis in the time interval t. Therefore, the induced spectrum consists of the convolution between the free rotator spectrum $G_r(\nu_j)$ and the pure translational profile $G_t(\nu-\nu_j)$ given by the Fourier transform of

$$\sum_{i \neq j; i \neq k} < \frac{15}{2} \frac{\left[\vec{r}_{ij}(0) \cdot \vec{r}_{ik}(t) \right]^3}{r_{ij}^7(0) \, r_{ik}^7(t)} - \frac{9}{2} \frac{\vec{r}_{ij}(0) \cdot \vec{r}_{ik}(t)}{r_{ij}^5(0) \, r_{ik}^5(t)} > \left(\frac{\alpha Q}{4\pi\varepsilon_o}\right)^2 \cdot$$

Recalling that the rotational lines which arise from the same in-

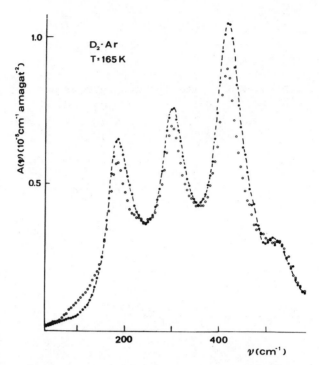

Fig. 1. Experimental absorption coefficients of D_2-Ar mixtures at
T=165K (• • • = 142 amagats; ○ ○ ○ = 665 amagats).

duction mechanism exhibit the same line shape and taking into
account the detailed balance principle we obtain the following relation

$$\Gamma(\nu) = \int_{-\infty}^{+\infty} \frac{G_R(\nu_j)}{(1+e^{-hc\nu_j/kT})} \cdot \frac{G_t(\nu - \nu_j)}{(1+e^{-hc(\nu-\nu_j)/kT})} \, d\nu_j \, , \qquad (2)$$

where $\Gamma(\nu) = A(\nu)/\nu(1-e^{-hc\nu/kT})$ and $A(\nu)$ is the measured absorption coefficient defined as

$$A(\nu) = \frac{1}{\ell \rho_{H_2} \rho_{Ar}} \, \ell n \left[I_o(\nu)/I(\nu) \right] \qquad (3)$$

where ℓ is the cell length, ρ_{H_2} and ρ_{Ar} are the densities of H_2 and
Ar respectively, and $I(\nu)$ and $I_o(\nu)$ are the intensities transmitted
with and without the sample, respectively. Since the free rotator
spectrum can be easily calculated, we can directly derive the pure
translational correlation function $C_t(t)$ from the measured $A(\nu)$.

In Fig. 1 we report the measured $A(\nu)$ at two different densi-

196

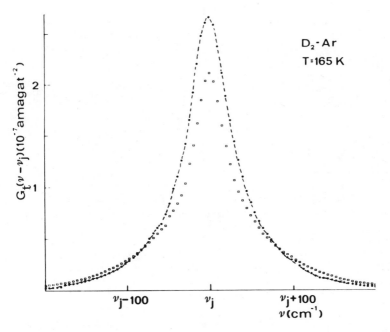

Fig. 2.   Experimental reduced lineshapes of the single rotational
line for D_2-Ar (• • • = 110 amagats; □□□ = 665 amagats).

ties for D_2-Ar mixtures. It is evident from the figure that with increasing density, the peaks narrow while the magnitude of the tails
increases. As evident in Fig. 2, the same density effects are much
more pronounced in the translational profiles $G_t(\nu-\nu_j)$, as obtained from the deconvolution of the experimental spectra. The deconvolution procedure, which takes into account also the small contributions to the spectrum due to the isotropic overlap induction mechanism, is discussed elsewhere (Buontempo et al., 1983).

To obtain a quantitative description of the density effects
with suitable parameters, it is convenient to perform the Fourier
transform of the measured $G_t(\nu-\nu_j)$ in order to derive the translational correlation function $C_t(t)$.

Fig. 3 shows the $C_t(t)$ as obtained at three different densities
in D_2-Ar mixtures. It is evident that the long time $C_t(t)$ decay is
exponential in shape at any density: therefore, it is possible to
define a characteristic time τ_t from the slope of $\ln C_t(t)$.
This characteristic time, which increases with increasing density,
is suitable to parametrize the density narrowing of the peak of the
translational profile $G_t(\nu-\nu_j)$.

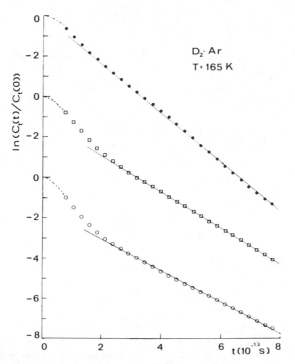

Fig. 3. Logarithmic plot of the normalized induced dipole moment
autocorrelation function $C_t(t)$ for D_2-Ar at T=165K
(● ● ● =110 amagats; □□□ =325 amagats; ○ ○ ○ =665 amagats).
The broken line at short times represents the portion of
$C_t(t)$ affected by the smoothing in the wings of the spectral profile. From the slope of the full straight lines
the characteristic times have been derived.

At short times $C_t(t)$ shows a rapidly decaying component, which
is negligible at low density and becomes increasingly significant
as the density increases. It is difficult to derive directly from
the measured $C_t(t)$ a parameter suitable to describe the rapidly
decaying component.

To derive information from the short time behaviour of $C_t(t)$
we try a different approach to the problem; the observed behaviour
of $C_t(t)$ suggests that the autocorrelation function can be represented by the sum of an exponential part and a rapidly decaying
component. This suggests that the translational line-shape $G_t(\nu-\nu_j)$
may be reproduced by a lorentzian peak superimposed on a broad component. In a previous analysis (Buontempo et al., 1983), in order
to describe the broad component, we have used a modified gaussian

$$\exp - \left[(\nu-\nu_j)/\nu_o \right]^2 \cdot \left[1+\varepsilon H_4 \left[(\nu-\nu_j)/\nu_o \right] \right]$$

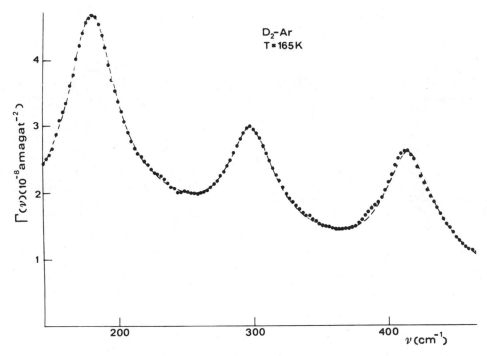

Fig. 4.   Experimental $\Gamma(\nu)$ of D_2–Ar at T=165K, ρ=665 amagats ($\bullet$ $\bullet$ $\bullet$) reproduced by Eq. (2), using the single line profile given by Eq. (3) ($---$).

where $H_4(x) = x^4 - 3x^2 + 3/4$ is the 4th order Hermite polynomial and ν_0 and ε are parameters. In those papers we have noted that the resulting fit is rather insensitive to large variation of the parameter ε. The value of the parameter ε affects the profile only in the high frequency region where large deconvolution errors are present. In order to reduce the number of the fit parameters, we prefer, as previously discussed (Buontempo et al., 1983), to model the broad component with a gaussian expression. Thus we use for $G_t(\nu - \nu_j)$ the following expression

$$G_t(\nu-\nu_j) = A\left[\frac{\delta^2}{\delta^2 + (\nu-\nu_j)^2} + f\,\exp-\left\{(\nu-\nu_j)/\nu_0\right\}^2\right] \text{ for } |\nu-\nu_j| \le p\delta$$

$$G_t(\nu-\nu_j) = A\left[B\,e^{-\frac{|\nu-\nu_j|/\nu^*}{}} + f\,\exp-\left\{(\nu-\nu_j)/\nu_0\right\}^2\right] \text{ for } |\nu-\nu_j| > p\delta$$

(3)

where B and ν^* are determined by the continuity requirement of the function and its derivative at $|\nu-\nu_j| = p\delta$, A, p, f, and ν_0 are adjustable parameters, and $\delta = 1/2\pi c\tau_t$ is obtained at any density from the long time decay of $C_t(t)$. The fit obtained by using Eq. (2) with $G_t(\nu-\nu_j)$ given by Eq. (3) is shown in Fig. 4.

Table 1. Values of δ, f, and ν_o for H_2-Ar and D_2-Ar.

H_2-Ar

ρ (amagat)[0]	δ (cm^{-1})	f	ν_o(cm^{-1})
90	44 ± 2	/	/
110	42 ± 2	.05 ± .05	130 ± 30
150	38 ± 2	.15 ± .05	130 ± 30
278	31 ± 2	.35 ± .05	150 ± 30
280	30 ± 2	.35 ± .05	130 ± 30
300	29 ± 2	.40 ± .05	150 ± 30
450	25 ± 2	.35 ± .05	180 ± 30
590	23 ± 2	.30 ± .05	180 ± 30
650	21 ± 2	.30 ± .05	180 ± 30

D_2-Ar

ρ (amagat)[0]	δ (cm^{-1})	f	ν_o(cm^{-1})
108	32 ± 1	.05 ± .05	130 ± 30
142	29 ± 1	.10 ± .05	130 ± 30
176	28 ± 1	.15 ± .05	120 ± 30
228	25 ± 1	.25 ± .05	120 ± 30
245	26 ± 1	.30 ± .05	120 ± 30
325	24 ± 1	.30 ± .05	120 ± 30
420	23 ± 1	.35 ± .05	120 ± 30
474	23 ± 1	.40 ± .05	120 ± 30
540	22 ± 1	.40 ± .05	120 ± 30
588	21 ± 1	.35 ± .05	150 ± 30
610	22 ± 1	.35 ± .05	130 ± 30
655	21 ± 1	.35 ± .05	130 ± 30

[0] The error in the calculated density of the system is less than 5%.

The values of the fit parameters ν_o and f, as well as the values of δ obtained from $C_t(t)$, are reported in Table 1 for the D_2-Ar mixtures. In the same table we report also the values of δ, ν_o and f obtained for H_2-Ar mixtures (Buontempo et al., 1983), by using the same procedure. We note that at low density the values of δ for the two isotopes are nearly proportional to the square root of the reduced mass of the colliding couple. This is the expected behaviour because at low density the motion of the couple is not affected by the medium (Buontempo et al., 1983). When the density increases, the values of δ decrease for both D_2-Ar and

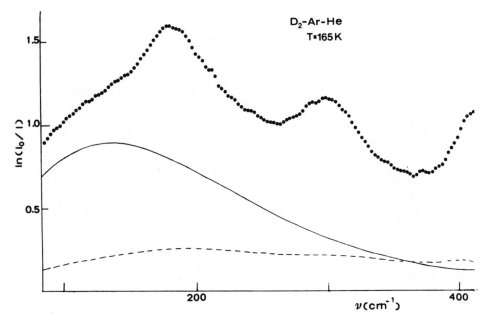

Fig. 5. Experimental absorption coefficient of D_2-Ar-He at T=165K and ρ=312 amagats ($\circ \circ \circ$). The full line and the broken line represent the contributions to the total spectrum of He-Ar and D_2-He, respectively.

H_2-Ar mixtures and they seem to reach the same value. The disappearance of the isotopic effect clearly indicates that at high density the long time decay process involves a many particle, correlated motion. On the contrary, the width of the broad component of the translational profile seems to be nearly density independent and also at high density its value scales with the square root of the masses. This fact indicates that at any density the broad component is related to the single particle motion. The relevance of this component increases with increasing density in the same way for the two systems (Buontempo et al., 1983).

D_2-Ar-He mixtures

As previously discussed, the translational component measured in D_2-Ar and H_2-Ar mixtures contains both two body and three body terms. Thus, the observed density effects can be attributed both to the cancellation between the two and three body terms of Eq. (1) and to the change of the two body component due to the change in the dynamics at high density. In order to derive the two body component we have performed a new experiment in a mixture of D_2 and Ar diluted by He.

201

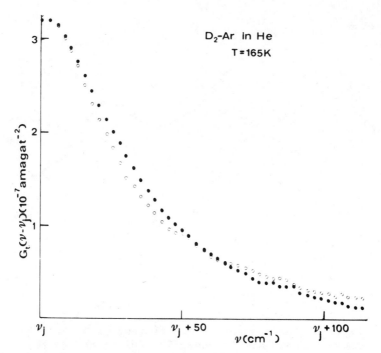

Fig. 6. Experimental reduced lineshapes of the single rotational
line for D_2-Ar in D_2-Ar-He ($\bullet\ \bullet\ \bullet$ = 217 amagats;
$\circ\ \circ\ \circ$ = 418 amagats).

For the three component mixture D_2-Ar-He, the total dipole
moment is given by

$$\vec{\mu} = \sum_{i \neq i'} \vec{\mu}_{ii'} + \sum_{ij} \vec{\mu}_{ij} + \sum_{ik} \vec{\mu}_{ik} + \sum_{jk} \vec{\mu}_{jk}$$

where i, j, k, run over the D_2, Ar, He, respectively. For dilute
solutions of D_2 the first term is negligible. Moreover, we assume,
as previously discussed, that the rotational and translational
motions are uncoupled and we study only low argon concentrations.
For these conditions, noting that the He atom has a polarizability
much smaller than argon, we can approximate the dipole moment autocorrelation function by

$$C_t(t) \cong \sum_{i \neq j} <\vec{\mu}_{ij}(0) \cdot \vec{\mu}_{ij}(t)> + \sum_{i, k \neq k'} <\vec{\mu}_{ik'}(0) \cdot \vec{\mu}_{ik}(t)> +$$

$$+ \sum_{j, k \neq k'} <\vec{\mu}_{jk}(0) \cdot \vec{\mu}_{jk'}(t)>$$

since the contribution to the measured spectrum of the other terms

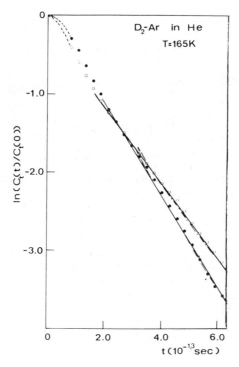

Fig. 7. Logarithmic plot of the normalized induced dipole moment
autocorrelation function $C_t(t)$ for D_2-Ar in D_2-Ar-He
(● ● ● =217 amagats; o o o =418 amagats). From the slope of
the full straight lines the characteristic times have been
derived. The broken lines represent the correlation function
$C_m(t)$, as obtained from the model.

is negligible for the experimental conditions we use (Birnbaum et
al., 1982).

In order to obtain from the measured spectrum the D_2-Ar absorption, we must subtract the D_2-He and Ar-He contributions. The latter
was measured under the same experimental conditions, while the D_2-He
spectrum, which does not contribute more than 20% to the total
absorption, can be evaluated from the data reported in the literature (Birnbaum et al., 1982). In Fig. 5 we present the total
spectrum of the three component mixture and the contributions to
be subtracted. The experimental procedure, as well as the details
of the analysis of the three components mixtures, will be presented
in forthcoming paper (Buontempo et al., 1984). From the pure two
body spectrum of D_2-Ar we can derive the translational component
$G_t(\nu-\nu_j)$ by the same analysis used in the D_2-Ar mixture. The
resulting $G_t(\nu-\nu_j)$ at two different densities are reported in Fig. 6
and the corresponding results for $C_t(t)$ are reported in Fig. 7. We
note that the density effect in the two body spectrum is to give a

Table 2. Values of δ, f, and ν_o for D_2-Ar in He.

ρ (amagat)[0]	δ (cm^{-1})	f	ν_o (cm^{-1})
217	32 ± 2	.02 ± .02	100 ± 30
312	28 ± 2	.10 ± .02	140 ± 30
418	26 ± 2	.12 ± .02	150 ± 30

[0] The error in the calculated density of the system is less than 5%.

narrowing of the peak with an increase of the tails of $G_t(\nu-\nu_j)$. These two effects reflect on the behaviour of $C_t(t)$ (see Fig. 7) as a slower exponential decay at long times and a faster decay at short times. The values of the parameters δ, ν_o and f, which are derived by following the same procedure used in the D_2-Ar case, are reported in Table 2. The density behaviour of δ, ν_o and f for the two body spectrum is similar to that observed in the total spectrum of D_2-Ar and H_2-Ar mixtures. This result indicates that also in those cases the density effects are essentially related to the change in the two body dynamics.

N_2 spectra

For a pure fluid the dipole moment autocorrelation function contains the two body and the three body terms, as well as the four body term. However, if we compare the pure N_2 absorption spectra with the absorption spectra of dilute solutions of N_2 in argon, we find that the two absorption coefficients are similar in shape (Buontempo et al., 1971). Moreover, taking into account the difference in polarizability of nitrogen and argon, the intensities also agree (Buontempo et al., 1979). Since in dilute mixtures of nitrogen in argon the dipoles induced in different couples ($i \neq j \neq k \neq \ell$) are not correlated, the four body term of $C(t)$ can be neglected. Moreover, the similarity of the two spectra indicates that the double transitions, which are absent in the mixture, are negligible in the case of pure N_2. This fact indicates that the effects of the anisotropy of the polarizability and of the potential are very small. According to the previous assumption, we use Eq. (1) for the $C(t)$ of N_2 and analyze the N_2 spectra following a procedure similar to that used in the previous cases. The details of the N_2 spectra analysis are reported elsewhere (Buontempo et al., 1983a). The single line profiles, derived from the experimental data, are shown in Fig. 8 at two different densities. In Table 3 we report the values of δ, ν_o and f. We note that the density effects are similar to those observed in the other systems we have studied.

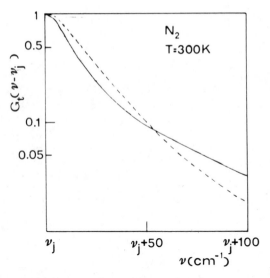

Fig. 8. The translational profiles at two different densities for the N_2 system at T=300K (- - - =55 amagats; ———=300 amagats).

For the analysis previously reported we have used the available experimental results for N_2 at 300 K and at densities ranging from 50 to 300 amagats. We have not analyzed in the same way the spectrum of liquid N_2 (Buontempo et al., 1971), because it is well known that at high density and low temperatures the anisotropy of the potential cannot be neglected (Sampoli et al., 1981). An attempt to calculate the rototranslational spectrum of liquid N_2 has been recently performed, taking into account also the anisotropy of the potential and qualitative agreement with the experimental results

Table 3. Values of δ, f, and ν_0 for the N_2 system.

ρ (amagats)[(0)]	δ (cm^{-1})	f	ν_0 (cm^{-1})
55	18 ± 2	.02 ± .02	110 ± 30
250	14 ± 2	.06 ± .02	100 ± 30
300	12 ± 2	.10 ± .02	100 ± 30

(0) The error in the calculated density of the system is less than 5%.

has been obtained (Guillot and Birnbaum, 1983, 1985).

MICROSCOPIC MODEL

The density behaviour of the measured $C_t(t)$ for each system considered here, suggests that in the low density limit, where only two body collisions are present, the autocorrelation function is essentially exponential in shape in the investigated time domain, so that a single time τ_o characterizes the phenomenon. From this characteristic time, which can be interpreted as the optical duration of a two body collision, we can obtain the value of the effective range R_o of the interaction from (Zaidi and Van Kranendonk, 1971).

$$R_o = \sqrt{<v^2>} \cdot \tau_o \tag{4}$$

where $<v^2> = 3KT/\mu$ is the mean square velocity and μ is the reduced mass of the colliding couple.

Two different characteristic times become well evident in the $C_t(t)$ when the density increases; this effect is qualitatively similar to that observed in the collision induced light scattering (CILS) experiments (Madden, 1978), as well as induced vibrational spectra (Madden and Cox, 1981, Madden and Tildesley, 1983). In all the cases the rapidly decaying part has been related to the rattling component of the motion of a molecule in a dense system, while the slow exponential decay reflects the diffusive motion at long times (An et al., 1979; Buontempo et al., 1983). As reported elsewhere (Buontempo et al., 1983a), the characteristic frequencies ν_o obtained from the fit of the broad component of the translational profile agree reasonably well with the rattling frequencies as calculated from the data reported in the literature. In spite of this agreement, we stress that the broad component cannot be interpreted as due uniquely to the rattling motion. In fact, this component also contains contributions from other short range induction mechanisms (Poll and Hunt, 1981) which we neglect in our analysis.

The experimental data clearly show that the long time decay of the translational correlation function is related to a many particle correlated motion. In discussing the microscopic origin of the transport coefficients, it has been shown that the density fluctuations play an important role in determining the dynamics of many correlated particles (Cohen and Turnbull, 1959; Ricci et al., 1977). We can expect that also in our case the long time decay is related to the appearance of density fluctuations on a distance scale of the order of the optical induction range R_o. The simplest model that we can suggest in order to describe the long time decay of $C(t)$ considers only two relevant conditions for the inducing molecule.
a) The free volume around the inducing molecule is larger than a characteristic volume V_o which is related to the range of the in-

duction mechanism. In this case, the time dependence of the induced dipole moment is due only to two body dynamics. Thus, the correlation function $C_a(t)$ is the same as in the low density limit and we have

$$C_a(t) \propto e^{-t/\tau_o}$$

b) The free volume around the inducing molecule is smaller than V_o. Thus, many particles are within the range R_o and the dynamics on a distance scale of the order of R_o involve many particles motions. Since at high density the measured correlation function is nearly exponential in shape at long times, we can assume

$$C_b(t) \propto e^{-t/\tau_1}$$

The parameter τ_1, which represents the duration of the induced dipole moment in the cluster, is determined by the relaxation of the concerted process. In principle, the value of τ_1 depends on the local density. Since R_o is smaller than the molecular diameter, the probability of having a local free volume appreciably smaller than V_o, is quite small, particularly at the triple point density ρ_t. Recalling that the measurements are performed at densities lower than in the triple point, we may model the experimental results by assuming τ_1 to be density independent.

Thus the translational autocorrelation function $C_m(t)$ can be expressed as

$$C_m(t) = A\, e^{-t/\tau_1} + B\, e^{-t/\tau_o}$$

where A and B represent the probability of having a local free volume smaller and larger than V_o, respectively. In order to give a numerical evaluation of $C_m(t)$ by using this model, we assume

$$V_o = \frac{4}{3}\, \pi\, R_o^3$$

and calculate the density fluctuation probability in the hard spheres approximation from

$$A = \frac{1}{V_F} \int_0^{V_o} e^{-V/V_F}\, dV \qquad \text{and } B = 1-A$$

where V_F is the mean free volume defined as $(1/n - \sigma^3/\sqrt{2})$. For the value of the induction range R_o for the different systems we use the data reported in the literature (Buontempo et al., 1975), derived from the low density spectroscopic measurements. The parameter τ_o is obtained from Eq. (4). Since no simple numerical evaluation of τ_1 is possible, we consider τ_1 as a free parameter in fitting the experimental results.

207

We note that $C_m(t)$ obtained with this model is not a single exponential. Nevertheless, in the time domain that is experimentally accessible, $C_m(t)$ given by our model decays nearly exponentially at long times and fits very well the long time decay of the experimental $C_t(t)$. In Fig. 7 we present the comparison between $C_m(t)$ and $C_t(t)$ for the D_2-Ar-He case. The agreement between $C_m(t)$ and $C_t(t)$ is good for all the systems considered here. The best fits of the measurements have been obtained with the following values for the parameter τ_1: $\tau_1 = 3.75 \times 10^{-13}$ sec for D_2-Ar and H_2-Ar mixtures, $\tau_1 = 3.01 \times 10^{-13}$ sec for D_2-Ar-He system, and $\tau_1 = 6.37 \times 10^{-13}$ sec for nitrogen. We note that the values of τ_1 as obtained for D_2-Ar and H_2-Ar systems coincide. This fact confirms that the process which determines τ_1 is related to a many particle, correlated motion.

From the computed $C_m(t)$ we can derive a characteristic time τ_m and thus $\delta_m = 1/2\pi c \tau_m$, which should be compared with the experimental $\delta = 1/2\pi c \tau_t$. In Fig. 9 we present the results obtained for D_2-Ar and H_2-Ar mixtures. Analogous results have been obtained for the other systems considered here; in all the cases the model reproduces very well the measured density behaviour of δ.

COMPARISON WITH DENSITY EFFECTS AS OBSERVED IN CILS SPECTRA

The similarity between the narrowing effect observed in the binary term as measured in D_2-Ar-He mixtures and that measured in D_2-Ar, H_2-Ar and N_2 systems suggests that, also in these last cases, the long time decay of $C_t(t)$ is related to the two body term of the translational correlation function.

As a matter of fact, we note that for this particular aspect the infrared spectra previously discussed and the CILS spectra in noble gases at high density behave differently. This happens because the dipole induced dipole (DID) mechanism, which is responsible for the CILS spectra, exhibits a weaker distance dependence than that of the quadrupolar induction mechanism, which is responsible for the infrared absorption. Indeed, as widely reported in the literature, the depolarized light scattering measurements in dense noble gases show at long times a large cancellation effect among the three terms due to the pair, triplet and quadruplet contributions (Ladd et al., 1979). Therefore the effect of the diffusive motion is hardly detectable from the total correlation function as derived from the CILS experiments.

In order to study the slow relaxation processes, molecular dynamics (MD) calculations of DID spectra of noble gases have been performed and the pair correlation function has been calculated (Ladd et al., 1979; Balucani et al., 1979; Balucani and Vallauri, 1979). From the long time decay of the pair correlation function we have derived the characteristic times τ_{MD} and thus the parameter $\delta_{MD} = 1/2\pi c \tau_{MD}$. Figure 10 shows the values of δ_{MD} obtained from the

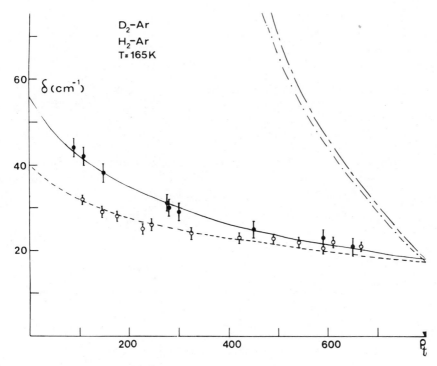

Fig. 9. The parameter δ versus ρ for D_2-Ar (o o o) and H_2-Ar
(• • •) systems. The full lines represent the δ_m behaviour
as obtained from the model. In the same figure we report
the values of δ_D for D_2-Ar (— · —) and for H_2-Ar (— - —)
as calculated from Eq. (5).

MD computations for argon at 300K at four different densities (Balucani et al., 1979; Balucani and Vallauri, 1979). In the same figure we also report the density dependence of δ_m as obtained from
our model; we have used for the induction range R_0^{DID} of the DID
mechanism the value $R_0^{DID} = 2.7$ Å, as calculated from Eq. (4)
by using for τ_0 the value $\tau_0 = 4.42 \times 10^{-13}$ sec. This value has been
derived from the zero density extrapolation of the CILS experiments
in argon at room temperature (Barocchi and Zoppi, 1980). As evident
from the figure the model gives a good description of δ_{MD}.

In conclusion, we note that the density dependence of δ is very
well reproduced by this simple model for infrared and computed two
body terms of CILS spectra. Indeed, in our opinion the model well
describes the density effect on the long time decay of C(t).

NARROWING EFFECT AND DIFFUSION COEFFICIENT

In the hypothesis that the long time decay of the translational
correlation function is related to the time evolution of the

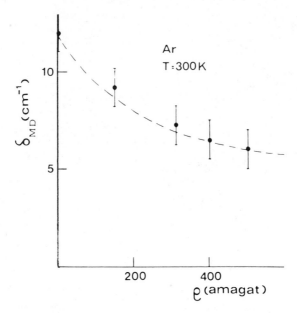

Fig. 10. Density effect of δ_{MD} obtained from the two body terms of CILS spectra (•) for argon at room temperature. The broken line represents δ_m as calculated by our model.

distance of two first neighbouring molecules, it is reasonable to expect that at high density δ is related to the induction range R_o by the expression (Zaidi and Van Kranendonk, 1971)

$$R_o^2 = 6D_r/2\pi c\delta \qquad (5)$$

where D_r is the relative diffusion coefficient, defined, as $D_r=D_a+D_b$, and D_a and D_b are the diffusion coefficients of the two interacting molecules. In fact, MD experiments have shown that at densities higher than the critical one we can consider the translational processes to be diffusive even at distances of the order of R_o (Rahman, 1964; Levesque and Verlet, 1970). The values of D_a and D_b can be derived from the diffusion coefficients of a Lennard-Jones fluid, as calculated from MD experiments (Levesque and Verlet, 1970). In order to evaluate the diffusion coefficient of the impurity in a mixture we have used an extension of the Macedo-Litovitz hybrid expression (Ricci et al., 1977) to take into account the differences in masses and Lennard-Jones parameters. Thus from Eq. (5) we can compute δ_D as a function of the density. The resulting values of δ_D for the D_2-Ar and H_2-Ar cases are shown in Fig. 9. This figure clearly indicates that the experimental δ seems to approach the value derived from

Eq. (5) only at the triple point density, while at densities lower than that one the experimental values are lower than those calculated from Eq. (5). The same discrepancy has been previously noted in the analysis of the CILS spectra of noble gases (An et al., 1979). For the other systems investigated no direct comparison between δ_D and the experimental value at ρ_t is possible, because the higher densities explored are much lower than ρ_t. Nevertheless, in these cases the values of δ at ρ_t extrapolated with the help of our model agree with the δ_D values, while their density dependence is strongly different.

To show the similarity between the four systems here discussed, we present in Fig. 11 δ/δ_m and δ/δ_D versus the reduced density ρ/ρ_t, in order to take into account the different values of masses, diameters and induction ranges for the different systems. We note that both these quantities behave in the same way for all the systems we have studied. Within the experimental errors, δ/δ_m is equal to one at any density, thus indicating that the proposed model well describes the observed density dependence of δ while δ/δ_D is strongly density dependent and approaches one at ρ_t.

The discrepancy between δ and δ_D could be related to the fact that the relative mean square displacement of a pair of molecules that are first neighbours at t=0 increases with time more slowly than predict by Eq. (5). However, the magnitude of such an effect as evaluated by MD calculations is too small to explain our results (Balucani et al., 1983). Moreover, by decreasing the density, the magnitude of this effect can be expected to decrease, while as evident from Fig. 11 the difference between δ and δ_D increases.

The discrepancy between δ and δ_D can be easily understood if we consider a fluid of hard spheres, where it is possible to define the free path of the molecule. It is evident that if the free path of the inducing molecule is longer than R_o, the contribution to δ is δ_o independently of the length of the free path, while the contribution to the diffusion coefficient is proportional to the length of the free path. At high densities, where the probability of having free paths longer than R_o is negligible, the molecular motion can be assumed diffusive even at distances of the order of R_o and thus δ and δ_D are similar. On lowering the density, the percentage of the free path longer than R_o increases and the diffusion coefficient gives an half-width much larger than that derived from the infrared experiments. In fact, MD calculations on hard spheres fluids (Alder and Einwohner, 1965) show that at ρ_t only a few percent of the free paths are longer than R_o, while on lowering the density the probability of having free paths longer than R_o strongly increases.

Since the concept of "collision" is not applicable in dense real fluids, the free path cannot be defined. Nevertheless, there are different criteria for dividing the trajectories into physical-

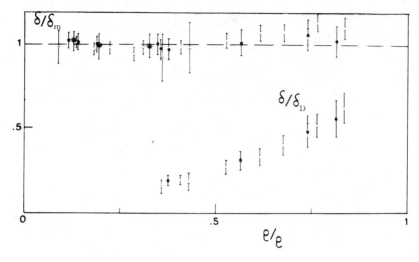

Fig. 11. Density behaviour of δ/δ_m and δ/δ_D for all systems here discussed. ($\bullet\ \bullet\ \bullet$: H_2-Ar at T=165K; $\circ\ \circ\ \circ$: D_2-Ar at T=165K; $\triangle\ \triangle\ \triangle$: N_2 at T=300K; $\ast\ \ast\ \ast$: D_2-Ar in D_2-Ar-He at T=165K).

ly meaningful subunits, which have the same physical meaning as the free path in the hard spheres fluids. MD experiments have been recently performed in Lennard-Jones fluids in order to derive the probability distribution of such "nearly free paths" (Murty and Singer, 1983). The results show also that in real fluids the probability of having nearly free paths longer than R_o is negligible at ρ_t, but strongly increases at lower densities.

CONCLUSIONS

The analysis presented here shows that it is possible to obtain from the induced absorption spectra of simple diatomic molecules parameters suitable to describe the density effects on the translational lineshape. In particular, from the long times decay of the translational correlation function we derive a characteristic time τ_t which reflects the observed narrowing effect of the rotational line. The density dependence of τ_t can be described by using a simple model. Moreover, the comparison of the results obtained in different systems suggests that the values of the parameter τ_t is related to the time evolution of the distance between pair of interacting molecules.

Molecular dynamics experiments using different induction ranges will be useful to test the model we propose and to clarify the relation between the diffusion and the long time decay of the translational correlation function. In order to give a detailed analysis of the density effects on the translational line-shape, theoretical treatments of the molecular motions in dense systems will be necessary, in addition to extensive measurements on different systems at various densities and temperatures.

ACKNOWLEDGEMENTS

The authors wish to thank F. P. Ricci, R. Vallauri, S. Cunsolo and P. A. Madden for many useful and stimulating discussions.

REFERENCES

Alder, B. J., and Einwohner, T., 1965, J. Chem. Phys., 43:3399

An, S. C., Fishman, L., Litovitz, T. A., and Montrose, C. J., 1979 J. Chem. Phys., 70:4626, and references therein

Bachet, G., Cohen, E. R., Dore, P., and Birnbaum, G., 1983, Can. J. Phys., 61:591

Balucani, U., Tognetti, V., and Vallauri, R., 1979, Phys. Rev., A 19:177

Balucani, U., Vallauri, R., 1979, Mol. Phys., 38:1115

Balucani, U., Vallauri, R., Murty, C. S., Gaskell, T., and Woolfson, M. S., 1983, J. Phys. Chem., 16:5605

Barocchi, F., and Zoppi, M., 1980, Intermolecular spectroscopy and dynamical properties of dense systems, Soc. Italiana di Fisica, Bologna, Italy

Birnbaum, G., Cohen, E.R., and Frommhold, L., 1982, J. Chem. Phys., 77:4933

Buontempo, U., Cunsolo, S., and Jacucci, G., 1971, Mol. Phys. 21:381

Buontempo, U., Cunsolo, S., Jacucci, G., and Weis, J.S., 1975, J. Chem. Phys., 63:2570

Buontempo, U., Cunsolo, S., Dore, P., and Maselli, P., 1979, Mol. Phys., 38:2111

Buontempo, U., Cunsolo, S., Dore, P., and Maselli, P., 1980, Intermolecular spectroscopy and dynamical properties of dense systems, Soc. Italiana di Fisica, Bologna, Italy

Buontempo, U., Cunsolo, S., Dore, P., and Maselli, P., 1981, Can. J. Phys., 59:1499

Buontempo, U., Codastefano, P., Cunsolo, S., Dore, P., and Maselli P., 1983, Can. J. Phys., 61:156

Buontempo, U., Maselli, P., and Nencini, L., 1983a, Can. J. Phys., 61:1498

Buontempo, U., et al., 1984, to be published

Cohen, M. H., and Turnbull, D., 1959, J. Chem. Phys., 31:1164

De Remigis, J., Mactaggart, J. W., and Welsh, H. L., 1971, Can. J. Phys., 49:381

Guillot, B., Bratos, S., Birnbaum, G., 1982, Phys. Rev., A25:773

Guillot, B., and Birnbaum, G., 1983, J. Chem. Phys., 79:686

Guillot, B., and Birnbaum, G., 1985, This volume

Keijser, R. A. J., Lombardi, J. R., Van Den Hout, K. D., Sanctuary, B. C., and Knapp, H. F. P., 1974, Physica 76:585

Keijser, R. A. J., Van Den Hout, K. D., De Groot, M., and Knaap, H. F. P., 1974a, Physica 75:515

Ladd, A. J. C., Litovitz, T. A., and Montrose, C. J., 1979, J. Chem. Phys., 71:4242

Levesque, D., and Verlet, L., 1970, Phys. Rev. A, 2:2514

Lewis, J. C., 1985, This volume

MacTaggart, J. W., De Remigis, J., and Welsh, H. L., 1973, Can. J. Phys., 51:1971

Madden, P. A., and Cox, T. I., 1981, Mol. Phys. 43:287

Madden, P. A., and Tildesley, D. J., 1983, Mol. Phys., 49:193

Murty, C. S., and Singer, K., 1983, Proc. R. Soc. Lond., A389:299

Poll, J. D., and Hunt, J. L., 1981, Can. J. Phys., 59:1448

Rahman, A., 1964, Phys. Rev. A, 136:405

Ricci, F. P., Ricci, M. A., and Rocca, D., 1977, J. Phys. Chem., 81:171

Sampoli, M., De Santis, A., and Nardone, M., 1981, Can. J. Phys. 59:1403

Van Kranendonk, J., and Gass, D. M., 1973, Can. J. Phys., 51:2428

Van Kranendonk, J., 1980, Intermolecular Spectroscopy and Dynamical Properties of Dense Systems, Soc. Italiana di Fisica, Bologna, Italy

Zaidi, H. R., and Van Kranendonk, J., 1971, Can. J. Phys., 49:385

INTERCOLLISIONAL INTERFERENCE - THEORY AND EXPERIMENT

John Courtenay Lewis

Physics Department
Memorial University of Newfoundland
St. John's, Newfoundland
A1B 3X7, Canada

ABSTRACT

This paper presents a review of all aspects of intercollisional interference, with emphasis on recent development. Both experiment and theory are discussed. The review concludes with a survey of important unresolved problems connected with intercollision interference.

INTRODUCTION

This paper constitutes a review of the current state of knowledge of the intercollisional interference effect, both of the phenomena as revealed by experimental investigation and of the theoretical approaches which have been used to understand it. It is appropriate to undertake such a review at the present time, as collision-induced absorption has been known now for thirty-five years[1], and Van Kranendonk's explanation of intercollisional interference is seventeen years old, so that the field has achieved a certain maturity; and yet is at present receiving ever-increasing interest.

The theory of intercollisional interference has been the subject of two earlier reviews, by Lewis (1980a) and by Van Kranendonk (1980). However, these concentrate on the basic principles of intercollisional interference, and on the kinetic theory developed jointly

---

[1] Welsh (1974) gives a good account of the development of collision-induced absorption up to 1974.

by Lewis and Van Kranendonk. In this paper, therefore, those topics will be only lightly touched upon. Later theoretical developments will be discussed in more detail, as will relevant computer simulations. In addition, experimental work specifically relating to intercollisional interference will be reviewed, I think for the first time. In the conclusion I will survey some of the important unresolved problems in the study of intercollisional interference.

The paper is organized on a quasichronological basis, although where theoretical and experimental developments overlapped they are usually treated separately. Also, the selection of the figures is non-chronological.

1. OBSERVATION OF INTERCOLLISIONAL INTERFERENCE, 1950'S
(Welsh and coworkers)

The recognition of a peculiar feature near the hydrogen fundamental vibrational frequency in the fundamental band of hydrogen collision-induced spectra goes back almost to the very beginning of the subject. In the first published work on H_2-rare gas mixtures, Crawford, Welsh, MacDonald and Locke (1950) noted the apparent presence of an unexplained "component X" at about 4100 cm^{-1}. More detailed studies by Chisholm and Welsh (Chisholm 1952, Chisholm and Welsh 1954) soon elucidated the main features of the phenomenon of intercollisional interference - the deep dip about the fundamental frequency, which broadens approximately linearly with increasing perturber density. This work was extended to higher densities - 5000 atm. - by Hare and Welsh (1958).

A diminution of intensity in the fundamental band about the vibrational frequency of the molecule was noted, and recognized as requiring explanation, in the earliest work on H_2. The dip was resolved and thoroughly studied over the next decade. It was then observed in deuterium (Reddy and Cho 1965b) and in deuterium-rare gas mixtures (Pai, Reddy and Cho 1966).

It was found in H_2-rare gas mixtures that the dip goes nearly to zero and that it broadens approximately linearly with increasing density. Fig. 1 shows the dip in D_2-He (for a change) over a range of densities (Pai, Reddy and Cho 1966); Fig. 2 shows the dip as it appears in an excellent spectrum from John Mactaggart's thesis (1977). Figures 3 show the fundamental band of hydrogen in H_2 - Ar mixtures (De Remegis 1971b). Fig. 3a shows the spectrum as it appears at low densities (essentially as in Fig. 2) with the dip not resolved and the lines from the van der Waals complexes in evidence; Fig. 3b shows the dip in a liquid mixture, with the central unsplit $Q_1(1)$ peak much in evidence, while Fig. 3c shows the fate of the dip in the solid.

216

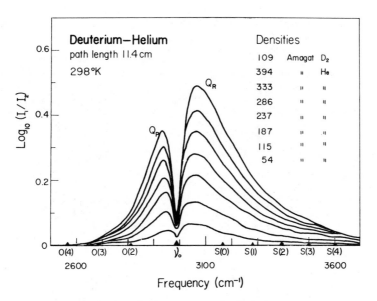

Fig. 1.   Intercollisional interference dips in the fundamental band
of D_2-He (after Pai, Reddy and Cho 1966).

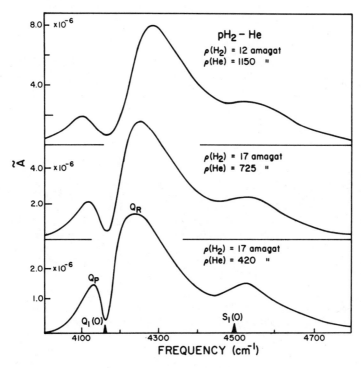

Fig. 2.   The fundamental band of pH_2-He (after Mactaggart 1971).

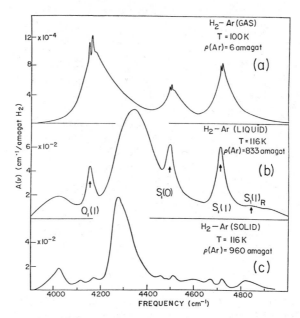

Fig. 3. The fundamental band of H_2-Ar; Fig. 3a, at low densities; Fig. 3b, in the liquid phase; Fig. 3c in the solid phase (after Mactaggart 1971).

The dip about the fundamental frequency is also known in N_2, from the work of Reddy and Cho (1965a). Fig. 4a shows the N_2-H_2 spectrum around the fundamental band, while Fig. 4b shows the enhancement due to H_2; a weak dip is evident. The dip is more pronounced, or at any rate cleaner, with He as the perturber (Figs. 5a and 5b). The effect is apparently absent or profoundly modified with Ar as the perturber (Figs. 6a and 6b), with a pronounced peak being present about the fundamental frequency, rather than a dip.

Identification of the intercollisional interference effect in far-infrared pure translational spectra came much later (Marteau, Vu and Vodar 1968, 1979); in fact, clear identification at moderately low densities (Cunsolo and Gush 1972) was subsequent to the first theoretical work on intercollisional interference; see also section 9 below.

2. EXPLANATION OF INTERCOLLISIONAL INTERFERENCE IN TERMS OF UNDERLYING FORCE CORRELATIONS, 1967-68. (Van Kranendonk)

The accepted explanation of intercollisional interference was first given in 1967 by J. Van Kranendonk (1967, 1968) as due to a time correlation in the intermolecular force on a molecule or group of molecules. Van Kranendonk developed his explanation after becoming

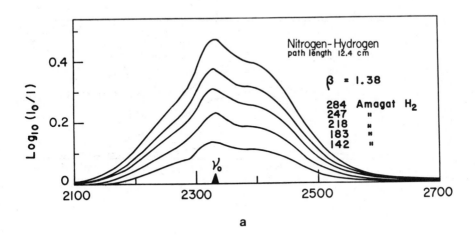

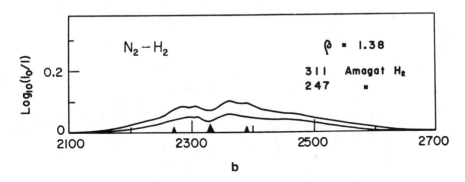

Fig. 4. The fundamental band of N_2-H_2; Fig. 4a, the N_2-H_2 fundamental; Fig. 4b, the enhancement (after Reddy and Cho 1965a). The "enhancement spectrum" is the difference between the absorption actually observed in the N_2 mixture and the absorption which would be observed in the same quantity of pure N_2.

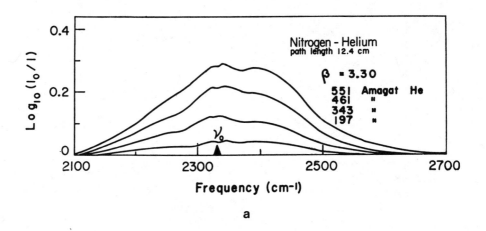

a

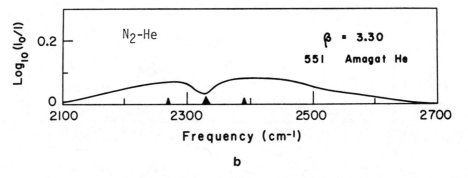

b

Fig. 5. The fundamental band of N_2-He; Fig. 5a, the N_2-He fundamental; Fig. 5b, the enhancement (after Reddy and Cho 1965a).

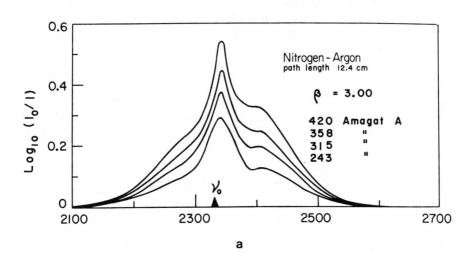

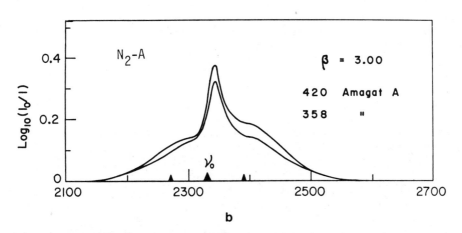

Fig. 6. The fundamental band of N_2-Ar; Fig. 6a, the N_2-Ar fundamental; Fig. 6b, the enhancement (after Reddy and Cho 1965a).

acquainted with some work of E. M. Purcell, who showed, in the context of a study (Purcell 1960) of nuclear electric dipole relaxation, that even at low densities the force pulses experienced by a molecule in a fluid cannot be treated as uncorrelated. The correlation is such that the power spectrum of the net intermolecular force on a molecule or group of molecules goes to zero at zero frequency; or, in time language, the autocorrelation function has a negative tail equal in area to the positive peak about zero lag[2]. Furthermore, the characteristic time for the decay of the negative tail, at least at low densities, is the mean time between collisions. Consequently, the negative tail in the autocorrelation function is shorter, and the dip in the power spectrum broader, the higher the density (Fig. 7).

As a point of notation, Van Kranendonk expressed the lineshape function in the region of the dip in the form

$$G(\omega) = \frac{1-\gamma+\omega^2\tau_c^2}{1+\omega^2\tau_c^2} \ G_{intra}(0) \tag{1}$$

Here τ_c is essentially the mean free time (more precisely it is the reciprocal of the mean collision frequency), and $G_{intra}(0)$ is the value which the lineshape function would assume at zero frequecny in the absence of any correlation among successive collisions. Hence the ratio of $G(0)$, the dip minimum, to $G_{intra}(0)$ is $1-\gamma$. A dip which goes exactly to zero, is given by $\gamma = 1$, while the absence of a dip is expressed by $\gamma = 0$. This somewhat confusing notation has been largely accepted by experimentalists.

The basic correctness of Van Kranendonk's picture received confirmation from the work of the Toronto group (McKellar 1968, McKellar, Mactaggart and Welsh 1975), who showed in a series of careful measurements on the Q branch of pH_2-He that the central frequency of the dip goes accurately to the unperturbed transition frequency of the H_2 molecule as perturber density goes to zero (see also section 4.5 below).

3. DEVELOPMENT OF A KINETIC THEORY OF INTERCOLLISIONAL INTERFERENCE, 1968-1971. (Lewis and Van Kranendonk)

The present author, working initially with J. Van Kranendonk,

---

[2] For the power spectrum to be zero at zero frequency, it is sufficient, but not necessary, that the system should be in thermal equilibrium (Lewis 1980a). The necessary conditions have not been explored; however, consideration of special cases leads one to the conclusion that the phenomenon is robust, so that a system may depart considerably from equilibrium and still show perfect negative correlation. In particular, it is not necessary for the diffusion coefficient to exist.

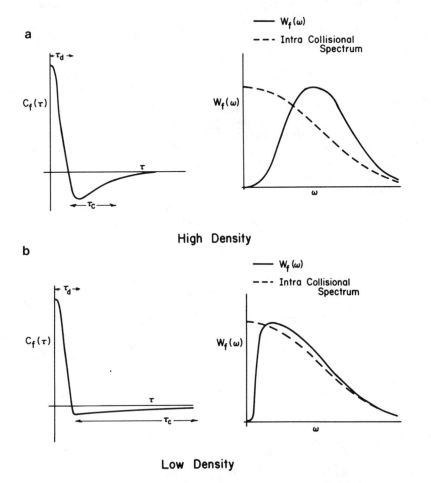

Fig. 7. Autocorrelation function and power spectrum of the net
intermolecular force on a molecule in an equilibrium fluid:
Fig. 7a, at low densities; Fig. 7b, at high densities. The
quantity τ_c is a time which is characteristic of the time
between collisions, and which is approximately proportional
to the density; τ_d is characteristic of the duration of a
collision, and is independent of the density. The intracollisional spectrum is that which could obtain if successive collisions were perfectly uncorrelated.

developed a kinetic theory of intercollisional interference applicable in gases at low and moderate densities. The theory was derived by Lewis (1971) and Lewis and Van Kranendonk (1972a), extended and applied by Lewis (1972, 1973, 1976, 1983 and 1985) and by Lewis and Van Kranendonk (1972b); and reviewed in some detail by Lewis (1980a).

The Principal Assumptions of the Kinetic Theory

The principal assumptions of the theory are:

1. The intermolecular force and induced dipole moment are pairwise additive with central pair force and pair induced dipole moment.

2. If the collisional history of a given molecule is followed, not only are ternary collisions and collisions of higher order negligible, but the density is sufficiently low that each binary collision is complete before the next begins, so that the time series of the dipole moment induced by each molecule can be expressed as the superposition of isolated (but not independent) binary collisions. This was called the "temporal superposition approximation" by Lewis and Van Kranendonk.

3. The intervals between successive collisions of a molecule are independently randomly distributed, with exponential distribution. Except in the Lorentz gas, it is usually additionally assumed that the collision frequency is velocity-independent, so that the collision times[3] of any given molecule form a homogeneous Poisson process. However, the theory in its most fully-developed form assumes that collision frequencies are velocity-dependent.

4. The gas mixture is infinitely dilute in one component. In vibrational transitions in pure hydrogen, the theory is applicable to single transitions in which the molecule making the transition plays the role of the infinitely dilute species.

Principal results of the theory

For definiteness let us call the dilute species A, and the other B. The principal result of the theory is an expression for the lineshape function which is valid in the neighborhood of the interference dip:

$$G(\omega) = \bar{\nu}_c \int_0^\infty dc_1 \, P(c_1) \, \{K(c_1) - 2\mathrm{Re} \, \frac{\nu_c(c_1)}{\nu_c(c_1)+i\omega} \, A(c_1)Q_c(\omega,c_1)\} \quad (2)$$

---

[3] The time of collision is defined as the time of closest approach of a colliding pair of molecules; this definition can be applied to soft interactions as well as to hard disks and spheres.

where $\bar{\nu}_c$ is the mean collision frequency of the molecule of type A with the B molecules, and $\nu_c(c_1)$ is the collision frequency of molecule A at speed c_1 with the B molecules; $P(c_1)$ is the probability density for AB collisions with A's initial speed being c_1; $K(c_1)$ is the intracollisional spectrum at zero frequency, per collision, with initial speed c_1; $A(c_1)$ is the mean projection of the integrated dipole moment induced by collisions with initial speeds c_1 on the velocity $\vec{c}_1$ of A before the collision; and $Q(\omega,c_1)$ is the solution to the integral equation

$$Q_c(\omega,c_1) = A(c_1) + \int_0^\infty dc_1' \; \frac{\nu_c(c_1')}{\nu_c(c_1')+i\omega} \; \Delta(c_1'|c_1)Q_c(\omega,c_1'). \quad (3)$$

The kernel $\Delta(c_1'|c_1)$ is a measure of the persistence of A's velocity in a collision with initial and final speeds c_1 and c_1' respectively. Expressions for $K(c_1), A(c_1)$, and $\Delta(c_1'|c_1)$ are given by Lewis (1972, 1980a).

If the dependence of $\nu_c(c_1)$ on c_1 is assumed to be insignificant, then eqs. (2) and (3) simplify to

$$G(\omega) = \bar{\nu}_c \int_0^\infty dc_1 \; P(c_1) \; \{K(c_1)-2\text{Re}\; \frac{\bar{\nu}_c}{\bar{\nu}_c + i\omega} \; A(c_1)Q(\omega,c_1)\} \quad (2a)$$

where $Q(\omega,c_1)$ is the solution of the integral equation

$$Q(\omega,c_1) = A(c_1) + \frac{\bar{\nu}_c}{\bar{\nu}_c + i\omega} \int_0^\infty dc_1' \; \Delta(c_1'|c_1)Q(\omega,c_1'). \quad (3a)$$

A further simplification can be obtained if it is assumed that the persistence-of-velocity kernel $\Delta(c_1'|c_1)$ acts as a delta-function. While this is a drastic approximation, the one detailed calculation which has been performed to date (Lewis 1971, 1972) indicates that it does not lead to gross errors in the present context.

$$\Delta(c_1'|c_1) \cong \tilde{\Delta} \; \delta(c_1'-c_1) \quad (4)$$

$\tilde{\Delta}$ is then a weighted average of $\Delta(c_1'|c_1)$. A simple choice of weighting leads to a $\tilde{\Delta}$ which is identical to the mean persistence-of-velocity ratio defined by Chapman and Cowling (1982). In any case, substitution of eq. (4) into eqs. (2a) and (3a) leads to an expression for γ,

$$\gamma = \frac{2\bar{A}^2}{\bar{K}(1-\tilde{\Delta})} \quad (5)$$

and for the lineshape function in the region of the interference dip,

$$G(\omega) = \left[1 - \frac{1}{1+[\omega/\bar{\nu}_c(1-\tilde{\Delta})]^2} \right] \bar{\nu}_c \bar{K}. \tag{2b}$$

Here

$$\bar{K} = \int_0^\infty dc_1 \, K(c_1)$$

and

$$\overline{A^2} = \int_0^\infty dc_1 \, A(c_1)^2.$$

The expression (2b) for the lineshape function is of the same form as eq. (1), Van Kranendonk's expression, remembering that $\tau_c = 1/\bar{\nu}_c$, except for the factor $1-\tilde{\Delta}$ in the halfwidth. Thus the halfwidth of the interference dip as given by eq. (2b) is

$$\omega_{1/2} = \bar{\nu}_c \, (1-\tilde{\Delta}) \tag{6}$$

The persistence-of-velocity correction $\tilde{\Delta}$ is quite significant for the dips in the Q branches of $H_2 - He$ and $H_2 - H_2$ (see section 4.1 below). In systems where the mass dissimilarity is greater, the accuracy of experimental work to date has not warranted the application of this correction in curve-fitting.

The Dip is Negative at all Frequencies

It will be seen that the interference dip as given by the approximate expression, eq. (2b), is always negative and negative at all frequencies. A detailed analysis shows that such is also the case for the interference dip as given by the more accurate expression, eqs. (2) and (2a); the kernel of the integral equations (3) and (3a) is positive definite. Now it is well-known experimentally that the ternary absorption coefficient may be of either sign; and, according to theory (Van Kranendonk 1957, 1959), it can be represented as the sum of two terms of opposite sign and the same order of magnitude (together with a third weaker term). The first of these terms, the intermolecular force effect in Van Kranendonk's terminology, comes from the density dependence of the pair correlation function, and is positive. The second, called by Van Kranendonk the cancellation effect, is negative, and is identifiable with the intercollisional interference effect. The third, smaller effect comes from the nonadditive three-body contribution to the induced dipole moment. The kinetic theory, as would be expected, gives the cancellation effect but not the intermolecular force effect. In fact the cancellation effect can be regarded as the integrated form of the intercollisional effect.

The Lorentz Gas

The Lorentz gas being simpler than a gas with arbitrary mass ratio, the kinetic theory can be taken farther than in the general case. For example, the ansatz (4) is exact for the Lorentz gas. For example, the speed variation of the collision frequency has been included in calculations of the dip lineshape. The result shows small deviations from the Lorentzian lineshape (see Lewis 1971 and Lewis and Van Kranendonk 1972):

$$G(\omega) \propto \omega^2 \, e^{\omega^2} \, E_3(\omega^2) \tag{7}$$

where E_3 is the exponential integral

$$E_3(x) = \int_1^\infty t^{-3} \, e^{-xt} \, dt.$$

More important, the lineshape at zero frequency has a simple closed form; for a monoenergetic Lorentz gas in two dimensions, it is

$$G(0) = \frac{\nu_c}{4c_1^2(1-\Delta)\sigma_c^2} \int_0^{\sigma_c} db \int_0^{\sigma_c} db' \, [\bar{\mu}(b)c(b') - \bar{\mu}(b')c(b)]^2 \tag{8}$$

where c_1 is the speed of the light particle at infinite separation from any of the fixed scatterers; b (and b') is the impact parameter for a collision, σ_c is the cutoff for integration over the impact parameter, ν_c is the collision frequency for a collision diameter of σ_c, and $\bar{\mu}(b)$ and $c(b)$ are time integrals of the induced dipole moment and force respectively, which are termed the "(time) integrated induced dipole moment" and "momentum transfer". To be precise, $\bar{\mu}(b)$ is the integral with respect to time of the dipole moment induced in an isolated binary collision with speed c_1 and impact parameter b, projected on the apse of the collision; $c(b)$ is obtained by integrating the force for the same binary collision, forming the projection of the integral on the apse, and dividing the result by the mass of the light particle. It is clear that if the induced dipole moment and force are proportional to each other, then $\bar{\mu}(b) \propto c(b)$ and the spectral density G is zero at zero frequency. The converse can also be demonstrated starting from this expression (see section 5 below).

The above equation can be written in an interesting alternative form. Introduce the inner product

$$(\phi,\psi) = \int_0^{\sigma_c} \phi(b)\psi(b)db \qquad (9)$$

and define the normalized integrated induced dipole moment and momentum transfer $\tilde{\mu}(b)$ and $\tilde{c}(b)$ respectively, to be

$$\tilde{\mu}(b) = \bar{\mu}(b)/(\bar{\mu},\bar{\mu})^{\frac{1}{2}}$$

$$\tilde{c}(b) = c(b)/(c,c)^{\frac{1}{2}}$$

Then the integrals in eq. (8) can be written as

$$G(0) = \frac{\nu_c}{2c_1{}^2(1-\Delta)\sigma^2{}_c} (c,c)(\bar{\mu},\bar{\mu}) [1 - (\tilde{c},\tilde{\mu})^2] \quad .$$

With a little further manipulation, this can be written as

$$G(0) = \frac{\nu_c}{4c_1{}^2(1-\Delta)\sigma^2{}_c} (c,c)(\bar{\mu},\bar{\mu}) [1 + (\tilde{c},\tilde{\mu})](\tilde{c}-\tilde{\mu},\tilde{c}-\tilde{\mu}), \qquad (10)$$

which is probably the form of the kinetic-theory expression for $G(0)$ which shows most clearly the manner in which differences between $c(b)$ and $\bar{\mu}(b)$ lead to filling-in of the interference dip, and thus express the spoiling of correlation resultant from nonproportionality of the force and induced dipole moment.

If $\tilde{c}-\tilde{\mu} = \delta$, where $\delta(b)$ is a function small with respect to 1, then eq. (10) shows that

$$G(0) \propto (c,c)(\bar{\mu},\bar{\mu})(\delta,\delta) + O(\delta^3)$$

This shows that if c and $\bar{\mu}$ have similar dependencies on the impact parameter b, the dip will be deep

Intercollisional Interference at Very Low Densities

At densities sufficiently low that the mean free path is comparable to the wavelengths of light taking part in a collision-induced transition, it is no longer valid to describe that transition as an electric dipole one if intercollisional interference is taken into account. The consequences are discussed briefly by Lewis (1971): qualitatively, as the density decreases, the dip shifts, departs from Lorentzian shape, and fills in. However, these changes have never been worked out quantitatively. Experimentally, the collision-induced fundamental bands of pure hydrogen and hydrogen mixtures are dominated by the line spectra of the van der Waals complexes at the requisite densities.

3.1. Application to Light Scattering

Lewis and Van Kranendonk (1970, 1972b); see also Lewis 1971 and 1980a) extended their kinetic theory to describe time correlations in the collision-induced anisotropy in the polarizability responsible for collision-induced light scattering. As the polarizability is tensorial rather than vectorial, the interference is constructive rather than destructive, and in that way resembles intracollisional interference in HD - perturber mixtures, which is a scalar interference phenomenon. To sum the infinite series of collisional correlations it was necessary to ignore four-body correlations. As the integrated induced anisotropy varies more rapidly with angle than the integrated induced dipole moment, the correlations among successive collisions are weaker in light scattering than in light absorption. The line-shape expressions were evaluated making the ansatz analogous to eq. (4) and by assuming that the time-integrated induced anisotropy depends on the collision parameters only through the momentum transfer in the collision, and is proportional to the momentum transfer. The resulting peak height is 25% of the intracollisional height. The analogous assumption about the integrated induced dipole moment in light absorption of course gives a 100% dip, and is realistic at temperatures above 80 K. Owing to the long-range character of the induced anisotropy, the assumption of isolated binary collisions will be true only at very low densities; the assumption about the relation-ship between the integrated induced anisotropy and the momentum transfer is probably a poor one. In any event intercollisional interference has not been observed to date in collision-induced light scattering, despite careful observation of scattered spectra close to the exciting lines.

4. EXPERIMENTAL WORK OF Mactaggart, De Remegis, McKellar AND Welsh, ca. 1968-1971.

An important body of experimental work in collision-induced absorption was carried out by three graduate students of H. L. Welsh in the late 1960's. While this was by no means confined to inter-collisional interference (their work included the first high-resolution study of the van der Waals complexes and the discovery of pressure narrowing, to mention a few other subjects), it was important for the theory. While much of this work has been published (Mactaggart and Welsh 1973; McKellar, Mactaggart and Welsh 1975), a good deal of it has not (particularly some of the beautiful experi-mental work of John Mactaggart), and is to be found only in the original theses[4] (McKellar 1968; De Remegis 1971b; Mactaggart 1971).

---

[4] These citations are of course intended to cover only the authors' work related to intercollisional interference; they are not otherwise comprehensive.

4.1. Confirmation of the Kinetic Theory, Including the Persistence-of Velocity Effect

Mactaggart (Mactaggart 1971; Mactaggart and Welsh 1973) studied the intercollisional interference dips in the Q branches of the fundamental bands of gas-phase H_2 - He, H_2 - Ar, H_2 - Xe, while De Remegis (1971b) studied hydrogen in liquid Ar, Kr and Xe and in the same gases a little above their critical points. They compared their observations with the kinetic theory of Lewis and Van Kranendonk using a hard sphere model to calculate the collision frequencies and the persistence of velocity. The gas-phase observations were in good agreement in the density ranges where the halfwidths are linear functions of density. The persistence-of-velocity effect is significant in H_2 - He; good agreement between observation and theory was obtained when it was properly taken into account but not otherwise. The liquid-phase results agreed

a): where the kinetic-theory dip lineshape adequately described the observed dip (see section 4.4 below);

b): at the lowest available liquid densities; at higher densities there were systematic deviations.

The experimental halfwidths showed significant deviations from linearity at moderately high perturber densities - above about 700 Amagat for H_2 - He and above about 250 Amagat for H_2 - Xe, with intermediate values for Ar and Kr. These deviations were usually positive - the one exception in their work is H_2 - He at 298 K; that is, the halfwidths were greater at such densities than those predicted by the kinetic theory.

Mactaggart and De Remegis modified the kinetic theory by using a high-density correction to the collision frequency derived by H.H. Thorne[5] for hard spheres. This improved the agreement between theory and experiment somewhat, although the halfwidths so calculated underestimate the nonlinearity actually observed.

In sum, the experimental results of McKellar, Mactaggart, De Remegis and Welsh indicate that the kinetic theory of Lewis and Van Kranendonk is correct in the density ranges for which its assumptions are valid.

4.2. Observation of Interference Dips in S Lines

A weak dip near the fundamental frequency of the $S_1(1)$ line was first observed by Hunt and Welsh (1964) in H_2 - He, and similar dips were observed in the same line of the H_2 - Ne enhancement spectrum by

---

[5] Thorne (Chapman and Cowling 1972) used the Enskog equation generalized for mixtures.

Reddy and Lee (1968), and by Prasad and Reddy (1976) in HD - Ne. However, systematic studies of the phenomenon were first carried out by John Mactaggart (Poll, Hunt and Mactaggart 1975), again in H_2 - He. His spectra are were of sufficiently high resolution to show the characteristic increase in dip width with increasing perturber density. A theoretical treatment of the phenomenon was given by Poll, Hunt and Mactaggart (1975), and is summarized in section 6 below.

4.3. Dip Shifting

Collisions of molecules with perturbers alter their frequencies. This is of course one of the mechanisms leading to line broadening of allowed transitions. In collision-induced vibrational absorption, it leads to shifting of the intercollisional interference dip, as well as to overall displacement of the S and Q branches. The shift of the interference dip was carefully studied by John Mactaggart (1971) in H_2 -- He, H_2 - Ar, H_2 - Kr and H_2 - Xe. His results are summarized in Fig. 8. He found that the shift was linear in perturber density at sufficiently low densities (1000 Amagat for He, 400 Amagat for Ar, 300 Amagat for Kr and 200 Amagat for Xe), going to zero (McKellar 1968) as the perturber density went to zero. The latter fact was initially thought to be paradoxical, as a collision-induced spectrum is formed entirely by emissions and absorptions from molecules in collision, so that the vibrational and rotational frequencies are always perturbed while being observed. This paradox was resolved by Lewis, who extended the kinetic theory of intercollisional interference to take into account phase shifting of the vibrational frequency. The shifting is accompanied by an asymmetry between the low-frequency and the high-frequency wings of the spectrum. See sections 7, 11 and 15 below.

4.4. Change in Form of Dip at High Densities

De Remegis noted in his thesis (1971b) that the intercollisional interference dip in the fundamental band of hydrogen-rare gas mixtures is no longer accurately described by a Lorentzian at liquid densities. Although a Gaussian dip proved more satsifactory than the Lorentzian form (De Remegis 1971a), the most satisfactory fits were obtained with the following lineshape:

$$
G(\omega) = \frac{\left(\dfrac{\omega^2}{\omega_0^2}\right)\tau\Phi(0)}{\left[1 - \dfrac{\omega^2}{\omega_0^2}\right]^2 + \omega^2\tau^2}
\tag{11}
$$

where ω is the frequency displacement from the fundamental frequency. This expression had in fact been obtained by Desai and Yip (1968) in their treatment of the velocity autocorrelation function and

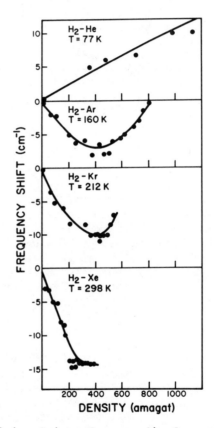

Fig. 8.   Intercollisional interference dip frequency shifts observed for four gas systems (after Mactaggart 1971).

the incoherent neutron scattering function[6]. Desai and Yip derived
eq. (11) using P. C. Martin's correlation function formalism, together
with a quite arbitrary truncation procedure. It had also been
obtained earlier by Berne, Boon and Rice (1966) using a memory function formalism, and an equally arbitrary truncation procedure. These
two formalisms are of course equivalent to each other, and to the
Zwanzig-Mori formalism, which Guillot, Bratos and Birnbaum have used
to extend the above expression (see section 12 below)[7].

In these approaches, it is found that τ is proportional to the
diffusion coefficient of a hydrogen molecule in the rare gas, and ω_0^2
is related to the mean square force acting on the hydrogen. Neither
Desai and Yip nor Berne et al. attempted to estimate these parameters
from first principles, although the former compared their expression
with molecular-dynamics simulations of liquid Ar. A succinct account
of their work, including application to inelastic neutron scattering
from hydrogen in liquid Ar, can be found in Desai and Yip (1969).

The physical picture underlying the above expression is that the
hydrogen molecule is an oscillating particle, with frequency ω_0, for
short times, but undergoes diffusive motion on a longer time scale.
Such a model has been referred to as an "itinerant oscillator" in the
literature of neutron scattering.

De Remegis used the above lineshape to fit the whole Q branch of
hydrogen in liquid Ne at 30 K, and of hydrogen in liquid Ar at 86 K
and 137 K. He used $\Phi(0)$, τ and ω_0 as arbitrary parameters, though his
fitted values of τ were checked against neutron scattering data. He
obtained good agreement, except in the high frequency wing, for Ne at
30 K and Ar at 86 K, but poor agreement for Ar at 137 K. However, for
the liquid Ar, he obtained good agreement using the kinetic theory
together with the Levine-Birnbaum lineshape to give both dip and the
band envelope.

As noted in section 4.1 above, at perturber densities of several
hundreds of Amagat, but low enough for the dip profile to be
Lorentzian, both Mactaggart and De Remegis found (De Remegis 1971b,
Mactaggart 1971, Mactaggart and Welsh 1973) the dip halfwidth became
a nonlinear function of the density.

4.5. The Intercollisional Interference Dip Fills in at Low Temperatures

In H_2 - He the interference dip partially fills in at low
temperatures (McKellar, Mactaggart and Welsh 1975). At a temperature

---

[6] They refer to it as the "interpolation model".

[7] In their later work, Desai and Yip (1969) explicitly use Zwanzig-
Mori formalism to derive the velocity autocorrelation function.

of 77 K, the dip parameter γ is 0.92, so that the dip goes almost to zero. At 61.5 K, γ has decreased to 0.8 (20% filled in), and falls to 0.5 (50% filled in) at 18 K. This was explained qualitatively by Lewis (1980b, 1985) on the basis of increased sensitivity to the non-proportionality of the induced dipole moment and intermolecular force in low-energy collisions. See section 10 below.

5. A ZERO DIP IMPLIES THAT THE FORCE IS PROPORTIONAL TO THE INDUCED DIPOLE MOMENT, 1972   (Lewis)

This work is described in Lewis (1973). It is based on the kinetic theory developed by Lewis and Van Kranendonk. The theorem was proved for low density Lorentz gases assuming pairwise additive central intermolecular forces and induced dipole moments. While it is plausible that the theorem is true even when these conditions do not apply, the theorem has not to date been proved in the general case.

The theorem allows the ratio of the dip height to the maximum of the intracollisional part of the spectrum to be used as a measure of the difference between the induced dipole moment and the inter-molecular force.

To what extent is the proportionality of force to induced dipole moment necessary as well as sufficient for a dip to extend to zero? A complete answer has not been given, but within the context of the kinetic theory, and for the Lorentz gas, it was shown by Lewis that a zero dip does indeed require the proportionality of force and induced dipole moment. There is no evident reason why this would not also apply to the case of gas mixtures of arbitrary mass ratio, the structure of the theory in the two cases being similar. However, the kinetic theory assumes that the induced dipole moment should be parallel to the force. If that requirement is relaxed, a zero dip can indeed be obtained without proportionality, as the following perhaps rather artificial example shows.

Let

$$\vec{\mu}(t) = \alpha\vec{f}(t)+\vec{\beta}\times\vec{f}(t) \tag{12}$$

where α is a constant of proportionality and $\vec{\beta}$ is a constant vector fixed in the laboratory frame of reference. Then it is a matter of simple vector algebra to show that

$$\vec{\mu}(t)\cdot\vec{\mu}(t+\tau) = \alpha^2\vec{f}(t)\cdot\vec{f}(t+\tau)+|\vec{\beta}|^2\vec{f}_\perp(t)\cdot\vec{f}_\perp(t+\tau) \tag{13}$$

where $\vec{f}_\perp(t)$ is the component of $\vec{f}(t)$ which is perpendicular to $\vec{\beta}$. If the power spectra of $\vec{f}_x$, $\vec{f}_y$, and $\vec{f}_z$ are then zero, as will be the case for all Cartesian components of $\vec{f}$, the power spectrum of $\vec{\mu}$

will also be zero. The relevance of this counterexample to realistic induced dipole moments, which are indifferent to the laboratory frame, is not clear, but at any rate it makes any facile generalization to the nonparallel case untenable.

While ordinarily the parallelism of the intermolecular pair force and the pair component of the induced dipole moment is sufficient to lead to a deep dip, usually experimentally indistinguishable from zero, there are three cases where the partially filled-in dip is found. The first, known experimentally, is hydrogen in helium at low temperatures (see section 4.5 above). The second, of considerable theoretical interest, is the hard disk or hard sphere system with a soft (typically exponential) pair induced dipole moment (see sections 8 and 13 below). The third is the liquid-density molecular dynamics simulation of Birnbaum and Mountain described in section 17 below.

6. THEORY OF INTERCOLLISIONAL INTERFERENCE IN S LINES, 1974-1975. (Poll, Hunt and Mactaggart)

Poll, Hunt and Mactaggart (1975) pointed out that the S lines can be regarded as the incoherent superposition of components, of which two dominate:

1. that which is due to the "anisotropic L=3" component of the induced dipole moment; at long ranges this is induced by the H_2 quadrupole, so that it behaves as R^{-4} asymptotically;

2. that which is due to the "anisotropic L=1" component of the induced dipole moment; that is induced by overlap at short distances and by dispersion forces at large distances; thus it is induced by the same mechanisms as the "isotropic L=1" component which is responsible for the Q branch absorption; the anisotropic L=1 induced dipole moment should therefore have approximately the same dependence on intermolecular separation as the isotropic L=1 component.

As noncentrality in the induced dipole moment is effective in destroying the negative correlation responsible for intercollisional interference, Poll et al. made the plausible assumption that all of the intercollisional interference in the S lines comes from the anisotropic L=1 component. They further assumed that, as the isotropic and anisotropic L=1 components are both central and have approximately the same dependence on intermolecular separation, the anisotropic L=1 component would show perfect negative correlation.

To determine the correctness of these assumptions, Poll et al. fit the $S_1(1)$ line intensity of H_2 - He at three different temperatures. The S(1) line intensity was obtained after removal of the Q branch intensity, as determined by Mactaggart and Welsh (1973) in the frequency region 4500 to 5000 cm^{-1}.

They used an unsplit Lorentzian[8] for the lineshape from the anisotropic L=3 component. For the anisotropic L=1 component, they used the same form as used in the analysis of the Q branch: a Levine-Birnbaum lineshape multiplied by the intercollisional interference lineshape (1) with $\gamma=1$, thus implementing the assumption of perfect negative correlation. The halfwidth of the Levine-Birnbaum lineshape was taken equal to the best-fit value from the Q branch analysis at that temperature. The strengths of the two components, the width of the L=3 component, and the interference halfwidth were taken as adjustable parameters.

The resulting fits were in good agreement with the measured line intensities. The interference halfwidth was found to be linear in perturber density, and equal to the values obtained for the Q branch. The intensity of the L=3 component at 78 K was in satisfactory agreement with a theoretical estimate.

In sum, the approach of Poll, Hunt and Mactaggart appears to give a satisfactory account of the intercollisional interference effect in S lines.

7. INCORPORATION OF PHASE SHIFTS INTO THE KINETIC THEORY, 1975. (Lewis)

As noted above, the intercollisional interference dips in collision-induced spectra undergo shifting which at sufficiently low density is proportional to the density. To account for this phenomenon, Lewis (1976) incorporated the collisional phase shifts into the kinetic theory of intercollisional interference described in section 3 above. While the resulting expressions for the lineshape are rather complicated in the general case, if the phase shifts $\bar{\eta}$ are small compared to 1 and persistence of velocity is negligible, the lineshape in the region of the dip reduces to

$$G(\omega)=G_{intra}(0)+\frac{\bar{\nu}_c}{2}\left\{\frac{2}{1+(\omega/\nu_c)^2}\left\langle\vec{\bar{\mu}}_i\cdot\vec{\bar{\mu}}_{i+1}\right\rangle_i+\frac{(\omega/\bar{\nu}_c)}{1+(\omega/\bar{\nu}_c)^2}\left\langle\vec{\bar{\mu}}_i\cdot\vec{\bar{\mu}}_{i+1}\bar{\eta}_i\right\rangle_i\right\}(14)$$

In the above equation, $\bar{\mu}_i$ and $\bar{\eta}_i$ are the integrated dipole moment and the phase shift induced in the ith collision sequence. $< \ldots >_i$ denotes the appropriate collisional average. Three things of interest follow from this expression:

1. The lineshape function is asymmetric. This asymmetry has been observed. See section 11 and 15 below.

---

[8] The lineshapes were, of course appropriately asymmetrized following the procedure of Mactaggart and Welsh (1973).

2. The pressure shift of the dip minimum is given by

$$\frac{\bar{\nu}_c}{2} \frac{\left\langle \vec{\bar{\mu}}_i \cdot \vec{\bar{\mu}}_{i+1} \bar{\eta}_i \right\rangle_i}{\left\langle \vec{\bar{\mu}}_i \cdot \vec{\bar{\mu}}_{i+1} \right\rangle_i} \qquad (15)$$

and is indeed linear in perturber[9] density.

3. The pressure shift given by eq. (15) above is the ratio of two collisionally averaged quantities, and cannot for that reason be reduced in any obvious way to a time average and then to a canonical average. In contrast, the Raman shift of the same line will be given by the expression

$$\bar{\nu}_c \left\langle \bar{\eta}_i \right\rangle_i$$

in the weak shifting limit used to obtain eq. (15). This in turn equals the time average of $\eta(t)$, the instantaneous phase shift, which, assuming ergodicity, equals the canonical average of η. Exploiting this fact, May et al. (1961, 1964) were able to obtain expressions for the Raman line shifts in H_2 which were valid at sufficiently high densities for the nonlinearities in the density dependence to be substantial. In contrast, it would seem that corresponding expressions for the intercollisional interference dip shift cannot exist, and that a kinetic theory of dense fluids would be necessary to calculate the density dependence of the shifting beyond the linear régime.

These considerations hold for the general case as well as for the case of weak shifting and negligible persistence of velocity.

8. FIRST APPLICATION OF MOLECULAR DYNAMICS TO INTERCOLLISIONAL INTER-FERENCE, 1975-1977. (Lewis and Tjon)

The first application of molecular dynamics to collision-induced absorption was made by Lewis and J. A. Tjon, at the University of Utrecht (Lewis and Tjon 1974, 1978). The model chosen for computer simulation was a two-dimensional Lorentz gas of hard disks, in which the light particle was of nonzero radius. The pair induced dipole moment used was central; two radial dependencies were studied, exponential and R^{-4}.

The first result obtained (Lewis and Tjon 1974) was the existence of a "caging spike" which develops in the interference dip at high

---

[9] In pure hydrogen, of course, the "perturber" molecules are simply the hydrogen molecules not involved in the transition.

densities owing to caging of the light particle in asymmetric cages. The asymmetry is necessary so that the time-averaged total induced dipole moment induced within a cage will be non-zero. However, this effect probably has more to do with pressure narrowing that with intercollisional interference.

The spectra obtained from the computer simulations were compared with those calculated from the kinetic theory (Lewis and Tjon 1978). Good agreement was found at the lowest densities studied (up to densities which roughly correspond to the order of 100 Amagat), except that even at the lowest densities the peaks of the spectra were noticeably sharper than predicted by theory. This may represent a three-body effect, as discussed in section 3 above. At higher densities, as would be expected, the kinetic theory became inapplicable. In particular it predicted interference dips which were shallower than those actually observed.

As there had been considerable discussion in the literature of rotational relaxation at that time of the possibility of extending low-density theories to higher densities simply by using a non-Poissonian distribution of collision times, with successive intervals independent but (higly) non-exponentially distributed (Frenkel, Wegdam and van der Elsken 1972, Frenkel, van Aalst and van der Elsken 1974 and Frenkel and Wegdam 1974), and they had also been used in describing translational correlations (Lindenberg and Cukier 1977), we fit the simulation spectra with spectra calculated from the theory of intercollisional interference, but with adjustable distributions of collision times. This procedure did indeed improve the fits, markedly so at high densities. However, the best-fit distributions bore little or no relationship to the actual distributions, which were, of course, accessible to us (Lewis and Tjon 1978, Lewis 1980c). The disagreement between the fitted and the actual distributions was particularly striking at low densities.

It could thus be concluded that the improved agreement obtained by allowing nonexponential distributions of collision times was spurious; and that the best-fit distributions were artifacts which did not correspond to reality. This view was strengthened by our observations in two model systems (Lewis 1980c) that successive intervals between collisions are only weakly correlated; it seems that the most important features of the collision time processes are insensitive to the static and dynamic correlations known to be present in dense fluids. One might say that simply tinkering with the distribution of collision times is too cheap a way to describe a dense fluid.

9. MICROWAVE STUDIES OF COLLISION-INDUCED ABSORPTION BY ARBITRARY MIXTURES OF RARE GASES, 1977-1978   (Dagg, Reesor and Wong)

Dagg, Reesor and Wong (1977, 1978; Wong 1978) studied

intercollisional interference in the translational spectra of rare gas mixtures by a microwave technique in which they measured the absorption at fixed frequencies (2.3 cm^{-1} and 4.5 cm^{-1}) and varied the total pressure of gas mixtures of constant composition. Owing to the weakness of the absorption, the mixtures were not dilute in either component (roughly 2:1; 1:1 and 1:2 in mole fraction). This preludes direct comparison with the kinetic theory outlined in section 3 above, although the results are in qualitative agreement with it. Wong attempted to extend the kinetic theory to mixtures of arbitrary composition, but could take into account only a small class of the relevant terms; he obtained good fits to the experimental data, but only for unphysical values of one of the parameters. See Campbell (1982) and section 14 below.

10. EXPLANATION OF THE FILLING-IN OF THE DIP AT LOW TEMPERATURES, 1978-1979 (Lewis)

The intercollisional interference dip in the Q branch of the fundamental band of collision-induced spectra of H_2 - He mixtures partially fills in at low temperatures (McKellar, Mactaggart and Welsh 1975; see section 4.5 above). In contradiction to claims that this is a quantum effect, Lewis (1980b, 1985) showed

1. that if the induced dipole moment is exactly proportional to the intermolecular force then the interference dip goes to zero at all temperatures, quantum-mechanically as well as classically;

2. that the filling-in of the dip is essentially a classical phenomenon and is due mainly to the discontinuity in the distance of closest approach during binary collisions as a function of impact parameter (see Figs. 9a and 9b). As was noted in section 3 above, the depth of the dip depends immediately upon the exactness of the proportionality of the integrated induced dipole moment $\bar{\mu}(b)$ to the collisional momentum transfer $c(b)$; as can be seen from the figures, $\bar{\mu}$ is sensitive to differences between the intermolecular force and the induced dipole moment for low-energy collisions but is insensitive for high-energy ones.

11. APPLICATION OF THE ASYMMETRICAL LINESHAPE FUNCTION INCORPORATING COLLISIONAL PHASE SHIFTS TO HD-Xe AND H_2-Xe, 1981 (Herman)

Independent of but subsequent to Lewis's work on intercollisional interference dip shifting and the associated asymmetry, R. M. Herman (1981a, 1981b) derived equivalent expressions for the lineshape function from a different viewpoint, which emphasizes similarities between intercollisional interference ("vector intercollisional interference" in Herman's terminology) and intracollisional interference ("scalar intercollisional interference") in HD - X enhancement spectra.

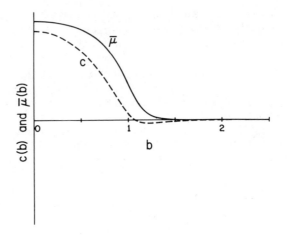

Fig. 9a. The momentum transfer $c(b)$ and integrated induced dipole
moment $\bar{\mu}(b)$ for a Lennard-Jones potential and exponential
induced dipole moment; the parameters have been chosen to
model H_2 - He; the relative velocity is that of a typical
collision at 416 K.

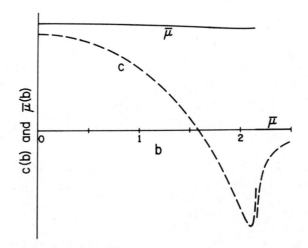

Fig. 9b. $c(b)$ and $\bar{\mu}$ for the same Lennard-Jones potential and induced
dipole moment as Figure 9a; the relative velocity is that of
a typical collision at 4.5 K. The drop in $\bar{\mu}$ about
$b = b_{orbit}$ amounts to six orders of magnitude.

240

According to Herman's scheme, intercollisional interference in collision-induced light scattering would be described as "tensor intercollisional interference".

Herman analysed the collision-induced spectra of H_2 - Xe and HD - Xe observed by S. P. Reddy and coworkers (Prasad and Reddy 1977, Varghese and Reddy 1969) using the asymmetrical dip lineshape. He found that with reasonable values of the parameters he could account for the long-standing puzzle of the symmetry in the absorption pro-files of these mixtures; a symmetry[10] which of course implies an asymmetry in the corresponding lineshape function G.

12. APPLICATION OF Zwanzig-Mori FORMALISM TO OBTAIN THE COMPLETE LINE-SHAPE FUNCTION, 1982. (Guillot, Bratos, and Birnbaum)

In 1982, Guillot, Bratos and Birnbaum (1982) published a theory of collision-induced absorption in dense binary rare-gas mixtures. The theory is also applicable at low densities, and, neglecting small anisotropies, to the Q branch of the fundamental band of hydrogen. A basic assumption is that the induced dipole moment is exactly propor-tional to the total force between molecules of the two species A and B comprising the mixture. Hence the lineshape function is exactly pro-portional to the power spectrum of the interdiffusion current fluctu-ation $\vec{J}$. They use Zwanzig-Mori formalism, truncating the continued-fraction expansion to give a lineshape of the form

$$G(\omega) = \frac{\left[\dfrac{\omega^2}{\omega_0{}^2}\right]\tau\Phi(0)}{\left[1-\dfrac{\omega^2}{\omega_0{}^2}\right]^2+\omega^2\tau^2\left[1-\dfrac{1-\dfrac{\omega^2}{\omega_0{}^2}}{1-\dfrac{\omega_1{}^4}{\omega_0{}^4}}\right]^2} \tag{16}$$

where τ is proportional to the mutual diffusion coefficient of the two species, and $\omega_0{}^2$ and $\omega_1{}^4$ depend on the static interspecies pair and triplet correlation functions g_{AB}, g_{AAB} and g_{ABB}, together with various derivatives of the interspecies pair potential. Using a lat-tice gas model from in their earlier related work on collision-induced light scattering (Guillot, Bratos and Birnbaum 1980), the authors are able to obtain a simple approximate expression for $\omega_1{}^4$ in

---

[10] Q_P is more intense than it should be, if the lineshape function were symmetric; Q_R is less intense.

terms of g_{AB} alone[11]. This they evaluate using the low-density limit of the pair correlation function, an approximation which should be adequate for their purposes, as the correlation function always occurs in their expressions multiplied by short-range functions involving the pair potential

The mutual diffusion coefficient, and hence τ, can be calculated by kinetic theory at low densities. The method used to estimate τ in eq. (16) is described in Guillot, Bratos and Birnbaum (1980) (Birnbaum 1984).

Their truncation of the continued-fraction expansion after the sixth power of ω in the denominator is justified by an appeal to the Kivelson-Keyes approximation procedure. Such a truncation is equivalent to using a basis set consisting of $\vec{J}$ and its first and second time derivatives. As these three collective variables provide a good description of the motions in the system, it is likely that no significant improvement would be obtained, except at high frequencies, by adding the third derivative of J to the basis set, i.e., in using a "four-variable" theory. This is consistent with the body of knowledge which has accumulated in the study of orientational relaxation in dense fluids (Kivelson and Keyes, 1972; Rothschild, 1984). It would, nevertheless, be interesting to compare explicitly the three-variable and four-variable approximate expressions for the lineshape function.

While the work of Guillot, Bratos and Birnbaum is closely related to the earlier work on neutron scattering (Berne, Boon and Rice 1966, Desai and Yip 1968); see section 4.4 above), it advances beyond it in three ways:

1. It treats arbitrary binary mixtures.
2. Their theory is of higher order than earlier work; they go high enough in frequency to cover all of the lineshape function except its high-frequency wings.
3. They evaluate the parameters in their expansion from first principles, albeit in a rather approximate way, and thus can predict the density behaviour of the lineshape from first principles.

To extend this theory so as accurately to describe the high-frequency wing of the lineshape function is obviously a formidable undertaking; any truncation procedure will give a rational function, and the line shape function is well known not to be describable asymptotically by any reciprocal power, except for certain model systems (see section 8 and 13). Consequently some summation procedure, whether an approximate summation of exact terms, or exact summation of

---

[11] They apparently do not use the Kirkwood superposition approximation.

242

approximate terms, is required, which will give at least an approximate estimate of the contributions of all orders in the frequency.
However, as far as intercollisional interference is concerned, the
work of Guillot, Bratos and Birnbaum constitutes a valuable approach.
Their formulation cannot be applied directly to induce dipole moments
which are not proportional to the intermolecular force, but Zwanzig-
Mori formalism can be applied, as they have shown in their earlier
work on collision-induced light scattering (Guillot, Bratos and
Birnbaum 1980). The expressions resulting are considerably more complex; they require four-body functions as well as the pair and triplet correlation functions used in the expression above; and intercollisional interference does not emerge in any obvious way; however,
their successes to date give hope for further progress with the
application of Zwanzig-Mori formalism to the problem of intercollisional interference in the future.

As with the lineshape of Desai and Yip discussed in section 4.1
above, the lineshape here is to be interpreted as originating in the
interplay of a dissipative, essentially diffusive mode with an oscillatory mode. Interestingly, the correlation function corresponding
to eq. (16) when evaluated for Ne in Ar shows a pronounced positive
secondary maximum at 90 K and 728 Amagat, while it assumes its
characteristic low-density form at 130 K and 280 Amagat. This is
consistent with the observations of De Remegis described in section
4.4. The coupling or interplay of the two modes, which separate at
low densities, is well described. Comparison between theory and
experiment for Ne in liquid Ar (90 K, 728 Amagat) and for Kr in
liquid Ar (135 K, 380 Amagat) shows good qualitative agreement; the
theoretical peak is too sharp, but occurs where it should; the interference dip is a little too broad, by about 20%, and the high-
frequency wing falls off a little too sharply. While it is outside
of the scope of this review, we note that their theory predicts some
pressure narrowing in going from Ne - Ar at 280 Amagat to Ne - Ar at
597 Amagat.

13. AN EXACTLY SOLVABLE CASE IN THE THEORY OF INTERCOLLISONAL INTER-
FERENCE, 1982   (Lewis)

It became evident in the course of the first molecular dynamics
simulations of collision-induced absorption by Lewis and Tjon (see
section 8 above) that hard disks with a soft induced dipole moment
gave a relatively shallow interference dip, with values of $\gamma \cong 0.5$,
depending somewhat on the form of the dipole moment. It was, of
course, possible that with an induced dipole moment of very short
range, that the dip might deepen. Even so, "hard" systems are
worthy of study more for the insights which they can provide into the
processes underlying the many-body effects of collision induced
absorption, and for the useful checks which they can provide on
theory, than for any capacity to model real fluids with a high degree

of fidelity. It has in fact been possible to find a class of "hard"
systems for which the dip height at zero frequency could be calculated
exactly (Lewis 1983), using the kinetic theory of intercollisional
interference described in section 3 above. These models are Lorentz
gases with disks or spheres as the fixed scatterers, and central pair
induced dipole moments

$$\mu(R) \propto R^{-2\nu}$$

varying as an inverse power of the intermolecular separation. For
these models, the integrated induced dipole moments $\bar{\mu}(b)$ and the relative dip heights $1-\gamma$ can be evaluated analytically and in closed form.
The interference dips are relatively shallow as, in each case, the
integrated induced dipole moment $\bar{\mu}(b)$ as a function of the impact
parameter b has a cusp about the point where b equals the collision
diameter (see Fig. 10). The largest values of $\bar{\mu}$ come from near-
grazing collisions, as in such collisions, whether for b smaller or
larger than the collision diameter, the moving particle spends a
longer time in regions where μ is large than is the case for values
of b substantially smaller or substantially larger than the collision
diameter.

The cusp in $\bar{\mu}(b)$ in fact becomes sharper as ν increases, that is
as the range of the induced dipole moment decreases. The increasing
sharpness of $\bar{\mu}$ is an immediate consequence of the decreasing range of
μ; if two induced dipole moments of different ranges are compared
along the same trajectory, at every point of the trajectory except the
point of collision itself, the dipole moment with shorter range makes
a smaller contribution.

As $\bar{\mu}(b)$ becomes sharper, its overlap with the momentum transfer
c(b) in a collision becomes less. According to the kinetic theory,
it is this overlap which directly determines the dip depth. In consequence the dip actually tends to fill in as the range of μ decreases.
An asymptotic analysis indicates that the dip will fill in completely
as ν increases, although the infill is slow;

$$\gamma = O(1/\ln \nu) \tag{17}$$

for sufficiently large ν. The same analysis can be applied with minor
modifications to exponential induced dipole moments, and shows that
the interference dips also fill in as the range goes to zero for these
systems.

The analytical calculation of the lineshapes at nonzero frequencies is much more difficult than at zero frequency for these models,
and to date it has not been accomplished.

Aside from the intrinsic interest which attaches to the exact
solution of any statistical mechanical model, this calculation negates

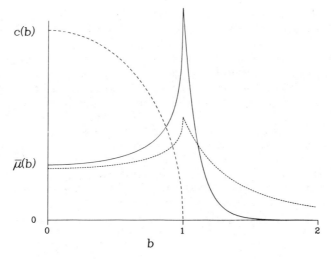

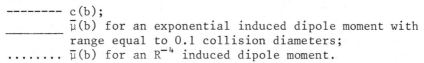

Fig. 10. The momentum transfer c(b) and integrated induced dipole
moment $\bar{\mu}$(b) for a hard disk or hard sphere gas:

    -------- c(b);
    _____ $\bar{\mu}$(b) for an exponential induced dipole moment with
              range equal to 0.1 collision diameters;
    .... $\bar{\mu}$(b) for an R^{-4} induced dipole moment.

the conjecture that a central pair force and pair induced dipole
moment necessarily imply a deep dip; it provides the most extreme of
the three known counter examples, the other two being the low-
temperature dip infilling (see sections 4.5 and 10 above) and the
high-density molecular dynamics simulation of Birnbaum and Mountain
(see section 17 below).

    The low temperature dip-infilling mechanism in H_2 - He depends
essentially on the attractive part of the intermolecular force. In
the "hard" models considered here, there is of course no attractive
force. However, for a real gas at sufficiently high temperatures the
attractive part of the pair potential becomes unimportant. In such a
case, the grazing mechanism responsible for the infilling in "hard"
systems could be significant, provided that if the induced dipole
moment varies rather more slowly than the force for energetic collisions. In systems where that obtains, dip infilling can be expected
at high temperatures as well as low ones.

14. EXTENSION OF THE KINETIC THEORY OF INTERCOLLISIONAL INTERFERENCE TO MIXTURES OF ARBITRARY COMPOSITION, 1981-1982   (Lewis and Campbell)

The kinetic theory of intercollisional interfence in collision-induced absorption as derived by Lewis and Van Kranendonk is applicable only to binary mixtures which are dilute in one component. Lewis and Campbell (Campbell 1982) attempted to extend the kinetic theory to mixtures of arbitrary composition: first, binary mixtures with arbitrary ratios concentration ratios, and then mixtures with arbitrary numbers of species. To carry this through it was necessary to neglect correlations among binary collisions with no common members (e.g. the correlation between a collision of two molecules 1 and 2 and a collision of molecules 3 and 4); otherwise the extension was straightforward in principle, though somewhat complicated in detail. This neglect of four-body correlations was also required to adapt the kinetic theory to collision-induced light scattering (see section 3.1 above).

M. Wong (1978) had earlier attempted such an extension of the kinetic theory. However, he considered only correlations among immediately successive collisions, whereas Lewis and Campbell took into account correlations among all collisions in the collision sequences of each molecule. This must be done, as the extent of correlation is determined by the persistence of velocity. In a mixture of two species where the molecular weight of one is much less than that of the other, and the mixture is infinitely dilute in the lighter species, then the persistence of velocity of molecules of the lighter species in collisions with the heavier molecules is small, and only correlations among immediately successive collisions need be considered. In all other cases, the persistence of velocity of at least one species will be nonnegligible, and correlations will extend over many collisions in the collision sequences of molecules of that species. Consequently the assumption that only immediately successive collisions are correlated is always incorrect in mixtures which are not very dilute in one component.

For binary mixtures of two species A and B, the Lewis and Campbell's expression for the lineshape function involves two integral equations, rather than the one necessary in the infinitely dilute case (eqs. (3) and (3a)). If the kernels are approximated by δ-functions, as in eq. (4), a generalization of eq. (2b) results, with two γ parameters rather than one. These two parameters are in fact the γ-values for the two infinitely dilute extremes [A] << [B] and [B] << [A]. All parameters can in principle be calculated from the pair forces and the pair induced dipole moment, but they can also be treated as adjustable, as in the infinitely dilute case.

If the two γ-values are taken equal to 1, so that the interference dip goes to zero in the infinitely dilute limiting cases, then it will deviate from zero by as much as 10% of the intracollisional spectral density at zero frequency for intermediate values of the mole fraction - i.e. the interference dip depth will constitute only about 90% of the intracollisional contribution, rather than 100%. Furthermore, the dip spectrum is conspicuously non-Lorentzian for intermediate mole fraction values.

If the persistence-of-velocity ratios are evaluated using hard-sphere models, the dip spectra can be compared with the microwave measurements of Dagg, Reesor and Wong (section 9 above). However, the agreement is not particularly good. It can thus be concluded that four-body correlations are important in intercollisional interference, even at low densities, and that a fully successful theory must take them into account.

15. HIGH-PRECISION MEASUREMENTS OF ASYMMETRY IN THE COLLISION-INDUCED LINESHAPE OF H_2, 1983   (Bragg)

As noted in sections 7 and 11 above, because of the phase shifts which hydrogen molecules undergo in collisions, the interference dip will undergo pressure shifting, and the lineshape will be asymmetric. S. L. Bragg et al. (1983) studied quadrupole-allowed and collision-induced fundamental band absorption in H_2 at densities between 1.3 and 2.7 Amagat at high resolution (0.009 cm^{-1}. The absorption dips for several Q and S branch transitions (Q(0), Q(1), Q(2) and S(0)) were, indeed, clearly observed to be asymmetric about their central frequencies. Combination of a dip lineshape incorporating the collisional phase shifts with a Galatry profile for the narrow quadrupole absorption features gave satisfactory fits. However, Bragg et al. use a form of eq. (14) above, without attribution, in which the phase shifts are assumed to be independent of the mean induced dipole moments, and the persistence-of-velocity correction is completely neglected. The former assumption is unlikely and the latter is wrong. For that reason their fitted parameters lack physical significance, beyond being of the correct order of magnitude. These are estimated independently of experiment using the intraintermolecular potential

$$V_1(r,R) = A \exp(r/2L) \exp(-R/L)$$

where r is the nuclear separation in a hydrogen molecule, and R is as usual the separation of the centres of mass of two molecules. L is a characteristic length, taken to be 0.2 Å. With this model, and a head-on classical trajectory, the mean phase shift can be estimated. The estimate is in reasonable agreement with the fitted value.

16. EXPERIMENTAL OBSERVATION OF INTERCOLLISIONAL INTERFERENCE IN S_1 IN THE PURE ROTATION SPECTRUM OF H_2 - He, 1983 (Bachet)

G. Bachet (1983) has recently published a study of the collision-induced spectrum of H_2 - He at 300 K in the far infrared, between 200 and 700 cm^{-1}, using Fourier transform spectroscopy. The gas mixture used was 15.6% H_2. A dip in the spectrum, amounting to 6% of the peak maximum, was found at the S_1 frequency. This constitutes the first observation of intercollisional interference in pure rotational spectra; previous investigations were at too low resolutions to observe the dips.

The dip in the S_0 band, if any, was of the same order of magnitude as the noise, and thus several times weaker than the S_1 dip.

The smallness of the interference dip, as well as its narrowness, precludes intercollisional interference as an explanation for features at the S_0 and S_1 frequencies in spectra of the upper Jovian atmosphere taken by Voyager 1.

17. MOLECULAR DYNAMICS STUDY OF THE COLLISION-INDUCED ABSORPTION IN RARE GAS LIQUID MIXTURES, 1983 (Birnbaum and Mountain)

Birnbaum and Mountain (1983) have recently carried out molecular dynamics calculations of considerable importance to the study of intercollisional interference. They simulated an Ar - Ne liquid mixture assuming pairwise additive forces and induced dipole moments, using the best available pair potentials and pair induced dipole moment. The resulting simulation spectrum was not in agreement with the observed spectrum in the high-frequency wing, and was not even in qualitative agreement at low frequencies, in the dip region.

These calculations used 450 Ar atoms and 50 Ne atoms; this is sufficient that finite size effects should not be significant in the collision-induced spectrum. The Beeman algorithm was employed for integration of the equations of motion. The simulation density and temperature were those of the mixture under its own vapour pressure at about 100 K. The potentials used for comparison with experiment were the HFD potentials of Ahlrichs, Penco and Scoles (1977). The induced dipole moment was that of Birnbaum, Brown and Frommhold (1981),

$$|\vec{\mu}(r)| = M_0 \exp(-\alpha r) - \frac{C_7}{r^7} \qquad (18)$$

fit to gas phase collision induced spectra using the Ne - Ar HFD potential to define the interaction.

The resulting spectrum dips only to about 50% of the peak maximum height, so that γ is only about 0.6 - 0.7. Also, the peak occurs at a substantially lower frequency. The zero of the best induced dipole moment occurs at a roughly 30% greater separation than that of the Ne – Ar force. If the dipole moment is then modified so that the zeros are coincident, then qualitative agreement between simulation and experiment is obtained. Birnbaum and Mountain did this in three different ways, with equivalent results: by decreasing M_0 by a factor of 4.7, by increasing α by a factor of 1.14, and by increasing C_7 by a factor of 4. In each case the dip minimum was about 5% of the peak maximum ($\gamma \cong 0.97$), and the peak maximum was located around 50 – 60 cm^{-1}. The changes required are thus substantial.

An ab initio calculation (Birnbaum, Krauss and Frommhold 1984) has supported the correctness of the dipole moment used in these molecular dynamics calculations.

Birnbaum and Mountain also carried out molecular dynamics computer calculations with a pure exponential (repulsive) pair force, and a pair dipole moment equal in magnitude to a power of the magnitude of the pair force. Thus, they used

$$|\vec{\mu}| = \mu_0 \ |\vec{f}|^n \tag{19}$$

with

$$\vec{f}(\vec{R}) = f_0 \ \hat{R} \ exp(-\alpha R) \tag{20}$$

where $\vec{f}$ is the force between unlike atoms, and μ_0 and f_0 are constants. They considered the cases n = 1, 3/4, 1/2, and 1/4. With n = 1 and 3/4 a deep dip was obtained (going to zero for n = 1); with n = 1/2 some infilling was observed ($\gamma \approx 0.8$) while n = 1/4 gave only a shallow dip ($\gamma \approx 0.35$). These calculations were used to provide some indication of the sensitivity of the interference to deviations from proportionality.

The molecular dynamics calculations of Birnbaum and Mountain are in qualitative accord with conclusions reached earlier about the relation of force and induced dipole moment in producing the interference dip: a deep dip will be produced if the induced dipole moment is approximately proportional to the intermolecular force; except at very low temperatures the dip is not highly sensitive to deviations from exact proportionality; large deviations will, however, cause a partial or even complete infilling of the dip, even if force and induced dipole moment are parallel. These points are discussed in sections 5, 10 and 13 above.

That said, however, it seems that the intercollisional interference phenomenon in Birnbaum and Mountain's simulations is more sensitive to differences between the induced dipole and the force than is the case in the gas phase. One reason for such an enhanced sensitivity could well be the fact that at liquid densities each molecule is simultaneously interacting with several others, whereas in the gas phase at sufficiently low densities only binary collisions are important. At such densities, if the pair force and induced dipole moments are not exactly proportional to each other, then the total force and total induced dipole moment on a given molecule will not be parallel, even if the total force and total induced dipole moment are pairwise additive with central pair forces and induced dipole moments. Deviations from parallelism are much more effective in destroying the negative correlation of collision-induced intercollisional interference than are deviations from proportionality, as the shallow or non-existent lines in the S bands in H_2 show. In other words, at liquid densities, deviations from proportionality will lead to deviations from parallelism. This effect would be expected to be particularly strong if there are substantial differences in the zero crossing separations of the pair force and the pair induced dipole moment[12]. The deviation from parallelism could easily be quantified in a molecular dynamics simulation – for example, by computing

$$Q = \overline{\hat{f}_i(t) \cdot \hat{\mu}_i(t)} \; ; \quad \hat{f}_i = \vec{f}_i / f_i \text{ and } \hat{\mu}_i = \vec{\mu}_i / \mu_i \tag{21}$$

where $\vec{f}_i(t)$ is the total force on molecule i at time t, and $\vec{\mu}_i(t)$ is the total induced dipole moment on i at t. This quantity Q equals 1 in the low density limit and would not expected to differ substantially from 1 until liquid densities are reached.

The discrepancy between the simulation results and experiment could possibly be due to an insensitivity of the gas phase results to the form of the induced dipole moment around the zero crossing of the force. This is, however, unlikely; for while early work (Brenner and McQuarrie 1971) indicated that substantially different induced dipole moments might lead to essentially the same spectrum, more recent work (Birnbaum et al. 1981, 1984) has eliminated major uncertainties in the form of the induced dipole moment in rare gas mixtures at low densities. Therefore, while the form of the pair induced dipole moment will no doubt be subject to further verification in the future, the changes necessary to resolve the discrepancy are improbably great. This is especially so in view of the ab initio calculation of $\vec{\mu}$ reported in Birnbaum, Krauss and Frommhold 1984. The most likely conclusion is that of Birnbaum and Mountain, that the discrepancy is due to the presence of irreducible three-body forces in the real liquid. Many-body forces have been clearly identified in Kr by comparison between neutron scattering data and Monte Carlo calculations using good pair potentials obtained from low-density thermodynamic and transport properties (Egelstaff et al. 1983; Teitsma and Egelstaff 1980).

It would be most interesting to see molecular dynamics

---

[12] On the other hand it should be least important in systems with pure repulsive, exponential forces and induced dipole moments, as in the second set of Birnbaum and Mountain's simulations.

simulations performed on Ar - Ne at a series of at lower densities, to make contact with gas phase experimental and theoretical results. This would serve as a check on the high-density work. More important, the onset of the irreducible many-body forces could be observed in detail. Indeed, these forces may be more significant at somewhat reduced densities than in the liquid, as there is some evidence for cancellation of three-body forces in liquids (Egelstaff et al. 1980, 1983; Hoheisel 1981). While molecular dynamics calculations, at, say, 1/10 of liquid density, are more difficult and more time-consuming than those at higher density, in this instance they would be well worthwhile.

18. NOTE: APPLICATIONS TO VIBRATIONAL RELAXATION

In some models of vibrational relaxation (Zwanzig 1961, Ormonde 1975), the interaction between oscillator and surroundings is taken as approximately proportional to the intermolecular force. The transition rate then is proportional to the power spectrum of the intermolecular force, at the natural frequency of the oscillator. This transition rate can, therefore, in suitable systems, exhibit intercollisional interference with changing density. Up to the time of Ormonde's review (Ormonde 1975), the methods developed for the study of intercollisional interference in collision-induced absorption had not been applied to vibrational relaxation. The author is not familiar with developments in the field subsequent to 1975.

19. CONCLUSIONS

19.1 Kinetic Theory

19.1.1. Calculations with realistic potentials and induced dipole moments. To date no calculations have been performed with the kinetic theory using good intermolecular potentials and induced dipole moments. The present author has done approximate calculations for a model with exponential force and induced dipole moment, where the difference in ranges was much smaller than the ranges (Lewis 1971, Lewis and Van Kranendonk 1972a), and have calculated the entire lineshape for hard repulsive potentials with exponential and inverse-power-law induced dipole moments (Lewis and Tjon 1978, Lewis 1983). Even these were carried out for a Lorentz gas, not a real gas.

These realistic calculations, which do require rather complex multidimensional integrals, are of particular importance for light scattering; or rather, to lead to understanding of why the effect has not been seen in light scattering.

19.1.2. Quantum mechanical calculations. The kinetic theory as developed is purely classical. It could be made partly quantum-

mechanical by use of quantum-mechanical scattering cross sections, but
that is not likely to be too helpful as it is not clear what is
required to replace the time integral of the induced dipole moment
along a classical path. In any case a full quantum-mechanical theory
will almost certainly be required to give an accurate rather than
merely qualitative picture of intercollisional interference, in particular the in-filling of the dip, at low temperatures as described by
McKellar, Mactaggart and Welsh (1975).

19.1.2. Kinetic theory for arbitrary gas mixtures. The problems
with the extension of the kinetic theory to mixtures of arbitrary composition by Lewis and Campbell have been described in section 14
above.

19.2. Intermediate Densities

The shift of the dip becomes nonlinear at intermediate densities.
While the corresponding Raman shift can be reduced to a canonical
average, and thus treated by the methods of equilibrium statistical
mechanics, the same cannot be said for the dip shift. It requires
extension of the kinetic theory (see section 7 above) to take into
account ternary and higher-order collisions. As the first deviations
from low-density behaviour are important, this might be a testing-
ground for higher-order kinetic theories.

19.3. High Densities

19.3.1. Theory. While a lineshape theory has been given by
Guillot, Bratos and Birnbaum, as discussed in section 12 above, that
theory assumes the proportionality of the induced dipole moment and
the intermolecular force. The molecular dynamics experiment of
Birnbaum and Mountain, on the other hand, seems to indicate that the
spectrum will in fact be quite sensitive to the difference. It is
necessary to develop a theory which will give the correct dip shape,
and it is not clear that that of Guillot, Bratos and Birnbaum does
so.

Finally, the place of non-additive interactions in high-density
lineshapes remains to be elucidated.

19.3.2. Experiment. It would be interesting to see spectra taken
around the critical point, to see if the spectra show any substantial
influence of the long-range correlations which play such a major role
there. This has been examined briefly by Mannik and Stryland (1972),
but is worthy of more detailed examination. Also in this regard, we
note that little has been done in collision-induced absorption at high
temperatures. It has been known since the earliest theoretical work
that the actual dip height was temperature - sensitive, even over
temperature ranges where the dip remains deep, and it was suggested by
Lewis (1983) that the dip might fill in at sufficiently elevated

temperatures. I am informed (Mactaggart 1972) that such experiments were carried out at the University of Toronto in 1971-1972 but were never analysed, much less published.

20. ACKNOWLEDGEMENTS

This work was supported by a grant from the Natural Sciences and Engineering Research Council of Canada.

I thank David Sells for his assistance in compiling the bibliography.

I wish to express my appreciation to Professor Rashmi C. Desai for discussing his work on velocity autocorrelation functions with me.

Above all, it is a pleasure to acknowledge the hospitality of the NATO Advanced Research Workshop, and the many stimulating discussions which took place there. In particular I wish to acknowledge numerous discussions with George Birnbaum about intercollisional interference prior to, during, and subsequent to the Workshop. This paper owes much to his encouragement and editorial patience during its protracted gestation.

REFERENCES

Ahlrichs, R., Penco, R., and Scoles, G., 1977, Chemical Physics 19, 119.

Bachet, G., 1983, Experimental Observation of the Intercollisional Interference Effect on the S_1 Pure Rotation Line of the Collision Induced Spectra of the H_2-He Mixture, J. Physique - Lettres 44, L-183-L-187.

Berne, B. J., Boon, J. P., and Rice, S. A., 1966, On the Calculation of Autocorrelation Functions of Dynamical Variables, J. Chem. Phys. 45, 1086-1096.

Birnbaum, G., Brown, M. S., and Frommhold, L., 1981, Lineshapes and Dipole Moments in Collision-Induced Absorption, Can. J. Phys. 59, 1544-1554.

Birnbaum, G., and Mountain, R. D., 1984, Molecular Dynamics Study of Collision-Induced Absorption in Rare-Gas Liquid Mixtures, J. Chem. Phys. 81, 2347-2351.

Birnbaum, G., Krauss, M., and Frommhold, L., 1984, Collision-Induced Dipoles of Rare Gas Mixtures, J. Chem. Phys. 80, 2669-2674.

Birnbaum, G., 1984, personal communication.

Bragg, S. L., and coworker, 1983, Asymmetry of the Intercollisional Interference Dips in the Collision-Induced Absorption Spectrum of Molecular Hydrogen, submitted to Phys. Rev. A. preprint, McDonnell Douglas Research Laboratories, St. Louis, Missouri.

Brenner, S. L., and McQuarrie, D. A., 1971, On the Theory of
    Collision-Induced Absorption in Rare Gas Mixtures, Can. J. Phys.
    49, (1971), 837-847.
Campbell, R. R. A., 1982, A Kinetic Theory of Intercollisional Inter-
    ference Effects in Arbitrary Gas Mixtures, (M.Sc. Thesis,
    Memorial University of Newfoundland).
Chapman, S., and Cowling, T. G., 1952, "The Mathematical Theory of
    Non-Uniform Gases", 2nd edition, Cambridge University Press.
Chisholm, D. A., 1952, (Ph.D. Thesis, University of Toronto).
Chisholm, D. A., and Welsh, H. L., 1954, Induced Infrared Absorption
    in Hydrogen and Hydrogen-Foreign Gas Mixtures at Pressures up to
    1500 Atmospheres, Can. J. Phys. 32, (1954), 291-312.
Crawford, M. F., Welsh, H. L., MacDonald, J. C. F., and Locke, J. J.,
    1950, Infar-red Absorption of Hydrogen Induced by Foreign Gases,
    Phys. Rev. 80, 469-470.
Cunsolo, S., and Gush, H. P., 1972, Collision-Induced Absorption of H_2
    and He-A Mixtures near λ = 1 mm, Can. J. Phys. 50, 2058-2059.
Dagg, I. R., Reesor, G. E., and Wong, M., 1977, Collision-Induced
    Microwave Absorption in Neon-Krypton Mixtures, Chem. Phys.
    Letters 51, 90-94.
Dagg, I. R., Reesor, G. E., and Wong, M., 1978, Collision-Induced
    Microwave Absorption in Ne-Xe and Ar-Xe Gaseous Mixtures, Can. J.
    Phys. 56, 1046-1056.
De Remegis, J., 1971a, personal communication.
De Remegis, J., 1971b, Induced Infrared Absorption of H_2, D_2 and N_2 in
    the Solid, Liquid and Highly Compressed Gas Phases of Ne, Ar, Kr
    and Xe., (Ph.D. Thesis, University of Toronto).
Desai, R. C., and Yip, S., 1968, Dynamical Correlations in Simple
    Liquids and Cold-Neutron Scattering by Argon, Phys. Rev. 166,
    129-138.
Desai, R. C., and Yip, S., 1969, A Stochastic Model for Neutron
    Scattering by Simple Liquids, in "Stochastic Processes in Chemi-
    cal Physics", K. E. Shuler (ed.), John Wiley and Sons, 129-136.
Egelstaff, P. A., Teitsma, A., and Wang, S. S., 1980, Phys. Rev. A 22,
    1702.
Egelstaff, P. A., Glaser, W., Litchinsky, D., Schneider, E., and Suck,
    J. B., 1983, Two-Body Time Correlations in (and the structure of)
    Dense Krypton Gas., Phys. Rev. A 27, 1106-1115.
Frenkel, D., Wegdam, G. H., and van der Elsken, J., 1972, Rotational
    Diffusion Model with a Variable Collision Distribution., J. Chem.
    Phys. 57, 2691-2697.
Frenkel, D., van Aalst, R. M., and van der Elsken, J., 1974, Inter-
    pretation of Far Infrared Spectra in Terms of a Collision Distri-
    bution, in "Molecular Motion in Liquids", J. Lascombe (ed.),
    Reidel, Dordrecht, pp. 647-653.
Frenkel, D., and Wegdam, G. H., 1974, Rotational Diffusion Model with
    a Variable Collision Distribution. II. The Effect of Energy
    Transfer., J. Chem. Phys. 61, 4671-4679.

254

Guillot, B., Bratos, S., and Birnbaum, G., 1980, Theoretical Study of Spectra of Depolarized Light Scattered from Dense Rare-Gas Fluids, Phys. Rev. A 22, 2230-2237.

Guillot, B., Bratos, S., and Birnbaum, G., 1982, Theoretical Study of Collision-Induced Far-Infrared Absorption of Dense Rare-Gas Mixtures, Phys. Rev. A 25, 773-781.

Hare, W. F. J., and Welsh, H. L., 1958, Pressure-Induced Infrared Absorption of Hydrogen and Hydrogen- Foreign Gas Mixtures in the Range 1500-5000 Atmospheres, Can. J. Phys. 36, 88-103.

Herman, R. M., 1981a, Scalar and Vector Collisional Interference in the Fundamental Absorption Band of HD and D_2 (preprint).

Herman, R. M., 1981b, Intercollisional Interference in the Translational and Vibrational Absorption Spectra of Molecular Hydrogen (preprint).

Hoheisel, C., 1981, Phys. Rev. A 23, 1998.

Hunt, J. L., and Welsh, H. L., 1964, Analysis of the Profile of the Fundamental Infrared Band of Hydrogen in Pressure-Induced Absorption, Can. J. Phys. 42, 873-885.

Kivelson, D., and Keyes, T., 1972, Unified Theory of Orientational Relaxation, J. Chem. Phys. 57, 4599-4612.

Lewis, J. C., and Van Kranendonk, J., 1970, Intercollisional Interference Effects in Collision-Induced Light Scattering, Phys. Rev. Lett. 24, 802-804.

Lewis, J. C., 1971, Theory of Intercollisional Interference Effects, (Ph.D. Thesis, University of Toronto).

Lewis, J. C., 1972, Theory of Intercollisional Interference Effects. II. Induced Absorption in a Real Gas, Can J. Phys. 50, 2881-2901.

Lewis, J. C., and Van Kranendonk, J., 1972a, Theory of Intercollisional Interference Effects. I. Induced Absorption in a Lorentz Gas, Can. J. Phys. 50, 352-367.

Lewis, J. C., and Van Kranendonk, J., 1972b, Theory of Intercollisional Interference Effects. III. Collision-Induced Light Scattering, Can. J. Phys. 50, 2902-2913.

Lewis, J. C., 1973, Theory of Intercollisional Interference Effects. IV. Does a Zero Minimum in Induced Absorption Imply the Proportionality of the Induced Dipole Moment to the Force?, Can. J. Phys. 51, 2455-2458.

Lewis, J. C., and Tjon, J. A., 1974, A Cage Effect in Collision-Induced Light Absorption from a Molecular Dynamics Calculation, Chem. Phys. Letters 29, 558-560.

Lewis, J. C., 1976, Theory of Intercollisional Interference Effects. V. Pressure Shift of the Interference Minimum in the Q Branch of H_2-Rare Gas Mixtures, Physica 82A, 500-520.

Lewis, J. C., and Tjon, J. A., 1978, Computer Simulation of Collision-Induced Absorption in a Two-Dimensional Lorentz Gas, Physica 91A, 161-201.

Lewis, J. C., 1980a, Intercollisional Interference Effects, in "Inter-molecular Spectroscopy and Dynamical Properties of Dense Systems", J. Van Kranendonk (ed.), Societa Italiana di Fisica, Bologna, Italy. Course LXXV, Enrico Fermi Summer Schools.

Lewis, J. C., 1980b, Intercollisional Interference at Low Tempera-tures, a paper given at the Conference on Collision Induced Phenomena: Absorption, Light Scattering, and Static Properties held in Florence, Italy on 2-5 September 1980.

Lewis, J. C., 1980c, Distributions of Collision Times for Rough Disks and for a Two-Dimensional Lorentz Gas with Non-Overlapping Fixed Scatterers, Chem. Phys. Letters 76, 96-100.

Lewis, J. C., 1983, Theory of Intercollisional Interference Effects. VI. An Exactly Soluble Model Exhibiting a Shallow Interference Dip, Can. J. Phys. 61, 440-450.

Lewis, J. C., 1985, Intercollisional Interference at Low Temperatures, to appear in Can. J. Phys.

Lindenberg, K., and Cukier, R. I., 1977, A Stochastic Theory of Trans-lational Correlation Functions in Gases and Liquids, J. Chem. Phys. 67, 568-578.

Mactaggart, J. W., 1971, Band Shapes in Pressure-Induced Infrared Absorption and Their Applications to the Molecular Dynamics of Dense Gases, (Ph.D. Thesis, University of Toronto).

Mactaggart, J. W., 1972, personal communication.

Mactaggart, J. W., and Welsh, H. L., 1973, Studies in Molecular Dyna-mics by Collision Induced Infrared Absorption in H_2-Rare Gas Mixtures. I. Profile Analysis and the Intercollisional Inter-ference Effect, Can. J. Phys. 51, 158-169.

Mannik, L., and Stryland, J. C., 1972, The ν_1 Band of Carbon Dioxide in Pressure-Induced Absorption. II. Density and Temperature Dependence of the Intensity; Critical Phenomena, Can. J. Phys. 50, 1355-1362.

Marteau, P., Vu, H., and Vodar, B., 1968, Probabilité de transition des bandes de translation pure des couples de gaz rare aux basses fréquences, Compt. rend. 266B, 1068.

Marteau, P., Vu, H., and Vodar, B., 1970, J. Quant. Spectr. Rad. Transfer 10, 283.

May, A. D., Degen, V., Stryland, J. C., and Welsh, H. L., 1961, Can. J. Phys. 39, 1769.

May, A. E., Varghese, G., Stryland, J. C., and Welsh, H. L., 1964, Can. J. Phys. 42, 1058.

McKellar, A. R. W., 1968, (M.Sc. Thesis, University of Toronto).

McKellar, A. R. W., Mactaggart, J. W., and Welsh, H. L., 1975, Studies in Molecular Dynamics by Collision Induced Infrared Absorption in H_2-Rare Gas Mixtures. III. H_2-He Mixtures at Low Temperatures and Densities, Can. J. Phys. 53, 2060-2067.

Ormonde, S., 1975, Vibrational Relaxation Theories and Measurements, Revs. Mod. Phys. 47, 193-258. See especially Section V.A.

Pai, S. T., Reddy, S. P., and Cho, C. W., 1966, Infrared Absorption of Deuterium in Deuterium- Foreign Gas Mixtures, Can. J. Phys. 44, 2893-2903.

Poll, J. D., Hunt, J. L., and Mactaggart, J. W., 1975, Inter-collisional Interference Lines in the S Lines of H_2-He Mixtures, Can. J. Phys. 53, 954-961.

Prasad, R. D. G., and Reddy, S. P., 1976, Infrared Absorption Spectra of Gaseous HD. II. Collision-Induced Fundamental Band of HD in HD-Ne and HD-Ar Mixtures at Room Temperature, J. Chem. Phys. 65, 83-88.

Prasad, R. D. G., and Reddy, S. P., 1977, Infrared Absorption Spectra of Gaseous HD. III. Collision-Induced Fundamental Banf of HD in HD-Kr and HD-Xe Mixtures at Room Temperature, J. Chem. Phys. 66, 707-712.

Purcell, E. M., 1960, Nuclear Spin Relaxation and Nuclear Electric Dipole Moments, Phys. Rev. 117, 828-831.

Reddy, S. P., and Cho, C. W., 1965a, Induced Infrared Absorption of Nitrogen and Nitrogen-Foreign Gas Mixtures, Can. J. Phys. 43, 2331-2343.

Reddy, S. P., and Cho, C. W., 1965b, Infrared Absorption of Deuterium Induced by Intermolecular Forces, Can. J. Phys. 43, 793-799.

Reddy, S. P., and Lee, W. F., 1968, Pressure-Induced Infrared Absorption of the Fundamental Band of Hydrogen in H_2-Ne and H_2-Kr Mixtures at Room Temperature, Can. J. Phys. 46, 1373-1379.

Rothschild, W. G., 1984, Dynamics of Molecular Liquids, John Wiley and Sons. See Chapter 2, Section A5, especially A5.8.

Teitsma, A., and Egelstaff, P. A., 1980, Three-Body- Potential Contribution to the Structure of Krypton Gas, Phys. Rev. A 21, 367-78.

Van Kranendonk, J., 1957, Theory of Induced Infra-red Absorption, Physica 23, 825-837.

Van Kranendonk, J., 1959, Induced Infrared Absorption in Gases - Calculation of the Ternary Absorption Coefficents of Symmetrical Diatomic Molecules, Physica 25, 337-342.

Van Kranendonk. J., 1967, Intercollisional Interference Effects in Pressure-Induced Infrared Spectra (unpublished MS).

Van Kranendonk, J., 1968, Intercollisional Interference Effects in Pressure-Induced Infrared Spectra, Can. J. Phys. 46, 1173-1179.

Van Kranendonk, J., 1980, Intercollisional Interference Effects, in "Intermolecular Spectroscopy and Dynamical Properties of Dense Systems", J. Van Kranendonk (ed.), Societa Italiana di Fisica, Bologna, Italy, 1980. Course LXXV, Enrico Fermi Summer Schools.

Varghese, G., and Reddy, S. P., 1969, Further Studies on the Collision-Induced Absorption of the Fundamental Band of Hydrogen at Room Temperature, Can. J. Phys. 47, 2745-2751.

Welsh, H. L., 1974, Evolution of an Idea, Physics in Canada 30, no. 6, 84-95, Canadian Association of Physicists.

Wong, M., 1978, Collision-Induced Microwave Absorption in Certain Inert Gas Mixtures, (Ph.D. Thesis, University of Waterloo, Waterloo, Canada).

Zwanzig, R., 1961, Theory of Vibrational Relaxation in Liquids, J. Chem. Phys. 34, 1931-1935.

WORKSHOP REPORT: INFRARED ABSORPTION IN

COMPRESSED GASES

J.D. Poll and J.L. Hunt

Guelph Waterloo Programme for Graduate Work in Physics

Guelph Campus, Guelph,Ontario, Canada N1G 2W1

INTRODUCTION

In this report we will briefly review the contributions made
to the session on infrared absorption in compressed gases; we
will only consider the review talks and not the contributions
which were concerned with specific topics. In addition, we will
make some remarks of a general nature which we hope will reflect
the actual discussions that took place during the workshop.

WORKSHOP REPORT

Absorption and light scattering are determined by the dipole
moment and the polarizability of the system being investigated.
In many cases it is sufficient to know the dipoles and polarizabilities of the isolated molecules only. When interaction induced effects are important this is no longer the
case, and it becomes necessary to introduce the dipole (or
polarizability) of a pair or of a cluster of molecules. In
practice, only pair-dipoles (and polarizabilities) have been
considered up to the present time.

Two papers reviewed ab-initio calculations of dipoles and
polarizabilities of pairs of molecules viz: those of Hunt
and of Meyer. As pointed out by Hunt, pair properties at
sufficiently large separation can be expressed in terms of the
properties of the isolated molecules. This part of the subject
is in principle well understood although many of the higher
polarizabilities have not yet been calculated. At shorter
distance, the full electronic wave function of the pair has to be

evaluated. As pointed out by Meyer, the most difficult part of such a calculation is to properly take electron correlation into account; this has been possible so far only for simple systems like $H_2 - H_2$.

Apart from the ab-initio calculations there is also theoretical work which is aimed at establishing the link between the experimental results and the fundamental pair properties like dipoles (μ) polarizabilities (α) and intermolecular potentials (V). Frommhold reviewed how the detailed lineshape, at low density and not too low frequency, is related to the pair properties μ, α and V. Lewis discussed the same situation at low frequencies where intercollisional interference effects are important. The conclusion was that, given the fundamental pair quantities, low density spectra can be calculated accurately. Because of the limited accuracy and range of experimental data the converse is not the case. What is most needed in low density experimental work is data over a very large frequency range, preferably taken at many different temperatures to enable a really reliable determination of pair properties. Very low frequency data, using microwave techniques, were reviewed by Dagg. The connection between static and dynamic measurements were reviewed by Bose. Light scattering data generally comprise about four decades in intensity; for absorption usually only two decades are measured. This allows more accurate moments to be obtained from light scattering data.

Accurate experimental work at high gaseous densities has been done for a number of systems; such experiments and their interpretation were discussed by Buontempo. For dense systems the link between experiment and the quantities μ, α, and V cannot be uniquely made. There are a number of approaches to the interpretation of high density systems. A reliable, but unambitious, approach is to use only spectral moments; not all of the detailed information present in the line shape can be effectively used in this way. Phenomenological theories of high density systems suffer from difficulty of interpretation in terms of molecular properties. Theories of the Mori type provide much physical insight but because of the necessity of a cutoff are not suitable for an accurate determination of μ, α and V. On the other hand, for systems in which quantum effects are small, molecular dynamics provide a very powerful approach. It turns out that, at high densities, there is considerable cancellation between two and three-body effects even using only pair interactions. For this reason high accuracy of the molecular dynamics calculation is required to obtain quantitative results. Ideally, reliable μ, α and V's are used in the calculation and any discrepancies from experiment are to be interpreted in terms of contributions beyond the pair interactions to the potential, and perhaps the dipole and the polarizability as well; this ideal is just beginning to be realized.

A general question discussed at the workshop concerned the reliability of μ, α and V determined from experimental data. Because different experiments are sensitive to quite different ranges of the intermolecular separation (R) it is often very hard, if not impossible, to make statements about the accuracy of a function like $\mu(R)$ at a particular R. In comparing $\mu(R)$, $\alpha(R)$ and V(R) obtained from different experiments, or in comparing them with theory, it may be difficult to interpret any discrepancies that are observed. Whenever possible it would be preferable to take an ab-initio set of two-particle quantities and calculate the spectrum directly from it. In such a case discrepancies can be related directly to the approximations in the theory. It is realized that such an approach is not always practical, but we are convinced that too often the use of empirical and phenomenological procedures of interpretation will impede instead of facilitate an understanding of the physics involved.

Finally, we want to make some remarks about the problems that, in our view, should be addressed in the immediate future. In low density systems, the field has progressed to the point where only a rather sophisticated analysis of experimental results is worthwhile. To assume, for example, that only the quadrupolar induction mechanism is operating in the absorption spectrum of a homonuclear gas is no longer adequate. In addition, it is necessary to take the anisotropic intermolecular interaction into account (particularly at low temperature). Low density work in the future will turn to more complicated molecules where very many rotational states are involved; semiclassical methods will have to be developed to deal with these.

At high density information about non-additive properties will be obtained from high accuracy molecular dynamics. An outstanding problem is the one of incorporating quantum effects into molecular dynamics calculations. Other important problems at high density are concerned with the corrections due to internal field effects and the possibility of making a density expansion at a fixed frequency.

We note that interaction-induced effects will always be present in allowed spectra and, in particular, in the wings of the lines. Little work has been done in this area. The induced dipoles that have been most thoroughly investigated are those due to induction by overlap and by quadrupoles and by higher multipoles.

More work involving induction by monopoles and dipoles is to be expected. In conclusion we note the increasingly important role of induced phenomena in the atmospheric sciences and in astrophysics.

AB INITIO AND APPROXIMATE CALCULATIONS OF COLLISION-INDUCED

POLARIZABILITIES

Katharine L. C. Hunt

Department of Chemistry
Michigan State University
East Lansing, MI 48824

ABSTRACT

The size and extent of optimization of the basis sets, the
numerical precision attained in the density matrices, inclusion
of correlation effects, and the use of function counterpoise, hyperpolarization, and size-consistency corrections all affect the
accuracy of *ab initio* calculations of collision-induced polarizabilities, as exemplified by calculations on H_2 in the triplet state,
inert-gas atom pairs, and pairs of hydrogen and nitrogen molecules.
The dipole-induced-dipole (DID) model provides a good first approximation to the polarizability anisotropy for inert-gas pairs, but the
collision-induced term in the trace differs qualitatively from DID
predictions. Approximate methods such as those based on a nonlocal
polarizability density model or label-free exchange perturbation
theory are useful in evaluating collision-induced properties near
the van der Waals minima of pair potentials; these methods include
the effects of the distribution of polarizable matter in the
interacting molecules, exchange, hyperpolarization, and correlation
in addition to the polarization effects represented in the DID model.

INTRODUCTION

Dielectric and optical properties of compressed gases and
liquids are affected by the changes in molecular polarizabilities
occurring when molecules collide (Gelbart, 1974). The collision-
induced polarizability anisotropy and the molecular pair potential
determine the intensities and lineshapes for two-body depolarized
light scattering spectra (Tabisz, 1979; Frommhold, 1981; Birnbaum,
1982), and the collision-induced anisotropy contributes to the second

virial coefficients for the Kerr effect (Buckingham and Pople, 1955a; Buckingham, 1955, 1962), and electric-field induced birefringence. Similarly the pair potential and the interaction-induced change in mean polarizability $\Delta\bar{\alpha}$ suffice to calculate second refractivity virial coefficients (Buckingham and Pople, 1956; Buckingham and Graham, 1974) and two-body polarized light scattering spectra (Proffitt et al., 1980; Frommhold and Proffitt, 1981; Dacre and Frommhold, 1981); both $\Delta\bar{\alpha}$ and orientational terms depending upon interaction-induced dipoles contribute to second dielectric virial coefficients for nonpolar substances (Buckingham and Pople, 1955b). As described in this paper, *ab initio* and approximate calculations have been performed to determine the effects of overlap, exchange, hyperpolarization, and electron correlation on the total polarizability of a pair of molecules interacting at short range. The quantitative results, tested by comparison of calculated and experimental values for the two-body properties listed above, should prove useful in extracting information on dynamics in dense media from collision-induced light scattering spectra.

MODELS VALID AT LONG RANGE

A good "back-of-the-envelope" approximation for collision-induced polarizabilities is provided by the dipole-induced-dipole (DID) model, in which each molecule is represented as a point dipole, polarized by an applied field and the field due to the polarization induced in neighboring molecules (Silberstein, 1917). For a pair of molecules A and B separated by a vector $\vec{R}$, self-consistent solution of the equations

$$\vec{\mu}^A = \overset{\leftrightarrow}{\alpha}_0^A \cdot (\vec{E}_0 + \overset{\leftrightarrow}{T}(\vec{R}) \cdot \vec{\mu}^B) \tag{1}$$

and

$$\vec{\mu}^B = \overset{\leftrightarrow}{\alpha}_0^B \cdot (\vec{E}_0 + \overset{\leftrightarrow}{T}(\vec{R}) \cdot \vec{\mu}^A) \tag{2}$$

yields

$$\overset{\leftrightarrow}{\alpha}^A = [\, \mathbf{1} - \overset{\leftrightarrow}{\alpha}_0^A \cdot \overset{\leftrightarrow}{T}(\vec{R}) \cdot \overset{\leftrightarrow}{\alpha}_0^B \cdot \overset{\leftrightarrow}{T}(\vec{R})]^{-1} \cdot (\overset{\leftrightarrow}{\alpha}_0^A + \overset{\leftrightarrow}{\alpha}_0^A \cdot \overset{\leftrightarrow}{T}(\vec{R}) \cdot \overset{\leftrightarrow}{\alpha}_0^B) \tag{3}$$

and

$$\overset{\leftrightarrow}{\alpha}^B = [\, 1 - \overset{\leftrightarrow}{\alpha}_0^B \cdot \overset{\leftrightarrow}{T}(\vec{R}) \cdot \overset{\leftrightarrow}{\alpha}_0^A \cdot \overset{\leftrightarrow}{T}(\vec{R})]^{-1} \cdot (\overset{\leftrightarrow}{\alpha}_0^B + \overset{\leftrightarrow}{\alpha}_0^B \cdot \overset{\leftrightarrow}{T}(\vec{R}) \cdot \overset{\leftrightarrow}{\alpha}_0^A), \tag{4}$$

where $\overset{\leftrightarrow}{\alpha}_0^A$ and $\overset{\leftrightarrow}{\alpha}_0^B$ are the polarizabilities of the isolated A and B molecules, $\mathbf{1}$ denotes the unit tensor, and $\overset{\leftrightarrow}{T}(\vec{R})$ is the dipole propagator: $\overset{\leftrightarrow}{T}(\vec{R}) = \overset{\leftrightarrow}{\nabla\nabla}(\frac{1}{R})$. In the DID model a pair of atoms or isotropically polarizable molecules exhibits a collision-induced polarizability anisotropy at first order in the molecular interaction (i.e., first order in $\overset{\leftrightarrow}{T}(\vec{R})$), but the interaction-induced change in mean polarizability $\Delta\bar{\alpha}$ vanishes at first order. At second order $\Delta\bar{\alpha}$ is positive. The DID model correctly predicts that the two-body depolarized light scattering spectra of the inert gases and gases composed of isotropically polarizable polyatomic molecules are substantially higher in intensity than the corresponding two-body polarized scattering spectra (Tabisz, 1979; Dacre and Frommhold, 1982). Discrepancies between the intensities of the two-body depolarized spectra calculated for the inert gases using the DID model and accurate intensity measurements by Frommhold, Proffitt, Hong and Keto (Frommhold, 1981; Proffitt et al., 1981) and by Barocchi and Zoppi (1978) are small at low frequency shifts ($\sim$10% discrepancy for Ar at $\omega = 100$ cm^{-1}); also at low frequency shifts the collision-induced depolarized scattering spectra of CH_4, CF_4, SF_6 (Buckingham and Tabisz, 1977, 1978) and H_2 (Borysow and Frommhold, 1985) agree well with DID-based calculations. At high frequency shifts, however the DID intensities are too large by factors of 3-5 for the inert gases (Dacre and Frommhold, 1982), and too small for CH_4, CF_4, and SF_6 (Buckingham and Tabisz, 1977, 1978). Two-body polarized scattering spectra are not well approximated by the DID model (Dacre and Frommhold, 1982), and for helium and neon the experimentally determined second dielectric virial coefficients B_ϵ are negative (Orcutt and Cole, 1967; Kirouac and Bose, 1976; Vidal and Lallemand, 1976, 1977), in contrast with the DID prediction of a small positive B_ϵ.

The DID model neglects long-range higher multipole induction and electron correlation, as well as short-range overlap and exchange. For a pair of tetrahedral molecules, the lowest-order correction to the DID polarizability anisotropy depends upon the dipole-quadrupole polarizability $\overset{\leftrightarrow}{A}$ and varies as R^{-4} in the separation between the molecular centers, while for octahedral molecules the correction depends upon the dipole-octopole polarizability $\overset{\leftrightarrow}{E}$ and varies as R^{-5}. The rotational Raman scattering associated with these correction terms accounts in part for the high-frequency wings of the depolarized Rayleigh scattering peaks of CH_4, CD_4, CF_4, and SF_6 samples (Buckingham and Tabisz, 1977, 1978). Higher multipole terms appear at second order in the interaction between atoms in S states: the applied field polarizes one atom, producing a field gradient that induces a quadrupole in the neighboring atom, thus contributing to the reaction field at the first atom. The resulting change in pair polarizability depends upon the atomic quadrupole polarizability C and varies as R^{-8} in the interatomic distance (Buckingham and Clarke, 1978). For a pair of H atoms at the van der Waals minimum R = 7.85 a.u., the contribution of the quadrupole-induced-dipole (QID) term to $\Delta\bar{\alpha}$ is only 3-4% of the total long-range R^{-6} term ($\sim$14% of the R^{-6} term in the DID model), but for argon, krypton, and xenon pairs, the QID contribution to $\Delta\bar{\alpha}$ at the van der Waals minimum is more than 10% of the total R^{-6} term (Logan and Madden, 1982).

To order R^{-6}, the differences between the DID values for the pair polarizability and the total long-range pair polarizability are attributable to electron correlation (Jansen and Mazur, 1955). Buckingham has developed a simple model that represents correlation effects as a change in intrinsic polarizability of one molecule in the presence of another, due to the hyperpolarization of the first by the applied field and the field due to the fluctuating multipoles of the second (Buckingham, 1956; Buckingham and Clarke, 1978). Recently Hunt, Zilles, and Bohr (1981) have derived integral expressions for collision-induced polarizabilities in a model based on Buckingham's work but differing in two regards: first, the frequency dependence of the γ hyperpolarizability is incorporated in the model and second, the mean-square fluctuating multipoles are determined from the fluctuation-dissipation theorem, replacing Buckingham's estimate based on the coefficients C_n in the asymptotic expansion of the van der Waals interaction energy. For two S-state atoms, separated by a distance R along the z axis, this model gives

$$\alpha_{zz} \equiv \alpha_\parallel = \alpha_0^A + \alpha_0^B + 4\alpha_0^A \alpha_0^B R^{-3} + 4(1+\mathscr{P}_{AB})(\alpha_0^A)^2 \alpha_0^B R^{-6}$$

$$+(1+\mathscr{P}_{AB})\frac{\hbar}{4\pi} R^{-6} \int_{-\infty}^{\infty} [2\gamma_{zzxx}^A(0,iu,-iu)+4\gamma_{zzzz}^A(0,iu,-iu)]\alpha_0^B(iu)du \quad (5)$$

$$+ \ldots$$

and $\quad \alpha_{xx} \equiv \alpha_\perp = \alpha_0^A + \alpha_0^B - 2\alpha_0^A \alpha_0^B R^{-3} + (1+\mathscr{P}_{AB})(\alpha_0^A)^2 \alpha_0^B R^{-6}$

$$+ (1+\mathscr{P}_{AB})\frac{\hbar}{4\pi} R^{-6} \int_{-\infty}^{\infty} [\gamma_{xxxx}^A(0,iu,-iu)+5\gamma_{xxzz}^A(0,iu,-iu)]\alpha_0^B(iu)du \quad (6)$$

$$+ \ldots$$

where $\mathscr{P}_{AB}$ permutes the indices A and B. Through order R^{-6}, Eqs. (5) and (6) have been proven equivalent to the results of two-center fourth-order perturbation theory for the pair polarizability. Analogous results for the van der Waals energy coefficients C_n have been derived previously by Dalgarno (1967) and by Mavroyannis and Stephen (1962), while a corresponding expression for the collision-induced dipole coefficient D_7 has been derived by Galatry and Gharbi with use of the fluctuation-dissipation theorem (1980) and by Craig and Thirunamachandran in a direct application of perturbation theory (1981). The hyperpolarizability $\overleftrightarrow{\gamma}(0,\omega,-\omega)$ fixes the first virial coefficient for the DC Kerr effect in inert-gas samples, but its values at imaginary frequencies are not well known from *ab initio* calculations. The integrals in Eqs. (5) and (6) may be approximated by assuming that the ratio of $\gamma(0,\omega,-\omega)$ to $\alpha(\omega)$ is frequency-independent, yielding (Hunt et al., 1981)

$$\alpha_{\parallel} = \alpha_0^A + \alpha_0^B + 4\alpha_0^A\alpha_0^B R^{-3} + 4(1+\mathscr{P}_{AB})(\alpha_0^A)^2\alpha_0^B R^{-6}$$

$$+ \frac{7}{18}(1+\mathscr{P}_{AB})C_6^{AB}\gamma^A/\alpha_0^A R^{-6} + \dots \qquad (7)$$

$$\alpha_{\perp} = \alpha_0^A + \alpha_0^B - 2\alpha_0^A\alpha_0^B R^{-3} + (1+\mathscr{P}_{AB})(\alpha_0^A)^2\alpha_0^B R^{-6}$$

$$+ \frac{2}{9}(1+\mathscr{P}_{AB})C_6^{AB}\gamma^A/\alpha_0^A R^{-6} + \dots . \qquad (8)$$

For inert-gas homodiatoms, polarizabilities from Eqs. (7) and (8) are equivalent to those obtained by Buckingham and Clarke (1978); however, for interacting species with excitation frequencies that differ substantially, Eqs. (7) and (8) may give more accurate results than Buckingham's model. In Table 1, the coefficients of R^{-6} ($A_{\parallel}^{(6)}$ and $A_{\perp}^{(6)}$) in the model are listed for comparison with results from accurate perturbation calculations for H-atom (Buckingham et al., 1973) and He-atom pairs (Certain and Fortune, 1971).

The discrepancies between the calculated and experimentally determined second dielectric virial coefficients for the inert gases are <u>increased</u> by the addition of these long-range corrections to the DID model as are the discrepancies between calculated and experimental second Kerr virial coefficients (Buckingham and Dunmur, 1968; Dunmur and Jessup, 1979; Dunmur et al., 1979) and between calculated two-body depolarized light scattering intensities and the accurate results of Frommhold et al. (Frommhold, 1981; Dacre and Frommhold, 1982). Further, the experimental Kerr virial coefficients, depolarization ratios, and scattering intensities are consistent (Dunmur et al., 1983). Clearly in calculating pair polarizabilities it is essential to include corrections for overlap and exchange, either by *ab initio* computation or by approximation.

AB INITIO COMPUTATIONS: FACTORS AFFECTING ACCURACY

In order to calculate pair polarizabilities accurately, large basis sets with carefully selected orbital exponents are generally required. Since computed pair polarizabilities depend sensitively upon the overlap between the interacting charge distributions, it is important to represent the wave function well in regions far from the molecular nuclei; but these regions are not heavily weighted in variational calculations. In addition, most *ab initio* calculations on molecules with two or more nuclei are performed with Gaussian basis sets (for computational convenience in the evaluation of two-electron exchange integrals), but Gaussian functions fall off too rapidly at large distances from the function origin. The resulting Gaussian truncation error proves more problematic in collision-induced property calculations than in interaction energy calculations, because the errors in calculated dipole moments and polarizabilities

Table 1. Coefficients of R^{-6} in long-range expansions of
$\alpha_\parallel$ and $\alpha_\perp$ (in atomic units)

	Perturbation Theory	Model	DID Approximation
H-atom pairs			
$A_\parallel^{(6)}$	2558	2227	730
$A_\perp^{(6)}$	1268	1038	183
He-atom pairs			
$A_\parallel^{(6)}$	60.09	57	22
$A_\perp^{(6)}$	28.43	26	5.7

are first order in the error in the wave function, while the errors in the energy are second order. Interest in the difference between the computed collision-induced polarizabilities and DID model values imposes an added requirement for accuracy.

Ab initio calculations can be assessed qualitatively by considering the size of the basis set, the types of functions included, the treatment of correlation effects, and the numerical precision attained in the density matrix. As explained below, function counterpoise, hyperpolarization, and size-consistency corrections reduce the errors in calculated pair polarizabilities.

Extended basis calculations typically begin with single-molecule bases optimized to give near Hartree-Fock energies in self-consistent field calculations. Functions representing radial and angular correlation (Shavitt, 1977) are then added to the basis along with polarization functions that bring the calculated single-molecule polarizabilities into good agreement with experiment. In specific cases, hyperpolarization functions, p and d functions with exponents chosen to minimize the energy of the pair at the van der Waals minimum, and additional diffuse functions (Dacre, 1982a,c,d) have been included. Gaussian truncation error can be minimized by contracting a sufficiently large number of Gaussian functions into Slater-type orbitals (STO's). Dacre's 1978 calculations of the helium pair polarizability show that the convergence of the STO expansion to results obtained with the corresponding Slater basis is relatively slow; in the published calculations (Dacre, 1978), each s function is represented by 6 Gaussians, and each p or d function is represented by 4 Gaussians, for a total of 212 primitive orbitals contracted into 48 STO's (5s,

3p, and 2d on each He atom). Although Slater-basis calculations by
Arrighini et al. (1976) had previously shown the expected agreement
between the DID values for $\alpha_\parallel$ and $\alpha_\perp$ and the long-range self-consistent field (SCF) results, Dacre's work was the first to show this
agreement in a Gaussian basis; cf. Lim et al. (1970), Buckingham and
Watts (1973), O'Brien et al. (1973), and Fortune and Certain (1974).
For two He atoms separated by R = 8.0 a.u., Dacre's 48 STO basis
yields an SCF value for the pair polarizability anisotropy $\alpha_\parallel - \alpha_\perp$
differing by more than 65% from the best previous result (O'Brien
et al., 1973). At R = 6.0 a.u., discrepancies among the *ab initio*
results are considerably smaller: the value for the SCF anisotropy
in the 48-STO basis differs by 6% from the result of Fortune and
Certain (1974) and by 14% from the result of O'Brien et al. (1973);
however, the difference between the SCF and DID anisotropies is only
15% at this internuclear separation, and inclusion of correlation
effects reduces the difference to 7%. In the most accurate work to
date on the helium pair polarizability, Dacre (1982a) has employed an
82-STO basis comprising 146 Gaussian primitives. The polarizability
anisotropy computed with the extended basis typically differs by $\sim$1-2%
from the previous results, with the largest difference (6%) found at
the smallest internuclear separation, R = 3.0 a.u. In contrast, the
interaction-induced change in mean polarizability,

$$\Delta\overline{\alpha} = \frac{1}{3}\,(\alpha_\parallel + 2\alpha_\perp) - 2\alpha_0 \,, \tag{9}$$

differs between bases by as much as 40% for R near the van der Waals
minimum (Dacre, 1978, 1982a). The greater variability of $\Delta\overline{\alpha}$ reflects
the relative importance of exchange, overlap and correlation effects
in determining the trace of the collision-induced polarizability
($3\Delta\overline{\alpha}$), since $\Delta\overline{\alpha}$ vanishes to first order in the DID model.

Consideration of the physical effects that influence the calculated pair polarizability directly or indirectly is important in basis
set selection. For example, approximate calculations of the polarizabilities of H_2 ($^3\Sigma_u^+$ state) and He_2 show that hyperpolarization terms
(i.e., the contributions to the polarizability due to the interaction
of the hyperpolarized charge distribution on one atom with the unperturbed charge distribution on the other) are significant in both the
anisotropy and the trace of the polarizability at short range (Clarke
et al., 1978; Oxtoby, 1978), so full sets of d orbitals must be
included in the basis. Although hyperpolarization effects are
expected to be less important for the heavier inert gases, f orbitals
are required to obtain definitive results. As a second example, in
configuration interaction calculations on diatoms, it is necessary
first to include p functions with exponents optimized to represent
angular correlation in a single atom, and then to add more diffuse
p orbitals to represent polarization by external fields (Dacre, 1978).
Basis sets used in calculations on H-atom and inert-gas atom pairs
are listed in Table 2.

Table 2. Basis sets used in pair polarizability calculations

Atom	Single-atom basis (Primitive orbitals/contracted functions)	Reference
H	(10s, 8p, 1d/4s, 3p, 1d)	(Hunt and Buckingham, 1980)
He	(10s, 11p, 6d/10s, 7p, 2d)	(Dacre, 1982a)
Ne	(12s, 8p, 3d/7s, 4p, 3d)	(Dacre, 1981,1982b)
	(14s, 6p, 3d/10s, 5p, 3d)	(Kress and Kozak, 1977)
Ar	(15s, 11p, 3d/5s, 4p, 3d)	(Dacre, 1982c)
Kr	(23s, 14p, 10d/10s, 7p, 7d)	(Dacre, 1982d)
Xe	(18s, 12p, 8d/11s, 9p, 5d)	(Dacre, 1982d)

Time required for computation (scaling roughly as n^5 in the number of basis functions n) is the major factor limiting the size of basis sets; but also, as the basis-set size is increased, near-linear dependence may eventually develop in the basis, signalled by near-singularity of the overlap matrix and resulting in loss of precision (Kołos and Wolniewicz, 1965). Werner and Meyer (1976) have provided a useful prescription for replacing single functions by sets of independent functions when extending a basis.

Other factors influencing the accuracy of. *ab initio* calculations include numerical precision of the density matrix, hyperpolarization effects, the application of function counterpoise corrections, and (in single plus double excitation CI calculations on molecules with three or more electrons) the application of size-consistency corrections. Numerical precision in the density matrix is important because the pair polarizability must be computed as a difference between the "supermolecule" polarizability and the sum of the isolated molecule polarizabilities, and the difference rarely exceeds 10%. In calculations by finite field techniques, convergence of the density matrix to ∿6 figures is typically needed in order to obtain results for the pair polarizability good to 3 figures, assuming that a field strength E = 0.001 a.u. is used in the calculations (Dacre, 1978, 1982a; Hunt and Buckingham, 1980).

Hyperpolarization effects are usually negligible in calculations on pairs when the "supermolecule" has a center of symmetry, since the hyperpolarization contribution to the induced dipole is then reduced in magnitude by E^2 relative to the linear term. In a finite-field calculation on two H atoms with E = 0.01 a.u. contributions from the estimated pair hyperpolarizability (Hunt, 1980) would result in an error of ∿2% in the calculated pair polarizability. Hyper-polarization errors may be larger in calculations on noncentrosym-metric molecular pairs, for which the induced dipole includes terms varying as E^2, as well as those proportional to E and E^3.

Function counterpoise corrections were introduced by Boys and Bernardi (1970) to compensate for the differences in adequacy of the representations of isolated molecules and interacting pairs by limited basis sets. The function counterpoise correction (also termed basis extension or "ghost orbital" correction) is obtained by carrying out a calculation on an isolated molecule in a basis consisting of the orbitals for that molecule and the orbitals for a second molecule at a fixed separation and relative orientation, in the absence of nuclei on the second "ghost" center. In polarizability calculations, two "ghost orbital" polarizabilities are determined, one for the left molecule of a pair and the other for the right molecule; the ghost-orbital corrected polarizability is then obtained by subtracting the sum of these polarizabilities from the polarizability for the inter-acting pair. Calculations by Ostlund and Merrifield (1976) have shown that closer agreement with results of large-basis calculations of the helium pair polarizability is obtained if ghost-orbital correc-tions are applied to results from small basis sets (Buckingham and Watts, 1973), but this correction procedure is not rigorously justi-fiable. In large-basis studies on helium pairs, Dacre has found substantially larger function counterpoise corrections at CI level than at SCF level (Dacre, 1978, 1982a); but in calculations on neon pairs (with fewer basis functions per electron), the SCF and CI coun-terpoise corrections are comparable (Dacre, 1982b).

Finally a correction for size inconsistency is needed if a calculation on a "supermolecule" with three or more electrons is performed at CI level with single and double excitations only; SCF calculations are size consistent, as are full CI calculations and CI calculations in the coupled cluster approximation (Chiles and Dykstra, 1981) developed by Čížek et al. (1966, 1969a,b, 1971) or in the random phase approximation (Szabo and Ostlund, 1977). Size inconsistency arises in single plus double excitation CI calculations because the wave function for the isolated molecules at infinite separation effectively includes triple and quadruple excitations not part of the pair wavefunction, and thus the polarizability of the pair at infinite separation is typically less than the sum of the isolated-molecule polarizabilities. Corrections for size inconsistency may be made by estimating the effect of the omitted triple and quadruple excitations (Diercksen et al., 1981). Dacre has also proposed two correction schemes: in the first (Dacre, 1978), the effective collision-induced polarizability $\Delta\overleftrightarrow{\alpha}(\vec{R},\Omega_1,\Omega_2)$ is computed as

$$\Delta \overset{\leftrightarrow}{\alpha}(\vec{R},\Omega_1,\Omega_2) = \overset{\leftrightarrow}{\alpha}_{PAIR}(\vec{R},\Omega_1,\Omega_2) - \overset{\leftrightarrow}{\alpha}{}^{\ell}(\vec{R},\Omega_1,\Omega_2) - \overset{\leftrightarrow}{\alpha}{}^{r}(\vec{R},\Omega_1,\Omega_2) \quad (10)$$

$$- [\overset{\leftrightarrow}{\alpha}_{PAIR}(R=\infty) - \overset{\leftrightarrow}{\alpha}_0(\Omega_1) - \overset{\leftrightarrow}{\alpha}_0(\Omega_2)] ,$$

where $\overset{\leftrightarrow}{\alpha}_{PAIR}(\vec{R},\Omega_1,\Omega_2)$ is the total polarizability of the pair, $\overset{\leftrightarrow}{\alpha}{}^{\ell}(\vec{R},\Omega_1,\Omega_2)$ and $\overset{\leftrightarrow}{\alpha}{}^{r}(\vec{R},\Omega_1,\Omega_2)$ are the polarizabilities of the left and right molecules respectively as obtained in ghost-orbital calculations, and $[\overset{\leftrightarrow}{\alpha}_{PAIR}(R=\infty) - \overset{\leftrightarrow}{\alpha}_0(\Omega_1) - \overset{\leftrightarrow}{\alpha}_0(\Omega_2)]$ is a pure size-consistency correction; Ω_1 and Ω_2 denote the Euler angles for molecules 1 and 2. In the second (Dacre, 1982a) the CI contributions to single-molecule polarizabilities from ghost orbital calculations are scaled by the ratio of the CI term in the polarizability of an infinitely separated pair to the sum of the CI terms in the polarizabilities of the isolated molecules. The scaled quantities are then subtracted from the correlation contribution to $\overset{\leftrightarrow}{\alpha}$ for the "supermolecule" to give the CI term in $\Delta\overset{\leftrightarrow}{\alpha}$. Differences between results computed with the two schemes are small. Figure 1 shows the relative magnitudes of the ghost-orbital corrections (GOC) and the size-consistency corrections (SCC) in Dacre's 1982 calculations of the CI contributions to the pair polarizability of helium for R = 3.0 a.u. and R = 6.0 a.u. It is essential to note that the size-consistency correction is not an estimate of the error in the computed pair polarizability; instead, the remaining error depends upon the difference between size-consistency corrections at R = ∞ and at finite R.

AB INITIO COMPUTATIONS: RESULTS

    Collision-induced polarizabilities have been computed in *ab initio* studies of H...H in the triplet state (Hunt and Buckingham, 1980), He...He (Dacre, 1982a gives the best results to date), Ne...Ne (Kress and Kozak, 1977; Dacre, 1981, 1982b), Ar...Ar (Dacre, 1982c; Lallemand et al., 1974), Kr...Kr, Xe...Xe (Dacre, 1982d), $H_2...H_2$ (Bounds, 1979) and $N_2...N_2$ (Bounds et al., 1981). In this section the calculations are reviewed, results are analyzed in comparison with the DID model, and the level of agreement between calculated and experimental results is discussed.

    For $^3\Sigma_u^+$ H_2 (Hunt and Buckingham, 1980), He...He (Dacre, 1978, 1982a), and Ne...Ne (Dacre, 1981, 1982b) *ab initio* computations including configuration interaction have been performed. The results show several common features: at SCF (or restricted Hartree-Fock) level the long-range polarizability anisotropy $\alpha_{\parallel}(R)-\alpha_{\perp}(R)$ approaches the DID value computed with the SCF polarizability, as expected. Electron correlation effects increase the anisotropy for all internuclear separations studied. At the van der Waals minimum, the total polarizability anisotropy falls below the DID value calculated with α^{CI} ($\sim$6% for H...H, 10% for He...He, and 20% for Ne...Ne), and the ratio of the actual anisotropy to the DID model value generally

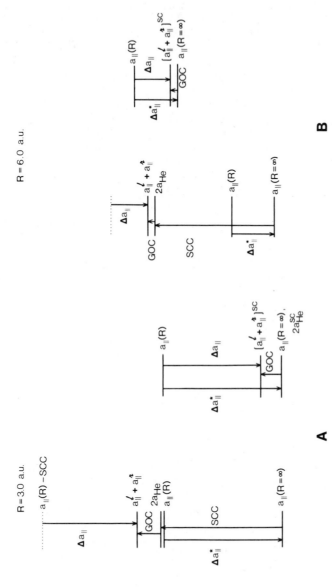

Fig. 1. Correlation contributions to the polarizabilities of helium pairs: $a_\parallel(R)$ denotes the correlation term in $\alpha_\parallel$ for a pair separated by R; a_{He}, the correlation term in the atomic polarizability (single-atom basis); and $a_\parallel^\ell + a_\parallel^r$, the sum of correlation terms in ghost-orbital calculations on the left and right atoms of a pair. For R = 3.0 (a) and R = 6.0(b) a.u., results obtained with separate size-consistency corrections (SCC) and ghost-orbital corrections (GOC) are compared with results obtained by scaling single-atom and ghost-orbital polarizabilities (indicated by superscript sc). In each case $\Delta a_\parallel^*$ is the apparent correlation term and $\Delta a_\parallel$, the collision-induced polarizability and $\Delta a_\parallel$, the corrected term.

273

decreases as the internuclear separation decreases. Though positive at long range, the trace of the collision-induced polarizability $3\Delta\bar{\alpha}$ is negative and relatively large in magnitude at the van der Waals minimum in each case; for smaller R the values of $\Delta\bar{\alpha}$ decrease further, thus showing little relation to the DID predictions. For $^3\Sigma_u^+$ H_2 correlation effects increase $\Delta\bar{\alpha}$ at all internuclear distances studied and for He...He correlation increases $\Delta\bar{\alpha}$ except at the smallest R values used (3.0 and 3.4 a.u.), but for Ne...Ne the correlation contribution to $\Delta\bar{\alpha}$ is negative for $R \leq 6.0$ a.u. Values for the collision-induced polarizability anisotropy and mean change in polarizability $\Delta\bar{\alpha}$ for helium and neon pairs are plotted in Fig. 2.

Comparison of the experimentally determined two-body depolarized light scattering spectra for $^3He_2$ and $^4He_2$ with the calculated spectra based on Dacre's results for the collision-induced polarizability anisotropy shows excellent agreement, except at the largest frequency shifts, $\omega \gtrsim 200$ cm^{-1} for $^4He_2$ (Dacre and Frommhold, 1982). Agreement between experimental and calculated results for the two-body contribution to the polarized scattering spectra is not as good, but uncertainties in the theoretical results are greater for the trace than for the anisotropy and experimental errors in the polarized scattering spectra are estimated at 50-60% (Dacre and Frommhold, 1982). The calculated second dielectric virial coefficient B_ϵ for helium at 294 K is $B_\epsilon = -0.062$ cm^6/mol^2, based on Dacre's values for $\Delta\bar{\alpha}$; this result is in excellent agreement with the experimental value reported in 1976 by Kirouac and Bose, $B_\epsilon = -0.059\pm0.009$ cm^6/mol^2 (see Table 3). For neon Dacre's CI calculations give $B_\epsilon = -0.15$ cm^6/mol^2 at 298 K. This value is smaller in absolute magnitude than the B_ϵ values obtained by Orcutt and Cole (1967) and by Vidal and Lallemand (1976,1977), but it agrees well with the most recent determination of B_ϵ by Bose (1985) and co-workers, $B_\epsilon = -0.17\pm0.01$ cm^6/mol^2 at 300 K. The polarizability anisotropy of neon pairs appears to be well determined in calculations at intermediate and long range since good agreement between experimental and calculated two-body depolarized scattering spectra is obtained for $\omega < 80$ cm^{-1} (Dacre and Frommhold, 1982). At short range, however, $\alpha_\parallel - \alpha_\perp$ shows an unexplained local maximum (Kress and Kozak, 1977; Dacre, 1982b); this may result from a reorganization of electron density in the region of significant charge overlap, but it may be an artifact of the basis set. A similar local maximum in the helium pair polarizability anisotropy near R = 3.0 a.u. was found by Buckingham and Watts (1973) in calculations with a 16-function basis on each atom. The minimum internuclear separation in Dacre's calculations on the helium pair is R = 3.0 a.u., so it is not certain whether the maximum is also found with a larger basis.

For Ar...Ar (Dacre, 1982c), Kr...Kr, Xe...Xe (Dacre, 1982d), H_2...H_2 (Bounds, 1979) and N_2...N_2 (Bounds et al., 1981), calculations have been carried out at SCF level only. Based on the results for helium and neon, Dacre has estimated the actual polarizability

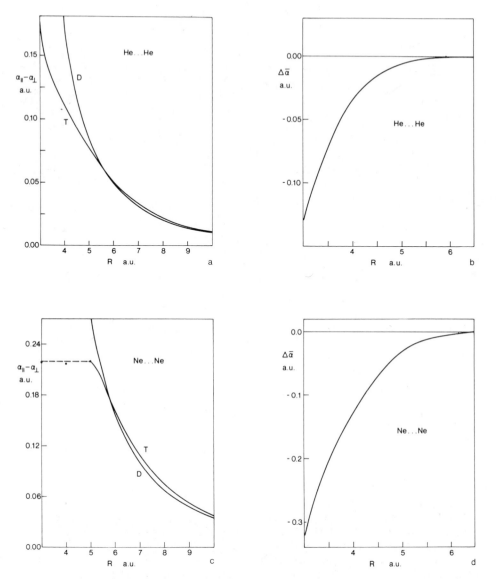

Fig. 2. Collision-induced polarizabilities for He and Ne pairs.
(a) Collision-induced polarizability anisotropy for He...He;
(b) collision-induced change in mean polarizability for He...
He; (c) collision-induced polarizability anisotropy for Ne...
Ne; (d) collision-induced change in mean polarizability for
Ne...Ne. D labels the DID curves computed with SCF polarizabilities and T labels the total anisotropy (SCF + CI). Calculated short-range results are indicated by solid circles in
(c).

275

Table 3. Comparison of experimental and calculated second dielectric
virial coefficients for helium and neon

Helium	B_ε (cm^6/mol^2)	T(K)
Experimental values		
Orcutt and Cole (1967)	−0.06±0.04	322
Kirouac and Bose (1976)	−0.059±0.009	294
Vidal and Lallemand (1976)	−0.11±0.02	298
Lallemand and Vidal (1977)	−0.08±0.01	298
Calculated values		
Dacre SCF (1982a)	−0.085	294
CI (1982a)	−0.062	294
Neon		
Experimental values		
Orcutt and Cole (1967)	−0.30±0.10	322
Vidal and Lallemand (1976)	−0.24±0.04	298
Lallemand and Vidal (1977)	−0.22±0.02	298
Calculated values		
Dacre SCF (1982b)	−0.14	298
CI (1982b)	−0.15	298

anisotropies for the heavier inert gases (including correlation
effects) by scaling the SCF anisotropies by $[\alpha(\omega)/\alpha_{SCF}]^2$, where
$\alpha(\omega)$ is the experimentally determined single-atom polarizability
at frequency ω and α_{SCF} is the SCF single-atom polarizability. This
scaling law applies exactly to the first-order DID contributions
to the anisotropy. Though other contributions to the anisotropy
do not scale in this way, for He pairs the discrepancy between the
actual CI results for the anisotropy and the SCF results scaled by
the square of the single-atom polarizability ratio α_{CI}/α_{SCF} is less
than 1% for the range R = 3.0-5.6 a.u. and less than 3% for all R
values. Unscaled SCF results, in contrast, are too small by 6-9%.
For neon the scaling procedure gives anisotropies larger than the
counterpoise-corrected CI results by $\sim$9%, but in better agreement
than SCF results. Dacre has also shown that the mean collision-
induced polarizability for helium pairs may be separated into an SCF
trace scaled by $(\alpha_{CI}/\alpha_{SCF})^3$ plus a long-range dispersion correction,
$\Delta\bar{A}R^{-6}$; the difference between the CI values of $\Delta\bar{\alpha}$ and the scaled

SCF results is close to 30 R^{-6} over the range of R values from
4.5-8.0 a.u.

The SCF polarizability anisotropies for Ar, Kr, and Xe pairs
(Dacre, 1982c, d) are slightly larger than the DID predictions at
long range, but smaller than DID results by 5-15% at the van der
Waals minima. The SCF traces $3\Delta\overline{\alpha}$ also exceed the DID values at long
range, with deviations most pronounced for xenon pairs. In each case,
as the internuclear separation is decreased $\Delta\overline{\alpha}$ goes through a maximum,
and at the van der Waals minimum R_{min} the counterpoise-corrected SCF
trace of the collision-induced polarizability is negative (though $\Delta\overline{\alpha}$
is near zero for Xe pairs). For $R < R_{min}$, $\Delta\overline{\alpha}$ is large and negative
except at very small R where $\Delta\overline{\alpha}$ rises sharply. Qualitatively the
behavior of $\Delta\overline{\alpha}$ is in accord with the predictions of Buckingham and
Watts (1973).

The two-body depolarized scattering spectra computed from the
scaled SCF results are in very good agreement with spectra recorded
by Proffitt et al. (1981) and by Barocchi and Zoppi (1978) (see Dacre
and Frommhold, 1982) for argon, krypton and xenon. Again discrepancies between experimental and calculated results are quite small
for low frequency shifts. For accurate calculations of polarized
light scattering spectra and second dielectric virial coefficients,
inclusion of correlation appears to be necessary: the SCF value of
B_ϵ for argon at 322 K is less than ten percent of the experimentally
determined B_ϵ (Orcutt and Cole, 1967; Bose and Cole, 1970; Lallemand
and Vidal, 1977).

Two SCF polarizability calculations for pairs of diatomic molecules have been reported, one for $H_2...H_2$ with a (3s,2p) Gaussian
basis on each H atom (Bounds, 1979) and one for $N_2...N_2$ with a
(5s,4p,1d) Gaussian basis on each N atom (Bounds et al., 1981).
The DID model represents the SCF results reasonably well for N_2
dimers in all relative orientations studied (rectangular, linear,
T-shape, and cross-T) when the separation between the molecular
centers is greater than $R \sim 8.0$ a.u.; discrepancies are greatest in
$\alpha_\perp$ values for collinear molecules. At short range the $N_2...N_2$
collision-induced polarizabilities are smaller in magnitude than the
DID values, as a result of overlap and exchange. Calculations with
larger bases (certainly feasible for $H_2...H_2$) are expected to preserve these qualitative features, though the numerical results may
differ (cf. Dacre, 1978, 1982a).

METHODS OF APPROXIMATING COLLISION-INDUCED PROPERTIES

Because of the extensive time requirements for *ab initio* calculations, there is interest in approximations for collision-induced
polarizabilities including overlap and exchange corrections. In this
section a nonlocal polarizability density model and a label-free
exchange perturbation model for collision-induced properties are

277

outlined. These models permit direct calculation of the interaction-induced changes in pair properties and also permit identification of different physical contributions to net pair properties.

Polarizability densities represent the distribution of polarizable matter throughout the interacting molecules (Jameson and Buckingham, 1980) and thus yield overlap corrections to the DID results. In the first models developed (Theimer and Paul, 1965; Oxtoby and Gelbart, 1975a, b), local dipole polarizability densities were used to describe the polarization induced at point $\vec{r}$ in a molecule by the applied field $\vec{F}(\vec{r})$ at the same point; however, since the shift in charge at one point in a molecule depends upon the charge shifts induced by the applied field elsewhere in the molecule (Clarke et al., 1978; Sipe and Van Kranendonk, 1978), these models are valid at best to first order in the intermolecular interaction. Models accurate to arbitrary order in electrostatic and induction interactions can be based on local polarizability densities if intramolecular contributions are included in computing the polarizing field at $\vec{r}$ (Frisch and McKenna, 1965; Orttung, 1977, 1978); only the response to applied fields need be considered if the model is based on local multipole polarizability densities of all orders (Oxtoby, 1980) or on nonlocal polarizability densities (Hunt, 1983, 1984).

The nonlocal polarizability density $\overleftrightarrow{\alpha}(\vec{r},\vec{r}';\omega)$ introduced by Maaskant and Oosterhoff (1964) gives the ω-frequency component of the polarization induced at point $\vec{r}$ in a molecule by application of a field $\vec{F}(\vec{r}',\omega)$ due to charges not part of that molecule:

$$\vec{P}(\vec{r},\omega) = \int \overleftrightarrow{\alpha}(\vec{r},\vec{r}';\omega)\cdot\vec{F}(\vec{r}',\omega)d\vec{r}' \ . \tag{11}$$

If the frequency of the applied field ω differs from the transition frequencies ω_{m0} between the ground state ϕ_0 and excited states ϕ_m, and if $\vec{F}(\vec{r},\omega)$ is derivable from a scalar potential,

$$\alpha_{\alpha\beta}(\vec{r},\vec{r}';\omega) = \frac{2}{\hbar}\sum_{n\neq0}\frac{\omega_{n0}}{\omega_{n0}^2-\omega^2}[P_\alpha(\vec{r})]_{0n}[P_\beta(\vec{r}')]_{n0}, \tag{12}$$

where the polarization operator $\hat{P}(\vec{r})$ (Power, 1964) is related to the charge density operator $\hat{\rho}(\vec{r})$ and the current density operator $\hat{j}(\vec{r})$ by

$$\vec{\nabla}\cdot\hat{P}(\vec{r}) = -\hat{\rho}(\vec{r}) \tag{13}$$

and

$$\dot{\hat{P}}(\vec{r}) = \hat{j}(\vec{r}) \ . \tag{14}$$

In Eq. (12) and below, Greek subscripts designate the Cartesian components of vectors and tensors, and the convention that repeated Greek subscripts imply summation over x, y, and z terms is used

278

throughout. In the derivation of Eq. (12), the functions ϕ_n are assumed to be purely real; and the spin current density is assumed to vanish.

From Eqs. (12) and (13) the longitudinal part of the spatial Fourier transform of the nonlocal polarizability density $\alpha_{kk'}(\vec{k},\vec{k}';\omega)$ is related to a known charge susceptibility density $\chi(\vec{k},\vec{k}';\omega)$ (Longuet-Higgins, 1965). This relation provides a means of computing $\alpha_{kk'}(\vec{k},\vec{k}';\omega)$ because $\chi(\vec{k},\vec{k}';\omega)$ can be evaluated using a function determined variationally (Koide, 1976), and in the Unsöld approximation $\chi(\vec{k},\vec{k}';\omega)$ is related to molecular form factors (Linder et al., 1980; Malinowski et al., 1981). Charge susceptibility densities have been determined to a good approximation for H, He, Ar, and Xe atoms (Krauss et al., 1979a, b, 1980, 1982).

To apply this model in computing collision-induced polarizabilities, it is necessary to add nonlinear response governed by the nonlocal hyperpolarizability densities $\beta(\vec{r},\vec{r}',\vec{r}'';\omega-\omega',\omega')$ and $\overset{\leftrightarrow}{\gamma}(\vec{r},\vec{r}',\vec{r}'',\vec{r}''';\omega-\omega'-\omega'',\omega',\omega'')$ (Hunt, 1984). The polarization at point $\vec{r}$ in one molecule of an interacting pair is then the sum of the polarization (both permanent and fluctuating) of the unperturbed molecule, the polarization produced by linear response to the effective field at other points $\vec{r}'$, the polarization induced nonlinearly by the effective fields at $\vec{r}'$ and $\vec{r}''$, and higher-order terms. The effective field acting on molecule A may be split into the external field $\vec{F}_0$ plus the field due to the polarization of the second molecule B; solving the equations for the polarization of molecules A and B self-consistently, computing the total dipole

$$\vec{\mu} = \int [\vec{P}^A(\vec{r}) + \vec{P}^B(\vec{r})]d\vec{r} , \qquad (15)$$

and selecting terms linear in the external field $\vec{F}_0$ gives the total pair polarizability. The model generates induction and dispersion terms in $\overset{\leftrightarrow}{\alpha}$, but an exchange correction must be added separately (Oxtoby and Gelbart, 1975b). The collision-induced polarizability $\Delta\overset{\leftrightarrow}{\alpha}$ satisfies

$$\Delta\overset{\leftrightarrow}{\alpha} = \Delta\overset{\leftrightarrow}{\alpha}{}^A_{IND} + \Delta\overset{\leftrightarrow}{\alpha}{}^A_{DISP} + \Delta\overset{\leftrightarrow}{\alpha}{}^B_{IND} + \Delta\overset{\leftrightarrow}{\alpha}{}^B_{DISP} + \Delta\overset{\leftrightarrow}{\alpha}_{EX} . \qquad (16)$$

The induction and dispersion terms are most conveniently written in terms of the Fourier transforms of reduced polarizability densities,

$$\hat{\alpha}_{\alpha\beta}(\vec{r},\omega) = \int \alpha_{\alpha\beta}(\vec{r},\vec{r}';\omega)d\vec{r}' \qquad (17)$$

$$\hat{\beta}_{\alpha\beta\gamma}(\vec{r},\vec{r}';\omega,\omega') = \int \beta_{\alpha\beta\gamma}(\vec{r},\vec{r}',\vec{r}'';\omega,\omega')d\vec{r}'' \qquad (18)$$

and

$$\hat{\gamma}_{\alpha\beta\gamma\delta}(\vec{r},\vec{r}',\vec{r}'';\omega,\omega',\omega'') = \int \gamma_{\alpha\beta\gamma\delta}(\vec{r},\vec{r}',\vec{r}'',\vec{r}''';\omega,\omega',\omega'')d\vec{r}''' , \qquad (19)$$

and doubly reduced hyperpolarizability densities $\hat{\hat{\beta}}(\vec{r};\omega,\omega')$ and $\hat{\hat{\gamma}}(\vec{r},\vec{r}';\omega,\omega',\omega'')$ obtained by integrating over two spatial coordinates. To first order in the A-B interaction there are two nonvanishing contributions to $\Delta\alpha^A_{IND}$, the change in the static polarizability of A due to induction effects (Hunt, 1984):

$$\alpha^A_{\alpha\beta}(1,1) = \frac{1}{(2\pi)^3}\int \hat{\alpha}^A_{\gamma\alpha}(-\vec{k};\omega=0)T_{\gamma\delta}(\vec{k})\hat{\alpha}^B_{\delta\beta}(\vec{k};\omega=0)d\vec{k} \qquad (20)$$

and

$$\alpha^A_{\alpha\beta}(2,1) = \frac{1}{(2\pi)^3}\int \hat{\hat{\beta}}^A_{\gamma\alpha\beta}(-\vec{k};\omega=0,\omega'=0)T_{\gamma\delta}(\vec{k})\overline{P}^B_{0\delta}(\vec{k})d\vec{k}, \qquad (21)$$

where $\overline{P}^B_{0\delta}(\vec{r})$ is the δ-component of the permanent polarization of B and $\overleftrightarrow{T}(\vec{k})$ is the Fourier transform of $\overleftrightarrow{T}(\vec{R})$. Three additional induction terms are found at second order in the A-B interaction, along with the lowest-order dispersion term,

$$(\alpha^A_{DISP})_{\alpha\beta} = \frac{\hbar}{(2\pi)^7}\int_0^\infty d\omega\int \hat{\hat{\gamma}}^A_{\gamma\delta\beta\alpha}(-\vec{k},-\vec{k}';i\omega,-i\omega,0)\alpha^B_{\epsilon\phi}(-\vec{k},-\vec{k}';i\omega)$$

$$T_{\gamma\epsilon}(\vec{k})T_{\phi\delta}(\vec{k}')d\vec{k}\ d\vec{k}'; \qquad (22)$$

overlap damping of the long-range (R^{-6}) correlation contribution to $\overleftrightarrow{\Delta\alpha}$ is included automatically in Eq. (22). The longitudinal part of $\overleftrightarrow{\alpha}(\vec{k},\vec{k}';\omega)$ suffices to evaluate the integrals in Eqs. (20) and (22).

For interacting closed-shell atoms (Oxtoby and Gelbart, 1975b; Lacey and Byers Brown, 1974) the exchange term in $\overleftrightarrow{\Delta\alpha}$ is approximated by

$$(\Delta\alpha_{EX})_{\alpha\beta} = \lim_{F_0\to 0}\frac{\partial}{\partial F_{0\beta}}[Tr(-2X^{AA}_\alpha S^{AB}S^{BA}-2X^{BB}_\alpha S^{BA}S^{AB}+4X^{AB}_\alpha S^{BA})]; \qquad (23)$$

the matrices S^{AB}, $\vec{X}^{AA}$, and $\vec{X}^{AB}$ have elements

$$S^{AB}_{ij} = \langle\psi^A_i|\psi^B_j\rangle, \qquad (24)$$

$$\vec{X}^{AA}_{ij} = \langle\psi^A_i|\vec{x}|\psi^A_j\rangle, \qquad (25)$$

and

$$\vec{X}^{AB}_{ij} = \langle\psi^A_i|\vec{x}|\psi^B_j\rangle, \qquad (26)$$

where ψ^A_i denotes the ith occupied orbital on atom A in the external field $\vec{F}_0$. (Effects of correlation on the exchange energy are not included in the theory from which Eq. (23) is derived. Thus the theory does not give the correct asymptotic form for the energy difference between the singlet and triplet states of H_2, for example (Jeziorski and Kołos, 1982); but numerical differences between results of the theory and an accurate asymptotic form (Herring and Flicker, 1964) are small for $R \lesssim 12$ a.u.).

Comparison of *ab initio* results for the polarizability of H_2 in the triplet state with results from the nonlocal polarizability density model taken to first order in the molecular interaction shows that the model may provide useful estimates of the overlap reductions in $\Delta\overset{\leftrightarrow}{\alpha}$ relative to DID values. It is also useful in approximating pair properties for planar molecules in "sandwich" configurations where overlap is small but the molecules are poorly represented by point-polarizable multipoles of low order.

If $\alpha(\vec{r},\vec{r}')$ is approximated in terms of the relay tensor $\overset{\leftrightarrow}{B}_{ij}$ (Applequist et al., 1972, 1977) by

$$\overset{\leftrightarrow}{\alpha}(\vec{r},\vec{r}') = \sum_{i,j} \overset{\leftrightarrow}{B}_{ij}\delta(\vec{r}-\vec{r}_i)\delta(\vec{r}'-\vec{r}_j) , \qquad (27)$$

then the nonlocal polarizability density model for molecular polarization reduces to Applequist's point-atom-polarizability approximation. Keyes and Ladanyi (1977, 1983), Posch (1985), and Buckingham and Hunt (1980) have applied Applequist's approximation to entire A-B "supermolecules" in order to determine the influence of the distribution of polarizable matter on collision-induced polarizabilities.

Obvious limitations of the nonlocal polarizability density model are the approximations in $\Delta\overset{\leftrightarrow}{\alpha}_{EX}$, the neglect of nonadditive exchange-induction and exchange-dispersion effects, and omission of changes in intramolecular correlation due to intermolecular electron correlation. These limitations can be removed in a complete calculation employing "label-free" exchange perturbation theory (Jansen, 1967; Ritchie, 1968a,b; Rumyantsev, 1974). In the label-free formalism, in contrast with the exchange perturbation theory developed by Murrell and Shaw (1967a,b, 1968), both the unperturbed Hamiltonian H_0 and the perturbation term V are explicitly cast in a form invariant under exchange of electrons between the two interacting molecules A and B:

$$H_0 = \sum_{i=1}^{p} [H_{A(i)} + H_{B(i)}]\Lambda_i \qquad (28)$$

and

$$V = \sum_{i=1}^{p} V_{(i)}\Lambda_i . \qquad (29)$$

In these equations p is the number of ways of assigning N_A electrons to molecule A and N_B to B, from a total of $N_A + N_B$, $H_{A(i)}$ is the A-molecule Hamiltonian for the ith assignment of electrons to A and B, and Λ_i is a projection operator for the ith electron assignment. (The definition is easily generalized to include projection operators for ionic terms in the wavefunction with $N_A + \Delta N$ electrons assigned to molecule A and $N_B - \Delta N$ assigned to B.) If ψ is a wavefunction antisymmetrized by summing over permutations σ of electrons between A and B,

$$\psi = \mathcal{N} \sum_{\sigma} (-1)^{\sigma} P_{\sigma} [\phi_A (1,2 \ldots N_A) \phi_B (N_A + 1, \ N_A + 2 \ldots N_A + N_B)]$$

$$= \sum_{i=1}^{p} c_i \phi_i \ , \tag{30}$$

then

$$\Lambda_i \psi = c_i \phi_i \ . \tag{31}$$

Mahanty and Majumdar (1982) have applied this formalism to "zeroth" order in calculating the He...H dipole; at this order the label-free exchange perturbation formalism is equivalent to the antisymmetrization approximation for heterodiatom dipoles derived by Lacey and Byers Brown (1974). Calculations using Murrell-Shaw exchange perturbation theory overestimate the negative overlap contributions to both the polarizability anisotropy and the trace of the polarizability for H_2 in the lowest triplet state (Hunt and Buckingham, 1980), but Hilton and Oxtoby (1981) have shown that this error can be significantly reduced by choosing a sufficiently large basis on each H center.

Harris, Heller and Gelbart (1974, 1975) have applied the electron gas model to compute polarizabilities for inert-gas atom pairs. The model includes linear electrostatic effects, hyperpolarization, exchange, and correlation effects (when the molecular charge distributions overlap), but since induction effects and full dispersion effects are not included it does not give the proper long range form for the pair polarizability. In electron gas calculations the electron density at each point in space is approximated as the sum of the densities of molecules A and B in an external field, but unperturbed by A-B interactions; this approximation is not made in either of the theoretical treatments discussed above.

Quantum Monte Carlo calculations (Reynolds, et al., 1982) have been suggested as a nonstandard *ab initio* means of computing pair polarizabilities, since the approach yields good results for He...He and H_2...H_2 pair potentials (Alder et al., 1982). In principle, polarizabilities could be determined in finite field calculations or by use of the fluctuation-dissipation theorem and a Kramers-Kronig relation.

COLLISION-INDUCED NONLINEAR RESPONSE TENSORS

Intermolecular interactions also affect the β and γ hyperpolarizabilities of molecular pairs. For atoms A and B in S states, the lowest-order contribution to the pair β hyperpolarizability varies as R^{-4} at long range. If atom B is located at a large distance R in the positive z direction from A,

$$\beta_{zzz}^{AB} = 6 (B^A \alpha^B - B^B \alpha^A)/R^4 + \mathcal{O}(R^{-7}) \tag{32}$$

and

$$\beta^{AB}_{zxx} = \beta^{AB}_{zyy} = 3(B^B\alpha^A - B^A\alpha^B)/R^4 + \mathcal{O}(R^{-7}) \ , \tag{33}$$

where the constant B (Buckingham, 1967) gives the atomic energy change ΔE quadratic in an applied field F_z and linear in an applied field gradient F'_{zz} $(F'_{zz} = -2F'_{xx} = -2F'_{yy})$,

$$\Delta E = -\frac{1}{4} B F'_{zz} F^2_z. \tag{34}$$

The dispersion contribution to the pair β hyperpolarizability varies as R^{-7}, as for the dispersion dipole. For the H...He pair, with $\alpha^H = 9/2$ a.u., $B^H = -213/2$ a.u., $\alpha^{He} = 1.38$ a.u., and $B^{He} = -6.587$ a.u. (Bhattacharya and Mukherjee, 1973), $\beta^{H\cdot He}_{zzz} \cong -704 \ R^{-4}$ a.u.

At long range, the collision-induced γ hyperpolarizability of a homodiatom pair (Hunt, 1980) is related to the single-atom polarizability α and hyperpolarizability γ by

$$\Delta\gamma_{zzzz} = 16\alpha\gamma R^{-3} + \mathcal{O}(R^{-5}) \tag{35}$$

$$\Delta\gamma_{xxxx} = -8\alpha\gamma R^{-3} + \mathcal{O}(R^{-5}) \tag{36}$$

$$\Delta\gamma_{xxzz} = \frac{4}{3} \alpha\gamma R^{-3} + \mathcal{O}(R^{-5}) \ . \tag{37}$$

Classical contributions varying as R^{-5} and R^{-6} and an estimate of the dispersion contribution varying as R^{-6} have been given by Hunt (1980). Since hyperpolarizabilities generally depend upon the perturbed charge distributions at greater distances from the nuclei than for polarizabilities, these properties are expected to show greater sensitivity to overlap effects.

REFERENCES

Alder, B. J., Ceperley, D. M., and Reynolds, P. J., 1982, Stochastic calculation of interaction energies, J. Phys. Chem., 86:1200.
Applequist, J., 1977, An atom dipole interaction model for molecular optical properties, Acc. Chem. Res., 10:79.
Applequist, J., Carl, J. R., and Fung, K.-K., 1972, An atom dipole interaction model for molecular polarizabilities. Application to polyatomic molecules and determination of atom polarizabilities, J. Am. Chem. Soc., 94:2952.
Arrighini, G. P., Guidotti, C., and Lamanna, U. T., 1976, Refractivity of He gas: An estimate of its second virial coefficient, Chem. Phys., 16:29.
Barocchi, F., and Zoppi, M., 1978, Collision-induced light scattering spectra and pair polarizability of gaseous argon, Phys. Lett., A66:99.

Bhattacharya, A. K., and Mukherjee, P. K., 1973, Coupled Hartree-Fock calculation of the uniform field quadrupole polarizabilities and shielding factors of S-state ions, Int. J. Quantum Chem., 7:491.

Birnbaum, G., 1982, The study of atomic and molecular interactions from collision-induced spectra, in: "Proceedings of the Eighth Symposium on Thermophysical Properties, Vol. I: Thermophysical Properties of Fluids", J. V. Sengers, ed., The American Society of Mechanical Engineers, New York.

Bose, T. K., 1985, this volume.

Bose, T. K., and Cole, R. H., 1970, Dielectric and pressure virial coefficients of imperfect gases. II. CO_2-argon mixtures, J. Chem. Phys., 52:140.

Bounds, D. G., 1979, The interaction polarizability of two hydrogen molecules, Molec. Phys., 38:2099.

Bounds, D. G., Hinchliffe, A., and Spicer, C. J., 1981, The interaction polarizability of two nitrogen molecules, Molec. Phys., 42:73.

Boys, S. F., and Bernardi, F., 1970, The calculation of small molecular interactions by the differences of separate total energies. Some procedures with reduced errors, Molec. Phys., 19:553.

Buckingham, A. D., 1955, Theoretical studies of the Kerr effect II: The influence of pressure, Proc. Phys. Soc., A68:910.

Buckingham, A. D., 1956, The polarizability of a pair of interacting atoms, Trans. Faraday Soc., 52:1035.

Buckingham, A. D., 1962, Frequency dependence of the Kerr constant, Proc. R. Soc., A267:271.

Buckingham, A. D., 1967, Permanent and induced molecular moments and long-range intermolecular forces, Advan. Chem. Phys., 12:107.

Buckingham, A. D., and Clarke, K. L., 1978, Long-range effects of molecular interactions on the polarizability of atoms, Chem. Phys. Letters, 57:321.

Buckingham, A. D., and Dunmur, D. A., 1968, Kerr effect in inert gases and sulphur hexafluoride, Trans. Faraday Soc., 64:1776.

Buckingham, A. D., and Graham, C., 1974, The density dependence of the refractivity of gases, Proc. R. Soc., A337:275.

Buckingham, A. D., and Hunt, K. L. C., 1980, The pair polarizability anisotropy of SF_6 in the point-atom-polarizability approximation, Molec. Phys., 40:643.

Buckingham, A. D., Martin, P. H., and Watts, R. S., 1973, The polarizability of a pair of hydrogen atoms at long range, Chem. Phys. Letters, 21:186.

Buckingham, A. D., and Pople, J. A., 1955a, Theoretical studies of the Kerr effect I: Deviations from a linear polarization law, Proc. Phys. Soc., A68:905.

Buckingham, A. D., and Pople, J. A., 1955b, The dielectric constant of an imperfect nonpolar gas, Trans. Faraday. Soc., 51:1029.

Buckingham, A. D., and Pople, J. A., 1956, Electromagnetic properties of compressed gases, Disc. Faraday Soc., 22:17.

Buckingham, A. D., and Tabisz, G. C., 1977, Collision-induced rotational Raman scattering, Optics Lett., 1:220.

Buckingham, A. D., and Tabisz, G. C., 1978, Collision-induced rotational Raman scattering by tetrahedral and octahedral molecules, Molec. Phys., 36:583.

Buckingham, A. D., and Watts, R. S., 1973, The polarizability of a pair of helium atoms, Molec. Phys., 26:7.

Certain, P. R., and Fortune, P. J., 1971, Long-range polarizability of the helium diatom, J. Chem. Phys., 55:5818.

Chiles, R. A., and Dykstra, C. E., 1981, An electron pair operator approach to coupled cluster wavefunctions. Application to He_2, Be_2, and Mg_2 and comparison with CEPA methods, J. Chem. Phys., 74:4544.

Čížek, J., 1966, On the correlation problem in atomic and molecular systems. Calculation of wavefunction components in Ursell-type expansion using quantum-field theoretical methods, J. Chem. Phys., 45:4256.

Čížek, J., 1969a, On the use of the cluster expansion and the technique of diagrams in calculations of correlation effects in atoms and molecules, Advan. Chem. Phys., 14:35.

Čížek, J., Paldus, J., and Sroubkova, L., 1969b, Cluster expansion analysis for delocalized systems, Int. J. Quantum Chem., 3:149.

Čížek, J., and Paldus, J., 1971, Correlation problems in atomic and molecular systems. III. Rederivation of the coupled-pair many-electron theory using the traditional quantum chemical methods, Int. J. Quantum Chem., 5:359.

Clarke, K. L., Madden, P. A., and Buckingham, A. D., 1978, Collision-induced polarizabilities of inert gas atoms, Molec. Phys., 36:301.

Craig, D. P., and Thirunamachandran, T., 1981, Elementary derivation of long-range moments of two coupled centrosymmetric systems, Chem. Phys. Letters, 80:14.

Dacre, P. D., 1978, A calculation of the helium pair polarizability including correlation effects, Molec. Phys., 36:541.

Dacre, P. D., 1981, A calculation of the neon pair polarizability including correlation effects, Can. J. Phys., 59:1439.

Dacre, P. D., 1982a, On the pair polarizability of helium, Molec. Phys., 45:17.

Dacre, P. D., 1982b, A calculation of the neon pair polarizability including correlation effects II. Inclusion of the configuration interaction basis extension corrections, Can. J. Phys., 60:963.

Dacre, P. D., 1982c, An SCF calculation of the pair polarizability of argon, Molec. Phys., 45:1.

Dacre, P. D., 1982d, Pair polarizabilities of the heavy inert gases II. SCF calculations of the pair polarizabilities of krypton and xenon, Molec. Phys., 47:193.

Dacre, P. D., and Frommhold, L., 1981, Spectroscopic examination of *ab initio* neon diatom polarizability invariants, J. Chem. Phys., 75:4159.

Dacre, P. D., and Frommhold, L., 1982, Rare gas diatom polarizabilities, J. Chem. Phys., 76:3447.

Dalgarno, A., 1967, New methods for calculating long-range intermolecular forces, Advan. Chem. Phys., 12:143.

Diercksen, G. H. F., Kramer, W. P., and Sadlej, A. J., 1981, Unlinked cluster effects in limited CI calculations of molecular properties, Chem. Phys. Letters, 82:117.

Dunmur, D. A., and Jessup, N. E., 1979, The influence of intermolecular interactions on the Kerr effect in gases I. Statistical theory for spherical top molecules, Molec. Phys., 37:697.

Dunmur, D. A., Hunt, D. C., and Jessup, N. E., 1979, The influence of intermolecular interactions on the Kerr effect in gases II. Experimental results for spherical top molecules, Molec. Phys. 37:713.

Dunmur, D. A., Manterfield, M. R., and Robinson, D. J., 1983, Depolarized light scattering studies of the collision-induced polarizability anisotropy of atoms and spherical top molecules, Molec. Phys., 50:573.

Fortune, P. J., and Certain, P. R., 1974, Dielectric properties of helium: The polarizability of diatomic helium, J. Chem. Phys., 61:2620.

Frisch, H. L., and McKenna, J., 1965, Double scattering of electromagnetic radiation by a fluid, Phys. Rev., 139:A68.

Frommhold, L., 1981, Collision-induced scattering of light and the diatom polarizabilities, Advan. Chem. Phys., 46:1.

Frommhold, L., 1985, this volume.

Frommhold, L., and Proffitt, M. H., 1981, The polarized Raman spectrum of the argon diatom, J. Chem. Phys., 74:1512.

Galatry, L., and Gharbi, T., 1980, The long-range dipole moment of two interacting spherical systems, Chem. Phys. Letters, 75:427.

Gelbart, W. M., 1974, Depolarized light scattering by simple fluids, Advan. Chem. Phys., 26:1.

Harris, R. A., Heller, D. F., and Gelbart, W. M., 1974, *A priori* calculation of collisional polarizabilities: $(He)_2$, $(Ne)_2$, and $(Ar)_2$, J. Chem. Phys., 61:3854.

Heller, D. F., Harris, R. A., and Gelbart, W. M., 1975, Density functional formulation of collisional polarizabilities: Application to homonuclear noble gas diatoms, J. Chem. Phys., 62:1947.

Herring, C., and Flicker, M., 1964, Asymptotic exchange coupling of two hydrogen atoms, Phys. Rev., 134:A362.

Hilton, P. R., and Oxtoby, D. W., 1981, Collisional pair polarizabilities calculated by exchange perturbation theory using electric field variant basis sets, J. Chem. Phys., 74:1824.

Hunt, K. L. C., 1980, Long-range dipoles, quadrupoles, and hyperpolarizabilities of interacting inert-gas atoms, Chem. Phys. Letters, 70:336.

Hunt, K. L. C., 1983, Nonlocal polarizability densities and van der

Waals interactions, J. Chem. Phys., 78:6149.

Hunt, K. L. C., 1984, Nonlocal polarizability densities and the effects of short-range interactions on molecular dipoles, quadrupoles, and polarizabilities, J. Chem. Phys., 80:393.

Hunt, K. L. C., and Buckingham, A. D., 1980, The polarizability of H_2 in the triplet state, J. Chem. Phys., 72:2832.

Hunt, K. L. C., Zilles, B. A., and Bohr, J. E., 1981, Effects of van der Waals interactions on the polarizability of atoms, oscillators, and dipolar rotors at long range, J. Chem. Phys., 75:3079.

Jameson, C. J., and Buckingham, A. D., 1980, Molecular electronic property density functions: The nuclear magnetic shielding density, J. Chem. Phys., 73:5684.

Jansen, L., 1967, Schrödinger perturbation formalism for exchange interactions between atoms or molecules, Phys. Rev., 162:63.

Jansen, L., and Mazur, P., 1955, On the theory of molecular polarization in gases I. Effects of molecular interaction on the polarizability of spherical nonpolar molecules, Physica, 21:193.

Jeziorski, B., and Kołos, W., 1982, Perturbation approach to the study of weak intermolecular interactions, in: "Molecular Interactions, Vol. 3", H. Ratajczak and W. J. Orville-Thomas, eds., Wiley, New York.

Keyes, T., and Ladanyi, B. M., 1977, The role of local fields and interparticle pair correlations in light scattering by dense fluids IV. Removal of the point-polarizability approximation, Molec. Phys., 33:1271.

Kirouac, S., and Bose, T. K., 1976, Polarizability and dielectric properties of helium, J. Chem. Phys., 64:1580.

Koide, A., 1976, A new expansion for dispersion forces and its application, J. Phys. B., 9:3173.

Kołos, W., and Wolniewicz, L., 1965, Potential-energy curves for the $x^1\Sigma_g^+$, $b^3\Sigma_u^+$, and $c^1\Pi_u$ states of the hydrogen molecule, J. Chem. Phys., 43:2429.

Krauss, M., and Neumann, D. B., 1979a, Charge overlap effects in dispersion energies, J. Chem. Phys., 71:107.

Krauss, M., Neumann, D. B., and Stevens, W. J., 1979b, The dispersion damping functions and interaction energy curves for He-He, Chem. Phys. Letters, 66:29.

Krauss, M., Stevens, W. J., and Neumann, D. B., 1980, The dispersion damping functions and interaction energy curves for Xe-Xe, Chem. Phys. Letters, 71:500.

Krauss, M., and Stevens, W. J., 1982, Ab initio determination of the ground-state potential energy curve for Ar_2, Chem. Phys. Letters, 85:423.

Kress, J. W., and Kozak, J. J., 1977, Determination of the pair polarizability tensor for the Ne diatom, J. Chem. Phys., 66:4516.

Lacey, A. J., and Byers Brown, W., 1974, Long-range overlap dipoles for inert gas diatoms, Molec. Phys., 27:1013.

Ladanyi, B. M., 1983, Molecular dynamics study of Rayleigh light scattering from molecular fluids, J. Chem. Phys., 78:2189.

Lallemand, P., David, D.-J., and Bigot, B., 1974, Calculs de polarisabilités atomiques et moléculaires I. Méthodologie et application à l'association Ar-Ar, Molec. Phys., 27:1029.

Lallemand, M., and Vidal, D., 1977, Variation of the polarizability of noble gases with density, J. Chem. Phys., 66:4776.

Lim, T.-K., Linder, B., and Kromhout, R. A., 1970, Polarizability and second dielectric virial coefficient of interacting He atoms, J. Chem. Phys., 52:3831.

Linder, B., Lee, K. F., Malinowski, P., and Tanner, A. C., 1980, On the relation between charge-density susceptibility, scattering functions, and van der Waals forces, Chem. Phys., 52:353.

Logan, D. E., and Madden, P. A., 1982, On the second dielectric virial coefficients of methane and the inert gases, Molec. Phys., 46:1195.

Longuet-Higgins, H. C., 1965, Intermolecular forces, Disc. Faraday Soc., 40:7.

Maaskant, W. J. A., and Oosterhoff, L. J., 1964, Theory of optical rotatory power, Molec. Phys., 8:319.

Mahanty, J., and Majumdar, C. K., 1982, Exchange-induced dipole moments in atom pairs, Phys. Rev.A, 26:2334.

Malinowski, P., Tanner, A. C., Lee, K. F., and Linder, B., 1981, Van der Waals forces, scattering functions, and charge density susceptibility. II. Application to the He-He interaction potential, Chem. Phys., 62:423.

Mavroyannis, C., and Stephen, M. J., 1962, Dispersion forces, Molec. Phys., 5:629.

Murrell, J. N., and Shaw, G., 1967a, Intermolecular forces in the region of small orbital overlap, J. Chem. Phys., 46:1768.

Murrell, J. N., and Shaw, G., 1967b, The He-He potential energy in the region of the van der Waals minimum, Molec. Phys., 12:475.

Murrell, J. N., and Shaw, G., 1968, The helium-helium potential in the region of the van der Waals minimum, Molec. Phys., 15:325.

O'Brien, E. F., Gutschick, V. P., McKoy, V., and McTague, J. P., 1973, Polarizability of interacting atoms: Relation to collision-induced light scattering and dielectric models, Phys. Rev. A, 8:690.

Orcutt, R. H., and Cole, R. H., 1967, Dielectric constants of imperfect gases. III. Atomic gases, hydrogen, and nitrogen. J. Chem. Phys., 46:697.

Orttung, W. H., 1977, Direct solution of the Poisson equation for bimolecules of arbitrary shape, polarizability density, and charge distribution, Ann. N. Y. Acad. Sci., 303:22.

Orttung, W. H., 1978, Extension of the Kirkwood-Westheimer model of substituent effects to general shapes, charges, and polarizabilities. Application to the substituted bicyclo [2.2.2] octanes, J. Am. Chem. Soc., 100:4369.

Ostlund, N. S., and Merrifield, D. L., 1976, Ghost orbitals and the basis set extension effects, Chem. Phys. Letters, 39:612.

Oxtoby, D. W., 1978, The calculation of pair polarizabilities through continuum electrostatic theory, J. Chem. Phys., 69:1184.

Oxtoby, D. W., 1980, Local polarization theory for field-induced molecular multipoles, J. Chem. Phys., 72:5171.

Oxtoby, D. W., and Gelbart, W. M., 1975a, Collisional polarizability anisotropies of the noble gases, Molec. Phys., 29:1569.

Oxtoby, D. W., and Gelbart, W. M., 1975b, Collisional polarizabilities of the inert gases. Second-order overlap, exchange, and correlation effects, Molec. Phys., 30:535.

Posch, H., 1985, this volume.

Power, E. A., 1964, "Introductory Quantum Electrodynamics", Longmans, London.

Proffitt, M. H., Keto, J. W., and Frommhold, L., 1980, Collision-induced spectra of the helium isotopes, Phys. Rev. Lett., 45:1843.

Proffitt, M. H., Keto, J. W., and Frommhold, L., 1981, Collision-induced Raman spectra and diatom polarizabilities of the rare gases – an update, Can. J. Phys., 59:1459.

Reynolds, P. J., Ceperley, D. M., Alder, B. J., and Lester, W. A., 1982, Fixed-node quantum Monte Carlo for molecules, J. Chem. Phys., 77:5593.

Ritchie, A. B., 1968a, Perturbation theory for exchange interactions between atoms and molecules. I, Phys. Rev., 171:125.

Ritchie, A. B., 1968b, Perturbation theory for exchange interactions between atoms or molecules. II, J. Chem. Phys., 49:2167.

Rumyantsev, A. A., 1974, Perturbation theory with allowance for exchange forces, Sov. Phys. JETP, 38:459.

Shavitt, I., 1977, The method of configuration interaction, in: "Methods of Electronic Structure Theory", H. F. Schaefer,III, ed., Plenum, New York.

Silberstein, L., 1917, Molecular refractivity and atomic interaction, Phil. Mag., 33:92, 521.

Sipe, J. E., and Van Kranendonk, J., 1978, Limitations of the concept of polarizability density as applied to atoms and molecules, Molec. Phys., 35:1579.

Szabo, A., and Ostlund, N. S., 1977, The correlation energy in the random phase approximation: Intermolecular forces between closed-shell systems, J. Chem. Phys., 67:4351.

Tabisz, G. C., 1979, Collision-induced Rayleigh and Raman scattering, in: "Molecular Spectroscopy, Vol. 6", R. F. Barrow, D. A. Long, and J. Sheridan, eds., The Chemical Society, London.

Theimer, O., and Paul, R., 1965, Anisotropic light scattering by inner-field fluctuations in a dense monatomic gas, J. Chem. Phys., 42:2508.

Vidal, D., and Lallemand, M., 1976, Evolution of the Clausius-Mossotti function of noble gases and nitrogen, at moderate and high density, near room temperature, J. Chem. Phys., 64:4293.

Werner, H.-J., and Meyer, W., 1976, PNO-CI and PNO-CEPA studies of electron correlation effects. V. Static dipole polarizabilities of small molecules, Molec. Phys., 31:855.

DEPOLARIZATION RATIO OF LIGHT SCATTERED

BY A GAS OF ISOTROPIC MOLECULES

M. Thibeau[a], J. Berrué[a], A. Chave[a], B. Dumon[a]
Y. Le Duff[b], A. Gharbi[c] and B. Oksengorn[d]

a-Laboratoire d'Optique des Fluides[+], Faculté des
Siences, bd Lavoisier, 49045 Angers Cédex, France
b-Département de Recherches Physiques[++], Université
Pierre et Marie Curie, 4, Place Jussieu, 75230 Paris
Cédex 05, France
c-Laboratoire de Spectroscopie Moléculaire, Faculté des
Sciences, Le Belvédère, Tunis, Tunisie
d-Laboratoire des Interactions Moléculaires et des
Hautes Pressions, C.N.R.S., Centre Universitaire
Paris-Nord, av. J.B. Clément, 93430 Villetaneuse
France

ABSTRACT

A general discussion is given about the depolarization ratio
of the collision-induced light scattering. In the high density
range, experimental results obtained for depolarized Rayleigh and
vibrational Raman scattering, in the case of atomic and isotropic
molecular fluids, are compared to theoretical results calculated in
the framework of the classical DID theory by using the lattice gas
model or molecular dynamics simulations. At low densities, a comparison is made between data obtained either from the depolarization
ratios, or from spectral line shapes, in the case of argon and
methane; experimental results are also compared to DID values. It
is found that there are some discrepancies which are discussed.

+ Equipe associée au C.N.R.S., U.A. n° 780
++ Laboratoire associé au C.N.R.S., U.A. n° 71

INTRODUCTION

Since the first observations of the collision-induced depolarized component of Rayleigh scattering, by measuring depolarization ratio on the one hand (Thibeau et al., 1966; Thibeau et al., 1967; Thibeau et al., 1968), and the spectral line shape on the other hand (Levine and Birnbaum, 1968; McTague and Birnbaum, 1968), many experiments have been made for all the rare gases and for several optically isotropic molecular fluids by using the two kinds of measurement. Moreover, the collision-induced depolarization effect has been observed in Raman spectra of optically isotropic molecules in the compressed gaseous and liquid states (Holzer and Le Duff, 1974; Le Duff and Gharbi, 1978); this phenomenon has also been studied recently in mixtures of atomic and molecular fluids (Le Duff et al., 1983). Finally, recall that the second virial collision-induced Kerr coefficient (Buckingham and Dunmur, 1968) is directly proportional to the integrated intensity of the depolarized Rayleigh component.

From the theoretical viewpoint, collision-induced light scattering has been predicted for many years to be due to field fluctuations, arising from molecular interactions (Silberstein, 1917; Yvon, 1937; Buckingham and Stephen, 1957), which give rise to a polarizability anisotropy in a pair of particles (long range dipole-induced dipole (DID) interaction). However, at short distance other contributions can play a role due to the distortion of the electronic clouds (electron overlap and/or electron exchange), or of the molecular frame.

The experimental results obtained by several groups during the last ten years have stimulated ab-initio calculations of the polarizability anisotropy and molecular dynamics simulations. Detailed discussions of the experiments and theories can be found in several review papers (Gelbart, 1974; Tabisz, 1979; Frommhold, 1981; Birnbaum et al., 1982).

In this paper, we present a brief description of the DID model for the depolarization ratio at low and high density for Rayleigh and Raman scattering. Then, we give some experimental results obtained with argon and several isotropic molecular fluids in a large density range. Finally, a detailed comparison is made between the different kinds of experiments and the DID model, for argon and methane at low density.

THEORETICAL CONSIDERATIONS

Consider the principle of a scattering experiment: a monochromatic, vertically polarized laser beam illuminates a cell containing a pure fluid of optically isotropic molecules, and the

light scattered at right angle is analyzed in the horizontal
scattering plane (Fig.1).

For isolated atoms and spherical molecules at very low
densities, there is no depolarized component and only the
vertically polarized Rayleigh component (I_{VV}) can be observed. However, at moderate and high densities, a weak horizontally depolarized Rayleigh component (I_{VH}) also appears, and it is possible to
define a depolarization ratio η_{Ray} equal to I_{VH}/I_{VV}. A modified
Rayleigh depolarization ratio can also be defined as

$$(\eta_m)_{Ray} = \eta_{Ray}\ \frac{RT\chi_T}{V_M} \qquad (1)$$

where the quantity $RT\chi_T/V_M$ is an interference factor which plays a
role in the usual polarized Rayleigh scattering (Fabelinskii,
1968), where R is the ideal gas constant, T is the absolute
temperature, χ_T is the isothermal compressibility, and V_M is the
molar volume. Similarly, a collision induced depolarization ratio
η_{Ram} can be defined in the case of a vibrational Raman band
associated with a totally symmetric mode. From the theoretical
point of wiew, using a pair approximation, we can write the general
formula of the depolarization ratio for N scattering particles as
follows (Thibeau et al., 1977)

$$\eta_m = \frac{1}{15N\alpha_o^2} \underset{h,1,m,n}{\overset{<}{\sum}}\ \beta^{hl}\ \beta^{mn}\ P_2(\vec{u}^{hl}.\vec{u}^{mn}) \qquad (2)$$

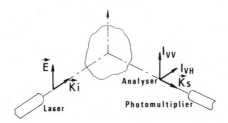

Fig. 1 Principle of the experimental procedure. I_{VH} is a
depolarized intensity, where "VH" indicates respectively the polarization of the incident and scattered
beams.

where β^{hl} is the anisotropic part of the polarizability of molecule h induced by molecule l, P_2 is the second Legendre polynomial, $\vec{u}^{hl}$ is the unit vector connecting the centers of molecules h and l and < > indicates a thermodynamic ensemble average. In the first order DID approximation with point dipoles, the Rayleigh collision-induced anisotropy (Silberstein, 1917; Yvon, 1937; Buckingham and Stephen, 1957), just as the Raman collision-induced anisotropy (Thibeau et al., 1977) are given respectively by

$$(\beta^{hl})_{Ray} = \frac{3\alpha_o^2}{4\pi\varepsilon_o} \frac{1}{(r^{hl})^3} \tag{3}$$

$$(\beta^{hl})_{Ram} = \frac{3\alpha_o}{4\pi\varepsilon_o} \frac{\partial\alpha_o}{\partial Q_1} (Q_1^h + Q_1^l) \frac{1}{(r^{hl})^3} \tag{4}$$

where α_o is the polarizability of the isolated particle, Q_1 is the normal coordinate associated with the totally symmetric mode ν_1 of spherical molecules and r^{hl} is the interparticle distance. Then by taking into account the coherence of the Rayleigh scattering and the incoherence of the Raman scattering, depolarization ratios (Thibeau et al., 1977; Berrué et al., 1978) can be written in the form

$$(\eta_m)_{Ray} = \frac{3}{5} (\alpha_o/4\pi\varepsilon_o\sigma^3)^2 (2 S^{II} + 4 S^{III} + S^{IV}) \tag{5}$$

$$(\eta_m)_{Ram} = \frac{3}{5} (\alpha_o/4\pi\varepsilon_o\sigma^3)^2 (4 S^{II} + 4 S^{III}) \tag{6}$$

where σ is the molecular diameter. The quantity S is given by

$$S = \frac{\sigma^6}{N} \sum_{h,l,m,n} <(r^{hl}r^{mn})^{-3} P_2(\vec{u}^{hl} \cdot \vec{u}^{mn})>$$

S^{II}, S^{III} and S^{IV} represent, respectively, the doublet (mn = kl), the triplet (m = h and n $\neq$ l) and the quadruplet (m $\neq$ h $\neq$ n $\neq$ l) contributions. Now, consider the evaluation of Eqs. (1) and (2) for the two domains of low and high densities.

Low Density

In this density range the contributions S^{III} and S^{IV} are negligible compared to S^{II}, which is proportional to the density of the gas. Then, it follows that

$$(\eta_m)_{Ray} = A_{Ray} \rho \tag{7}$$

$$(\eta_m)_{Ram} = \eta_{Ram} = A_{Ram}\,\rho \qquad (8)$$

where ρ is the gas density (in Amagat units). The coefficient A_{Ray} is given by the general formula

$$A_{Ray} = \frac{2n_o}{15\alpha_o^2} \int \left[\beta(r)\right]^2 g(r)d\tau \qquad (9)$$

where $g(r)$ is the pair distribution function, $d\tau$ is a volume element, and n_o is the NTP number density. At low densities, $g(r)$ is accurately approximated by the Boltzmann factor, and by using the DID value of $\beta(r)$ the coefficient A_{ray} becomes

$$A_{Ray} = \frac{6}{5}\frac{n_o}{(4\pi\varepsilon_o)^2}\,\alpha_o^2 \int r^{-6}\exp(-W/kT)d\tau \qquad (10)$$

where W is the intermolecular potential. In the case of Raman scattering, one obtains

$$A_{Ram} = 2A_{Ray} \qquad (11)$$

Then, since S^{II} is proportional to the density, it follows that the intensity of the collision-induced depolarized light scattering is proportional to the square of the gas density in the low density range.

Futhermore, as has been shown recently (Le Duff and Sergiescu, 1984), the ratio A_{Ram}/A_{Ray} is independent of the intermolecular potential only in the case of the DID approximation, and may be a good test of this theory.

Collision-induced scattering has been also studied for gas mixtures of two kinds of isotropic molecules (Le Duff et al., 1983). Consider the Raman scattering intensity I^{Ram} for molecules B, at the frequency of the ν_1 mode, and the Rayleigh scattering intensity I^{Ray} for the mixture of molecules A and B. In this case, Eqs. (5) and (6) must be modified in the following way

$$\eta_{Ram} = I_{VH}^{Ram}/I_{VV}^{Ram}(B) = \eta^{Ram}(B,B) + \eta^{Ram}(A,B) \qquad (12)$$

$$\eta^*_{Ray} = (I^{Ray}_{VH}/I^{Ram}_{VV}(B))\ (\frac{\partial \alpha_B}{\partial Q_1})^2\ \frac{\langle Q_1^2 \rangle}{\alpha_B^2} \tag{13}$$

We obtain from these equations

$$\eta_{Ram} = 4N_A\ \alpha_A^2\ s^{II}(A,B) + 4N_B\ \alpha_B^2\ s^{II}(B,B) \tag{14}$$

$$\eta^*_{Ray} = 4N_A\ \alpha_A^2\ s^{II}(A,B) + 2\ \frac{N_A^2 \alpha_A^4}{N_B \alpha_B^2}\ s^{II}(A,A) + 2N_B \alpha_B^2\ s^{II}(B,B) \tag{15}$$

where N_A and N_B are the number densities of molecules A and B, respectively, and

$$s^{II}(A,B) = \langle (r^{ij})^{-6} \left[\frac{3(r^i_V - r^j_V)(r^i_H - r^j_H)}{(r^{ij})^2} \right]^2 \rangle \tag{16}$$

Here i and j label molecules A and B, respectively, and V and H refer to vertical and horizontal axes (See Fig.1). In Eqs. (14) and (15) the contributions from unlike pairs are found to be equal. Measurements of collision-induced Raman and Rayleigh scattering from mixtures of rare gases and spherical molecules have been made for Ar-CF$_4$(Le Duff et al, 1983). Comparison of experimental results with DID values calculated with Eqs. (14) and (15) has shown that this model is not accurate for this pair of molecules.

High Density

In the high density range, the contributions of three and four particles clusters become important (Thibeau et al., 1968), and the depolarisation ratios differ appreciably from their low density values. It is useful to define a parameter F (Le Duff and Gharbi, 1978) by the ratios

$$F_{Ray} = (\eta_m)_{Ray}/(A_{Ray}\rho) \tag{17}$$

$$F_{Ram} = (\eta_m)_{Ram}/(A_{Ram}\rho) \tag{18}$$

which vary between the values 1 (low density) and zero (high density). This parameter is mainly an interference factor, describing the partial cancellation of the induced polarizability effect due to the higher symmetry of the fluid as density increases (Levine and Birnbaum, 1968; Thibeau et al., 1968; An et al., 1979).

This cancellation effect is less important in Raman scattering, because the state characterized by vibrational phase differences between all molecules is equivalent to a state with unlike molecules. Consequently, we can write

$$1 \geqslant F_{Ram} \geqslant F_{Ray} > 0$$

Three methods have been used to obtain F values:
1) from models describing dense media, it is possible to calculate a theoretical value. The lattice gas model has been often used (Thibeau et al., 1967; Thibeau et al., 1968; Thibeau et al., 1977);
2) from molecular dynamics calculations which give the different contributions S^{II}, S^{III} and S^{IV} (Alder et al., 1973; Alder et al., 1979; Ladd et al., 1980);
3) determination of S^{II} from experimental results on the depolarization ratio at moderate densities (Gelbart, 1972; Gray and Ralph, 1970; Ralph and Gray, 1974), or from spectral intensities (McTague et al., 1972).

For a simple and quantitative physical interpretation of the parameter F one may use the lattice gas model. We suppose that the possible positions of the molecules are restrained to the sites of a fictitious lattice which is partially occupied. Position fluctuations of the real fluid are represented by occupation fluctuations of the lattice sites. The modification of the average degree of occupation is correlated with the variation of density. This model has been discussed and improved (Sergiescu, 1979; Guillot et al., 1980). Although it is rather crude, it nevertheless gives the approximate behaviour for collision induced quantities as a function of density. The parameter F is given in this model by

$$F_{Ray} = (1 - \rho/\rho_o)^2 \tag{19}$$

$$F_{Ram} = \sqrt{F_{Ray}} = (1 - \rho/\rho_o) \tag{20}$$

where ρ_o is an empirical parameter, characteristic of the solid state density, and ρ/ρ_o is the probability of a site occupation correlated to the microscopic structure of dense medium (Berrué et al., 1978; Chave, 1982).

In the range of liquid state densities, where the molecular dynamics calculations with the first order DID approximation (Alder et al., 1973) predict a depolarized intensity much higher than the experimental results, some authors argued that multiple higher order scattering must be taken into account (Keyes et al., 1979; Keyes, 1979). However, since it is hard to estimate precisely this contribution, a particle-hole approach has been developed either by using a dielectric continuum model (Keyes, 1980) or a lattice gas model (Keyes and Madden, 1981). In the first case, the depolarized intensity at high density is found to be proportional to

$$I_{dep} \propto \alpha_o^4 \ f(\varepsilon,\rho^*) \ \rho_h^2$$

where ε is the dielectric constant of the liquid, ρ^* is the dimensionless particle density, and ρ_h the hole density. For the second case, a general and exact relation can be written

$$I_{dep} \propto \rho_h^2 \ \sum_{j \neq 1} \left[(\alpha_{1j}^h)^{xz} \right]^2 \ g_{1j}^h$$

where α^h is the polarizability of a pair of holes, and g^h is the hole pair distribution function. However, the hole pair polarizability is unknown and difficult to compute.

EXPERIMENTS AND RESULTS

For measuring depolarization ratios in a large density range, we have used two types of experimental devices.
1) With a four branch high pressure cell and a retractable half-wave plate, the depolarization ratio is determined from I_{HH}/I_{VV}(Fig. 2) (Berrué et al., 1977). It has been observed that the depolarized component I_{HH} was perturbed very little by the pressure-induced birefringence in the cell windows, or by the stray light of the polarized component (Oksengorn, 1983).
2) With a six branch high pressure cell (Fig. 3) and two photomultipliers (PM) (Berrué et al., 1979), the depolarization ratio is determined by the ratio $I_{zy}^{(z)}/I_{xz}^{(z)}$, where the upper index labels the polarization of the laser beam, the first lower index, X or Z, labels the scattering direction (PM axes), and the second lower index labels the polarization of the scattered component. In this case, there is no reproducibility problem regarding the polarization state of the incident laser beam.

The constants A (see Eqs. 17 and 18) for the two-body contribution, can be determined by a least-squares fit of the experimental data. Thus the results depend on the theoretical value of the parameter F used. With a correct theory, A must remain constant for a large range of densities up to the liquid state. For

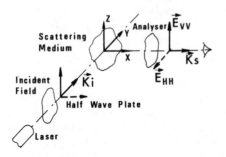

Fig. 2 Geometry of 4 branch cell: a typical arrangement
with one scattering branch, a retractable half-wave
plate changing the polarization of the incident beam.

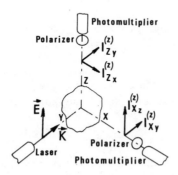

Fig. 3 Geometry of 6 branch cell: a typical arrangement
with two scattering branches and the polarization
of the incident beam fixed.

example, in Fig. 4 are plotted values of A_{Ray} versus the density for argon. Curves are drawn for no correction (F=1) and for values of F determined from molecular dynamics calculations (Alder et al. 1973) and from the lattice gas model (Thibeau et al., 1968). It can be seen that the molecular dynamics calculations and the lattice gas model give a rather good description of the interference factor F in a large range of densities. However, it appears that the lattice gas model gives a quantitative description of the depolarzed intensity once ρ_0 is chosen, as shown in Fig.5 for compressed argon, and in Fig. 6 for liquid neopentane.

Finally, Fig. 7 shows a comparison between experimental and theoretical determinations of the factor F_{Ray} for several fluids at moderate densities. The best agreement is obtained with the molecular dynamics calculations, but any precise comparison is not possible owing to the use of the hard sphere potential. Thus, for instance, calculations made at the triple point of argon with an accurate intermolecular potential show an important difference with those made with a Lennard-Jones potential (Vermesse et al., 1982).

For Raman scattering on the other hand, the experiment is in rather good agreement with the theoretical relation (see Eq. 20) connecting the interference factors F_{Ram} and F_{Ray} (Fig.8).

In the moderate and high density range, it is well known that the determination of the effect of the local field is very important for the measurement of the absolute scattered intensities (Fabelinskii, 1968), particularly in the case of the depolarized component I_{VH}. Figure 9 shows the density dependence of the factor Q proportional to the ratio $(I_{VV})^{exp}/(I_{VV})^{theo}$, determined by using different theories of this effect (Berrué et al, 1981; Dumon, 1982). The comparison is in favour of Einstein's formula (Einstein, 1901), which gives a constant ratio Q as a function of density, while formulas obtained by others authors (Ramanathan, 1927; Rocard, 1928; Cabannes, 1929) (RCC) are not verified by experiment. Moreover, a dynamical and fluctuating Onsager model has been developed (Thibeau et al., 1981; Dumon, 1982), with which the solution of the problem of local field is obtained, including the fluctuations of the external and local fields, together with the intensity of the scattered light. These results are in contradiction with those given by RCC theories, which suppose that there is no fluctuation in these fields.

Comparison between experiment and DID theory for the pair polarizability anisotropy of Ar and CH_4

As is well known, it is possible to compare the three kinds of experiments:
1) depolarization ratio;

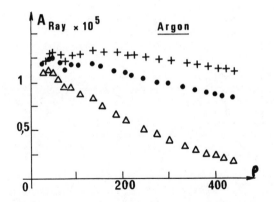

Fig. 4 Dependence of the coefficient A_{Ray} versus gas
density in Amagat. A_{Ray} values are deduced from
experimental data (Thibeau et al., 1968) with no
correction ($\triangle$), or corrected by different
interference factors F, calculated by molecular
dynamics (+) (Alder et al., 1973), and in the
framework of the lattice gas model ($\bullet$) (Thibeau et
al., 1967; 1968).

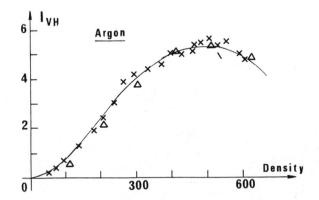

Fig. 5 Density dependence of I_{VH} (in arbitrary units) for
gaseous argon: values deduced from experimental
data (Thibeau et al., 1968) (x); values calculated
in framework of the lattice gas model, with
ρ_o=1000 Amagat ($\triangle$).

301

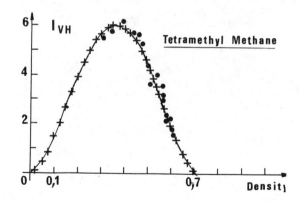

Fig. 6 Dependence of I_{VH} (in arbitrary units) versus density
(in g/cm³) for liquid tetramethylmethane:experimental data
(Perrot, private communication, 1983)(·); calculated values
in the framework of the lattice gas model, with ρ_o=0.735g/cm³(+).

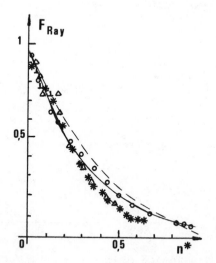

Fig. 7 Dependence of the interference factor F_{Ray} versus reduced
density $n^* = n_o \rho \sigma^3$ for several gases. Experimental data :
(Δ)Ar, ($*$)CH₄, (o)CF₄, ($\perp$)SF₆, (Chave, 1982).
Calculation (——) molecular dynamics (Alder et al; 1973),
(----) lattice gas model (Thibeau et al., 1968).

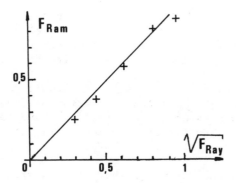

Fig. 8 Fitting of the theoretical relation $F_{Ram} = \sqrt{F_{Ray}}$ calculated in the framework of the lattice gas model (Thibeau et al., 1968), with experimental data of CF_4 (Le Duff and Gharbi, 1978; Charbi, 1978).

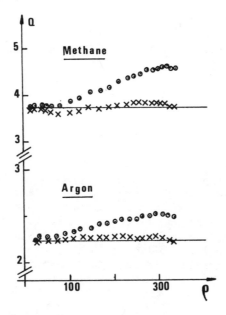

Fig. 9 Ratio Q between the experimental and theoretical polarized intensities (in arbitrary units), versus gas density (in Amagat units).(⊚) RRC theories;(x) Einstein's theory.

2) zeroth moment or absolute depolarized intensity at a given laser frequency, deduced from the spectral line shape;
3) the second virial collision-induced Kerr effect, with the corresponding values calculated with the DID model.

This comparison is done here for an atomic gas such as argon, for which many available results have been obtained by different groups, and accurate interaction potentials have been determined. We consider also an isotropic molecular fluid such as methane, which has been studied as often as argon.

Table 1 gives the ratio r between the experimental and theoretical DID values of the pair polarizability anisotropy of argon for the different kinds of experiments. As can be seen, there is an important difference of about 30% between the previous measurements of the zeroth moment, those of the depolarization ratio or the induced Kerr effect, and the recent measurements of the zeroth moment (Shelton and Tabisz, 1980; Shelton and al., 1981). Nevertheless, a recent measurement of the depolarization ratio for argon by Dunmur et al. (1983) gives satisfactory agreement with the recent zeroth moment measurements. Furthermore, these authors have reanalyzed the earlier data on the Kerr effect (Buckingham and Dunmur, 1968; Dunmur et al., 1979) by taking into account the calculated DID three-body term and have found rather good agreement between the new virial Kerr coefficient, the latest spectral studies, and their depolarization ratio measurements. However, it seems to us that this analysis is not totally correct, because the effect of the three-body correction term appears to be somewhat overestimated (see Table 1).

On the other hand, these discrepancies might be accounted for by some sort of instrumental effect related to the large aperture used in spectral studies. This should give rise to an additional contribution at low frequency for the depolarized component (Oksengorn, 1983).

In the case of methane, Table 2 shows that there exists also discrepancies between the different kinds of experiments and the DID theory, but these differences are not so important as for argon. Moreover, the major discrepancy appears between light scattering and the Kerr effect. Finally, note that the theoretical value of the pair polarizability anisotropy is dependent in a large measure on the intermolecular potential that is chosen.

CONCLUSION

In this paper we have presented a general description of depolarized Rayleigh and Raman scattering for optically isotropic medium in the low and high density range and from the point of view

Table 1. Ratio $r = \langle\beta^2\rangle_{exp} / \langle\beta^2\rangle_{DID}$ for Argon.

Method	Ref.	r
depolarization (analysis of high pressure data)	Chave (1982) Berrué et al.(1976) Thibeau et al.(1968)	0.88 0.91 0.85a
depolarization at low density (3-20Am)	Oksengorn (1983)	0.85
depolarization at relatively low density (4-80Am)	Dunmur et al. (1983)	1.03
spectral line shape	Shelton and Tabisz (1980)	1.08
	Proffitt and Frommhold (1979)	1.04
	Lallemand (1971)	0.70
	Barrochi et al. (1977)	1.01
	McTague et al. (1972)	0.54
Kerr effect	Buckingham and Dunmur (1968)	0.64b
	Dunmur et al. (1983)	1.09c

a Value corrected by a better numerical analysis.
b Without three-body correction.
c With three-body correction.

Table 2. Collision-induced coefficient A_{Ray} and ratio r, for methane.

Theoretical DID values of A_{Ray} $\times 10^5$ Am^{-1}		Experimental values of A_{Ray} $\times 10^5$ Am^{-1}		r
$\alpha_o = 2.6010^{-24}$ cm^3 ; L.J.6-12 potential Ref: Hirschfelder et al. (1964)	2.49	depola- rization ratio	Chave (1982) 2.60	1.04-0.80
$\alpha_o = 2.64210^{-24}$ cm^3; same L.J. pot.	2.57	analysis of high pressure data.	Berrué et al. (1976) 2.65	1.06-0.81
$\alpha_o = 2.64210^{-24}$ cm^3; potential calculated by Matthews and Smith (1976)	3.26	depola- rization at low density	Watson and Rowell (1974) 2.84	1.14-0.87
			Tabisz et al. (1984) 2.72	1.09-0.83
			Barocchi and Zoppi (1978) 3.30	1.33-1.01
		spectral line shape	Lallemand (1971) 2.43	0.98-0.75
			Proffitt and Frommhold (1979) 2.42	0.97-0.74
			Gharbi and Le Duff (1977))) 2.56 Gharbi (1978))	1.03-0.79
			Prengel and Gornall (1976) 2.42	0.97-0.74
		Kerr effect	Dunmur et al. (1979)	1.40

of experiment and theoretical determinations of the depolarization ratios. A significant feature of this work is the rather good agreement obtained between theory based on the DID model and experiment. In addition, the lattice gas model is found to account for the density dependence of the depolarized intensities in a reasonably satisfactory way.

Our feeling is that the depolarization ratio measurements of Rayleigh and Raman scattering in a large range of density, combined with the spectral line shape and Kerr effect studies, are powerful tools for providing insights on the collision-induced polarizabilities, and/or on the microscopic structure of dense media. However, some discrepancies should be reduced between different kinds of experiments, and new comparisons should be made, particularly by studying the temperature dependence in a large range of temperature (Bose, 1984). This should be very important for obtaining a precise description of the non-DID part of the collision-induced polarizability anisotropies. It would be also very interesting to perform such measurements with gas mixtures.

Finally, measurements of the depolarization ratios for anisotropic molecules as a function of density and temperature may provide new insights into the interference terms between permanent and collisional polarizability anisotropies, and the angular part of the intermolecular potential.

REFERENCES

Alder, B. J., Weis, J. J., and Strauss, H. L., 1973, Phys. Rev. A7:281
Alder, B. J., Beers, J. C., Strauss, H. L., and Weis, J. J., 1979, J.C.P., 70:4091.
An, S. C., Fischman, L., Litovitz, T. A., Montrose, C. J., and Posch, H. A., 1979, J.C.P., 70:4626.
Barrochi, F., Zoppi, M., and Shelton, D. P., 1977, Can. J. Phys., 55:1962.
Barrochi, F., and Zoppi, M., 1978, Phys. Lett. A., 66:99.
Berrué, J., Chave, A., Dumon, B., and Thibeau, M., 1976, J. Phys., (Paris), 37:84.
Berrué, J., Chave, A., Dumon, B., and Thibeau, M., 1977, Rev. Phys. Appl., 12:1743.
Berrué, J., Chave, A., Dumon, B., and Thibeau, M., 1978, C.R. Acad. Sci. Paris, 287B:269.
Berrué, J., Chave, A., Dumon, B., and Thibeau, M., 1979, Optics Comm., 31:317.
Berrué, J., Dumon, B., Sergiescu, V., and Thibeau, M., 1981, Phys. Lett., 83A:123.
Birnbaum, G., Guillot, B., and Bratos, S., 1982, Adv. in Chem. Phys., 51:49.
Bose, T. K., 1985, this volume.

Buckingham, A. D., and Dunmur, D. A., 1968, Trans. Farad. Soc., 547:1778.

Buckingham, A. D., and Stephen, M. J., 1957, Trans. Farad. Soc., 53:884.

Cabannes, J., 1929, La diffusion de la lumière (P.U.F., Paris).

Chave, A., 1982, Thesis, Angers.

Dumon, B., 1982, Thesis, Angers.

Dunmur, D. A., Hunt, D. C., and Jessup, N. E., 1979, Mol. Phys., 37:713.

Dunmur, D. A., Manterfield, M. R., and Robinson, D. J., 1983, Mol. Phys., 50:573.

Einstein, A., 1901, Ann. Physik, 33:1275.

Fabelinskii, I. L., 1968, Molecular Scattering of Light, Plenum Press, New York.

Frommhold, L., 1981, Adv. in Chem. Phys., 46:1.

Gelbart, W. H., 1972, J.C.P., 57:699.

Gelbart, W. H., 1974, Adv. in Chem. Phys., 26:1.

Gharbi, A., and Le Duff, Y., 1977, Physica A, 87:177.

Gharbi, A., 1978, Thesis, Paris.

Gray, G. C., and Ralph, H. S., 1970, Phys. Lett., 33A:165.

Guillot, B., Bratos, S., and Birnbaum, G., 1980, Phys. Rev., A22:2230.

Hirschfelder, J. O., Curtiss, C. F., and Bird, R. B., 1964, Molecular Theory of Gases and Liquids, Wiley, New York.

Holzer, W., and Le Duff, Y., 1974, Phys. Rev. Lett., 32:205.

Keyes, T., Ladanyi, B. M., and Madden, P. A., 1979, Chem. Phys. Lett., 64:479.

Keyes, T., 1979, J.C.P., 70:5438.

Keyes, T., 1980, Chem. Phys. Lett., 70:194.

Keyes, T., and Madden, P. A., 1981, Can. J. Phys., 59:1560.

Ladd, A. J. C., Litovitz, T. A., Clarke, J. H. R., and Woodcock, L. V., 1980, Chem. Phys., 72:1759.

Lallemand, P., 1971, J. Phys. (Paris), 32:119.

Le Duff, Y., and Gharbi, A., 1978, Phys. Rev. A, 17:1729.

Le Duff, Y., Gharbi, A., and Othman, T., 1983, Phys. Rev. A., 28:2714.

Le Duff, Y., and Sergiescu, V., 1984, Physica, to be published.

Levine, H. B., and Birnbaum, G., 1968, Phys. Rev. Lett., 20:439.

McTague, J. P., and Birnbaum, G., 1968, Phys. Rev. Lett., 21:661.

McTague, J. P., Ellenson, W. D., and Hall, L. H., 1972, J. Phys. (Paris), 33:C1-247.

Matthews, J. B., and Smith, E. B., 1976, Molec. Phys., 32:1719.

Oksengorn, B., 1983, Chem. Phys. Lett., 102:429.

Prengel, A. T., and Gornall, W. S., 1976, Phys. Rev. A, 13:253.

Proffitt, M. H., and Frommhold, L., 1979, J.C.P., 36:197.

Ralph, H. Y., and Gray, G. C., 1974, Mol. Phys., 27:1683.

Ramanathan, K., 1927, Indian J. Phys., 1:413.

Rocard, Y., 1928, Ann. de Physique, 10:158.

Sergiescu, V., 1979, Physica, 97C:292.

Shelton, D. P., and Tabisz, G. C., 1980, Mol. Phys., 40:285.

Shelton, D. P., and Tabisz, G. C., 1980, Mol. Phys., 40:299.

Shelton, D. P., Tabisz, G. C., Barrochi, F., and Zoppi, M., 1982, Mol. Phys., 46:21.

Silberstein, L., 1917, Lond. Edinb., Dubl. Phil. Mag., 92:521.

Tabisz, G. C., 1979, Specialist Periodical Reports, Chem. Soc. London, 6:156.

Tabisz, G. C., Penner, A., and Meinander, N., 1985, this volume.

Thibeau, M., Dumon, B., Chave, A., and Sergiescu, V., 1981, Physica A, 105:219.

Thibeau, M., Gharbi, A., Le Duff, Y., and Sergiescu, V., 1977, J. Phys. (Paris), 38:641.

Thibeau, M., Oksengorn, B., and Vodar, B., 1966, C.R. Acad. Sci., Paris, 263B:135.

Thibeau, M., Oksengorn, B., and Vodar, B., 1967, C.R. Acad. Sci., Paris, 265B:722.

Thibeau, M., Oksengorn, B., and Vodar, B., 1968, J. Phys. (Paris), 29:287.

Vermesse, J., Levesque, D., and Weis, J. J., 1982, Chem. Phys. Lett., 85:120.

Watson, R. C., and Rowell, R. L., 1974, J.C.P., 61:2666.

Yvon, J., 1937, Act. Sci. et Ind., (éditeur Hermann et Cie, Paris), n° 542-543.

DEPOLARIZED INTERACTION INDUCED LIGHT SCATTERING EXPERIMENTS IN

ARGON, KRYPTON AND XENON

F. Barocchi
Dipartimento di Fisica, Università di Firenze
Largo E.Fermi, 3, Firenze (Italy)
and

M. Zoppi
Istituto di Elettronica Quantistica, CNR
Via Panciatichi 56/30, Firenze (Italy)

INTRODUCTION

This paper will be devoted to review the latest experimental results of the Depolarized Interaction-Induced Light Scattering (DILS) and their interpretation in the noble gases argon, krypton, xenon. We restrict ourselves to these systems for two reasons: 1) because they can be interpreted in the framework of classical mechanics (quantum corrections for the interpretation of the spectra begin to be appreciable only for argon at high frequency, i.e. in the region of the fourth moment at room temperature and of the second moment near to the triple point (Barocchi et al., 1981 a; Barocchi et al., 1983));2) because the results which have been obtained by several groups (Frommhold et al., 1978; Barocchi and Zoppi, 1978 a; Barocchi and Zoppi, 1978 b; Shelton and Tabisz, 1980; Proffit et al., 1981; Barocchi et al., 1981 b, Zoppi et al., 1981) during the last few years have converged and are now widely accepted. Furthermore, they have been recently confirmed by experiments of a different nature, like depolarization ratio and Kerr-effect measurements (Dunmur et al., 1983).

Sect.I will briefly report the theoretical background needed to discuss the experimental results over a wide density range. Sect.II will be devoted to a) our measurements at low density in Ar, Kr, Xe; b) the derivation of an empirical pair-polarizability anisotropy; c) the discussion of the experimental three-body correlation spectrum of argon; d) the discussion of the experimental results in high density argon, both in the gas and liquid phases. Since for the correct interpretation of the DILS spectra, and for the comparison between theoretical calculations and experimental results, absolute intensity measurements have played a crucial role, we discuss in Appendix A some details of the intensity measurement procedures.

SECTION I. THEORETICAL BACKGROUND

Let us consider a system of N identical atoms contained in a scattering volume which is irradiated by photons of energy $h\nu_0$, wave vector $\vec{k}_0$ and intensity n_0 (number of photons per unit time per unit area). In the case in which only pair polarizabilities are important and the experiment is performed in the depolarized geometry, i.e. when $\vec{k}_0$ is along the z axis and both polarization of the incoming light and direction of the scattering detection are along the y axis of an orthogonal reference frame, the total number of photons scattered per unit time at the energy $h\nu_s$ and wave vector k_s per unit frequency and unit solid angle is given by (Gelbart, 1974; Varshneya et al., 1981)

$$\mathcal{N}_{\parallel}(\nu_s) = 2 K_0 K_s^3 n_0 \int_{-\infty}^{+\infty} dt \, e^{-i\omega t} \left\langle \sum_{i>j} \left[\hat{y} \cdot \tilde{\tilde{\alpha}}(ij,t) \cdot \hat{x} \right] \cdot \right. \quad (1)$$

$$\left. \cdot \sum_{k>\ell} \left[\hat{y} \cdot \tilde{\tilde{\alpha}}(k\ell,0) \cdot \hat{x} \right] \right\rangle ,$$

where $\omega = 2\pi(\nu_0 - \nu_s)$, $\tilde{\tilde{\alpha}}(ij,t) = \tilde{\tilde{\alpha}}\left[r(ij,t)\right]$ is the interaction-induced polarizability of the pair of atoms (ij) at time t which in turn is a function only of the pair separation $r(ij,t)$. The summations are performed over all pairs of atoms with the restriction i > j and k > 1.

A. The Low Density Limit and the Two-Body Spectrum

If we consider the low density limit, where only the contributions of binary encounters are considered important for the scattering process, and the atoms are all identical, expression (1) can be written as

$$\mathcal{N}_{\shortparallel}(\nu_s) = K_o K_s^3 n_o \, N(N-1) \int_{-\infty}^{+\infty} dt \; e^{-i\omega t} \left\langle \alpha_{xy}(12,t)\, \alpha_{xy}(12,0) \right\rangle_o^{(2)}. \tag{2}$$

Therefore, the differential scattering cross section for a single pair of interacting atoms is given by

$$\frac{d\sigma_{\shortparallel}^2(12)}{d\Omega \, d\nu_s} = 2 K_o K_s^3 \int_{-\infty}^{+\infty} dt \; e^{-i\omega t} \left\langle \alpha_{xy}(12,t)\, \alpha_{xy}(12,0) \right\rangle_o^{(2)}. \tag{3}$$

Here $\langle \ldots \rangle_o^{(2)}$ indicates that the average is independent of the density of the system and will be specified below, $\alpha_{xy}(12,t)$ is the xy component of the polarizability tensor $\widetilde{\widetilde{\alpha}}(12,t)$. If the atoms can be treated as classical particles interacting with central forces, the dynamics of the pair can be easily analyzed by means of Newton's law. Therefore, once the impact parameter b and the relative velocity v are given, the time dependence of the polarizability $\alpha_{xy}(12,t)$ can be explicitly described by the functional dependence $r(12,t)$. The correlation function which appears in (3) can be calculated as an average over all possible conditions for the colliding pair. This correlation function of $\alpha_{xy}(12,t)$ can also be written by means of intrinsic variables of the colliding pair i.e., the polar coordinates $r(12,t)$ and $\phi(t)$, which are defined as usual in the colliding plane, and the polarizability anisotropy $\beta_{12}(t) =$ $= \alpha_{\shortparallel}(12,t) - \alpha_{\perp}(12,t)$ which is a function only of $r(12,t)$. The $\alpha_{\shortparallel}$ and $\alpha_{\perp}$ are the components of the polarizability parallel and perpendicular to the internuclear axis.

In this case the pair correlation function

$$C_o(t) = \left\langle \alpha_{xy}(12,t)\, \alpha_{xy}(12,0) \right\rangle_o^{(2)} \tag{4}$$

can be given in terms of the anisotropy $\beta_{12}(t)$. This transformation is a straightforward tensor algebra calculation which leads to (Barocchi and Zoppi, 1978 b)

$$C_o(t) = \frac{1}{15} \left\langle \beta_{12}(t)\beta_{12}(0) \, P_2 \left[\cos \vartheta_{12}(t)\right] \right\rangle_o^{(2)}. \tag{5}$$

In this expression P_2 is the second Legendre polynomial and $\theta_{12}(t)$ is the angle of the interatomic axis at time t relative to that at time t = 0. For comparison between theory and experiments it is convenient to define a depolarized spectrum $D_{\parallel}(12,\nu)$ as

$$D_{\parallel}(12,\nu) = V \frac{d^2\sigma_{\parallel}(12)}{d\Omega \, d\nu_s} \tag{6}$$

which by means of Eqs.(3) and (5) can be written as

$$D_{\parallel}(12,\nu) = \frac{6}{45} K_0 K_s^3 \int_0^\infty d\nu \, P(\nu) \int_0^\infty db \, 2\pi b\nu \, \Gamma(\omega) , \tag{7}$$

where

$$\Gamma(\omega) = \frac{3}{2}\left\{\int_0^\infty \beta_{12}(t) \cos[2\phi(t)+\omega t]\,dt\right\}^2 + \left\{\int_0^\infty \beta_{12}(t) \cos\omega t \, dt\right\}^2 +$$
$$+ \frac{3}{2}\left\{\int_0^\infty \beta_{12}(t) \cos[2\phi(t)-\omega t]\,dt\right\}^2 . \tag{8}$$

Expressions (7) and (8) can be used to calculate the DILS spectrum within the classical framework once a suitable models for the pair interaction potential, $U(r)$, and the anisotropy, $\beta(r)$, are chosen; here r is the pair distance $r(12)$.

Alternatively, the comparison between theory and experiments can be done by using the moments of $D_{\parallel}(12,\omega)$ which are defined as:

$$M_{2n}^{(2)} = \int_{-\infty}^{+\infty} d\omega \, \omega^{2n} D_{\parallel}(12,\omega) = \int_{-\infty}^{+\infty} d\nu \, (2\pi\nu)^{2n} D_{\parallel}(12,\nu) . \tag{9}$$

For most practical cases of interest we can approximate $k_0 \simeq k_s$ in Eq.(6). Therefore from Eqs.(9), (4), and (6), the moments can be written as:

$$M_{2n}^{(2)} = (-i)^{2n}\left[\frac{d^{2n}}{dt^{2n}} A(t)\right]_{t=0} , \tag{10}$$

where $A(t) = 2Vk_0^4 c_0(t)$. By means of Eqs.(5) and (10) we can write explicit expressions for the first three even moments in terms of $\beta(r)$, $U(r)$ and their first (β', U') and second (β'') derivatives with respect to r. For the sake of completeness we will give here the expression for the "reduced" moments $\overline{M}_0^{(2)}$, $\overline{M}_2^{(2)}$, and $\overline{M}_4^{(2)}$ (Barocchi and Zoppi, 1978 b) with $M_{2n} = (2/15)k_0^4 \, \overline{M}_{2n}^{(2)}$

$$\overline{M}_0^{(2)} = V \langle \beta^2 \rangle_0 , \tag{11}$$

$$\overline{M}_2^{(2)} = V \frac{kT}{\mu} \left\langle (\beta')^2 + 6 \frac{\beta^2}{r^2} \right\rangle_0 , \tag{12}$$

$$\overline{M}_4^{(2)} = V \left\{ \left(\frac{kT}{\mu}\right)^2 \left\langle 3(\beta'')^2 + 4 \frac{\beta'\beta''}{r} - 12 \frac{\beta\beta''}{r^2} + 32 \left(\frac{\beta'}{r}\right)^2 - 96 \frac{\beta\beta'}{r^3} + \right. \right.$$

$$\left. + 120 \frac{\beta^2}{r^4} \right\rangle_0 - \frac{2kT}{\mu} \left\langle \frac{U'\beta'}{\mu} \left(\beta'' + 2 \frac{\beta'}{r} - 6 \frac{\beta}{r^2} \right) \right\rangle_0 +$$

$$\left. + \left\langle \left(\frac{U'\beta'}{\mu}\right)^2 \right\rangle_0 \right\} , \tag{13}$$

where μ is the reduced mass of the pair and the averages indicate:

$$\langle \dots \rangle_0 = \frac{4\pi}{V} \int_0^\infty dr \; r^2 \, g_0(r) \dots . \tag{14}$$

In this expression $g_0(r) = \exp\{-U(r)/kT\}$, is the low-density pair distribution function. For a given system of atoms both line shape (Frommhold, 1981) and moments can be calculated by means of a computer, once the model form for the interaction potential $U(r)$ and anisotropy $\beta(r)$ are chosen. The line shape calculation requires, first of all, the integration of the equation of motion of the pair and a Fourier transformation, followed by the integration with respect to the parameters v,b. Moments are calculated by a simple integration.

We mention that spectra computed on the basis of classical mechanics are symmetric, $D_s(\omega) = D_s(-\omega)$. By contrast, measured spectra obey detailed balance

$$D(-\omega) = \exp\left(-\frac{\hbar\omega}{kT}\right) D(\omega) , \qquad (15)$$

which renders them unsymmetric. Although wave mechanical spectra can be computed (Frommhold, 1981) which satisfy Eq.(15), there are cases in which it is sufficient to "unsymmetrize" classically calculated spectra by multiplication with a suitable function as in

$$D(\omega) = 2\left(1 + \exp\left(-\frac{\hbar\omega}{kT}\right)\right)^{-1} D_s(\omega) . \qquad (16)$$

In this way classical lineshapes can be compared with experiment. Furthermore, even moments of the spectral function can be shown to equal the even moments of the unsymmetrized function. Odd moments of the classical function vanish identically. This procedure is often useful since it avoids a full quantum treatment of the line-shape computation, which is much more complex. It must be noted, however, that the unsymmetrization Eq.(16) is valid only when $h\nu/kT$ is sufficiently small to allow the neglect of the quantum properties of the particular spectrum under study (Barocchi et al., 1982).

B. Spectrum of the Triplet

If the density of the system is slowly increased from the low-density limit, polarizability correlations of triplets of atoms and their dynamics start to contribute to the DILS spectra. Therefore, they must be considered and used, in particular, to study three-body interactions.

Recent MD calculations (Weis and Alder, 1981; Zoppi and Spinelli, 1984) indicate that, at liquid density, the contribution due to three-body irreducible polarizability (Weis and Alder, 1981) and potential (Zoppi and Spinelli, 1984) is negligible. We will assume that this is true also for the gas phase and we will limit to consider only pairwise additive polarizabilities and potentials. In this case Eq.(1) can be written (Gelbart, 1974) ($\omega_s = 2\pi\nu_s$):

$$\mathcal{N}(\omega_s) = 2K_0 K_s^3 V n_0 \frac{1}{2\pi} \int_{-\infty}^{+\infty} dt \left[G_2(t) + G_3(t) \right] e^{-i\omega t} , \qquad (17)$$

where

$$G_2(t) = \frac{N(N-1)}{2} \frac{1}{V} \left\langle \alpha_{xy}(12,t)\alpha_{xy}(12,0) \right\rangle_0^{(2)} = \frac{V}{2} \rho^2 C_0(t) \qquad (18)$$

and

$$G_3(t) = \frac{N(N-1)}{2} \frac{1}{V} \left\langle \alpha_{xy}(12,t)\alpha_{xy}(12,0) \right\rangle_1^{(2)} +$$

$$\qquad (19)$$

$$+ N(N-1)(N-2) \frac{1}{V} \left\langle \alpha_{xy}(12,t)\alpha_{xy}(13,0) \right\rangle_0^{(3)} .$$

The averages $\langle \cdots \rangle_0^{(2)}$, $\langle \cdots \rangle_0^{(3)}$ are performed with respect to
the "pure" pair and triplet distribution in $G_2(t)$ and $G_3(t)$, re-
spectively, while $\langle \cdots \rangle_1^{(2)}$ is performed with respect to the part
of the pair distribution function which depends on the presence
of a third particle. From Eqs.(17), (18) and (19) the scattering
cross section per unit scattering volume for a system of N particles is, therefore,

$$\frac{1}{V} \frac{d^2\sigma_\parallel}{d\Omega\, d\nu_s} = 2K_0 K_s^3 \frac{1}{2\pi} \int_{-\infty}^{+\infty} dt\ e^{-i\omega t} \left\{ V \frac{\rho^2}{2} \left[\left\langle \alpha_{xy}(12,t) \right. \right. \right.$$

$$\qquad (20)$$

$$\alpha_{xy}(12,0) \right\rangle_0^{(2)} + \left\langle \alpha_{xy}(12,t)\alpha_{xy}(12,0) \right\rangle_1^{(2)} \right] + V^2 \rho^3 \left\langle \alpha_{xy}(12,t) \right.$$

$$\alpha_{xy}(13,0) \right\rangle_0^{(3)} \right\} = \frac{\rho^2}{2} D_\parallel(12,\omega) + \rho^3 D_\parallel(123,\omega) ,$$

where $D_\parallel(12,\omega)$ is the pair spectrum and

$$D_\parallel(123,\omega) = 2 K_0 K_s^3 \frac{1}{2\pi} \int_{-\infty}^{+\infty} dt\, e^{-i\omega t}\, \frac{G_3(t)}{\rho^3} =$$

$$= 2 K_0 K_s^3 \frac{1}{2\pi} \int_{-\infty}^{+\infty} dt\, e^{-i\omega t} \left[\frac{V}{2\rho} \left\langle \alpha_{xy}(12,t)\alpha_{xy}(12,0) \right\rangle_1^{(2)} + V^2 \left\langle \alpha_{xy}(12,t)\alpha_{xy}(13,0) \right\rangle_0^{(3)} \right] \tag{21}$$

is the ternary spectrum. We will call it the three-body correlation spectrum. We point out that $D_\parallel(123,\omega)$ is composed of two terms, the second of which can be considered an interaction induced depolarized three-body spectrum while the first one is the contribution of the part of the two body spectrum which originates from dynamical correlations with the third particle. Similarly to Eq.(5) $D_\parallel(123,\omega)$ can be written in terms of the anisotropy of the pair, $\beta(ij)$.

In this case $D_\parallel(123,\omega)$, assumes the form (Barocchi et al., 1977)

$$D_\parallel(123,\omega) = \frac{2}{2\pi} K_0 K_s^3 \int_{-\infty}^{+\infty} dt\, e^{-i\omega t} \left\{ \frac{V}{30\rho} \left\langle \beta_{12}(t)\beta_{12}(0) P_2(\cos\vartheta_{12}(t)) \right\rangle_1^{(2)} + \right.$$

$$\left. + \frac{V^2}{15} \left\langle \beta_{12}(t)\beta_{13}(0) P_2(\cos\vartheta_{23}(t)) \right\rangle_0^{(3)} \right\}, \tag{22}$$

where $\theta_{23}(t)$ is the polar angle of the pair (1,2) at time t, relative to that of (1,3)at time t = 0.

The moments of the three body correlation spectrum are defined as

$$M_{2n}^{(3)} = \int_{-\infty}^{+\infty} d\omega\, \omega^{2n}\, D_\parallel(123,\omega). \tag{23}$$

Again, we can approximate k_s by k_0 and derive explicit expression for $M_0^{(3)}$ and $M_2^{(3)}$ in terms of pair polarizability anisotropy and pair potential. We give here the expression of the reduced moments $\overline{M}_{2n}^{(3)}$ with $M_{2n}^{(3)} = 2/15\, k_0^4\, \overline{M}_{2n}^{(3)}$ (Barocchi et al., 1977):

$$\overline{M}_0^{(3)} = \frac{V^2}{2} \left[\left\langle \beta_{12}^2 \right\rangle_1 + 2 \left\langle \beta_{12} \beta_{13} P_2 (\cos \theta_{23}) \right\rangle_0 \right] , \tag{24}$$

$$\overline{M}_2^{(3)} = \frac{V^2}{2} \frac{KT}{\mu} \left[\left\langle \left(\frac{d\beta_{12}}{d\eta_{12}} \right)^2 + 6 \left(\frac{\beta_{12}}{\eta_{12}} \right)^2 \right\rangle_1 + \left\langle \left(\frac{d\beta_{12}}{d\eta_{12}} \right) \left(\frac{d\beta_{13}}{d\eta_{13}} \right) \right. \right.$$

$$\cos \theta_{23} P_2 (\cos \theta_{23}) \Big\rangle_0 + 6 \left\langle \left(\frac{d\beta_{12}}{d\eta_{12}} \right) \left(\frac{\beta_{13}}{\eta_{13}} \right) \sin^2 \theta_{23} \right. \tag{25}$$

$$\left. \cos \theta_{23} \right\rangle_0 + 6 \left\langle \left(\frac{\beta_{12}}{\eta_{12}} \right) \left(\frac{\beta_{13}}{\eta_{13}} \right) \cos^3 \theta_{23} \right\rangle_0 \Bigg] .$$

In expressions (24) and (25) the averages indicate:

$$\left\langle \cdots \right\rangle_1 = \frac{(4\pi)^2}{V^2} \int_0^\infty d\eta_{13} \int_0^{\eta_{13}} d\eta_{23} \int_{\eta_{13}-\eta_{23}}^{\eta_{13}+\eta_{23}} d\eta_{12} \cdots g_0(\eta_{12}) f(\eta_{13}) f(\eta_{23}) \eta_{12} \eta_{13} \eta_{23} \tag{26}$$

and

$$\left\langle \cdots \right\rangle_0 = \frac{(4\pi)^2}{V^2} \int_0^\infty d\eta_{12} \int_0^{\eta_{12}} d\eta_{13} \int_{\eta_{12}-\eta_{13}}^{\eta_{12}+\eta_{13}} d\eta_{23} \cdots g_0(\eta_{12}) g_0(\eta_{13}) g_0(\eta_{23}) \eta_{12} \eta_{13} \eta_{23} \tag{27}$$

while

$$f(r_{ij}) = g_0(r_{ij}) - 1 \tag{28}$$

is the Ursell-Mayer function and $r_{ij} = r(ij,0)$.

C. The High Desity Fluid

When the density of the fluid is increased up to the point that contributions to the DILS intensity from complexes with more than three atoms cannot be neglected, a density expansion of the spectral intensity is not useful any more and the correlation function which appears in Eq.(1) must be calculated taking into account the contributions from all the possible clusters. In order to compare experiments and theories, due to the complexity of the N-particle system, the calculation of the spectral DILS properties can be done only with statistical methods which relay on computer simulation techniques like "Molecular Dynamics" (M.D.). Such comparisons are usually limited to many-body classical systems. Even though calculations for "almost classical" systems have been recently performed (Barocchi et al., 1983), we will limit ourselves to consider only classical M.D. For the case of a high density fluid it is convenient to write Eq.(1) in the form:

$$\mathcal{N}_{\parallel}(\omega_s) = 2 K_0 K_s^3 V n_0 I(\omega) , \tag{29}$$

where the spectrum $I(\omega)$ is the Fourier transform

$$I(\omega) = \frac{1}{2\pi} \int_{-\infty}^{+\infty} dt \, e^{-i\omega t} G(t) \tag{30}$$

and

$$G(t) = \frac{1}{V} \left\langle \sum_{i>j} \left[\hat{y} \cdot \tilde{\alpha}(ij,t) \cdot \hat{x} \right] \sum_{\kappa\ell} \left[\hat{y} \cdot \tilde{\alpha}(\kappa\ell,0) \cdot \hat{x} \right] \right\rangle . \tag{31}$$

The pair polarizability $\tilde{\alpha}(ij,t)$ is defined as:

$$\tilde{\alpha}(ij,t) = 2 \alpha_0^2 \, \tilde{T}(ij,t) . \tag{32}$$

320

Here α_0 is the polarizability of an isolated atom and $\widetilde{\widetilde{T}}(ij,t)$ is the electric field propagator of the atoms i and j. When one is dealing with the depolarized component of the scattering it can be assumed, without lack of generality, that $\widetilde{\widetilde{T}}(ij,t)$ is only the symmetric, traceless part of the field propagator. In this case, it can be written:

$$\widetilde{\widetilde{T}}(ij,t) = \frac{\beta(r_{ij}(t))}{6\alpha_0^2} \left[\widetilde{\widetilde{I}} - 3 \frac{\vec{r}_{ij}(t)\,\vec{r}_{ij}(t)}{r_{ij}^2(t)} \right]. \tag{33}$$

$\widetilde{\widetilde{I}}$ is the unity tensor and $\vec{r}\vec{r}$ is a second order dyadic. In particular, if $\beta(r_{ij})$ is expressed by means of the lowest order DID approximation (i.e., $\beta(r) = 6\alpha_0^2/r^3$)), $\widetilde{\widetilde{T}}(ij,t)$ coincides with the total dipole field propagator tensor. By means of Eqs.(31-33) one can calculate the correlation function G(t) for a given model of the pair anisotropy $\beta(r)$. At intermediate and high densities this is usually done by means of MD.

It is worthwhile to point out that in the low density limit G(t) reduces to:

$$G(t) = G_2(t) + G_3(t) + \dots. \tag{34}$$

Once again spectral moments are defined by:

$$M_{2n} = \int_{-\infty}^{+\infty} d\omega\, \omega^{2n}\, I(\omega) = (-i)^{2n} \left[\frac{d^{2n}}{dt^{2n}} G(t) \right]_{t=0}. \tag{35}$$

The expression of the zeroth moment is immediately obtained from Eq.(31). The expression of the second moment is given by (Barocchi et al., 1983)

$$M_2 = \frac{KT}{mV} \left\langle \left(\nabla \left[\sum_{i>j} \hat{y}\cdot\widetilde{\widetilde{\alpha}}(ij,0)\cdot\hat{x} \right] \right)^2 \right\rangle, \tag{36}$$

where m is the mass of the atom and the operator ∇ is the vector gradient in the 3N-dimensional space of the configurations of the N-particles system.

SECTION II : EXPERIMENTAL RESULTS FOR Ar, Kr, Xe AT LOW DENSITY

A. The Two-Body Spectra

The measurements of the low-density spectra have been performed in the past in two similar ways which give the same results (Barocchi et al., 1981b).

One measurements obtains the density dependence of $N_{\parallel}(\omega)$ and establishes, for each system, a density region in which the spectra depend only on density squared and cubed as in Eq.(20). From such measurements the two-body spectrum $D_{\parallel}(12,\omega)$ and the triplet correlation spectrum $D_{\parallel}(123,\omega)$ are obtained with a least-squares

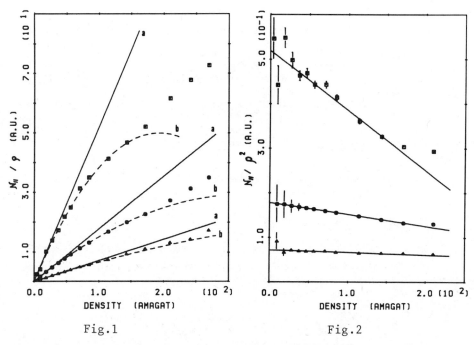

Fig.1

Fig.2

Behaviour of the intensity $N_{\parallel xy}$ $(\nu)/\rho$ as a function of the density ρ for three different frequencies. The lines A) and B) represent a linear and a quadratic fit to the data points, ▫ 10 cm^{-1}, o 20 cm^{-1}, ▲ 30 cm^{-1}.

Behaviour of the intensity $N_{\parallel xy}$ $(\nu)/\rho^2$ as a function of the density ρ ; the lines represent a linear fit to the data points, ▫ 10 cm^{-1}, o 20 cm^{-1}, ▲ 30 cm^{-1}.

322

fit procedure. The useful density region for Ar, Kr, Xe at room temperature ranges from ~ 5 to ~100 Amagat.

The other method obtains $D_{\parallel}(12,\omega)$ directly at densities where ternary contributions are negligible, usually ~ 2-5 Amagat for Ar, Kr, Xe. The first method is more complex in the analysis of the data but has the advantages of yielding both $D_{\parallel}(12,\omega)$ and $D_{\parallel}(123,\omega)$ and of permitting measurements of the spectra at very high frequencies (Barocchi and Zoppi, 1978b). Moreover, since in this case very small detection solid angles can be used, interference from the polarized spectra is easily minimized.

The features of the experimental apparatus used in these measurements have been reported elsewhere (Barocchi and Zoppi, 1978b).

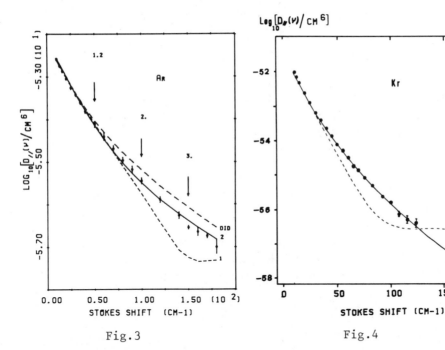

Fig.3

Fig.4

Comparison of the stokes side of the measurement pair spectrum of Argon (dots) and the computed ones. I,2,DID label three different anisotropy models for a pair (see Table 2).

Comparison of the stokes side of the measured pair spectrum of Kr (dots) and two computed line shapes. 1 and 5 label two different anisotropy models for a pair (see Table 3).

323

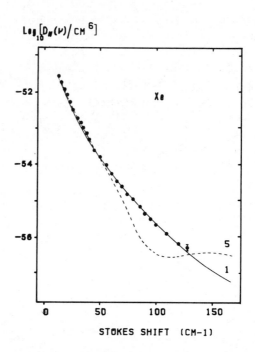

$$\text{Log}_{10}\left[D_{\scriptstyle N}(\nu)/\text{cm}^{6}\right]$$

Xe

STOKES SHIFT (CM-1)

Fig.5

Comparison of the stokes side of the measured pair spectrum of Xenon (dots) and two computed lineshapes. 1 and 5 label two different
anisotropy models for a pair (see Table 4).

Fig.1 and 2 show an example of the typical density behaviour
of the spectrum $N_{\scriptstyle ||}(\nu)/\rho$ for the case of argon, from which the vali-
dity of Eq.(20) is experimentally demonstrated in the density re-
gion up to $\sim$ 100 Amagat.

The above mentioned procedures have permitted the determination
of the two-body spectra of Ar, Kr, Xe (Barocchi and Zoppi, 1978a;
Zoppi et al., 1981a) which are reported, in absolute units, in Figs.
3,4,5.

B. Determination of the Pair Anisotropy $\beta(r)$ from the Two-Body
   Spectra

In principle, binary DILS spectra can be used to derive information on both pair polarizability anisotropy $\beta(r)$ and pair potential U(r). From the comparison of measured and calculated spectra
and moments model functions for U(r) and $\beta(r)$ could be determined.
However, since two-body spectra have been experimentally deter-

324

mined only at one temperature, there is not enough information to explore both quantities. The case of the noble gases Ar, Kr, Xe is, therefore, of particular interest because very good semi-empirical pair potentials do exist (Bobetic and Barker, 1970; Aziz and Chen, 1977; Aziz, 1979; Barker et al., 1974). Assuming the pair potentials as known quantities, reliable information concerning the pair polarizabilities can be derived. It has been shown that a variation of the potential function (for example, when comparing results for argon based on such potential models as Bobetic-Barker (Barocchi and Zoppi, 1978b), Smith (Shelton and Tabisz, 1980), Aziz (Frommhold et al., 1978)) affects the computed profiles and low-order moments by only a few percent, an amount comparable to the experimental uncertainty of present measurements. By contrast, a variation of the induced anisotropy model affects moment and profiles considerably, particularly in the far wings, as we will see below.

Historically, the first model which has been used for $\beta(r)$ is the so called first order Dipole-Induced-Dipole (DID) approximation

$$\beta_{DID}(r) = 6\alpha_o^2 r^{-3}. \tag{37}$$

This model gives a fair agreement with the experimental results for the calculation of the zeroth-moment $M_0^{(2)}$ for the three noble gases. However it fails completely in describing the behaviour of the spectra at high frequencies.

An example of this fact is given in Fig.3, where together with the experimental two-body spectrum of Argon, also the one calculated on the basis of the DID model is reported for comparison. In this case the calculation of the classical lineshape has been performed by means of Eqs.(7,8) using the Bobetic-Barker potential for Argon. The calculated spectra are always unsymmetrized with the procedure Eq.(16) here and in what follows.

In Fig.3 the quantitative difference between the experimental result and the DID calculation is stressed, which does not seem to be too serious in the logaritmic plot employed. However, this difference amounts roughly to factors of 1.2, 2 and 3 in the spectral region around 50, 100, 150 cm^{-1}, respectively, and is clearly outside the experimental uncertainties.

Table 1 also shows this difference with reference to the first three even moments of $D_{\parallel}(12,\omega)$

Since the comparison of the DID calculated lineshapes and moments on one hand, and the experimental results on the other, shows a large discrepancy for all three gases Ar, Kr, Xe, the DID model for those systems must be rejected and improved anisotropy models be derived.

Table 1. Comparison between experimental and calculated moments for the pair spectra of Ar, Kr, Xe.

Moments	Experiment	DID theory		Exp
		LJ potential	B potential	DID-B
Ar[a] $10^{51}M_0^{(2)}(cm^5)$	1.45 ± 0.09	1.28	1.35	1.07
$10^{49}M_2^{(2)}(cm^3)$	3.53 ± 0.42	3.95	4.25	0.83
$10^{45}M_4^{(2)}(cm)$	0.99 ± 0.16	1.53	1.63	0.61
Kr[a] $10^{51}M_0^{(2)}(cm^5)$	5.75 ± 0.62	6.05	6.44	0.89
$10^{49}M_2^{(2)}(cm^3)$	6.73 ± 0.67	7.87	8.54	0.79
$10^{45}M_4^{(2)}(cm)$	0.68 ± 0.10	1.34	1.44	0.47
Xe[a] $10^{50}M_0^{(2)}(cm^5)$	3.74 ± 0.19	3.21	4.11	0.91
$10^{48}M_2^{(2)}(cm^3)$	2.34 ± 0.18	2.05	2.97	0.79
$10^{45}M_4^{(2)}(cm)$	1.51 ± 0.12	1.77	2.92	0.52

(a) $\alpha_0(5145\ \text{Å})_{Ar} = 1.674\ \text{Å}^3$; $\alpha_0(5145\ \text{Å})_{Kr} = 2.540\ \text{Å}^3$;
$\alpha_0(5145\ \text{Å})_{Xe} = 4.164\ \text{Å}^3$

(b)   values obtained from Ref.5
(c)   values obtained from Ref.9

We have proposed (Barocchi et al., 1978) that a possible model for $\beta(r)$, which describes the available experimental data, is a three parameter model of the form

$$\beta(r) = 6\alpha_0^2 r^{-3} + A r^{-6} - B e^{-r/r_0}. \tag{38}$$

The method for the derivation of values A,B and r_0 from the experimental spectral data is described in detail elsewhere (Bafile et
al., 1983); here we will only outline it briefly. We start by adopting a dependable pair potential model and rewriting the three parameter model $\beta(r)$, Eq.(38), in reduced form

$$\beta(x) = \frac{6\alpha_0^2}{b^3}\left(x^{-3} + A^* x^{-6} - B^* e^{-x/x_0}\right),$$

(39)

where $x = r/b$ and b is the distance parameter of the potential.

The substitution of Eq.(39) in the expression of the zeroth,
second and fourth moments of the DILS pair spectrum (Eqs.(11), (12),
(13)) and the comparison with their experimental values leads to
a set of three simultaneous equations for the parameters A, B, x_0.
Once a potential is adopted, we solve the equations with the help
of a computer and find sets of the three parameters which are in
agreement with the experimental moments. We have used the pair
potentials for argon, krypton and xenon by Aziz and Barker and coworkers (Bobetic and Barker, 1970; Aziz, 1979; Barker et al., 1974)
together with the following values for the atomic polarizability of
argon, krypton and xenon: 1.674 $\mathring{A}^3$, 2.540 $\mathring{A}^3$ and 4.164 $\mathring{A}^3$. These
values are slightly different from the ones given by Dalgarno and
Kingston (1960) since we have used the correct values for the density of the gases at normal conditions (Michels et al., 1949;
Trappeniers et al., 1966; Michels et al., 1954).
Tables 2-4 give all solutions found. The experimental values of the
zeroth, second and fourth moment we have used are reported in Table
1. The sixth column of Tables 2, 3 and 4 gives the mean relative
deviation Δ_1 between the experimental and theoretical moments for

Table 2. Mean relative deviations Δ_1 and Δ_2 between the experimental and theoretical moments and lineshapes respectively
for the pair polarizabilities found for Ar (b = 3.7630 $\mathring{A}$).

Model	A^*	B^*	x_0	$r_0(\mathring{A})$	$\Delta_1(\%)$	$\Delta_2(\%)$
1	1.81×10^{-1}	2.61×10^4	8.13×10^{-2}	0.31	1.4	40
2	6.16×10^{-1}	8.48×10^2	1.38×10^{-1}	0.52	2.0	14

each parameter set, which we define as

$$\Delta_1 = \left[\sum_{n=0}^{2} \frac{\left[M_{2n}(\exp) - M_{2n}(calc) \right]^2}{M_{2n}^2(\exp)} \frac{1}{\delta_{2n}^2} \right]^{\frac{1}{2}} \cdot \left[\sum_{n=0}^{2} \frac{1}{\delta_{2n}^2} \right]^{-\frac{1}{2}}, \qquad (40)$$

Table 3. Mean relative deviation Δ_1 and Δ_2 between the experimental and theoretical moments and lineshapes respectively, for the pair polarizabilities found for Kr (b = 4.0067 Å)

Model	A^*	B^*	x_0	r_0(Å)	Δ_1(%)	Δ_2(%)
1	2.16×10^{-1}	9.64×10^{2}	1.20×10^{-1}	0.48	6.5	7.6
2	7.93×10^{-1}	4.28×10^{4}	7.48×10^{2}	0.30	6.5	35.0
3	1.14×10^{-1}	3.62×10^{2}	1.32×10^{-1}	0.53	6.6	17.4
4	6.85×10^{-1}	8.33×10^{2}	1.42×10^{-1}	0.57	9.3	21.5
5	1.80×10^{-1}	1.19×10^{4}	8.97×10^{-2}	0.36	9.5	50.9

where M_{2n} is the even moment of order 2n, $M_{2n}(\exp)$ and δ_{2n} are the experimental values of the moment and its relative error and M_{2n} (calc) is the value of the moment calculated with the given values for A^*, B^*, x_0. Since the values of Δ_1 in all cases are not significantly different, we have then calculated the classical lineshapes for all the parameter sets reported in Tables 2,3 and 4.

The reliability of all computer lineshape calculations has been carefully analyzed by means of: a) the convergence of lineshape values as a function of the increasing precision of the calculation of the pair dynamics, and b) the consistency of the theoretical values of the moments compared to those of the calculated lineshapes.

The reliability of our calculated classical lineshapes as discussed in a previous paper (Bafile er al., 1983), is not acceptable below ~ 10 cm^{-1}; therefore the reported values are always limited to frequencies higher than 10 cm^{-1}.

Figs.3,4 and 5 give the comparison of some calculated lineshapes with the experimental ones for frequencies higher than 10 cm^{-1}.

From these figures we note that, even though the chosen polari-

Table 4. Mean relative deviations Δ_1 and Δ_2 between the experimental and theoretical moments and lineshapes respectively for the pair polarizabilities found for Xe (b = 4.3623 Å).

Model	A^*	B^*	x_0	$r_0(\text{Å})$	$\Delta_1(\%)$	$\Delta_2(\%)$
1	1.24×10^{-2}	6.31×10^{2}	1.10×10^{-1}	0.48	1.8	11.4
2	1.33×10^{-2}	2.80×10^{3}	9.17×10^{-2}	0.40	2.3	14.7
3	1.60×10^{-1}	4.44×10^{2}	1.31×10^{-1}	0.57	2.9	12.6
4	3.82×10^{-2}	6.10×10^{5}	5.96×10^{-2}	0.26	7.8	40.9
5	1.70×10^{-1}	6.94×10^{2}	1.21×10^{-1}	0.53	8.3	16.4
6	5.59×10^{-2}	7.39×10^{4}	6.88×10^{-2}	0.30	12.2	29.8

zability models are in agreement with the moments, they give substantially different high-frequency spectra. In order to have a numerical measure of the difference between the experimental and computed lineshapes, we have calculated a mean relative deviation with the various polarizability models given in Tables 2, 3 and 4,

$$\Delta_2 = \left[\sum_{n=1}^{N} \frac{\left[I_{exp}(\nu_n) - I_{calc}(\nu_n) \right]^2}{I_{exp}^2(\nu_n)} \frac{1}{\delta_n'^2} \right]^{1/2} \cdot \left[\sum_{n=1}^{N} \frac{1}{\delta_n'^2} \right]^{-1/2} \tag{41}$$

For simplicity we have defined $I = D_\parallel$ which is given in Eq.(7) and $I_{calc}(\nu_n)$ is the calculated lineshape at the frequency $\nu_n(\text{cm}^{-1})$ while $I_{exp}(\nu_n)$ and δ_n' are the absolute experimental values of lineshape and the relative errors at the frequency ν_n, respectively. The summation in Eq.(41) is extended over all the frequencies at which the lineshape has been calculated.

The last column of Tables 2, 3 and 4 gives the values of Δ_2 for argon, krypton and xenon when the lineshape is calculated with the values of the various polarizability parameters.

329

The comparison of the Δ_1 and Δ_2 shows that, once various sets of the three parameters are found from moment analysis, lineshape calculations can greatly aid in separating the physical from unphysical solutions.

Since the quantities Δ_1^2 and Δ_2^2 are proportional to the statistical χ^2 parameter, the set which minimizes Δ_1 and Δ_2 minimizes also χ^2 and gives, therefore, the triplet of values, A^*, B^* and x_0, which is most consistent with the experiments.

Table 5. Most probable values of pair polarizabilities for Ar, Kr, and Xe.

Gas	A^*	B^*	x_0	$r_0(\overset{\circ}{A})$	$b(\overset{\circ}{A})$
Ar	6.16×10^{-1}	8.48×10^2	1.38×10^{-1}	0.52	3.7630
Kr	2.16×10^{-1}	9.64×10^2	1.20×10^{-1}	0.48	4.0067
Xe	1.24×10^{-2}	6.31×10^2	1.10×10^{-1}	0.48	4.3623

These most consistent values are reported in Table 5. The comparison between the argon, krypton and xenon polarizability parameters shows that the "overlap contribution" decay constant r_0 is very similar in the three cases, while A^* decreases very strongly from a high value for argon to much lower values for krypton and xenon.

This strong decrease of A^* shows that the intermediate contribution to the interaction-induced polarizability-anisotropy becomes less and less important with respect to the lowest order DID one $(6\alpha_0^2/b^3)x^{-3}$ when increasing the size and mass of the interacting atoms. It is also interesting to note that the second-order DID contribution $(6\alpha_0^2/b^3)A_{DID}^*$, with $A_{DID}^* = \alpha_0/b^3$, gives for A_{DID}^* the values: 3.2×10^{-2}, 3.9×10^{-2}, 5×10^{-2} for argon, krypton and xenon, respectively. The values of A we found are all very different from A_{DID}^*. However we point out that a direct comparison between A^* and A_{DID}^* is meaningless since in the model Eq.(39) A^* accounts effectively for all possible intermediate-range effects, for example multipoles, which are present in the pair-polarizability anisotropy.

The comparison between the behaviour of our experimentally determined $\beta(r)$ with Dacre's ab initio calculations (Dacre, 1982) is given in Figs.6, 7, 8 where for the sake of clarity only the extra

DID polarizabilities $\beta(x) - \beta_{DID}(x)$ are reported. The agreement is quite good for xenon while increasing differences are present for krypton and argon. This differences are due to "intermediate range" effects which are present in the experimental data while they seem not to be sufficiently accounted for by the theoretical calculation.

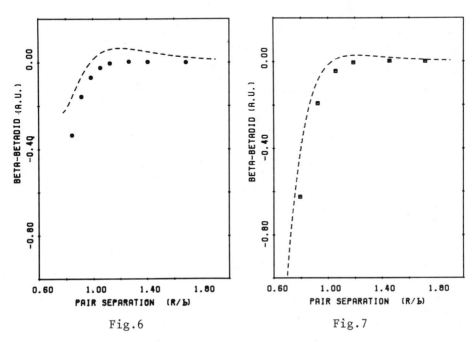

Fig.6

Fig.7

Extra DID contribution in the pair anisotropy for Argon. The line represents the model 2 of Table 2 whereas the circles are the SCF calculation of Dacre (Dacre, 1982).

Extra DID contribution to the pair anisotropy for Krypton. The line represents the model 1 of Table 3, whereas the squares are the SCF calculations of Dacre (Dacre, 1982).

C. The Three Body Correlation Spectrum

The spectra of moderately dense gases have been analyzed repeatedly with the purpose of deriving the properties of colliding pairs from the two-body spectra. Spectral features due to three and even four-body correlation have been shown to be also experimentally accessible (Lallemand, 1971; Mc Tague et al., 1971; Barocchi et al., 1977b ; Barocchi and Zoppi, 1978c; Shelton et al., 1982). As we have seen in Sect.I the three-body correlation spectrum $D(123,\omega)$

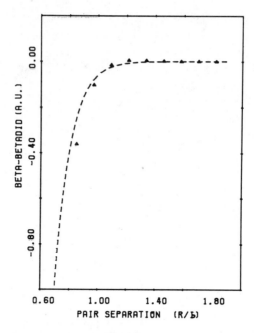

Fig.8

Extra DID contribution to the pair anisotropy for Xenon. The line represents the model 1 of Table 4, whereas the triangles are the SCF calculations of Dacre (Dacre, 1982).

can yield, in principle, valuable information in three-body inter-actions.

In practice, however, only few experimental results have been derived up to now from the three-body spectra and compared with theoretical predictions (Barocchi et al., 1977b; Barocchi and Zoppi, 1978c; Shelton et al., 1982). In particular, for noble gases only the spectrum of argon has been measured (Barocchi and Zoppi, 1978c; Shelton et al., 1982) while for krypton and xenon there are data for the third depolarization virial coefficient (Dunmur et al., 1983). Fig.9 shows the behaviour of $D_{||}(123,\omega)$ for argon (Barocchi and Zoppi, 1978c; Shelton et al., 1982), while Table 6 gives the values of the zeroth and second moments. These are compared to their theoretical values which are calculated with Lennard-Jones and Bobetic-Barker potentials within the DID approximation for the pair polarizability anisotropy.

The principal conclusions which one can derive from the analy-sis of the three-body correlation spectral moments are the follow-

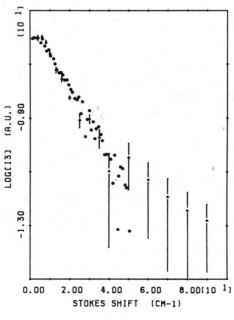

Fig.9

The three-body spectrum of argon, after Barocchi and Zoppi (1978c)
and Shelton et al. (1982).

Table 6. Values of the zeroth and second moment of the three-body
intensity for argon.

		$-M_0^{(3)} \times 10^{74}$ (cm^8)	$-M_2^{(3)} \times 10^{72}$ (cm^6)
Experiment	Barocchi & Zoppi	7.4 ± 0.7	$10. \pm 4.$
	Shelton & Tabisz	7.6 ± 0.6	$10. \pm 4.$
Theory (DID)	Hard Sphere	5.77	0
	Lennard Jones	7.30	7.88
	Bobetic & Barker	7.56	9.54

ing: first, the DID model and the available refined empirical potential describe very well the zeroth and second moments within the actual experimental errors, which is a result confirmed also for the zeroth moment of krypton and xenon (Dunmur et al., 1983). This is not surprising if one thinks that in a low density gas the biggest contribution to the triplet spectrum should come from clusters where only two bodies can be at short-range while the third body is relatively distant. Secondly, the second moment of $D(123,\omega)$ seems to be much more sensitive to the details of the pair potential. This is confirmed from calculations which have been performed for Ar, Kr, Xe at various temperatures (Barocchi et al., 1977a) and from calculations which have been performed for polyatomic isotropic molecules (Shelton et al., 1982). This feature can be advantageously used to investigate those systems, for which pair potentials are not known with sufficient precision.

D. The High Density System

For the interpretation of high density DILS spectra it is of primary importance to compare experimental results and theoretical calculations on an absolute scale. Even though several measurements have been performed in the past (Fleury and Mc Tague, 1969; Gornall et al., 1970; Fleury et al., 1971; Volterra et al., 1971; An et al., 1976), only recently reliable absolute values of high density spectra in argon have been published (Vershneya et al., 1981; Zoppi et al., 1981b). Therefore, here we will refer only to these last ones.

Figures 10 and 11 show the behaviour of the zeroth and second moments of argon at room temperature as a function of density up to 500 amagat. The experimental results reported here are given in absolute units, the calibration has been performed with the method of the internal standard as described in the Appendix A both in the gas and in the liquid phases.

Table 7 gives the results for the measurements in the liquid near to the triple point.

The theoretical values which are reported in Figs. 10, 11 and in Table 7 have been derived by means of Eqs.(31-36) with the application of the molecular dynamics technique.

In the gas phase the molecular dynamics simulation has been performed at T = 298 K, for the densities 100, 200, 300, 400, 500 amagat with a system of 500 atoms while in the liquid phase we used a system with 864 atoms at T = 90.8 K and at a density of 770

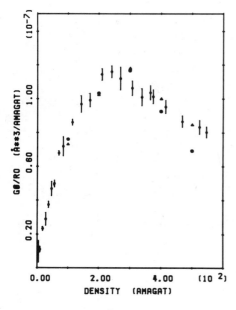

Fig.10

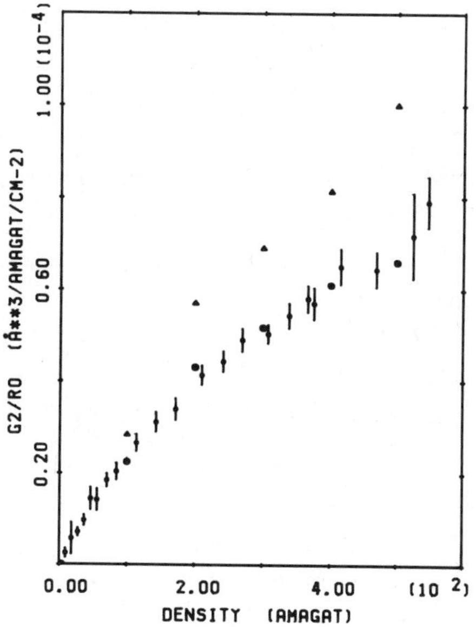

Fig.11

Density behaviour of $G^{(0)}(\rho)/\rho$ for argon gas at room temperature. The dots with error bars are the experimental points. The circles and the triangles are evaluated by means of computer simulation using model 2 of Table 2 and the DID respectively.

Density behaviour of $G^{(2)}(\rho)/\rho$ for argon gas at room temperature. The dots with error bars are the experimental points. The circles and triangles have the same meaning as in Fig.10.

amagat. For all densities the cut-off radius of the interaction potential was 2.5 σ while the cut-off radius for the interaction polarizability in the calculations of the scatterd intensity has been set equal to 5σ, where σ is the distance of the zero value of the potential. This choice for the polarizability cut-off corresponds to a value of r for which both the radial distribution function g(r) and the reduced integrated intensity $G^{(0)}$ approach their asymptotic values (Vershneya et al., 1981). The average of Eq.(31) has been performed over 6000 and 4000 time steps of 2 x 10^{-14}s in the gas phase and in the liquid, respectively.

Table 7. Molecular-dynamics results for the reduced integrated intensity $G^{(0)}/\rho$ and the reduced second moment $G^{(2)}/\rho$ in the liquid phase and comparison with experiments.

Model	Density (Amagat)	Temperature (°K)	$G^{(0)}/\rho \times 10^8$ (Å^3 amagat^{-1})	$G^{(2)}/\rho \times 10^5$ (Å^3 amagat^{-1}cm^{-2})
DID	770	90.8	3.12[b]	2.40[b]
2[a]	770	90.8	2.17[b]	1.37[b]
Experiment	770 ± 5	90.8 ± 1.5	1.57 ± .22[c]	1.13 ± 0.10[d]

(a) the label is the same as in Table 2
(b) value from Barocchi et al. (1982b)
(c) value from Vershneya et al. (1981)
(d) value from Zoppi et al. (1981b)

Two induced polarizability anisotropy forms have been used in the calculations, the DID form given in Eq.(39) and the three parameter form given in Eq.(40) with the values of the parameters given in Table 5 for argon. The potential was the Bobetic-Barker(1970).

The comparison between experiments and calculations as given in Figs. 10, 11 and in Table 7 shows that the DID model gives as good account of the results for the zeroth moment in the gas phase as the three-parameter polarizability anisotropy. However it fails completely in describing the behaviour of the second moment in the gas and of both moments in the liquid. Other empirical models, which have been proposed in the past for the $\beta(r)$ of argon, have also been shown not to be able to describe the high density experimental results like the DID model (Barocchi et al., 1982b). The pair-polarizability anisotropy we have derived from the low density spectrum of argon is, up to now, the one which best describes the overall behaviour of the experimental data both in the gas and in the liquid (Barocchi et al., 1982b). However, also in this case the data of the liquid mantain a disagreement of ~ 27% and ~17% for the zeroth and second moment, respectively, which are much higher than the experimental errors. This remaining discrepancy could be ascribed to various causes, among which: 1) the high sensitivity of the liquid behaviour to the details of both pair-polarizability and pair-potential forms, 2) the role played by three-body irreducible properties, 3) the quantum behaviour which for the case of the second moment of argon at triple point could amount to ~10% (Barocchi et al., 1983).

For the above reasons we believe that the case of the liquid should be further investigated even though the present three-parameters polarizability anisotropy brings the discrepancy between experiment and calculation from a factor 2, as it was for the DID model, to ~27% and ~17%.

It is worth noticing here that in order to distinguish properly between the various models for $\beta(r)$ in the liquid it is of crucial importance to perform the comparison between the experimental and calculated values on an absolute scale. In fact, if we would have considered, as this is sometimes done by various authors, only the relative value of the second moment, i.e. the ratio between the second and zeroth moment, we would have found .77 x 10^3, .63 x 10^3, .72 ± .3 x 10^3 cm^{-2} for the DID model, the empirical model and the experiment, respectively, which would have shown a better agreement between the experiment and the DID than the empirical model.

We think that in order to describe properly the behaviour of the DILS spectra in high density fluids, either atomic or molecular, comparison on absolute values must be performed.

APPENDIX A1

As we have seen in the text, the measurement of the absolute DILS intensity is of fundamental importance for a correct interpretation of the experimental results, as well as for determining a reliable empirical model for the induced pair anisotropy.

Here we will critically discuss the techniques which are used in this kind of experiment, relying essentially on a number of experimental facts.

The absolute intensity measurement of DILS spectra in gases was first introduced by Lallemand (1970), who added a small amount of hydrogen to the gaseous sample in order to calibrate the measured depolarized intensities with respect to the rotational lines of H_2. Since then this technique of comparing the relative intensities of DILS scattering and rotational Raman lines of known cross section has been extensively used. Practically, one can distinguish between two main calibration techniques. In the first one, the hydrogen (or any other calibration gas) is added as an impurity to the sample under study, in such a quantity that its presence does not appreciably change the behaviour. In the second one, the comparison is made on pure samples at different times by changing the content of the scattering cell. Both methods have advantages and disadvantages.

In the first method the intensity standard is added internally to the sample and therefore the two measurements are performed exactly in the same macroscopic condition, i.e. same temperature, same refractive index and same geometrical configuration of the scattering volume. However, one has to deal with a mixture and therefore has to face problems which involve the interactions of the two molecular species connected either with the possible change of the local field around the scattering center due to the substitution of some of its neighbours, or with the collisional contribution to the intensity of the reference line.

By using the second method the comparison is made on two different samples. Even if one can make the calibration on the two samples at the same temperature (which is not always possible), the refractive index will never be exactly the same. The implications of this fact are manifold. The most important is that by changing the refractive index one also changes the local field (l.f.) seen by the individual scattering center. On the other hand, the functional dependence of the l.f. upon the refractive index does not seem to be well established in the literature. In fact the Lorentz-Lorenz factor for the local field has been interpreted in different ways by different researchers (Burnham et al., 1975; Keyes and Landanyi, 1977; Frenkel and Mc Tague, 1980) and moreover the Lorentz-Lorenz function itself has been questioned and some corrections have been proposed (Sullivan and Deutch, 1976). Apart from this, any change in the refractive index also influences both the transmittivity of the windows and the magnitude of the scattering collection angle in a way which is not easily predictable and must be carefully analyzed in every single experiment.

In the case of low density measurements, since the refractive index does not appreciably change from one, the two methods are completely equivalent as it has been demonstrated in previous works (Barocchi and Zoppi, 1978b; Shelton and Tabisz, 1980; Barocchi et al., 1981b).

Here we will not discuss the low density case in detail and also we will not describe the important step of the absolute calibration of the detection system which has been already done (Barocchi and Zoppi, 1978b)

The aim of this Appendix is to show the influence of the different effects on the calibration procedures in high density case and to demonstrate on an experimental basis, that the measurement with the internal standard (mixture) can be very reliable once the experimental parameters are carefully chosen. In order to achieve this goal, we will discuss the results of the calibration of the integrated intensity of the Rayleigh scattering (polarized) of a gaseous sample of argon. It is well known that this intensity is related to the fluid compressibility $\beta_T(\rho)$ by means of the following expression:

$$I(ray) = K \cdot \beta_T(\rho)\rho^2 \qquad (A1)$$

where K is a normalization constant and ρ is the density of the gas. Moreover, since in this measurement the depolarization ratio around the Rayleigh line is less than a few fractions of a percent, the collisional contribution to the intensity can be easily neglected or eventually accounted for in the experimental error. We have measured the density behaviour of the polarized Rayleigh scattering of a mixture of hydrogen and argon at room temperature at various argon densities, keeping fixed the density of the hydrogen in the cell. In particular, we have filled the scattering cell with 1 atm. of H_2 and gradually added some amount of argon to reach pressures, almost evenly spaced, up to more than 1000 atmospheres. Since the amount of H_2 was always very small (at most ~2% at the lowest pressure) the calculation of the argon densities was made simply by subtracting 1 atm. from the reading of the gauge and deriving the densities from previous work (Michels and Botzen, 1949). The integrated intensity is obtained from the ratio between the Rayleigh intensity due to argon and the Raman intensity due to the rotational transition j = 1 → j = 3 of molecular hydrogen. Since the amount of hydrogen is a constant, the ratio can change only because of the change of the Rayleigh cross section (compressibility) or because of the change of the collisional contribution to the rotational Raman line. By comparing the experimental results with the function $\beta_T(\rho)\rho^2$ one can plot the quantity K, defined in Eq.(A1), as a function of the density and verify which are the limitations on the validity of the above assumptions; i.e. to neglect the collisional contribution to the Raman line of H_2 and to verify the equality of

Table A1. Measured values of the normalization constant K as defined in Eq.(A1) for various argon densities. $\bar{K}$ and s.d.
are the mean and standard deviation of the sample.

ρ(amagat)	K(a.u.)	ρ(amagat)	K(a.u.)	ρ(amagat)	K(a.u.)
273	.119	384	.120	467	.131
308	.124	413	.125	482	.132
339	.127	433	.129	496	.135
367	.127	451	.131	505	.126
				524	.135

$\bar{K}$ = .128 ; s.d. = .005

the local field on the two scattering centers. Table A1 shows the
results of the experiment and indicates that both assumptions are
fulfilled within ± 4% which is also the actual precision of the measurements. The value of $\beta_T(\rho)$ in the previous calculation has been
derived from the data already published (Michels and Botzen, 1949).

In order to further investigate the validity of the Lorentz-
Lorenz expression for the l.f. correction, we have also taken some
collision-induced experimental data on the same mixture of argon-H_2.
In this experiment the frequency shift was kept constant at 40 cm^{-1}
and only the density of argon was changed. Figure A1 shows the comparison between the intensity calibrated with respect to the S(0) line
of H_2 compared with the same intensity which has been corrected by
means of the Lorentz-Lorenz local field factor

$$LF = \left[(n^2 + 2)/3 \right]^4 \tag{A2}$$

and by the change of the collection solid angle. Open circles represent the crude experimental data while the triangles represent
the same data reduced by the factor $1/n^2$ (change of the collection
solid angle) (Nestor and Lippincot, 1973). Figure A2 shows the same
comparison when the l.f. factor has been substituted by

$$LF = \left[(n^2 + 2)/3 \right]^2 \tag{A3}$$

which is the Lorentz-Lorenz expression for any first order effect
(for example absorption), and by

$$LF = \left[(n^2 + 2)/3 \right]^8 \cdot 1/n^4 \tag{A4}$$

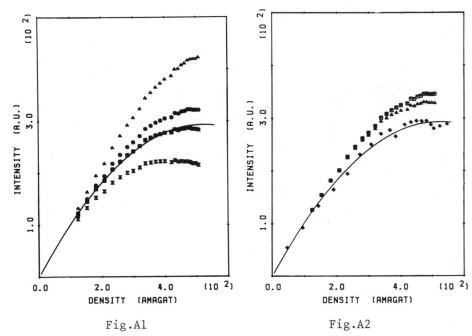

Fig.A1

Fig.A2

Density behavior of the different corrections to the experimental intensity. The circles represent the measured data. The correction for the l.f. only (Eq.A2) gives the crosses while the correction for the collection solid angle only generates triangles. The squares are obtained by using both the corrections and the full line is the best fit of the experimental data normalized to the H_2 rotational line (see Fig. A2 for the experimental points).

The effect of the different l.f. corrections. The experimental points normalized to the rotational S(O) line of H_2 are represented by diamonds, while the full line is the best fit. Triangles and squares represent the measured data corrected both for l.f. change and collection solid angle. Triangles and squares represent the l.f. correction as given in Eqs.(A4) and (A3), respectively.

which was recently proposed by Frankel and McTague (1980). The coincidence shown in Fig. A1 indicates that in our case the Lorentz-Lorenz local field factor given by Eq.(A1) is the one that should be used. Even if this is the case, however, our method of calibration avoids the need of considering any explicit local field correction.

REFERENCES

An, S.C., Montrose, C.J., and Litivitz, T.A., 1976, J.Chem.Phys.,
  64: 3717.
Aziz, R.A. and Chen, H.H., 1977, J.Chem.Phys. 67: 5719.
Aziz, R.A., 1979, Mol.Phys. 38: 177.
Bafile, U., Magli, R., Barocchi, F., Zoppi, M., and Frommhold, L.,
  1983, Mol.Phys. 49: 1149.
Barker, J.A., Watts, R.O., LEE, J.K., Schafer, T.P., and Lee, X.T.,
  1974, J.Chem.Phys. 61: 3081.
Barocchi, F., Neri, M. and Zoppi, M., 1977 a, Mol.Phys. 34: 1391.
Barocchi, F., Zoppi, M., Shelton, D.P., and Tabisz, G.C., 1977 b,
  Can.J.Phys. 55: 1962.
Barocchi, F., and Zoppi, M., 1978 a, Phys.Lett. 66A: 99.
Barocchi, F., and Zoppi, M., 1978 b, Proceedings of the Internatio-
  nal School of Physics "E.Fermi", Course LXXV, Varenna, Italy
Barocchi, F., and Zoppi, M., 1978 c, Phys.Lett. A69: 187.
Barocchi, F., Neri, M., and Zoppi, M., 1978, Chem.Phys.Lett. 59: 537.
Barocchi, F., Moraldi, M., and Zoppi, M., 1981 a, Mol.Phys. 43: 1193.
Barocchi, F., Zoppi, M., Proffit, M.H., and Frommhold, L., 1981 b,
  Can.J.Phys. 59: 1418.
Barocchi, F., Moraldi, M., and Zoppi, M., 1982 a, Mol.Phys. 45: 1285.
Barocchi, F., Spinelli, G., and Zoppi, M., 1982 b, Chem.Phys.Lett.
  90: 22.
Barocchi, F., Zoppi, M., and Neumann, M., 1983, Phys.Rev. A27: 1587.
Bobetic, M.V., and Barker, J.A., 1970, Phys.Rev. B2: 4149.
Burnham,A.K., Alms, G.R., and Flygare, W.H., 1975, J.Chem.Phys. 62:
  •3289.
Dacre, P.D., 1982, Mol.Phys. 45: 1 ; 47: 193.
Dalgarno, A., and Kingston, A.E., 1960, Proc.Roy.Soc. A259: 424.
Dunmur, D.A., Manterfield, M.R., and Robinson, D.J., 1983, Mol.Phys.
  50: 573.
Fleury, P.A., and Mc Tague, J.P., 1969, Opt.Comm. 1: 164.
Fleury, P.A., Daniels, W.B., and Worlock, J.M., 1971, Phys.Rev.Lett.
  27: 1493.
Frenkel, D., and Mc Tague, J.P., 1980, J.Chem.Phys. 72: 2801.
Frommhold, L., Hong, K.H., and Proffit, M.H., 1978, Mol.Phys. 35:
  665.
Frommhold, L., 1981, Adv.Chem.Phys. 46: 1.
Gelbart, W.L., 1974, Adv.Chem.Phys. 26: 1.
Gornall, W.S., Howard-Lock, H.E., and Stoicheff, B.P., 1970, Phys.
  Rev. A1: 1288.
Keyes, T., and Landanyi, B., 1977, Mol.Phys. 33: 1063.

Lallemand, P.M., 1970, Phys.Rev.Lett. 25: 1079.

Lallemand, P.M., 1971, J. de Physique 32: 119.

Mc Tague, J.P., Ellenson, W.D., and Hall, L.H., 1971, J.de Physique 33: 241.

Michels, A., Wijker, H., and Wijker, H.K., 1949, Physica XV: 627.

Michels, A., Wassenaar, T., and Louwerse, P., 1954, Physica XX: 99.

Michels, A., and Botzen, A., 1949, Physica XV: 769.

Nestor, J.R., and Lippincot, E.R., 1973, J.Raman Spectr. 1: 305.

Proffit, M.H., Keto, J.W., and Frommhold, L., 1981, Can.J.Phys. 59: 1459.

Shelton, D, and Tabisz, G.C., 1980, Mol.Phys. 40: 285.

Shelton, D.P., Tabisz, G.C., Barocchi, F., and Zoppi, M., 1982, Mol.Phys. 46: 21.

Sullivan, D.E., and Deutch, J.M., 1976, J.Chem.Phys. 64: 3870.

Trappeniers, N.J., Wassenaar, T., and Wolkers, G.J., 1966, 32: 1503.

Vershneya, D., Shirron, S.F., Litovitz, T.A., Zoppi, M., and Barocchi, F., 1981, Phys.Rev. A23: 77.

Volterra, V., Bucaro, J.A., and Litovitz, T.A., 1971, Phys.Rev.Lett. 26: 55.

Weis, J.A., and Alder, B.J., 1981, Chem.Phys.Lett. 81: 113.

Zoppi, M., Moraldi, M., Barocchi, F., Magli, R., and Bafile, U., 1981 a, Chem.Phys.Lett. 83: 294.

Zoppi, M., Barocchi, F., Vershneya, D., Neumann, M., and Litovitz, T.A., 1981 b, Can.J.Phys. 59: 1475.

Zoppi, M., and Spinelli, G., 1984, Proceedings of the IX International Conference on Raman Spectroscopy (Tokyo).

INTERACTION INDUCED ROTATIONAL LIGHT SCATTERING IN MOLECULAR GASES

G.C. Tabisz*
Division of Chemistry, National Research Council of
Canada,** Ottawa, Canada. K1A OR6

N. Meinander and A.R. Penner
Department of Physics, University of Manitoba, Winnipeg
Manitoba, Canada. R3T 2N2

ABSTRACT

The theory of induced rotational light scattering by molecular
gases is reviewed and its application to experimental studies of
tetrahedral and octahedral molecules is discussed. The success of
the theoretical description based on a long-range interaction is
assessed.

INTRODUCTION

This paper reviews interaction induced rotational light scattering in molecular gases. Elsewhere in this volume, H. Posch (1985)
discusses induced rotational scattering in liquids. The phenomenon
is describable in terms of a long-range mechanism involving dipoles
induced by field gradients and consequently involving high order
molecular multipole polarizabilities. The paper begins with an
historical introduction, reviews the theory of induced rotational
scattering, discusses its application to specific molecules and
concludes with some summarizing comments.

HISTORICAL BACKGROUND

The first experiments on interaction induced Raman scattering
were performed in the mid-seventies (Holzer and LeDuff, 1974; Holzer

---

*Permanent address: Dept. of Physics, University of Manitoba.
**submitted as NRCC contribution No. 23087

and Ouillon, 1974,1976) on the molecules CF_4, SF_6 and CO_2; they explained their observation of depolarized components to ν_1 vibrational bands by analogy to induced depolarized Rayleigh scattering. Essentially they proposed a DID mechanism involving $\partial\alpha/\partial q$. Thibeau et al. (1977) elucidated this mechanism, making a thorough and general comparison between the depolarization ratio for Rayleigh and for Raman scattering by a fluid composed of isotropic molecules. Such an approach, however, could not explain the observation of completely forbidden vibrational bands. Samson, Pasmanter and Ben-Reuven (1976; Samson and Ben-Reuven, 1976) proposed a theory to account for these which formally included effects due to the electric-dipole electric-quadrupole ($\overset{\leftrightarrow}{A}$) and electric-dipole magnetic-dipole ($\overset{\leftrightarrow}{G}$) polarizabilities. To our knowledge this theory has not been developed to the point where it may be used for detailed analysis of experiment.

At this time, Buckingham and Ladd (1976) extended the theory of collision induced absorption in the far infrared region to include the contribution of the dipole moment induced in a molecule by the gradient of the field due to the permanent multipole moments of its neighbours. This theory is based on the following expressions for the total multipole moments of a molecule in an external electric field $\vec{F}$ (Buckingham, 1967):

$$\mu_\alpha = \mu_\alpha^{(0)} + \alpha_{\alpha\beta}F_\beta + \frac{1}{2}\beta_{\alpha\beta\gamma}F_\beta F_\gamma + \frac{1}{6}\gamma_{\alpha\beta\gamma\delta}F_\beta F_\gamma F_\delta + \frac{1}{3}A_{\alpha\beta\gamma}F'_{\beta\gamma} + \frac{1}{15}E_{\alpha\beta\gamma\delta}F''_{\beta\gamma\delta} + \cdots$$

$$\Theta_{\alpha\beta} = \Theta_{\alpha\beta}^{(0)} + A_{\alpha\beta\gamma}F_\gamma + C_{\alpha\beta\gamma\delta}F'_{\gamma\delta} + \frac{1}{15}H_{\alpha\beta\gamma\delta\epsilon}F''_{\gamma\delta\epsilon} + \cdots\cdots$$

$$\Omega_{\alpha\beta\gamma} = \Omega_{\alpha\beta\gamma}^{(0)} + E_{\alpha\beta\gamma\delta}F_\delta + \frac{1}{3}H_{\alpha\beta\gamma\delta\epsilon}F'_{\delta\epsilon} + R_{\alpha\beta\gamma\delta\epsilon\phi}F''_{\delta\epsilon\phi} + \cdots\cdots \tag{1}$$

$\vec{\mu}$, $\overset{\leftrightarrow}{\Theta}$, $\overset{\leftrightarrow}{\Omega}$ are the dipole, quadrupole and octopole moments, respectively; the subscripts refer to components of the tensor in any Cartesian reference frame. The superscript zero denotes a permanent moment. $\overset{\leftrightarrow}{\alpha}$ is the dipole polarizability; $\overset{\leftrightarrow}{\beta}$, $\overset{\leftrightarrow}{\gamma}$ etc. are hyperpolarizabilities describing departures from a linear polarization law. $\overset{\leftrightarrow}{A}$, $\overset{\leftrightarrow}{E}$, etc. appear because derivatives of the field (F', F", etc.) may induce moments in the molecule.

These tensors $\overset{\leftrightarrow}{A}$ and $\overset{\leftrightarrow}{E}$ are central to the present discussion. Note that $\overset{\leftrightarrow}{A}$, the dipole-quadrupole polarizability, describes both the dipole induced by a field gradient and the quadrupole induced by the field. Similarly, the dipole-octopole polarizability $\overset{\leftrightarrow}{E}$ describes the dipole induced by the second derivative of the field as well as the field-induced octopole. For a tetrahedral molecule, the magnitudes of both $\overset{\leftrightarrow}{A}$ and $\overset{\leftrightarrow}{E}$ may be specified by single parameters, denoted as A and E, respectively. For an octahedral molecule $\overset{\leftrightarrow}{A}$ vanishes and again $\overset{\leftrightarrow}{E}$ may be specified by a single parameter. $\overset{\leftrightarrow}{A}$ and $\overset{\leftrightarrow}{E}$ are anisotropic; thus there are rotating induced dipoles coupling the incident electric vector to the molecular rotations.

Effects due to $\overset{\leftrightarrow}{A}$ and $\overset{\leftrightarrow}{E}$ have, however, not been clearly identified in absorption spectra. See, for example, the work of Birnbaum and Sutter (1981) on SF_6 and of Birnbaum et al. (1983) on CH_4. The reason is that these tensors give rise to weak contributions to the rotational spectrum which lie largely in the same frequency region as those due to the principal induction mechanism, which involves the dipoles induced by the field of the permanent multipole moments of the collision partners. In interaction induced light scattering in the Rayleigh region, a significant part of the induced rotational spectrum may be displaced to frequencies higher than the intense translational spectrum and is thus more readily identifiable.

THEORY OF INDUCED ROTATIONAL SCATTERING

The theory of induced pure rotational scattering was developed by Buckingham and Tabisz (1977, 1978). To appreciate the proposed interaction consider a pair of molecules 1 and 2 separated by a distance R and in the exciting light beam. The electric field $\overset{\rightarrow}{\mathcal{E}}$ associated with the light beam induces a dipole $\overset{\rightarrow}{\mu}$ in 1 and the field $\vec{F}$ of $\overset{\rightarrow}{\mu}_1$ induces a dipole $\alpha_2 \vec{F}$ in 2. This interaction yields the DID contribution in R^{-3} to the pair polarizability. The field gradient $\vec{F}'$ also acts on 2 to induce a dipole moment $(1/3)\overset{\leftrightarrow}{A}_2 : \vec{F}'$; moreover the external field $\overset{\rightarrow}{\mathcal{E}}$ induces a quadrupole moment $\overset{\leftrightarrow}{\theta}_1 = \overset{\leftrightarrow}{A}_1 \cdot \overset{\rightarrow}{\mathcal{E}}$ in 1 and its field induces a dipole in 2. These two interactions yield a pair polarizability varying as R^{-4} and rotating with the molecules.

For a scattering geometry in which the laser beam propagates along the X-axis, polarized in the Z-direction, with observations made along the Y-axis, the XZ and ZZ components of the mean square polarizability are of interest; these are given for tetrahedral and octahedral (A=0) symmetry by the following:

$$\langle \alpha_{XZ}^2 \rangle = \frac{12}{5} (\alpha_1 \alpha_2)^2 \ R^{-6} + \frac{48}{35} \left[(\alpha_1 A_2)^2 + (\alpha_2 A_1)^2 \right] R^{-8} \qquad (2)$$

$$+ \frac{62912}{4725} (A_1 A_2)^2 \ R^{-10} + \frac{11}{9} \left[(\alpha_1 E_2)^2 + (\alpha_2 E_1)^2 \right] R^{-10} + \dots .$$

$$\langle \alpha_{ZZ}^2 \rangle = (\alpha_1 + \alpha_2)^2 + \frac{16}{5} (\alpha_1 \alpha_2)^2 \ R^{-6} + \frac{592}{105} \left[(\alpha_1 A_2)^2 + (\alpha_2 A_1)^2 \right] R^{-8}$$

$$+ \frac{95616}{4725} (A_1 A_2)^2 \ R^{-10} + \frac{52}{9} \left[(\alpha_1 E_2)^2 + (\alpha_2 E_1)^2 \right] R^{-10} + \dots .$$

$\langle \dots \rangle$ denotes an average over all orientations of 1 and 2 and of the intermolecular vector. $(\alpha_1 + \alpha_2)^2$ gives the polarized Rayleigh scattering; the terms in R^{-6} are the first order DID contributions while those in R^{-8} and R^{-10} yield the induced rotational scattering. The term in $(\alpha A)^2 R^{-8}$ gives a rotational spectrum following the selection rule

$$\Delta J_i = 0 \quad, \qquad \Delta J_j = 0, \pm1, \pm2, \pm3 \quad, \qquad (J_j + J_{j'}) \geqslant 3$$

(single A spectrum),

where J is the total angular momentum quantum number and the subscripts (i,j) refer to pair (1,2) or (2,1). The term $(\alpha E)^2 R^{-10}$ follows the selection rule,

$$\Delta J_i = 0, \qquad \Delta J_j = 0, \pm1, \pm2, \pm3, \pm4, \qquad J_j + J_{j'} \geqslant 4$$

(single E spectrum).

The term $(A\,A)^2 R^{-10}$ describes a spectrum of double transitions:

$$\Delta J_i = 0, \pm1, \pm2, \pm3, \qquad \Delta J_j = 0, \pm1, \pm2, \pm3, \qquad J_i \pm J_{i'} \geqslant 3, \qquad J_j + J_{j'} \geqslant 3$$

(double A spectrum).

This theory was derived with the assumption of no translation-rotation coupling, the rigid rotor approximation, the neglect of nuclear spin effects and the use of symmetric top wave functions.

Recall that the expression for the total dipole moment μ_α in Eq. (1) contains non-linear terms. For tetrahedra, $\overset{\leftrightarrow}{\beta}$, $\overset{\leftrightarrow}{A}$ and $\overset{\leftrightarrow}{\Omega}$ have the same transformation properties and therefore the term $(1/2)\beta F^2$ in Eq. (1) will give rise to a rotational spectrum following the same selection rules as the $A^4 R^{-10}$ term in Eq. (2), where the field is that of the light beam plus that of a permanent octopole moment of a neighbour. For CH_4, it can, however, be shown (Buckingham and Tabisz, 1977) that this contribution to the intensity is less than 2% of that in $A^4 R^{-10}$ and is thus negligible. As $\overset{\leftrightarrow}{\gamma}$ is taken to be isotropic for tetrahedra, the term $(1/6)\,\gamma F^3$ does not give a rotational spectrum.

Posch (1979,1980) has put the theory in correlation function formalism and extended its application to the case of dense fluids. This requires rotational correlation functions of $\overset{\leftrightarrow}{A}$ and $\overset{\leftrightarrow}{E}$, which are respectively third and fourth rank tensors, as well as third and fourth rank tensors to describe the relative translational motion. The spectra are then expressed as the Fourier transforms of four point correlation functions which contain the number density and the orientational density of the particles. For CCl_4, he numerically evaluated the contributions to the integrated intensity of the two- and three-body collisions and showed that the cancellation between the positive pair and negative triplet terms is not nearly as effective as for the DID case and that at the liquid density their sum remains positive; this fact should facilitate the observation of induced rotational scattering at high densities.

Each induced rotational line is translationally broadened.

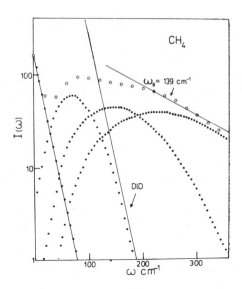

Fig. 1. The calculated envelopes of the four rotational branches of
CH$_4$ at 295K for single A transitions (•••). The solid line
(——) is the estimated DID spectrum and the curve (ooo) is
the experimental spectrum (Buckingham and Tabisz, 1977,
1978).

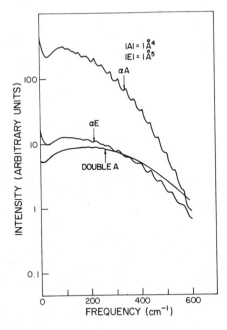

Fig. 2. The calculated translationally broadened spectra of CH$_4$ at
295K for single A, single E and double A transitions.
(A=1 Å^4, E=1 Å^5). (Penner, 1983; Penner et al., 1984).

Posch (1982) has computed lineshapes describing the broadening due to a translational tensor of rank ℓ associated with a contribution to the pair polarizability varying as (1/R) to the power ($\ell+1$). He assumed free classical trajectories and rotations and, thus, excluded the effects of bound dimers. Interestingly, as the order of the interaction increases the line shape is affected the most at low frequency with the shape of the nearly exponential tail not significantly altered.

The theory (Buckingham and Tabisz, 1977,1978) together with these broadening functions may be used to generate theoretical spectra. Figure (1) shows the smoothed envelope of the four rotational branches due to single A transitions for CH_4. Note that the spectrum extends well beyond the region where the translational DID spectrum is important. Figure (2) shows the broadened spectra for the single A, single E and double A transitions for A=1 A^4 and E=1 A^5. Note that the single A spectrum is dominant. Let us now consider comparison of the theory with experimental data.

SPECIFIC APPLICATIONS

CH_4
___

CH_4 has received the most attention and evidence for the existence of induced rotational scattering is perhaps most direct from a comparison of the spectra of CH_4 and CD_4. The shape of the translational spectra should differ only slightly due to the 10% difference in molecular velocity at a given temperature. However the rotational constant is 1/2 as large for CD_4 as for CH_4 and the width of its rotational spectrum should be reduced by a factor of 2. Indeed, at low frequency the spectra are observed to be nearly identical but the high frequency wing of CD_4 falls off much more rapidly (Fig. 3) (Shelton, Tabisz, 1980).

Figure (4) shows the spectrum of CH_4 compared with theory (Penner, 1983; Penner et al. 1984); there is excellent reproduction of the wing beyond 200 cm^{-1} where the rotational spectrum dominates, even to the extent that the partially resolved rotational structure appears to be accounted for. This structure is significant and reproducible; only about 50% of the error bars shown are due to photon statistics; the remainder results from uncertainties in the intensity calibration and normalization procedures. The spectrum was taken at densities sufficiently low that all but two-body interactions are negligible. The total intensity can be determined with an accuracy of 7%. Figure 5 shows the spectrum due to CH_4-Xe encounters. As the perturber is changed and double transitions eliminated (A=E=0 for a sphere), the spectrum is still reproduced. These mixture spectra are weaker and inherently noisier; any rotational structure is thus masked. The spectral intensity may be

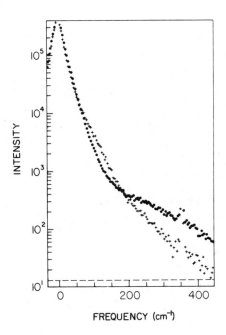

Fig. 3. CH_4 ($\cdots$) and CD_4 (+++) spectra (75 atm, 295K). The peak at 350 cm^{-1} is H_2 S(0). Spurious rise of the CD_4 spectrum at 100 cm^{-1} is due to air, (Shelton and Tabisz, 1980).

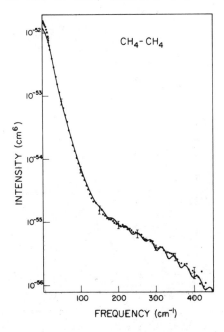

Fig. 4. The two-body CH_4 spectrum at 295K ($\cdots$ experimental, theoretical). (Penner, 1983; Penner et al., 1984).

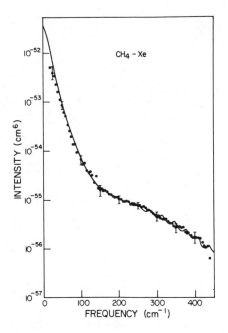

Fig. 5. Spectrum due to CH_4-Xe encounters at 295K ($\bullet\bullet\bullet$ experimental, —— theoretical). (Penner, 1983; Penner et al. 1984).

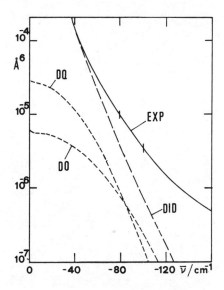

Fig. 6. The two-body spectrum of $C(CH_3)_4$ at 295K (+++) compared with the calculated components due to single A (DQ) and single E(DO) transitions and to the first order DID interaction. (Posch, 1982).

Table 1. Magnitude of $\overset{\leftrightarrow}{A}$ for CH_4

	Potential	$\|A\|$ $(\text{Å})^4$
CH_4-CH_4	Righini et al. (1981)	0.90 ± 0.07
CH_4-Ar	Buck et al. (1981)	0.84 ± 0.10
CH_4-Xe	Kr–Xe, Lee et al. (1975)	0.87 ± 0.10
	Average:	0.88 ± 0.05
Amos (1975) (SCF)		0.82
(CI)		0.79
John et al. (1980) (SCF)		0.81
Rivail and Cartier (1979) (SCF)		0.79
bond model (Buckingham 1967)		0.97

used to obtain estimates of $\|A\|$. These are given in Table 1, together with ab initio calculations of the static value.

There is consistency among the values deduced from the different spectra and excellent agreement with calculation. The best computed value must be taken to be the CI result of Amos.

$C(CH_3)_4$

Posch (1982) has made an extensive study of neopentane, assuming the molecule has T_d symmetry and neglecting the possible effects of internal rotation. From a study of the spectral intensity he obtains upper bounds for $\|A\|$ and $\|E\|$ (Table 2). There is, however, a good deal of unexplained intensity at high frequency (Fig. 6).

An interesting aspect of induced rotational scattering is the depolarization ratio, which differs from that for the first order DID interaction:

$$\rho \equiv \langle \alpha_{XZ}^2 \rangle / \langle \alpha_{ZZ}^2 \rangle$$

$$\rho_{DID} = 3/4 \quad \text{(pure first order DID)}$$

$$\rho_A = 9/37 \quad \text{(pure single A)}$$

$$\rho_E = 11/52 \quad \text{(pure single E)}$$

Posch studied the frequency dependence of the polarization ratio q' defined as $(I_{ZZ}+I_{ZY})/(I_{XZ}+I_{XY})$ which can be expressed in terms of the differential cross sections for the various interactions:

$$q' = \frac{\partial^2 ((\tfrac{4}{3}+1)\sigma_{XZ}^{DID} + (\tfrac{37}{9}+1)\sigma_{XZ}^A + (\tfrac{52}{11}+1)\sigma_{XZ}^E)/\partial\Omega\partial\nu}{2\,\partial^2(\sigma_{XZ}^{DID} + \sigma_{XZ}^A + \sigma_{XZ}^E)/\partial\Omega\partial\nu} \ .$$

He finds that q' increases with increasing frequency from the DID value of 1.17 at low frequency to above 1.3 beyond 100 cm^{-1} (Fig. 7). Again estimates of A and E may be obtained from this data and they are lower than those deduced from the intensity measurements (Table 2). This result demonstrates the usefulness of polarization ratio measurements. The measurement of the spectral intensity depends markedly on the intensity calibration while that of q' does not. Like CH_4, the bond polarizability estimates are greater than the experimental values.

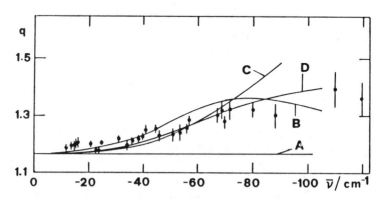

Fig. 7. The polarization ratio q' at 295K as a function of frequency for $C(CH_3)_4$. Curve A is drawn for a pure first order DID interaction; curves B,C,D are drawn for various choices of A and E. (Posch, 1982).

CF_4, SF_6, SiH_4, H_2S

Shelton and Tabisz (1980) have observed the spectra of CF_4 and SF_6 and find an excess of intensity at high frequency. An air impurity and the presence of Raman difference bands has complicated the analysis of these spectra and they are currently under reinvestigation. Chave and Thibeau (Chave, 1982) have made spectral intensity and frequency dependent depolarization ratio measurements on CH_4, CF_4,

Table 2. Magnitude of $\overset{\leftrightarrow}{A}$ and $\overset{\leftrightarrow}{E}$ for $C(CH_3)_4$

	$\|A\|$ A^4	$\|E\|$ A^5
Intensity	3.0	10
q'	2.0	5.2
bond model	6.0	10.7

354

and SiH_4. They attempt to gain physical insight into the interaction process by considering a model of colliding conducting spheres and conclude that many more terms in the multipole polarizability series have to be taken into account in order to explain their results. Evidence for induced rotational scattering in liquid H_2S has been seen (Mazzacurati et al., 1983) and a qualitative attempt has been made to explain it in terms of mechanisms involving tensors $\overset{\leftrightarrow}{A}$ and $\overset{\leftrightarrow}{B}$ (De Santis and Sampoli, 1983).

SUMMARY AND COMMENTS

Let us first consider the case where the effect is clearly identified and the theory appears to apply well – namely, CH_4.

Successes (CH_4)

(i)   The spectral shape of the high frequency wing is well reproduced with theoretical spectra generated assuming a long-range interaction mechanism.

(ii) There is consistency between the values of $|A|$ obtained from the spectra of the pure gas and the mixtures and these agree closely with calculation. The spectral intensities are thus shown to scale with α and the average of R^{-n} as predicted. The effect of further terms in the multipole polarizability series or of an anisotropic overlap interaction would make a very small contribution to the total intensity.

(iii) Even the partially resolved rotational structure present in the theoretical spectrum of CH_4 broadened assuming a long-range interaction appears to be confirmed by experiment. Spectra due to an anisotropic overlap interaction would presumably be much broader and any structure would be more obscure or even smeared out entirely. This is further evidence that the long-range interaction dominates the spectrum.

(iv) These results conspire to give confidence in the long-range mechanism. One can then obtain the pure translational component to the spectrum by subtracting the rotational component from the total spectrum, with the aid of the theory in the extrapolation through to zero frequency. The profile and spectral moments of this translational component may then be analyzed in the same way as the inert gas spectra in order to derive an expression for the pair polarizability responsible for it (Bafile et al., 1983, Meinander et al., 1984).

(v)   It appears that induced rotational scattering is a better way to estimate $|A|$ than methods based on the anisotropic dispersion correction to the intermolecular potential (Isnard et al.,

1976). Admittedly the choice of potential causes an uncertainty in $|A|$ of the order of $\pm 10\%$. It has been shown, however, that the determination of $|A|$ from pressure virial coefficient data is very sensitive to the isotropic potential; a change in well- depth of only a few percent can cause a change in $|A|$ by a factor of two or three (Meinander and Tabisz, 1983).

Problems

The principal problem is the unexplained intensity at high frequency in the spectra of the heavier molecules CF_4, SF_6, $C(CH_3)_4$ and, even, CH_4 beyond 600 cm^{-1} (Shelton and Tabisz, 1980). There are several possibilities for the source of the intensity.

(i)   Perhaps more multipole polarizability terms are required. For example, Logan and Madden (1982) have shown that the gradient induced quadrupole term (CF') in Eq. (1) makes a 12% contribution to the dielectric second virial coefficient at room temperature. The role of $\overset{*}{C}$ in the light scattering problem has not been investigated but Chave and Thibeau (Chave, 1982) suggest it is important. Little is known, however, about still higher multipole polarizabilities. If many more are necessary to reproduce the spectra, physical insight will be lost.

(ii)   Anisotropic overlap may be important. Such an interaction is usually described by a term having the symmetry of the lowest multipole moment of the molecules involved and a very marked dependence on R. For example, Birnbaum and Sutter (1981) and Posch and Litovitz (1976) in the analysis of their SF_6 spectra have respectively included an R^{-28} term in the pair dipole moment and R^{-29} term in the pair polarizability. Birnbaum and Cohen (1975) have studied the effect of anisotropic overlap on the spectral moments of the CH_4 absorption spectrum. The difficulty is that the sign and magnitude of this term are uncertain and the analysis becomes tentative. It is interesting to note that for this reason, and because of its presumed small contribution, Birnbaum et al. (1983) have rejected the inclusion of such a term in their latest treatment of the spectrum of CH_4.

(iii) In certain cases, for example $C(CH_3)_4$, some of this excess intensity may be due to the translational component. More careful truncation of the DID series and treatment of the isotropic overlap interaction are required (Posch, 1982).

Suggestions for Future Work

(i)   Careful measurements of the very high frequency wings are needed to resolve these uncertainties. The experiments will, in general, be very time consuming. The CH_4 spectra shown in

Figs. (4) and (5) took about 150 hours of scanning time and the higher frequency wing is, of course, still weaker.

(ii) Polarization ratio studies as a function of frequency have been shown to be valuable and should be extended to more molecules.

(iii) Studies of the temperature dependence of induced rotational scattering are all but missing.

(iv) An investigation of the effect of the inclusion of an anisotropic overlap interaction in the analysis should be made.

(v) Elsewhere in this volume, Borysow and Frommhold (1985) demonstrates the relevance of dimers, and the concomitant quantum mechanical line shape, to the CH_4 absorption spectrum. Such a line shape should be used in the analysis of the scattering spectrum as well.

(vi) The molecules SiH_4 and GeH_4, which are heavy, have a relatively large rotational constant and should have a large $\stackrel{*}{A}$, are ideal candidates for serious experimental study of induced rotational scattering.

ACKNOWLEDGEMENTS

This paper was prepared while GCT was a Visiting Scientist at the National Research Council of Canada. He wishes to thank Dr. W. Siebrand and the Division of Chemistry for their warm and generous hospitality.

REFERENCES

Amos, R.D., 1979, Molec. Phys. 38:33.
Bafile, U., Maglie, R., Barocchi, F., Zoppi, M. and Frommhold, L., 1983, Molec. Phys. 49:1149.
Birnbaum, G. and Cohen, E.R., 1975, J. Chem. Phys., 62:3807.
Birnbaum, G. and Sutter, H., 1981, Molec. Phys., 42:21.
Birnbaum, G., Frommhold, L., Nencini, L. and Sutter, H., 1983, Chem. Phys. Letters, 100:292.
Borysow, J., and Frommhold, L., 1985, this volume.
Buck, U., Schleusener, J., Malik, D.J. and Secrest, J., 1981, J. Chem. Phys., 74:1707.
Buckingham, A.D., 1967, Adv. Chem. Phys., 12:107.
Buckingham, A.D. and Ladd, A.J.C., 1976, Can. J. Phys., 54:611.
Buckingham, A.D. and Tabisz, G.C., 1977, Optics Letters, 1:220.
Buckingham, A.D. and Tabisz, G.C., 1978, Molec. Phys., 36:583.
Chave, A., 1982, Thèse de Doctorat d'Etat, Angers.

De Santis, A. and Sampoli, M., 1983, Chem. Phys. Letters, 102:425.

Holzer, W. and LeDuff, Y., 1974, Phys. Rev. Letters, 32:205.

Holzer, W. and Ouillon, R., 1974, Chem. Phys. Letters, 24:589; 1976, "Proceedings of the Fifth International Conference on Raman Spectroscopy," E.D. Schmid, ed., Schulz, Freiburg, 424.

Isnard, P., Robert, D. and Galatry, L., 1976, Molec. Phys., 31:1789.

John, I.G., Bacskay, G.B. and Hush, N.S., 1980, Chem. Phys. 51:49.

Lee,J.K., Henderson, D. and Barker, J.A., 1975, Molec. Phys., 29:429.

Logan, D.E. and Madden, P.A., 1982, Molec. Phys., 46:1195.

Mazzacurati, V., Ricci, M.A., Ruocco, G. and Nardonne, M., 1983, Molec. Phys., 50:1083.

Meinander, N. and Tabisz, G.C., 1983, J. Chem. Phys., 79:416.

Meinander, N., Penner, A.R., Bafile, U., Barocchi, F., Zoppi, M., Shelton, D.P., and Tabisz, G.C., 1984, Molec. Phys.

Penner, A.R., 1983, M.Sc. Thesis, University of Manitoba.

Penner, A.R., Meinander, N. and Tabisz, G.C., 1984, to be published.

Posch, H. A., 1979, Molec. Phys., 37:1059.

Posch, H. A., 1980, Molec. Phys., 40:1137.

Posch, H. A., 1982, Molec. Phys., 46:1213.

Posch, H. A., 1985, this volume.

Posch, H.A. and Litovitz, T.A., 1976, Molec. Phys., 32:1559.

Righini, R., Maki, K. and Klein, M.L., 1981, Chem. Phys. Letters, 80:301.

Rivail, J.L. and Cartier, A., 1979, Chem. Phys. Letters, 61:469.

Samson, R. and Ben-Reuven, A., 1976, J. Chem. Phys., 65:3586.

Samson, R., Pasmanter, R.A. and Ben-Reuven, A., 1976, Phys. Rev., A14:1224 and 1238.

Shelton, D.P. and Tabisz, G.C., 1980, Mol. Phys., 40:299.

Thibeau, M., Gharbi, A., LeDuff, Y. and Sergiescu, V., 1977, J. Phys. (Paris), 38:641.

WORKSHOP REPORT: LIGHT SCATTERING IN

COMPRESSED GASES

Yves Le Duff

Département de Recherches Physiques, Tour 22
Université Pierre et Marie Curie
4, place Jussieu - 75230 Paris Cedex 05 - France

Since the first observation in the late sixties of the interaction induced light scattering (IILS) in gaseous argon (McTague and
Birnbaum, 1968; Thibeau et al., 1968) much work has been performed
in this field. IILS has appeared as a new tool to study atomic and
molecular interactions in gases and liquids. In particular at low
densities IILS studies yield information on: (1) induced pair polarizability due to molecular interactions, (2) intermolecular potential. At high densities IILS gives indications on the various
many-body effects.

At the present time the IILS <u>low density</u> Rayleigh spectra are
quite well known at room temperature for all the rare gases as well
as for several optically isotropic molecules. For low density and
room temperature rare gases it is now established after many discussions that point dipole-induced dipole (DID) anisotropy accounts for
the observed integrated intensities with generally a precision of
about 10%, the contribution of shorter range interactions not exceeding ~ 10%. Concerning the lineshape, DID anisotropy gives the
general shape of the spectrum though an exchange term is needed to
obtain an accurate fit with experimental spectra (Frommhold, 1981).
Ab-initio calculations, including both long and short range interactions, have been performed and yield better lineshapes in particular
for helium (Dacre, 1982; Dacre and Frommhold, 1982). For molecules
the situation is not so satisfying since available theoretical induced anisotropies and intermolecular potentials are not so accurate. Moreover, specific effects such as higher induced multipole
polarizabilities contribute to the high frequency induced spectrum
(Tabisz, 1979). At <u>high densities</u> the IILS studies on compressed
gases are scarcer. The discussions during this conference also show
this tendency. Although the density behavior of the spectral mo-

359

ments are theoretically understood, there has been no progress in developing a theory of lineshape at the higher densities.

Now many results have been accumulated in this field but new studies seem necessary to go further. For isotropic molecules the discrepancies between experiment and theory (DID interaction and Lennard Jones potential) are still relatively high (from 50% up to 600%) for the integrated depolarized intensities of the heaviest molecules like CF_4, SF_6 and $C(CH_3)_4$. For these molecules the lack of an accurate intermolecular potential constitutes a serious difficulty which prevents any accurate experimental determination of the pair polarizability. However, as pointed out at this conference, the DID model may be tested in a comparison between the induced Rayleigh scattering and the induced vibrational Raman scattering (Le Duff and Sergiescu, 1984). Thus, for DID interaction and only in this case, the ratio of the ν_1 Raman depolarization ratio divided by the Rayleigh depolarization ratio for isotropic molecules is equal to 2 for any intermolecular potential. This criterion may be used to show the existence of non-DID interactions.

The IILS experiments in compressed gases have been conducted mostly with particles of a single type. However, the study of gaseous mixtures greatly increases the scope of the IILS experiments. Indeed recent gas mixtures studies (Le Duff et al., 1983) have shown that it is possible to determine the IILS from a given particle perturbed by particles of different kinds. Moreover in this kind of experiment the possibility to change the interaction acting on one particle may give some indication of the reliability of the intermolecular potential.

The many-body correlations have received some attention (Barocchi and Zoppi, 1985; Thibeau et al., 1985) although further work would be valuable. It may be emphasized at high densities when molecules are involved that the simultaneous study of induced Rayleigh and vibrational Raman intensities would help to determine the high-order correlations contributions. Indeed because of the different coherence properties of the Rayleigh and the Raman scattering the various many-body contributions occur differently in the two scatterings.

Finally some remarks may be made on a recent extension of these studies to anisotropic molecules. In this case the depolarized intensities observed in the Rayleigh band include several contributions: (1) the specific part due to the permanent anisotropy β_p, (2) the pure collisional contribution due to the pure induced anisotropy β_c and (3) and interference term due to both β_p and β_c. The experimental separation of these different contributions cannot be achieved easily. The use of density as a parameter and the measurement of the spectral depolarization ratio would help to solve this problem. We would also suggest the use of the resonance effect by using an excitation wavelength near an absorption line. Indeed since the different contributions depend in a different way on the permanent anisotropy β_p and the isotropic polarizability of the molecule, the modification of these contributions must be different when the excitation wavelength approaches an absorption line. This might be a way to discriminate between the different contributions to the depolarized intensity.

REFERENCES

Barocchi, F., and Zoppi, M., 1985, this volume.
Dacre, P.D., 1982, Molec. Phys., 45:17.
Dacre, P.D., and Frommhold, L., 1982, J. Chem. Phys., 76:3447.
Frommhold, L., 1981, Adv. Chem. Phys., 46:1.
Le Duff, Y., Gharbi, A., and Othman, T., 1983, Phys. Rev. A., 28:2714.
Le Duff, Y., and Sergiescu, V., 1984, Physica A, 127:347.
McTague, J.P., and Birnbaum, G., 1968, Phys. Rev. Lett., 21:661.
Tabisz, G.C., 1979, Molecular Spectroscopy, v. 6, edited by Barrow, R.F., Long, D.A., and Sheridan, J., (The Chemical Society, London), p. 136.
Thibeau, M., Oksengorn, B., and Vodar, B., 1968, J. Phys. (Paris), 29:287.
Thibeau, M., Berrue, J., Chave, A., Dumon, B., Le Duff, Y., Gharbi, A., Oksengorn, B., 1985, this volume.

THEORY OF COLLISION-INDUCED LIGHT SCATTERING

AND ABSORPTION IN DENSE RARE GAS FLUIDS

S. Bratos and B. Guillot
Laboratoire de Physique Théorique des Liquides[*]
Université Pierre et Marie Curie, Paris, France

and

G. Birnbaum
National Bureau of Standards
Washington, D.C. 20234

ABSTRACT

Studies of collision-induced light scattering in rare gas liquids and absorption in liquids of rare gas mixtures are reviewed. For each phenomena, the status of the electronic theory of the induced property is described (induced polarizability for light scattering and induced dipole for absorption). Next, the results of statistical theories, which includes computer simulation and generalized Langevin-type theories, are considered. Although not all problems have been solved, it is concluded that at least semi-quantitative theoretical descriptions of collision-induced processes are available.

INTRODUCTION

The purpose of the present article is to review the studies of both collision-induced absorption and light scattering in dense rare-gas fluids. No review of this subject has yet been published; see, however, the reviews of Gelbart (1974, 1980), Weiss (1976), Frommhold (1981), and Birnbaum et al., (1982) describing low density gases. There are two major reasons which justify this effort. The first is that since the interpretation of several aspects of the data has remained controversial for many years, it seemed interest-

---

*Equipe Associée au CNRS

ing to review the present state of the art from the theoretical point of view. The second is that rare-gas fluids represent a sort of prototype which merits careful examination. This is particularly important at the present time when considerable effort is being made to study collision-induced processes occuring in the more complex molecular fluids. This review shows that after ten or more years of careful experimental and theoretical work a coherent description of collision-induced processes in atomic liquids has been achieved. The language of liquid state physics is employed, since problems and unnecessary difficulties may arise when oversimplified models are borrowed from the low pressure work.

The basic formulas of the theory relate the infrared absorption coefficient $\alpha(\omega)$ and the differential cross-section $\partial^2\sigma/\partial\omega\partial\Omega$ of depolarized light scattering to the appropriate correlation functions. If $\vec{M}$ denotes the total dipole moment of the system, $\overleftrightarrow{\varepsilon}$ its macroscopic polarizability tensor, ω the frequency of the incident infrared radiation and $\Delta\omega$ the frequency difference between the incident and the scattered light, one finds (Gordon, 1965a, 1965b; Gelbart, 1974)

$$
\begin{aligned}
G(\omega) &= \left[\frac{4\pi}{3\hbar cnV}\,\omega\,\tanh\frac{\beta\hbar\omega}{2}\right]^{-1}\alpha(\omega)\\
&= \int_{-\infty}^{+\infty}dt\;e^{-i\omega t}\,\frac{1}{2}\left[\langle\vec{M}(0)\cdot\vec{M}(t)\rangle + \langle\vec{M}(t)\cdot\vec{M}(0)\rangle\right]
\end{aligned}
\tag{1}
$$

$$
\frac{\partial^2\sigma}{\partial\omega\partial\Omega} = \frac{1}{2\pi}\left(\frac{\omega_0}{c}\right)^4\int_{-\infty}^{+\infty}dt\;e^{-i\Delta\omega t}\langle\varepsilon^{xz}(0)\varepsilon^{xz}(t)\rangle
\tag{2}
$$

In Eq. (1), $G(\omega)$ is the reduced absorption coefficient. In Eq. (2), the z-axis is taken to be parallel to the direction of the polarizer and the x-axis to that of the analyser. $G(\omega)$ is expressed in terms of a symmetrized correlation function (CF), which is a real, even function of time; it is often approximated by its classical analogue. First quantum corrections to the spectrum and spectral moments of dense fluids have been discussed (Barocchi et al., 1981, 1982, 1983).

It is generally assumed that the total dipole moment $\vec{M}$ of a mixture of rare gas atoms can be suitably approximated by the sum of dipole moments $\vec{m}_{ij}$ of all possible pairs of atoms of different species which may be formed by collisions. Similarily, the total polarizability tensor $\overleftrightarrow{\varepsilon}$ of a pure rare gas fluid is generally taken to be the sum of polarizability tensors $\overleftrightarrow{\varepsilon}_{ij}$ associated with all possible pairs which can exist in the system. Within the limits of the present state of the art, this approximation is believed to be compatible with the existing experimental results. It should be pointed out, however, that its validity has been questioned by a number of authors; see the papers by Keyes (1979, 1980), Keyes et al., (1979), Keyes and Madden (1981) and Birnbaum and Mountain (1984). *The experimental results are not yet able to settle this matter.

DEPOLARIZED LIGHT SCATTERING IN DENSE RARE GAS FLUIDS

Generalities

The theory contains two conceptually and technically different parts. The first concerns the calculation of noble gas diatom polarizabilities and employs quantum chemical ab-initio techniques. Systematic investigations of this kind were undertaken in the early seventies and are now nearing maturity. Its second part refers to spectral profiles of the collision-induced light scattered from dense fluids and utilizes standard techniques of statistical mechanics, including computer simulation. Systematic investigations started in the late sixties and still are under way.

Electronic theory of rare gas polarizabilities

Long-range theories. It is convenient to start the description by examining the problem for large atom-atom separations where the theory has its simplest form. Many years ago, Silberstein (1917) using classical theory, presented the well-known dipole-induced dipole (DID) expressions for the incremental mean polarizability $\Delta\alpha$ and the anisotropy β of the pair. If $\alpha_{\parallel}$ and $\alpha_{\perp}$ denote the components of the polarizability tensor parallel and perpendicular, respectively, to the intermolecular axis, α the atomic polarizability and R the internuclear separation, then

$$\Delta\alpha(R) = \frac{1}{3}\left[\alpha_{\parallel}(R) + 2\alpha_{\perp}(R)\right] - 2\alpha = 4\alpha^3 R^{-6} + \cdots$$

$$\beta(R) = \alpha_{\parallel}(R) - \alpha_{\perp}(R) = 6\alpha^2 R^{-3} + 6\alpha^3 R^{-6} + \cdots$$

$$(3)$$

Subsequently, Jansen and Mazur (1955) and Buckingham (1956) determined quantum corrections to this simple formula; these corrections are due to a hyperpolarization of one atom by the fluctuating dipolar field of the other. The corrected expressions for $\Delta\alpha(r)$ and $\beta(R)$ still preserve the general form of Eq. (3), but the coefficients of the R^{-6} term are different. Certain and Fortune (1973) calculated them for helium by using an accurate ground state wave function and found

$$\Delta\overline{\alpha}(R) = 14.86\alpha^3 R^{-6} + \cdots$$

$$\beta(R) = 6\alpha^2 R^{-3} + 12.07\alpha^3 R^{-6} + \cdots$$

$$(4)$$

Moreover, useful estimates were provided by models due to Buckingham and Clarke (1978) and to Hunt et al., (1981). The conclusion is that the leading term of β(R) is still given by the DID model, but that of Δα(R) is not. This result suggests Δα(R) to be intrinsically more difficult to calculate than β(R) and further work amply confirmed this conjecture (Mayer, 1976).

Intermediate and short-range theories. The most straightforward method of calculating the incremental polarizability and the anisotropy of a rare gas atom pair is to employ the Hartree-Fock method, or if a better accuracy is required, the configuration interaction method. The Hartree-Fock method can be applied to the present problem in two different ways. In its first version, one solves the coupled Hartree-Fock equations in the presence of a finite external electric field F and calculates the dipole moment M(F). The polarizability tensor may then be obtained by calculating numerically the first derivative of M(F) with respect to F. In practice, one identifies the polarizability with the ratio M(F)/F for small values of F. This method was proposed by Cohen and Roothaan (1965) and is called the finite field coupled Hartree-Fock method. In its second version, the coupled Hartree-Fock equations perturbed by a small external field F are solved with the help of second order perturbation theory. This alternative method, invented by Dalgarno (1959) and by several other authors, is generally termed the Hartree-Fock perturbation method. Both methods are equivalent to each other. They permitted the calculation of Δα(R) and β(R) of the helium diatom (Lim et al., 1970; O'Brien et al., 1973; Buckingham and Watts, 1973; Fortune and Certain, 1974), of the neon diatom (Kress and Kozak, 1977), of the argon diatom (Lallemand et al., 1974; Dacre, 1982a), and the krypton and xenon diatoms (Dacre, 1982b). The discussion of the configuration interaction method is similar in many respects to that of the Hartree-Fock method. However, only the finite field method was employed in the published configuration interaction work. These calculations invariably are large scale calculations, since the number of configurations introduced into the theory is typically of the order of 10^5. This method, always combined with the Hartree-Fock method representing the first level of description, was used to calculate the incremental mean polarizability Δα(R) and the anisotropy β(R) for the helium diatom (Dacre, 1978, 1982c) and for the neon diatom (Dacre, 1981).

In addition to the Hartree-Fock and the configuration interaction methods, two other treatments of the problem were attempted. Harris et al., (1974) and Heller et al., (1975) proposed a density functional treatment of the nobel gas diatom polarizabilities. This method, which is based on the Hohenberg and Kohn expression for the ground state energy of any system of electrons and nuclei, involves a universal functional of density. Then, by assuming the total electronic density of the pair to be a superposition of free atom

densities and approximating the universal functional of density by
the energy functional of a homogeneous electron gas, the authors
were able to calculate $\alpha_{\parallel}$ (R) and $\alpha_{\perp}$ (R) for $(He)_2$, $(Ne)_2$, and
$(Ar)_2$. However, results from these calculations are at variance
with the ab-initio calculations at short range. There is also some
difficulty in matching results at intermediate range to the proper
asymptotic form. Another approach was developed by Oxtoby and
Gelbart (1975a, 1975b) in which a local polarizability density is
assigned to the atoms and the system is treated by analogy with
macroscopic dielectrics. The basic equation of this theory is

$$\vec{m}(\vec{r}) = \overleftrightarrow{\alpha}(\vec{r})\vec{F}_0 + \overleftrightarrow{\alpha}(\vec{r})\int d\vec{r}\,'\overleftrightarrow{T}(\vec{r} - \vec{r}\,')m(\vec{r}\,') \tag{3}$$

where $\vec{m}$ is the dipole moment density, $\overleftrightarrow{\alpha}$ is the polarizability density, and $\overleftrightarrow{T}$ is the static dipole propagator. This equation is
solved iteratively to give the polarization of the diatom system.
Unfortunately, a number of unjustifiable approximations were introduced into Eq. (5) making the theory unacceptable; see the papers by
Sipe and Van Kranendonk (1978), Clarke et al., (1978), Oxtoby (1978),
and the more recent work by Oxtoby (1980) and Hunt (1984). These
papers showed how to circumvent the difficulties and to render
this approach operational. The polarizabilities of the helium and
argon diatoms were determined in this way. Still, in spite of the
efficacy of approximate methods, Hartree-Fock and configuration
interaction theories surpass in power all competing theories.

Results and discussion. The following results have been
obtained from the theory. (1) The anisotropy $\beta(R)$ is well reproduced by the average self-consistent field and the Hartree-Fock
description is satisfactory. On the other hand, the electron correlation effects are essential to the understanding of the properties of the incremental mean polarizability $\Delta\alpha(R)$, particularly for
large values of R. This finding confirms the conjecture mentioned
in the previous discussion of long-range theories. (2) Electronic
overlap does not contribute much to the reduction of the anisotropy
$\beta(R)$ from its DID value (Fig. 1). The opposite view prevailed for
many years and was the source of much controversy. (3) The incremental mean polarizability $\Delta\alpha(R)$ exhibits a complicated R-dependence
(Fig. 2). It expresses the progressive reorganization of the electronic cloud of the diatom when going from the united atom to the
separate atoms.

Statistical theory of depolarized light scattering from dense rare
gas fluid

Theoretical methods. The early work on the theory of line shape
in compressed gases is due to Levine and Birnbaum (1968); and Thibeau
et al., (1968), and in liquids is due to McTague et al., (1969) and

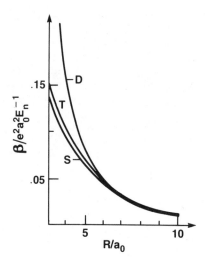

Fig 1. The helium anisotropy versus the internuclear separation: D, DID model; S, Hartree-Fock results; and T, configurations interaction results (Dacre, 1982c). In this and the following figure, a_0 and E_n denote atomic units for charge, distance and energy.

Bucaro and Litovitz (1971) who employed various approximate methods to study this problem. It soon became evident that the problem in the liquid may conveniently be treated by combining computer simulation techniques and generalized Langevin-type theories. The combined use of these two methods represents one of the most powerful approaches actually available for analyzing N-body problems.

Molecular dynamics calculations. This direction of research was initiated by Alder et al., (1973a, 1973b) and Berne et al., (1973). The liquid sample was replaced by several hundred particles interacting with Lennard-Jones, hard-sphere, or square-well potentials. The induction mechanism was assumed to be the simple DID type. Although the correct density dependence of the integrated intensity and reasonable spectral band shapes were generated by these calculations, unfortunately the integrated intensity was at variance with the experimental data (Fleury and McTague, 1969). New calculations by Alder et al., (1979) with modified pair polarizabilities where the effect of electron overlap was included still could not reproduce the experimental value of the integrated intensity of argon near the triple point. However, three independent low pressure experiments due to Barocchi and Zoppi (1978), Frommhold et al., (1978) and Shelton and Tabisz (1980) showed fair agreement with the integrated intensity predicted by the DID model. The same conclu-

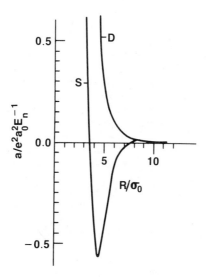

Fig 2.   The argon mean polarizability versus the internuclear separation: D, DID model; S, Hartree-Fock results (Dacre, 1982a).

sion was reached theoretically by Clarke et al., (1978) and by Dacre (1981).   Varshnaya et al., (1981) remeasured the dense argon spectrum and recalculated it with a collision-induced anisotropy drawn from the dilute gas experiment, which was based on the DID model with some corrections, and with the Bobetic-Barker argon-argon pair potential.   The agreement between the calculated and experimental integrated intensity was then found to be within the experimental error.

Balucani and Vallauri (1979a, 1979b) examined the density dependence of the zeroth and second spectral moments, whereas Ladd et al., (1980) investigated the effect of truncation of the pair polarizability anisotropy on calculated spectral properties.   Ladd et al., (1979) and Balucani et al., (1975) analyzed two-, three- and four-body contributions to the total correlation function and found their decay slow with respect to that of the total correlation function.   At short times the ratio of pair, triplet and quadruplet contributions turned out to be close to 1,-2, 1, which is reminiscent of the perfect solid situation.

Generalized Langevin-type theories. Molecular dynamics calculations described in the preceeding section have been complemented by generalized Langevin type calculations.   Theories of this class were published by Madden (1977, 1978) and Guillot et al., (1980) (see

also Bratos and Guillot (1982), and Evans (1977)). These theories
are based on the Zwanzig-Mori theory of Brownian motion but differ
in the choice of basic variables. In Madden's theory this choice
was dictated by the decision to use neutron scattering data to construct the transport matrix. The correlation function which enters
into Eq. (2) and which involves the polarizability tensor ε is thus
expressed in terms of the number density n, the variable characterizing the neutron scattering process. In order to deal with a
workable expression for the spectrum, several approximations were
made. Finally, the following approximate expression was obtained

$$\frac{\partial^2 \sigma}{\partial \omega \partial \Omega} \sim \int_0^\infty d\vec{k}'k'^2(Z(k'))^2 \lim_{k \to 0} \langle n(\vec{k} - \vec{k}', \omega)$$
$$x \cdot n(\vec{k}', \omega)n(-\vec{k} + \vec{k}',0)n(-\vec{k}',0)\rangle \qquad (6)$$

where $n(\vec{k}, \omega)$ is the spatial and temporal Fourier transform of
$n(\vec{r},t)$. This theory employs a basic set of six variables comprising
all possible products of the number density, and its first and second time derivatives. The use of this complicated basic set is
necessary if one wishes to calculate the correlation function which
occurs in Eq. (6) and involves four space and two time points.
The transport matrix may then be calculated and the neutron scattering data, after some extrapolations, may be incorporated.

The theory by Guillot et al., (1980) employs a much simpler
basic set composed of three variables, the XZ component of the
polarizability tensor and its first and second time derivatives.
Although the transport matrix associated with this basic set cannot
be deduced from neutron scattering data, its density dependence may
be determined theoretically, for example, with the help of the lattice gas model, a choice suggested by its successful application by
Thibeau et al., (1970). Although admittedly crude, this model retains the important statistical fluctuations which dominate the
critical behavior. If sufficiently developed, it may be cast into a
form equivalent to that of the Ising model and may be employed to
study phase transitions. Adopting this approach as well as the
dipole-induced dipole pair polarizability anisotropy then leads to
the following correlation function

$$\langle \varepsilon^{xz}(0)\varepsilon^{xz}(t) \rangle = Ae^{-\lambda t} + Be^{-\mu t} + Ce^{-\nu t} \qquad (7)$$

where A, B, C, λ, μ, ν are known functions of thermodynamic variables of the system. The quantities λ, μ, ν represent the eigenvalues of the transport matrix; the first quantity is real whereas
the other two are complex conjugates of each other. The polarizability correlation function thus decays in three relaxation modes,
one dissipative and two doubly degenerate oscillatory modes.

Results and discussion. The following results may be reached
from the statistical theories. (1) All observed spectral features
can be interpreted, within the accuracy of the currently available
experimental data, in terms of standard pair potentials and slightly
modified DID pair polarizability anisotropies. (2) The band shape
comprises a low frequency lorentzian and a high frequency wing
(Fig. 3). The low frequency lorentizian, which is described either
by the small k' portion of the integral occuring in Eq. (6) or by
the dissipative mode term of the correlation function of Eq. (7), is
produced by diffusion-type atomic motions. The high frequency wing,
containing a small shoulder, which is described either by the large
k' portion of the integral of Eq. (6) or by the oscillatory mode
terms of the correlation function of Eq. (7), is generated by rat-
tling-type atomic motions. These features of the band shape were
not understood prior to these theories. (3) Two-, three-, and four-
body correlation functions all contribute in an essential way to the
spectrum of scattered light. However, as demonstrated by molecular
dynamics simulations, a significant cancellation of these terms

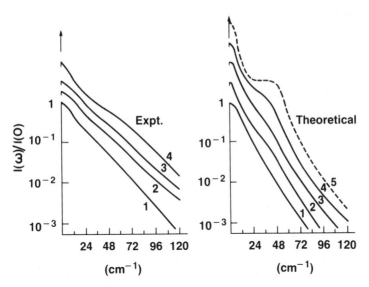

Fig 3.   (a) Experimental spectra of depolarized light scattered from
         dense argon: (1) 144K and 524 amagat; (2) 120K and 664
         amagat; (3) 106K and 723 amagat; and (4) 89K and 784 ama-
         gat (An et al., 1976). (b) Theoretical spectra for dense
         argon: (1) 150K and 433 amagat; (2) 120K and 664 amagat;
         (3) 106K and 723 amagat; (4) 84K and 925 amagat, and (5)
         84K and 984 amagat. The last two states are just below and
         above the liquid-solid transition of argon (Guillot et al.
         1980).

occurs. This is an excluded volume effect, as easily shown by the lattice gas model. (4) The irreducible three- and four-body contributions to the polarizability anisotropy have not yet been identified experimentally. More elaborate techniques would be required for their detection.

COLLISION-INDUCED ABSORPTION IN DENSE MIXTURES OF RARE GASES

Generalities

The theory of collision-induced absorption in rare-gas mixtures contains two parts, one dealing with the quantum-chemical calculations of the rare-gas diatom dipole moment and another describing the statistical theory of band shapes produced by this mechanism. The investigations relative to the first problem started in the mid sixties whereas those associated with the second were initiated for dense systems nearly ten years later. At the present time, ab-initio calculations for the induced dipole are less advanced than those for the induced polarizability (see, however, Meyer this volume).

Electronic theory of collision-induced rare-gas diatom dipole moments

Long-range theories. The interaction of two different atoms in their totally symmetrical ground states gives rise to a dipole moment directed along the internuclear axis. It arises from two sources, an overlap contribution due to the electron exchange between the atoms and subsequent distortion, and a dispersion contribution due to inter-electron correlation. The simplest theory of this effect neglects the electron overlap and calculates the diatom dipole moment $\vec{m}$ by means of standard quantum mechanical perturbation theory. Proceeding in this way, Buckingham (1955) found that

$$m(R) = \frac{D_7}{R^7} + \frac{D_9}{R^9} + \cdots \tag{8}$$

and, by using the Unsöld closure approximation, he gave an explicit expression for D_7. Later, Byers (1973) and Whisnant and Byers Brown (1973) developed a new theory of D_7 by applying the Rayleigh-Schrödinger perturbation method and the resolvent operator technique. The dependence of D_7 on the frequency-dependent polarizabilities and quadratic hyperpolarizabilities of atoms was brought out by Galatry and Gharbi (1980) (see also Giraud and Galatry (1980), Levine (1968) and Bentley (1979)). Finally, Gray and Lo

(1974), Martin (1974), Bruch et al., (1978) and Brunch and Osawa (1980) presented a calculation of the long range induced dipole moment of three interacting atoms by using the perturbation scheme developed by Byers Brown and Whisnant (1973).

Intermediate and short-range theories. At short distances, the electronic clouds of two colliding atoms are pushed outward with respect to their nuclei as a consequence of the exclusion principle and a net atomic moment is induced in each atom. If the atoms are different, a molecular moment appears because each induced atomic moment differs in magnitude. The effect was studied by Matcha and Nesbet (1967) and Birnbaum et al., (1984) in the frame of the Hartree-Fock theory. The dipole moments were calculated for the He-Ne, He-Ar, Ne-Ar, Ne-Kr, and Ar-Kr pairs. The polarity was found to be He^-Ne^+, He^+Ar^-, and Ne^+Ar^-. Moreover, Lacey and Byers Brown (1974) investigated the dipole moment of rare gas diatoms at intermediate internuclear separations. Their ground state is described by an antisymmetrized product of two Hartree-Fock determinants and the dipole moment expression is expanded in terms of overlap integrals. Six heteroatoms formed from He, Ne, Ar, and Kr were treated by this procedure. In conclusion, it is now possible to evaluate the dipole moments at the Hartree-Fock level of approximation for any pair of rare gas atoms. To our knowledge, the electron correlation effects have not yet been systematically investigated [see, however, the review by Meyer (1984)].

Results and discussion. The following results may be deduced from these theories. (1) The dipole moment of a rare gas diatom can be reasonably well described by the formula

$$m(R) = Ce^{-R/\rho} + \frac{D}{R^7} \tag{9}$$

where C, D, and ρ are constants. However, a quadratic term is sometimes added to the argument of the exponent (Birnbaum et al., 1984). Representative values of the second term of this equation are smaller by an order of magnitude than those of the first term. (2) The sign of C most often is opposite to that of D. The short and the long-range contributions to $\vec{m}$ thus cancel each other partially (Fig. 4). (3) The R-dependence of the dipole moment $\vec{m}(R)$ of a diatom XY is similar to that of the force $\vec{F}(R)$ acting between X and Y; this conclusion may be drawn from Eq. (9) and Fig. (4). Although it provides the physical basis of the currently used approximation due to Van Kranendonk (1968) who wrote $\vec{m} = const \vec{F}$, it may be inferred from the work of Birnbaum et al., (1984) that this proportionality is never entirely exact.

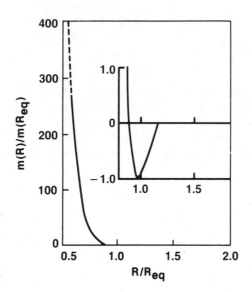

Fig 4. The reduced pair dipole moment $m(R)/m(R_{eq})$ of a rare gas pair. The inset gives enlarged view of the region around the dipole minimum. R_{eq} is the equilibrium internuclear distance (Weiss, 1976).

Statistical theory of collision-induced absorption in dense rare gas fluids.

Theoretical methods. The preliminary work on this problem is due to Gray et al., (1976) and Hamer et al., (1977). These authors calculated the lowest spectral moments and their density dependence by applying standard methods of statistical mechanics. Later, computer simulation techniques and Langevin-type theories for describing the line shape in liquids were developed. Complete molecular dynamics calculations appeared only recently, presumably because of the inherent difficulties in performing computer simulations of solutions.

Computer simulation. The first attempt in this direction is due to Lewis and Tjon (1978) who investigated the problem for a two dimensional Lorentz gas. This system consists of a light particle moving through an assembly of fixed scatterers. Both, the light particle and the fixed scatterers are assumed to be hard disks and the induced dipole moment is given an exponential form. The configurations of fixed scatterers were then generated using the standard Monte Carlo technique. The direction of the light particle was chosen at random and its trajectory was followed for a time t. These calculations were performed for various densities up to the hard disk "fluid" range. The main result of Lewis and Tjon (1978) is the prediction of the existence of a low frequency dip in the power spectrum of $\vec{M}$. The shorter the range of $\vec{M}$, the deeper is the dip which broadens with increasing density. Weiss et al., (1979) compared the experimentally determined dipole moment correlation function of various rare gas mixtures with the computer generated force correlation function of liquid argon. The latter was obtained by differentiating its velocity correlation function twice with respect to time. It was concluded that the induced dipole and the force are strikingly similar to one another and may be proportional. Finally, Birnbaum and Mountain (1984) described a complete molecular dyanmics calculation of a system consisting of 450 atoms of Ar and 50 atoms of Ne. Several potentials and dipole moment functions were tested. The essential conclusion of this calculation is that the force law and dipole moment determined for the low density gas are incapable of producing a low frequency dip in agreement with the measured Ar-Ne spectrum. The effective and the free pair dipole moment and/or potential thus may be quite different.

Generalized Langevin-type theories. The early investigations in this direction preceded, chronologically, the computer simulation work; the opposite development took place in studying collision-induced light scattering. Two Langevin-type theories were proposed, a semi-empirical approach due to Buontempo et al., (1980, 1981) and a Zwanzig-Mori approach due to Guillot et al., (1981, 1982). See also the papers by Bratos and Guillot (1982) and Buontempo (1984). The former of these theories considers for simplicity a mixture in which only one of the rare-gas atoms is present as an impurity. It is then assumed that the resultant force acting on the impurity is proportional to the total dipole moment associated with it. The dipole moment correlation function can thus be represented by the force correlation function. This is calculated from a generalized Langevin equation with a Gaussian kernel similar to that used to describe the velocity correlation function. The frequency ω_0 that characterizes the rattling component of the motion of the impurity in the liquid is explicitly introduced. The self-diffusion coefficient of the impurity can also be derived from the experimental value of ω_0 using the Rice-Allnatt theory.

The theory by Guillot et al., (1982) is the counterpart of the theory the authors used to describe the collision-induced light scattering. It is assumed that the collision-induced dipole moment $\vec{m}$ of a pair of dissimilar atoms is proportional to the force $\vec{F}$ acting between them. Then, using the action-reaction law, it may be shown rigorously, that the total dipole moment is

$$\vec{M} = \text{const} \left[\frac{1-x}{m_A} + \frac{x}{m_B} \right]^{-1} \frac{d\vec{J}}{dt} \tag{10a}$$

$$\vec{J} = (1 - x) \sum_{i=1}^{N_A} \vec{v_i} - x \sum_{i'=1}^{N_B} \vec{v_i} , \qquad (10b)$$

$$x = N_A/(N_A + N_B) \qquad (10c)$$

where N_A is the number of atoms of species A, N_B is that of species B, and $\vec{J}$ is the interdiffusion current fluctuation. Its presence in this problem emphasizes the role of mutual diffusion of atoms in the collision-induced absorption. The remainder of the description is similar to that given in the section on depolarized light scattering. A Zwanzig-Mori theory is constructed with the variable $\vec{J}$ and its first and second time derivatives. The transport matrix is calculated with the help of the lattice-gas model. The resulting correlation function $\langle\vec{J}(0)\vec{J}(t)\rangle$ conserves the general form of Eq. (7) but the parameters A, B, C, λ, μ, ν have totally different values. In spite of these differences, this correlation function decays, as does the correlation function Eq. (7), in three relaxation modes, one dissipative and two doubly degenerate oscillatory modes.

Results and discussion. (1) The profile $G(\omega)$ presents a low frequency dip as well as a high frequency wing (Fig. 5). This spectral behavior is due to the interplay of diffusive and rattling atomic motions in the system. The oscillatory mode generates the wing whereas the small amplitude diffusive mode generates an inverted Lorentzian which, coupled to the oscillatory mode, produces the dip. (2) The profile of $G(\omega)$ in the dip region strongly depends on the form of m(R) (Birnbaum and Mountain, 1984). If $\vec{m}$ = const $\vec{F}$, the

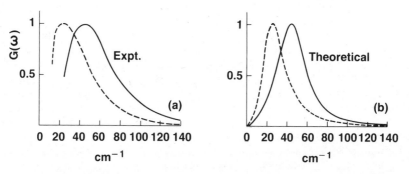

Fig 5. (a) Experimental reduced absorption coefficient $G(\omega)$: neon in liquid argon with x_{Ar} = 0.989, T = 90K and ρ = 728 amagat; krypton in liquid argon with x_{Ar} = 0.85, T = 135K (Buontempo et al., 1971). (b) Theoretical spectra: neon-argon mixture with x_{Ar} = 0.989; T = 90K and ρ = 728 amagat; krypton-argon mixture x_{Ar} = 0.85, T = 135K and ρ = 380 amagat. All spectra are normalized (Guillot et al., 1982).

spectral density $G(\omega)$ vanishes at $\omega = 0$. A non-vanishing value of $G(0)$ is found otherwise. (3) The profile varies with density. In dilute solutions, the shift of $G_{max}(\omega)$ is proportional to the square root of the mass of the dilute atom. At low densities the dip narrows, due essentially to the density dependence of the mutual diffusion coefficient.

CONCLUDING REMARKS

One of the essential contributions of the theory of collision-induced light scattering and absorption in dense rare gas fluids is the identification of the role of diffusive and rattling motions in producing band shapes. This view has been occasionally questioned. Are the time scales of the experiment compatible with this interpretation? Are the above statements consistent with data obtainable from other sources? A partial answer to these questions may be given by noticing that the half-width of a quasi-elastic incoherent neutron scattering spectrum of an atomic liquid is of the order of 10 cm^{-1} for wave vectors of the order of a few inverse Angstroms. The translational diffusion of atoms thus creates spectral densities comparable to those associated with the Lorentzian component of a light scattering spectrum. From the other side, representative values of the Einstein frenquency in solids are of the order of 50 cm^{-1} which is comparable to the rattling frequencies observed in collision-induced spectra. These values are thus entirely consistent with the present interpretation. Diffusive and oscillatory modes are detectable, in principle at least, by collision-induced spectroscopies.

Another relevant goal is the explanation of the difference between the spectra of collision-induced light scattering and absorption. This difference is due, in main lines, to the difference in the range of $\beta(R)$ and $\vec{m}(R)$. The former has a long range and permits the observation of atomic motions over large distance, whereas the latter has a short range and limits the observation of atomic motions to short distances. A light scattering spectrum thus contains a Lorentzian component produced by diffusive atomic motions as well as a wing generated by rattling atomic motions. The rattling motions are more pronounced in absorption due to the short range of $\vec{m}(R)$. The spectral density in absorption at low frequencies is very small because of a cancellation between the diffusive and oscillatory modes whose contributions to $G(\omega)$ have opposite signs.

This review may be concluded by briefly comparing the theories discussed above to those due to Lewis (1980) and Van Kranendonk (1980). These authors provided the first interpretation of the collision-induced light scattering and absorption in moderately dense gases. The description of the scattering process is based on kinetic considerations, where the temporal superposition of the polarizability tensors induced in successive collisions produces an interference and generates a Lorentzian feature peaked at zero frequency deviation. This spectral density is convoluted with that related to the remainder of the profile to obtain an estimate of the complete spectrum. A similar description applies, mutatis mutandis, to the absorption spectra. These kinetic theories are valid at moderate densities, whereas theories covered in this review apply to high densities. A correspondence can be established between them. For example, the mean collision time responsible in kinetic theories for the dip width is replaced in theories of dense fluids by the correlation time of the interdiffusion current fluctuation. A description of collision-induced process is thus available for dilute as well as for dense systems.

REFERENCES

Alder, B. J., Beers, J. C., Strauss, H. L., and Weis, J. J., 1979, J. Chem. Phys., 70:4091.
Alder, B. J., Strauss, H. L., and Weis, J. J., 1973a, J. Chem. Phys., 59:1002.
Alder, B. J., Weis, J. J., and Strauss, H. L., 1973b, Phys. Rev., A7:281.
An, S. C., Montrose, C. J., and Litovitz, T. A., 1976, J. Chem. Phys., 64:3717.
Balucani, V., Tognetti, V. and Vallauri, R., 1975, Phys. Rev., A19:177.
Balucani, V., and Vallauri, R., 1979a, Mol. Phys., 38:1099.
Balucani, V., and Vallauri, R., 1979b, Mol. Phys., 38:1115.
Barocchi, F., and Zoppi, M., 1978, Phys. Letters, 66 A:99.
Barocchi, F., Moraldi, M., and Zoppi, M., 1981, Mol. Phys., 43:1193.
Barocchi, F., Moraldi, M., and Zoppi, M., 1982, Phys. Rev. A26:2168.
Barocchi, F., Moraldi, M., and Zoppi, M., 1983, Phys. Rev. A27:1587.
Bentley, J., 1979, J. Chem. Phys., 70:3125.
Berne, B.J., Bishop, M., and Rahman, A., 1973, J. Chem. Phys., 58:2696.
Birnbaum, G., Frommhold, L., and Krauss, M., 1984, J. Chem. Phys., 80:2669.
Birnbaum, G., and Mountain, R.D., 1984, J. Chem. Phys., 81:2347.
Birnbaum, G., Guillot, B., and Bratos, S., 1982, Adv. Chem. Phys., 51:49.
Bratos, S., and Guillot, B., 1982, J. Mol. Structure, 84:195.
Bruch, L. W., Corcoran, C. T., and Weinhold, F., 1978, Mol. Phys., 35:1205.
Bruch, L. W., and Osawa, T., 1980, Mol. Phys., 40:491.
Bucaro, J. A., and Litovitz, T. A., 1971, 54:3846.
Buckingham, A. D., in "Properties Optiques et Accoustiques des Fluides Comprimes", Editions du C.N.R.S., Paris 1955, p. 57.
Buckingham, A. D., 1956, Trans Faraday Soc., 52:1035.

Buckingham, A. D., and Clarke, K. L., 1978, Chem. Phys. Letters, 57:321.

Buckingham, A. D., and Watts, R. S., 1973, Mol. Phys., 26:7.

Buontempo, U., Cunsolo, S., Dore, P., and Maselli, P., 1981, Can. J. Phys., 39:1499.

Buontempo, U., Cunsolo, S., Dore, P., and Maselli, P., in "Intermolecular Spectroscopy and Dynamical Properties of Dense Systems", J. Van Kranendonk Editor, North Holland Publ. Co. Amsterdam (1980), p. 211.

Buontempo, U., 1984, J. Mol. Structure, to be published.

Byers Brown, W., and Whisnant, D. M., 1973, Mol. Phys., 25:1385.

Certain, P. R., and Fortune, P. J., 1973, J. Chem. Phys., 55:5818.

Clarke, K. L., Madden, P. A., and Buckingham, A. D., 1978, Mol. Phys., 35:579.

Cohen, H. D., and Roothaanm, C. C. J., 1965, J. Chem. Phys., 43:534.

Dacre, P. D., 1982a, Mol. Phys., 45:1.

Dacre, P. D., 1982b, Mol. Phys., 47:193.

Dacre, P. D., 1982c, Mol. Phys., 45:17.

Dacre, P. D., 1978, Mol. Phys., 36:541.

Dacre, P. D., 1981, Can. J. Phys., 59:1439.

Dalgarno, A., 1959, Proc. Roy. Soc., A 251:282.

Evans, M., 1977, J. Chem. Soc. Faraday Trans., 2, 73:485.

Frommhold, L., Hong Hong, K., and Profitt, M. H., 1978, Mol. Phys., 35:665.

Frommhold, L., 1981, Adv. Chem. Phys., 46:1.

Fortune, P. J., Certain, P.R., 1974, J. Chem. Phys., 61:2630.

Galatry, L., and Gharbi, T., 1980, Chem. Physics Letters, 75:427.

Gelbart, W. M., 1974, Adv. Chem. Phys., 26:1.

Gelbart, W. M., 1980, in "Intermolecular Spectroscopy and Dynamical Properties of Dense Systems", J. Van Kranendonk, Editor, North Holland Publ. Co., Amsterdam, p 1.

Giraud, N., and Galatry, L., 1980, Chem. Physics Letters, 76:18.

Gordon, R. G., 1965a, J. Chem. Phys., 42:3658.

Gordon, R. G., 1965b, J. Chem. Phys., 43:7307.

Gray, C. G., Gubbins, K. E., Lo, B. W. N., and Poll, J. D., 1976, Mol. Phys., 32:989.

Gray, C.G., and Lo, B.W.N., 1974, Chem. Phys. Letters, 25:55.

Guillot, B., Bratos, S., and Birnbaum, G., 1982, Phys. Rev. A, 25:773.

Guillot, B., Bratos, S., and Birnbaum, G., 1980, Phys. Rev. A, 22:2230.

Hammer, D., Freasier, B. C., and Bearman, R. J., 1977, Chem. Phys., 21:239.

Harris, R. A., Heller, D. F., and Gelbart, W. M., 1974, J. Chem. Phys., 61:3854.

Heller, D. F., Harris, R. A., and Gelbart, W. M., 1975, J. Chem. Phys., 62:1947.

Hunt, K. L. C., Zilles, B. A., and Bohr, J. E., 1981, J. Chem Phys., 75:3079.

Hunt, K. L. C., 1984, J. Chem. Phys., 80:393.

Jansen, L., and Mazur, P., 1955, Physica, 21:193, 208.

Keyes, T., 1979, J. Chem. Phys., 70:5438.

Keyes, T., Ladany, B. M., and Madden, P. A., 1979, Chem. Phys. Letters, 64:479.

Keyes, T., 1980, Chem. Phys. Letters, 70:194.

Keyes, T., and Madden, P. A., 1981, Chem. J. Phys., 59:1560.

Kress, J. W., and Kozak, J. J., 1977, J. Chem. Phys., 66:4516.

Lacey, A. J., and Byers Brown, W., 1974, Mol. Phys., 27:1013.

Ladd, A. J. C., Litovitz, T. A., Clarke, J. R. H., and Woodcock, L. V., 1980, J. Chem. Phys., 72:1759.

Ladd, A. J. C., Litovitz, T. A., and Montrose, C. J., 1979, J. Chem. Phys., 71:4242.

Lallemand, P., David, D., and Bigot, B., 1974, Mol. Phys., 27:1029.

Levine, H. B., 1968, Phys. Rev. Letters, 21:1512.

Lewis, J. C., and Tjon, J. A., 1978, Physica, 91A:161.

Lewis, J. C., and Van Kranendonk, J., 1972a, Can J. Phys., 50:352.

Lewis, J. C., and Van Kranendonk, J., 1972b, Can J. Phys., 50:2902.

Lewis, J. C., 1972, Can. J. Phys., 50:2881.

Lewis, J. C., 1980, in: "Intermolecular Spectroscopy and Dynamical Properties of Dense Systems," J. Van Kranendonk, ed., North Holland Publishing Co., Amsterdam, p. 91.

Lim, T. K., Linder, B., and Kromhout, R. A., 1970, J. Chem. Phys., 52:3831.

Madden, P. A., 1977, Chem. Phys. Letters, 47:174.

Madden, P. A. 1978, Mol. Phys., 36:365.

Martin, P. H., 1974, Mol. Phys., 27:129.

Matcha, R. L., and Nesbet, R. K., 1967, Phys. Rev., 166:72.

McTague, J. P., Fleury, P. A., and DuPré, D. B., 1969, Phys. Rev., 188:303.

Meyer, W., 1976, Chem. Phys., 17:27.

Meyer, W., 1976, this volume.

O'Brien, E. F., Gutschick, V. P., McKoy, V., and McTague, J. P., 1973, Phys. Rev. A, 8:650.

Oxtoby, D. W., and Gelbart, W. M., 1975a, Mol. Phys., 29:1569.

Oxtoby, D. W., and Gelbart, W. M., 1975b, Mol. Phys., 30:535.

Oxtoby, D. W., 1978, J. Chem. Phys., 69:1184.

Oxtoby, D. W., 1980, J. Chem. Phys., 72:5171.

Shelton, D., and Tabisz, G. C., 1980, Mol. Phys., 40:785.

Silberstein, L., 1917, Phil. Mag., 33:521.

Sipe, J. E., and Van Kranendonk, J., 1978, Mol. Phys., 35:579.

Stephen, M. J., 1969, Phys. Rev., 187:279.

Thibeau, M., Tabisz, G. C., Oksengorn, B., and Vodar, B., 1970, J. Quant. Spectrosc. Rad. Transfer, 10:839.

Thibeau, M., Oksengorn, B., and Vodar, B., 1968, J. Physique, 29:287.

Thibeau, M., and Oksengorn, B., 1968a, Mol. Phys., 15:579.

Thibeau, M., and Oksengorn, B., 1968b, J. Physique., 30:47.

Van Kranendonk, J., 1980, in: "Intermolecular Spectroscopy and Dynamical Properties of Dense Systems," ed., J. Van Kranendonk, North Holland Publishing Co., Amsterdam, p. 77.

Varshnaya, D., Shirron, S. F., Litovitz, T. A., Zoppi, M., and
    Barocchi, F., 1981, Phys. Rev. A, 23:77.
Volterra, V., Bucaro, J. A., and Litovitz, T. A., 1971, Phys. Rev.
    Letters, 26:55.
Weiss, S., 1976, Can. J. Phys., 54:584.
Weiss, S., Strauss, H. L., and Alder, B. J., 1979, Mol. Phys.,
    38:1749.
Whisnant, D. M., and Byers Brown, W., 1973, Mol. Phys., 26:1105.

CALCULATION OF SPECTRAL MOMENTS FOR INDUCED ABSORPTION IN LIQUIDS

C.G. Joslin and C.G. Gray

Department of Physics
University of Guelph
Guelph, Ontario N1G 2W1 Canada

ABSTRACT

We review the methods which have been used to calculate CIA spectral moments in atomic and molecular liquids and liquid mixtures.

INTRODUCTION

Theoretically calculated spectral moments have a number of important uses in general, including (i) for comparison with experimental moments, to test the theory, (ii) for comparison with computer simulation results, to provide a check on the expensive simulations, (iii) to determine intermolecular interaction parameters (particularly useful for gases), (iv) for use as input to certain line shape theories. The latter use is particularly relevant for liquids in view of the paucity of reliable adjustable-parameter-free theories of line shape in liquids.

The moments M_n, $n = 0,1,2,\ldots$, of the line shape function $I(\omega)$ are defined by Eq. (2.7). By expanding the exponential $\exp(i\omega t)$ in the Fourier transform relation (cf. Eq. (2.2))

$$C(t) = \int_{-\infty}^{+\infty} d\omega \, e^{i\omega t} \, I(\omega) \tag{1.1}$$

where $C(t) = \langle \vec{\mu}(0) \cdot \vec{\mu}(t) \rangle$ is the correlation function for the system dipole moment $\vec{\mu}$, we get

$$C(t) = \sum_{n=0}^{\infty} M_n \frac{(it)^n}{n!} , \qquad (1.2)$$

so that the spectral moments M_n are essentially the Taylor series expansion coefficients of $C(t)$.

Given $I(\omega)$ we can calculate the M_n from the definition, Eq. (2.7). We are interested in the converse problem: given the M_n, what is $I(\omega)$? This is a classic 'inverse problem' which has been studied for over a century. (For references to the classical literature, see Kendall and Stuart (1969), Feller (1971), Shohat and Tamarkin (1963), Vorobyev (1965) and Akhiezer (1965). For reviews, extensions and references to more recent work, see Langhoff (1980), Nickel (1974), Reinhardt (1982) and Nadler and Schulten (1983). For the information theory (IT) approach see the general references Jaynes (1957, 1979), Powles and Carazza (1970) and Berne and Harp (1970), and Gburski et al. (1983) and Joslin and Gray (1984a, 1984b) for applications to CIA. Mori theory using only moments for closure is discussed by Berne and Harp and has been applied to CIA by Gburski et al. (1984) and Joslin et al. (1984). A comparison of the IT approach with more traditional solutions to the inverse problem has recently appeared (Mead and Papanicolaou, 1984).) We see from Eq. (1.2) that knowledge of all the moments M_n, $n = 0,1,2,...,\infty$ would determine $C(t)$ and hence determine the spectrum $I(\omega)$ uniquely (actually, there are some restrictions on the validity of this statement). It is true if the moments M_n do not increase more rapidly with n than n! (Kendall and Stuart, 1969; Feller, 1971).) In practice we can calculate only a finite, and usually small, number of moments (often only M_0, M_2, M_4, M_6). What approximations to the spectrum can we then make given only this limited information? Relevant to the CIA field, we note the recent work based on information theory (Gburski et al., 1983; Joslin and Gray, 1984a, 1984b) and on Mori theory (Gburski et al., 1984; Joslin et al., 1984). In these theories the spectrum is estimated directly from a small number of the M_n, and contains no adjustable parameters.

CALCULATIONS OF THE MOMENTS IN LIQUIDS

The absorption of radiation at angular frequency ω is measured by the absorption coefficient, $A(\omega)$. An isolated molecule in the gas phase experiences only the electric field $\vec{E}_0$ of the exciting radiation, and in this case one can derive a rigorous theoretical relationship between $A(\omega)$ and the spectral intensity $I(\omega)$, which is the Fourier transform, or power spectrum, of the total dipole moment autocorrelation function $C(t)$. One finds

$$A(\omega) = \frac{4\pi^2}{3\hbar cV} \omega\left(1 - e^{-\beta\hbar\omega}\right) I(\omega) , \qquad (2.1)$$

where V is the system volume, c is the speed of light, $\hbar$ is Planck's constant, $\beta = (kT)^{-1}$, and

384

$$I(\omega) = \frac{1}{2\pi} \int_{-\infty}^{+\infty} dt\ e^{-i\omega t}\ C(t) \tag{2.2}$$

where

$$C(t) = \langle \vec{\mu}(0) \cdot \vec{\mu}(t) \rangle \ . \tag{2.3}$$

In Eq. (2.3) the angular brackets denote an equilibrium ensemble average in the absence of the radiation field. When one considers the absorption of light by the molecules of a liquid, however, one finds that the simple relationship Eq. (2.1) no longer holds. This is because each absorbing unit (such as is constituted by a pair of molecules at low density) now no longer experiences only the field $\vec{E}_0$, but also the fluctuating electric fields generated by the time-dependent dipoles, and higher multipoles, that $\vec{E}_0$ induces in neighbouring molecules. One is at once confronted by a many-body problem for which there is no exact or rigorous solution. One can however proceed in an approximate manner using Lorentz's concept of the local field. This relates the average or local field $\vec{E}_\ell$ acting on an absorber in the condensed phase to $\vec{E}_0$ by an equation of the form

$$E_\ell^2 = \kappa E_0^2 \ , \tag{2.4}$$

in which

$$\kappa = \frac{1}{n} \left(\frac{n^2 + 2}{3}\right)^2 \ , \tag{2.5}$$

where n can be taken (when discussing absorption in the infrared region of the spectrum) as the high-frequency (optical) refractive index of the sample. The quantity κ defined in Eq. (2.5) is often referred to as the Polo-Wilson factor (Polo and Wilson, 1955; Van Kranendonk, 1957). Since $A(\omega)$ is now proportional to E_ℓ^2 rather than to E_0^2, Eq. (2.1) is replaced by the approximate relation

$$A(\omega) \approx \kappa \frac{4\pi^2}{3\hbar cV} \omega\left(1 - e^{-\beta\hbar\omega}\right) I(\omega) \ . \tag{2.6}$$

n is typically about 1.4 - 1.5, so that Eq. (2.6) predicts an increase in the intensity of absorption at a given frequency of about 30% due to the κ factor.

In a theoretical calculation of the line shape, the quantity that is computed directly is $I(\omega)$. We stress that (however difficult this may prove in practice) a rigorous theoretical evaluation of $I(\omega)$ via the methods of statistical mechanics is always possible. The errors and uncertainties inherent in the use of local fields enter only through Eq. (2.6), which relates $I(\omega)$ to the experimentally accessible $A(\omega)$. Essentially, κ serves as a filter which is applied to the experimental (or simulated) absorption coefficient to sift out the grosser effects of many-body interactions, so that a direct comparison of experiment and theory becomes possible.

When the methods discussed in the introduction are applied, the problem of calculating $I(\omega)$ reduces to the calculation of the spectral moments

$$
\begin{aligned}
M_n &= \int_{-\infty}^{+\infty} d\omega \; \omega^n \; I(\omega) \\[2mm]
&= (-i)^n \left. \left\langle \frac{d^n}{dt^n} \; C(t) \right|_{t=0} \right\rangle \\[2mm]
&= (-i)^n \langle \vec{\mu} \cdot \vec{\mu}^{(n)} \rangle \; . \tag{2.7}
\end{aligned}
$$

In Eq. (2.7) $\vec{\mu}^{(n)}$ denotes the nth time derivative of $\vec{\mu}$, evaluated at t=0. In the classical limit, with which we shall be exclusively concerned, we can use $\langle A\dot{B} \rangle = - \langle \dot{A}B \rangle$ to show that

$$
M_{2n+1} = 0 \; , \tag{2.8a}
$$

$$
M_{2n} = \langle \vec{\mu}^{(n)2} \rangle \; . \tag{2.8b}
$$

Odd moments vanish in the classical limit.

We will now review the various methods that have been used to calculate the even moments, M_0, M_2, M_4 etc., of CIA spectra in liquids. For a non-polar fluid the dipole moment μ can be written as a sum of terms representing the induced dipoles of pairs of molecules, triplets, etc. Thus

$$
\vec{\mu} = \sum_{i<j} \vec{\mu}(ij) + \sum_{i<j<k} \vec{\mu}(ijk) + \dots \tag{2.9}
$$

In Eq. (2.9) $\vec{\mu}(ij)$ denotes the dipole moment that the isolated pair of molecules i and j induce in one another. Only very rough estimates are at present available for the three-body term $\vec{\mu}(ijk)$, and none of the treatments discussed attempts to take any account of these terms. The precise importance of three-body corrections in liquids is unclear, and remains an intriguing question. In the pairwise-additive approximation the moments of Eq. (2.8b) become the sum of two-, three- and four-body terms. Thus for the zeroth spectral moment we have

$$
M_0 \sim \underbrace{\sum \langle \vec{\mu}(12)^2 \rangle}_{\text{two-body term}} + \underbrace{\sum \langle \vec{\mu}(12) \cdot \vec{\mu}(13) \rangle}_{\text{three-body term}}
$$

$$+ \sum < \vec{\mu}(12) \cdot \vec{\mu}(34) > \quad , \qquad (2.10)$$

$$\underbrace{\phantom{+ \sum < \vec{\mu}(12) \cdot \vec{\mu}(34) >}}_{\text{four-body term}}$$

with similar expressions for the higher moments (except that in M_2, the four-body term vanishes identically because the velocities of molecules 1, 2, 3 and 4 are uncorrelated).

Gray et al. (1976) have computed the zeroth and second moments of the far-infrared translational absorption band of rare gas liquid mixtures. They applied their results to the case of a dilute mixture of neon (A) in argon (B), and showed that

$$M_0 = \rho_A \rho_B \, V \int d\vec{r}_{12} \, g_{AB}(12) \, \vec{\mu}(12)^2 +$$

$$\rho_A \rho_B{}^2 \, V \int d\vec{r}_{12} \, d\vec{r}_{13} \, g_{ABB}(123) \, \vec{\mu}(12) \cdot \vec{\mu}(13) \quad , \qquad (2.11)$$

and

$$M_2 = \rho_A \rho_B \, V\left(\frac{kT}{m_{AB}}\right) \int d\vec{r}_{12} \, g_{AB}(12) \left[\mu'(12)^2 + \frac{2\vec{\mu}(12)^2}{r_{12}{}^2}\right]$$

$$+ \rho_A \rho_B{}^2 \, V\left(\frac{kT}{m_A}\right) \int d\vec{r}_{12} \, d\vec{r}_{13} \, g_{ABB}(123) \quad \times$$

$$\left[\mu'(12)\mu'(13) \cos^2\alpha_1 + \left(\frac{\mu'(12)\mu(13)}{r_{13}} + \frac{\mu(12)\mu'(13)}{r_{12}}\right)\left(1 - \cos^2\alpha_1\right)\right.$$

$$\left. + \frac{\mu(12)\mu(13)}{r_{12}r_{13}} \left(1 + \cos^2\alpha_1\right)\right] \quad . \qquad (2.12)$$

In these equations ρ is the density, m_A is the mass of an A molecule, m_{AB} is the reduced mass of an AB pair, $\mu'(r) = d\mu/dr$, and $g_{AB}(12)$ and $g_{ABB}(123)$ are the two- and three-particle correlation functions for an AB pair and an ABB triplet, respectively. α_1 is the angle at molecule 1 formed by the triangle (123), so that

$$\cos\alpha_1 = \frac{r_{12}{}^2 + r_{13}{}^2 - r_{23}{}^2}{2 \, r_{12}r_{13}} \quad . \qquad (2.13)$$

Gray et al. assumed an exponential model for the dipole $\mu(12) \equiv \mu(r_{12})$, viz.

$$\mu(r) = \mu_0 \exp(-r/\rho) \quad , \qquad (2.14)$$

where the parameters μ_0 and ρ were obtained by fitting to the moments of the gaseous Ne-Ar CIA spectrum. For the intermolecular interactions between like molecules they used a Lennard-Jones potential with parameters obtained from second virial data; for unlike interactions, the standard combining rules were used.

To estimate the triplet function $g_{ABB}(123)$ Gray et al. used the superposition approximation

$$g_{ABB}(123) \approx g_{AB}(12) \, g_{AB}(13) \, g_{BB}(23) \quad , \tag{2.15}$$

which is known to give good results for the integrals involved in thermodynamic properties.

$g_{BB}(r)$ was calculated using the perturbation scheme of Verlet and Weis (1972), which is based on the Weeks-Chandler-Andersen approach, which involves the approximation

$$g_{BB}(r) \approx g_{BB}^{ref}(r) \quad , \tag{2.16}$$

where $g_{BB}^{ref}(r)$ is the pair function for molecules interacting with the repulsive part of the potential $u_{BB}(r)$ (Weeks et al., 1971). $g_{BB}^{ref}(r)$ is then related to the hard sphere pair correlation function using the prescription of Verlet and Weis for $r > d$ and of Henderson and Grundke (1975) for $r < d$ (where d is a hard sphere diameter). This procedure gave a good estimate of $g_{BB}(r)$ in the vicinity of $r \approx \sigma$, which is where the principal contribution to the integrals in Eqs. (2.11) and (2.12) comes from. (Since this calculation was performed, better estimates of $g_{BB}(r)$ from computer simulation have become available.)

For the mixed pair function $g_{AB}(r)$, the conformal solution approximation

$$g_{AB}(r) \equiv \exp\left(-\beta u_{AB}(r)\right) y_{AB}(r)$$

$$\approx \exp\left(-\beta u_{AB}(r)\right) y_{BB}(r) \tag{2.17}$$

was used, where $y(r)$ is the indirect correlation function, which takes into account the effect of other molecules on the correlation of a given pair. It is defined by

$$g_{BB}(r) = \exp\left(-\beta u_{BB}(r)\right) y_{BB}(r) \quad . \tag{2.18}$$

The results are compared with experimental data obtained by Buontempo et al. (1970) in Table 1. Agreement is probably as good as can be expected in view of the large number of approximations made. Use of the superposition approximation, Eq. (2.15), is probably the major source of error in the theory.

Buontempo et al. (1979) have calculated M_0 and M_2 for the translation-rotation spectrum of N_2 gas at densities near the critical density. They assumed that the induction mechanism is quadrupolar, so that

Table 1. Experimental and theoretical values of the zeroth and second spectral moments for a dilute solution of Ne in liquid Ar at 90K. ρ_{Ne} = 8 Agt and ρ_{Ar} = 720 Agt (Gray et al., 1976).

| Moment | theory | | | |
	two–body contribution	three–body contribution	total	experiment
$(M_0/V)/10^{-27}$ J	12.6	−5.7	6.9	5.0 ± 0.5
$(M_2/V)/J\ s^{-2}$	0.82	0.15	0.97	0.73 ± 0.04

$$\vec{\mu}(12) = \frac{1}{3} \overset{\leftrightarrow}{\alpha}_1 \cdot \overset{\leftrightarrow}{T}^{(3)}(\vec{r}_{12}) : \overset{\leftrightarrow}{Q}_2 - \frac{1}{3} \overset{\leftrightarrow}{\alpha}_2 \cdot \overset{\leftrightarrow}{T}^{(3)}(\vec{r}_{12}) : \overset{\leftrightarrow}{Q}_1 \quad , \qquad (2.19)$$

where $\vec{r}_{12} = \vec{r}_2 - \vec{r}_1$ is the intermolecular vector, and $\overset{\leftrightarrow}{T}^{(3)}(\vec{r})$ is the symmetric, traceless, third-rank tensor

$$\overset{\leftrightarrow}{T}^{(3)}(\vec{r}) = \vec{\nabla}\,\vec{\nabla}\,\vec{\nabla}\,(1/r) \quad . \qquad (2.20)$$

$\overset{\leftrightarrow}{Q}$ and $\overset{\leftrightarrow}{\alpha}$ denote, respectively, the quadrupole and polarizability tensors: $\overset{\leftrightarrow}{\alpha}$ was assumed to be isotropic.

Buontempo et al. further neglected the relatively small anisotropy in the N_2 intermolecular pair potential. With these assumptions they could write the dipole autocorrelation function as the product of a single-molecule free-rotor correlation function and a translational correlation function:

$$C(t) = C_{rot}(t)\,C_{tr}(t) \quad . \qquad (2.21)$$

The statement of Eq. (2.21) in frequency space is that the spectrum is the convolution of a rotational and a translational band.

$C_{rot}(t)$ is given by $\langle P_2(\cos\theta(t))\rangle$, where P_2 denotes the second Legendre polynomial, and $\theta(t)$ is the angle between the symmetry axis of the N_2 molecule at time t and its position at time 0. $C_{rot}(t)$ can be evaluated exactly for a free rotor; its moments are given by

$$M_0^{rot} = 1 \quad , \qquad (2.22a)$$

$$M_2^{rot} = 6\,(kT/I) \quad , \qquad (2.22b)$$

etc.

$C_{tr}(t)$ is given by

$$C_{tr}(t) = 3\alpha^2 Q^2 \Big[\underbrace{N(N-1) \langle P_3\big(\cos\theta_{12}(t)\big) \, r_{12}(t)^{-4} \, r_{12}(0)^{-4} \rangle}_{\text{two-body term}}$$

$$+ \underbrace{N(N-1)(N-2) \langle P_3\big(\cos\alpha_1(t)\big) \, r_{12}(t)^{-4} \, r_{13}(0)^{-4} \rangle}_{\text{three-body term}} \Big] \qquad (2.23)$$

In Eq. (2.23) N is the number of N_2 molecules in the sample, P_3 is the third Legendre polynomial, and $\theta_{12}(t)$ and $\alpha_1(t)$ denote, respectively, the angles between the intermolecular vectors $\vec{r}_{12}(t)$ and $\vec{r}_{12}(0)$ and between $\vec{r}_{12}(t)$ and $\vec{r}_{13}(0)$. The absence of four-body terms from Eq. (2.23) is a consequence of the neglect of the anisotropic component of the polarizability.

Buontempo et al. calculated M_0^{tr} and M_2^{tr} and obtained

$$M_0^{tr} = 3\alpha^2 Q^2 V \Big[\rho^2 \int d\vec{r}_{12} \, g(r_{12}) \, r_{12}^{-8} +$$

$$\rho^3 \int d\vec{r}_{12} \, d\vec{r}_{13} \, g(r_{12}r_{13}r_{23}) \, P_3(\cos\alpha_1) \, r_{12}^{-4} \, r_{13}^{-4} \Big] \quad , \quad (2.24a)$$

$$M_2^{tr} = 84\alpha^2 Q^2 V (kT/m_{12}) \Big[\rho^2 \int d\vec{r}_{12} \, g(r_{12}) \, r_{12}^{-10} +$$

$$\tfrac{1}{2} \rho^3 \int d\vec{r}_{12} \, d\vec{r}_{13} \, g(r_{12}r_{13}r_{23}) \, P_4(\cos\alpha_1) \, r_{12}^{-5} \, r_{13}^{-5} \Big] \, . \quad (2.24b)$$

Here m_{12} is the reduced molecular mass, half the mass of an N_2 molecule; α_1 is as defined in Eq. (2.13). These expressions were evaluated assuming the molecules interacted with a Lennard-Jones potential. The pair correlation function $g(r_{12})$ was calculated numerically by solving the Percus-Yevick equation, and the superposition approximation was used for $g(r_{12}r_{13}r_{23})$.

The moments M_0 and M_2 of the composite lineshape were then computed using

$$M_0 = M_0^{rot} M_0^{tr} = M_0^{tr} \qquad (2.25a)$$

and

$$M_2 = M_0^{rot} M_2^{tr} + M_2^{rot} M_0^{tr} = M_2^{tr} + 6(kT/I)M_0^{tr} \quad , \quad (2.25b)$$

as follows from Eqs. (2.21) and (2.22).

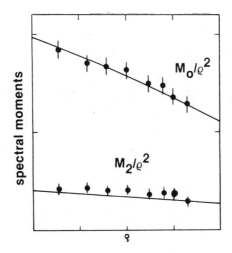

Fig. 1. The zeroth and second moments of the N_2 FIR spectrum as a
function of density. The axes are in arbitrary units:
the maximum on the density scale is close to the critical
density. $T \approx 300$ K (Buontempo et al., 1979).

The results of these calculations are displayed in Fig. 1.
Agreement with experiment was found to be very good for M_0, but
somewhat less satisfactory for M_2. An adjustable quadrupole moment
Q was used to improve the fit.

Guillot and Birnbaum (1983) have studied the FIR absorption of
liquid N_2 at densities above the critical density. They followed
Buontempo et al. (1979) in assuming that the induction mechanism is
quadrupolar, and in neglecting the anisotropies in the molecular
polarizability and in the intermolecular potential. They thus
arrived at a correlation function C(t) identical to that of Eqs.
(2.21) and (2.23). Their subsequent evaluation of the translational moments was however different. These were calculated
using a lattice gas model, in which the integrations over the

configurational space were replaced by discrete summations over small elementary volumes v, which define a reference density $\rho_0 = v^{-1}$. The n-body correlation functions $g_n(\vec{r}_1,\vec{r}_2,\ldots\vec{r}_n)$ involved in the calculations were treated so as to forbid multiple occupancy of a given elementary volume, and to render all remaining possibilities of occupation equally probable. For M_0^{tr} and M_2^{tr} they thus obtained

$$M_0^{tr} = 3\alpha^2 Q^2 v \, \rho^2 (1 - \rho/\rho_0) \int d\vec{r}_{12} \, g(r_{12}) \, r_{12}^{-8} \qquad (2.26a)$$

and

$$M_2^{tr} = 84\alpha^2 Q^2 v (kT/m_{12}) \, \rho^2 \left(1 - \frac{1}{2}\rho/\rho_0\right) \times$$

$$\int d\vec{r}_{12} \, g(r_{12}) \, r_{12}^{-10} \, , \qquad (2.26b)$$

which may be compared with Eqs. (2.24a) and (2.24b), respectively. In evaluating these expressions they replaced the pair correlation function $g(r_{12})$ by its low-density limit. They also computed an expression for the fourth translational moment M_4^{tr} by making further approximations.

There is some degree of uncertainty in the value one assigns to ρ_0. This must lie between the close-packing density and the solid density. Guillot and Birnbaum chose $\rho_0 = 800$ Agt.

The results of these calculations are displayed in Fig. 2. This is a plot of the reduced translational moments $\hat{M}_2^{tr} = M_2^{tr}/M_0^{tr}$ and $\hat{M}_4^{tr} = M_4^{tr}/M_0^{tr}$ as a function of density. These ratios increase fairly slowly until $\rho \sim \rho_0$, and then they increase much more rapidly. These results are in moderately good agreement with experiment.

Steele and Birnbaum (1980) have also calculated M_0 and M_2 for the CIA spectrum of liquid N_2. They assumed a quadrupolar induction mechanism. However, the treatment differed from that of Buontempo et al. (1979) and Guillot and Birnbaum (1983) in two respects. Firstly, they did not entirely neglect the anisotropy in the molecular polarizability. Secondly, and more importantly, they sought to take some account of anisotropy in the molecular correlations associated with (a) the non-spherical electrostatic (quadrupolar) forces, and (b) the short-range shape-dependent forces (for which a di-Lennard-Jones form was assumed). Instead of using a radially-symmetric pair correlation function, they wrote

$$g(r_{12} \, \omega_1' \, \omega_2') = \sum_{\ell \ell' m} g(\ell \ell' m; r_{12}) \, Y_{\ell m}(\omega_1') \, Y_{\ell' \bar{m}}(\omega_2') \qquad (2.27)$$

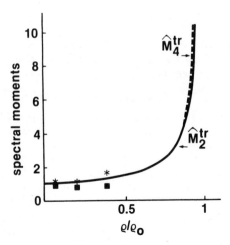

Fig. 2. The reduced second and fourth moments of the N₂ FIR translational spectrum as a function of density. Scale on the vertical axis is arbitrary. Experimental data (■ , $\hat{M}_2^{tr}$; *, $\hat{M}_4^{tr}$) are from Buontempo et al. (1979). T ≈ 300 K (Guillot and Birnbaum, 1983).

where ω'_1 and ω'_2 denote the orientations of molecules 1 and 2 with respect to the intermolecular vector, $Y_{\ell m}(\omega)$ is a spherical harmonic, and $\bar{m} = -m$. The expansion in Eq. (2.27) runs formally over all even values of ℓ and ℓ' (Gray and Gubbins, 1983). However, Steele and Birnbaum retained only those terms for which $\ell + \ell' \leq 4$.

The two-body contributions to the moments depend on integrals of the form

$$I_n(\ell\ell'm) = \int_0^\infty dr_{12} \; r_{12}^{-n} \; g(\ell\ell'm; r_{12}) \quad , \qquad (2.28)$$

where n = 8 or 10, which demonstrates that the behaviour of $g(\ell\ell'm; r_{12})$ at short distances is more important in determining the moments than the variation at large distances. Steele and Birnbaum therefore calculated the $g(\ell\ell'm;r_{12})$ using blip function theory, neglecting the attractive part of the pair potential (including the quadrupolar interactions), and assuming that the repulsive part of the potential could be represented by a hard-sphere interaction with suitably chosen d.

To calculate the three-body contributions to the moments Steele and Birnbaum used the superposition approximation in the form

$$g(123) \;=\; (4\pi)^{-3} \; g(000;r_{12}) \; g(000;r_{13}) \; g(000;r_{23}) \;\; , \quad (2.29)$$

which amounts to a complete neglect of all angular correlations in the interactions of triplets of molecules. The effect of this assumption is to eliminate certain three-body terms. Recent simulations have shown that while these terms are small, their omission can lead to substantial errors in the calculated moments because of the extensive cancellation that occurs (Steele, 1984).

When the intermolecular pair potential is anisotropic, there are also significant four-body contributions to M_0 (though not to M_2, as explained above) (Steele, 1984). Steele and Birnbaum neglected these terms.

Values of M_0 and M_2 calculated in this way for both liquid N_2 and for the dilute gas are listed in Table 2. Agreement with experiment is very good for the gas at 300K; the poor agreement at 124K may be attributable to experimental difficulties in extrapolating the measured spectrum to zero frequency (Buontempo et al., 1975). In the liquid phase the calculated and experimental M_0 agree closely, but the values for M_2 differ by 50%. Part of the reason for this discrepancy can be attributed to the near cancellation of two- and three-body contributions to M_2, which are given by

$$M_2(\text{two-body}) \;=\; 671 \;\; ,$$

$$\quad (2.30a)$$

$$M_2(\text{three-body}) \;=\; -472 \;\; ,$$

yielding a net moment

$$M_2 \;=\; 199 \;\; , \quad\quad\quad\quad\quad\quad\quad\quad\quad\quad (2.30b)$$

and the concomitant magnification of errors this introduces.

Steele and Birnbaum found they could improve this agreement by using instead $g(\ell\ell'm;r_{12})$ obtained directly from computer simulations in which the model potential included the quadrupolar energy. However, this worsened the agreement found for M_0.

Table 2. Comparison of calculated and experimental (Buontempo et al., 1975) values for the zeroth and second moments of the CIA spectrum of gaseous and liquid nitrogen (arbitrary units) (Steele and Birnbaum, 1980).

	$\beta M_0 / \rho^2$		$\beta^2 M_2 / \rho^2$	
	theory	experiment	theory	experiment
N_2 gas, 300 K	131	117	146	154
N_2 gas, 124 K	413	279	459	346
N_2 liquid, 76 K	150	143	199	297

Steele and Birnbaum's study emphasises the importance of considering the effects of anisotropy in the intermolecular potential in an accurate evaluation of CIA spectral moments of molecular liquids.

Madden and Tildesley (1983) have used computer simulation to study FIR absorption by carbon disulphide. The CS_2 pair potential was modelled as a three-centre atom-atom Lennard-Jones interaction; neglect of the quadrupole-quadrupole coupling was justified on the grounds that although CS_2 has a relatively large Q, it is the reduced moment $Q^* = Q/(kT\sigma^5)^{1/2}$ which effectively determines the magnitude of u_{QQ}, and this is quite small because of the large molecular size.

Madden and Tildesley assumed a quadrupolar induction mechanism. They did not neglect the anisotropy in the polarizability: for CS_2 this is very large $(\gamma = \alpha_\| - \alpha_\perp \sim \alpha)$. They could compute M_0 simply by computing ehe mean square dipole moment of the sample in the MD run. They calculated a mean square moment per molecule of

$$M_0^{calc}/\rho V = 3.3 \times 10^{-61} c^2 m^2 , \qquad (2.31a)$$

at 295K, which compares with an experimental value of

$$M_0^{expt}/\rho V = 4.9 \times 10^{-61} c^2 m^2 \qquad (2.31b)$$

at the same temperature (calculated from the data of Davies and Evans, 1976).

The discrepancy between the calculated and observed moments clearly cannot be blamed on an inherently inadequate treatment of the molecular correlations: no superposition approximation is employed in a simulation, and the anisotropy of the model potential was fully accounted for. Madden and Tildesley suggest the difference is probably associated with the use of the Polo-Wilson local field factor (vide supra). However, it is by no means obvious that their intermolecular potential, which was fitted to thermodynamic properties of the liquid, should necessarily reproduce $\langle \mu^2 \rangle$ accurately. Neglect of three-body terms in the potential may not be altogether justified. It is also possible their induction mechanism is oversimplified: omitted terms which could be significant include dipoles arising from frame distortion in the liquid, hexadecapole and higher permanent moments, and hyperpolarizability effects.

Madden and Tildesley found that two-, three- and four-body contributions to M_0 were all of approximately equal importance (see their table 2).

Madden and Tildesley also simulated the FIR CIA line shape. However, this lies outside the scope of our discussion.

In the course of preparing this review, several other papers have appeared. Joslin et al. have calculated M_0^{tr} and M_2^{tr} for liquid nitrogen (1985a), liquid methane (1985b) and liquid tetrafluoromethane (1985c), and Joslin and Gray (1985) have calculated these moments for dilute solutions of methane in liquid argon.

CONCLUSIONS

It is seen that using standard liquid state theoretical methods reasonable estimates of the moments can now be made, and that improved methods are being developed. As discussed in the introduction, these moments can now be used directly in certain line shape theories for both gases (Gburski et al., 1983, 1984; Joslin and Gray, 1984; Joslin et al., 1984, 1985d) and liquids (Joslin and Gray, 1985; Joslin et al., 1985a,b,c). These theories are free of adjustable parameters.

REFERENCES

Akhiezer, N. I., 1965, "The Classical Moment Problem," Oliver and Boyd, Edinburgh.
Berne, B. J., and Harp, G. D., 1970, Adv. Chem. Phys., 17:63.
Buontempo, U., Cunsolo, S., and Jacucci, G., 1970, Phys. Letts. A, 31:128.
Buontempo, U., Cunsolo, S., Jacucci, G., and Weis, J.J., 1975, J. Chem. Phys., 63:2570.
Buontempo, U., Cunsolo, S., Dore, P., and Maselli, P., 1979, Molec. Phys., 38:2111.
Davies, G. J., and Evans, M., 1976, J. Chem. Soc. Faraday 2, 72:1194.

Feller, W., 1971, "An Introduction to Probability Theory and its Applications," Vol. 2, 2nd. ed., Wiley, New York, p. 227.

Gburski, Z., Gray, C. G., and Sullivan, D. E., 1983, Chem. Phys. Letts., 100:383.

Gburski, Z., Gray, C. G., and Sullivan, D. E., 1984, Chem. Phys. Letts., 106:55.

Gray, C. G., Gubbins, K. E., Lo, B. W. N., and Poll, J. D., 1976, Molec. Phys., 32:989.

Gray, C. G., and Gubbins, K. E., 1984, "Theory of Molecular Fluids," Vol. 1, Oxford.

Guillot, B., and Birnbaum, G., 1983, J. Chem. Phys., 79:686.

Henderson, D., and Grundke, E. W., 1975, J. Chem. Phys., 63:601.

Jaynes, E. T., 1957, Phys. Rev., 106:620 and 108:171.

Jaynes, E. T., 1979, in: "The Maximum Entropy Formalism," R. D. Levine and M. Tribus, eds., MIT Press, Cambridge, MA.

Joslin, C. G., and Gray, C. G., 1984, Chem. Phys. Letts., 107:249.

Joslin, C. G., and Gray, C.G., 1985, Molec. Phys., to be published.

Joslin, C. G., Gray, C. G., and Gburski, Z., 1984, Molec. Phys., 53:203.

Joslin, C. G., Singh, S., and Gray, C. G., 1985a, Can. J. Phys., to be published.

Joslin, C. G., Singh, S., and Gray, C. G., 1985b, Molec. Phys., to be published.

Joslin, C. G., Singh, S., and Gray, C. G., 1985c, Chem. Phys. Letts., to be published.

Joslin, C. G., Gray, C. G., and Singh, S., 1985d, Molec. Phys., to be published.

Kendall, M. G., and Stuart, A., 1969, "The Advanced Theory of Statistics," Vol. 1, 3rd ed., Hafner, New York, p. 109.

Langhoff, P. W., 1980, in: "Theory and Applications of Moment Methods in Many-Fermion Systems," B. J. Dalton et al., eds., Plenum, New York, p. 191.

Madden, P. A., and Tildesley, D. J., 1983, Molec. Phys., 49:193.

Mead, L. R., and Papanicolaou, N., 1984, J. Math. Phys., 25:2404.

Nadler, W., and Schulten, K., 1983, Phys. Rev. Letts., 51:1712.

Nickel, B. G., 1974, J. Phys. C, 7:1719.

Polo, S. R., and Wilson, M. K., 1955, J. Chem. Phys., 23:2376.

Powles, J. G., and Carazza, B., 1970, in: "Magnetic Resonance," C. K. Coogan et al., eds., Plenum, New York, p. 133.

Reinhardt, W. P., 1982, Int. J. Quant. Chem., 21:133.

Shohat, J. A., and Tamarkin, J. D., 1963, "The Problem of Moments," 2nd. ed., Amer. Math. Soc., Providence.

Steele, W. A., and Birnbaum, G., 1980, J. Chem. Phys., 72:2250.

Steele, W.A., 1984, private communication.

Van Kranendonk, J., 1957, Physica, 23:825.

Verlet, L., and Weis, J. J., 1972, Phys. Rev. A, 5:939.

Vorobyev, Yu. V., 1965, "Method of Moments in Applied Mathematics," Gordon and Breach, New York.

Weeks, J. D., Chandler, D., and Andersen, H. C., 1971, J. Chem. Phys., 54:5237.

INTERACTION-INDUCED VIBRATIONAL SPECTRA IN LIQUIDS

P. A. Madden

Physical Chemistry Laboratory
South Parks Road
Oxford   OX1 3QZ
U.K.

1.   INTRODUCTION

In this article I will survey the way in which the study of induced vibrational spectra in liquids can complement more conventional Rayleigh and far infra-red work and describe the results which have been obtained recently. I will deal only with vibrational spectra which are forbidden by some selection rule for the isolated molecule; the issue of the interference of the molecular and induced components of an allowed band is discussed elsewhere (Lascombe and Perrot; Jonas; Madden; this volume). The work I shall describe is concerned with infra-red and Raman spectra of fundamental vibrational transitions. It should not be forgotten, however, that numerous other possibilities are offered by the title. For example vibrational circular dichroism (Barron, 1978) and hyper-Raman scattering (Long, 1977) offer possible induced processes which (to my knowledge) have not been examined. Besides the fundamental, overtones, combination bands, simultaneous transitions on different molecules and induced Fermi resonance may also be studied.

Much of the work published before 1980 (principally on infrared spectra) has been reviewed (Birnbaum, 1980). Here, after a general survey, I will present an account of recent attempts to interpret the lineshapes of infra-red and Raman spectra on a common basis.

2.   SURVEY

There are a number of compelling reasons for a more widespread study of induced vibrational spectra; to some extent these have been exploited in work to date.

i)   The class of molecules for which a spectroscopic phenomenon which
is unambiguously interaction-induced is enlarged, more complex fluids
become accessible.   In recent years a number of polyatomics have been
studied: CO_2 (Holzer and Ouillon, 1978; Cox and Madden, 1984),
CS_2 (Cox and Madden, 1980, 1981A), CF_4 (Le Duff and Gharbi, 1978),
SF_6 (Holzer and Ouillon, 1974) and C_2H_6 (Baglin et al., 1984).

ii)   The range of induced phenomena which may be studied for a given
material is greatly enhanced.   For CS_2 or CO_2, for example, the i.r.
absorption of ν_1 and the isotropic and anisotropic Raman spectra of
ν_2 and ν_3 may be set alongside the far i.r. spectrum.   The reason
why this point is significant is that for the kind of molecule
mentioned in i) the liquid is too complex for a direct attack on
interpreting a single lineshape (as may be possible for argon, for
example).   However, if a range of lines is available a great deal
may be learnt by contrasting their behaviour under different
physical and chemical (see v)) conditions.

iii) Perhaps the most valuable information to emerge from the
vibrational studies to date has come about through the obvious fact
that the centre of the line appears at a vibrational frequency.
This makes it easy to study the low frequency characteristics of
the induction process (in contrast to Rayleigh and far i.r. spectra).
If we regard the objective of the study of induced spectra in liquids
to be to gain insight into local structural relaxation, and thereby
transport processes, then this type of information is particularly
valuable.   For example, such a transport coefficient as the friction
coefficient is

$$\xi \; \alpha \; \lim_{\omega \to 0} \; Re \int_{0}^{\infty} dt \; e^{i\omega t} \; <\underline{f}(t).\underline{f}(o)> \tag{1}$$

where $\underline{f}$ is the random force on a particle which is determined by
the same kind of intermolecular fluctuation event as is responsible
for induced spectra.   The relevant point is that ξ is determined by
the spectrum of this force at zero frequency.   (Some transport
coefficients, notably those involving energy relaxation rates of
molecular resonances involve the spectra density at the resonance
frequency.)

iv) A corollary of iii) is that induced effects can be studied in
"messy" samples.   For example, good Raman scattering lineshapes can
be obtained in polycrystalline samples or glasses.   Such spectra can
be usefully contrasted with liquid state data (Cox and Madden, 1981B).

v)   It also follows from iii) that the effect of one component of a
solution on another may be identified.   Rayleigh and far infra-red
spectra of solutions are a composite of all interactions present.
Solution studies have been helpful in identifying the electrodynamic mechanisms responsible for the induction process.

Solution studies also make it possible to study interaction-induced spectra involving molecules of low symmetry, which possess no forbidden transitions of their own, through their influence on the forbidden spectra of high symmetry molecules. For example, by dissolving small amounts of strongly polar CH_3CN in CS_2 Weiss and Dinur (1983) have examined the mechanism for the infra-red absorption of ν_1 in CS_2. The concentration dependence of the induced intensity was consistent with a multipole model for the vibrationally modulated induced dipole of CS_2, i.e.

$$\hat{m}^i_\alpha = \hat{\alpha}^i_{\alpha\beta} [\sum_{j(CH_3CN)} T^{(2)}_{\beta\gamma} (\underline{r}^{ij}) \mu^j_\gamma + \sum_k T^{(3)}_{\beta\gamma\delta} (\underline{r}^{ik}) \theta^k_{\gamma\delta}]$$

$$+ \sum_k \alpha^k_{\alpha\beta} T^{(3)}_{\beta\gamma\delta} (\underline{r}^{ki}) \hat{\theta}^i_{\gamma\delta} , \qquad (2)$$

(where $\underline{T}^{(2)}(\underline{r}) = \underline{\nabla}\underline{\nabla} \, r^{-1}$, $\underline{T}^{(3)} = \underline{\nabla}\underline{T}^{(2)}$; μ^i, α^i and θ^i are the dipole polarizability and quadrupole moment of molecule i and $\hat{\alpha}^i$, $\hat{\theta}^i$ are their vibrationally modulated parts). Similarly Cox and Madden (1981A) dissolved solutes of different polarity and polarizability in CS_2 to distinguish between two possible mechanisms for the interaction-induced ν_2 and ν_3 Raman bands. Two terms occur in the same order in the mulitpole expansion for the induced polarizability of these u-symmetry vibrations:-

$$\hat{\Pi}^i_{\alpha\phi} = \hat{A}^i_{\alpha\beta,\gamma} \sum_j T^{(3)}_{\gamma\delta\epsilon} (\underline{r}^{ik})\alpha^j_{\epsilon\phi} + \beta^i_{\alpha\phi\gamma} [\sum_{j \neq CS_2} T^{(2)}_{\gamma\delta} (\underline{r}^{ik}) \mu^k_\delta$$

$$+ \sum_j T^{(3)}_{\gamma\delta\epsilon} (\underline{r}^{ij}) \theta^j_{\delta\epsilon}], \qquad (3)$$

(where $\hat{A}$ and $\hat{\beta}$ are the vibrationally modulated parts of the dipole-quadrupole polarizability and first hyperpolarizability). The relative importance of these terms is of general interest because they refer to effects of different character in the influence of the environment of a molecule on its electrodynamic properties. The first term may be viewed as a correction to the DID model due to the distribution of polarizable matter in the molecule and the second to the distortion of the polarizability of a molecule by the permanent charge distribution of another. The A-tensor term was found to dominate; a similar result was found for CO_2 by different means (Amos et al, 1980).

vi) Because the interaction between the normal coordinates of different molecules is usually sufficiently weak to be neglected (this is particularly true of infra-red forbidden transitions) the correlation functions involved in induced vibrational spectra tend to be somewhat simpler than corresponding non-vibrational spectra. Contrast, for example, the DID mechanism for the depolarised Rayleigh and ν_1 Raman spectra of a tetrahedral molecule (Le Duff and Gharbi, 1978). In the Rayleigh case the induced polarizability is

$$\Pi_{xz}^i = \alpha^2 \sum_j T_{xz}^{(2)} (\underline{r}^{ij}) \tag{4}$$

and the intensity is determined by

$$< \sum_i \Pi_{xz}^i \sum_j \Pi_{xz}^j > = \alpha^4 \{ 2N^2 <T_{xz}^{(2)} (\underline{r}^{12}) T_{xz}^{(2)} (\underline{r}^{12}) > \tag{5}$$

$$+ 4N^3 <T_{xz}^{(2)} (\underline{r}^{12}) T_{xz}^{(2)} (\underline{r}^{13}) > + N^4 <T_{xz}^{(2)} (\underline{r}^{12}) T_{xz}^{(2)} (\underline{r}^{34}) > \}$$

whereas, in the Raman case

$$\hat{\pi}_{xz}^i = 2\alpha\hat{\alpha}^i \sum_j T_{xz}^{(2)} (\underline{r}^{ij}) \tag{6}$$

which gives for the intensity

$$< \sum_i \hat{\pi}_{xz}^i \sum_j \hat{\pi}_{xz}^j > = N < |\hat{\pi}_{xz}^1|^2 >$$

$$= (\alpha\hat{\alpha})^2 \{ 4N^2 < |T_{xz}^{(2)} (\underline{r}^{12})|^2 >$$

$$+ 4N^3 <T_{xz}^{(2)} (\underline{r}^{12}) T_{xz}^{(2)} (\underline{r}^{13}) > \} \tag{7}$$

where all terms involving averages like $<\hat{\alpha}^1\hat{\alpha}^2 ...>$ have been neglected. Thus whilst the Rayleigh intensity involves the well known 2-, 3- and 4-body terms the Raman involves only 2- and 3-body correlation functions. The consequences of this difference for the evolution of the Rayleigh and Raman intensities with density were studied by Le Duff and Gharbi (1978). Equation (7) shows that there should be a close similarity between the Raman intensity for a spherical top and the DID contributions to the departure of the refractivity from the Clausius-Mossotti formula.

The significance of the different degrees of "coherence" of vibrational and non-vibrational spectra for liquid studies is not clear. For infra-red spectra and for the Raman spectra of non-spherical molecules there are (as we shall see below) other contributions to "incoherence" of orientational origin. However, one practical consequence is that it is much easier to simulate

402

vibrational spectra as the four-body correlation function (which makes the simulation of Rayleigh and far i.r. spectra very time consuming) is not present (Vallauri, this volume).

Whilst it is clear from this list that induced vibrational spectra can add significantly to the understanding of inter-molecular interactions in liquids there are limitations for detailed quantitative studies. One arises from the limited knowledge of many of the vibrationally modulated properties which have entered the expressions above, however many are now within range of ab initio calculation (Amos, 1980). A second arises from the fact that for the type of polyatomic fluid mentioned in i) above the polarizability is quite large so that "local field" effects become a problem. The most suitable candidates for quantitative studies are the depolarised Raman spectra of totally symmetric vibrations of spherical molecules (Le Duff and Gharbi, 1978); intensity studies of these bands would be useful to resolve many body contributions to DID spectra. The particular advantage of these spectra is that the isotropic spectrum provides a very convenient, internal intensity standard; the local field effects on the intensity of the isotropic line may be expected to be very small (Ladanyi, this volume).

3. LINESHAPES IN MOLECULAR LIQUIDS

Some progress has been made towards interpreting the shapes of induced spectra in liquids of anisometric molecules through a detailed study of CS_2. For the forbidden DID spectra of spherical top molecules the problem of modelling the lineshape is substantially the same as modelling that of argon (Bratos, this volume) except that a number of extra-DID terms also appear (Posch, this volume). The fundamental problem in devising a theory for molecular liquids is that the induced dipoles and polarizabilities depend upon the relative orientation of molecules as well as their relative position; this extra degree of complexity may preclude a general theory and only be overcome by developing theories specialised for particular relative rates of translational and rotational motion. Amongst the liquids whose induced spectra have been extensively studied to date, CS_2 is exceptional in the extent to which the rate of reorientational motion is slower than that of structural relaxation (Madden, this volume). At the opposite extreme is the case of N_2 for which the rates of reorientational and intermolecular motion are substantially the same (Sampoli, this volume). However, in a general survey of dense molecular liquids it is CS_2 which appears typical, with a well packed local environment which inhibits reorientation. By contrast, liquid N_2 appears like a dense gas; indeed the far infra-red spectrum has been interpreted as the convolution of a translational and free rotor spectrum (Birnbaum et al., 1982). To illustrate this point I shall also refer to the application of the CS_2 "theory" to the case of liquid CO_2, which is similar to N_2 in many regards.

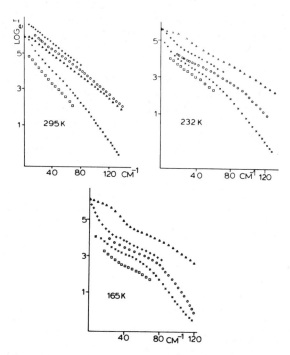

FIGURE 1. Induced spectra of CS_2:- +++ ν_2 Raman, $\triangle\triangle\triangle$ ν_3 Raman, ooo far i.r., xxx Rayleigh, $\square\square^2$ ν_1 Raman.

A variety of induced spectra for CS_2 are shown in figure 1 at three temperatures along the SVP curve (Madden and Cox, 1981). As well as various forbidden spectra the figure also shows the collision-induced parts of the depolarised Rayleigh and Raman lines. The spectra are most conveniently discussed in terms of their behaviour in three frequency regimes: low ($\omega < 30$ cm^{-1}), intermediate ($30 < \omega < 90$ cm^{-1}) and high ($\omega > 90$ cm^{-1}). In the latter two regions the spectra are strongly reminiscent of the depolarised Rayleigh spectrum (DRS) of argon in the same frequency domain (An et al, 1976), they are piecewise exponential and only weakly temperature dependent. Furthermore, there is a remarkable similarity between all the forbidden spectra and between the ν_1 Raman and Rayleigh spectra. The exponent which characterises the high frequency wings of the ν_1 Raman and Rayleigh spectra is about eight tenths of that of the forbidden spectra. At low frequencies the molecular spectra behave quite differently to the argon DRS. They show a pronounced feature which becomes more intense and narrows as the temperature is lowered; in contrast the argon spectrum shows a relatively weak low frequency peak which loses intensity and broadens as the triple point is approached. The low frequency infra-red and Raman spectra are unambiguously shown to be much more sharply peaked ("cusped") than a lorentzian. The induced spectra of CS_2 have been calculated in computer

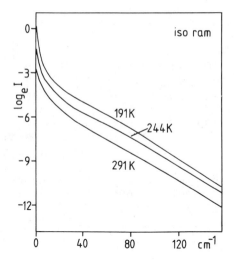

FIGURE 2.   Isotropic ν_1 Raman spectra of CS_2 from computer simulation.

simulations using the multipole models for the induced properties given in eqns. 2, 3, 5 and 7 (Madden and Tildesley, 1983, 1984). The calculated spectra agree well with the experimental ones, where comparison is possible.   The pronounced low frequency feature is found in the calculated collision-induced isotropic DID spectra (these spectra could not be observed experimentally), as illustrated in figure 2.   This suggests that the feature is a property of CS_2 as an anisometric molecular liquid rather than due to the difference between the induction mechanisms involved in the forbidden CS_2 spectra and the DRS of argon.

It is now well recognised (Madden, 1984; Bratos, this volume) that the cancellation between 2-, 3- and 4-body contributions to the spectrum plays an important role in determining the shape of the DRS in dense argon.   The cancellation occurs because the local environment of each atom is well ordered because the triple point density necessitates (almost) close packing.   Ladd et al (1979) showed that the separate 2-, 3- and 4-body correlation functions contained slowly decaying tails, due to the relative diffusion of atoms over the range of the $\underline{\underline{T}}^{(2)}$ tensor, but that these terms cancel each other with increasing perfection as the triple point is approached.   The remnant is responsible for the diminishing low frequency peak seen in the spectrum.   At high frequencies the shapes of the 2-body and total spectrum were found to be similar.

This essential aspect of cooperativity can be built into a theory of the DRS by modelling the relaxation of local density fluctuations in the fluid (Madden, 1978). This theory can be adapted to account for the spectra in molecular fluids. The different relaxation characteristics of fluctuations of different types (contrast a fluctuation which arises from an overfilled coordination shell with one in which a member of an intact shell is slightly displaced from its equilibrium position) are distinguished by calculating the spectrum of a fluctuation of a given wavelength (subspectrum). The total spectrum is a superposition of all sub-spectra weighted by a factor which follows from the form of the $\underline{\underline{T}}^{(2)}$ tensor. The subspectrum at a given wavelength (λ) may be thought of as reflecting the relative motion of atoms over a distance of order λ. Short wavelength subspectra ($\lambda \leq \sigma/4$, where σ is an atomic diameter) may therefore be relaxed by motions which do not disturb the coordination shells of the fluid. These motions are gas-like for very small λ and develop an oscillatory character for $\lambda \sim \sigma/4$ because in moving over this distance atoms encounter their surrounding cage and rebound from it. Such subspectra dominate the shape of the total spectrum at high and intermediate frequency. For longer λ ($\sigma \gtrsim \lambda \gtrsim \sigma/4$) to relax the density fluctuation atoms must push past each other; this must be an activated process and much slower than the "in-shell" motions. At larger λ the relative motion is diffusional. These motions dominate the low frequency total spectrum. Because of the cancellation effect subspectra with wavelengths longer than σ are of negligible amplitude. It should be noted that this description of the spectrum and the underlying motion arises from the concept of a well defined co-ordination shell and is therefore appropriate to dense liquids.

To extend this description to the case of molecular spectra the local density is replaced by a local orientation density which is resolved into fourier components as above (Madden and Cox, 1981). The different molecular spectra are associated with orientation densities which differ in the rank of the molecular orientation variables they contain, due to the fact that the induced dipoles and polarizabilities (Eqns. 2, 3, 5, 7) depend upon molecular tensors of differing rank.

This extended description may be used to account for the behaviour of the molecular spectra at high and intermediate frequencies. Since the orientation densities involved differ in their dependence on the molecular orientation variables the outstanding problems are to explain why the slopes of the semilog plots of the forbidden and of the DID spectra should be so similar and why the forbidden spectra should be broader than the DID ones (figure 1). Both may be explained (Madden & Cox, 1981) if, as in the case of argon, the high and intermediate frequency spectra are dominated by the behaviour of subspectra associated with short wavelength fluctuations in the orientation density and if these are pre-

dominantly relaxed by translational motion. That is, these short
wavelength fluctuations are relaxed by elementary translations and
in-shell oscillations without any significant change in the relative orientation of the molecules. This would seem to be plausible
for liquid CS_2 where the dense packing strongly inhibits reorientation (between the boiling point and the triple point the second rank
orientation time of CS_2 ranges from 1.5 ps to 10 ps).

To test this point in detail the spectra of the autocorrelation
functions of the following terms:

$$(3,2)\underline{\hat{\Pi}}^i = \sum_j {}^{(3)}\underline{\underline{A}}^i . \underline{\underline{T}}^{(3)}(\underline{r}^{ij}) . {}^{(2)}\underline{\underline{\alpha}}^j$$

and

$$(1,0)\underline{\hat{\Pi}}^i = \sum_j {}^{(1)}\underline{\underline{A}}^i . \underline{\underline{T}}^{(3)}(\underline{r}^{ij}) . {}^{(0)}\underline{\underline{\alpha}}^j$$

have been calculated (Madden and Tildesley, 1983), they are shown in
figure 3. These terms contribute to the interaction-induced
polarizability responsible for the Raman spectra (c.f. eqn (3)).
The experimental spectra involve a complicated superposition of
such terms but they may be examined individually in simulation data.
${}^{(n)}\underline{\underline{A}}$ and ${}^{(n)}\underline{\underline{\alpha}}$ denote the nth rank spherical tensor parts of the
polarizability. ${}^{(3,2)}\underline{\underline{\Pi}}$ depends much more strongly upon the molecular
orientation than does ${}^{(1,0)}\underline{\underline{\Pi}}$. However, their spectra are found to
be almost identical at frequencies greater than about 40 cm^{-1}, the
curves labelled B and D give the ${}^{(3,2)}\underline{\underline{\Pi}}$ and ${}^{(1,0)}\underline{\underline{\Pi}}$ spectra
respectively (these labels were inadvertently reversed in the
original paper). The finding that the high frequency spectra of
these very dissimilar terms are so closely related strongly supports
the simple model discussed in the preceding paragraph.

The analysis of the argon DRS suggests that the low frequency
spectrum should be affected by translation over distances of order
σ, but this occurs on the same timescale as molecular reorientation
(diffusion of the ends of a molecule over a similar distance) and
so both processes should contribute to the lineshape. At first
sight it might be thought that the effect of the orientational
degrees of freedom would be to broaden the low frequency spectrum,
since they provide additional relaxation channels. However, as
noted in discussing figure 1, the opposite tendency seems to
occur. Madden and Cox (1981) argued that this was due to
"uncancelled two-body" contributions to the molecular spectra.
They postulated that imperfect orientational correlation in molecular
fluids led to a much lower degree of cancellation between 2- and
3-body correlation functions so that the molecular spectra were
more strongly affected by the slowly relaxing 2-body correlation
functions than an atomic fluid at the same density. To illustrate

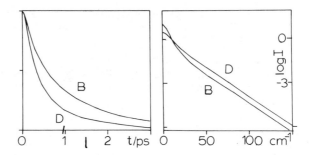

FIGURE 3. Correlation functions and spectra of the $^{(1,0)}\Pi(D)$ and $^{(3,2)}\Pi$ (B) polarizabilities.

the point consider the following correlation functions which contribute to the ν_1 infra-red spectrum of CS_2:

$$A(t) = \sum_{jk} < \underline{m}^{1j}(t) . \underline{m}^{1k} >$$

and

$$C(t) = \sum_{jk} < \underline{m}^{j1}(t) . \underline{m}^{k1} >$$

where

$$\underline{m}^{1j} = {}^{(0)}\underline{\underline{\alpha}}^1 . \underline{\underline{T}}^{(3)} (\underline{r}^{1j}) : {}^{(2)}\underline{\underline{\theta}}^j$$

and the (n) superscript again indicates tensorial rank. Notice that both correlation functions involve exactly the same molecular tensors but combined in different ways. In particular, for the 3-body (j≠k) of A to be non-zero there must be orientational correlation between the 2nd rank tensors on molecules j and k; this is not so for the 3-body contribution to C (denoted C3), it requires only positional correlation between molecules j and k. The 2-body contributions to the two correlation functions are identical. If there were no orientation correlation between molecules then A(t) would simply be a 2-body term and would relax slowly, in exactly the same way as the 2-body part of C(t) (denoted C2(t)). However, since C3 does not require orientational correlation and may be expected to be non-zero we expect C(t) to relax more rapidly than A(t) due to a cancellation between C2 and C3 at long times. These functions, taken from a computer simulation (Madden and Tildesley, 1983), are shown in figure 4,

408

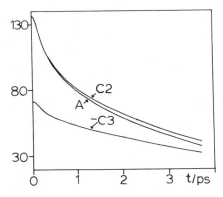

FIGURE 4.   The A(t) and C(t) induced dipole correlation functions
             (see text).

their behaviour is described rather well by these simple ideas.
The simulation thus confirms that there are important, slowly
relaxing contributions to the spectrum as a result of the imperfect
correlation of the orientational degrees of freedom.

   Madden and Cox (1981) proposed a simple model which leads to
a prediction for the shape of the low frequency peak. They
suggested that it should be modelled as the spectrum of the uncancelled two-body contributions alone, these were found by
neglecting all orientational correlation but assuming that positional correlation was perfect. The two-body spectrum was modelled
by assuming that both the rotational and translational motions were
diffusive and independent. Under these assumptions the spectrum
is a convolution of a sharply peaked translational spectrum (the
associated correlation function decays as $t^{-5/2}$ for forbidden
spectra and $t^{-3/2}$ for DID spectra) and a lorentzian re-orientational
spectrum.   It was assumed that the widths of these spectra were
governed by the normal translational and rotational diffusion
coefficients; the low frequency lineshape is then predicted,
without adjustable parameters.

   The comparison of prediction and experiment is shown in
figure 5. The non-lorentzian shape of the line is predicted rather
well. The linewidth is also very good close to the triple point
(165K - the lower curve) but the prediction becomes too broad at
higher temperatures (the upper curve is at 309K). This finding

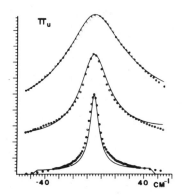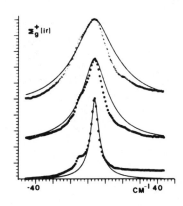

FIGURE 5. The low frequency regions of the ν_1 i.r. and ν_2 Raman spectra of CS_2 compared with the two-body diffusion model.

is very reminiscent of Buontempo's report (Buontempo, this volume) on the width of the induced rotational lines in the far infra-red spectrum of H_2. In that case it was found that a diffusion model (using the bulk diffusion coefficient) was in good agreement with experiment at high densities but that the predicted line-widths were too large at lower densities. An explanation of this behaviour, based upon a failure of the diffusion model to describe short-range translation at low densities, has been offered (Buontempo, this volume).

As has been stressed, the model of the CS_2 spectra is firmly based on description of intermolecular motion in a dense fluid. The model works at a semiquantitative level along the coexistence curve over the normal fluid range (165K - 310K), the density variation over this range is not large (1.45 to 1.24 x 10^3 kg m^{-3}). It is there-fore of some interest to see if the same description can be applied to liquid CO_2. As argued elsewhere (Madden, this volume) CO_2 crystallizes at low densities relative to CS_2 and the lower part of the liquid range is cut off. Only at the triple point (~ 222 K) does the reduced density of CO_2 approach that of CS_2 at its boiling point.

The interaction-induced light scattering spectra of liquid CO_2 along the SVP curve have been recorded by Cox and Madden (to be published). There have been other studies of the Rayleigh spectra in the liquid (Versmold, 1981; Konynenberg and Steele, 1975; Perrot et al, 1978) and of the forbidden Raman spectra in the compressed gas (Holzer and Ouillon, 1978). There is also a far

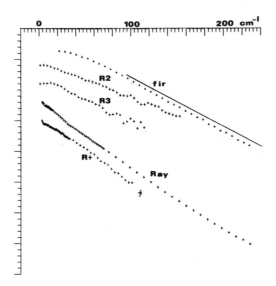

FIGURE 6.   Semilogarithmic plots of the forbidden Raman (R2 and R3)
and far i.r. spectra of CO_2. Also shown are the
Rayleigh and ν_1 spectra.

infra-red spectrum of liquid CO_2 under its vapour at 273K (Birnbaum
et al, 1971). In figure 6 semilog plots of the forbidden Raman
(R2 and R3 for ν_2 and ν_3), the far infra-red (fir) and the Rayleigh
(Ray) and ν_1 Raman spectra (R+ - actually the high frequency side
of the Fermi doublet) are shown. The light scattering spectra are
at 295K but the far i.r. is at 273K, the solid line is an attempt
to scale the far i.r. data for the temperature difference but now
allowance can be made for the effect of the (large) difference
in densities on the lineshape. The Rayleigh and ν_1 Raman data are
the total spectra, no attempt has been made to separate an
interaction-induced component (as in the case of the CS_2 data
shown in a comparable plot in figure 1). Computer simulation
results (Ladanyi, 1983; Madden, this volume) do not suggest that
such a separation is possible for CO_2 at 295K. Indeed it seems
unlikely that the Ray and R+ curves actually represent interaction induced spectra.

With this limited experimental data it is dangerous to draw
firm conclusions. However, it does seem that the slopes of the
high frequency forbidden spectra are less similar to each other
than are the corresponding spectra in CS_2. Since, as argued above,
the similarity in CS_2 arises because the high frequency spectra
are predominantly affected by translational motion, as a result of
dense packing in the fluid, it would appear that a similar

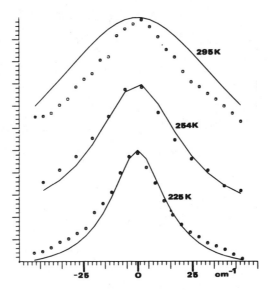

FIGURE 7.   The low frequency ν_2 Raman spectra of CO_2 compared
with the two-body diffusion model.

conclusion does not hold for CO_2 at 295K. Recall that at this
temperature the CO_2 is close to its critical point (304K).

The "uncancelled two-body", diffusion model for the low
frequency lineshape (Madden and Cox, 1981) is compared with the
experimental data on the ν_2 Raman band of CO_2 in figure 7. As
in the case of CS_2 the model reproduces the lineshape rather
well at 225K and 254K and at these temperatures the width of
the line is also well represented. However, the disagreement
between the predicted and observed linewidths at 295K is very
marked. As already noted in the case of CS_2 this is probably due
to a failure of the diffusion model in the low density liquid,
for the same reasons as discussed by Buontempo (this volume).

Overall, the CO_2 results suggest that the CS_2 analysis and
the underlying description of the intermolecular motion may be
appropriate close to the triple point for CO_2 as well. However,
to describe CO_2 near the critical point it appears that some new
concepts may be required. More extensive experimental data on
CO_2 would be valuable; for this liquid a large range of liquid
densities can be scanned at room temperature.

REFERENCES

Amos, R. D., Buckingham, A. D., and Williams, J. H., 1980, Molec. Phys., 39:1579.

An, S-C., Montrose, C. J., and Litovitz, T. A., 1976, J. Chem. Phys., 64:3717.

Baglin, F. G., Zimmerman, V., and Versmold, H., 1984, Molec. Phys., 52:877.

Barron, L. D., 1982, Molecular Light Scattering and Optical Activity (Cambridge University Press).

Birnbaum, G., Ho, W., and Rosenberg, A., 1971, J. Chem. Phys., 55:1039.

Birnbaum, G., 1980, in: "Vibrational Spectroscopy of Molecular Liquids and Solids," S. Bratos and R. M. Pick, eds., p. 147, Plenum Press, New York.

Birnbaum, G., Guillot, B., and Bratos, S., 1982, Adv. Chem. Phys., 51:49.

Cox, T. I., and Madden, P. A., 1980, Molec. Phys., 39:1437.

Cox, T. I., and Madden, P. A., 1981A, Molec. Phys., 43:307.

Cox, T. I., and Madden, P. A., 1981B, Chem. Phys. Lett., 77:511.

Cox, T. I., and Madden, P. A., 1984, Molec. Phys., to be published.

Holzer, W., and Ouillon, R., 1974, Phys. Rev. Lett., 32:205.

Holzer, W., and Ouillon, R., 1978, Molec. Phys., 36:817.

Ladanyi, B. M., 1983, J. Chem. Phys., 78:2189.

Ladd, A. J., Litovitz, T. A., and Montrose, C. J., 1979, J. Chem. Phys., 71:4242.

LeDuff, T., and Gharbi, A., 1978, Phys. Rev. A, 17:1729.

Long, D. A., 1977, Raman Spectroscopy (McGraw-Hill).

Madden, P. A., 1978, Molec. Phys., 36:365.

Madden, P. A., and Cox, T. I., 1981, Molec. Phys., 43:287.

Madden, P. A., and Tildesley, D. J., 1983, Molec. Phys., 49:193.

Madden, P. A., and Tildesley, D. J., 1984, Molec. Phys., submitted for publication.

Madden, P. A., 1984, in: "Molecular Liquids," A. J. Barnes, ed., D. Reidel Pub. Co., Dordrecht, The Netherlands.

Perrot, M., Devaure, J., and Lascombe, J., 1978, Molec. Phys., 36:921.

Van Konynenberg, P., and Steele, W. A., 1975, J. Chem. Phys., 62:230.

Versmold, H., 1981, Molec. Phys., 43:383.

Weiss, S., and Dinur, S., 1983, Chem. Phys. Lett., 99:197.

FAR INFRARED INDUCED ABSORPTION

IN HIGHLY COMPRESSED ATOMIC AND MOLECULAR SYSTEMS

Ph. Marteau

Laboratoire des Interactions Moléculaires et des Hautes
Pressions - C.N.R.S., Université Paris-Nord
Avenue J.B. Clément, 93430 Villetaneuse, France

ABSTRACT

The combination of far infrared spectroscopy and high pressure
techniques creates many experimental problems and measured spectra
are affected more or less by instrumental artifacts that must be
corrected. The role of high pressure absorption measurements for
helping our understanding of the collision-induced process is
discussed. In rare gas mixtures, observed translational absorption
bands show density effects at low frequencies. Theoretical
calculations of spectral moments and line shapes are reviewed. For
non-polar molecules, strong density dependences of the trans-
lational/rotational band are observed that can be studied with
advantage in liquids. New results in liquid nitrogen are presented.

INTRODUCTION

Collision-induced dipole moments are orders of magnitude
smaller than the dipole moments of typical polar molecules. For the
recording of useful spectra one needs, therefore, long absorption
paths or high pressures. Here, we are interested in the use of high
pressures which, of course, means that many-body induction
processes are important. Density variations in the high-pressure
regime show interesting many-body contributions of the induced
absorption spectra which will concern us here.

Accurate measurements in this field are difficult and only a
few laboratories attempt these because of the considerable
complexity of measurement and analysis. Nevertheless, progress in
this field is indispensable for several reasons : 1) By pressure
variations, the parameters of the unit cell in molecular crystals

415

are modified and moreover phase transitions can occur. The corresponding induced spectra reveal a great detail about intermolecular interactions which are invaluable for the modelling of induction operators. 2) Nonpolar molecules, especially in the liquid state, show induced spectra which depend to a surprisingly high degree on density; the observable spectra change shape drastically as the pressure is increased from the low-density limit to high densities where many-body interactions completely dominate the scene. Valuable information concerning molecular interactions in the dense states is to be gained from the study of such pressure variations. 3) Even near the low-pressure limit where binary interactions prevail, one cannot ignore many-body contributions totally: intercollisional interference and other many-body processes often affect the appearance of recorded spectra, and the concept of binary collisions may be an oversimplification of an actually more complicated situation. For all these reasons, a detailed investigation of induced spectra at high pressures appears to be most desirable.

Since collision-induced absorption in atomic and molecular systems has been extensively studied in numerous other publications, we restrict ourselves here to the review of high-pressure experiments. The liquid state will be emphasized at the expense of phonon spectra of solids, although they have been studied, in particular solid rare gases (Keeler and Batchelder, 1972), methane (Obriot et al., 1978), nitrogen (Fondère et al., 1981; Medina, 1982) and hydrogen halides (Obriot et al., 1983).

FAR INFRARED SPECTROSCOPY AND HIGH PRESSURE

Work at pressures up to hundreds of kilobars has been known in the near infrared. However, in the far infrared all work is restricted to lower pressures, typically below 10 Kbar, owing to practical or technical limitations. In general, the clear aperture of a window will have to be smaller the higher the maximum pressure of a given cell design. This may conflict with the requirement that the beam diameter be much greater than the wavelength of light. Thus one must compromise between the maximum pressure allowed and the amount of transmitted intensity, even if lasers are employed. In this way a practical limit to measurements at high pressure is set by diffraction effects. In a recent paper, Adams et al. (1981) have shown spectra above 100 cm^{-1} recorded with a diamond anvil cell of 0.4 mm diameter aperture. Work at lower frequencies and high pressures would require an enormously costly apparatus and is unlikely to be performed in the near future.

If the complete spectral profile is needed so that the spectral moments of the translational/rotational band can be obtained accurately, for all practical purposes useful pressures seem to be limited to a range from 1 to 10,000 bar or so. For such

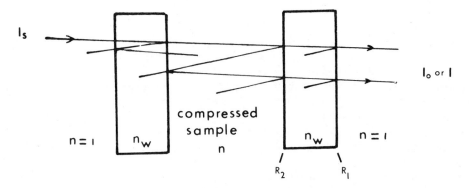

Fig. 1.   Transmitted light through a high pressure cell with highly
reflecting windows.

pressures, proven sample cell designs exist, as reported by Ferraro
et al. (1974), and one has to solve only the problem of the
windows. All useful materials have been effectively used, such as
crystalline quartz (Lowndes and Rastogi, 1976), silicon
(Bukhtoyarova and Tonkov, 1977), sapphire (Keeler and Batchelder,
1972; Obriot et al., 1978; Medina, 1980), and diamond (Marteau et
al., 1969). Even though sapphire cannot be used at room temperature
because of strong absorption due to multiphonon processes, it is
very useful at low temperatures (4.2 K) where the cut-off frequency
is shifted to higher values as reported by Hadni (1964). For quartz
and silicon, the useful range of frequencies strongly depend on
sample thickness. Diamond has no infrared absorption except from
5 - 8 micron and would be ideal if large flats were available. Most
of our experiments have been performed with diamond windows 5 mm
thick, with a clear aperture of 4 mm.

A detailed analysis of the technical problems is beyond the
scope of the present review, but we remind the reader that,
especially in the far infrared and at high pressures, spectroscopic
measurements are subject to systematic errors. One such problem is
related to the high reflectivity of suitable window materials. We
note that refractive indices are 2.10, 2.375, 3.06, 3.41 and 4.06
for quartz (Roberts and Coon, 1962), diamond (Edwards and Ochoa,
1981), sapphire (Roberts and coon, 1962), silicon (Aronson and
Mclinden, 1964) and germanium (Decamps and Hadni, 1960). In
deriving the absorption coefficient A from the recorded signals,
one must take into account the multiple passes of light due to
reflections at the window-sample and window-vacuum interfaces if
parallel windows are used, Fig.1. The reflections at the high
pressure sides are a function of the filling pressure. The
necessary corrections that must be applied to the measured signals
to get the true absorption coefficient are well known. Under the
assumption of low spectral resolution, so that interference effects

can be neglected, Quazza et al. (1973) have shown that the apparent absorption coefficient A^* can be related to the true value A by :

$$A^* = A + d^{-1} \ln \frac{(1 - R_1R_2)^2 - (R_1+R_2 - 2R_1R_2)^2 e^{-2Ad}}{(1 - R_2)^2 (1 - R_1) (1 + 3R_1)} \qquad (1)$$

Here, d is the absorption path length, and R_1 and R_2 are the reflection coefficients of the window-vacuum and window-sample surfaces, respectively. This relation (1) has been verified by measurement in the case of zero absorption, A = 0, in pure rare gases. With increasing density, R_2 decreases and becomes smaller than R_1. In this case, the logarithmic term in (1) becomes a negative number. Experimentally, one observes an enhancement of the transmitted signals in the order of 10% for argon at 500 Am. Considerable errors are possible when broad induced absorption bands are recorded if the exact baseline is not carefully determined. Similar corrections to Eq. (1) were proposed by Jones (1970) and by Chamberlain (1972) on the basis of slightly different approximations. It must be pointed out, however, that the final result of Jones is not in agreement with ours because only the first reflected ray has been considered at the innermost interfaces instead of summing, as we did, over the complete set of rays.

Equation (1) allows for a correction of multipassing if the beam is well collimated and shows minimal diffraction or defocussing. In all other cases, the measurement must be referenced to a standard "background" spectrum obtained with a non-absorbing (rare gas) medium of the same refractive index. This procedure doubles the time required for a measurement. A perfect match of the refractive indices is not always possible because of pressure limitations, but approximate matches can give useful results. We note in conclusion that the background referencing does not eliminate the need for a multipass correction. One can show that in this case Eq. (1) is replaced by :

$$A^* = A + d^{-1} \ln \frac{1 - R^2 e^{-2Ad}}{1 - R^2} \qquad (2)$$

where $R = (R_1+R_2-2R_1R_2)/(1-R_1R_2)$ is the total reflection of one window. The logarithmic term is a small correction and may often be ignored.

INDUCED ABSORPTION IN COMPRESSED RARE GASES

Translational spectra of rare gas mixtures were discovered by Kiss and Welsh in 1959 and are the subject of numerous investigations up to this date. A bibliography on induced

absorption, virtually complete up to the year 1975, has been
compiled (Rich and McKellar, 1976). Discussions of more recent work
can be found in the book edited by van Kranendonk (1980) and also
in the October 1981 issue of the Canadian Journal of Physics which
is devoted to the subject of collision – induced phenomena and
contains many valuable references of interest here. Apparently, the
binary absorption process is well understood. Absorption profiles
have been computed from first principles on the basis of Newtonian
mechanics (McQuarrie and Bernstein, 1968) and, more recently,
quantum mechanics (Birnbaum et al., 1981; Raczinski, 1982, 1983);
the agreement of measurements with the fundamental theory is
typically at the 10% level or better since the ab initio dipole
data of systems containing neon were corrected (Birnbaum et al.,
1984). Only for heavier systems (Ar-Kr, etc.) is the agreement
slightly poorer, perhaps 20% or so, for reasons believed to be
related to the oversimplification of Eq.(3). The intercollisional
interference process, on the other hand, is less well studied in
the rare gases and much work remains to be done, as is the case
with the many-body spectra beyond the binary pairs.

A general expression describes approximately the variation of
the induced dipole moment as function of separation, R, of the
binary pair,

$$\mu(R) = \mu_0 \exp (-R/\rho) + C_7/R^7 \tag{3}$$

In the past, many different values of the strength, range and
dispersion parameters, μ_0, ρ and D_7, have been derived from the
fundamental theory, or from measurements by moment or line shape
analysis. At first sight, the variation observed is bewildering;
not much if any consistency of the three parameters is observed.
The observed differences are to a certain extent understandable and
are in part due to unreliable approximations of computational
procedures, inadequate potential functions (such as the
Lennard-Jones model when much better models are available), the
inadequacy of Eq. (3) for heavier systems, and the use of
procedures which are not necessarily the most discriminating.
Closer examination indicates, however, that the induced dipole
functions do in fact agree at least for the better evaluations,
over the range of separations where the spectroscopic interactions
take place in spite of the drastically different sets of parameters
(see, as an example, Fig. 3 in the article of Birnbaum et al.,
1981). An error of the previous ab initio calculations affecting
all systems containing neon atoms (Wishnant and Byers Brown, 1973;
Lacey and Byers Brown, 1974) was also discovered (Birnbaum et al.,
1981) and recently corrected (Birnbaum et al., 1984). Summarizing,
one may assume that accurate binary induction dipoles are known for
most of the dissimilar rare gas pairs. Spectral profiles which
approximate known measurements at the 10% level can be computed
from these if the most accurate potential models are used. While
binary spectra (obtainable at low pressures) are thus understood,

this cannot be said of the spectra at higher densities where intercollisional interference and ternary etc. interactions influence the spectra.

The zeroth moment of an absorption spectrum is of great significance for the analysis of a measurement. Unfortunately, it is a quantity that is very difficult to determine experimentally, for two reasons: 1) its main contribution is at the low frequencies where intercollisional interference affects the measurement most ; and 2) the classical interferometric method is not accurate below 25 cm^{-1}. As a consequence, the low-frequency part of the induced spectra must be investigated by other methods such as polarized interferometry recently developed by Benson et al. (1983), microwave spectroscopy as used by Dagg et al. (1978)

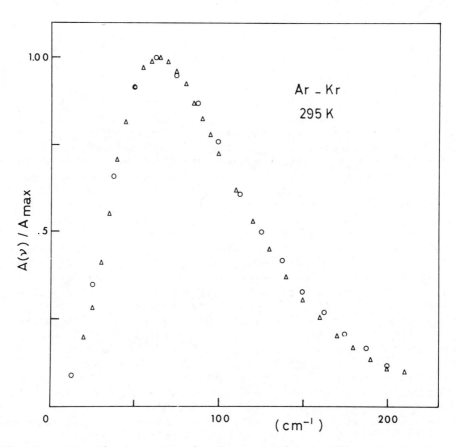

Fig. 2. Normalized translational absorption profiles for Ar-Kr mixtures. o: Low density spectrum (Buontempo et al., 1977); Δ: high pressure spectrum (see text) ρ_{Kr} = 152 Am ρ_{Ar} = 508 Am.

and infrared lasers (Dagg et al., 1982). By combining the results
of all these methods one can obtain the most dependable data to
close the low-frequency gap. For that purpose, it would be useful
to establish a research program among the various laboratories.
Experience shows that otherwise separate studies do not complement
each other because either different systems or different
temperatures are commonly considered.

New Developments

There has been enormous progress in recent years in computing
spectral line shapes, especially of the binary systems, see the
very detailed review article by Birnbaum et al. (1982). The new
quantum calculations based on the best interaction potentials and
dipole models show good consistency with measurements at low
pressures, although small inconsistencies at low frequencies seem
to persist. However, with increasing pressure stronger deviations
from the computed binary profiles are noticeable, apparently on
account of the increasing significance of the intercollisional
interference effect and many-body interactions. Valuable
information concerning these can be extracted from measurements at
such higher densities. If we are concerned with the spectral line
shape only, with no regard to absolute absorption intensities, we
may consider the normalized profile $A(\nu)/A_{max}$ which are relatively
accurately obtainable. Apart from the significant variations of a
small low-frequecy part of the spectra related probably to
intercollisional interference, we find the normalized profiles
essentially invariant over the whole range of densities, from 150
to 750 Am. Furthermore, our He-Ar and Ne-Ar profiles agree with
Bosomworth and Gush's normalized profiles which were obtained at
much lower densities, from 60 to 90 Am, and which were shown to be
essentially identical with the binary profiles. Data of $A(\nu)/A_{max}$
for Ne-Ar, Ne-Kr, Ar-Kr, and Ar-Xe are given in App. 1. Figures 2
and 3 show that the reduced lineshapes are invariant with respect to
the density. This is particularly well illustrated in Fig. 2. Small
distortions appear in Fig. 3 which may be ascribed to experimental
uncertainties. High pressure spectra shown in Figs. 2 and 3 originate in a new compilation of the results previously obtained by
Marteau et al., (1970) and Quazza et al., (1976). Apparently, the
inconsistencies which some of the quantum profiles show when compared with measurements cannot be considered three-body effects as
suggested recently by Raczynski (1982). Instead, it appears that
more accurate potential models, and perhaps improved induced dipole
models than Eq. (3), are needed for better agreement as shown elsewhere (Birnbaum et al., 1981; 1984).

Many-body spectra can be computed by molecular dynamics
calculations. A new theory based on the Mori method was also
recently advanced by Guillot et al. (1982) which reveals separate
spectral contributions of the "diffusive" and the "oscillatory"
modes of motion of an atom in the liquid. With the assumption of

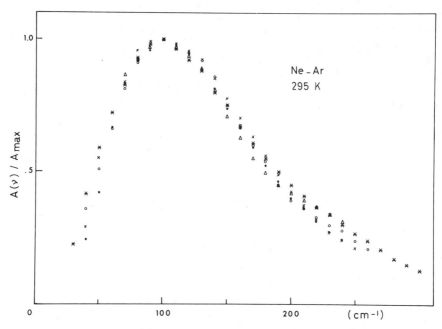

Fig. 3. Normalized translational absorption profiles for Ne-Ar mixtures. Stars are for the low density spectrum as observed by Bosomworth and Gush (1965). In the high pressure experiments (see text) the density of neon has been kept constant : 77 Am. The argon densities are the following: o (416 Am); × (488 Am); Δ (530 Am); • (553 Am).

the induced dipole being proportional to the interaction force, the intercollisional dip to zero intensity at zero frequency is obtained. However, the induced dipole is not proportional to force (Birnbaum et al., 1984), and a computer simulation shows for Ne-Ar that a zero intensity dip at zero frequency is not obtained (Birnbaum and Mountain, 1984).

Another development concerns the calculations of high order spectral moments of binary systems. Some recent work is due to Evans (1981) and Gburski et al., (1983). Although a direct comparison of these moments with measurements is not possible, Joslin and Gray (1985) points out that these may be useful for the construction of accurate spectral profiles on the basis of the Zwanzig-Mori method.

Integrated Intensities

For the integrated intensity, a virial expansion exists (Poll and van Kranendonk, 1961):

$$\alpha = \int_0^\infty A(\nu) \; d\nu = \alpha_1 \; \rho_1 \; \rho_2 + \alpha_2' \; \rho_1^2 \; \rho_2 + \alpha_2'' \; \rho_1 \; \rho_2^2 + \ldots \quad (4)$$

Gray et al. (1976) have calculated the exact 2- and 3-body terms for the zeroth and second moments for a dense system, Ne in liquid Ar, which was experimentally investigated by Buontempo et al. (1970). The standard liquid superposition approximation is used. Recently, Freasier and Hamer (1981) have computed these moments for the He-Ar pair using a density-dependent pair distribution function. The cubic term of the zeroth moment is found negative (sometimes positive for exotic choices of the dipole parameters); it is always positive for the second moment. The density correction amounts to about 10% at 200 Am, roughly as observed by Bukhtoyarova and Tonkov (1977). (Lowndes and Rastogi (1977) have recorded the spectra of equimolar mixtures of He and Ar at pressures up to 5.17 kbar. Unfortunately, their restricted frequency range does not allow computation of the moments).

Numerical calculations of spectral moments in the intermediate pressure range are often done for the light pairs. It is much easier for the experimentalist to obtain accurate measurements for the more massive pairs, owing to their more limited frequency bands. As a consequence, valuable work is as yet untested. We have measured the integrated intensities for five rare gas pairs (Ne-Ar, Ne-Kr, Ne-Xe, Ar-Kr, and Ar-Xe) as a function of the density products, in the range from 5,000 to 80,000 Am^2. Numerical data are listed in Appendix 2. Figure 4 shows these results together with a least squares fits of the data. If the density of constituent a is kept constant, we can write :

$$\alpha = \rho_a \; \rho_b \; (a_1 + a_2 \; \rho_b + a_3 \; \rho_b^2 + \ldots) \quad (5)$$

where a_1 is the sum of all ρ_a dependent terms. If, furthermore, ρ_a is sufficiently small, the a_1 coefficient should be given essentially by the binary expression. Accordingly, the term containing $(\rho_a\rho_b)^2$ has not been written out and its contribution, if not negligible, is included in the a_2 coefficient. Since we could not obtain a satisfactory fit with a cubic polynominal, a fourth-order term was added. Higher order polynomials did not improve the quality of the fit and could not be used except in the case of Ne-Ar for which low-density points were available from Bosomworth and Gush (1965). However, the addition of a higher order term did not affect the lower-order coefficients. Moreover, its contribution at 670 Am amounted to only 1% of those of the lower order terms. The values of the adjusted coefficients are given in Table 1. Although the constant neon density of the Ne-Ar system is not very low, namely 77 Am, the a_1 value is in reasonable agreement with the one derived by Bosomworth and Gush (1965) from the low-density measurements for the binary coefficient, $1.6 \; 10^{-4} \; cm^{-2} \; Am^{-2}$. The cubic term is negative for every pair considered which contradicts the experimental results of Bukhtoyarova and Tonkov (1977)

Table 1. Values of the coefficients in Eq.(5).

Pair	a_1	a_2	a_3
	$cm^{-2} Am^{-2}$	$cm^{-2} Am^{-3}$	$cm^{-2} Am^{-4}$
	10^{-4}	10^{-7}	10^{-10}
Ne–Ar	1.10	– 1.68	4.3
Ne–Kr	2.59	– 4.82	12.9
Ar–Kr	0.43	– 0.24	1.3
Ar–Xe	3.09	– 8.33	16.7

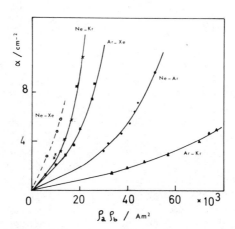

Fig. 4. Integrated intensities as a function of density products
for rare gas pairs at room temperature.

for the He-Ar case. We add, however, that we can also get positive
values if the polynomial expansions are limited to an insufficient
third order as they did. We state, furthermore, that our work does
not support the computational results of Freasier and Hamer (1981).

Other Interacting Atomic Systems

Pure induced translational absorption spectra have been
measured in mixed rare gases only. However, theoretical
computations of the binary spectra for alkali-rare gas systems have
been carried out by Bottcher et al. (1972). It is interesting to
compare their results with some empirical relations that were found
useful for the rare gas pairs (Quazza et al., 1976; Marteau et
al., 1970; Bar-Ziv and Weiss, 1976). For example, the frequency at
which the absorption is a maximum was seen to be simply proportional to $(KT/m\sigma^2)^{1/2}$. Similarly, the maximum absorption intensity
was found to be proportional to $(\alpha_1 - \alpha_2)$, where α_1, α_2 are the
polarizabilities of colliding atoms. Table 2 shows that the
"predicted" peak frequency is twice the computed, and the predicted
absorption is only one fifth of the theoretical one. Although the
agreement is not good, it is clear that the spectra are measurable.
For the He-Cs system the absorption can be accurately measured with
a 25 cm path cell if 260 Am of helium and 0.4 Am of cesium is used;
the required temperature for the latter is 700°C.

Fifteen years ago we tried to record the translational
absorption spectrum of Ar-Rb without success. With our experimental
conditions, the absorption was too weak to be measured by a factor
of 30. A change in temperature from 300°C to 450°C should have
increased the vapor pressure enough to record a spectrum. The
problem in such measurements is the low alkali vapor pressure,
although this is expected to be compensated for by the high
polarizability of these atoms. The polarizability will be even
greater in some excited states which can be populated by using
high power laser radiation. For example, the metastable first

Table 2. Translational absorption in Na-He mixture.

	calculated values (Bottcher et al., 1972)	expected empirical values See text
ν_{max} (cm^{-1})	90	180
$A(\nu)_{max}$ (cm^{-1} Am^{-2})	$4 \ 10^{-4}$	$0.8 \ 10^{-4}$

triplet state of calcium, has a lifetime of $3.85 \, 10^{-4}$ s. The first excited state of cesium has the polarizability values, 196 $\mathring{A}^3$ and 273 $\mathring{A}^3$, respectively. Finally the Cesium 7 P $^{3/2}$ state should have a polarizability close to 6000 $\mathring{A}^3$ according to the calculations of Granier et al. (1973).

The feasibility of such experiments has not been demonstrated. Possibly modulated laser sources with photoacoustic detectors should be used so that absorption of much less than 1% can be detected.

INDUCED ABSORPTION IN COMPRESSED MOLECULAR LIQUIDS

Starting from pure induced translational absorption in rare gas mixtures, the complexity of the induction mechanisms can be gradually increased by replacing one of the two atoms by a non-polar molecule and then by considering a collision between two such molecules. It has been shown in such systems that the induced spectrum is both rotational and translational in origin and that the dipole moment induced in a molecule is mainly due to the multipolar field of its neighbours. On the basis of these assumptions one can fairly well reconstruct the induced spectrum which is experimentally observed in the gas phase at moderate densities. The situation is more complex in the liquid phase because the approximation of pair interaction is no longer valid and one has to take into account, in general, three and four-body interactions.

Molecular liquids have been studied for a long time and experimental (Birnbaum et al., 1971; Buontempo et al., 1975; Arning et al., 1982) and theoretical results (Ryckaert and Bellemans, 1981; Steele and Birnbaum, 1980; Guillot and Birnbaum, 1983) continue to appear. There are promises of further advances from molecular dynamics calculations.

Evidence for density effects in the induced spectra of liquids is usually deduced by comparing estimated profiles with recorded ones. Even in cases where experimental variations of the liquid density are obtained by moving along the coexistence curve, density effects do not appear clearly since the rotational intensity distribution is modified due to the temperature change. The only simple way to see density effects is to compress the liquid at constant temperature.

To our knowledge there are no examples of far infrared studies of liquids under pressure except a recent work on liquid nitrogen that has been performed in our laboratory. The preliminary results presented below show that in a dense phase spectra showing interesting density effects can be obtained from an investigation of the effect of pressure applied to the liquid.

Nitrogen

We shall not present an exhaustive review of the studies made during the last twenty years on the far infrared spectrum of nitrogen, but rather start with the important work performed by Buontempo et al. (1971, 1975, 1979). (A rather extensive bibliography on previous work can be found in these papers). The situation can be summarized in the following way. The spectrum of the gas phase is very close to that expected from the pure rotational lines due to the quadrupolar induction. In the liquid phase, however, the spectrum exhibits a large deviation from that expected for the gas at the same temperature. Cancellation effects in the induced dipole arise in the dense phase, as well as the possible increased importance of overlap induction. The results of molecular dynamics calculations (Buontempo et al., 1975) have shown that quadrupolar induction is still the main induction process and that it can explain the whole spectrum, including the strong absorption in the high frequency wing. However, a large discrepancy was observed between experiment and calculations regarding the intensity.

Recently two papers have been published on the subject of liquid diatomic spectra. One is concerned with the calculation of the zeroth and first spectral moments with the assumptions of quadrupolar induction (Steele and Birnbaum, 1980). It was found that agreement between experiment and theory is obtained when the large cancellations due to three-body interactions is included in the calculation. The other paper gives a derivation of the absorption profile induced by a quadrupolar mechanism (Guillot and Birnbaum, 1983). For the sake of simplicity, the intermolecular potential is first assumed to be isotropic, and then an anisotropic component is introduced as a perturbation. This calculation clearly shows the respective roles played by rotational and translational contributions. Only the translational part is density dependent. Furthermore two modes reflecting the collective behaviour of the molecules are found which arise from a diffusive motion whose effect appears at rather low frequencies, and an oscillatory motion which dominates at intermediate and high frequencies. A strong dependence of the spectral shape on density is predicted for the spectrum of the liquid phase.

New Results

Experiments have been performed using one of our high pressure cells equipped with diamond windows, and with a pathlength of 1 cm. The temperature was stabilized by immersing the cell in a liquid argon bath (87.3 K). At this temperature gas-liquid and liquid-solid phase transitions occur at pressures respectively equal to 4 and 1250 bar. We could thus record the spectra for densities ranging from 610 to 742 Amagats.

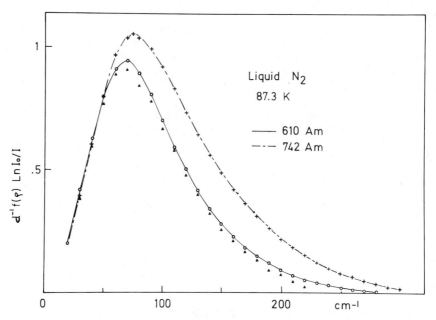

Fig. 5. Optical density of compressed liquid nitrogen at 87.3 K.
Triangles represent the result obtained at 90 K by
Buontempo et al. (1971).

Spectra were recorded in the 10–300 cm^{-1} frequency range.
Since the accuracy becomes rather poor below 25 cm^{-1}, results
recently obtained by Benson et al. (1983) in the 4–28 cm^{-1} region
were used. All our spectra have been scaled by the Polo–Wilson
factor $f(\rho)$ to take into account the local field effect (van
Kranendonk, 1957). Absorption profiles corresponding to extreme
values of the density are shown in Fig.5. The low density spectrum
(610 Am) can be favorably compared to that obtained by Buontempo et
al. (1971) at 90 K (triangles). The two spectra differ only by an
intensity factor of 1.05. The main part of this discrepancy could
be due to a difference in the liquid densities since at 90 K the
lowest value one can obtain is only 597 Am. If intensities are
normalized the agreement between the two recordings is found to be
better than 2% except in the very high frequency part where our
spectrum exhibits slightly more absorption.

As the density is increased, one observes a shift of the band
towards high frequencies and a rise of the absorption, particularly
apparent at moderate and high frequencies. In contrast, the low
frequency part of the spectrum remains apparently unchanged. The
band width is clearly density dependent and this definitely
confirms the conclusion that Buontempo et al. (1975) reached in
comparing the liquid spectrum to that expected for the gas phase.

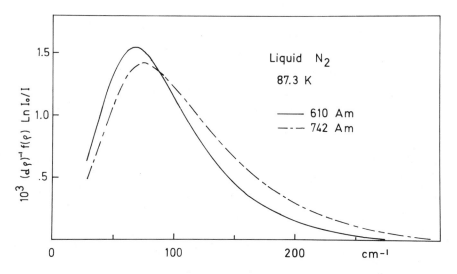

Fig. 6.   Spectra of compressed liquid nitrogen, normalized with
respect to the same number of molecules.

Fig. 5. shows the optical density $d^{-1}f(\rho)\ln I_0/I$. In the
binary approximation the intensity of the induced spectrum is
expected to vary as ρ^2 since in the volume V, N active molecules
are perturbed by (N-1) molecules. By applying pressure on the
liquid, one increases the density and therefore the number of
active molecules. A better examination of the density effect can be
made if one first normalizes the spectra with respect to the same
number of active molecules. This has been achieved by representing
$(\rho d)^{-1} f(\rho) \ln I_0/I$, as shown in Fig. 6. It becomes then clear that
the low frequency wing is strongly affected by cancellation effects
while absorption is enhanced at higher frequencies. The shift of
the band must be understood as a consequence of these two opposite
behaviours. The theory of Guillot and Birnbaum (1983) qualitatively
accounts for the type of density dependence shown in Fig. 6.

Integrated Intensity

A detailed analysis of spectral moments is still in progress.
So far, integrated intensity has been measured for several density
values. Here α is defined in the usual way as in Eq.(4). Results
are shown in Fig. 7, where α has been plotted as a function of ρ.
The triangles are experimental values while the full line is the
best fit obtained from a power series expansion,

$$\alpha = \alpha_1 \rho^2 + \alpha_2 \rho^3 , \qquad (6)$$

with $\alpha_1 = 3.62 \ 10^{-4}$ cm^{-2} Am^{-2} and $\alpha_2 = - 1.79 \ 10^{-7}$ cm^{-2} Am^{-3}

deduced from a least square calculation.   It is likely that an

429

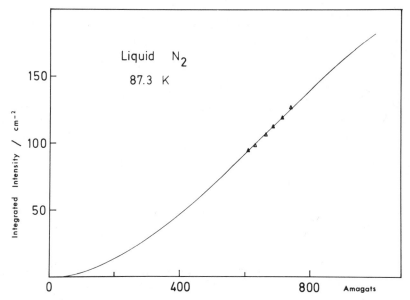

Fig. 7.   Integrated intensity. The full line represents the
polynomial fitting defined by rel. (7).

extension to higher order terms is necessary, although it does not
seem reasonable to do this here, because of the limited density
range we can investigate at this low temperature. A larger
variation of the liquid density could be obtained at some elevated
temperature. Although we intend do this in a near future, the
present results clearly show the departure from the simple binary
behaviour. Furthermore the ratio $\alpha_1/2\alpha_2$, approximately equal to
1000, is in good agreement with the value of the reference density
for the lattice gas model used by Guillot and Birnbaum (1983).
Finally a comparison of our results with the theoretical
calculations of Steele and Birnbaum (1980) can tentatively be made.
Starting from their spectral invariants and assuming our experimental conditions of temperature and density, we find that the
integrated absorption is expected to be close to 78 cm^{-2} while the
experimental value is 95 cm^{-2}. However it should be noticed that
calculation and experiments have been performed at different
temperatures, 77 K and 87.3 K, respectively, and that the integrals
involved in the calculation are somewhat temperature dependent.

CONCLUSION

    Because of the correspondence between photon energy and

molecular thermal energy in the far infrared region, spectroscopy
in this region has been extensively used for the study of collision
induced phenomena. However it is noticeable that there is only
little work on the collision-induced absorption as a function of
density. This fact is related to the considerable experimental
difficulties which, for instance, lead to a critical increase of
the time required to obtain the data. Even when experimental data
were tediously collected, these have sometimes not been analyzed.
Several reasons can be put forward to explain this state of
affairs.

1. Many body contributions in molecular liquids were not
treated theoretically until recent time.
2. As a consequence of experimental difficulties, the accuracy
of the results could occasionally have been rather poor, and thus
experimental data may have been considered with some suspicion.
3. Most of the time a typical high pressure device is
associated with a single spectroscopic system. As a consequence one
can only record part of the spectrum although the whole spectrum is
needed.
4. Up to a recent time calculations were usually performed on
light pairs while spectra of heavy pairs are more easily recorded.
A typical case is that of the He-Ne system for which many
calculations have been made although, at least until now, no
measurable absorption could be detected.

Nevertheless a considerable amount of work has already been
done, leading to interesting conclusions. In the future, it seems
that the efficiency of the investigations could be improved by
different investigators working simultaneously on the same
molecular system to collect a complet set of data over an extended
frequency range. Adequate spectroscopic devices now exist but the
far infrared high pressure apparatus is still not very common.

On the theoretical level, a better understanding of the
spectroscopic properties in dense fluids can be expected from the
new possibilities of computer simulations.

Acknowledgments

The author wishes to thank Drs. F. Fondère and J. Obriot for
their cooperation and for making their results on compressed
liquid nitrogen available prior to publication. He is also indebted
to Dr. F. Schuller for valuable discussions during the writing of
the manuscript.

431

REFERENCES

Adams, D. M., Berg, R. W., and Williams, A. D., 1981, J. Chem.
    Phys., 74:2800.
Arning, H. J., Samios, J., Tibulski, K., and Dorfmüller, Th., 1982,
    Chem. Phys. 67:177.
Aronson, J. R., and McLinden, H. G., 1964, Phys. Rev. 135A:785.
Bar-Ziv, E., and Weiss, S., 1976, J. Chem. Phys. 64:2412.
Benson, J., Fischer, J., and Boyd, D. A, 1983, Int. J. IR and MM
    Waves, 4:145.
Birnbaum, G., Ho, W., and Rosenberg, A., 1971, J. Chem. Phys.,
    55:1039.
Birnbaum, G., Brown, M. S., Frommhold, L., 1981, Can. J. Phys.,
    59:1544.
Birnbaum, G., Guillot, B., Bratos, S., 1982, Adv. Chem. Phys., 51:49.
Birnbaum, G., Krauss, M., Frommhold, L., 1984, J. Chem. Phys.,
    80:2669.
Birnbaum, G., and Mountain, R. D., 1984, J. Chem. Phys., 81:2347.
Bosomworth, R. D., and Gush, H. P., 1965, Can. J. Phys. 43:751.
Bottcher, C., Dalgarno, A., and Wright, E. L., 1972, Phys. Rev. A.
    7:1606.
Bukhtoyarova, V. I., and Tonkov, M. V., 1977, Opt. Spectrosc. 42:14.
Buontempo, U., Cunsolo, S., and Jacucci, G., 1970, Phys. Lett.
    31A:128.
Buontempo, U., Cunsolo, S., Jacucci, G., 1971, Mol. Phys. 21:381.
Buontempo, U., Cunsolo, S., Jacucci, G., and Weiss, J. J., 1975,
    J. Chem. Phys., 63:2570.
Buontempo, U., Cunsolo, S., Dore, P., and Maselli, P., 1977, J.
    Chem. Phys., 66:1278.
Buontempo, U., Cunsolo, S., Dore, P., and Maselli, P., 1979, 38:2111.
Chamberlain, J., 1972, Inf. Phys. 12:145.
Dagg, I. R., Reesor, G. E., and Wong, M., 1978, Can. J. Phys.,
    56:1046.
Dagg, I. R., Read, L. A. A., and Vanderkooy, J., 1982, Rev. Sci.
    Inst., 53:187.
Decamps, E. and Hadni, A., 1960, C.R. Acad. Sc. Paris, 250:1827.
Edwards, D. F., and Ochoa, E., 1981, J.O.S.A. Lett., 71:607.
Evans, M. W., 1981, Chem. Phys., 62:179.
Ferraro, J. R., and Basile, L. J., 1974, Appl. Spectrosc., 28:505.
Fondère, F., Obriot, J., Marteau, Ph., Allavena, M., and Chakroun, H.,
    1981, J. Chem. Phys., 74:2675.
Freasier, B. C., and Hamer, N. D., 1981, Chem. Phys., 58:347.
Gburski, Z., Gray, C.G. and Sullivan, D.E., 1983, Chem. Phys.
    Lett., 95:430.
Granier, J., and Granier, R., 1973, J. Quant. Spectrosc. Radiat.
    Transfer, 13:473.
Gray, C. G., Gubbins, K. E., Lo, B. W. N., and Poll, J. D., 1976,
    Mol. Phys., 32:989.
Gray, C. G., 1985, This volume.

Guillot, B., Bratos, S., and Birnbaum, G., 1982, Phys. Rev. A., 25:773.

Guillot, B., and Birnbaum, G., 1983, J. Chem. Phys., 79:686.

Hadni, A., 1964, Phys. Rev., 136A:758.

Jones, M. C., 1970, April. N.B.S. Technical Note 390.

Keeler, G. J., and Batchelder, D. N., 1972, J. Phys. C. 5:3264.

Keeler, G. J., and Batchelder, D. N., 1972, J. Phys. E. 5:931.

Kiss, Z. J., and Welsh, H. L., 1959, Phys. Rev. Lett., 2:166.

Lacey, A. J., Byers Brown, W., 1974, Mol. Phys., 27:1013.

Lowndes, R. P., and Rastogi, A., 1976, Phys. Rev. B., 14:3598.

Lowndes, R. P., and Rastogi, A., 1977, J.O.S.A., 67:905.

Marteau, Ph., Vu, H., and Vodar, B., 1969, Rev. Phys. Appliquée, 4:463.

Marteau, Ph., Vu, H., and Vodar, B., 1970, J. Quant. Spectrosc. Radiat. Transfer, 10:283.

McQuarrie, D. A., Bernstein, R. B., 1968, J. Chem. Phys., 49:1958.

Medina, F. D., 1980, Inf. Phys., 20:297.

Medina, F. D., 1982, J. Chem. Phys., 77:4785.

Obriot, J., Fondère, F., and Marteau, Ph., 1978, Inf. Phys., 18:607.

Obriot, J., Fondère, F., Marteau, Ph., Vu, H., and Kobashi, K., 1978, Chem. Phys. Lett., 60:90.

Obriot, J., Fondère, F., Marteau, Ph., and Allavena, M., 1983, J. Chem. Phys., 79:33.

Poll, J. D., and van Kranendonk, J., 1961, Can. J. Phys., 39:189.

Quazza, J., Marteau, Ph., and Vu, H., 1973, Inf. Phys., 13:245.

Quazza, J., Marteau, Ph., Vu, H., and Vodar, B., 1976, J. Quant. Spectrosc. Radiat. Transfer, 16:491.

Raczynski, A., 1982, Chem. Phys., 72:321.

Raczynski, A., 1983, Chem. Phys. Lett., 96:9.

Rich, N., and McKellar, A. R. W., 1976, Can J. Phys., 54:486.

Roberts, S., and Coon, D. D., 1962, J.O.S.A., 52:1023.

Ryckaert, J.P., and Bellemans, A., 1981, Mol. Phys., 44:979.

Steele, W. A., and Birnbaum, G., 1980, J. Chem. Phys., 72:2250.

van Kranendonk, J., 1957, Physica, 23:825.

van Kranendonk, J., 1980, "Intermolecular Spectroscopy and Dynamical Properties of Dense Systems", Soc. Italiana di Fisica, Bologna.

Wishnant, D. M., Byers Brown, W., 1973, Mol. Phys., 26:1105.

APPENDIX 1.   Reduced absorption profiles of rare gas mixtures.

ν cm^{-1}	$10^2\ A(\nu)/A_{max}$				
	Ne–Ar	Ne–Kr	Ne–Xe	Ar–Kr	Ar–Xe
20				19.4	22.44
25			21.06	28.1	37.21
30	13.84	24.14	30.30	41.4	55.91
35			43.24	54.9	69.53
40	33.30	33.79	54.41	70.4	80.74
45			64.71	81.5	88.98
50	53.02	61.33	73.66	91.6	95.34
55				97.2	98.72
60	70.53	78.38	86.22	99.1	100.00
65				100.0	98.63
70	84.50	90.76	94.93	99.1	94.51
75				96.3	89.92
80	92.70	98.00	99.18	92.6	83.94
85				87.0	78.03
90	97.51	100.00	98.73	82.4	71.45
95				77.8	65.74
100	100.00	97.14	94.74	72.2	60.40
110	97.66	91.60	88.65	62.2	49.77
120	95.06	85.57	81.13	53.1	40.98
130	90.65	78.02	72.83	44.9	33.63
140	83.44	71.39	64.28	36.9	28.17
150	74.44	64.74	58.23	30.7	23.53
160	66.92	58.63	51.86	25.4	19.93
170	59.47	54.06	45.26	20.2	16.94
180	53.08	48.77	38.70	16.8	13.32
190	46.24	44.00	33.10	13.4	10.93
200	40.85	39.81	27.89	10.9	8.81
210	36.70	36.73	21.67	10.0	6.35
220	32.72	33.91	18.97		4.29
230	29.66	30.25	14.91		2.49
240	26.89	27.45	11.26		1.55
250	22.77	24.70			1.03
260	21.35	22.55			
270		18.42			
280		15.41			
290		13.49			
300		12.20			

APPENDIX 2. Integrated intensity values. α unit is cm^{-2}.

Ne -Ar ρ_{Ne} = 77 Am		Ne – Kr ρ_{Ne} = 31 Am		Ne – Xe ρ_{Ne} = 46.5 Am	
ρ_{Ar}	α	ρ_{Kr}	α	ρ_{Xe}	α
390	3.24	303	2.64	137	2.8
416	3.84	316	2.96	228	4.8
488	4.64	387	3.16	258	5.8
530	5.44	439	4.12		
553	6.48	535	5.76		
574	7.16	594	8.24		
670	9.68	677	10.84		

Ar – Kr ρ_{Kr} = 152 Am		Ar – Xe ρ_{Xe} = 50 Am	
ρ_{Ar}	α	ρ_{Ar}	α
221	1.44	112	1.32
260	1.84	200	2.12
310	2.28	280	2.92
374	2.96	348	3.72
460	4.00	400	5.04
489	4.80	496	7.44
508	4.96	520	8.68

THEORETICAL INTERPRETATION OF THE FAR INFRARED

ABSORPTION SPECTRUM IN MOLECULAR LIQUIDS: NITROGEN

B. Guillot
Laboratoire de Physique Theórique des Liquides[*]
Université Pierre et Marie Curie, 4, place Jussieu
Paris, France

        and

G. Birnbaum
National Bureau of Standards
Washington, D.C. 20234

ABSTRACT

    The far infrared absorption due to quadrupole induced dipoles of
a liquid of homonuclear diatomic molecules is calculatd for an intermolecular potential which is only slightly anisotropic and is
applied to liquid N_2. The profile is described as the convolution
of a translational spectrum and a rotational spectrum assumed to be
free. The former, which is calculated from the Zwanzig-Mori theory,
is characterized by two translational modes, a diffusive low-frequency mode, and an oscillatory high-frequency mode. The parameters
in the theory are given analytically; the effect of density is obtained by the lattice-gas model. The results of this calculation
are compared with experimental and computer simulations.

INTRODUCTION

    Although the collision-induced translational band shapes in rare
gas liquids are rather well understood (Bratos et al., 1985), the
situation is quite different for the collision-induced spectra in
molecular liquids. The additional degrees of freedom in these liquids, which are mostly coupled, complicate the theoretical analysis

---

[*]Equipe Associée au C.N.R.S.

in a significant manner. Nevertheless, the far infrared (FIR) absorption spectrum of liquid N_2 seems to be a good candidate for theoretical investigation because a number of studies have been made in the gas phase (Heastie and Martin, 1962; Bosomworth and Gush, 1965; Maryott and Birnbaum, 1962; Rastogi and Lowndes, 1977), and in the liquid phase (Stone and Williams, 1965; Buontempo et al., 1975). Liquid N_2 also has been investigated by other experimental techniques like Raman and Rayleigh spectroscopy (de Santis et al., 1978; Sampoli et al., 1981; Medina and Dugas, 1981), by neutron scattering (Dore et al., 1975; Carneiro and McTague, 1975; Egelstaff et al., 1978; Pedersen et al., 1982), and by computer simulations (Barojas et al., 1973; Schoen, 1975; Levesque and Weis, 1975; Weis and Levesque, 1976). The purpose of this study is to present a theory which describes the FIR spectrum of a liquid of diatomic molecules like N_2 and which provides a simple interpretation of the band shape and its density dependence. The influence of weak anisotropic forces on the spectrum is also considered thanks to a perturbation treatment of the correlation function.

THEORY OF THE QUADRUPOLE-INDUCED-DIPOLE ABSORPTION SPECTRUM

In infrared spectroscopy, the absorption coefficient per unit path length, $\alpha(\omega)$, of a sample of volume V at temperature T is given by linear response theory,

$$\alpha(\omega) = \frac{4\pi}{3hcV} \omega \tanh \frac{\beta\hbar\omega}{2} \int_{-\infty}^{+\infty} dt \, e^{-i\omega t} \, G_+(t) \tag{1}$$

where $G_+(t)$ is the symmetrized correlation function associated with the total dipole moment M of the fluid. For a pure molecular fluid, the total dipole moment may be conveniently written as the sum of pair contributions,

$$\vec{M} = \sum_{i \neq j} \vec{\mu}_{ij} \tag{2}$$

where $\vec{\mu}_{ij}$ is the dipole moment induced in molecule i by its interaction with molecule j. We do not consider irreducible multibody interactions.

In the case of N_2, some investigations in the gaseous and liquid phase (Buontempo et al., 1975; Poll and Hunt, 1981) have pointed out the predominant role played by the quadrupolar induction mechanism. In this paper, neither higher multipole contributions (e.g., hexadecapole) nor short range induction (overlap) will be considered, although they could be formally included in the theory. According to these prescriptions, the induced dipole moment is,

$$\vec{\mu}_{ij} = \overleftrightarrow{\alpha}\vec{E}_{ij} \qquad (2a)$$

$$E_{ij}^{\alpha} = -\frac{Q}{2}\sum_{\beta\gamma} u_i^{\beta}u_i^{\gamma} \left\{ \frac{3}{r_{ij}^7}[5r_{ij}^{\alpha}r_{ij}^{\beta}r_{ij}^{\gamma} - r_{ij}^2(\delta_{\alpha\beta}r_{ij}^{\gamma} \right.$$

$$\left. + \delta_{\alpha\gamma}r_{ij}^{\beta} + \delta_{\beta\gamma}r_{ij}^{\alpha})] \right\} \qquad (2b)$$

where $\alpha = (1/3)(\alpha_{\parallel} + 2\alpha_{\perp})$ is the isotropic polarizability, E_{ij}^{α} is the α cartesian component (α = x, y, z) of the quadrupolar field E_{ij}, Q is the quadrupole, u_i^{β} is the β component of a unitary vector which lies along the axis of the molecule i, and r_{ij}^{γ} is the γ component of $\vec{r}_i - \vec{r}_j$, the distance between the centers of mass. It must be emphasized that generally $\vec{\mu}_{ij} \neq \vec{\mu}_{ji}$ due to the different orientations of the two molecules i and j. Thus the correlation function of the total dipole moment is expressed by

$$G(t) = \sum_{\substack{i,j \\ i \neq j}}^{N} \sum_{\substack{k,l \\ k \neq l}}^{N} \langle \vec{\mu}_{ij}(t)\cdot\vec{\mu}_{kl}(0)\rangle = N(N-1)[\langle\vec{\mu}_{12}(t)\cdot\vec{\mu}_{12}(0)\rangle$$

$$+ \langle\vec{\mu}_{12}(t)\vec{\mu}_{21}(0)\rangle] + N(N-1)(N-2)[\langle\vec{\mu}_{12}(t)\cdot\vec{\mu}_{13}(0)\rangle$$

$$+ \langle\vec{\mu}_{12}(t)\vec{\mu}_{23}(0)\rangle + \vec{\mu}_{12}(t)\vec{\mu}_{32}(0)]$$

$$+ N(N-1)(N-2)(N-3)\langle\vec{\mu}_{12}(t)\cdot\vec{\mu}_{34}(0)\rangle \qquad (3)$$

where the induced dipole moments $\vec{\mu}_{ij}$ are given by Eqs. (2a) and (2b). In Eq. (2b) there are two types of space variables, the bimolecular variables $\vec{r}_{ij}$ which describe the mutual translation of two colliding molecules and the monomolecular variables $\vec{u}$ which describe the intrinsic rotation of each molecule. In the autocorrelation function G(t), these two types of variable are coupled via the anisotropic part of the potential interaction, thus ruling out the possibility of a complete analytical calculation of the spectrum. Nevertheless, by noting the weak molecular asymmetry of N_2 we assume, in a first approximation, that the pair potential is isotropic. Both computer simulation (Levesque and Weis, 1975) and neutron scattering (Egelstaff et al., 1978) have emphasized that the equilibrium and the dynamical structure factor of liquid nitrogen at the triple point are almost identical to the structure factor of a system of spherical molecules. Moreover, a computer simulation study (Weis and Levesque, 1976) of orientational motions in fluids composed of slightly elongated molecules shows that the orientational correlations between neighbouring molecules are small.

Then we can decouple the rotational variables $\vec{u}_i$ from the translational variables $\vec{r}_{ij}$ and perform separate averages in G(t) to obtain (see also Buontempo et al., 1979)

$$G(\omega) = \frac{(\alpha Q)^2}{4} \sum_{\substack{i,j,k \\ i \neq j \\ i \neq k}} < 30 \frac{(\vec{u}_{ij}(t) \cdot \vec{u}_{ik}(0))^3}{r_{ij}^4(t) r_{ik}^4(0)} - 18 \frac{\vec{u}_{ij}(t) \vec{u}_{ik}(0)}{r_{ij}^4(t) r_{ik}^4(0)} >$$

$$\times \; <P_2(\vec{u}_i(t) \cdot \vec{u}_i(0))> \tag{4}$$

where P_2 represents the second order Legendre polynomial. Because the rotational motion of the molecules are uncorrelated due to the assumption of an isotropic potential, one finds: (1) the following terms vanish,

$$<\vec{\mu}_{12}(t) \cdot \vec{\mu}_{21}(0)>, \quad <\vec{\mu}_{12}(t) \cdot \vec{\mu}_{23}(0)>, \quad <\vec{\mu}_{12}(t) \cdot \vec{\mu}_{32}(0)>,$$

$$<\vec{\mu}_{12}(t) \cdot \vec{\mu}_{34}(t)(0)>$$

(2) since the molecules rotate freely,

$$<P_2(\vec{u}_i(t) \cdot \vec{u}_i(0))>$$

must be written in its free rotation limit; and (3) the total correlation function G(t) is expressed as the product of a translational correlation function, $G_{tr}(t)$, and a rotational correlation function, $G_{rot}(t)$, namely,

$$G(t) = \frac{\overline{\alpha Q}}{2}^2 G_{tr}(t) \times G_{rot}(t)$$

To develop an analytical theory of the FIR absorption spectrum of dense fluids composed of nearly spherical diatomic or linear molecules, the translational correlation function $G_{tr}(t)$ is calculated via the generalized Langevin type theory (Mori, 1965), which has demonstrated its ability to describe translational motions in atomic liquids (Bratos et al., 1985). According to this theory, we obtain (Guillot and Birnbaum, 1983)

$$G_{tr}[\omega] = 2ReG_{tr}[\omega] = \frac{2G(0)\tau}{1 - \left(\dfrac{\omega^2}{\omega_0^2}\right)^2 + (\omega\tau)^2 \left(1 - \left(\dfrac{1 - \omega^2/\omega_0^2}{1 - \omega_1^4/(\omega_0^2)}\right)^2\right)} \tag{5}$$

Here $G_{tr}[\omega]$ is the Laplace transform of $G(t)$ and τ, ω_0^2, ω_1^4 are the correlation time, the second and fourth normalized moments, respectively, of $G_{tr}(t)$. All the density dependence of the FIR spectrum is contained in the parameters τ, ω_0^2 and ω_1^4. Their evaluation involves integrations over the phase space product of the momentum space and the configurational space. The integrations over velocities are trivial due to the Maxwell-Boltzmann distribution function. By contrast, at liquid densities the configurational integrals involve many body correlations. More precisely, the three moments $G_{tr}(0)$, $G_{tr}^{(2)}(0)$ and $G_{tr}^{(4)}(0)$ contain two- and three-body correlations. Their respective contributions are estimated thanks to a lattice gas model used elsewhere (Bratos et al., 1985). The lattice gas model is useful because it allows an approximate evaluation of the sums involved in computing the moments and gives the explicit density dependencies of these sums. However, these sums may be evaluated by other approximate methods to obtain values for the spectral moments and the relaxation time.

According to the lattice gas model, the configurational space is divided in small elementary volumes v which define a reference density $\rho_0 = v^{-1}$ (Thibeau et al., 1977). The n-body distribution functions $g_n(\vec{r}_1, \vec{r}....\vec{r}_n)$ involved in the calculations are treated to prevent the multiple occupation of a given elementary volume, and to render all remaining possibilities of occupation equally probable. The translational correlation time is calculated in the framework of a stochastic approximation for which the memory function is assumed to decay much more rapidly than its corresponding correlation function (which is expected for diffusive type motions). Finally, we obtain

$$G_{tr}(0) = 12V\rho^2(1 - \frac{\rho}{\rho_0}) \int d\vec{r}_{12}(r_{12})^{-8}g(r_{12}) \tag{6a}$$

$$-G_{tr}^{(2)}(0) = 336\left(\frac{kT}{m_{12}}\right) V\rho^2(1 - \frac{\rho}{2\rho_0}) \int d\vec{r}_{12}(r_{12})^{-10}g(r_{12}) \tag{6b}$$

$$G_{tr}^{(4)}(0) = \frac{V\rho^2}{m_{12}^2} \left[192(1-\frac{\rho}{\rho_0}) \int d\vec{r}_{12}(r_{12})^{-10}e^{-\beta V(r_{12})} \left(\frac{\partial V(r_{12})}{\partial r_{12}}\right)^2 \right.$$
$$\left. + 97920(kT)^2 \left(1 - \frac{71\rho}{272\rho_0}\right) \int d\vec{r}_{12}(r_{12})^{-12}e^{-\beta V(r_{12})} \right] \tag{6c}$$

$$\tau = \frac{1 - \dfrac{\rho}{\rho_0}}{28D^*\left(1 - \dfrac{\rho}{2\rho_0}\right)} \quad \text{x} \quad \frac{\int d\vec{r}_{12}(r_{12})^{-8}g(r_{12})}{\int d\vec{r}_{12}(r_{12})^{-10}g(r_{12})} \tag{6d}$$

In these equations m_{12} represents the reduced mass of a pair of molecules, ρ is the number density of the fluid, $V(r_{12})$ is the isotropic pair potential, and D^* is the relative diffusion coefficient. A useful estimate of Eqs. (6a) to (6d) is obtained by calculating all the integrals with the low density expression of the radial distribution function

$$g(r) = e^{-\beta V(r)}$$

An improvement can be obtained by introducing a density dependent $g(r)$ given by computer simulation.

The absolute values of the moments and τ depend on the choice of the isotropic potential and on the reference density ρ_0. For a perfect solid, the reference density ρ_0 is known. Thus for a FCC lattice the density of close packing is $\rho_0 = \sqrt{2}/\sigma^3$, but the density for which the particle can just escape from a cage formed by the nearest neighbors is $1/2\sigma^3$ (see Hirschfelder, 1954). A practical value of ρ_0 for atomic liquids might be that close to the solid density ρ_s ($\sim 1/\sigma^3$). In the case of N_2, an analysis of the spectral moments of a recent measurement of the FIR absorption spectrum (Marteau, 1984) suggests the value $\rho_0 = 950$ amagat ($\sim \rho_s$). In addition to the uncertainty of the value of ρ_0 there is the question of the accuracy of the lattice gas model. An analysis of this model in its application to collision-induced Rayleigh scattering has been presented and extended to the next order of approximation by taking into account the short-range order, i.e., multiple position correlations (Sergiescu, 1979). It would be useful to examine the relevance of this treatment in the present case.

INTERPRETATION OF THE BAND SHAPE

The FIR absorption spectrum of N_2 has been extensively investigated in the last fifteen years, at low gaseous densities (Bosomworth and Gush, 1965; Maryott and Birnbaum, 1962; Heastie and Martin, 1962; high gaseous densities (Buontempo et al., 1979, 1983; Rastogi and Lowndes 1977) and liquid densities (Stone and Williams, 1965; Buontempo et al., 1975; Jones, 1970; Benson et al., 1983). At low densities the experimental profile

$$I(\omega) = \alpha(\omega)/\omega \tanh(\beta \hbar \omega/2)$$

shows a low frequency peak (below $20 \sim 30 \text{cm}^{-1}$), a pronounced should-

er at intermediate frequencies (roughly 50 cm^{-1}), and a high frequency wing (100 cm^{-1} and beyond). At liquid densities and low
temperatures (Fig. 1), the shoulder becomes less pronounced and the
spectrum is shifted to the lower frequencies. This last change is
due essentially to the effect of the lower temperature in reducing
the mean rotational frequency. At the same time the density dependence of the zeroth and second moment shows a cancellation effect due
to three-body collisions (see Figs. 4 and 5). It must be pointed
out that the profile I(ω) below ~30 cm^{-1} is not accurately known
(see Fig. 1), due to experimental difficulties in this region, although some improvement by using laser techniques may be expected.

At high frequencies, i.e., above roughly 80 cm^{-1}, the theoretical spectrum is seen in Fig. 1 to diverge from the experimental
spectrum. Although there are a number of factors which may contribute to inaccuracy in the theoretical spectrum, i.e., inaccuracy due
to truncation of the Mori continued fraction solution of the generalized Langevin equation, inaccuracy of the lattice gas model, estimate of the relaxation time, and neglect of anisotropy in the potential, we mention at this point only the neglect of quantum effects
in the theory. Although we have written the correlation function
$G_+(t)$ in symmetric form and thereby introduced the detailed balance
factor $[1 + \exp(-\hbar\omega/kT)]^{-1}$ in Eq. (1), $G_+(t)$ is in reality a quantum mechanical function, which has been computed classically. It
has been recently emphasized that this type of symmetrization procedure is in principle incorrect and starts to fail at the second
order in $\hbar$ (Barocchi et al., 1982). Consequently, one should expect
the liquid N_2 spectrum to exhibit substantial quantum effects, particularly at high frequencies.

In the theory described here, the absorption spectrum (Fig. 1)
results from the convolution of a rotational spectrum and a translational spectrum, namely

$$G[\omega] = \left(\frac{\bar{\alpha}Q}{2}\right)^2 \int_{-\infty}^{+\infty} d\omega' G_{tr}[\omega'] G_{rot}[\omega - \omega'] \tag{7}$$

where $G_{tr}[\omega]$ is given by Eq. (5) and where the free rotational spectrum for a linear molecule with moment of inertia I, is

$$G_{tr}[\omega] = \frac{3I}{32kT} |\omega| e^{-\omega^2/(8kT/I)} + \frac{1}{4} \delta(\omega)$$

The rotational spectrum (Fig. 2) characterizes the free rotations of
the N_2 molecules in the fluid and presents a Q branch ($\Delta J = 0$) and a
broad rotational band ($\Delta J = \pm 2$), whose spectral contribution is
temperature but not density dependent. By contrast, the translational spectrum is highly density dependent, Figs. 3a and 3b, and exhibits two modes, a diffusive mode due to the translational diffusion

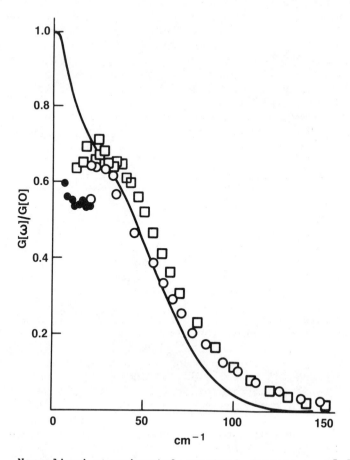

Figure 1. Normalized experimental spectral densities, $I[\omega]/I[0]$,
where $I[\omega] = \alpha(\omega)/\omega\tanh(\beta\hbar\omega/2)$, of liquid nitrogen measured by several authors; □ □ Buontempo et al., (1975) (T
= 66 K), ooo Jones (1970) (T = 76.4 K), ••• Benson (1983)
(T = 77 K). The theoretical (solid line) spectrum (T =
79 K and ρ = 635 amagat) is calculated with ρ_0 = 950
amagat and a Lennard-Jones pair potential (ε/k = 98 K,
σ = 3.6 A). The relative diffusion coefficient D^* (~ 2D)
is calculated from Cheung and Powles (1975). The data of
Buontempo et al., (1985) was multiplied by 0.95 to bring
them into agreement with the data of Jones (1970) near
30 cm^{-1}. This latter data and that of Levesque et al.,
(1984) are in good agreement (Marteau, 1984).

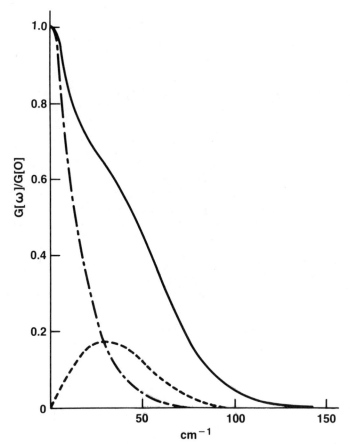

Figure 2. Spectral contributions to the theoretical profile: ——
total spectrum; —·—·— translational spectrum; ....
rotational spectrum. For clarity, the intensity of the
rotational spectrum was multiplied by a factor of 4
(Guillot and Birnbaum, 1983).

of the molecules in the fluid and an oscillatory mode generated by
their local oscillations. The diffusive mode creates a low frequency Lorentzian feature whose half-width is of the order of $1/\tau$ (see
Eq. (6d)). The oscillatory mode is responsible for the translational spectrum at intermediate and high frequencies. Its spectral
behavior is governed by the fourth moment $G_{tr}^{(4)}(0)$ which depends
explicitly on the forces acting between molecules (Eq. (6c)). However, the Mori procedure employed here necessarily leads to a spectral function which is a ratio of polynomials and which therefore
cannot quantitatively describe the exponential wings characteristic

of collision-induced absorption. This is because, as usual, it is
necessary to truncate the Mori continued fraction solution of the
generalized Langevin equation.

One notes that the convolution mixes both spectra and not in a
trivial manner. Thus, at low densities, the profile mainly results
from the rotational contribution which produces a shoulder (characteristic of free rotations) at intermediate frequencies. At liquid
densities, the role of the translational contribution is much increased. The low temperatures involved at liquid densities tend to
shift the rotational spectrum towards low frequencies, whereas the
structural ordering strengthens the translational spectrum at intermediate frequencies (oscillatory mode). Moreover, it is interesting
to note that the rather complex density dependence of τ is almost
governed by D^* (the relative diffusion coefficient) which decreases
rapidly when the density increases. The present theory predicts a
narrowing of the low frequency part of the translational spectrum
(due essentially to increasing τ) and a broadening of its high frequency part (due to the cage effect) when the density increases, as
shown in Fig. 3. A recent experimental investigation of compressed N_2 (Buontempo et al., 1983) shows clearly this phenomena.

The role which the translational component plays in the total
spectrum can also be seen from the analysis of the spectral moments.
In the theory described here, the density dependence of the moments
comes exclusively from the translational correlation function. The

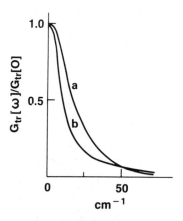

Figure 3.   Theoretical density effect of the translational spectrum.
The curves (a) and (b) correspond to the thermodynamical
states, respectively, T = 100 K, ρ = 640 amagat and T =
100 K, ρ = 715 amagat. The arrow indicates the maximum of
the absorption due to the free rotational spectrum.

446

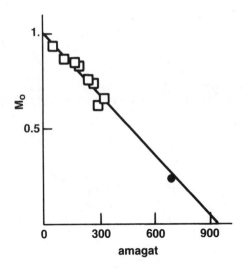

Figure 4. Density dependence of the normalized zeroth moment M_o = $G(0)/(G(0)_{\rho \to 0})$. The straight line corresponds to the theoretical prediction $G_{tr}(0)/(G_{tr}(0)_{\rho \to 0})$, the squares are the experimental data given by Buontempo et al., (1979), and the black dot is from the calculation of Steele and Birnbaum (1980). The value of ρ_o is the same as in Fig. 1.

observed cancellation effect for the normalized zeroth moment (Fig. 4) and the increasing of the normalized second moment, $-G^{(2)}(0)/G(0)$, with density (Fig. 5) are reasonably well reproduced by the theory, indicating the important role played by the translational dynamics at liquid densities.

The assumption of an isotropic pair potential, although admittedly approximate, has shown its ability to describe the main features of the absorption spectrum in liquid N_2. However, we go further and estimate the influence of anisotropic forces on the band shape. In the case of a pair potential that is weakly anisotropic, as is expected for N_2, a perturbation treatment of the correlation function should prove satisfactory in accordance with our aim here to obtain a semi-quantitative grasp of the spectrum. This type of approach has been extensively used to calculate thermodynamic quantities (Hansen and McDonald, 1976; Gubbins and Gray, 1972; Ananth et al., 1974) and spectral moments (Gray et al., 1974; Cohen, 1976). Although for dynamical properties the situation is more complex due to the presence of a time propagator in these quantities (Watts, 1971; Harris, 1971), a first order expansion can be obtained. One may proceed as follows. The pair potential V_{12} is written,

$$V_{12} = V_{12}^{iso} + V_{12}^{ani}$$

where V_{12}^{iso} is the spherical interaction and V_{12}^{ani} is the anistropic interaction. Then the first order expansion calculated in the appendix yields the following expression for $G(t)$,

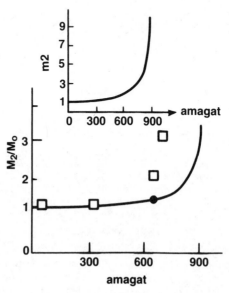

Figure 5. Density dependence of the normalized second moment M_2/M_0 $= -G^{(2)}(0)/G(0)$. The ordinate must be multiplied by $6kT/I$. The squares are the experimental data of Buontempo et al., (1979), the black dot is from the calculation of Steele and Birnbaum (1980), and the curve is computed from

$$M_2/M_0 = - [G_{tr}^{(2)}(0)/G_{tr}(0)] + 6kT/I$$

The inset shows the theoretical density dependence of the normalized second translational moment

$$m_2 = - [G_{tr}^{(2)}(0)/G_{tr}(0)]/[G_{tr}^{(2)}(0)/G_{tr}(0)]_{\rho \to 0}$$

The normalized fourth translational moment is, at the scale of the figure, indistinguishable from the second moment. The density dependence is calculated by the lattice gas model. All the theoretical curves are calculated with the parameters given in Fig. 1.

$$G(t) = \langle \sum_{i \neq j} \sum_{k \neq l} \vec{\mu}_{ij}(t) \cdot \vec{\mu}_{kl}(0) \rangle_o - \frac{1}{kT} \langle U^{ani} \sum_{i \neq j} \sum_{k \neq l} \vec{\mu}_{ij}(t) \cdot \vec{\mu}_{kl}(0) \rangle_o$$

where   (8)

$$U^{ani} = \frac{1}{2} \sum_{i \neq j} V_{ij}^{ani}$$

represents the anistropic part of the total potential and where $\langle \ldots \rangle_o$ signifies an averaging over the isotropic potential. An important consequence of the anisotropic potential is to allow correlations which previously vanished (see Eq. 4) such as

$$\langle \vec{\mu}_{12}(t) \cdot \vec{\mu}_{21}(0) \rangle, \quad \langle \vec{\mu}_{12}(t) \cdot \vec{\mu}_{23}(0) \rangle, \quad \langle \vec{\mu}_{12}(t) \cdot \vec{\mu}_{32}(0) \rangle,$$

$$\langle \vec{\mu}_{12}(t) \cdot \vec{\mu}_{34}(0) \rangle.$$

Although formal, Eq. (8) gives some insight concerning the spectral modifications due to the anisotropic forces. The perturbation term clearly has a shorter range than the zero order term because $V^{ani}(r)$ multiplies the induced dipole function in the former. Thus, in the case of the Pople potential investigated previously (Guillot and Birnbaum, 1983), the distance dependence in the perturbation term is $r_{ij}(t)^{-4} r_{ik}(0)^{-16}$ whereas it is $r_{ij}(t)^{-4} r_{ik}(0)^{-4}$ in the zero order term. Because of the shorter range of the former, one expects that it will effect the line shape preferentially at intermediate and high frequencies. Due to the presence of P_2 terms in the functional form of the Pople potential, the rotational correlation function $\langle P_2(\vec{u}_i(t) \cdot \vec{u}_i(0)) \rangle$ is involved in the correction to $G(t)$ as in the unperturbed part. With another choice of anisotropic potential, other rotational correlation functions would appear.

CONCLUDING REMARKS

The FIR absorption spectrum of N_2 is described in the present theory as the convolution of a translational spectrum and a rotational spectrum. The latter expresses the free rotations of N_2 molecules, whereas the former is characterized by two translational modes, a diffusive mode and an oscillatory mode. The translational spectrum is found to be responsible for the density dependence of the absorption spectrum at high densities and contributes significantly to the profile at all frequencies, whereas at low densitites the rotational spectrum is predominant. A recent experimental investigation (Buontempo et al., 1983) confirms this analysis. The ability of the theory to reproduce the main features of the spectrum emphasizes the important role played by a "sphericalized" pair potential (isotropic potential) in the case of slightly elongated molecules. Then the influence of the noncentral forces, which is expected to be significant in the high frequency part of the spectrum, can be estimated thanks to a perturbation expansion of the correlation function. Also induction due to overlap forces are expected to be significant at high frequencies.

Recently, two investigations by molecular dynamics (MD) simulation (Levesque et al., 1984; Steele, 1984) have pointed out that the deconvolution approximation with free rotation leads to good agreement with a full simulation of the N_2 spectrum. However, Steele (1984) noticed that the deconvolution approximation with an hindered rotation model fitted the spectrum nearly as well, although the theoretical justification for this procedure is unclear. The MD simulations confirm the strong cancellation that arises between the two- and three-body contributions in the translational spectrum, as stressed here. The anisotropy of polarizability does not appear to significantly affect the spectral shape which offers some support of our neglect of this effect (Steele and Birnbaum, 1980).

It has been reported that the FIR absoprtion spectrum of liquid N_2 is very similar to that of N_2-Ar liquid mixtures in which the anisotropic forces are small (Buontempo et al., 1971). This can be understood with the help of the present theory. During a N_2-Ar collision, the predominant induction mechanism is quadrupolar (overlap and hexadecapolar induction are much smaller). Then, in the case of a dilute mixture of N_2 in liquid Argon, Eq. (4) holds and the spectrum is the convolution of a rotational spectrum for the N_2 molecules which rotates freely and of a translational spectrum which expresses the mutual translation of the N_2-Ar pair. Because of the similarity of the polarizabilities, reduced mass, and molecular diameters of N_2 and Ar, the FIR absorption spectra of pure liquid N_2 and N_2-Ar liquid mixtures are expected to have similar shapes. The small differences between the corresponding anisotropic forces, and, in particular, the absence of quadrupolar interactions when N_2 is diluted in liquid Ar, does not change appreciably this statement.

APPENDIX. PERTURBATION THEORY OF THE CORRELATION FUNCTION

The purpose of this appendix is to develop a perturbation theory for the general correlation function,

$$\langle A(t)A(0)\rangle = \frac{1}{Z}\int dPdQe^{-\beta H(P,Q)}A(t)A(0) \tag{A.1}$$

where Z is the partition function and P, Q represent the generalized coordinates and momenta, respectively, of the system composed of N molecules. The value of the variable $A(P,Q)$ at time t is deduced from its value at time zero with the help of the time propagator,

$$A(P,Q;t) = e^{iL(P,Q)t}A(P,Q;0) \tag{A.2}$$

where L(P,Q) is the Liouvillian of the system. The basic step is to define a reference system in such a way that the Hamiltonian of the reference system, H_1, is the perturbation operator, and λ is an expansion parameter. By analogy, one can define, $L = L_0 + \lambda L_1$. Then, to develop a perturbation theory for $\langle A(t)A(0) \rangle$, one makes an expansion of the operators, $\exp(-\beta H)$ and $\exp(iLt)$, and introduces them in Eq. (A.1). This is trivial for $\exp[-\beta(H_0 + \lambda H_1)]$ and consequently for Z, and one readily obtains,

$$e^{-\beta H} = e^{-\beta H_0}(1 - \lambda \beta H_1 + O(\lambda^2) \ldots) \tag{A.3}$$

$$Z = Z_0(1 - \lambda \beta \langle H_1 \rangle_0 + O(\lambda^2) \ldots) \tag{A.4}$$

where the index o indicates an average taken over the reference system. On the contrary, the expansion of the time propagator, $\exp(iLt)$, presents some difficulties which arise from the non commutativity between L_0, L_1 and the comutator $[L_0, L_1]$. In fact this non-commutativity prevents the equality,

$$e^{iLt} = e^{iL_0 t} \times e^{iL_1 t}$$

This equality is replaced by a more complicated one due to Zassenhaus (see Magnus, 1954),

$$e^{iLt} = e^{iL_0 t + i\lambda L_1 t} = e^{iL_0 t} \times e^{i\lambda L_1 t} \times \prod_{n=2} e^{t^n C_n} \tag{A.5}$$

where the C_n coefficients can be deduced by a recurrence formula which gives, for example,

$$C_2 = -\frac{1}{2}[iL_0, i\lambda L_1]$$

$$C_3 = -\frac{1}{3}[[iL_0, i\lambda L_1], i\lambda L_1] - \frac{1}{6}[[iL_0, i\lambda L_1], iL_0]$$

$$C_4 = -\frac{1}{24}[[[iL_0, i\lambda L_1], i\lambda L_1], i\lambda L_1] + \frac{1}{4}[C_3, iL_0 + i\lambda L_1]$$

If we are interested in the first order (λ) expansion, one can show that

$$e^{iLt} = e^{iL_0 t}\left(1 + i\lambda L_1 t - \frac{1}{2}t^2[iL_0, i\lambda L_1]\right.$$

$$\left. - \sum_{n \geq 3} \frac{t^n}{n!}\left([iL_0, i\lambda L_1], (iL_0)^{n-2}\right) + O(\lambda^2) \ldots\right) \tag{A.6}$$

where the superbracket { } is defined as

$$\left\{ C_2, (iL_0)^n \right\} = [[\cdots[C_2, iL_0]iL_0\cdots iL_0]$$

Finally by introducing the expansions (A.3), (A.4) and (A.6) in Eq. (A.1), one obtains the first order expansion of the autocorrelation function, namely,

$$\langle A(t)A(0)\rangle = \langle e^{iL_0 t}A(0)A(0)\rangle_0(1+\lambda\beta\langle H_1\rangle_0) - \lambda\beta\langle H_1 e^{iL_0 t}A(0)A(0)\rangle_0$$

$$+ \lambda t\langle e^{iL_0 t}iL_1 A(0)A(0)\rangle_0 - \lambda\frac{t^2}{2}\langle e^{iL_0 t}[iL_0,iL_1]A(0)A(0)\rangle_0$$

$$-\lambda\sum_{n\geq 3}^{\infty}\frac{t^n}{n!}\langle e^{iL_0 t}\{[iL_0,iL_1],(iL_0)^{n-2}\}A(0)A(0)\rangle_0 \qquad (A.7)$$

Equation (A.7) can be written in a more compact form deduced by Harris (1971) from the perturbation formula due to Feynman, (1951). Since for any operators x and y the following relation holds,

$$e^{-x}ye^{x} = y + \{y,x\} + \cdots + \frac{1}{n!}\{y,x^n\} \qquad (A.8)$$

the following identity is obtained,

$$\int_0^1 dt e^{-xt}ye^{xt} = \int_0^1 dt(y + \{y,x\}t + \cdots + \frac{t^n}{n!}\{y,x^n\})$$

$$= y + \frac{1}{2}\{y,x\} + \cdots + \frac{1}{(n+1)!}\{y,x^n\} \qquad (A.9)$$

The introduction of the identity (A.9) in Eq. (A.7), gives the equivalent form,

$$\langle A(t)A(0)\rangle = \langle e^{iL_0 t}A(0)A(0)\rangle_0(1+\lambda\beta\langle H_1\rangle_0) - \lambda\beta\langle H_1 e^{iL_0 t}A(0)A(0)\rangle_0$$

$$+ \lambda\int_0^t dt'\langle e^{iL_0(t-t')}iL_1 e^{iL_0 t'}A(0)A(0)\rangle_0 \qquad (A.10)$$

The application of Eq. (A.7) or Eq. (A.10) to the anisotropic potential is straightforward. The total potential of the fluid is written as

$$U(R^N,\Omega^N) = U^{iso}(R^N) + U^{ani}(R^N,\Omega^N) \qquad (A.11)$$

where R^N represent the center of mass coordinates of the molecules and Ω^N their Euler angles. Then according to the above prescription one defines $H_0 = T + U^{iso}$ and $H_1 = U^{ani}$, where T is the kinetic part of the Hamiltonian, $H = H_0 + H_1$. With these definitions, the

Liouvillian L can be splitted in two parts, $L = L_0 + L_1$, namely

$$L_0 = - i \sum_j \left(\frac{\partial H_0}{\partial p_j} \frac{\partial}{\partial R_j} + \frac{\partial H_0}{\partial p_{\Omega_j}} \frac{\partial}{\partial \Omega_j} - \frac{\partial H_0}{\partial R_j} \frac{\partial}{\partial p_j} \right) \tag{A.12}$$

$$L_1 = i \sum_j \left(\frac{\partial U^{ani}}{\partial R_j} \frac{\partial}{\partial p_j} + \frac{\partial U^{ani}}{\partial \Omega_j} \frac{\partial}{\partial p_{\Omega_j}} \right) \tag{A.13}$$

Next, we introduce these definitions in Eq. (A.7), and write the correlation function $G(t)$ of the total dipole $M(R^N, \Omega^N)$,

$$G(t) = \langle \vec{M}(t) \cdot \vec{M}(0) \rangle = \langle e^{iL_0 t} \vec{M}(0) \cdot \vec{M}(0) \rangle_0$$

$$- \lambda (\beta \langle U^{ani} e^{iL_0 t} \vec{M}(0) \cdot \vec{M}(0) \rangle_0 - \frac{t^2}{2} \langle e^{iL_0 t} [iL_0, iL_1] \vec{M}(0) \cdot \vec{M}(0) \rangle_0$$

$$- \sum_{n \geq 3}^{\infty} \frac{t^n}{n!} \langle e^{iL_0 t} \{[iL_0, iL_1], (iL_0)^{n-2}\} \vec{M}(0) \cdot \vec{M}(0) \rangle_0) \tag{A.14}$$

In this relation, the average $\langle \ldots \rangle_0$ is taken over the isotropic potential, which annulus the term $\langle H_1 \rangle_0$ by construction. Nevertheless, although the term in Eq. (A7)

$$\langle e^{iL_0 t} iL_1 \vec{M}(0) \cdot \vec{M}(0) \rangle_0$$

does not figure in Eq. (A.14) by virtue of $iL_1 \vec{M}(R^N, \Omega^N; 0) = 0$, because $\vec{M}(t=0)$ is independent of the p_j's and p_{Ω_j}'s, the summation beyond this term subsists. However, at small times ($t \to 0$) the term,

$$\langle U^{ani} e^{iL_0 t} \vec{M}(0) \cdot \vec{M}(0) \rangle_0$$

is predominant in the parenthesis of Eq. (A.14) and affects significantly the intensity $G(0)$. At greater times the correlation function involved in the summation decays more rapidly with the order of the summation (the higher the value of n, the shorter the range of the correlations, due to the action of $(iL_0)^n$ and $(iL_1)^n$), and may redistribute the spectral density at high frequencies. Thus a useful first order expression for $G(t)$ can be obtained, and is given by Eq. (8). The infinite sum in Eq. (A.14) is impossible to evaluate, although it may be feasible to develop some procedure for truncating and modelling such sums (Allen and Diestler, 1980).

REFERENCES

Allen, J. W., and Dietler, D. J., 1980, J. Chem. Phys., 73:4597.
Ananth, M. S., Gubbins, K. E., and Gray, C.G., 1974, Mol. Phys., 28:1005.

Barocchi, F., Moraldi, M., and Zoppi, M., 1982, Mol. Phys., 45:1285.

Barojas, J., Levesque, D., and Quentrec, B., 1973, Phys. Rev., A7:1092.

Benson, J., Fisher, J., and Boyd, J. A., 1983, Int. J. of I.R. and M.W., 4:145.

Bosomworth, D. R., and Gush, H. P., 1965, Can. Phys., 43:751.

Bratos, S., Guillot, B., and Birnbaum, G., 1985, this volume.

Buontempo, U., Cunsolo, S., Dore, P., and Maselli, P., 1979, Mol. Phys., 38:2111.

Buontempo, U., Cunsolo, S., and Jaccuci, G., 1971, Mol. Phys., 21:381.

Buontempo, U., Cunsolo, S., Jaccuci, G., and Weis, J.J., 1975, J. Chem. Phys., 63:2570.

Buontempo, U., Maselli, P., and Nencini, L., 1983, Can. J. Phys., 61:1498.

Carneiro, K., and McTague, J. P., 1975, Phys. Rev., A11:1744.

Cheung, P. S. Y., and Powles, J. G., 1975, Mol. Phys., 30:921.

Cohen, E. R., 1976, Can. J. Phys., 54:475.

de Santis, A., Sampoli, M., Morales, P., and Signorelli, G., 1978, Mol. Phys., 35:1125.

Dore, J. C., Walford, G., and Page, D.I., 1975, Mol. Phys., 29:565.

Egelstaff, P. A., Litchinsky, D., McPherson, R., and Hahn, L., 1978, Mol. Phys., 36:445.

Feynman, R. P., 1951, Phys. Rev., 84:108.

Gray, C. G., Wang, S. S., and Gubbins, K. E., 1974, Chem. Phys. Lett., 26:610.

Gubbins, K. E., and Gray, C. G., 1972, Mol. Phys., 23:187.

Guillot, B., and Birnbaum, G., 1983, J. Chem. Phys., 79:686.

Hansen, J. P., and McDonald, I. R., 1976, in "Theory of Simple Liquids", Academic Press, ch. 6.

Harris, S., 1971, Mol. Phys., 21:933.

Heastie, R., and Martin, D.H., 1962, Can. J. Phys., 40:122.

Jones, M. C., 1970, National Bureau of Standards, Tech. Note 390, Washington, D.C.

Levesque, D., and Weis, J. J., 1975, Phys. Rev., A12:2584.

Levesque, D., Weis, J. J., Marteau, Ph., Obriot, J., and Fondére, F., to be published.

Magnus, W., 1954, Comm. Pure Appl. Math., 7:649.

Marteau, P., 1984, private communication.

Maryott, A. A., and Birnbaum, G., 1962, J. Chem., 36:10126.

Medina, F. D., and Dugas, J. M., 1981, J. Chem. Phys., 75:3252.

Mori, H., 1965, Prog. Theor. Phys. (Kyoto), 34:399.

Pederson, K. S., Carneiro, K., and Hansen, F.Y., 1982, Phys. A, 25:3335.

Poll, J. D., and Hunt, J. L, 1981, Can. J. Phys., 59:1448.

Pople, G. A., 1954, Proc. Roy. Soc. London Ser. A, 221:498.

Rastogi, A., and Lowndes, R. P., 1971, J. Phys. B, 10:495.

Sampoli, M., de Santis, A., and Nardone, N., 1981, Can. J. Phys., 59:1403.

Schoen, P. E., Cheung, P. S. Y., Jackson, D. A., and Powles, J.G., 1975, Mol. Phys., 29:1197.

Sergiescu, V., 1979, Physica, 97C:292.

Spurling, T. H., and Mason, E. A., 1967, J. Chem. Phys., 46:322.

Steele, W. A., and Birnbaum, G., 1980, J. Chem. Phys., 72:2250.

Steele, W. A., 1985, to be published.

Stone, N. W. B., and Williams, D., 1965, Mol. Phys., 10:85.

Thibeau, M., Gharbi, A., Le Duff Y., and Sergiescu, V., 1977, J. de Physique, 38:641.

Watts, R. O., 1971, Mol. Phys., 20:765.

Weis, J. J., and Levesque, D., 1976, Phys. Rev., A13:450.

MOLECULAR DYNAMICS STUDIES OF INTERACTION INDUCED ABSORPTION AND LIGHT SCATTERING IN DIATOMIC SYSTEMS

Renzo Vallauri

Istituto di Elettronica Quantistica del CNR
Via Panciatichi 56/30
I-50127 Firenze - Italy

ABSTRACT

A review of the more recent studies of spectroscopic properties of diatomic systems carried out by computer simulation is presented. The limitations imposed by the use of periodic boundary conditions are discussed in detail.

INTRODUCTION

Computer simulation is largely used at present in the study of spectroscopic properties of molecular fluids, as a unique tool to solve the classical statistical problem of many interacting particles. In particular the Molecular Dynamics (MD) method has been exploited to evaluate those correlation functions which, in the framework of the linear response theory, are directly connected with the experimental spectra. Whilst the measured frequency spectrum contains information about a global property of the system, computer simulation allows the separate study of different contributions, providing a guide to any meaningful theoretical approach. This route has been proved succesful in the analysis of collision induced light scattering (CILS) from monatomic fluids, in terms of two, three and four body contributions (Ladd et al., 1979; Balucani and Vallauri, 1979). Such an analysis made it possible to distinguish how the underlying physical processes are reflected in the measured spectrum.

In the present article we intend to give a review of the more recent studies of infrared absorption and light scattering from diatomic systems, carried out by MD technique. Some of the processes are completely interaction induced, whereas for some others the interaction induced contribution is superimposed on an allowed spectrum. We shall not deal with dipolar fluids since the long range nature of the interaction makes it difficult to separate the induced contributions: in fact little has been done in this area in the last years. On the other hand we have to include in our discussion some examples of triatomic linear molecules (e.g. CO_2) although the results of the extensive study of CS_2 are left to another paper of the present book (Madden, 1984).

The present article is organized as follows: firstly we present a general discussion of the computer simulation method, stressing its limitation in the evaluation of properties which depend on long range interactions. The following section will deal with the work done in the study of spectroscopic properties, during the last few years. For a detailed account of the previous work we refer to the Proceedings both of the 1978 Summer School on "Intermolecular Spectroscopy" and to the 1980 Conference on "Collision Induced Phenomena" (Van Kranendonk ed., 1980; Poll ed., 1980). Finally we shall summarize the results and try to give some hints for future work.

COMPUTER SIMULATION

Nowadays computer simulation is so commonly used that there is no need to describe the method in detail. However we think that some attention must be paid to the limitations of the method, because of the systematic errors which are intrinsic to the system under investigation. In particular, we shall discuss those aspects connected with the use of periodic boundary conditions. Other sources of error and limitation in the use of the MD results have been reported by Frenkel (1980); namely, the restriction on the time over which the correlation functions can be followed in a MD run, due to possible spurious correlation set up by the periodic boundary conditions, and the estimate of the statistical error due to the finite time averaging in the evaluation of both single particle or bulk properties. In the last few years other limitations of the MD method have been pointed out, mainly regarding the simulation of molecular fluids for which angular correlations are as important as center of mass correlations in determining every physical quantity.

The structure of an ensemble of N interacting particles reflects the form of the interaction potential and in this respect computer simulation can only work on model fluids, but in any case on well defined models. The comparison between experimental and calculated values of particular properties can give reliability to the computer simulation technique only if one can be sure that no spurious effects are introduced by the method. In fact angular correlations can exist that are only due to the periodic boundary conditions as discussed by Impey et al. (1981), in connection with the evaluation of the g_2 factor

$$g_2 = \frac{1}{N} \left\langle \sum_i \sum_j P_2(\cos\theta_{ij}) \right\rangle \qquad (1)$$

where θ_{ij} is the angle between the molecular axes of i and j. The argument is as follows: let us consider an arrangement of particles as illustrated in Fig.1 for linear molecules. Molecule 1' is the image of 1 in the neighboring box and is perfectly correlated with it, thus having the same orientation. An artificial orientational correlation between 1 and 3 can occur through particle 4 (chain 1 - 1' - 4 - 3) if the size of the box is small enough so that 4 and 1' are still orientationally correlated. This artifact leads to a value of g_2 which depends on the choice of a cut-off distance R_{ij} between i and j. By varying R_{ij} Impey et al. (1981) found that g_2 reaches a plateau value after which it decreases, and suggested that the plateau value gives the correct estimate of the quantity under investigation.

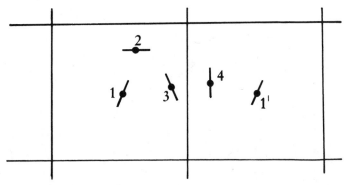

Fig.1. A particular arrangement of four linear molecules which can introduce spurious correlations. Particle 1' is the image of 1 in the neighboring box.

The case discussed above points out the limits of simulating a real system through a finite number of particles, when the process has a range of interaction comparable with the size of the box. Similar limitations were discussed in connection with the evaluation of the depolarized light scattering intensities due to the dipole induced dipole mechanism (DID) in monatomic liquids (Clarke and Woodcock, 1981). Under this approximation the measured intensity is proportional to the mean square fluctuation of the dipole moment induced in the sample:

$$S^{zz} = \frac{\sigma}{N}^6 \left\langle \sum_i \beta_i^{zz}(R_c) \sum_k \beta_k^{zz}(R_c) \right\rangle \tag{2}$$

where

$$\beta_i^{zz}(R_c) = \sum_{j \neq i} T_{ij}^{zz}(R_c) \tag{3}$$

and

$$T_{ij}^{zz}(R_c) = \left[\frac{1}{r_{ij}^3}\left(1 - 3\frac{z_{ij}z_{ij}}{r_{ij}^2}\right) \right] r_{ij} \leq R_c \tag{4}$$

r_{ij} is the distance between atoms i and j, and it has been emphasized that the field on atom i, $\beta_i(R_c)$ is evaluated neglecting the interactions with particles more distant than R_c. Since we deal with a finite system, the maximum value of R_c can be set equal to L/2 where L is the box length. We show here that if we choose $R_c = L/2$ and extend the sum in Eq.(2) over i and k to all the particles in the system (as has been done in most of the simulations), the result for S^{zz} is affected by a systematic error. In particular the four body contribution, which is present in S^{zz}, reads:

$$S_4^{zz} = \frac{\sigma}{N}^6 \left\langle \sum_i \sum_{j \neq i} \sum_{k \neq i,j} \sum_{\ell \neq k,i,j} T_{ij}^{zz}(R_c)T_{k\ell}^{zz}(R_c) \right\rangle \tag{5}$$

The evaluation of Eq.(5) implies an everage over a four-body distribution function $g_4(\vec{R}_1, \vec{R}_2, \vec{R}_3, \vec{R}_4)$. Let us suppose now that the four particles 1,2,3, and 4 are disposed as depicted in Fig.2: the quantity $T_{12}^{zz}T_{34}^{zz}$ is evaluated taking the distance R_{12} and R_{34}' indicated in Fig.2, but this term is weighted by g_4 relative to the distribution of (1,2,3,4), which is the only one accessible, and not with the proper distribution of the four particles (1,2,3,4').

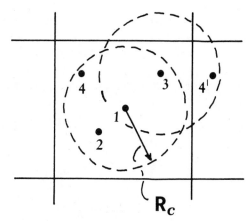

Fig.2. A disposition at four atoms in the evaluation of the local
field on particles 1 and 3. 4' is the image of particle 4.

In order to avoid this error one can proceed as follows: i) set the
cut-off radius for the evaluation of the local field to $R_c = L/2$;
ii) write Eq.(2) as

$$S^{zz} = \frac{\sigma^6}{N} \left\langle \Sigma_i \, \beta_i^{zz}(R_c)\beta_i^{zz}(R_c) + \Sigma_i \Sigma_{k \neq i} \beta_i^{zz}(R_c)\beta_k^{zz}(R_c) \right\rangle_{R_{ik} \leq L/2}$$

(6)

thus truncating the cross contribution at a distance $R_{ik} = L/2$. In
such a way, the four body term contains particles which are all in
the central box without resorting to the least image convention for
the evaluation of the local field.

Coming back to the simulation of diatomic fluids, any information concerned with infrared and Rayleigh spectra is derived, in
general, by the calculation of correlation functions of the collective orientational fluctuations:

$$C_{\ell,m}(t) = \left\langle \Sigma_i \Sigma_j \left(Y_\ell^m(\Omega_i) \right)_o \left(Y_\ell^{mx}(\Omega_j) \right)_t \right\rangle$$

(7)

where $Y_\ell^m(\Omega_i)$ is the ℓ-th order spherical harmonic and Ω_i indicates
the angular variable of molecule i. The extension of the double sum
over i and j has to be taken with particular care in order to avoid
spurious effects introduced by the use of periodic boundary conditions. Fortunately enough the angular correlations have been demonstrated to extend no farther than a first shell of neighbours so

that a reasonable cut-off can be set for the distance R_{ij} so to avoid this intrinsic limit. Nevertheless the evaluation of Eq.(7) is still affected by a statistical noise of the type discussed by Zwanzig and Ailawadi (1969) and by Frenkel (1980). According to this analysis the root mean square error of the correlation function evaluated over a finite sampling time T is:

$$\frac{<\sigma^2>^{\frac{1}{2}}}{<C(t)>} = \left[\frac{2a(t)t_c}{T}\right]^{\frac{1}{2}} \frac{<C(0)^2>}{<C(t)>} \tag{8}$$

where t_c is a correlation time defined as:

$$t_c = \frac{\int_0^\infty ds c(s)^2}{<c(0)^2>} \tag{9}$$

and $a(t) = 2$ for $t = 0$ and $a(t) = 1$ for $t \gg t_c$.

The only possible way to improve the statistics seems confined to an increase of the time T over which the averages are performed. This leads to very long MD runs (of the order of 100,000 time steps) and it is a particularly severe restriction to any reasonable budget. A possible way to improve the accuracy without resorting to longer and longer simulations was devised by Madden and Tildesley (1983). The correlation function (5) is written as:

$$\lim_{q \to 0} C_{\ell,m}(q,t) = \lim_{q \to 0} <\sum_i \sum_j \left[Y_\ell^m(\Omega_i)\exp(i\vec{q}.\vec{R}_i)\right]_o x$$
$$\left[Y_\ell^{m*}(\Omega_j)\exp(-\vec{q}.\vec{R}_j)\right]_t> \tag{10}$$

The correlation function of the Fourier transform of $C_{\ell,m}$ is then evaluated for all the smallest values of the vector $\vec{q}$, accessible to the simulation. Since $\vec{q}$ is defined by

$$\vec{q} \equiv \frac{2\pi}{L}(1_1,1_2,1_3) \tag{11}$$

where L is the box length, there are three vectors of magnitude $q_1 = 2\pi/L$, six with $q_2 = \sqrt{2}(2\pi/L)$ and four of magnitude $q_3 = \sqrt{3}(2\pi/L)$. The three values of $|q|$ are taken as an estimate of the limit as $|q|$ tends to zero. An average is then performed over the values of the corresponding correlation functions, which are considered as independent samples. Another advantage of this method is that the exponential factors in $C_{\ell,m}$ reduce the correlations at long ranges by a factor $\sin(qR_{ij})/qR_{ij}$, thereby eliminating the spurious correlations which might occur at the edge of the box.

INTERACTION INDUCED EFFECTS IN DIATOMIC SYSTEM

Light Scattering

Let us now examine what computer simulation has added to the interpretation of the role of interaction induced phenomena in systems composed of diatomic molecules.

Experimentally one can measure either the spectrum of the scattered light or the absorption coefficient both in the Rayleigh and in the Raman frequency region. In the framework of the linear response theory, the analysis of these spectra is based on the well known result that

$$I(\nu) \propto \frac{1}{2\pi} \int_0^\infty <\vec{\mu}(0).\vec{\mu}(t)> e^{i\nu t} \, dt \tag{12}$$

i.e. the frequency content is obtained as the Fourier transform of the correlation function of the total dipole moment of the sample. Both for Rayleigh and Raman scattering the dipole moment $\vec{\mu}(t)$ is written as

$$\vec{\mu}(t) = \sum_i \overleftrightarrow{\alpha_i}(t).\vec{E}_i(t) \tag{13}$$

where $\overleftrightarrow{\alpha_i}(t)$ is the proper polarizability of each molecule and $\vec{E}_i(t)$ is the external field acting on it. The sum is over all the particles of the sample. In the present context we indicate by "proper polarizability" the polarizability of a molecule imbedded in the field of all the other molecules, so that the bare contribution is corrected for the influence of the local field. Such an influence has been evaluated by resorting to several physical assumptions: i) the local field is the sum of pair terms, ii) multipole effects give the overwhelming contribution, and iii) quantum mechanical effects can be taken into account in a perturbative scheme of classical mechanics framework. Pointed brackets have now the meaning of statistical averages over a suitable ensemble which is the microcanonical one if use is made of the molecular dynamics method. Under these assumptions the polarizability $\overleftrightarrow{\alpha_i}(t)$ is written as

$$\overleftrightarrow{\alpha_i} = \overleftrightarrow{\alpha_i}^{(o)}(t) + \overleftrightarrow{\alpha_i}^{(o)}.\sum_{j \neq i} \overleftrightarrow{T}_{ij}(t).\overleftrightarrow{\alpha_i}^{(o)}(t) =$$
$$= \overleftrightarrow{\alpha_i}^{(o)}(t) + \overleftrightarrow{\Delta\alpha_i} \tag{14}$$

T_{ij} is the DID tensor defined in Eq.(4). Effects of the second order DID interaction have been discussed (Kielich, 1982) and found not negligible by an approximate calculation (Bancewicz, 1984), but no estimate of their importance in diatomic fluids have been given by MD method.

The scatterd light can be analyzed in terms of the two components of the electric field, parallel and perpendicular to the linearly polarized incident field. Both components are influenced by the collisional polarizability $\overleftrightarrow{\Delta\alpha_i}$ in two ways: the first is a static effect by which an effective polarizability, which determines the total scattering intensity, can be defined; the second effect is a dynamical one and reflects the time dependence of $\overleftrightarrow{\Delta\alpha_i}(t)$. In the absence of interaction induced effects, the scattering of the light is determined by the fluctuation of the total polarizability

$$\overleftrightarrow{\alpha}^{(o)}(t) = \sum_i \overleftrightarrow{\alpha}_i^{(o)}(t) = \sum_i \{ \alpha\overleftrightarrow{I} + \frac{2}{3}\gamma\overleftrightarrow{Q}_i(t) \} \tag{15}$$

where α is the mean polarizability of a molecule and is equal to $1/3(\alpha_{//} + \alpha_{\perp})$ whereas γ is the anisotropic part $\alpha_{//} - \alpha_{\perp}$. The tensor $\overleftrightarrow{Q}_i(t)$ is defined by

$$\overleftrightarrow{Q}_i = \frac{1}{2}(3\vec{u}_i\vec{u}_i - \overleftrightarrow{I}) \tag{16}$$

where $\vec{u}_i$ is the unit vector along the intermolecular axis. Thus the polarized scattering is due to the number density fluctuation in the infinitesimal scattering volume, whereas the depolarized component of the Rayleigh spectrum reflects the time dependence of the fluctuations of the collective angular variable

$$\overleftrightarrow{Q}(t) = \sum_i \overleftrightarrow{Q}_i(t) \tag{17}$$

On the other hand, the interaction induced polarizability as written in Eq.(14) depends both on the angular variable $Q_i(t)$ as well as on the distance between two molecules. If one wants to distinguish the effect of the time dependence of the interaction induced part it is useful to perform a projection of the induced polarizability over the collective variable $\overleftrightarrow{Q}(t)$, (Frenkel and McTague, 1980). This projection leads to a definition of the anisotropic polarizability

$$\overleftrightarrow{\alpha}_{anis} = \frac{2}{3}\gamma_{eff}\overleftrightarrow{Q}(t) + \overleftrightarrow{\Delta\alpha}_{CI}^{(2)}(t) \tag{18}$$

where

$$\gamma_{eff} = \gamma + \frac{3}{2}\frac{\langle Q(0)\Delta\alpha(0)\rangle}{\langle Q(0)Q(0)\rangle} \tag{19}$$

464

Similarly an effective isotropic polarizability can be defined as

$$\alpha_{eff} = \alpha + \frac{1}{N} < \Delta\alpha(0) > \qquad (20)$$

The effective polarizabilities account for the interaction induced contribution as a static effect. The time dependent part, on the other hand, can modify both the integrated intensity and the shape of the spectrum. In evaluating the spectrum (for example for the depolarized component) it is now important to know whether it can be separated into two distinct parts: the first due to the fluctuations of the orientational correlations and the second one ruled by the interaction induced term. Frenkel and McTague (1980) have shown that this simple picture by no means is valid for a large variety

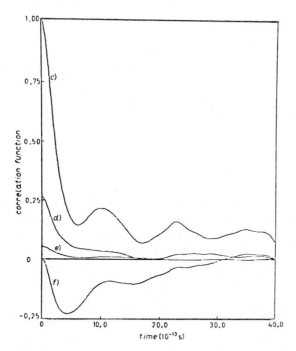

Fig.3. Different contributions to the correlation function of the polarizability for Cl_2: (c) the total anisotropic part; (d) collision induced anisotropic term; (e) collision induced isotropic part; (f) cross correlation between orientational and collision induced terms (Frenkel 1980)

465

of diatomic fluids (N_2, O_2, Cl_2) as well as for fluids composed of linear molecules such as CO_2. They found that a cross contribution between the two terms is important, leading to the conclusion that any attempt of separating the interaction induced contribution from the total spectrum by this simplifying assumption is misleading.

The computer simulation was carried out using 108 molecules in a standard way. Very long runs were performed in order to reduce the statistical noise. A typical result is shown in Fig.3 for Cl_2. The usefulness of the MD method is evident: it enabled the separate study of different contributions, showing in particular that the purely interaction induced correlation function decays to zero on the same time scale as the orientational fluctuations. No attempt has been made untill now to study separately the contributions of the two, three and four body terms or to analyse in more detail the influence of the cut-off in the interaction either on the correlation functions or, more simply, on the integrated intensities.

The most recent study of the light scattering properties of homonuclear diatomics has been performed by Ladanyi (1983), who considered the effect of a distributed polarizability model (Keyes and Ladanyi , 1977), according to which the molecule is not a point polarizable object but the polarization is distributed on the single atoms (site-site model). For homonuclear diatomics it can be demonstrated that the model leads to an interaction tensor which reads

$$\overset{\leftrightarrow}{D}_{ij} = \frac{1}{4} \ \sum_{\alpha\beta} \overset{\leftrightarrow}{T}_{i\alpha,j\beta} \tag{21}$$

where the sum runs over the two atoms. The effect is found to be quantitatively significant for CO_2, whereas in other case studied, namely O_2, the difference between the two models is irrelevant. About the time scale separation between orientational and collision induced contributions, no major differences are found by Ladanyi (1983) between the two models, except for the fact that collision induced correlation time in the site-site model is weakly density dependent, leading to an increase in the time scale separation. In general, the effective polarizabilities show a stronger dependence on density than on temperature: the difference between the two models diminishes with increasing the temperature, whereas they show an opposite beheviour with increasing density.

Despite the accurate study of the consequences of the two models, no comparison has been made with the experimental data which might support one against the other. We think that accurate measurements

of the light scattering spectra should be undertaken, both by varying the density at constant temperature and vice versa in order to
confirm the validity of the theoretical predictions.

Infrared Absorption

Infrared absorption by homonuclear diatomic fluids is attributed to the dipole moment induced on a molecule by the quadrupole
moment of the neighbouring particles. This induction mechanism has
been proved successful in the case of N_2 as far as the line shape
is concerned and was the subject of an early computer simulation
(Buontempo et al. 1975).

The dipole moment induced in the sample is written as

$$\vec{\mu}(t) = \sum_i \overleftrightarrow{\alpha}_i . T_{ij}^{(3)} : \overleftrightarrow{\theta}_j \tag{22}$$

where $T_{ij}^{(3)}$ is the third rank tensor which gives the electric field
on molecule i produced by the quadrupole moment $\overleftrightarrow{\theta}_j$ of molecule j,
and

$$\overleftrightarrow{\theta}_j = \tfrac{1}{2}\theta_o \overleftrightarrow{Q}_j \tag{23}$$

Little effort has been devoted in recent years to clarify the
effect of different contributions to the correlation function of
Eq.(22), (i.e. from two and three body terms). Computer simulation
has been carried out to study the quadrupole induced dipole infrared
absorption around the Raman line (near infrared absorption or near
IR). In this case, the dipole moment is written as

$$\vec{\mu}(t) = \sum_i \sum_{j \neq i} (\overleftrightarrow{\alpha}_i' . T_{ij}^{(3)} : \overleftrightarrow{\theta}_j + \overleftrightarrow{\alpha}_j . T_{ji}^{(3)} : \overleftrightarrow{\theta}_i') q_i \tag{24}$$

where the primes indicate the derivative with respect to the normal
coordinate q_i. Two distinct contributions are present in Eq.(24):
the first one, $\alpha_i' . T_{ij}^{(3)} : \overleftrightarrow{\theta}_j$ accounts for the effect of the local field
$T_{ij}^{(3)} : \overleftrightarrow{\theta}_j$ which induces a dipole moment modulated at the Raman frequency through the derivative of the polarizability $\overleftrightarrow{\alpha}_i'$; the second
one accounts for the dipole moment modulated by the component of the
local field $T_{ji}^{(3)} : \overleftrightarrow{\theta}_i'$, oscillating at the Raman frequency. Under the
reasonable assumption of statistical independence of the vibrational
motion of different molecules, the IR spectrum turns out to be proportional to the Fourier transform of a single particle correlation
function $\vec{\mu}_i(t)$, which can be evaluated with sufficient accuracy by
averaging over some 12,000 ÷ 15,000 time steps. If one separate the

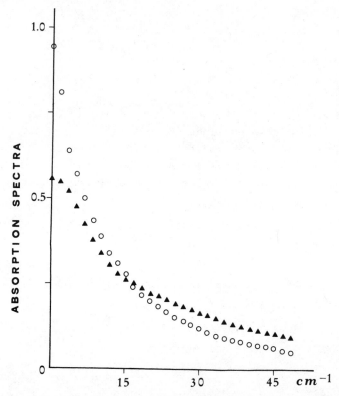

Fig. 4. Near IR spectra of liquid Cl_2 at T∿ 240°K : (▲ ▲ ▲ ▲) experimental data ; (o o o o) computer simulation results for
the quadrupole induced dipole mechanism. The spectra are
normalized to unit area. (Murthy et al., 1982)

isotropic and anisotropic parts of $\overset{\leftrightarrow}{\alpha}$, making use of Eqs.(15) and (16)
the expression for $\vec{\mu}_i(t)$ reads

$$\vec{\mu}_i(t) = \tfrac{1}{2}\Theta_o\alpha \sum_{j \neq i} \{ \frac{\alpha'}{\alpha}[^{ij}\vec{m}^{(0,2)}(t) + \frac{\gamma'}{3\alpha'}{}^{ij}\vec{m}^{(2,2)}(t)] +$$

$$\frac{\Theta'_o}{\Theta_o}[^{ji}\vec{m}^{(0,2)}(t) + \frac{\gamma'}{3\alpha'}{}^{ji}\vec{m}^{(2,2)}(t)] \} \qquad (25)$$

where

$$ij \overrightarrow{m}(0,2) = T^{(3)}_{ij} : \overleftrightarrow{Q}_j \tag{26a}$$

$$ij \overrightarrow{m}(2,2) = \overleftrightarrow{Q}_i \cdot T^{(3)}_{ij} : \overleftrightarrow{Q}_j \tag{26b}$$

$$ji \overrightarrow{m}(0,2) = T^{(3)}_{ji} : \overleftrightarrow{Q} \tag{26c}$$

$$ji \overrightarrow{m}(2,2) = \overleftrightarrow{Q}_j \cdot T^{(3)}_{ji} : \overleftrightarrow{Q}_i \tag{26d}$$

Recently Murthy et al. (1982) have evaluated the correlation function of eq.(25) for the two models of liquid Cl_2 and compared these with the experimental findings. One of the Cl_2 models is the two Lennard-Jones centers implemented by Singer et al. (1977), the second one has in addition a quadrupolar interaction. The relative merits of the two models have been discussed (Murthy et al., 1983); from our point of view no big changes are found for the correlation functions under examination, due to the fact that the major difference between the two models is reflected in the structural properties, leaving the dynamical ones virtually unchanged.

The agreement with the experimental data is not particularly good, as shown in Fig.4.

Apart from possible errors introduced in the extraction of the $^{35}Cl_2$ contribution from the rough spectrum as shown in Fig.5, the comparison between the computer simulation and the experimental spectrum suggests that short range induction mechanisms can be present which can account for the high frequency part of the spectrum.

The correlation function of Eq.(25) contains two and three body contributions. In Table I we report the values at $t = 0$ of the various terms normalized to the value of $<ij\overrightarrow{m}(0,2)(0) \cdot ij\overrightarrow{m}(0,2)(0)>$. In parentheses is reported the two body contribution which shows that the three body term is very small, at least for those terms which contribute to the total correlation function (namely $(0,2)(0,2)$ and $(2,2)(2,2)$. A larger cancellation between two and three body contributions is present in the mixed terms (i.e. $(0,2)(2,0)$); in fact Steele and Birnbaum (1980) evaluated, by an approximate method, the three body contribution to the far IR absorption of N_2 and O_2 and found that in this case the cancellation effect is even more important. A recent computer simulation of the near IR absorption

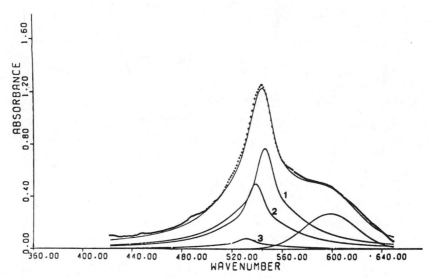

Fig. 5. The experimental near IR absorption spectra ($\cdot$ $\cdot$ $\cdot$ $\cdot$) and its bands: (1) $^{35}Cl_2$; (2) $^{35}Cl_2$$^{37}Cl_2$; (3) $^{37}Cl_2$ respectively. (Murthy et al.,1982).

Table 1. Normalized contributions to the total intensity of the quadrupole induced dipole near infrared absorption in Cl_2

a \ b	(0,2)(0,2)	(0,2)(2,2)	(2,2)(0,2)	(2,2)(2,2)
(i,j)(i,k)	1.0(1.0)	-0.04(-0.13)		1.93(2.02)
(j,i)(k,i)	0.79(1.05)	-0.06(-0.13)		2.03(2.02)
(i,j)(k,i)	-0.17(-0.13)	-0.34(-0.37)	-0.31(-0.37)	-1.99(-2.08)

a) labels of the pair of particles
b) labels of the particular dipole moment contribution as indicated in Eqs. (26a÷d) (Murthy et al.,1984)

in CS_2 performed by Madden and Tildesley (1983) is in agreement
with the present results: they also demonstrated that the time
evolution of the two body correlation function is very close to
that of the total. This supports the hypothesis that angular correlations play a minor role in the overall effect. The small cancellation of the three body terms seems a confirmation that, even for
Cl_2 angular correlation between three molecules can be disregarded.

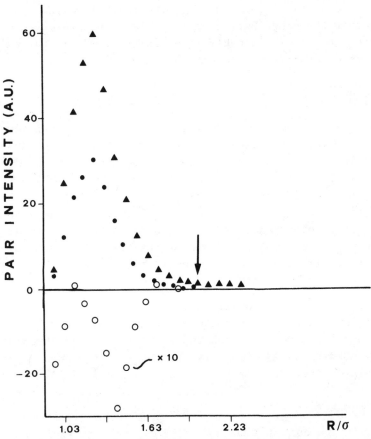

Fig. 6 Distance dependence of the pair contribution to the functions:
$<{}^{ij\vec{}}_m(0,2)(0).{}^{ij\vec{}}_m(0,2)(0)>$(triangles);$<{}^{ij\vec{}}_m(2,2)(0).{}^{ij\vec{}}_m(2,2)(0)>$
(dots);$<{}^{ij\vec{}}_m(0,2)(0).{}^{ij\vec{}}_m(2,2)(0)>$ (open circles); for Cl_2 and
quadrupole induced dipole mechanism. The arrow indicates the
distance at which the integrated intensities reach 98% of
their values (Murthy et al.,1984).

As a final remark we wish to point out that in the case of quadrupole induced dipole mechanism the finite size of the computer simulated system does not limit the estimate of the effect. As already noted the major contribution to the correlation function of Eq.(25) comes from the two body part: we can therefore study how molecules at a given distance from a central one contribute to the value of different terms in the correlation function. In Fig.6 is reported the result of this analysis for the following terms: $<^i j_m^\rightarrow(0,2)_{(0)} \cdot ^i j_m^\rightarrow(0,2)_{(0)}>$, $<^i j_m^\rightarrow(2,2)_{(0)} \cdot ^i j_m^\rightarrow(2,2)_{(0)}>$ and the cross contribution $<^i j_m^\rightarrow(0,2)_{(0)} \cdot ^i j_m^\rightarrow(2,2)_{(0)}>$, (Murthy et al., 1984). It appears that the contribution of molecules whose relative distance is greater than 2.5 σ is negligible; in fact, 98% of the pair intensity is taken at distances of the order of 2 σ.

CONCLUSION

In this paper we tried to illustrate what computer simulation has added to the understanding of the effect of the various processes ruling the spectroscopic properties of homonuclear diatomic systems. We have discussed the more recent results in the field. Particular attention has been devoted to the problem of the simulation of an infinite system by a finite number of molecules when the physical process under examination has a range of interaction of the order or greater than half of the box length. The DID mechanism for the light scattering process is a well known but still not completely solved example.

For molecular fluids all interaction mechanisms involve also the rotational degree of freedom of the particles and we have pointed out that spurious effects can be introduced through periodic boundary conditions. Fortunately the range of distances over which the angular correlations are important is sufficiently short, not extending much beyond a first shell of neighbours. We have shown this in connection with the study of near IR absorption in Chlorine.

We wish to conclude the paper by giving some example of what could be usefully done by computer simulation in order to gain a deeper insight into the process responsible for the interaction induced part to the spectroscopic properties of diatomic fluids.

A first suggestion is to study separately the many body contribution to the quadrupole induced dipole mechanism in analogy with the DID analysis in monoatomic systems. This calculation in the case of CS_2 has been proved useful to assess the reliability of simplifying assumptions.

472

Computer simulation should then help in describing the relative motion of a pair of molecules which is the ruling dynamics of interaction induced effects. The extension of the analysis performed in monatomic fluids (Haan, 1979; Balucani and Vallauri, 1980), to molecular ones is, of course, considerably more intricate, involving many variables and should somewhat be simplified. As a first attempt one might understand how to extend the Smoluchoski equation (Haan, 1979), to include rotational variables. In particular, the importance of translational-rotational coupling should be made clear.

The improvement achieved in recent years in the field of interaction potential models for molecular fluids should stimulate comparison between computer simulation and experiments, which at present has been carried out only for a few systems.

REFERENCES

Balucani U., and Vallauri R., 1979, Collision induced scattering at intermediate densities. I. The integrated density. II. The second frequency moment, Mol.Phys. 38: 1099; 1115.

Balucani U., and Vallauri R., 1980, Relative motions in atomic fluids: a molecular dynamics investigation, Physica 102 A: 70.

Bancewicz T., 1983, Rayleigh scattering by liquids composed of interacting anisotropic molecules. Spherical tensor approach within the second order approximation of the DID model, Mol. Phys. 50: 173.

Buontempo U., Cunsolo S., Jacucci G., and Weiss J.J., 1975, The far infrared absorption spectrum of N_2 in the gas and liquid phases. J.Chem.Phys. 63: 2570.

Clarke J.H.R. and Woodcock L.V., 1981, Boundary problems in the calculation of the light scattering intensities from liquids using computer simulation, Chem.Phys.Letters 78: 121.

Frenkel D., 1980, Intermolecular spectroscopy and computer simulation, in: "Intermolecular spectroscopy and dynamical properties of dense systems", J.Van Kranendonk Ed., North Holland Publ. Company, Amsterdam, New York, Oxford.

Frenkel D., and McTague J.P., 1980, Molecular dynamics studies of orientational and collision-induced light scattering in molecular fluids, J.Chem.Phys. 72: 2801.

Haan S., 1979, Dynamic behaviour of pairs of atoms in simple liquids, Phys.Rev. 20: 2516.

Impey R.W., Madden P.A., and Tildesley D., 1981, On the calculation of the orientational correlation parameter g_2, Mol.Phys. 44: 1319.

Keyes T., and Ladanyi B.M., 1977, The role of local fields and interparticle pair correlations in light scattering by dense fluids. IV. Removal of the point polarizability approximation. Mol.Phys. 33: 1271.

Kielich S., 1982, Coherent light scattering by interacting anisotropic molecules with variable dipolar polarizability, J.Phys. 43: 1749.

Ladd A.J., Litovitz T.A., and Montrose C.J., 1979, Molecular dynamics studies of depolarized light scattering from argon at various fluid densities, J.Chem.Phys. 71: 4242.

Ladanyi B.M., 1983, Molecular dynamics study of Rayleigh light scattering from molecular fluids, J.Chem.Phys. 78: 2189.

Madden P.A., and Tildesley D., 1983, The interaction-induced spectra of liquid CS_2: a computer simulation study, Mol.Phys. 49: 193.

Madden P.A., 1984, This volume.

Murthy C.S., Singer K., Vallauri R., Tindle J.J., Steele D., 1982, Interaction-induced infrared absorption in liquid Cl_2: an experimental and molecular dynamics investigation, Chem.Phys. Letters 90: 95.

Murthy C.S., Singer K., and Vallauri R., 1983, Computer simulation of liquid Chlorine, Mol.Phys. 49: 803.

Murthy C.S., Singer K., and Vallauri R., 1984, unpublished results.

Poll J.D., Ed., 1980, Collision induced phenomena: absorption, light scattering and static properties, Can.J.Phys. 59: special issue.

Singer K., Taylor A., Singer J.V.L., 1977, Thermodynamic and structural properties of liquid modelled by "2-Lennard-Jones centers" pair potential, Mol.Phys. 33: 1757.

Steele W.A., and Birnbaum G., 1980, Molecular calculations of moments of the induced spectra for N_2, O_2 and CO_2. J.Chem.Phys. 72: 2250.

Van Kranendonk J., 1980,"Intermolecular spectroscopy and dynamical properties of dense systems",North Holland Publ.Company, Amsterdam, New York, Oxford.

Zwanzig R., and Ailawadi N.K., 1969, Statistical error due to finite time averaging in computer experiments, Phys.Rev. 182:280

INTERACTION INDUCED LIGHT SCATTERING

FROM TETRAHEDRAL MOLECULES

M. Neumann and H.A. Posch

Institut für Experimentalphysik der Universität Wien
Strudlhofgasse 4
A-1090 Vienna, Austria

ABSTRACT

Collision induced light scattering from tetrahedral molecules
is an highly collective N-body process and depends - in principle -
on the full charge distribution of the molecules and, consequently,
on the full orientation dependent pair potentials and induced pair
polarizabilities. The pair potential is usually treated in terms
of many-center Lennard-Jones potentials. For the calculation of the
collision induced pair polarizabilities an interacting point atom
polarizability model is introduced, the properties of which are
discussed. It may be cast into a form most suitable for molecular
dynamics simulations of condensed phases. As an illustration of
the applicability of these models a computer simulation for dense
fluids resembling CF_4 (for two different densities) and CCl_4 are
presented.

THE PROBLEM

Since the early days of collision induced (CI) light scattering (Levine and Birnbaum, 1968) considerable attention has been
awarded to fluid systems composed of tetrahedral molecules. Studies
on compressed gaseous states of methane have been carried out by
Lallemand (1970), Barocchi and McTague (1974, 1975) and Prengel
and Gornall (1976), whereas CF_4 has been treated by Shelton and
Tabisz (1975) and Shelton et al. (1975). For more recent work on
these gases the results by Barocchi et al. (1977), Shelton et
al. (1982) and Gharbi and Le Duff (1977, 1980, 1981) are to be
mentioned. Early light scattering studies from the respective
liquids have been performed by Leite et al. (1965), Gabelnick and

Strauss (1968) and Gornall et al. (1970). Later work is discussed in the articles by Bucaro and Litovitz (1971), Ho and Tabisz (1973), and Howard-Lock and Taylor (1974). The reason for this interest derives from the fact that the polarizability tensor of noninteracting molecules of this type is spherical and that – to lowest order – the mechanism for CI scattering is very similar to that of noble gas fluids which serve as reference fluids for the formulation of the theory.

Two body CI light scattering from atomic gases at low densities is now well understood (Frommhold, 1981, 1984). The classical dipole-induced dipole (DID) model for the polarizability tensor of an interacting particle pair appropriately corrected for atomic wave function overlap (electron overlap, EO) has been identified as the basic mechanism in this case leading to very close agreement between experiment and theory. Even at large fluid densities such as liquid argon, for which three- and four particle correlations contribute significantly, reasonable agreement between experiment and molecular dynamics simulations has been obtained (Ladd et al.,1979; Varshneya et al., 1981).

At first sight the CI spectra of tetrahedral molecular fluids look similar to those of the noble gases. A closer examination, however, reveals differences, which are significant particulary at high frequency shifts, and which are due to the particular electric charge distribution within the molecules (Buckingham and Tabisz, 1977, 1978). For the case of two body collision induced spectra at low gas densities these experimental differences may be summarized as follows (Barocchi et al., 1977; Shelton and Tabisz, 1980; Posch, 1979, 1980, 1982):

a) At large frequency shifts the observed spectral density exceeds that predicted by the DID model. This disagreement cannot be removed by the application of EO-corrections which would cause the theoretical spectrum to be even smaller in that frequency range. As a consequence the total intensity ratio $I/I_{DID} > 1$.

b) The polarization ratio is frequency dependent and larger than the DID-value 4/3. This signals the involvement of interaction tensors of rank higher than 2.

Theoretically, Buckingham and Tabisz (1977, 1978) have suggested a point multipole expansion for the induced pair polarizability

$$\overset{\leftrightarrow}{\alpha}(\vec{r},\vec{\Omega}_1,\vec{\Omega}_2) = \overset{\leftrightarrow}{\alpha}_{DID}(\vec{r}) + \overset{\leftrightarrow}{\alpha}_{DQ}(\vec{r},\vec{\Omega}_1,\vec{\Omega}_2) + \overset{\leftrightarrow}{\alpha}_{DO}(\vec{r},\vec{\Omega}_1,\vec{\Omega}_2) + \ldots \qquad (1.1)$$

where $\vec{r} = |r,\vec{\Omega}|$ denotes the center of mass separation vector and $\vec{\Omega}_1, \vec{\Omega}_2$ the orientation of the interacting molecules. The first and most prominent term is the DID-effect, and the remaining terms constitute the collision induced rotational Raman effect (CIRR). The terms labelled DQ, DO etc. describe the response of a molecule in field gradients of ascending order and are characterized by the dipole quadrupole polarizability $\overset{\leftrightarrow}{A}{}^{(3)}$, dipole octopole polarizability $\overset{\leftrightarrow}{E}{}^{(4)}$, etc. This theory has been reformulated in terms of spherical coordinates and correlation functions (Posch, 1979, 1980, 1982) and has been tested for a small number of molecular gases of tetrahedral (T_d) and octahedral (O_h) point group symmetry (Buckingham and Tabisz, 1978; Shelton and Tabisz, 1980; Posch, 1982). A more detailed account is contained in the article by G.C.Tabisz in this volume.

From this work it may be concluded that the expansion Eq.(1.1) provides a good description for the CI spectral density of gaseous methane over a very large range of frequency shifts. For the heavier molecular gases, however, the convergence of this expansion for the pair polarizability is poor and necessitates the inclusion of terms of higher order than the DQ- or DO-effects for an explanation of the high frequency wings.

An alternative way of calculating the induced pair polarizability is the substitution of a polarizability model for each of the two interacting molecules by which the molecular shape and hence their spatial charge distribution is explicitly taken into account. One of the most promising models of this type is the interacting point atom polarizability (PAP) approximation which has been introduced into the literature under a variety of names (Applequist et al.,1972; Applequist, 1977; Ladanyi and Keyes, 1979; Prasad and Nafie, 1979). It consists in a replacement of the polarizable charge distribution of a molecule by point polarizabilities located at the position of the atoms forming the molecule. In an electric field all point polarizabilities within a molecule are dynamically coupled to infinite order through DID interactions. In this formulation the model has been used for the calculation of permanent molecular polarizabilities (Applequist et al., 1972; Applequist, 1977; Ladanyi and Keyes, 1979), dipole multipole polarizabilities (Applequist, 1977; Prasad and Nafie, 1979) and Raman optical activity parameters (Prasad and Nafie, 1979).

For the calculation of the induced pair polarizability an additional coupling between atoms of different molecules must be introduced. In contrast to the intramolecular coupling mentioned previously, the intermolecular interaction is only of first order in the DID-approximation. Through this feature the desirable property of pairwise additivity for the polarizability of a macroscopic sample is retained. It is demonstrated in the following that this model may be cast into a form which is most suitable for molecular dynamics simulations of light scattering from molecular fluids. This is true not only for the globular molecules of tetrahedral (or octahedral) symmetry of concern for this paper, but also for stiff molecules of any shape (Keyes and Ladanyi, 1977). This approach has been used recently by B.Ladanyi (1983) in her molecular dynamics study of Rayleigh light scattering from fluids of homonuclear diatomic.

Another problem entering the analysis of CI spectra of molecular fluids is that of the angle dependent pair potential. The most suitable and widely used potential for MD simulations is a many center Lennard Jones potential. Such a potential is also used for the computer simulations reported below, where the potential parameters are adjusted to reproduce the second virial coefficients over the whole range of temperatures. For the evaluation of the spectra or moments from the point multipole expansion method based on Eq.(1.1), effective spherical potentials are frequently used (Buckingham and Tabisz, 1977, 1978; Shelton and Tabisz, 1980; Posch, 1979, 1980, 1982). It will be argued in the following that such a potential is most easily obtained from the many center LJ-potential by angle averaging of the respective Boltzmann factor. This approach has been tested for a number of tetrahedral and octahedral molecules (Posch, 1982; Treitl et al., 1984) and yields theoretical zeroth moments for CI two-body scattering in dilute gases in close agreement with experimental data.

For the atomic liquids such as argon, Mori-type theories have been formulated by Madden (1977, 1978) and Guillot et al.(1980) permitting a semi-quantitative description of collision induced spectra. No such theory is available at present for the calculation of CI-line shapes and intensities of dense molecular fluids. One has to rely on computer simulations of the N-body dynamics for that purpose. Such a molecular dynamics simulation is presented in this paper. Two different states resembling carbon tetrafluoride (CF_4) and one state of carbon tetrachloride (CCl_4) close to the triple point have been studied. Both the pure DID - and the interacting PAP-models have been tested. A comparison of these results with the available experimental data is presented below.

THE PAP-MODEL FOR MOLECULES

The interacting point atom polarizability model has been originally used for the calculation of optical properties of single molecules (Applequist et al., 1972; Applequist, 1977; Ladanyi and Keyes, 1979). It consists in a replacement of the molecular charge distribution by isotropic point polarizabilities, which are located at the atomic sites and interact dynamically through the DID-interaction to all orders. For further reference we shall briefly review the essentials of this theory.

We consider an m-atomic molecule in a possibly inhomogenous electric field. Let $\vec{E}_i$ denote this field at the location $\vec{r}_i$ of atom i, to which a point polarizability $\alpha_i^0 \overleftrightarrow{1}$ has been assigned. The dipole moment $\vec{\mu}_i$ induced in this atom due to the field and the interaction with all other point polarizabilities is given by

$$\vec{\mu}_i = \alpha_i^0 \left[\vec{E}_i + \sum_{j \neq i}^m \overleftrightarrow{T}_{ij} \cdot \vec{\mu}_j \right] , \qquad (2.1)$$

where

$$\overleftrightarrow{T}_{ij} \equiv \overleftrightarrow{T}(\vec{r}_{ij}) = \frac{3}{r_{ij}^3} \left(\frac{\vec{r}_{ij} \vec{r}_{ij}}{r_{ij}^2} - \frac{1}{3} \overleftrightarrow{1} \right) \qquad (2.2)$$

is the dipole interaction tensor acting along

$$\vec{r}_{ij} = \vec{r}_i - \vec{r}_j \qquad (2.3)$$

The sum in Eq.(2.1) is over all other atoms $j \neq i$ of the molecule. In block vector notation

$$\vec{\mu} = \begin{bmatrix} \vec{\mu}_1 \\ \vec{\mu}_2 \\ \vdots \\ \vec{\mu}_m \end{bmatrix} , \quad \vec{E} = \begin{bmatrix} \vec{E}_1 \\ \vec{E}_2 \\ \vdots \\ \vec{E}_m \end{bmatrix} ; \quad \overleftrightarrow{B} = \begin{bmatrix} \overleftrightarrow{B}_{11} \cdots \overleftrightarrow{B}_{1m} \\ \vdots \qquad \vdots \\ \overleftrightarrow{B}_{m1} \cdots \overleftrightarrow{B}_{mm} \end{bmatrix} \qquad (2.4)$$

with tensor components

$$\overleftrightarrow{B}_{ij} = (\alpha_i^0)^{-1} \overleftrightarrow{1} \delta_{ij} - \overleftrightarrow{T}_{ij} (1 - \delta_{ij}), \qquad (2.5)$$

the Eq.(2.1) may be written as

$$\overleftrightarrow{B} \cdot \vec{\mu} = \vec{E} . \qquad (2.6)$$

Eq.(2.6) represents a set of 3m linear equations, which may be solved according to

$$\vec{\mu} = \overleftrightarrow{A} \cdot \vec{E} , \qquad (2.7)$$

with

$$\overset{\leftrightarrow}{B}{}^{-1} = \overset{\leftrightarrow}{A} = \begin{bmatrix} \overset{\leftrightarrow}{A}_{11} & \cdots & \overset{\leftrightarrow}{A}_{1m} \\ \vdots & & \vdots \\ \overset{\leftrightarrow}{A}_{m1} & \cdots & \overset{\leftrightarrow}{A}_{mm} \end{bmatrix} . \tag{2.8}$$

In real space Eq.(2.7) assumes the form

$$\vec{\mu}_i = \sum_{j=1}^{m} \overset{\leftrightarrow}{A}_{ij} \cdot \vec{E}_j . \tag{2.9}$$

Our initial problem of calculating $\vec{\mu}_i$ for all atoms i of the molecule has thus been reduced to a matrix inversion of a 3m x 3m matrix $\overset{\leftrightarrow}{B}$.

The matrix $\overset{\leftrightarrow}{A}$ is called the relay matrix. Its physical interpretation is readily seen from Eq.(2.9): if a field $\vec{E}_j$ is applied at the position of j, which vanishes everywhere else, the induced dipole at the location of atom i is given by $\overset{\leftrightarrow}{A}_{ij} \cdot \vec{E}_j$. If the field does not vanish at the other m-1 atomic sites, the full dipolar response at i is simply obtained by adding the corresponding m-1 partial responses. As is obvious from Eqs.(2.8) and (2.5), $\overset{\leftrightarrow}{A}_{ij}$ is a molecular property. It contains all direct and mediated interactions between the sites i and j. It is a sum of all possible chains of dipole tensors such as $\alpha_i^o \overset{\leftrightarrow}{T}_{ik} \cdot \alpha_k^o \cdot \overset{\leftrightarrow}{T}_{kl} \; \alpha_1^o \ldots \alpha_m^o \cdot \overset{\leftrightarrow}{T}_{mj} \; \alpha_j^o$ starting at j and ending at i. Since the dipole tensor $T_{ij,\alpha\beta}$ is symmetric with respect to an interchange of both the sites i,j and the components α, β, inverting the direction of any chain of $\overset{\leftrightarrow}{A}_{ij}$ yields another chain contributing to $\overset{\leftrightarrow}{A}_{ji}^T$, where T denotes the transposed matrix. Thus,

$$\overset{\leftrightarrow}{A}_{ij} = \overset{\leftrightarrow}{A}_{ji}^T \tag{2.10}$$

For the special case of a constant external electric field, $\vec{E}_i = \vec{E}_o$, Eq.(2.9) may be rewritten as

$$\vec{\mu}_i = \overset{\leftrightarrow}{\tilde{\alpha}}_i \cdot \vec{E}_o , \tag{2.11}$$

where

$$\overset{\leftrightarrow}{\tilde{\alpha}}_i = \sum_{j=1}^{m} \overset{\leftrightarrow}{A}_{ij} \tag{2.12}$$

is a local anisotropic atomic polarizability located at i, which for brevity we shall refer to as a "local polarizability". The

480

total molecular polarizability is obtained by a sum over all atomic contributions:

$$\overset{\leftrightarrow}{\alpha} \;=\; \sum_{i}^{m} \overset{\approx}{\alpha}_{i} \;=\; \sum_{i}^{m}\sum_{j}^{m} \overset{\leftrightarrow}{A}_{ij} \qquad\qquad (2.13)$$

It is important to note that in general the local polarizabilities $\overset{\leftrightarrow}{\alpha}_i$ defined by Eq.(2.12) are nonsymmetrical tensors, $\overset{\leftrightarrow}{\alpha}_i \neq \overset{\leftrightarrow}{\alpha}_i^T$, which distinguishes them from the bond polarizabilities commonly used in bond polarizability models of the molecular polarizability (Prasad and Nafie, 1979; Barron and Buckingham, 1975). For highly symmetrical molecules, however, these tensors become symmetrical, $\overset{\leftrightarrow}{\alpha}_i = \overset{\leftrightarrow}{\alpha}_i^T$, as is the case for the molecules of interest in this paper. This will be taken adventage of in the following section.

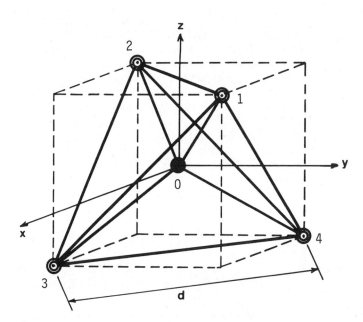

Fig. 1. Standard frame of reference for tetrahedral molecules. The YY-distance is denoted by d. Site 0 is occupied by X, sites 1 to 4 by Y-atoms, respectively.

Summarizing, we want to emphasize also the difference between the originally assigned spherical point polarizabilities $\alpha_i^0 \overset{\leftrightarrow}{1}$ and the anisotropic local polarizabilities $\overset{\leftrightarrow}{\tilde{\alpha}}_i$. The original spherical point polarizabilities $\alpha_i^o \overset{\leftrightarrow}{1}$ are all dynamically coupled through chains of dipolar interactions. This information is contained in the relay tensor $\overset{\leftrightarrow}{A}_{ij}$. No such coupling, however, exists between the local polarizabilities $\overset{\leftrightarrow}{\tilde{\alpha}}_i$ containing the same information. The price to pay is their increased complexity: anisotropy and possibly non-symmetry.

For an application of this theory the local polarizabilities $\overset{\leftrightarrow}{\tilde{\alpha}}_i$ must be expressed in terms of the original isotropic point polarizabilities α_i^o. The desired relation is obtained by placing the molecule into a homogeneous field, $\vec{E} = \vec{E}_i$. Substitution of Eq. (2.11) into Eq.(2.1) yields the desired result:

$$\overset{\leftrightarrow}{\tilde{\alpha}}_i = \alpha_i^o \overset{\leftrightarrow}{1} + \alpha_i^o \sum_{j \neq i}^{m} \overset{\leftrightarrow}{T}_{ij} \cdot \overset{\leftrightarrow}{\tilde{\alpha}}_j \qquad (2.14)$$

For tetrahedral and octahedral molecules Eq.(2.14) may be easily evaluated analytically (Neumann, 1984). As an illustration the re-sult for the local polarizabilities of CF_4 and CCl_4-molecules are summarized in Table 1. X and Y denote central and peripheral sites, respectively, and the symbols $\parallel$ and $\perp$ are labels for the eigenvalues of $\overset{\leftrightarrow}{\tilde{\alpha}}_Y$ and refer to the C_{3v}-symmetry axis passing through Y. d is the molecular YY-separation (see Fig.(1)). The anisotropy of the local $\overset{\leftrightarrow}{\tilde{\alpha}}_F$- and $\overset{\leftrightarrow}{\tilde{\alpha}}_{Cl}$-tensors is clearly seen, whereas the central $\overset{\leftrightarrow}{\tilde{\alpha}}_C$-tensor is, of course, isotropic.

Table 1 : Polarizability parameters for the CF_4 and CCl_4 molecule. d is the YY-distance and α is the total molecular polarizability.

XY_4	CF_4	CCl_4
d / Å	2.15	2.89
α_X^o / Å^3	0.878[a]	0.878[a]
α_Y^o / Å^3	0.32[a]	1.91[a]
$\tilde{\alpha}_X$ / Å^3	1.613	2.045
$\tilde{\alpha}_Y^{\parallel}$ / Å^3	0.821	3.970
$\tilde{\alpha}_Y^{\perp}$ / Å^3	0.104	1.208
α / Å^3	2.99	10.59

[a] This value is taken from Applequist et al. (1972).

APPLICATION OF THE PAP-MODEL TO CI-SCATTERING

The calculation of the dipole induced in a molecule A due to the presence of another molecule B proceeds in 3 steps (Neumann, 1984):

a) We consider a molecule B in the electric field $\vec{E}_0$ of the incoming light, which may be taken constant. The primary dipoles induced at any of the atomic sites b of B are obtained from the PAP-model applied to molecule B. From Eq.(2.11) we find:

$$\vec{\mu}_b (B) = \overset{\leftrightarrow}{\underset{\sim}{\alpha}}_b (B) \cdot \vec{E}_0 \tag{3.1}$$

b) The electric field at the position of site a of molecule A originating from all dipoles in Eq.(3.1) of molecule B is given by

$$\vec{E}_a(A) = \sum_b^m \overset{\leftrightarrow}{T}_{A a, B b} \cdot \vec{\mu}_b (B) \tag{3.2}$$

where the notation

$$\overset{\leftrightarrow}{T}_{A a, B b} \equiv \overset{\leftrightarrow}{T} (\vec{r}_a (A) - \vec{r}_b (B)) \tag{3.3}$$

obviously implies a dipole tensor coupling between site a of molecule A and site b of molecule B. The restriction to first order coupling for the intermolecular interactions preserves the pairwise additivity of the total macroscopic polarizability of the sample.

c) From the inhomogeneous secondary field $\vec{E}_a(A)$ at the position of all sites of A the secondary dipoles induced at sites a' of molecule A are again obtained by application of the PAP-model. From Eq.(2.9) one has

$$\vec{\mu}_{a'} (A) = \sum_a^m \overset{\leftrightarrow}{A}_{a'a} (A) \cdot \vec{E}_a (A) \tag{3.4}$$

Insertion of (3.2) and (3.1) and summation over all atoms a of A finally yields for the induced total polarizability $\overset{\leftrightarrow}{\alpha}(A)$ due to the presence of B:

$$\overset{\leftrightarrow}{\alpha} (A) = \sum_a^m \sum_b^m \left[\sum_{a'}^m \overset{\leftrightarrow}{A}_{a'a} (A) \right] \cdot \overset{\leftrightarrow}{T}_{A a, B b} \cdot \overset{\leftrightarrow}{\underset{\sim}{\alpha}}_b (B) \tag{3.5}$$

Making use of the symmetry relation (2.10) and the definition (2.12) gives

$$\overset{\leftrightarrow}{\alpha} (A) = \sum_a \sum_b \overset{\leftrightarrow}{\underset{\sim}{\alpha}}_a^T (A) \cdot \overset{\leftrightarrow}{T}_{A a, B b} \cdot \overset{\leftrightarrow}{\underset{\sim}{\alpha}}_b (B) . \tag{3.6}$$

A further summation of A and B over the assembly of N molecules yields the total induced polarizability of the sample due to inter-molecular interactions:

$$\Delta \overset{\leftrightarrow}{A} = \sum_{A}^{N} \sum_{B \neq A}^{N} \sum_{a}^{m} \sum_{b}^{m} \overset{\approx}{\alpha}_a{}^{T}(A) \cdot \overset{\leftrightarrow}{T}_{Aa,Bb} \cdot \overset{\approx}{\alpha}_b(B) \ . \qquad (3.7)$$

For the special case of homonuclear diatomics, Eq.(3.7) has been used by Ladanyi (1983).

It is interesting to note that the collision induced tensorial contributions of rank 1 to Eq.(3.7) and hence CI optical activity vanishes only for molecules with high enough symmetry, for which the bond polarizabilities $\overset{\approx}{\alpha}_i$ are symmetrical:

$$\overset{\approx}{\alpha}_i = \overset{\approx}{\alpha}_i{}^{T} \qquad (3.8)$$

This is the case for the molecules of type XY_4 of our interest, for which each atomic site is passed through by at least one C_{3v} axis of symmetry. For this particular case all $\overset{\approx}{\alpha}_i$ are also symmetric with respect to this axis as has been mentioned in the previous section. If $\overset{\approx}{\alpha}_i$ is decomposed into isotropic (rank 0) and anisotro-pic (rank 2) tensorial parts, one obtains (Posch, 1979; Ladanyi, 1983)

$$\overset{\approx}{\alpha}_i = \overline{\alpha}_i \overset{\leftrightarrow}{1} + \frac{2}{3} \overline{r}_i \overset{\leftrightarrow}{Q}_i \ , \qquad (3.9)$$

where

$$\overline{\alpha}_i = \frac{1}{3} Tr (\overset{\approx}{\alpha}_i) \qquad (3.10)$$

is the isotropic contribution, and

$$\overline{r}_i = \overset{\sim}{\alpha}_i{}^{\parallel} - \overset{\sim}{\alpha}_i{}^{\perp} \qquad (3.11)$$

is the anisotropy of the local polarizability with respect to the direction of its axis of symmetry. $\overset{\leftrightarrow}{Q}_i$ is a traceless tensor of second rank,

$$\overset{\leftrightarrow}{Q}_i = \frac{1}{2} (3 \hat{u}_i \hat{u}_i - 1) \ , \qquad (3.12)$$

and $\hat{u}_i$ is a unit vector in the direction of the symmetry axis. In-sertion of Eq.(3.9) into Eq.(3.7) yields the desired decomposition into isotropic (1 = 0) and anisotropic (1 = 2) contribution of $\Delta \overset{\leftrightarrow}{A}$:

$$\Delta \overset{\leftrightarrow}{A} = \Delta A^{(o)} \overset{\leftrightarrow}{1} + \Delta \overset{\leftrightarrow}{A}^{(2)} \qquad (3.13)$$

$$\Delta A^{(0)} = \frac{1}{3} Tr \left\{ \sum_{A}^{N} \sum_{B \neq A}^{N} \sum_{\alpha}^{m} \sum_{b}^{m} \left[\bar{\alpha}_{\alpha}(A) \overset{\leftrightarrow}{T}_{A\alpha,Bb} \cdot \frac{2}{3} \bar{\tau}_{b} \overset{\leftrightarrow}{Q}_{b}(B) + \right. \right.$$

(3.14)

$$\left. \left. + \frac{2}{3} \bar{\tau}_{\alpha} \overset{\leftrightarrow}{Q}_{\alpha}(A) \cdot \overset{\leftrightarrow}{T}_{A\alpha,Bb} \bar{\alpha}_{b}(B) + \frac{2}{3} \bar{\tau}_{\alpha} \overset{\leftrightarrow}{Q}_{\alpha}(A) \cdot \overset{\leftrightarrow}{T}_{A\alpha,Bb} \frac{2}{3} \bar{\tau}_{b} \overset{\leftrightarrow}{Q}_{b}(B) \right] \right\}$$

$$\Delta \overset{\leftrightarrow}{A}^{(2)} = \sum_{A}^{N} \sum_{B \neq A}^{N} \sum_{\alpha}^{m} \sum_{b}^{m} \left[\bar{\alpha}_{\alpha}(A) \overset{\leftrightarrow}{T}_{A\alpha,Bb} \bar{\alpha}_{b}(B) + \right.$$

(3.15)

$$+ \bar{\alpha}_{\alpha}(A) \overset{\leftrightarrow}{T}_{A\alpha,Bb} \cdot \frac{2}{3} \bar{\tau}_{b} \overset{\leftrightarrow}{Q}_{b}(B) + \frac{2}{3} \bar{\tau}_{\alpha} \overset{\leftrightarrow}{Q}_{\alpha}(A) \cdot \overset{\leftrightarrow}{T}_{A\alpha,Bb} \bar{\alpha}_{b}(B) +$$

$$\left. + \frac{2}{3} \bar{\tau}_{\alpha} \overset{\leftrightarrow}{Q}_{\alpha}(A) \cdot \overset{\leftrightarrow}{T}_{A\alpha,Bb} \cdot \frac{2}{3} \bar{\tau}_{b} \overset{\leftrightarrow}{Q}_{b}(B) \right] - \Delta A^{(0)} \overset{\leftrightarrow}{1} .$$

The spectral density for depolarized collision-induced light scattering is proportional to

$$I_{xz}(\omega) = \frac{1}{10} \cdot \frac{1}{2\pi} \int_{-\infty}^{\infty} \exp(-i\omega t) \, F^{(2)}(t) \, dt \, , \tag{3.16}$$

where the correlation function $F^{(2)}(t)$ for anisotropic scattering is defined by

$$F^{(2)}(t) = \langle \Delta \overset{\leftrightarrow}{A}^{(2)}(0) \odot \Delta \overset{\leftrightarrow}{A}^{(2)}(t) \rangle . \tag{3.17}$$

Equations (3.14 - 3.17) have been used for the molecular dynamics simulations of XY_4-type molecular fluids at liquid densities, which are reported below.

THE MOLECULAR PAIR POTENTIAL

For the MD-simulations of dense fluids composed of tetrahedral molecules a four center LJ-potential is used,

$$\varepsilon(\vec{r}, \vec{\Omega}_1, \vec{\Omega}_2) = \sum_{\alpha=1}^{4} \sum_{b=1}^{4} 4 \, \varepsilon_{\alpha b} \left[\frac{\sigma_{\alpha b}^{12}}{|\vec{r}_{\alpha}(A) - \vec{r}_{b}(B)|^{12}} - \frac{\sigma_{\alpha b}^{6}}{|\vec{r}_{\alpha}(A) - \vec{r}_{b}(B)|^{6}} \right] \tag{4.1}$$

where a,b are summed over all peripheral atomic sites of molecules A,B respectively. The parameters ε and σ are determined from a fit of the second virial coefficient over the whole available range of temperatures. In Table 2 these parameters are listed for CF_4, CCl_4 and $C(CH_3)_4$. For reasons of comparison respective parameters for SF_6 and the linear molecules F_2 and Cl_2 are also included in this table.

Table 2: Multi center LJ potential parameters for the interaction of peripheral sites taken by F, Cl and (CH_3).

Molecule	$\varepsilon_{YY}/k_B |K|$	$\sigma_{YY} |\overset{\circ}{A}|$
CF_4	70	2.77
SF_6	77	2.75
F_2	55	2.80
CCl_4	200	3.41
Cl_2	120	3.82
$C(CH_3)_4$	104	3.9

For the evaluation of binary properties the full orientation dependent pair distribution is needed. If this quantity is expanded in terms of rotation matrices followed by an angle averaging over $\vec{\Omega}_1$ and $\vec{\Omega}_2$, the angle independent first term of this expansion is given by

$$g^{00}_{000}(r) = \exp\left(-\varepsilon_{eff}(r)/k_B T\right) =$$
$$= \frac{1}{(8\pi^2)^2} \iint d\vec{\Omega}_1\, d\vec{\Omega}_2 \exp\left(-\varepsilon(\vec{r},\vec{\Omega}_1,\vec{\Omega}_2)/k_B T\right) \quad (4.2)$$

This equation may serve as a definition for the effective spherical potential $\varepsilon_{eff}(r)$, which is obtained by angle averaging of the Boltzmann factor. Eq.(4.1) may be used in Eq.(4.2) for the evaluation of $\varepsilon_{eff}(r)$. The resulting isotropic effective potential has been successfully applied for the analysis of binary CI-light scattering data from dilute gases of $C(CH_3)_4$ (Posch, 1982), CCl_4 and SF_6 (Treitl et al., 1984).

486

MOLECULAR DYNAMICS SIMULATIONS FOR CF_4 AND CCl_4-FLUIDS

Simulations were carried out for molecular systems resembling CF_4 at two different thermodynamic states and CCl_4 close to the triple point. The states are listed in Table 3 along with the internal energy, the diffusion coefficient D and a second rank tensor reorientational correlation time τ_2. These numbers may be used to judge the performance of the intermolecular potential models of Table 2. 108 particles (432 LJ centers) and periodic boundary conditions have been used. The (spherical) cutoff radius R_c of forces as well as pair polarizabilities has always been taken to be equal to half the box length, which at liquid densities corresponds to roughly 2.5 molecular diameters. The timestep chosen has been $\Delta t = 0.005 \ (m_Y \sigma_{YY}^2 / \varepsilon_{YY})^{1/2}$, where m_Y is the mass of the Y-atom, and σ_{YY}, ε_{YY} are listed in Table 2.

Let us consider the intensities first. According to Eqs.(3.16) and (3.17), the total depolarizedly scattered intensity per molecule is proportional to

$$S_{XZ} = \frac{1}{10 \, N} \, F^{(2)}(0) = \frac{1}{10 \, N \, \alpha^4} \left\langle \Delta \overset{\leftrightarrow}{A}{}^{(2)} \odot \Delta \overset{\leftrightarrow}{A}{}^{(2)} \right\rangle \qquad (5.1)$$

where α is the (spherical) molecular polarizability in Eq.(2.13).

As usual, S_{XZ} may be decomposed into terms involving only pair-, three particle and four particle correlations (Ladd et al., 1979, 1980):

$$S_{XZ} = 2 \, S_{2,XZ} + 4 \, S_{3,XZ} + S_{4,XZ} \qquad (5.2)$$

These terms have been evaluated separately

a) for the pure DID-model, for which the total induced CI polarizability is given by

$$\Delta \overset{\leftrightarrow}{A}{}^{(2)} = \sum_{A}^{N} \sum_{B \neq A} \alpha(A) \, \overset{\leftrightarrow}{T}_{AB} \, \alpha(B) \, , \qquad (5.3)$$

where α is the spherical molecular polarizability, and $\overset{\leftrightarrow}{T}_{AB}$ is the dipole tensor connecting the centers of mass of A and B,

b) for the PAP-model introduced above, for which $\Delta \overset{\leftrightarrow}{A}{}^{(2)}$ is given by Eq.(3.15).

The results are also included in Table 3. It is seen that for the dense systems of CF_4 and CCl_4 similar cancellations of two-, three- and four-body terms take place as in the case of liquid argon (Ladd et al., 1979, 1980). At the present stage, a comparison of the simulation results for S_{XZ} with corresponding experimental data,

Table 3: Molecular dynamics results for the three model fluids studied. ρ is the density, T the temperature, U the internal energy, D the diffusion coefficient and τ_2 a second rank tensor orientational correlation time, respectively. The intensity parameters S are defined in the text.

XY_4	CF_4		CCl_4	
State	I	II		Model
$\rho \lvert g\ cm^{-3}\rvert$	0.156	1.505	1.593	
$T\ \lvert K\rvert$	239	165	300	
$U/Nk_B\ \lvert K\rvert$	–	–1170	–4180	
$10^5.D\lvert cm^2 s^{-1}\rvert$	–	3.88	1.27	
$\tau_2\lvert ps\rvert$	–	0.70	2.0	
$10^4.S_{2,xz}\lvert Å^{-6}\rvert$	0.684	5.88	1.94	DID
	0.612	5.24	1.55	PAP
$10^4.S_{3,xz}\lvert Å^{-6}\rvert$	–0.066	–4.83	–1.76	DID
	–0.055	–4.34	–1.40	PAP
$10^4.S_{4,xz}\lvert Å^{-6}\rvert$	–0.074	8.29	3.28	DID
	–0.068	7.44	2.64	PAP
$10^4.S_{xz}\lvert Å^{-6}\rvert$	1.03	0.72	0.146	DID
	0.934	0.54	0.086	PAP
$10^4.S_{exp}\ Å^{-6}$	1.04[a]	1.09[b]	–	

[a] From Shelton and Tabisz (1980).

[b] This number was estimated from unpublished data of An (1975).

however, is unconclusive with respect to the validity of any of the
two theoretical models. This is in   part a consequence of the
rather poor accuracy of the experimental figures quoted in Table 3
(the possible error for state II of CF_4 is estimated to be about
30%), but is also due to the deficiencies of the simulation. For
argon close to the triple point it has been shown by Ladd et al.
(1980) that truncation of the DID-interaction at the distance corresponding to a minimum of the pair distribution function g(r), leads
to an underestimation of the integrated intensity by as much as 25%.
A similar result is also found for dense molecular fluids. In Fig.2
we have plotted the intensity $S_{xz}(R_C)$ as a function of the cutoff-
radius R_C used for the truncation of the intermolecular dipole
interaction. From the strong oscillatory behaviour of the DID-model
curve in particular, one may conclude that, for liquid densities,
the DID-intensity of an infinite system would be somewhat larger
than the number given in Table 3. The PAP-model, on the other hand,
is seen to be much less sensitive to the magnitude of the cutoff-
radius R_C, so that the corresponding number in Table 3 is probably
reasonably close to that of an infinite system.

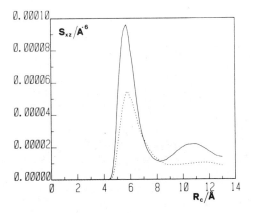

Fig.2: Dependence of the intensity function S_{xz} on the cutoff-
radius R_C for CCl_4. The smooth line is for the DID-model,
the dashed line for the PAP-approximation.

According to Table 3 the integrated intensity of the PAP-model is smaller than the DID intensity in spite of the same molecular polarizability $\overleftrightarrow{\alpha} = \alpha \overleftrightarrow{1}$ used for the calculation. As expected, this difference is much larger for liquid CCl_4 than for CF_4.

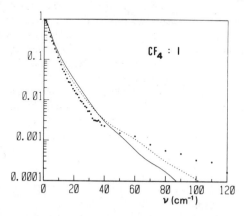

Fig.3: Calculated and experimental line shapes (in arbitrary units) for the low density state I of CF_4. The experimental points are normalized to coincide with the DID-result at $\omega = 0$. The relative magnitude of the DID-(smooth curve) and PAP-spectra (dashed) is preserved. The experimental data have been privately communicated by D.Varshneya and M.Zoppi.

Distributing the polarizability closer to the surface of the molecule, rather than localizing it at its center, obviously leads to a reduction of the overall intensity. Since the PAP-model is asymptotically (i.e. for large molecular separations) equivalent to DID, this difference can only originate from small clusters of closely spaced particles. In fact, $S_{xz}(R_c)$ in Fig.2 shows that it is the contribution from nearest neighbours (note the drastically reduced first peak), which eventually causes the decrease of the total intensity. It should be noted, however, that this loss of intensity is not due to the particular orientational correlations between molecules and/or the higher multipole polarizabilities also implicit in the PAP-model, but to the spatial distribution of polarizable matter over the molecule. A similar conclusion has been reached also by Buckingham and Hunt (1980) from calculations of CI polarizability anisotropies of SF_6-molecular pairs. The same physical situation has also been encountered by Oxtoby (1978) in his attempt to explain the breakdown of the DID-model at small interparticle separations of monatomic systems. The introduction of a polarizability density "spread out" all over the atom leads to a decrease of the CI pair anisotropy of atomic dimers.

As mentioned in the introduction, the point-multipole expansion Eq.(1.1) may be used for the calculation of correction terms taking care of the spatial charge distribution in the molecules. For the dilute gas case the first term of this CIRR-theory involves the dipole-quadrupole polarizability $\overset{\leftrightarrow}{A}{}^{(3)}$ and adds a positive contribution to the DID-intensity (Buckingham and Tabisz, 1978; Shelton and Tabisz, 1980; Posch, 1982). Even for liquid CCl_4 this first correction term has been found to be positive (Posch, 1980). In contrast to this result, the PAP-intensities are lower than the pure DID.

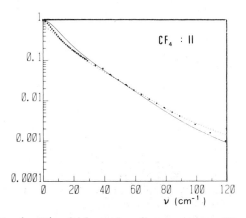

Fig.4: As in Fig.3 for the dense state II of CF_4

In Figs.(3) to (5) the calculated line shapes are compared to available experimental data. The relative intensities of the DID- and PAP-results are preserved in these figures, the experimental line shapes, however, are normalized to coincide with the DID-curves at $\omega = 0$. It is evident from these pictures that the gross appearance of the spectra is very similar to those of dense fluid noble gases (An et al., 1976, 1979). At low frequency shifts the line shapes are nearly Lorentzian (plus a constant background) and contain dynamical information arising from highly collective fluctuations of the bilinear polarizability density with wave vectors k, $\sim 2\pi/\sigma$, where σ is a molecular diameter. The high frequency wings, however, are nearly exponential and reflect the combined activity of larger wave vector modes.

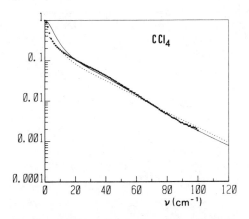

Fig.5: As in Fig.3 for liquid CCl_4.

The relative intensities of the low and high frequency domains are rather well reproduced by the simulations. This is particulary true for the slopes of the exponential wings, which are recovered equally well both by the DID- and the PAP-models. The worst disagreement is found for the width of the central Lorentzian. This frequency range, however, is most difficult to study both experimentally and by the simulation technique. Its experimental determination is always hampered by straylight corrections around $\omega = 0$, through which significant errors may be introduced. The simulation results, on the other hand, are very sensitive to the truncation procedure for the pair polarizabilities mentioned above. Truncation at a minimum of g ($\vec{r}$, $\vec{\Omega}_1$, $\vec{\Omega}_2$) as in our case may lead to an overestimation of the half width of the central Lorentzian, whereas the high frequency wings are hardly affected (Ladd et al., 1980). Increasing the size of the sample would thus bring the simulated spectrum to closer agreement with the experimental one for small frequency shifts.

OUTLOOK

The problem of calculating CI spectral lineshapes and intensities for molecular fluids in condensed states is far from being solved. Some models and methods have been discussed in this report, which in our opinion may become fruitful for further work in this field. In this respect the point atom polarizability model (PAP) is of particular interest for at least two reasons:

1) it offers an attractive though approximative method of taking the spatial charge distribution within a molecule into account;

2) it may be reformulated for CI-studies such to be most suitable for molecular dynamics simulations of condensed phases.

At present the results are not conclusive yet with respect to the accuracy and applicability of the models considered. In particular, the correct pair potentials and possible irreducible three body contributions to the potential and/or the polarizability impose additional problems, which have not been solved satisfactorily. But it is hoped that improved numerical procedures and new precise experimentation will eventually bridge the gap.

REFERENCES

An, S. C., 1975, Depolarized Rayleigh scattering in simple fluids, Dissertation, The Catholic University of America, Washington D.C.

An, S. C., Montrose, C. J., and Litovitz, T. A., 1976, Low-frequency structure in the depolarized spectrum of argon, J. Chem. Phys., 64:3717.

An, S. C., Fishman, L., Litovitz, T. A., Montrose, C. J., and Posch, H. A., 1979, Depolarized light scattering from dense noble gases, J. Chem. Phys., 70:4626.

Applequist, J., Carl, J. R., and Fung, K. K., 1972, An atom dipole interaction model for molecular polarizability. Application to polyatomic molecules and determination of atom polarizabilities, J. Am. Chem. Soc., 94:2952.

Applequist, J., 1977, An atom dipole interaction model for molecular optical properties, Accts. Chem. Res., 10:79.

Barocchi, F., and McTague, J. P., 1974, Binary collision induced light scattering in liquid CH_4, Opt. Commun., 12:202.

Barocchi, F., and McTague, J. P., 1975, Collision induced light scattering in gaseous CH_4, Phys. Lett., A53:488.

Barocchi, F., Zoppi, M., Shelton, D. P., and Tabisz, G. C., 1977, A comparison of the spectral features of the collision-induced light scattering by the molecular gases CH_4 and CF_4 and by argon, Can. J. Phys., 55:1962.

Barron, L. D., and Buckingham, A. D., 1975, Rayleigh and
    Raman optical activity, Ann. Rev. Phys. Chem., 26:381.

Bucaro, J. A., and Litovitz, T. A., 1971, Rayleigh scattering:
    collisional motions in liquids, J. Chem. Phys., 54:3846.

Bucaro, J. A., and Litovitz, T. A., 1971, Molecular motions
    in CCl_4: light scattering and infrared absorption,
    J. Chem. Phys., 55:3585.

Buckingham, A. D., and Tabisz, G. C., 1977, Collision-induced
    rotational Raman scattering, Optics Letters, 1:220.

Buckingham, A. D., and Tabisz, G. C., 1978, Collision-induced
    rotational Raman scattering by tetrahedral and octahedral
    molecules, Molec. Phys., 36:583.

Buckingham, A. D., and Clarke Hunt, K. L., 1980, The pair pola-
    rizability anisotropy of SF_6 in the point-atom-polarizabi-
    lity approximation, Molec. Phys., 40:643.

Frommhold, L., 1981, Collision-induced scattering and the
    diatom-polarizabilities, Adv. Chem. Phys., 46:1.

Frommhold, L., 1984, this volume.

Gabelnick, H. S., and Strauss, H. L., 1968, Low-frequency
    motions in liquid carbon-tetrachloride. II The Raman
    spectrum, J. Chem. Phys., 49:2334.

Gharbi, A., and Le Duff, 1977, Collision-induced scattering
    for molecules, Physica, 87A:177.

Gharbi, A., and Le Duff, 1978, Line shape of the collision-
    induced scattering in CF_4, Physica, 90A:619.

Gharbi, A., and Le Duff, 1980, Many-body correlations for
    Raman and Rayleigh collision induced scattering,
    Molec. Phys., 40:545.

Gornall, W. S., Howard-Lock, H. E., and Stoicheff, B. P., 1970,
    Induced anisotropy and light scattering in liquids,
    Phys. Rev. A, 1:1288.

Guillot, B., Bratos, S., and Birnbaum, G., 1980, Theoretical
    study of spectra of depolarized light scattering from
    dense rare-gas fluids, Phys. Rev. A, 22:2230.

Ho, J. H. K., and Tabisz, G. C., 1973, Collision-induced light
    scattering in liquids and the binary collision model,
    Can. J. Phys., 51:2025.

Howard-Lock, H. E., and Taylor, R. S., 1974, Induced anisotropy
    and light scattering in liquids. II., Can. J. Phys.,
    52:2436.

Keyes, T., and Ladanyi, B. M., 1977, The role of local fields
    and interparticle pair correlations in light scattering
    by dense fluids II. The depolarized spectrum for non-
    spherical molecules, Molec. Phys., 33:1099.

Ladanyi, B. M., and Keyes, T., 1979, Effect of internal fields
    on depolarized light scattering from n-alkane gases,
    Molec. Phys., 37:1809.

Ladanyi, B. M., 1983, Molecular dynamics study of Rayleigh
    light scattering from molecular fluids, J. Chem. Phys.,
    78:2189.

Ladd, A. J. C., Litovitz, T. A., and Montrose, C. J., 1979, Molecular dynamics studies of depolarized light scattering from argon at various fluid densities, J. Chem. Phys., 71:4242.

Ladd, A. J. C., Litovitz, T. A., Clarke, J. H. R., and Woodcock, L. V., 1980, Molecular dynamics simulations of depolarized Rayleigh scattering from liquid argon at the triple point, J. Chem. Phys., 72:1759.

Lallemand, P. M., 1970, Spectral distribution of double light scattering by gases, Phys. Rev. Lett., 25:1079.

Leite, R. C. C., Moore, R. S., and Porto, S. P. S., 1964, Use of gas lasers in studies of the depolarization of the Rayleigh scattering from simple liquids, J. Chem. Phys., 40:3741.

Levine, H. B., and Birnbaum, G., 1968, Collision-induced light scattering, Phys. Rev. Lett., 20:439.

Madden, P. A., 1977, The lineshape of the depolarised Rayleigh scattering from liquid argon, Chem. Phys. Lett., 47:174.

Madden, P. A., 1978, The depolarized Rayleigh scattering from fluids of spherical molecules, Molec. Phys., 36:365.

Neumann, M., 1984, in preparation.

Oxtoby, D. W., 1978, The calculation of pair polarizabilities through continuum electrostatic theory, J. Chem. Phys., 69:1184.

Posch, H. A., 1979, Collision-induced light scattering from fluids composed of tetrahedral molecules. I. Molec. Phys., 37:1059.

Posch, H. A., 1980, Collision induced light scattering from fluids composed of tetrahedral molrcules. II. Intensities, Molec. Phys., 40:1137.

Posch, H. A., 1982, Collision induced light scattering from fluids composed of tetrahedral molecules. III. Neopentane vapour, Molec. Phys., 46:1213.

Prasad, P. L., and Nafie, L. A., 1979, The atom dipole interaction model of Raman optical activity: Reformulation and comparison to the general two-group model, J. Chem. Phys., 70:1979.

Prengel, A. T., and Gornall, W. S., 1976, Raman scattering from colliding molecules and Van der Waals dimers in gaseous methane, Phys. Rev. A, 13:253.

Shelton, D. P., and Tabisz, G. C., 1975, Moment analysis of collision-induced light scattering from compressed CF_4, Phys. Rev. A., 11:1571.

Shelton, D. P., Mathur, M. S., and Tabisz, G. C., 1975, Collision-induced light scattering by compressed CF_4 and CF_4-He mixtures, Phys. Rev. A, 11:834.

Shelton, D. P., and Tabisz, G. C., 1980, Binary collision-

induced light scattering by isotropic molecular gases.
II. Molecular spectra and induced rotational Raman
scattering, Molec. Phys., 40:299.

Shelton, D. P., Tabisz, G. C., Barocchi, F., and Zoppi, M.,
1982, The three body correlation spectrum in collision
induced light scattering by isotropic molecular gases,
Molec. Phys., 46:21.

Treitl, K., Pleich, R., and Posch, H. A., 1984, in preparation.

Varshneya, D., Shirron, S. F., Litovitz, T. A., Zoppi, M., and
Barocchi, F., 1981, Collision-induced light scattering:
Integrated intensity of argon, Phys. Rev. A, 23:77.

LOCAL FIELDS IN LIQUIDS*

Branka M. Ladanyi[#]

Department of Chemistry
Colorado State University
Fort Collins, CO 80523

ABSTRACT

In this article the present state of theory and experiments designed to determine local field effects on light scattering and induced birefringence in liquids of optically anisotropic molecules is reviewed. Attention is focused on the effective polarizabilities, which measure the deviation of local field contributions to the observed intensities from the isotropic Lorenz-Lorentz forms. Results of measurements of effective polarizabilities in isotropic and depolarized light scattering (DLS) from pure liquids and dilute solutions are described. Molecular theory, which explains the observed behavior of effective polarizabilities in terms of the anisotropy of the short range fluid structure and dipole-induced dipole intermolecular interactions, is presented. It is shown how the molecular theory relates the effective polarizabilities observed in DLS, Kerr effect, and Cotton-Mouton effect. The dielectric cavity theory for effective polarizabilities is derived from the molecular theory. The results of this theory along with those of other approximations are compared to the computer simulation results. Theoretical basis and accuracy of two modern experimental methods for measuring effective anisotropic polarizabilities are discussed. Some problems in need of further investigation are briefly described.

---

*Work supported in part by the National Science Foundation.

[#]Alfred P. Sloan Foundation Fellow and Camille and Henry Dreyfus Teacher-Scholar.

INTRODUCTION

The effects of local fields on the optical response of liquids are usually large and have to be properly taken into account when analyzing experimental data in terms of fundamental fluid structure and dynamics. In a review, which will appear shortly, Keyes and Ladanyi (1984) explain in detail the molecular theory of local field effects in light scattering and induced birefringence in liquids and in dilute solutions of flexible molecules. In order to minimize overlap with this review, the scope of the present article will be limited, for the most part, to pure liquids and solutions containing small, rigid, optically anisotropic molecules. The particular topic, which will be emphasized herein, and which is addressed only briefly by Keyes and Ladanyi (1984), is the question of accuracy and reliability of experimental and theoretical methods which are being used to estimate the local field contributions to depolarized light scattering (DLS) and induced birefringence intensities. This question is important, since one of the main goals of these optical response experiments is the determination of the static second rank orientational correlation, g_2. In the case of non-associated fluids, where long range intermolecular interactions are relatively weak, measurement of g_2 requires a very accurate determination of the local field contribution to DLS or birefringence intensities.

In the Background section, we review briefly some of the experimental results which led to the development of our present understanding of local field effects in liquids. In the following section we outline the molecular theory of optical response of fluids its application to Rayleigh scattering, Raman scattering, Kerr effect and Cotton-Mouton effect. We then describe approximations used in evaluating the local field contributions to these phenomena and compare them to the results of computer simulation. In the next section we show how the continuum dielectric cavity theory of local field effects is related to the molecular theory and discuss the limitations of the continuum theory. Following that we describe the main experimental methods used in local field measurements and discuss the theoretical basis and experimental tests of these methods. We conclude the article by summarizing the present state of our understanding of the local field problems in liquids and by indicating some areas which need to be investigated further.

BACKGROUND

Light scattering and related optical response phenomena in liquids arise from the fluctuations in the local dielectric tensor in the medium. In the case of light scattering, $\delta \vec{s}$, the fluctuating source of scattered light within the scattering volume, V, is related to the fluctuations in the polarization, $\vec{P}$, and in the field, $\vec{E}$, by

$$\delta\vec{s} = \delta\vec{P} - \left(\frac{\varepsilon - 1}{4\pi}\right)\vec{E} \tag{1}$$

where ε is the optical dielectric constant (Fixman, 1955), defined by $\varepsilon = \text{Tr}\langle\overset{\leftrightarrow}{\varepsilon}\rangle/3$. $\overset{\leftrightarrow}{\varepsilon}$ is the instantaneous dielectric tensor and δ denotes a fluctuation. $\vec{P}$ is related to $\vec{E}$ by

$$\vec{P} = (\overset{\leftrightarrow}{\varepsilon} - \overset{\leftrightarrow}{1})/4\pi \cdot \vec{E}.$$

Using this expression, Eq. (1) becomes

$$\delta\vec{s} = \frac{\delta\overset{\leftrightarrow}{\varepsilon}}{4\pi}\cdot\langle\vec{E}\rangle, \tag{2}$$

where $\langle\vec{E}\rangle$ is the average Maxwell field in the sample. For incident light of wavelength λ polarized along direction $\hat{n}_i$, with intensity I_0, and scattered light polarized along $\hat{n}_f$, the scattered intensity at R is given by

$$I_{if} = \frac{I_0 16\pi^4}{R^2\lambda^4} \left\langle \left|\frac{\delta\varepsilon_{fi}}{4\pi}\right|^2 \right\rangle. \tag{3}$$

In the case of small molecule liquids and away from critical points, two independent components of I_{if} exist. For $\hat{n}_i$ perpendicular to the scattering plane and $\hat{n}_f$ in the scattering plane, I_{if} becomes I_{VH}, the anisotropic or DLS intensity. For both $\hat{n}_i$ and $\hat{n}_f$ perpendicular to the scattering plane, I_{if} becomes the polarized scattering intensity

$$I_{VV} = I_{is} - \frac{4}{3} I_{VH}, \tag{4}$$

where I_{is} is the isotropic intensity. An excellent theory for I_{is} was developed in the beginning of this century by Einstein (1910) and Smoluchowski (1908). They evaluated isotropic fluctuations in ε by applying the thermodynamic fluctuation theory to the equation of state for $\varepsilon(\rho,T)$. Usually the dependence of ε on temperature, T, is much weaker than that on the number density, ρ, and the isotropic Rayleigh ratio, R_{is}, at the scattering angle of $90°$ becomes

$$R_{is}(90°) = \frac{R^2 I_{is}}{I_0} = \frac{16\pi^4}{\lambda^4} k_B T \kappa_T \left[\frac{\rho}{4\pi}\left(\frac{\partial\varepsilon}{\partial\rho}\right)_T\right]^2, \tag{5}$$

where κ_T is the isothermal compressibility. This expression takes on a more familiar form if the Clausius-Mossotti equation of state for ε is used, namely

$$R_{is}(90°) = \frac{16\pi^4}{\lambda^4} k_B T \kappa_T (\alpha_0 \rho)^2 \left(\frac{\varepsilon+2}{3}\right)^4,$$ (6)

where α_0 is the isotropic molecular polarizability. The above expression differs from $R_{is}(90°)$ in an ideal gas at the same T by the presence of a factor dependent on the intermolecular pair correlation, h,

$$k_B T \kappa_T / \rho = 1 + \rho \tilde{h}(0),$$ (7)

where $\tilde{h}(k)$ is the Fourier transform of the pair correlation, h(r), and the Lorenz-Lorentz local field factor, $\lfloor(\varepsilon + 2)/3\rfloor^4 = L_{LL}$. A more general formulation is obtained by replacing the Lorenz-Lorentz local field factor by a more general one, L_{is}, which may correspond to a different equation of state for ε. Thus, using Eq. (7) and L_{is},

$$R_{is}(90°) = \frac{16\pi^4}{\lambda^4} \alpha_0^2 \rho \lfloor 1 + \rho \tilde{h}(0) \rfloor L_{is}$$ (8)

In the case of DLS due to molecular orientational relaxation in a fluid of axially symmetric molecules, an analogous expression for $R_{VH}^{OR}(90°)$ may be written

$$R_{VH}^{OR}(90°) = \frac{16\pi^4}{15\lambda^4} \Delta\alpha^2 \rho \ g_2 \ L_{an}$$ (9)

where $\Delta\alpha$ is the molecular polarizability anisotropy, L_{an} the anisotropic local field factor and

$$g_2 = 1 + \sum_{j\neq1}^{N} \langle P_2(\hat{u}_j \cdot \hat{u}_1)\rangle$$ (10)

where $\hat{u}_j$ is a unit vector along the symmetry axis of jth molecule and P_2 the second order Legendre polynomial.

As can be seen from Eqs. (9) and (10), the local field factors L_{is} and L_{an} can be obtained from light scattering intensity measurements if the other parameters in R_{is} and R_{VH}^{OR} are determined from other experiments. Burnham, Alms, and Flygare (1975), carried out such measurements on several molecular fluids and obtained the results shown in Table 1. The results are expressed in terms of "effective" polarizabilities, which are defined as follows

500

$$\alpha_0^2 \, L_{is} = \alpha_{0,eff}^2 \, L_{LL} \qquad\qquad (11)$$

and

$$\Delta\alpha^2 \, L_{an} = \Delta\alpha_{eff}^2 \, L_{LL} \qquad\qquad (12)$$

They are the isotropic and anisotropic polarizabilities a molecule would have if we assumed that both L_{is} and L_{an} are represented by L_{LL}. Theoretical justification exists for this assumption in the case of isotropic scattering, but is lacking in the case of DLS. However, until quite recently, experimental data were analyzed by using either L_{LL} or $L_{LL}^{1/2}$ to represent L_{an}. If the effective polarizabilities turn out to be almost the same as the gas phase polarizability components, then we may conclude that intermolecular correlations and anisotropies in molecular shape and polarizability make a negligible contribution to the L_{is} and L_{an}, namely that the Lorenz-Lorentz model applies. As can be seen from Table 1, $\alpha_{0,eff}/\alpha_0$ is quite close to unity, which means that such a conclusion is reasonable for isotropic Rayleigh scattering. This is, however, not the case for depolarized scattering, given that the observed $\Delta\alpha_{eff}$ in all the fluids studied so far is substantially smaller than $\Delta\alpha$.

Burnham et al. (1975) interpreted their data in terms of local field anisotropy which is due to the anisotropy in the molecular shape. They showed that their data are consistent with L_{an} obtained from anisotropic dielectric cavity theories, such as the Onsager-Scholte theory (Onsager, 1936; Scholte, 1949) or the Lorentz-Raman-Krishnan (LRK) theory (Lorentz, 1952; Raman and Krishnan, 1928), but definitely did not fit any isotropic dielectric cavity theories. Similar conclusion had earlier been reached by

Table 1. Effective Polarizabilities of Several Liquids at Room Temperature.

Molecule[a]	$\alpha_{0,eff}/\alpha_0$	$\Delta\alpha_{eff}/\Delta\alpha$
benzene	0.899	0.540
chloroform	0.906	0.474
CS_2	0.857	0.660
chlorobenzene	0.968	0.655
toluene	0.902	0.603
nitrobenzene	0.939	0.608

[a]Data from Burnham et al. (1975) and Burnham (1977).

Malmberg and Lippincott (1968), Kielich (1967), and Buckingham, Stiles and Ritchie (1971). Further evidence supporting this conclusion is provided by the measurements of R_{VH}^{OR} as a function of the refractive index, $n = \epsilon^{1/2}$, in dilute solutions of optically anisotropic molecules in isotropic molecule solvents carried out by Gierke and Flygare (1974), Alms et al. (1974) and Burnham et al. (1975). In these systems $g_2 = 1$, so that R_{VH}^{OR} vs. n is proportional to L_{an}. These results are depicted in Fig. 1. As can be seen from this figure, DLS intensity never increases with increasing n as fast as $\sqrt{L_{LL}}$. For highly elongated molecules such as p-methylbenzylidene-n-butylaniline (MBA) and p-ethylbenzylidene-n-butylaniline (EBA), it actually <u>decreases</u>

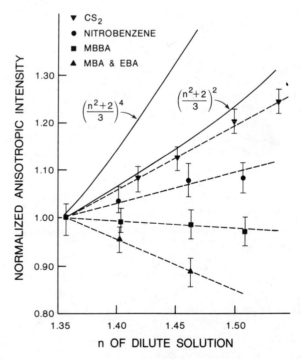

Fig. 1. Depolarized light scattering intensity as a function of refractive index of dilute solution. (Fig. reproduced from Burnham, 1977; data from Burnham et al., 1975 and from Alms et al., 1974).

with increasing n. This behavior is due to the fact that a molecule
is polarized more strongly along its short axis than along its long
one. L_{an} evaluated for a molecule inside an ellipsiodal
dielectric cavity in a uniform dielectric continuum predicts this
type of behavior.

MOLECULAR THEORY OF LOCAL FIELD EFFECTS

Molecular theory allows us to understand how intermolecular
interactions and fluid structure contribute to effective
polarizabilities and to develop accurate methods for evaluating
these quantities. Keyes and Ladanyi (Ladanyi and Keyes, 1977a,b;
Keyes and Ladanyi, 1977a,b) developed such a theory by generalizing
the Yvon theory (1937) to the optical response of anisotropically
polarizable molecules. The theory considers fluctuations in a system
where light propagates in a medium with optical dielectric constant
ε. The field experienced by a molecule at $\vec{r}_i$ is the Lorentz field,
$\vec{E}^{Lo}(\vec{r}_i)$, which includes polarization by other molecules, but
excludes self-polarization. In operator notation, the polarization
is

$$\vec{P} = A \, \vec{E}^{Lo},$$ (13)

where A is the polarizability density operator. It is an integral
tensor operator, with position space matrix elements

$$(A)(\vec{r},\vec{r}') = \overset{\leftrightarrow}{\alpha}(\vec{r}) \, \delta(\vec{r} - \vec{r}'),$$ (14)

and $\overset{\leftrightarrow}{\alpha}(\vec{r})$ is the polarizability density

$$\overset{\leftrightarrow}{\alpha}(\vec{r}) = \sum_{i=1}^{N} \overset{\leftrightarrow}{\alpha}_i \, \delta(\vec{r} - \vec{r}_i).$$ (15)

The Lorentz field is defined as

$$\vec{E}^{Lo} = \vec{E}_0 + L'\vec{P}$$ (16)

where $\vec{E}_0$ is the applied field,

$$L' = L + \frac{4\pi}{3} I$$ (17)

is the "cut out" dipole tensor operator (Boots, Bedeaux, and Mazur,
1975) with I the unit operator,

$$(I)(\vec{r},\vec{r}') = \overset{\leftrightarrow}{1} \, \delta(\vec{r} - \vec{r}'),$$

and

$$(L)(\vec{r},\vec{r}') = \overset{\leftrightarrow}{T}(\vec{r} - \vec{r}').$$ (18)

$\overset{\leftrightarrow}{T}$ is the dipole tensor

$$\overset{\leftrightarrow}{T}(\vec{r}) = 3\vec{r}\vec{r}/r^5 - \overset{\leftrightarrow}{1}/r^3.$$
(19)

The Maxwell field, $\vec{E}$, is given by

$$\vec{E} = \vec{E}_0 + L\vec{P}.$$
(20)

Using Eqs. (13), (16), and (20) to express $\delta\vec{P}$ and $\delta\vec{E}$ in terms of $\langle\vec{E}\rangle$ and substituting the resulting expressions into Eq. (1) the following expression for δs is obtained

$$\delta\vec{s} = \left(\frac{\varepsilon + 2}{3}\right)^2 (I + \langle G\rangle L)^{-1} \, \delta G \, (I + L'\langle G\rangle)^{-1} \, \langle\vec{E}\rangle,$$
(21)

where
$$G = (I - AL')^{-1}A.$$
(22)

Within the context of the dipole-induced dipole (DID) model, Eq. (21) is exact. In order to actually evaluate light scattering intensities from this source, it is necessary to use a perturbation expansion of Eq. (21). The most straightforward expansion is in powers of the DID interaction, L'. This expansion is the Yvon series

$$\delta\vec{s} = \left(\frac{\varepsilon + 2}{3}\right)^2 (\delta A + \delta AL'\delta A + \delta AL'AL'\delta A + \ldots.) \langle\vec{E}\rangle$$
(23)

Other expansions, based on expansion of Eq. (21) in powers of renormalized propagators instead of powers of L', have been proposed (Boots et al., 1975; Felderhof, 1974; Hynne, 1977; Frenkel and McTague, 1980). None of these expansions have so far been successfully applied to optical response of fluids of anisotropically polarizable molecules. In applications of the molecular theory, the contributions to the intensities from higher order terms in Eq. (23) have so far not been evaluated. The contribution from the third term in this equation has only recently been approximately evaluated (Bancewicz, 1983).

The expression for $\delta\vec{s}$, given in Eq. (21) can be generalized in a different way, in taking into account the fact that molecular charge distributions are delocalized and deviations from the center-center DID model are expected at short intermolecular separations. A way of modelling these deviations, which has been pioneered by Buckingham and coworkers (1967), is by using the multipole expansion approach and including into δs the contributions of field gradient terms. Another way of modelling this is to assume that dipole moments are induced at several sites within a molecule (Applequist, Carl, and Fung, 1972; Applequist, 1977) and that

504

intermolecular DID interactions occur between these sites (Keyes and Ladanyi, 1977b; Ladanyi and Keyes, 1978; Ladanyi, et al. 1980). The form of $\delta \vec{s}$ in the latter model, the interacting atom model (IAM), is the same as Eq. (21), with A and L' representing now, respectively, site polarizability density and site-site DID interaction operators. Some specific predictions of the IAM will be discussed in the following section.

The DLS spectrum at frequency ω, for the scattering geometry for which the scattered field is polarized along the x-axis and $\langle \vec{E} \rangle$ along the z-axis is

$$I_{VH}(\omega) \sim \frac{1}{2\pi} \int_0^\infty dt \; e^{i\omega t} \int_V d\vec{r} \int_V d\vec{r}' \; \langle \delta s^x(\vec{r},0) \; \delta s^x(\vec{r}',t) \rangle.$$

$$(24)$$

In order to evaluate the DLS spectrum due to molecular reorientation, the part of $\delta \vec{s}$, which has the time dependence of xz component of the collective second rank orientational variable, $\vec{Q}$, has to be identified and separated from the remainder of $\delta \vec{s}$, which is due to collision induced (CI) light scattering. As was shown by Keyes, Kivelson, and McTague (1971), this separation is effected by projecting δs^x along Q^{xz} and orthogonal to Q^{xz}. δs^x_{OR}, the part of $\delta \vec{s}$ along Q^{xz} is (Ladanyi and Keyes, 1977a).

$$\delta s^x_{OR} = \lfloor \langle \delta s^x \; Q^{xz} \rangle / \langle (Q^{xz})^2 \rangle \rfloor \; Q^{xz}.$$

$$(25)$$

where

$$\vec{Q} = \sum_{i=1}^N \vec{Q}_i$$

$$(26)$$

and

$$\vec{Q}_i = \hat{u}_i \hat{u}_i - \frac{1}{3} \vec{1}.$$

$$(27)$$

δs^x_{CI} is then simply

$$\delta s^x_{CI} = \delta s^x - \delta s^x_{OR}.$$

$$(28)$$

This separation of $\delta \vec{s}$ is only useful if orientational relaxation is substantially slower than intermolecular dynamics which gives rise to CI light scattering and if the cross correlations between δs^x_{OR} and δs^x_{CI} are negligible. Experimental (Burnham et al., 1975; Cox, Battaglia, and Madden, 1979) and computer simulation (Tildesley and Madden, 1983) evidence indicate that these conditions are met in the case of fluids of relatively large and highly anisotropic molecules. These conditions are not met in the case of small diatomic and triatomic molecules (Frenkel and McTague, 1980; Schoen, Cheung, Jackson, and Powles, 1975; Ladanyi, 1983). We will assume that these conditions are met in the cases of interest and that the DLS

505

spectrum can be separated into two clearly distinguishable contributions

$$I_{VH}(\omega) = I_{VH}^{OR}(\omega) + I_{VH}^{CI}(\omega).$$ (29)

$R_{VH}^{OR}(90°)$ is then obtained by integrating $I_{VH}^{OR}(\omega)$ over ω. Using Eq. (21) or (23), and Eq. (25) we can express δs_{OR} in terms of the effective polarizability density

$$\delta s_{OR}^{x} = \left(\frac{n^2+2}{3}\right)^2 \delta\alpha_{eff}^{xz} \langle E\rangle.$$ (30)

From Eq. (23) it is clear that $\delta\alpha_{eff}^{xz}$ differs from $\delta\alpha^{xz}$ because of the presence of contributions to it from fluctuations in intermolecular DID interactions. Using Eq. (30), the Rayleigh ratio for incident light at frequency ω_0 is

$$R_{VH}^{OR}(90°) = \frac{16\pi^4}{15\lambda^4}\left(\frac{n^2+2}{3}\right)^4 \lfloor\Delta\alpha_{eff}(\omega_0)\rfloor^2 \rho\, g_2$$ (31)

where n is the refractive index at ω_0.

Phenomena related to DLS are the Kerr effect, which is birefringence induced by a static electric field, $\vec{E}_1$, and the Cotton-Mouton effect, birefringence induced by a static magnetic field, $\vec{H}$. The molar Kerr constant, $_mK$ is defined by (Bottcher and Bordewijk, 1978)

$$_mK = (2nN_A/27\rho)\lim_{E_1\to 0}\frac{n_{||} - n_{\perp}}{\lfloor(n^2+2)/3\rfloor^2\lfloor(\varepsilon_1+2)/3\rfloor^2 E_1^2}$$ (32)

where N_A is Avogadro's number, ε_1 the static dielectric constant, and $n_{||}$ and $n_{\perp}$ are, respectively, refractive indices parallel and perpendicular to $\vec{E}_1$. For a fluid of optically anisotropic, axially symmetric, nonpolar molecules, $_mK$ is given by (Buckingham and Raab, 1957; Ladanyi and Keyes, 1977c)

$$_mK = (4\pi N_A/405)\lfloor\Delta\alpha_{eff}^{K}(\omega_0)\,\Delta\alpha_{eff}^{K}(0)g_2/(k_BT) + 5\gamma_{eff}^{K}\rfloor$$
$$+ _mK^{CI}$$ (33)

Here γ_{eff}^{K} and $\Delta\alpha_{eff}^{K}$ are the effective hyperpolarizability and polarizability appropriate to the Kerr experiment and $_mK^{CI}$

506

the collision induced contribution. An analogous expression is obtained for the molar Cotton-Mouton constant, $_mC$

$$_mC = (4\pi N_A/405) \, [\Delta\alpha^C_{eff}(\omega_0)\Delta\chi_{eff}(0)g_2/(k_BT) + 3\eta_{eff}/2]$$
$$+ \, _mC^{CI} \tag{34}$$

$\Delta\alpha^C_{eff}$ is the effective polarizability anisotropy appropriate to the Cotton-Mouton experiment, $\Delta\chi_{eff}$ is the effective magnetizability anisotropy, η_{eff} the term giving the modification in the effective polarizability by an applied magnetic field, and $_mC^{CI}$ the collision induced contribution.

Application of the molecular theory to $_mK$ (Keyes and Ladanyi, 1979a) and $_mC$ (Madden, 1979) has led to the conclusion that at a given frequency, ω_0,

$$\Delta\alpha^K_{eff} = \Delta\alpha^C_{eff} = \Delta\alpha_{eff}. \tag{35}$$

In addition, Madden (1979) pointed out that the magnitudes of the molecular coefficients in the Cotton-Mouton experiment are such that it is reasonable to assume that

$$\Delta\chi_{eff} = \Delta\chi, \tag{36a}$$

where $\Delta\chi$ is the magnetizability anisotropy of an isolated molecule,

and

$$|_mC^{CI}/_mC| \ll 1, \tag{36b}$$

$$|3\eta_{eff}/2| \ll \left|\frac{\Delta\alpha\Delta\chi}{k_BT}\right|. \tag{36c}$$

Under these assumptions, $_mC$ simplifies considerably to

$$_mC = (4\pi N_A/405) \, \Delta\alpha_{eff}(\omega_0)\Delta\chi(0)g_2/(k_BT). \tag{37}$$

By comparing Eqs. (31) and (37), we note that $\Delta\alpha_{eff}(\omega_0)$ may be obtained from the measurements of $R^{OR}_{VH}(90°)$ and $_mC$

$$\Delta\alpha_{eff}(\omega_0) = R^{OR}_{VH}(90°)/_mC \, [\lambda^4 N_A\Delta\chi/(108\pi^3\rho k_BT)] \, [3/(n^2+2)]^4 \tag{38}$$

Once $\Delta\alpha_{eff}$ has been found in this way, g_2 can be determined from either $_mC$ or $R^{OR}_{VH}(90°)$. This method of measuring g_2 was first used by Battaglia et al. (1979) and will be discussed in greater detail in the section on measurements of effective polarizability anisotropies.

It is not possible to make an analogous set of simplifications in the case of the Kerr effect.

APPROXIMATE EVALUATION OF EFFECTIVE POLARIZABILITIES

In this section we discuss the results obtained by evaluating exactly and approximately the effective polarizabilities, using the first order DID model.

To first order in the DID interactions, using the expansion of $\vec{\delta s}$ given in Eq. (23), we find the following expressions for $\alpha_{0,eff}$ and $\Delta\alpha_{eff}$

$$\alpha_{0,eff}/\alpha_0 = 1 + K/\alpha_0, \tag{39}$$

where

$$K = \frac{1}{3} \sum_{j=2}^{N} \langle \mathrm{Tr}(\overset{\leftrightarrow}{\alpha}_1 \overset{\leftrightarrow}{T}_{1j} \overset{\leftrightarrow}{\alpha}_j) \rangle, \tag{40}$$

and

$$\Delta\alpha_{eff}/\Delta\alpha = 1 + L/\Delta\alpha, \tag{41}$$

where

$$L = \sum_{i=1}^{N} \sum_{j \neq i}^{N} \langle Q^{xz} (\overset{\leftrightarrow}{\alpha}_i \overset{\leftrightarrow}{T}_{ij} \overset{\leftrightarrow}{\alpha}_j)^{xz} \rangle / \langle (Q^{xz})^2 \rangle. \tag{42}$$

Using a Wigner function expansion of the intermolecular pair distribution function, g, expressions for $\alpha_{0,eff}$ and $\Delta\alpha_{eff}$ in terms of radial coefficients of g can be developed (Ladanyi and Keyes, 1977a,b). We review these results here, since they are essential in understanding the subsequent approximations involved in dielectric cavity theories. As can be seen from the above equations, K involves an average over a pair of molecules, while L contains both 2 and 3 molecule correlations. Thus if only the pair distribution function, g, is known, $\alpha_{0,eff}$ can be evaluated exactly, but the 3 molecule contribution to $\Delta\alpha_{eff}$ has to be approximated. Using the expansion of the distribution of molecules 1 and 2 in Wigner functions (Rose, 1957), D^{ℓ}_{mn}

$$g(r_{12}, \Omega_1, \Omega_2) = \sum_{\ell m n} \sum_{\ell' m' n'} g_{\ell m n, \ell' m' n'}(r_{12}) D^{\ell}_{mn}(\Omega_1) D^{\ell'}_{m'n'}(\Omega_2) \tag{43}$$

Here r_{12} is the distance between the molecular centers and Ω_i $(i=1,2)$ symbolizes the set of Euler angles specifying the orientation of molecule i in the intermolecular reference frame (Steele, 1963). Using Eq. (43), K is found to be

$$K = \frac{2\rho}{15} \lfloor 2\alpha_0 \Delta\alpha \tau_{20} - \frac{(\Delta\alpha)^2}{15} \tau_{22} \rfloor \qquad (44)$$

where

$$\tau_{20} = 4\pi \int_0^\infty \frac{dr}{r} g_{200,000}(r) \qquad (45)$$

and

$$\tau_{22} = 4\pi \int_0^\infty \frac{dr}{r} \lfloor 2g_{200,200}(r) + g_{210,2-10}(r) - g_{220,2-20}(r) \rfloor \qquad (46)$$

The 3 molecule averages in L were evaluated in the "product" approximation. This approximation consists of using the superposition approximation to the 3 molecule correlation function. In addition, "connected" terms, which cannot be factored into one dimensional radial integrals, are neglected. The resulting L, denoted by, L_p, is

$$L_p = \frac{6}{5}\rho \left[\alpha_0^2 \tau_{20} + \frac{\alpha_0 \Delta\alpha}{3}(\tau_{20} - \frac{1}{5}\tau_{22}) + \left(\frac{\Delta\alpha}{3}\right)^2 (2\tau_{20} - \frac{1}{5}\tau_{22}) \right]. \qquad (47)$$

K' and L', the counterparts of K and L in Raman scattering, have been derived by Madden (1979) and by De Santis and Sampoli (1984). Here 2 molecule correlations only are involved, so both K' and L' are exact for the first order DID model. They are given by

$$K' = \frac{4\rho}{15} \lfloor (\alpha_0'\Delta\alpha + \Delta\alpha'\alpha_0)\tau_{20} - \frac{\Delta\alpha'\Delta\alpha}{15} \tau_{22} \rfloor \qquad (48)$$

and

$$L' = \frac{6}{5}\rho \left[(\alpha_0'\alpha_0 + \frac{\Delta\alpha'\alpha_0}{3})\tau_{20} - \frac{\alpha_0'\Delta\alpha}{15} \tau_{22} + \frac{\Delta\alpha\Delta\alpha'}{9} (2\tau_{20} - \frac{1}{5}\tau_{22}) \right], \qquad (49)$$

where α_0' and $\Delta\alpha'$ are polarizability derivatives with respect to the appropriate Raman active vibrational normal coordinate.

Calculation of $\alpha_{0,eff}$ and $\Delta\alpha_{eff}$ for several states of diatomic liquids and CS_2 led to results in agreement with experimental trends shown on Table 1. Frenkel and McTague (1980), using an interpolation of their molecular dynamics results, found that the approximation, defined by Eq. (47), underestimated $\Delta\alpha_{eff}$. Results of our own direct simulations (Ladanyi, 1983; Gierke, 1976) confirm their findings, but the differences between the approximate and exact $\Delta\alpha_{eff}$ are smaller than their estimate seemed to indicate. Results of molecular dynamics simulation of $\Delta\alpha_{eff}$ for 2 densities of a model for liquid CO_2 are given in Table 2. As can be seen from the table, the difference between L_p and L is appreciable, indicating that the three molecule correlations are not modelled accurately by the "product" approximation. The table also shows, however, that both L_p and L are nearly linear in ρ in this density range. Thus, Eq. (47) predicts correctly the density dependence of $\Delta\alpha_{eff}$.

The molecular theory described in Sec. III and the "product" approximation of this section, were extended to the optical response of fluids of anisometric molecules by Gierke (1976), Gierke and Burnham (1980), and Gierke and Alms (1982). This extension is conceptually straightforward, but, as these authors have demonstrated, data analysis is quite complex, due to the lack of molecular symmetry.

The effects of delocalization of molecular charge distributions on the effective polarizabilities have been studied (Ladanyi and Keyes, 1978; Ladanyi et al., 1980; Ladanyi, 1983; Ladanyi and Levinger, 1984), using the IAM. The resulting $\Delta\alpha_{eff}$ and $\alpha_{0,eff}$ are found to be somewhat larger than those obtained.

Table 2. First Order Effective Polarizability Anisotropies: Comparison between Exact and "Product" Approximation Results[a] for CO_2 at $k_B T/\epsilon_\ell = 1.6$.

$\rho^* = \rho\sigma^3$	$(\Delta\alpha_{eff}/\Delta\alpha - 1)/\rho^* = \dfrac{L}{\Delta\alpha\rho^*}$		
	Exact	"Product" Approx.	% Difference
0.36	-0.70	-0.88	21%
0.46	-0.68	-0.90	32%

[a] Data based on results of Ladanyi (1983) and Ladanyi and Levinger (1984) for a 2 interaction site model of CO_2. Site-site Lennard-Jones potential parameters: $\sigma = 2.99$ Å, $\epsilon_\ell/k_B = 163.6$ K; bond length: $l/\sigma = 0.793$; polarizabilities: $\alpha_0/\sigma^3 = 0.0985$, $\Delta\alpha/\alpha_0 = 0.7986$.

Table 3. First Order Effective Polarizability and Polarizability
Derivative Anisotropies: Comparison between Center-center
(c) and Site-site (s) Model Results[a] for CO_2 at $k_B T/\varepsilon_\ell$
= 1.6.

	$(\Delta\alpha_{eff}/\Delta\alpha - 1)/\rho^* = \dfrac{L}{\Delta\alpha\rho^*}$			$(\Delta\alpha'_{eff}/\Delta\alpha' - 1)/\rho^* = \dfrac{L'}{\Delta\alpha'\rho^*}$		
$\rho^* = \rho\sigma^3$	(c)	(s)	% Diff.	(c)	(s)	% Diff.
0.36	−0.70	−0.54	24%	−0.62	−0.52	16%
0.46	−0.68	−0.51	24%	−0.65	−0.51	22%

[a]Data based on results of Ladanyi (1983) and Ladanyi and
Levinger (1984) for a 2 interaction site model for CO_2. In
the (s) model, DID interaction sites coincide with Lennard-Jones
potential centers. Polarizability derivatives: $\alpha'_0/\sigma^3 = 0.00211$,
$\Delta\alpha'/\alpha'_0 = 0.439$. Other parameters are as in Table 2.

using the center-center DID model. In the case of two site
molecules, the differences between the two models increase with
increasing bond length. Results obtained for the two site model for
CO_2, described in Table 2, are shown in Table 3. In this case L
and L' for the two models differ by about 20%. In the case of
oxygen, where the the bond length is 0.420σ, the difference drops
to around 10% (Ladanyi, 1983; Ladanyi and Levinger, 1984). The
effects of the polarizability delocalization are certainly important
in fluids of large polyatomic molecules. In these systems the
molecular theory is difficult to apply and the continuum dielectric
theory might represent a more promising approach.

The discussion in this section has dealt with the first order
DID approximation to the effective polarizabilities. Very little
work has been done so far in trying to estimate the importance of
the higher order terms in the Yvon series. There are several reasons
to believe that these terms will be non-negligible. First, an
approximate calculation of the second order DID terms for a fluid of
diatomic molecules has recently been carried out by Bancewisz
(1983). The structural averages were evaluated using a low order
spherical harmonic expansion of the pair distribution function, so
that the approximations involved were more severe than those used in
the "product" approximation. The resulting second order contribution
to $\Delta\alpha_{eff}$ was found to be substantially smaller than the first
order one, but still appreciable. Second, one type of interaction
appearing at the second order level is a reaction field term. It
corresponds to a molecule polarizing its surroundings, which in turn

polarize the molecule. Dielectric cavity theories indicate that such local field contributions are often important (Bottcher, 1973). Finally, as can be seen from the data presented so far, the first order local field effects on effective polarizability anisotropies are large, indicating that the Yvon series for $\Delta\alpha_{eff}$ does not converge rapidly. Further investigation of higher order local field contributions, using computer simulation methods, would thus be of great interest. Resummation of the Yvon series, which would take into account some important higher order terms, while avoiding explicit evaluation of four molecule averages, also appears to be a promising area for further investigation.

DIELECTRIC CAVITY THEORIES

Dielectric cavity theories combine molecular and continuum pictures of optical response. Local field at a molecule is evaluated by considering the molecule inside a cavity within a continous, uniform dielectric medium. The size and the shape of the cavity are usually related to molecular dimensions. As was mentioned earlier, reasonable models for the local field effects on light scattering from fluids of non-spherical molecules are all based on a field experienced by a molecule inside a non-spherical cavity. The cavity shape is taken to be ellipsoidal, since the electrostatic problem is tractable in this case.

In order to understand how these theories are related to the molecular picture, it is instructive to derive from the molecular theory the effective polarizabilities in one of them, the LRK theory. We choose this particular dielectric cavity theory, since neither this theory nor the first order DID approximation to the molecular theory contains any reaction field contributions.

It is appropriate to start the derivation from the "product" approximation, since the irreducible 3 molecule correlations do not exist in any dielectric cavity theory. Since only a single molecule inside spheroidal cavity is considered, all the contributions to K and L_p, which are due to interactions between two anisotropically polarizable molecules are absent. Thus

$$\tau_{22} = 0$$

and

$$\tau_{20} = \tau_{20}^c = \frac{10\pi}{3} \Delta S,$$

(50)

where ΔS is the difference between depolarizing factors parallel and perpendicular to the cavity symmetry axis (Bottcher, 1973). It depends only on the cavity shape. For example, in the case of a prolate spheroid with semi-major axis a and semi-minor axis b, ΔS depends only in the axial ratio d=a/b

$$\Delta S = -\frac{1}{2}(d^2+2)/(d^2-1) + \frac{3}{2}\lfloor d/(d^2-1)^{3/2}\rfloor \ln\lfloor d + (d^2-1)^{1/2}\rfloor .$$

$$(51)$$

Since the tagged molecule interacts only with a uniform dielectric continuum, the contribution to L_p from interactions between pairs of anisotropically polarizable molecules, proportional to $(\Delta\alpha)^2$, should be neglected. Thus in the LRK theory, Eqs. (44) and (47) become

$$K_{LRK} = \frac{8}{9}\pi \alpha_0 \rho \Delta S$$

$$(52)$$

and

$$L_{LRK} = 4\pi\rho\Delta S (\alpha_0^2 + \frac{1}{3}\alpha_0\Delta\alpha) .$$

$$(53)$$

A better approximation to L is obtained by just substituting the dielectric cavity forms of τ_{20} and τ_{22} into Eq. (47). This results in

$$L_c = L_{LRK} + \frac{8}{9}\pi \rho (\Delta\alpha)^2\Delta S .$$

$$(54)$$

The above equation is properly regarded as a molecular theory expression, with the pair distribution given by the cavity approximation, expressed by Eqs. (50). In order to illustrate more clearly the nature of approximations involved in Eqs. (50), we plot in Fig. 2 the integrand of Eq. (45) as a function of r for two thermodynamic states of a liquid of diatomic molecules (Tildesley and Streett, 1976) and for a hard spheroidal particle in an unstructured medium. The latter case corresponds to τ_{20}^c for a dielectric cavity with d = $1+l/\sigma$ (See Table 2 for definitions of l and σ.). In the case of diatomics, Wigner functions in Eq. (43) are replaced by spherical harmonics (Steele, 1963). ℓ, ℓ', and m are sufficient to label the radial coefficients, since n = n' = 0 and m' = -m. Figure 2 shows that $g_{200}^c(r)$ (Keyes and Ladanyi, 1977c) is quite different from $g_{200}(r)$ for a molecular fluid, indicating that short range structural correlations between neighboring molecules are important. It shows also that the differences between g_{200} and g_{200}^c decrease with decreasing density. Dielectric cavity theory should be a better approximation in describing local field effects on the optical response of a large anisotropic molecule in a solvent composed of small isotropic molecules. In that case τ_{22} would vanish and we would expect g_{200} to closely resemble g_{200}^{c22}.

In Table 4, we compare τ_{20}^c for d = $1+l/\sigma$ = 1.793 to values of τ_{20} at 4 densities of the two site model for CO_2, described in Table 2. The table shows that τ_{20}^c is

513

substantially smaller than τ_{20}. Note, however, that τ_{20} is only weakly density dependent, in spite of the fact that g_{200} changes considerably with density, as Fig. (2) illustrates. Thus it is reasonable to assume, as is done in the LRK theory, that d and the resulting τ_{20}^c are independent of density.

The important question is how well does the LRK theory predict the effective polarizabilities. It is at present impossible to answer this question for an arbitrary fluid, although the foregoing discussion should provide some useful guidelines. In Table 5, we compare the exact results for first order DID effective polarizabilities, obtained from molecular dynamics simulation of CO_2 liquid, to those obtained from LRK dielectric cavity theory. We also include the results for $\Delta\alpha_{eff}$ obtained using Eq. (54). The data in Table 5 indicate that the dielectric cavity theory

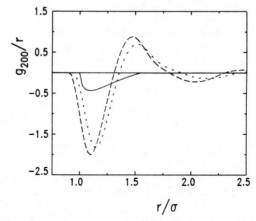

Fig. 2. Integrand of Eq. (45) as a function of separation, r, between molecular centers. Dashed and dotted lines represent the results of molecular dynamics simulation (Tildesley and Streett, 1976) on a fluid of diatomics interacting by a 2-site Lennard-Jones potential with parameters $\sigma = 3.63$ A, $\varepsilon_\ell/k_B = 245.70$ K, and bond length $l/\sigma = 0.5471$. Dashed lines are for the state $\rho^* = 0.60$, $k_B T/\varepsilon_\ell = 1.663$, and dotted lines for $\rho^* = 0.50$, $k_B T/\varepsilon_\ell = 0.930$. The full line is for a spheroid with semi-minor axis b = σ and semi-major axis a = $\sigma + l$.

Table 4. Comparison between Exact[a] and LRK Dielectric Cavity Theory[b] Results for τ_{20} of CO_2.

ρ^*	Exact	LRK
0.32	-4.72	
0.36	-4.74	-2.18
0.42	-4.80	
0.46	-4.89	

[a] Data based on results of Ladanyi and Levinger (1984) for a two interaction site model for CO_2 at $k_BT/\varepsilon_\ell = 1.6$. See Table 2 for definition of model parameters.
[b] Obtained from Eqs. (52) and (53) with $d = 1+l/\sigma = 1.793$, independent of ρ^*.

Table 5. First Order Effective Polarizabilites: Comparison between Exact[a] and LRK Dielectric Cavity Theory[b] Results for CO_2 at $k_BT/\varepsilon_\ell = 1.6$.

ρ^*	$(\Delta\alpha_{eff}/\Delta\alpha - 1)/\rho^* = \dfrac{L}{\Delta\alpha\rho^*}$			$(\alpha_{0,eff}/\alpha_0 - 1)/\rho^* = \dfrac{K}{\alpha_0\rho^*}$	
	Exact	LRK	Eq. (55)	Exact	LRK
0.36	-0.70	-0.41	-0.45	-0.092	-0.046
0.46	-0.68	-0.41	-0.45	-0.096	-0.046

[a] Data based on results of Ladanyi (1983) for a two interaction site model for CO_2. See Table 2 for definition of model parameters.
[b] Obtained from Eqs. (52) and (53) with $d = 1+l/\sigma = 1.793$.

underestimates the local field contribution to $\Delta\alpha_{eff}$ by about 40% and to $\alpha_{0,eff}$ by about 50%. Improved agreement with the molecular theory for $\Delta\alpha_{eff}$ is obtained if Eq. (54) is used instead of the LRK theory. Note that better agreement between the molecular theory and the LRK theory would have been obtained had we chosen d to be larger than $1+l/\sigma$. Table 5 also shows that the LRK theory predicts correctly that the effective polarizabilities are linear in density.

The dielectric cavity treatment of local field problems presents several advantages over the molecular theory:

(a) The local field problem can be solved exactly, including the reaction field contributions. This has recently been done by Brot, who has applied the dielectric cavity theory to several local field problems in fluids of axially symmetric and anisometric molecules. In particular, he considered the DLS intensity (1980), the Kerr constant of non-polar fluids (1980), the refractive index (1981), and the dielectric constant of polar molecule fluids (1982).

(b) Simple, analytic expressions for effective polarizabilities are obtained.

(c) Several experimental trends are correctly predicted. These include the decrease of effective polarizabilities with increasing density, refractive index, and cavity anisotropy.

The main disadvantages of the theory are the following:

(a) The effective polarizabilities are not usually sufficiently accurate to determine g_2.

(b) Important 2 and 3 molecule correlations are neglected.

(c) Cavity dimensions are ill defined. This type of problem occurs with all models which consider a single molecule embedded in an unstructured fluid medium. Stokes-Einstein theory for the self-diffusion constant of a molecule in a liquid presents another example of this problem. In practice, cavity dimensions are usually taken to be molecular dimensions (Bottcher, 1973).

MEASUREMENTS OF EFFECTIVE POLARIZABILITY ANISOTROPIES

Two main methods are presently used to measure $\Delta\alpha_{eff}$. They are the "dilution" experiments and determination of $\Delta\alpha_{eff}$ from measurements of the Cotton-Mouton constant, $_mC$, and depolarized Rayleigh ratio, $R_{VH}^{OR}(90°)$. We will discuss briefly both of these methods.

(A) "Dilution" Experiment

This is the older of the two methods and has been used by several research groups (Burnham et al., 1975; Gierke and Flygare, 1974; Alms et al., 1974; Bertucci, Burnham, Alms, and Flygare, 1977; Bauer, Brauman, Pecora, 1975; Brown, McGuire, and Swinton, 1978), usually with the goal of measuring g_2. In this method, $R_{VH}^{OR}(90°)$ is measured for a solution of anisotropic molecule solute A in isotropic molecule solvent B. $R_{VH}^{OR}(90°)$ is then due only to the solute molecules. The anisotropic local field factor, L_{an}, or, alternatively $\Delta\alpha_{eff}/\Delta\alpha$, is assumed to be a function of the refractive index n of the solution, but to be independent of other properties of B. Under this assumption, g_2, for a mole fraction X_A of the solute is

$$g_2(X_A) = \frac{R_{VH}^{OR}(90°;X_A)/\ L_{an}\lfloor n(X_A)\rfloor\ _A(X_A)}{\lim_{X_A \to 0}\ R_{VH}^{OR}(90°;X_A)/\ L_{an}\lfloor n(X_A)\rfloor\ _A(X_A)} \tag{55}$$

The molecular theory indicates that the assumption, $L_{an} = L_{an}\lfloor n(X_A)\rfloor$, is an approximation which ignores specific structural correlations among A and B molecules Keyes and Ladanyi, 1979b). It is, however, consistent with the dielectric cavity theory. For example, the LRK theory, described in the previous section leads to the following results

$$\Delta\alpha_{eff}/\Delta\alpha = 1 + 4\pi\rho\Delta S(\alpha_{0,A}X_A + \alpha_{0,B}X_B)(\alpha_{0,A}/\Delta\alpha + \tfrac{1}{3}), \tag{56}$$

and

$$\frac{n^2-1}{n^2+2} = \frac{4\pi\rho}{3}\ (\alpha_{0,A}X_A + \alpha_{0,B}X_B)(1 + \frac{8\pi}{3}\ \Delta S X_A \Delta\alpha_A). \tag{57}$$

Substituting Eq. (57) into Eq. (56) and neglecting higher order terms in ΔS

$$L_{an} = \left(\frac{n^2+2}{3}\right)^4 (\Delta\alpha_{eff}/\Delta\alpha)^2 = \left(\frac{n^2+2}{3}\right)^4 [1 + \left(\frac{n^2-1}{n^2+2}\right)\Delta S(3\alpha_{0,A}/\Delta\alpha_A + 1)]^2 \tag{58}$$

The above expression for L_{an} can be seen to have the desired form. In order to derive $L_{an}\lfloor n(X_A)\rfloor$ from the molecular theory, several approximations have to be made. As was shown by Keyes and Ladanyi (1978), they are analogous to the ones involved in the derivation of the LRK theory from the "product" approximation, namely

$$\tau_{20}^{AA} = \tau_{20}^{AB}, \tag{59}$$

$$|\tau_{22}^{AA}/3| \ll |\tau_{20}| \tag{60}$$

and

$$\frac{2}{9} (\Delta\alpha_A/\alpha_{0,A})^2 \ll 1. \tag{61}$$

Eqs. (59) - (61) may, in fact, be quite reasonable approximations for solutions which are reasonably close to being ideal. Eq. (59) has never been tested for solutions, but as Table 4 shows, τ_{20} for a pure liquid is nearly independent of density. For a mixture, it may then be insensitive to the identity of neighbors of an A molecule. Eqs. (60) and (61) are found to be reasonable approximations in cases of pure liquids studied so far (Ladanyi and Keyes, 1977a,b; Ladanyi and Levinger, 1984).

(B) Combination of Cotton-Mouton and DLS Experiments

This method is relatively recent and we are aware of only a few examples of its use (Battaglia et al., 1979; Madden, Battaglia, Cox, Pierens, and Champion, 1980). The assumptions involved in using it to determine $\Delta\alpha_{eff}$ and g_2 have already been discussed. They are summarized in Eqs. (36) and depend on the magnitudes of the components of the molecular magnetizabilities and of the effective magnetic field induced "hyperpolarizability", η_{eff}. They appear to be reasonable for many liquids (Madden, 1979). This method has the advantage over the previous one in that it involves measurements only on the system of interest. In the "dilution" experiment, the properties of the A - B mixture are used to deduce properties of pure A.

The accuracy of these two methods for determining $\Delta\alpha_{eff}$ and g_2 is at present best assessed by comparing the results obtained in using them. Such a comparison was made by Battaglia, Cox, and Madden (1979). These authors obtained values of g_2 in liquids CS_2, benzene, and hexafluorobenzene using the measurements of C_m and $R_{VH}^{OR}(90°)$ and compared their results to those of the earlier "dilution" experiments. They found that the results of the two methods were in agreement in the cases where the "dilution" experiment validity criteria, discussed in part (A) of this section, were properly met. In particular, $L_{an} = L_{an}[n(X_A)]$ was <u>experimentally</u> determined for a range of n values, rather than assumed to have a specific functional form, such as, for example, $L_{an} = L_{LL}^{1/2}$, and strong solute - solvent interactions were absent.

SUMMARY AND DISCUSSION

We have described the present state of theoretical understanding and experimental methods in the area of local field effects on light scattering and induced birefringence in liquids of optically anisotropic molecules. These effects may be characterized in terms of effective polarizabilities. Most of the effort in recent years has gone into determining $\Delta\alpha_{eff}$, which is more strongly affected by fluid structure and intermolecular DID interactions than $\alpha_{0,eff}$. Much progress has been made through a combination of experimental, theoretical, and computer simulation methods. Molecular theory and calculations based on it have shown that the local field contribution to $\Delta\alpha_{eff}$ is negative in all cases where the long axis of the molecular polarizability tensor is the same as the corresponding molecular axis. This contribution appears to have an approximately linear density dependence and increases in magnitude as the anisotropy in the molecular shape increases. The same trends are predicted by continuum theories, which approximate the local field at a molecule by a field inside an anisotropic dielectric cavity. These theories can only make qualitative predictions about $\alpha_{0,eff}$ and $\Delta\alpha_{eff}$ since the actual effective cavity shape is determined by the short range liquid structure and is not simply related to the shape of a single molecule. Molecular theory of optical response of non-polar anisotropic molecule fluids has established connections among DLS, Kerr effect, and Cotton-Mouton effect. These connections have been successfully exploited in developing an ingenious new method for measuring $\Delta\alpha_{eff}$ and g_2.

Several outstanding problems, most of which have already been mentioned, readily come to mind. The first one is the evaluation of higher order terms in the Yvon series, especially for $\Delta\alpha_{eff}$, where this series converges slowly. The most straightforward approach is to calculate the second order terms by computer simulation. A more efficient method would be resum the Yvon series to include, for example, the reaction field contribution to $\Delta\alpha_{eff}$ at the first order level. Another problem in need of further investigation is that of the importance of polarizability delocalization and of the best way of modelling intermolecular interactions induced by an external electric field. The article by K.C.L. Hunt (1984) addresses this question in greater detail. Recent calculations of $\Delta\alpha_{eff}$ indicate that this quantity is strongly density dependent. Experimental investigations of this quantity for liquids of relatively simple polyatomic molecules, accesible to computer simulation studies, would be very helpful in testing various models for $\Delta\alpha_{eff}$. Given the fact that the only alternative to using dielectric cavity theories to evaluate effective polarizabilities is now computer simulation, it would be desirable to try to develop a simple and reliable method for choosing the correct cavity shapes.

Progress in all these areas is possible using the present computer and experimental technologies and will enhance our understanding of the optical response of molecular fluids.

REFERENCES

Alms, G.R., Gierke, T.D., and Flygare, W.H., 1974, Depolarized Rayleigh scattering in liquids: The density and temperature dependence of the orientational pair correlations in liquids composed of anisometric molecules, J. Chem. Phys., 61:4083.

Applequist, J., Carl, J.R., and Fung, K.K., 1974, An atom dipole model for molecular polarizability. Application to polyatomic molecules and determination of atom polarizabilities, J. Am. Chem. Soc., 94:2952.

Applequist, J., 1974, An atom dipole interaction model for molecular optical properties, Acc. Chem. Res., 10:79.

Bancewicz, T., 1983, Rayleigh light scattering by liquids composed of interacting anisotropic molecules. Spherical tensor approach within the second order approximation and the DID model, Molec. Phys., 50:173.

Battaglia, M.R., Cox, T.I., and Madden, P.A., 1979, The orientational correlation parameter for liquid CS_2, C_6H_6 and C_6F_6, Molec. Phys., 37:1413.

Bauer, D.R., Brauman, J.I., and Pecora, R., 1975, Depolarized Rayleigh scattering and orientational relaxation of molecules in solution. IV. Mixtures of hexafluorobenzene and benzene with mesitylene, J. Chem. Phys., 63:53.

Bertucci, S.J., Burnham, A.K., Alms, G.R. and Flygare, W.H., 1977, Light scattering studies of orientational pair correlations in liquids composed of anisometric molecules, J. Chem. Phys., 66:605.

Boots, H.M.J., Bedeaux, D., and Mazur, P., 1975, On the theory of multiple scattering I, Physica, A76:397.

Bottcher, C.J.F., and Bordewijk, P., 1978, "Theory of Electric Polarization", Vol. II, Elsevier, Amsterdam.

Bottcher, C.J.F., 1973, "Theory of Electric Polarization", Vol. I, Elsevier, Amsterdam.

Brot, C., 1980a, Anisometric molecules in dense fluids. I. The depolarized light scattering intensity by anisometric molecules in solution, Molec. Phys., 39:683.

Brot, C., 1980b, Anisometric molecules in dense fluids. II Kerr constant of non-polar anisometric molecules in solutions, Molec. Phys., 41:1195.

Brot, C, 1981, Anisometric molecules in dense fluids. III Permitivité non polaire et refractivité des solutions diluées et des liquides purs à molecules anisometriques, Molec. Phys., 43:1021.

Brot, C, 1982, Anisometric molecules in dense fluids. VI. The static permitivity of solutions of ellipsoidal polar

molecules: extension of the Onsager model, Molec. Phys.,
45:543.

Brown, N.M.D., McGuire, J.F., and Swinton, F.L., 1978, Depolarized
Rayleigh scattering from binary mixtures composed of
optically anisotropic molecules, Faraday Discuss. Chem. Soc.,
66:244.

Buckingham A.D., 1967, Permanent and induced molecular moments
and long-range intermolecular interactions, Adv. Chem. Phys.
12:107, and references therein.

Buckingham, A.D., Stiles, P.J., and Ritchie, G.L.D., 1971, Theory
of the solvent effect on the molar refraction, polarization,
Kerr and Cotton-Mouton constants of non-polar solutes,
Trans. Faraday Soc., 67:577.

Buckingham, A.D., and Raab, R.E., 1957, A molecular theory of the
electro-optical Kerr effect in liquids, J. Chem. Soc.,
2341 (1957).

Buckingham, A.D., and Pople, J.A., 1956, A theory of magnetic double
refraction, Proc. Phys. Soc., B 69:1133.

Burnham, A.K., Alms, G.R., and Flygare, W.H., 1975, The local
electric field. I. The effect on isotropic and anisotropic
Rayleigh scattering, J. Chem. Phys., 62:3289.

Burnham, A.K., 1977, "Light Scattering and Electric Birefringence
Studies of Gases and Liquids and Magnetic Studies of
Aromaticity", Ph. D. Thesis, University of Illinois,
unpublished.

Cox, T.I., Battaglia, M.R., and Madden, P.A., 1979, Properties of
liquid CS_2 from the allowed light scattering spectra,
Molec. Phys., 38:1539.

De Santis, A, and Sampoli, M., 1984, Raman spectra of fluid N_2.
Temperature and density behavior of the second moment,
Molec. Phys., 51:97.

Einstein, A., 1910, Theory of the opalescence of homogeneous liquids
and liquid mixtures in the neighborhood of the critical
state, Ann. Physik, 33:1275.

Felderhof, B.U., 1974, On the propagation and scattering of light in
fluids, Physica, A76:486.

Fixman, M., 1955, Molecular theory of light scattering, J. Chem.
Phys., 23:2074.

Frenkel, D., and McTague, J.P., 1980, Molecular dynamics studies of
orientational and collision induced light scattering in
molecular fluids, J. Chem. Phys., 72:2801.

Gierke, T.D., 1976, Dynamic orientational pair correlations in
symmetric tops and static orientational pair correlations
in anisometric molecules, J. Chem. Phys., 65:3873.

Gierke, T.D., and Alms, G.R., 1982, Analysis of the depolarized
Rayleigh light scattering spectrum of liquids composed of
anisometric molecules: Nitrobenzene, J. Chem. Phys.,
76:4809.

Gierke, T.D., and Burnham, A.K., 1980, A comparison of effective
polarizabilities from electro-optical experiments using

microscopic and macrocsopic theories of the local field,
J. Chem. Phys., 73:4822.

Gierke, T.D., and Flygare, W.H., 1974, Depolarized Rayleigh
scattering in liquids. Molecular reorientation and pair
correlations in nematic liquid crystal: MBBA, J. Chem.
Phys., 61:2231.

Hunt, K.C.L., 1985, this volume.

Hynne, F., 1977, Dielectric screening and susceptibility
fluctuations in optical scattering, Molec. Phys., 34:681.

Keyes, T., Kivelson, D., and McTague, J.P., 1971, Theory of
k-independent depolarized Rayleigh wing scattering in liquids
composed of anisotropic molecules, J. Chem. Phys., 55:4096.

Keyes, T., and Ladanyi, B.M., 1984, The internal field problem
in depolarized light scattering, Adv. Chem. Phys., in press.

Keyes, T., and Ladanyi, B.M., 1977a, The role of local fields and
interparticle pair correlations in light scattering by
dense fluids. II Depolarized spectrum for nonspherical
molecules, Molec. Phys., 33:1099.

Keyes, T., and Ladanyi, B.M., 1977b, The role of local fields and
interparticle pair correlations in light scattering by
dense fluids. IV. Removal of the point polarizability
approximation, Molec. Phys., 33:1271.

Keyes, T., and Ladanyi, B.M., 1977c, Can dielectric theories and
measurements be used to predict depolarized light
scattering intensities?, Molec. Phys., 34:765.
The expression in Eq. (23) of this paper should be multiplied by -1/2. In the present notation, d=a/b and r is in
units of b.

Keyes, T., and Ladanyi, B.M., 1979a, The relation of the Kerr effect
to depolarized Rayleigh scattering, Molec. Phys., 37:1643.

Keyes, T., and Ladanyi, B.M., 1979b, Light scattering from two
component systems, an analysis of the 'dilution experiment',
Molec. Phys., 38:605.

Kielich, S., 1967, Role of intermolecular interaction in anisotropic
light scattering by liquids, J. Chem. Phys., 46:4090.

Ladanyi, B.M., 1983, Molecular dynamics study of Rayleigh light
scattering from molecular fluids, J. Chem. Phys., 78:2189.

Ladanyi, B.M., and Keyes, T., 1977a, The role of local fields and
interparticle pair correlations in light scattering by dense
fluids. I. Depolarized intensities due to orientational
fluctuations, Molec. Phys., 33:1063.

Ladanyi, B.M., and Keyes, T., 1977b, The role of local fields and
interparticle pair correlations in light scattering by
dense fluids. III. Polarized scattering by nonspherical
molecules, Molec. Phys., 33:1247.

Ladanyi, B.M., and Keyes, T., 1977c, Theory of the static Kerr
effect in dense fluids, Molec. Phys., 34:1643.

Ladanyi. B.M., and Keyes, T., 1978, The intensity of light scattered
by liquid CS_2, J. Chem. Phys., 68:3217.

Ladanyi, B.M., Keyes, T., Tildesley, D.J., and, Streett, W.B.,

1980, Structure and equilibrium optical properties of liquid CS_2, Molec. Phys., 39:645.

Ladanyi, B.M., and Levinger, N.E., 1984, Computer simulation of Raman scattering from molecular fluids, J. Chem. Phys., 81:2620.

Lorentz, H.A., 1952, "Theory of Electrons", Dover, New York.

Madden, P.A., 1979, unpublished results.

Madden, P.A., Battaglia, M.R., Cox, T.I., Pierens, R.K., and Champion, J.V., 1980, The orientational correlation parameter g_2 of symmetrical benzene derivatives, Chem. Phys. Lett., 76:604.

Malmberg, M.S., and Lippincott, E.R., 1969, Evidence of molecular interactions in Rayleigh light scattering, J. Colloid Interface Sci., 27:591.

Onsager, L., 1936, Electric moments of molecules in liquids, J. Am. Chem. Soc., 58:1486.

Raman, C.V., and Krishnan, K.S., 1928, Theory of light scattering in liquids, Phil. Mag., 5:498.

Rose, M.E., 1957, "Elementary Theory of Angular Momentum", Wiley, New York.

Schoen, P.E., Cheung, P.S.Y., Jackson, D.A., and Powles, J.G., 1975, The properties of liquid nitrogen. III. The light scattering spectrum, Molec. Phys., 29:1197.

Scholte, T.G., 1949, Theory of the dielectric constant of polar liquids, Physica, 15:437.

Steele, W.A., 1963, Statistical mechanics of nonspherical molecules, J. Chem. Phys., 39:3197.

Smoluchowski, M., 1908, Ann. Physik, 25:205.

Tildesley, D.J., and Madden, P.A., 1983, Time correlation functions for a model of liquid carbon disulfide, Molec. Phys., 48:129.

Tildesley, D.J., and Streett, W.B., 1976, Computer simulations of polyatomic molecules. I. Monte Carlo studies of hard diatomics, Proc. Roy. Soc. London, A 348:485.

Yvon, J., 1937, "Recherches sur la théorie cinétique des fluides. I. Fluctuations en densité. II. La propagation et la diffusion de la lumière", Hermann & Cie, Paris.

PRESSURE - AN ESSENTIAL EXPERIMENTAL VARIABLE IN SPECTROSCOPIC

STUDIES OF LIQUIDS

Jiri Jonas

Department of Chemistry, School of Chemical Sciences
University of Illinois
Urbana, IL 61801

ABSTRACT

The results of Raman experiments on molecular liquids at high pressure are reviewed. The density and temperature effects on vibrational dephasing in tetramethylsilane and isobutylene are discussed in terms of current theoretical models. Selected results of high pressure Rayleigh and Raman experiments on collision induced scattering in spherical molecules CH_4, SF_6 and triatomics CS_2, COS and CO_2 demonstrate well the essential role of high pressure in studying collision induced spectra.

INTRODUCTION

The main goal of this article is to show that pressure is an essential experimental variable in all spectroscopic studies which attempt to improve our basic understanding of the liquid state. The use of high pressure to investigate the density effects on various dynamic processes provides the common theme in this article which covers several different topics which illustrate the range of problems that can be studied. This article is organized as follows. First, as an introduction I shall give several specific examples to illustrate the main reasons why we perform Raman experiments at high pressure. Second, I shall review the main results of our studies of vibrational dephasing focusing on tetramethylsilane and isobutylene. These studies will illustrate well the importance of isothermal density dependence experiments. Third, I shall discuss our current work on collision induced scattering covering both Rayleigh and Raman scattering. I shall review some of our results on density and temperature effects on depolarized Rayleigh scattering in spherical top molecules such as CH_4 and SF_6, and also mention our Rayleigh and Raman experiments on triatomics CS_2, COS and CO_2. These experiments deal both with collision induced scattering contribution to allowed Raman bands and collision induced forbidden Raman bands. The results so far obtained provide convincing evidence that the investigation of density effects is essential in this specific area of interaction induced spectra.

There are several fundamental reasons for performing experiments on liquids at high pressures. If one investigates the temperature dependence of some dynamic process in a liquid at atmospheric pressure, the experimental data reflect both the change of the kinetic energy of the molecules and the change in the average volume available for the motion of the molecule. Only by carrying out a high pressure experiment one can separate the effect of temperature and density on the molecular motions and interactions in a liquid. In order to provide a rigorous test of a theoretical model of a liquid or a model of a specific dynamic process, one has to perform isobaric, isochoric, and isothermal experiments. The importance of the separation of the effects of temperature and density on molecular motions and interactions have been amply demonstrated in a number of NMR (Jonas, 1982) and Raman (Jonas, 1984) studies carried out in our laboratory. In addition, the use of pressure enables one to investigate liquids well above their normal boiling point and also allows the study of supercritical dense fluids. The temperature and density range covered in such high pressure experiments is very broad (Lamb and Jonas, 1981).

Our recent studies of intermolecular interactions and Fermi resonance in several systems may serve as yet another example of the important role of high pressure experiments. At this point I only mention one aspect of our Raman studies of liquid ethylene carbonate (C_{2v} symmetry) 1-3-dioxalan-one, a dipolar liquid, with a large permanent dipole moment (4.9 Debye), and of NH_3 and ND_3.

The Fermi resonance between the carbonyl stretching (ν_2) and the first overtone of the ring breathing vibration ($2\nu_7$) have been studied in liquid ethylene carbonate (Schindler et al., 1984) in the pressure range between 1 and 3000 bar and at temperatures from $40°C$ to $160°C$. Fig. 1 shows the pressure change of relative intensities of the two isotropic lines comprising the $\nu_2 + 2\nu_7$ bands which are in Fermi resonance.

Since Fermi resonance parameters are sensitive to intermolecular potential, we can change them by varying temperature and pressure. When this is done, the transition dipole moments of the $\nu_2 + 2\nu_7$ bands are found to vary and the Fermi resonance treatment enables us to estimate the changes in their relative magnitude. The high pressure experiments provided the critical spectroscopic information needed for the theoretical analysis of intermolecular

526

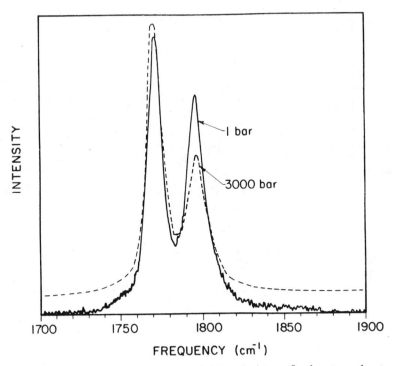

Fig. 1. The change in relative intensities of the two isotropic
lines in liquid ethylene carbonate. The $\nu_2 + 2\nu_7$ bands
are coupled by Fermi resonance. At constant temperature
of $80°C$ the pressure is changed from 1 bar (full line) to
3000 bar (dashed line).

interactions in the dipolar liquid of ethylene carbonate.

Another example is the Fermi resonance coupled ν_1 and $2\nu_4$ modes
in ND_3 occurring in the region 2340 cm^{-1} to 2410 cm^{-1} (Bradley,
et al, 1984). The degree of coupling is governed by the anisotropic part of the intermolecular potential which is modulated by
the intermolecular interactions and thus changes with density and
temperature. Fig. 2 shows the changes in relative intensities of
these Fermi resonance coupled bands for the extreme density range of
our measurements. Again, for ND_3 liquid the availability of spectroscopic data at high pressure proved essential for the theoretical
analysis. These two specific examples show clearly the value of the

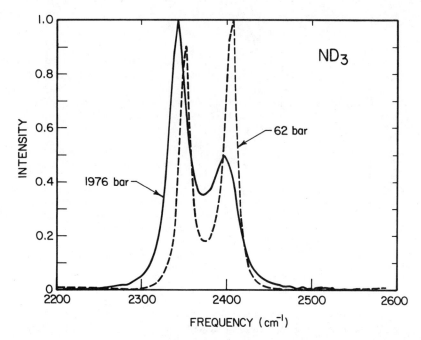

Fig. 2. Density effects on the relative intensity of the isotropic $\nu_1 + 2\nu_4$ Fermi resonance lines in ND_3. The full line denotes density $\rho = 0.457g \ cm^{-3}$ (T = 100°C; P = 62 bar) and the dashed line denotes density $\rho = 0.730g \ cm^{-3}$ (T = 0°C; P = 1967 bar).

pressure variable in studies of various spectroscopic phenomena in fluids.

VIBRATIONAL DEPHASING

The broadening of isotropic Raman band shapes may be influenced by several mechanisms. The two dominant ones involve energy relaxation via inelastic collisions and phase relaxation via quasi-elastic collisional processes. In the inelastic collisional process the energy levels of the molecule change, whereas the quasi-elastic collisions cause only a phase shift in the wave function, while the molecule remains in the same energy level. Although energy relaxation and dephasing are concepts initially created for the framework of the gaseous state, where collision processes are well defined and isolated, their extension to dense fluids is possible and the mechanisms will retain their original meaning. Both mechanisms have been investigated experimentally for a number of molecules, and it was found that phase relaxation occurs much faster than energy relaxation. In all cases discussed in this review, the broadening of the isotropic Raman lineshapes arises from a dephasing process.

General models which lead to dephasing of molecular vibration in the liquid state has been extensively reviewed (Oxtoby, 1979). We have focused our interest on four different models selected for their success in describing vibrational dephasing in the liquid state and which can be compared to experimental results on a quite simple basis.

The first one is the isolated binary collision (IBC) model of Fischer-Laubereau (1975). This model extended by Oxtoby (1979) gives the dephasing time, τ_{ph}, as

$$\tau_{ph}^{-1} = \frac{kT}{\omega^2 L^2 \tau_c} \frac{\mu(\gamma_A^4 + \gamma_B^4) B}{M^2} , \qquad (1)$$

where B represents the correction for anharmonicity, L is the range of interaction of the intermolecular potential, ω the frequency of the oscillator, τ_c the collision time, μ, γ_A, γ_B, M are mass factors.

The vibrational correlation time τ_v which can be obtained from the experimental half width at half height Γ (cm^{-1}) of the isotropic Raman profile is related to the dephasing time τ_{ph} by $\tau_v = 2\tau_{ph} = (2\pi c \Gamma)^{-1}$. Oxtoby (1979) has developed a hydrodynamic model for vibrational dephasing of an anharmonic diatomic oscillator A-B which is nonlinearly coupled to the thermal bath. Wertheimer (1978) has developed a model for vibrational relaxation which combines both dephasing and resonance contributions into a single expression. Finally Lynden-Bell (1977) has proposed a theory for vibrational linewidth in which dephasing is due to very rapidly varying fluctuations in intermolecular forces resulting from relative translational motion. The expected vibrational correlation time is

$$\tau_v^{-1} = A' \frac{\rho}{D} , \qquad (2)$$

where A' is a constant, ρ the density and D the self diffusion coefficient.

In the measurements of isotropic lineshapes of the C-H, C-D and C-C stretching modes in a variety of simple molecular liquids we found that the IBC model, which considers only the repulsive part of the intermolecular potential in calculating the dephasing rate, reproduces the general trends of the experimental data.

As a part of our systematic studies of vibrational dephasing we have recently investigated (Sharko et al., 1983) the ν_3 Si-CH$_3$ stretching mode in neat liquid tetramethylsilane (TMS). This choice was convenient for a number of reasons. TMS is a spherical molecule and the ν_3 mode is infrared inactive. As a consequence, neither dipolar nor inductive interactions, are present. Furthermore, as the dipolar effects which generally give rise to the most important contribution in the resonant energy transfer mechanism are non-existent, we suspect that this last contribution in TMS is neglible. From a purely experimental point of view, the Raman profile associated with the ν_3 mode can be easily studied as it is well isolated from other Raman peaks, and as this mode is completely polarized, the isotropic Raman profile is readily obtained without correction for the anisotropic one. Finally, extensive measurements of density, viscosity, self diffusion coefficients and hard sphere diameters were reported in a previous study by Parkhurst and Jonas (1975). These data are essential for a detailed comparison of experimental results with the theoretical models available.

We calculated at constant temperature the relative variation of linewidth $\Gamma(\rho)/\Gamma(\rho_0)$ as a function of reduced density ρ/ρ_0 where ρ_0 is the density at 4 kbar. We find this type of representation used by Schweizer and Chandler (1982) very convenient since the theoretical expressions contain parameters which are not easily obtainable. However, we prefer here to use as "reference" point the Γ obtained at high pressures instead of the low pressure Γ', since the high pressure lineshapes are broader and consequently the measured linewidth is more accurate. This avoids a systematic error in the relative ratio of the linewidths. The results for the two extreme values of the temperature range investigated are given in Figure 3. It appears that at constant temperature and increasing density, the relative ratio of linewidths increases. At constant temperature the Lynden-Bell theory (Lynden-Bell, 1977) predicts a trend of the relative linewidth proportional to $\rho D_0/\rho_0 D$. From the Wertheimer theory (Wertheimer, 1978) and the Oxtoby hydrodynamic model (Oxtoby, 1979) we expect a trend which is given by D_0/D and η/η_0, respectively. It is clear from Figure 3 that the general trend of the variation of the relative Γ obtained from these different models is the same as that observed. Furthermore, as we can expect from an examination of the corresponding theoretical expression of $\Gamma(\rho)/\Gamma(\rho_0)$, the results obtained from the different models are close to each other. However, these models do not give a satisfactory description of our experimental results. This disagreement is observed at all temperatures investigated.

The IBC model predicts at constant temperature a relative linewidth change proportional to $\tau_c(\rho)/\tau_c(\rho_0)$. The collision time τ_c is closely related to the Enskog collision time, τ_E $\tau_c^c = 2/3 \ \tau_E$. The results for the IBC model are also given in Figure 3. experimental error we find that this model predicts remarkably well

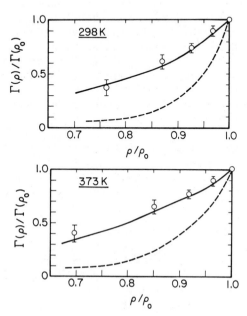

Fig. 3. Dependence of the experimental linewidth (o) $\Gamma(\rho)/\Gamma(\rho_0)$ upon the reduced density, ρ/ρ_0, (ρ_0 is the density at 4 kbar), for TMS at 298K and 373K. The full line denotes the theoretical prediction of the IBC model. The hydrodynamic model, the Wertheimer model and the Lynden-Bell model give predictions too close to be distinguished on the scale of this figure and are therefore represented by the single dashed line.

the experimental density dependence of the relative linewidth at all temperatures investigated.

In view of the fact that for several bands, particularly at lower frequency, the predictions using the IBC model differ from experimental data, we decided to extend our systematic investigations to additional liquids. Isobutylene (3-methylpropene) appeared to be a good candidate for such a study because it shows two strongly polarized Raman bands with intermediate frequencies. The Raman lineshapes of the ν_4 (A_1) symmetric C=CH$_2$ stretching mode of 1657 cm^{-1} and the ν_9 (A_1) symmetric C-CH$_3$ stretching mode of 805 cm^{-1} in isobutylene were measured (Schindler and Jonas, 1980) as a function of pressure from vapor pressure to 0.8g cm^{-1}, over the temperature range from 248 K to 348 K. For both bands studied, within experimental error, the frequencies of the peak maxima coincide for polarized and depolarized spectra. The frequencies depend only on density and are independent of temperature at a given density as shown in Figure 4.

A very different behavior of these two bands is observed. There is a large red shift from the gas to the liquid (at $\rho=2\rho_{crit}$) for the C=CH$_2$ band, while frequency hardly changes over the measured liquid range. The opposite is true for the C-CH$_3$ band, which shows the lowest frequency at approximately the critical density, so that the gas-liquid ($\rho=2\rho_{crit}$) shift is nearly zero, while we see a large blue shift when the density of the liquid is increased. A quantitative interpretation of these facts must await further experimental results and theoretical progress, but a qualitative explanation of the different behavior of the two vibrations can already be presented now considering that the ν_9 and ν_4 vibrations differ in two distinct ways. One can clearly expect that these differences also influence the half-widths of the bands.

First, the C=CH$_2$ vibration is strongly infrared active, while the C-CH$_3$ vibration is inactive. Secondly, the classical vibrational amplitudes show that the repulsive forces of the bath may affect more the C-CH$_3$ vibration. If only Lennard-Jones forces are considered, vibrational frequencies are expected to increase with density. It is the effect of $(d\alpha/d\ell)$ and of $(d\mu/\ell d)$ which can produce a red shift, where α is the polarizability, μ the dipole moment, and ℓ the bond length. The large dipole moment change of the C=CH$_2$ vibration, therefore, is connected with the large gas-liquid

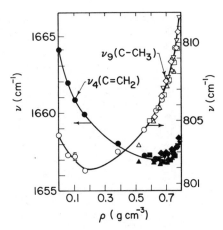

Fig. 4. Density dependence of the isotropic band frequency for the
$C=CH_2$ and the $C-CH_3$ stretching modes in liquid isobutylene
over the temperature range $-25°C$ to $75°C$ (no detectable
temperature effect).

frequency shifts. The $C-CH_3$ vibration, on the other hand, due to
the large vibrational amplitudes of the end groups, is strongly
affected by the hard core repulsive forces predominant in the
liquid. These short-ranged forces, which lead to increasing force
constants and increasing vibrational frequencies, become more effective with increasing density. Figure 5 shows the density dependence
of the experimental halfwidth $\Gamma = (2\pi c \tau_V)^{-1}$, where τ_V is the dephasing time and Γ is proportional to the dephasing rate. From
Figure 5 we see that increasing density, at constant temperature,
affects the bandwidths of the two vibrations in a qualitatively
different way. The $C-CH_3$ stretching bandwidth increases with increasing density, a behavior found for many other modes in liquids.
This basic trend can be predicted in terms of a IBC model based on
rapidly varying repulsive interactions. The most interesting result
of this study was the observed decrease of the bandwidth of the
$C=CH_2$ stretching mode (strongly infrared active band) with increasing density. To our best knowledge, this was the first experimental observation of a decrease in dephasing rate with increasing density in a liquid. It appears that this band is inhomogeneous-

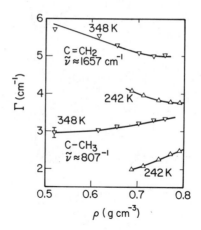

Fig. 5. Density dependence of the halfwidth at half maximum
intensity Γ (cm^{-1}), for the C=CH$_2$ and the C-CH$_3$
stretching modes in liquid isobutylene at 248K and
348K.

ly broadened as it is affected by environmentally induced frequency
fluctuations. These fluctuations are due to dispersion, induction,
and electrostatic forces which depend on the dipole (0.5 D) and
polarizability of the molecule. The decay of the inhomogeneous
invironment around a molecule results in motional narrowing. The
correlation function modeling (Rotschild, 1976) which used the Kubo
stochastic lineshape theory was in agreement with our experimental
data. In further studies we found a similar decrease in bandwidth
for the C=O stretching mode in liquid acetone (Schindler et al., 1982)
as shown in Figure 6.

Again the attractive interactions influence the dephasing process and are responsible for the density behavior of the bandwidth.
The Raman experiments on isobutylene and acetone have been discussed
in a theoretical study of dephasing by Schweizer and Chandler (1982)
who analyzed in detail the relative role of slowly varying attractive interactions and rapidly varying repulsive interactions on the
frequency shifts and dephasing in liquids. Their theoretical model
correctly predicts the isothermal density dependence of the C=CH$_2$
bandwidth in isobutylene and the C=O bandwidth in acetone.

From the experimental results discussed, it is evident that high
pressure experiments, and in particular the isothermal density dependence of a specific dynamic process, are essential for a meaningful
test of theoretical models of a various dynamic processes in liquids.

534

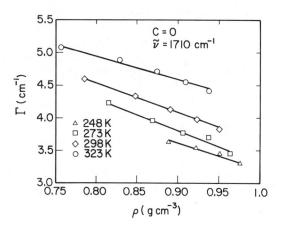

Fig. 6. Density and temperature dependence of Γ (cm^{-1}) of the isotropic carbonyl band in liquid acetone.

COLLISION INDUCED SCATTERING

The overwhelming majority of Raman studies of the dynamic processes in liquids dealt with the investigation of the properties of individual molecules. The reorientational and vibrational relaxation reflect only indirectly the influence of intermolecular interactions. In the past decade, the problem of collision induced scattering (CIS) has attracted both theoretical and experimental interest (Gelbart, 1974; Birnbaum, 1980). It has been observed that collisions in dense liquids or gases produce depolarized Rayleigh spectra in fluids composed of atoms or molecules of spherical symmetry. Collision induced Raman spectra forbidden by selection rules (symmetry) have been investigated in polyatomic molecular liquids as well as collision induced contributions to the allowed Raman bands. The origin of these collision induced spectra lies in the polarizability changes produced by intermolecular interactions. It is clear that studies of CIS can provide direct information about intermolecular interactions. The CIS represents though a very difficult theoretical problem because the scattered intensity depends on the polarizability change in a cluster of interacting molecules, and the time dependence of this change is a function of the intermolecular potential.

In analogy with the Raman studies of vibrational dephasing and reorientational motions in dense liquids, one may expect that studies of CIS at high pressure will contribute in a major way towards a better understanding of these phenomena and help to establish a sound experimental basis for further theoretical work. Since few studies of CIS in polyatomic molecular liquids have so far appeared, we have started systematic high pressure experiments dealing with CIS in dense liquids. Our interest focuses on three main areas: first, for molecules of spherical symmetry, we follow the effects of density and temperature on the depolarized Rayleigh scattering. Second, we investigate the CIS contribution to allowed Raman bands. Third, we study the density and temperature behavior of collision induced forbidden Raman bands.

Depolarized Rayleigh spectra (DRS) in particular have attracted much experimental and theoretical interest. Of course, atomic fluids (Bratos et al., 1985) represent the simplest systems available for the study of DRS because all of the polarizability anisotropy for atomic fluids may be attributed to multi-body interactions (i.e. it is entirely collision induced). As in the case of atomic fluids, the DRS for molecules with spherical symmetry are also entirely collision induced. Methane is one of the simplest spherical molecules and the DRS has been studied by a number of investigators. Buckingham and Tabisz (1978) and Shelton and Tabisz (1980) studied the DRS of methane at low densities. From their analysis it was shown that the spectra can be separated into two distinct regions. The first region extends from the exciting line out to approximately 150 cm^{-1} This region is due to the dipole induced dipole (DID) mechanism.

The second region (200 - 500 cm^{-1}) is due to the collision induced rotational Raman (CIRR) effect. This effect is caused by the interaction of two colliding molecules through their dipole-quadrupole tensors.

Medina and Daniels (1977, 1978) have also studied the DRS of methane over a much smaller spectral range (0-200 cm^{-1}) but at much higher densities than in previous studies. In this study, the effect of density on the DRS of methane at 240 K (ρ = 75 to ρ = 780 amagat) was investigated. The spectra were divided into low, middle and high frequency region. Each region was characterized respectively by the decay constants, Δ_1, Δ_2, Δ_3, i.e., a section of the spectra could be described by the equation

$$I(\omega) \propto \exp [-\omega/\Delta_n], \quad n = 1, 2, 3, 4 \quad . \tag{3}$$

No particular mechanism was ascribed to any of the three regions; the division was used simply to characterize the spectra.

In our study of methane (Baker and Jonas, 1984) we investigated DRS over a wide range of densities and temperatures. The density ranged from 180 to 500 amagat and the temperature range was from -25°C to 50°C. I shall mention only one specific result of our study of methane related to the density and temperature dependence of the exponential decay constant Δ for the 25 to 85 cm^{-1} region corresponding to the DID mechanism.

Figure 7 gives the density dependence of Δ in methane over a range of temperatures and compares the experimental data to the theoretical prediction using the theoretical model developed by Ballucani and Vallauri (1979). While these authors point out that their theory will break down in the limit of high densities, they obtained good results in comparing their calculated values of Δ to the experimental values obtained by Fleury et al. (1971, 1973) for argon at densities up to 600 amagat.

In comparing the theoretical predictions of Δ using Ballucani and Vallauri's expressions, we see that the theoretical estimated are 5 - 7 cm^{-1} greater than the experimental Δ's. However, the density dependence of Δ is reproduced quite well. This result is similar to the result of Ballucani and Vallauri when they compared Δ values for argon; again, the theory overestimates the Δ values, but the density trends are well reproduced.

In contrast to the strong density dependence of Δ, the theoretical model predicts that Δ should increase linearly with $T^{1/2}$. In Figure 8 we show Δ plot vs. $T^{1/2}$ of methane at different constant densities. However, the relatively large error in the experimental data did not permit an unambiguous determination of the functional

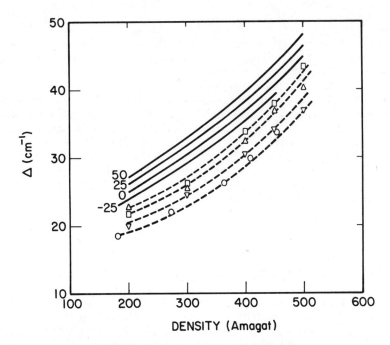

Fig. 7. Density dependence of the exponential decay constant Δ for DRS in methane at several temperatures; dashed lines; O=25°C; ∇ 0°C; Δ 25°C; □ 50°C. A comparison with the theoretical prediction using the model by Ballucani and Vallauri is also given (full line).

dependence of Δ upon temperature. The only statement one can make is that Δ changes as T^X where X is between 0.2 and 1.0.

In our study (Baker and Jonas, 1984) of SF_6 we have also found that the theory of Ballucani and Vallauri predicts well the density dependence of Δ but overestimates the Δ values by 2 ~ 3 cm^{-1}. Figure 9 compares the density dependence of the experimental Δ's for SF_6 to the theoretical prediction using the model of Ballucani and Vallauri (1979).

As already mentioned, the great advantage of studying spherical molecules lies in the fact that the entire DRS of these fluids may be attributed to collision induced effects. For linear triatomics the interpretation of the DRS is necessarily more complicated as the time

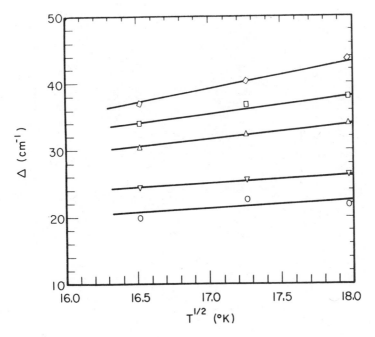

Fig. 8. Temperature dependence of Δ in methane at several constant densities: O 200 amagat; ∇ 300; $\triangle$ 400; $\square$ 450; and $\square$ 500 amagat.

dependence of the polarizability anisotropy of the molecule will contain contributions from both the permanent anisotropy of the molecule, whose time dependence arises from molecular reorientation, and the induced polarizability which arises from multi-body inter-actions. The part arising from the permanent anisotropy may be re-ferred to as the allowed part and the induced component as the non-allowed part. Despite thes complications, significant progress has been made in the study of collision induced effects on the DRS of linear triatomics (Madden, 1985, Sampoli, 1984).

Much of this work has been based on the rather complete studies of Madden (1985) on carbon disulfide. Madden has shown that in the case of CS_2 the DRS could be divided into a central region dominated by the allowed reorientational processes and the wings which were

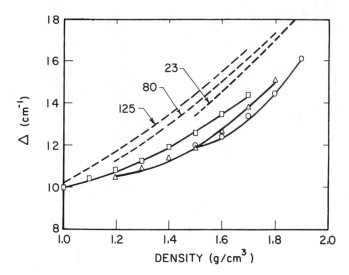

Fig. 9. Density dependence of Δ for DRS in SF_6 at several temperatures (full lines); $\bigcirc$ 23°C; $\square$ 80°C; $\triangle$ 125 C. A comparison with the theoretical prediction using the model by Ballucani and Vallauri is also given (dashed lines).

dominated by the non-allowed collision induced effects. The collision induced wings were analyzed using Madden's theory for the DRS of atomic liquids. It was shown that the features of the collision induced portion of the DRS were readily explained by this theory and the dipole-induced dipole (DID) model for the polarizability anisotropy. This set of experiments on liquid CS_2 were done along the liquid-vapor coexistence line with T = 165K to 309K. With this set of conditions both the density and the temperature changed in going from one thermodynamic state of another. This let to a certain amount of ambiguity in as far as ascertaining what was a temperature effect and what was a density effect. This ambiguity was resolved in our laboratory by Hegemann et al. (1984) in their high pressure light scattering experiment on liquid CS_2, where the effect of density on the collision induced DRS was shown to generally predominate over the effect of temperature. Similar high pressure light scattering studies by Hegemann and Jonas (1984) on carbonyl sulfide gave analogous results.

A typical DRS lineshape of liquid CS_2 is shown in Figure 10. Four distinct regions are apparent and have been labelled. Region I is the symmetry allowed portion of the DRS lineshape, which in the case of CS_2 can be meaningfully separated from the collision induced Regions II, III and IV (Cox et al., 1979; Tildesley and Madden, 1983). Since we are interested in CIS, the allowed DRS represented by Region I will not be further discussed.

Regions II and III have been seen previously in CS_2 (Cox and Madden, 1976; Madden and Cox, 1981) and are explained in terms of the dipole–induced–dipole (DID) interaction mechanism. Region II has been attributed to solid–like oscillatory motions (Madden and Cox, 1981) (although in the sense of motion of the interacting molecules relative to each other rather than motion relative to a fixed lattice point (An et al., 1979), while Region III is attributed to

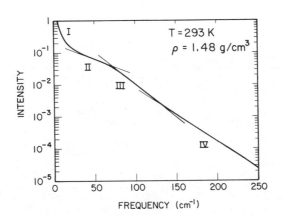

Fig. 10. The four observed regions of the DRS lineshape for liquid CS_2 (temperature $20^{\circ}C$; density $\rho = 1.48 g/cm^3$).

gas-like translation motions. Region IV has not been previously reported in liquid CS_2.

Each of the Regions II–IV was characterized by the exponential fit parameter Δ ($I(\omega) = e^{-\sqrt{\omega}/\Delta}$). Typical examples of the pure temperature and pure density effects on the measured Δ values are shown in Figures 11 and 12, respectively. Similar behavior is found over all temperature and density ranges investigated. Two aspects of this behavior require particular emphasis.

First, we find that Δ_{II} is insensitive to temperature and strongly dependent on density. Such behavior has not been previously suspected or directly observed. This result will have important implications on future quantitative theoretical work, which is presently lacking for this lineshape region. Secondly, the behavior of Δ_{III} and Δ_{IV} with temperature and density is strikingly similar, which strongly suggests a common dynamic origin for their behavior. As their trends with temperature and density are consistent with those predicted for gas-like translational motions through a multipole interaction mechanism, (Madden and Cox, 1981; Madden and Tildesley, 1983) it would appear that Region III does arise from a

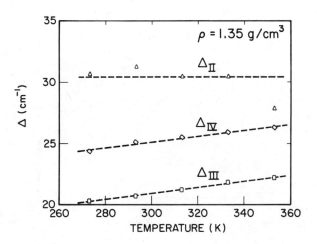

Fig. 11. Representative example of pure temperature effect on measured Δ values of DRS lineshape for liquid CS_2 (ρ = 1.35g/cm^3).

DID mechanism, and that Region IV arises from a higher order multi-pole expansion term, e.g. quadrupole-induced-dipole, with gas-like translational dynamics responsible for the observed behavior of both regions. This assignment for Region IV is further supported by the theoretically predicted and previously observed increase in Δ values for a higher-order multipole mechanism relative to the DID mechanism for gas-like translational motions (Madden and Cox, 1981). This result has important implications for future discussions of high frequency DRS lineshapes in dense liquids, the origin of which has sometimes alternatively been suggested to be electron overlap or frame distortion mechanisms.

In our study of ν_1, ν_2 and ν_3 Raman mode lineshapes in CS_2 as a function of temperatures ($0°C$ to $80°C$) and density (1.25 to 1.48 g cm^{-3}), we had to resort to a qualitative discussion of the experimental data because a quantitative comparison between theory and experiment was not possible. However, even a qualitative approach of discussing the physical interactions which give rise to the observed CIS lineshape behavior is quite useful. It was our hope

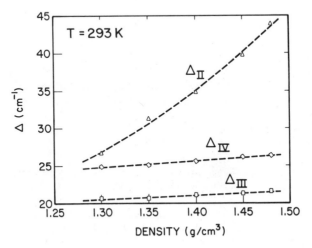

Fig. 12. Representative example of pure density effect on measured Δ values of DRS lineshape for liquid CS_2 (ρ = 1.35g/cm^3).

that quantitative experimental results obtained obtained in this study of separate temperature and density effect of dense fluid CIS lineshape behavior will stimulate further theoretical work. Work is presently in progress on the analysis of the experimental lineshapes for COS where the Rayleigh lineshape and the ν_1 mode Raman lineshape at 858 cm^{-1} have been investigated over a range of densities (1.10 to 1.22 g cm^{-1}) and over a range of temperatures ($-30^{\circ}C$ to $90^{\circ}C$).

Because of the results on CIS in linear triatomics, we also decided to study the effects on the observed DRS of carbon dioxide in the dense fluid state (Baker, 1984). While other work on the DRS of CO_2 as dense fluid has been reported (Versmold, 1981, Versmold and Zimmermann, 1983) elsewhere, we felt that the effect of CIS on the DRS has not been adequately dealt with. This is because these prior studies dealt primarily with the reorientational motion of the carbon dioxide molecule and, at most, dealt with the collision induced component as a complication.

In this overview I shall only mention one interesting result - namely the absence of Region IV at high frequencies (Baker, 1984). A typical DRS lineshape is shown in Figure 13 which is for CO_2 at $20^{\circ}C$ and ρ = 1.2 g/cm^3. Here, it is shown how the spectra have been divided into three regions; moreover, it is apparent how the beginning and end of regions I and II, respectively, correspond to distinct changes in the slope of the spectrum. A similar change in slope is evident between regions II and III.

In Figure 14 the density dependence of Δ_{II} and Δ_{III}, at 293K is shown. Δ_{II} increases more rapidly with increasing density than does Δ_{III} and actually is larger than Δ_{III} at all but the lowest densities. The precision for both Δ_{II} and Δ_{III} is $\pm$ .3 cm^{-1}. I would like to point out that no Region IV has been observed by us in the DRS of dense carbon dioxide as opposed to our results on CS_2 where Region IV was detected and attributed to a dipole-quadrupole interaction. This may be due to the fact that the dipole-quadrupole interaction is a shorter range interaction, varying as r^{-4}, than as the DID interaction which varies as r^{-3}. This is apparent when the reduced densities $\rho^* = \rho/\rho$ of the two experiments are compared. For our experiment on CO_2 the highest reduced density was ρ^* = 2.56 whereas for CS_2 the lowest reduced density was ρ^* = 2.79. Thus, we may have not been at sufficiently high enough densities to observe the dipole-quadrupole interaction in CO_2.

The results taken from our systematic high pressure experiments on CIS in molecular liquids illustrate well the fundamental role of the density variable in studies of CIS. Even though no quantitative theoretical analysis of the experimental data was so far carried out we tried to establish a firm experimental basis which will stimulate the development of new theoretical models for CIS.

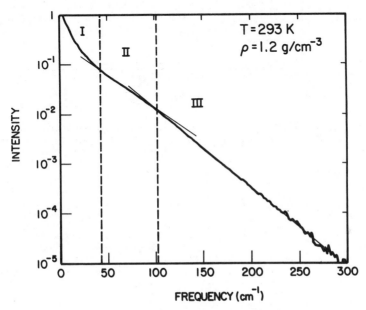

Fig. 13. Experimental DRS lineshape for CO_2 at $\rho = 1.2 \text{g/cm}^3$ and $20°C$. See the text for detail.

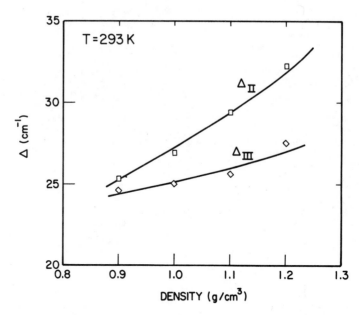

Fig. 14. Density dependence of the exponential decay constants Δ_{II} and Δ_{III} of DRS for CO_2 at 20°C.

ACKNOWLEDGMENTS

The authors wish to thank Professor S. Bratos and Dr. G. Birnbaum for bringing to their attention the problem of collision induced spectra. This research was supported in part by the NSF under Grant NSF CHE 81-11176 and NSF DMR 83-16981.

REFERENCES

An, S. C., Fishman, L., Litowitz, T. A., Montrose, C. J., and
    Posch, H. A., 1979, J. Chem. Phys., 70:4626.
Ballucani, V, and Vallauri, R., 1979, Mol. Phys., 38:1099,1115.
Baker, K. H., 1984, Ph.D. Thesis, University of Illinois, Urbana,
    Illinois, U.S.A..
Baker, K. H., and Jonas, J., Manuscript in preparation.
Birnbaum, G., 1980, "Collision-Induced Vibrational Spectroscopy in
    Liquids" in "Vibrational Spectroscopy of Molecular Liquids

and Solids," S. Bratos and R.M. Pick, Eds., Plenum Press, New York.

Buckingham, A. D., Tabisz, G. C., 1978, Mol. Phys., 36:583.

Bradley, M., Zerda, T. W., Jonas, J., 1984, Unpublished results.

Bratos, S., Guillot, B., and Birnbaum, G., 1985, This volume.

Cox, T. I., Battaglia, M. R., and Madden, P. A., 1979, Mol. Phys., 38:1539.

Cox, T. I., and Madden, P. A., 1976, Chem. Phys. Lett., 41:188.

Fischer, S. F., Lauberau, A., 1975, Chem. Phys. Lett., 35:6.

Fleury, P. A., Daniels, W. B., Worlock, S. M., 1971, Phys. Rev. Lett., 27:1493.

Fleury, P. A., Worlock, J. M., 1973, Phys. Rev. Lett. 30: 591.

Gelbart, W. M., 1974, Adv. Chem. Phys., 26:1.

Hegemann, B., Baker, K. H., and Jonas, S., 1984, J. Chem. Phys., 80:570.

Hegemann, B., and Jonas, J., 1984, Unpublished results.

Jonas, J., 1982, Science, 216:1179.

Jonas, J., 1984, Acc. Chem. Res., 17:74.

Lamb, W. J., Jonas, J., 1981, J. Chem. Phys., 74:913.

Lynden-Bell, R. M., 1977, Mol. Phys., 33:907.

Madden, P., 1985, This volume.

Madden, P. A., and Cox, T. J., 1981, Mol. Phys., 43:287.

Madden, P. A., and Tildesley, D. J., 1983, Mol. Phys., 49:193.

Medina, F., Daniels, W., 1977, J. Chem. Phys., 66:2228.

Medina, F., Daniels, W., 1978, Phys. Rev., A17:1474.

Oxtoby, D. W., 1979, Adv. Chem. Phys., 40:1.

Parkhurst, Jr., H. G., Jonas, J., 1975, J. Chem. Phys., 63:2698,2705.

Rotschild, W. G., 1976, J. Chem. Phys., 65:455.

Schindler, W., Jonas, J., 1980, J. Chem. Phys., 72:5019.

Schindler, W., Sharko, P. T., Jonas, J., 1982, J. Chem. Phys., 76:3493.

Schindler, W., Zerda, T. W., Jonas, J., 1984, J. Chem. Phys., 81:in press.

Schweizer, K. S., Chandler, D., 1982, J. Chem. Phys., 76:2296.

Sharko, P. T., Besnard, M., Jonas, J., 1983, J. Phys. Chem., 87:5197.

Shelton, D. P., Tabisz, G. C., 1980, Mol. Phys., 40:285,299.

Tildesley, D. J., and Madden, P. A., Mol. Phys., 48:129.

Versmold, H., 1981, Mol. Phys., 43:383.

Versmold, H., and Zimmermann, V., 1983, Mol. Phys., 50:65.

Wertheimer, R. K., 1978, Mol. Phys., 35:257.

WORKSHOP REPORT:

LIQUIDS AND LIQUID STATE INTERACTIONS

W. A. Steele[a] and H. A. Posch[b]

[a]Department of Chemistry, 152 Davey Laboratory
Pennsylvania State University
University Park, PA 16802

[b]Institut für Experimentalphysik der Universität Wien
Strudlhofgasse 4
A-1090 Vienna, Austria

The presentations dealing with induced phenomena in liquids
clearly demonstrate the need for further careful work in the fields
of experiment, computer simulation, and theory. The history of rare
gas collisional pairs discussed by Borysow and Frommhold (1985),
Lewis (1985), and Barocchi and Zoppi (1985) may serve as an example.
It shows how the interplay between improved experimental techniques,
resulting in reliable intensity and line shape data for collision
induced light scattering (CILS) at moderately low density, and a
thorough theoretical treatment of this problem, including the use of
the most accurate pair potentials and ab initio generated pair polarizabilities, may lead to a remarkable agreement between theory and
experiment of the order of 10% (Frommhold, 1981; Proffitt et al.,
1981; Dacre et al., 1981 and 1982). In the case of compressed fluids
composed of noble gases, good agreement has been obtained between experimental and computed zeroth spectral moments in absorption (Joslin
and Gray, 1985) and light scattering (Ladd et al., 1979 and 1980;
Varshneya et al., 1981; Zoppi et al., 1981; Clarke and Bruining,
1981). Guillot et al. (1980, 1981, 1983) have utilized Mori theory
to obtain the entire spectral band shape from calculations of a few
spectral moments. Other than this, difficulties arising from the
many-body nature of the induction process in liquids have been a
serious barrier to a quantitative theoretical description of the
complete spectrum.

EXPERIMENTAL

a) Accurate absolute intensity measurements should be made both in CILS and collision induced absorption (CIA). For the calibration the admixture of a small amount of H_2 to the sample (using the rotational lines of H_2 as a standard) seems to be the most promising method in the case of CILS of isotropic molecular gases (Barocchi et al., 1981). For systems (such as $CC\ell_4$), for which good H_2-solubility data are available, the same method could be applied to liquids thus avoiding the serious corrections due to internal fields, changes in the refractive index and the scattering geometry that are inherent to an external standard procedure.

b) Accurate line shape measurements over large frequency and intensity ranges in CILS will necessitate the use of novel experimental methods such as computer aided multichannel techniques.

c) The work of Cox et al., (1979, 1980) and Tildesley and Madden (1981, 1983) on the theory, experiment and computer simulation of the forbidden and allowed spectral band shapes in liquid CS_2 shows very clearly that such extensive studies can give great insight into the complex many-body rotational and coupled vibration-rotation dynamics that govern the observations (Madden, 1985). Thus, the measurement of a variety of forbidden vibrational spectra for a single system should be given considerable attention in the future.

d) The various intermolecular interactions reflect tensorial properties of different rank. The study of higher rank tensors through non-linear optical phenomena seems a promising though experimentally difficult task (Maker, 1970; Kielich, 1983; Birnbaum, 1985). Furthermore, the computer studies of Ladanyi (1983) and the experimental-theoretical work of Neumann (1984), and Neumann and Posch (1985) on molecules larger than diatomics indicate that it will be necessary to extend the point-polarizability models that have been reasonably successful for atoms and small diatomics to include "distributed polarizabilities" (Applequist, 1972, 1977) such as those discussed by K. Hunt (1985a; Buckingham et al., 1980).

e) So far most of the experiments in molecular liquids have been performed for thermodynamic states along the coexistence curve and over a moderate range of densities. Data on the pure density dependence of CI-phenomena are comparatively sparse (Adams et al., 1981; Fondere et al., 1981; Obriot et al., 1983; Marteau, 1985), opening up a wide field for further experimental work both in CILS and CIA.

f) CILS and CIA of solutions have some uniquely interesting aspects. For example, the dynamics of dipoles induced in atomic solvents (such as Ar) by quadrupolar molecules (such as H_2 or N_2) can be simplified as compared to the spectra for the neat liquids by going to low concentrations, where four-body terms are absent. The main feature of these spectra are reviewed by Barnabei et al. (1985), who also discussed the molecular dynamics underlying the phenomena

550

(Buontempo et al., 1982, 1983). More work on the concentration, solvent and temperature dependence of such spectra would be of great value.

g) Härtl and Versmold (1984a, b, and c) are investigating dilute dispersions of loaded polystyrene spheres by intensity fluctuation spectroscopy. They find phenomena analogous to collision induced scattering in molecular systems. By variation of the surface charges and concentrations, both ordered lattices and disordered "liquid" structures are being studied. In contrast to the molecular case, the whole range of interesting wave vectors is accessible to light scattering techniques. This provides unique model systems for detailed examination of the wave vector dependence of three and four-point correlation functions.

h) Studies of large molecules such as those presented by Dorfmüller (1985) also necessitate the consideration of collision induced intramolecular dynamical processes such as the relative motion of molecular subgroups and conformational transitions. This is another example where a joint effort of experiment and various computer simulation techniques may prove particularly fruitful.

SIMULATION

The second "experimental" branch for the study of many body effects in liquids is that of computer simulations of $10^2 - 10^4$ particles. Vallauri (1985) has reviewed this work and has pointed out some of the difficulties involved. In spite of problems with statistics and boundary conditions, simulation provides a unique opportunity of studying clean and well defined systems and of "measuring" quantities not accessible by true experiments. Still, further refinements and improvements are needed that again are listed in a more suggestive than exhaustive manner below:

a) The statistical quality of many body simulation data need further improvement (Smith and Wells 1984) and careful examination by the use of faster computers such as the matrix processors becoming available at present.

b) In spite of these improvements in the hardware, standard simulation procedures also need refinement and consideration. These include, for example, the effect of boundary conditions and cutoff problems, Ewald sum, reaction field (Neumann and Steinhausen, 1983a and b).

THEORY

For the theoretician, one of the most important findings of the simulation studies has been that CI spectra not directly involving forbidden vibrational modes are essentially many-body phenomena

(Madden, 1977). That is, the basic theoretical expressions that contain two-, three-, and four-body terms cannot be simplified by neglecting any of them (Ladd et al., 1979). Theoretical treatments of such many-body dynamics are still in their infancy; whereas it seems possible to formulate a theory for the simple two-body relative translational dynamics needed to evaluate the first term in the CILS for rare gases (Posch et al., 1984), the three- and four-body translational dynamics are not understood even qualitatively. Indeed, one may speculate that the extensive cancellation observed in simulations might be best handled in a totally different way wherein the dynamics of the total induced dipole or the polarizability is somehow followed directly, thus by-passing the problem of dealing with the relative displacements of two, three and four molecules.

In the case of induced effects in molecular liquids, the problem is even more difficult because of the effects of molecular rotation on the time-dependence of the induced dipole and/or polarizability. The cancellation found in liquid rare gas simulation persists, although perhaps not as complete for molecules. Here, it is hard to generalize because of the very wide range of moments of inertia (which partly determine relative translational and rotational time scales) and of molecular shape (that determines the hindrance to rotation and, thus, is the other determining factor in the time-scale problem). It is important to realize that the line shapes are sensitive to the coupled translation-rotation of groups of two, three and four molecules, since both separation distance and orientation determine the magnitude and direction of an induced dipole or polarizability tensor element (Levesque et al., 1985; Steele, 1985).

Independent of these dynamical problems, there are several aspects of the basic induction mechanism that need closer examination, particularly for molecular fluids. Current theory is primarily (but not entirely) based on multipolar expansions in which the leading terms are taken to be responsible for the induced effects; examples are the DID approximation for induced light scattering and the quadrupole-induced-dipole equation for the far infrared absorption of non-polar linear molecules. One is not surprised to find other induction mechanisms, when the molecules are in close contact as in a liquid. As discussed by Hunt (1985), Buckingham et al., (1977, 1978), Posch (1982), Shelton et al., (1980b) and Tabisz (1985), these can arise from higher terms in the multipolar series involving hyperpolarizabilities as well as induction by higher permanent electric multipoles; a problem being considered by Hunt (1985a) is the distortions of molecular electron density due to overlap in strong collisions that may lead to significant induced dipoles or polarizabilities; and finally, nuclear frame distortions due to collisions, particularly in molecules that are relatively flexible to start with, can also affect the induction process. None of these phenomena are satisfactorily handled by current theories, with the possible exception of deviations from the DID model for noble gas atoms.

Finally, the emphasis given here to spectra does not mean that theoretical and simulation studies of induced effects upon thermo-dynamic and transport properties of liquids are unimportant. This is particularly true of calculations of the pressure exerted by a liquid. Over much of the "normal liquid" range, this quantity is nearly zero because of a delicate balance between repulsive and at-tractive forces in the fluid. Even a relatively small contribution due to induction may alter this balance significantly. One might speculate that the viscosity, which theoretically is related to off-diagonal terms in the pressure tensor, may also be surprisingly sen-sitive to induced interactions.

The papers presented at this conference indicate that re-searchers are certainly aware of the experimental, simulational, and theoretical problems discussed here. However, a successful qualita-tive understanding and quantitative modelling of the many body dynamics of collision induced phenomena of liquids will rely on a concerted action of many widespread and seemingly different research efforts such as ab initio quantum mechanical calculations of mole-cular properties, the employment of the most sophisticated spectros-copic experiments and large scale computer simulations. The importance of such a joint effort has also been recognized by workers in the area and important contributions along the lines sketched above may be expected in the future.

REFERENCES

Adams, D.M., Berg, R.W., and Williams, A.D., 1981, "Vibrational spectroscopy at very high pressures, Part 28, Raman and far infrared spectra of some complex chlorides A2MCℓ6 under hydrostatic pressure", J. Chem. Phys. 74:2800.
Applequist, J., Carl, J.R., and Fung, K.K., 1972, "An atom dipole interaction model for molecular polarizability. Application to polyatomic molecules and determination of atom polarizabi-litites", J. Am. Chem. Soc. 94:2952.
Applequist, J., "An atom dipole interaction model for molecular optical properties", Accts. Chem. Res. 10:79.
Barnebei, M., Buontempo, U., and Maselli, P., 1985, "Molecular motions in dense fluids from induced rotational spectra", this volume.
Barocchi, F., and Zoppi, M., 1985, "Depolarized interaction induced light scattering experiments in argon, krypton, and xenon", this volume.
Barocchi, F., Zoppi, M., Proffitt, M.H., and Frommhold, L., 1981, "Determination of the collision induced depolarized Raman light scattering cross section of the argon diatom", Canad. J. Phys. 59:1418.
Birnbaum, G., 1985, "Comments on hyper-Rayleigh scattering", this volume.
Borysow, J., and Frommhold, L., 1985, "Infrared and Raman line shapes of pairs of interacting molecules", this volume.

Buckingham, A.D., and Tabisz, G.C., 1977, "Collision induced rotational Raman scattering", Optics Letters 1:220.

Buckingham, A.D., and Tabisz, G.C., 1978, "Collision induced rotational Raman scattering by tetrahedral and octahedral molecules", Mol. Phys. 36:583.

Buckingham, A.D., and Clarke Hunt, K.L., 1980, "The pair polarizability anisotropy of SF_6 in the point-atom-polarizability approximation", Mol. Phys. 40:643.

Buontempo, U., Cunsolo, S., Dore, P., and Nencini, L., 1982, "Far infrared absorption spectra in liquid and solid H_2", Canad. J. Phys. 60:1422.

Buontempo, U., Codastefano, P., Cunsolo, S., Dore, P., and Maselli, P., 1983, "New analysis of the density effects observed on the rotational line profile of induced spectra of H_2 and D_2 dissolved in argon", Canad. J. Phys. 61:156.

Buontempo, U., Maselli, P., and Nencini, L., 1983, "Density effects on the translational motion from infrared induced rotational spectra of N_2", Canad. J. Phys. 61:1498.

Clarke, J.H.R., and Bruining, J., 1981, "The absolute intensity of depolarized light scattering from liquid argon", Chem. Phys. Letters 80:42.

Cox, T.I., Battaglia, M.R., and Madden, P., 1979, "Properties of liquid CS_2 from the allowed light scattering spectra", Mol. Phys. 38:1539.

Cox, T.I., and Madden, P., 1980, "A comparative study of the interaction induced spectra of liquid CS_2. I. Intensities", Mol. Phys. 39:1487.

Dacre, P.D., and Frommhold, L., 1981, "Spectroscopic examination of ab initio neon diatom polarizability invariants", J. Chem. Phys. 75:4159.

Dacre, P.D., and Frommhold, L., 1982, "Rare gas diatom polarizabilities", J. Chem. Phys. 76:3447.

Dorfmüller, T., 1985, "Interaction induced spectra of 'large' molecules in liquids", this volume.

Fondere, F., Obriot, J., Marteau, Ph., Allavena, M., and Chakroun, H., 1981, "Far infrared spectroscopy and empirical potential for N_2 under pressure", J. Chem. Phys. 74:2675.

Frommhold, L., "Collision induced scatttering and the diatom polarizabilities", Adv. Chem. Phys. 46:1.

Guillot, B., Bratos, S., and Birnbaum, G., 1980, "Theoretical study of spectra of depolarized light scattered from dense rare gas fluids", Phys. Rev. A22:2230.

Guillot, B., Bratos, S., and Birnbaum, G., 1981, "Theory of collision induced absorption in dense rare gas mixtures", Mol. Phys. 44:1021.

Guillot, B., and Birnbaum, G., 1983, "Theoretical study of the far infrared absorption spectra of dense nitrogen", 1983, J. Chem. Phys. 79:686.

Härtl, W., and Versmold, H., 1984a, "An experimental verification of incoherent light scattering", J. Chem. Phys. 80:1387.

Härtl, W., and Versmold, H., 1984b, "Temperature dependence of the

structure factor S(Q) of liquid-like ordered colloidal
    dispersions", J. Chem. Phys. 81:2507.
Härtl, W., and Versmold, H., 1984c, "Dynamic light scattering:
    Brownian dynamics of colloidal dispersions in the presence of
    structure forming and structure breaking ions", J. Phys. Chem.
    139:247.
Hunt, K.L.C., 1983, "Nonlocal polarizability densities",
    J. Chem. Phys. 78:6149.
Hunt, K.L.C., 1985a, "Ab initio calculations of collision induced po-
    larizabilities", this volume.
Hunt, K.L.C., 1985b, "Classical multipole models: comparison with ab
    initio and experimental results", this volume.
Joslin, C.G., and Gray, C.G., 1985, "Calculation of spectral moments
    for induced absorption in liquids", this volume.
Kielich, S., 1983, "Multiphoton scattering molecular spectroscopy",
    Progress in Optics 20:155, editor Wolf, E.
Ladanyi, B.M., 1983, "Molecular dynamics study of Rayleigh light
    scattering from molecular fluids", J. Chem. Phys. 78:2189.
Ladd, A.J.C., Litovitz, T.A., and Montrose, C.J., 1979, "Molecular
    dynamics studies of depolarized light scattering from argon at
    various fluid densities", J. Chem. Phys. 71:4242.
Ladd, A.J.C., Litovitz, T.A., Clarke, J.H.R., and Woodcock, L.V.,
    1980, "Molecular dynamics simulations of depolarized Rayleigh
    scattering from liquid argon at the triple point",
    J. Chem. Phys. 72:1759.
Levesque, D., Weis, J.J., Marteau, Ph., Obriot, J., and Fondere, F.,
    1985, "Collision induced far infrared spectrum of liquid N_2.
    Comparison between computer simulations and experiment", to
    appear in Mol. Phys..
Lewis, J.C., 1985, "Intercollisional interference - theory and exper-
    iment", this volume.
Madden, P.A., 1977, "The line shape of the depolarized Rayleigh scat-
    tering from liquid argon", Chem. Phys. Letters 47:174.
Madden, P.A., 1985, "The interference of molecular and interaction
    induced effects in liquids", this volume.
Maker, P.D., 1970, "Spectral broadening of elastic second-harmonic
    light scattering in liquids", Phys. Rev. A1:923.
Marteau, Ph., 1985, "Far infrared induced absorption in highly
    compressed atomic and molecular fluids", this volume.
Neumann, M., and Steinhauser, O., 1983a, "On the calculation of the
    dielectric constant using the Ewald-Kornfeld tensor",
    Chem. Phys. Letters 95:417.
Neumann, M., and Steinhauser, O., 1983b, "On the calculation of the
    frequency dependent dielectric constant in computer
    simulation", Chem. Phys. Letters 102:508.
Neumann, M., and Posch, H.A., 1985, "Interaction induced light scat-
    tering from tetrahedral molecules", this volume.
Neumann, M., 1984, "Collision induced light scattering by globular
    molecules: Applequist's atom dipole interaction model and its
    implementation in computer simulation", Mol. Phys. 53:187.
Obriot, J., Fondere, F., Marteau, Ph., and Allavena, M., 1983, "An
    experimental and theoretical investigation of the far infrared

spectra of HC and HBr crystals under pressure at 4.2 K",
    J. Chem. Phys. 79:33.

Posch, H.A., 1982, "Collision induced light scattering from fluids
    composed of tetrahedral molecules. III. Neopentane vapor",
    Mol. Phys. 46:1213.

Posch, H.A., Balucani, V., and Vallauri, R., 1984, "On the relative
    dynamics of pairs of atoms in simple liquids", Physica
    123A:516.

Proffitt, M.H., Keto, J.W., and Frommhold, L., 1981, "Collision
    induced Raman spectra and diatom polarizabilitites of the rare
    gases - an update", Canad. J. Phys. 59:1459.

Shelton, D.P., and Tabisz, G.C., 1980, "Binary collision induced
    light scattering by anisotropic molecular gases.
    II. Molecular spectra and induced rotational scattering",
    Mol. Phys. 40:299.

Smith, E.B., and Wells, B.H., 1984, "Estimating errors in molecular
    simulation calculations", Mol. Phys. 53:701.

Steele, W.A., 1985, "Computer simulation of the forbidden absorption
    spectra of liquid nitrogen", subm. to Mol. Phys..

Tabisz, G.C., Meinander, M., and Penner, A.R., 1985, "Interaction
    induced rotational light scattering in molecular gases", this
    volume.

Tildesley, D.J., and Madden, P., 1981, "An effective pair potential
    for liquid carbon disulphide", Mol. Phys. 42:1137.

Tildesley, D.J., and Madden, P., 1983, "Time correlation function for
    a model of liquid carbon disulphide", Mol. Phys. 48:129.

Vallauri, R., 1985, "Study of interaction induced absorption and
    light scattering in diatomic systems by molecular dynamics",
    this volume.

Varshneya, D., Shirron, S.F., Litovitz, T.A., Zoppi, M., and
    Barocchi, F., 1981, "Collision induced light scattering:
    Integrated intensity of argon", Phys. Rev. A23:77.

Zoppi, M., Barocchi, F., Varshneya, D., Neumann, M., and Litovitz,
    T.A., 1981, "Density dependence of the collision induced light
    scattering spectral moments of argon", Canad. J. Phys.
    59:1475.

STUDY OF THE COLLECTIVE EXCITATIONS IN H_2

AS OBSERVED IN FAR INFRARED ABSORPTION

Salvatore Cunsolo, Paolo Dore and Luca Nencini

Dipartimento di Fisica - Università di Roma "La Sapienza"
P.le Aldo Moro, 2 - 00185 Roma, Italy

ABSTRACT

We discuss the far infrared absorption spectra measured in liquid para H_2 and in solid H_2 at different ortho concentrations. The similarity between the liquid and solid para H_2 spectra indicates that phonon-like collective modes are present in the liquid phase. The excitonic absorption is the dominant feature of the S(0) line measured in solid H_2 at low ortho concentrations, but still survives when the ortho concentration is relevant.

INTRODUCTION

In this paper we present some results (Van Kranendonk 1959; Van Kranendonk 1983; Gush et al. 1960; Bhatenagar et al. 1962; Treffler et al., 1969) of the measurements of the far i.r. absorption spectra of liquid and solid H_2 (Buontempo et al. 1982; Buontempo et al., 1983). As is well known, the collective excitations present in solid para H_2 are, besides phonons, the rotational and vibrational excitons (Van Kranendonk 1959; Van Kranendonk 1983; Gush et al., 1960; Bhatenagar et al., 1962; Treffler et al., 1969). In particular, the far i.r. absorption in solid para H_2 is due either to the simultaneous creation of phonons and a rotational exciton (phonon branch) or to a zero moment rotational exciton (S(0) line).

Our aim is to study how the introduction of disorder in the system affects the collective excitations observed in our spectra. We discuss here the results obtained both in liquid para H_2 (at 18 K) and in solid samples (at 4 K) at different ortho concentrations. Indeed these two ways to break the translational invariance

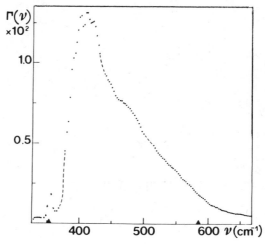

Fig. 1. Line shape of solid para-H_2. The solid triangles indicate the free molecule rotational frequencies (354.4 and 587.0 cm^{-1}).

in the system differently affect the collective excitations characteristic of solid para H_2.

In the analysis of the experimental results, it is convenient to introduce the line shape $\Gamma(\nu)$ from the measured absorption coefficient $A(\nu)$. $\Gamma(\nu)$ is proportional to the net probability of absorption and is defined as

$$\Gamma(\nu) = A(\nu) \left[\nu(1 - e^{-hc\nu/kT}) \right]^{-1} .$$

The experimental apparatus and the procedure used to derive the absorption coefficient $A(\nu)$ are reported in Buontempo et al. (1982).

ANALYSIS OF THE SPECTRA IN LIQUID AND SOLID H_2

In Fig. 1 we report the line shape $\Gamma(\nu)$ of pure para H_2 in the solid phase at 4 K, as obtained with a resolution of 5 cm^{-1} by Buontempo et al., 1982. It is evident that the spectrum is composed of a line peaked at about 355 cm^{-1}, followed by a broad band. The line, much sharper than the resolution, is the S(0) line associated with the creation of a zero moment rotational exciton (Van Kranendonk 1960). The broad band is the phonon branch associated with the simultaneous production of one rotational exciton and one or more

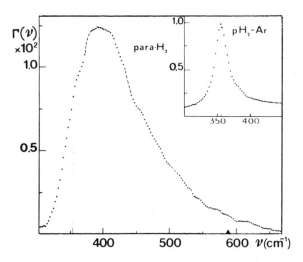

Fig. 2. Line shape of liquid para-H_2. The ν_o position is indicated by the vertical bar. The $\Gamma(\tilde{\nu})$ of para-H_2 dissolved in liquid Ar in the insert is in arbitrary units.

phonons, so that the momentum conservation law is respected. The fine features on the top of the band, studied by the authors at higher resolution, are mainly related to the presence of peaks in the phonon and exciton density of states. The rise of the phonon branch also depends on the increase, with increasing frequency, of the relative displacements of adjacent molecules and hence on the increase of the change in the induced dipole moment.

Our aim is to study the effect of disorder on the collective excitations present in the system. We start by studying para H_2 in the liquid phase: in this case the translational invariance of the system fails due to desordering of only the molecular positions. Fig. 2 shows the line shape of liquid para H_2 at about 18 K. The spectrum consists of a single large band, with a maximum shifted by about 40 cm^{-1} from the free molecule rotational frequency (Stoicheff, 1957) ($\nu_o = 354.4$ cm^{-1}), in agreement with the result by Jones (1970). At the ν_o frequency the presence of a shoulder in the line shape is evident. We point out that our data indicate that the detailed balance principle is satisfied around ν_o. In the insert of the figure we report for comparison the $S(0)$ line of para H_2 dissolved in liquid Argon (Buontempo et al., 1975). This spectrum consists of a much sharper line centered at ν_o. Indeed, in this case, the absorption is essentially due to the excitation

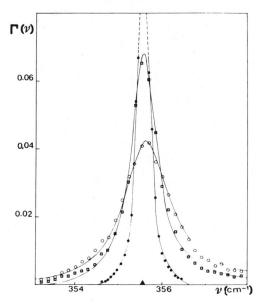

Fig. 3. S(O) line shapes at different c_o values.
(•••• : para H_2 ;□ □ □: c_o=3%; o o o: c_o=7%)
The solid lines represent the best fit with the
lorentzian profile.

of localized motions which produce relative displacements of the
light H_2 impurity with respect to the surrounding Ar atoms.

The comparison between these two spectra suggests that, in
the spectrum of liquid para H_2, a narrow component is present
centered at ν_o, associated with the motions localized around the
molecule which undergoes the rotational transition. To this component, responsible for the observed shoulder at ν_o, is superimposed
a much broader band. This indicates that in liquid para H_2, in
spite of the spatial disorder of the molecules, phonon like propa-
gating modes are present (Buontempo et al., 1982), which give rise
to a broad absorption band, in the same way as phonons and excitons
do in the solid phase. This result is in agreement with that
obtained from inelastic neutron scattering data of liquid para H_2
(Carneiro et al., 1973).

ANALYSIS OF THE S(O) LINE IN SOLID H_2

The second way to introduce disorder in the system is to add
ortho impurities in the solid. Indeed, in this way the translational invariance of the system fails because of the orientational
disorder of the ortho molecules. We have studied this effect measuring the S(O) line at high resolution, initially at low ortho

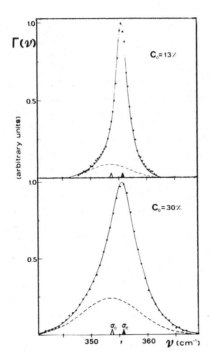

Fig. 4.   S(0) line shapes at c_o = 13% and c_o = 30%. The solid line
represents the best fit profile, the broken line repre-
sents the broad non excitonic band.

concentrations (c_o) (Buontempo et al., 1982). In Fig. 3 we report
the measured line shapes up to c_o=7%. We found that the experimental line shapes of the S(0) lines could be successfully described
by means of a lorentzian profile, at least within the experimental
accuracy of the data. In the case of pure para H_2, the absorption
was so intense that we could not measure the shape of the S(0) line
around the peak. However, by fitting the data with the lorentzian
profile, we found that the line is peaked at the rotational exciton
frequency, theoretically determined to be ν_e = 353.7 cm^{-1} (Van
Kranendonk, 1959), and that its half width is no larger than the
resolution (0.1 cm^{-1}). Increasing the ortho concentration, the line
broadens; indeed the lifetime of the exciton decreases because its
propagation is limited by the ortho impurities. At low c_o values
(c_o < 10%) the half width of the excitonic line seems to follow a
linear dependence on c_o, i.e. $\delta=\delta_0+ac_o$. δ_0 can be interpreted as
due to radiation or phonon damping, as suggested by J. Van
Kranendonk (private communication); our data indicate δ_0= 0.1 cm^{-1}.

Increasing the ortho H_2 concentration, it was found (Buontempo et al., 1983) that the rotational exciton picture, which was
quite satisfactory at low c_o values, no longer holds. Indeed the
S(0) line broadens with increasing c_o, but the measured line shapes
cannot be described by a simple lorentzian profile. In Fig. 4 we
report the S(0) lines at c_o=13% and c_o=30%; it is evident that an

extra contribution arises in the low frequency part of the line and increases with increasing c_o. A similar effect has already been observed in the fundamental band around the excitonic $S_1(0)$ line (Gush, 1961), associated with the vibrational transition ($v = 0$, $j = 0 \to v = 1$, $j = 2$) of a para molecule. In this case, the anisotropic interaction between an ortho molecule ($v = 0$, $j = 1$) and a nearby excited para molecule ($v = 1$, $j = 2$) removes the degeneracy of the excited state of the ortho-para couple (Gush, 1961; Gush and Kranendonk, 1962). This effect gives rise to weak satellite peaks, which were observed besides the $S_1(0)$ line at very low c_o values; when the ortho H_2 concentration is increased, the peaks broaden and merge into a large band.

It is reasonable to expect the same effect around the $S(0)$ line. We have therefore computed a stick spectrum, centered around the rotational frequency of the "free" molecule in the solid $\nu_s = 353.7$ cm^{-1} (Van Kranendonk, 1960), analogous to the one reported for the $S_1(0)$ line (Gush and Van Kranendonk, 1962). By convoluting the stick spectrum with a gaussian profile, we have derived the broad band which must be added to the lorentzian excitonic contribution in order to describe the experimental profiles. The results of this fitting procedure are reported in Fig. 4, where the dashed lines represent the broad non excitonic contribution to the absorption profiles.

In Fig. 5 we report the values of the half width δ_L of the lorentzian component as derived from the fits; for comparison we also report the full widths at half maximum (Δ), directly obtained from the experimental profiles. It is evident that the $S(0)$ line broadens because of both the broadening of the exciton line and the increasing of other contributions.

Our procedure gives satisfactory results up to c_o values of about 40%; indeed at high ortho concentration the failure of such a picture has to be expected because any para molecule has several ortho neighbours.

At high ortho concentration the measured profiles are very different from those observed at low c_o values. As is evident in Fig. 6, the $S(0)$ line is given by the superposition of two large contributions peaked, respectively, at about 351 and 356 cm^{-1}. The low frequency contribution, associated with the rotational excitation of isolated para molecules surrounded by several ortho neighbours, increases with increasing c_o. The reason why its peak is shifted to a frequency lower than ν_s is not clear. The second contribution, peaked at about the exciton frequency, decreases with increasing c_o, but is still present in normal H_2 ($c_o = 75\%$). A possible explanation of this feature could be that an excitonic absorption is still surviving at high ortho concentration.

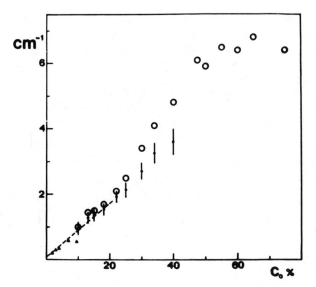

Fig. 5. Characteristic widths of the S(0) lines vs c_o. (OOO : half
full widths at half maximum (△); ••• : half widths of
the lorentzian component (δ_L); ▲ ▲ ▲: half widths from
Buontempo et al., (1982). The broken line at low c_o values
represents the linear behaviour $\delta=\delta+ac_o$.

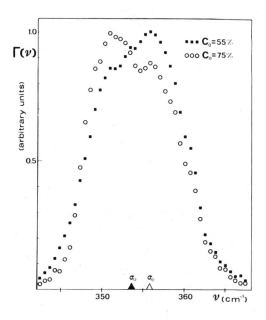

Fig. 6. S(0) line shapes at c_o= 55% (■■■■) and c_o= 75% (oooo).

This hypothesis is also supported by the results obtained from the vibrational Raman Q-lines measured at different ortho concentrations (Soots et al., 1965). These results indicate that a travelling vibrational excitation (vibron) associated with the ortho molecules can be sustained down to $c_0 = 20\%$. The corresponding result can be inferred for the vibrons associated with the para molecules. It should also be noted that this value of 20% corresponds to the calculated percolation threshold for an hcp lattice (Kirkpatric et al., 1973).

New information on the nature of the absorption feature centered at about 356 cm^{-1} could be brought in by new measurements in ortho enriched H_2. In fact this contribution will be clearly associated with the rotational exciton if it will appear just above the percolation threshold for para molecules imbedded in an ortho matrix ($c_0 = 20\%$).

CONCLUDING REMARKS

A remarkable result of our experiments is that in solid para H_2 the excitonic S(0) line is extremely narrow; its half width is not larger than 0.1 cm^{-1} and is probably entirely due to radiation or phonon damping. This result indicates that in pure para H_2 the rotational excitons decay in photons or phonons. Adding ortho H_2 impurities, the S(0) line broadens; however, the rotational excitons survive up to appreciable ortho H_2 concentrations. In this case it is not clear how these excitations decay.

A second remarkable conclusion is that in the case of liquid ra H_2 dissolved in liquid Argon (Buontempo et al., 1975) This still ordered enough at least in the short range, to allow for the existence of phonon-like translational collective modes, similar to those observed in the solid phase.

REFERENCES

Bhatenager, S. S., Allin, E. J., and Welsh, H., 1962 Can. J. Phys. 40:9.
Buontempo, U., Cunsolo, S., and Dore, P., 1975 J. Chem. Phys., 62:4062.
Buontempo, U., Cunsolo, S., Dore, P., and Nencini, L., 1982 Can. J. Phys., 60:1422.
Buontempo, U., Cunsolo, S., Dore, P., and Nencini, L., 1983 Can. J. Phys., 61:1401.
Carneiro, K., Nielsen, M., and McTague, J. P., 1973, Phys. Rev. Lett., 30:481.
Gush, H. P., Hare, W. F. J., Allin, E. J., and Welsh, H. L., 1960, Can. J. Phys., 38:176.
Gush, H. P., 1961, J. Phys., Radium 22:149.
Gush, H. P., and Van Kranendonk, J., 1962, Can. J. Phys. 40:1461.

Jones, M. C., 1970 Nat. Bur. Stand. US Tech. Note, TN390.

Kirkpatrick, 1973, Rev. Modern Phys., 45:574.

Soots, W., Allin, E. J., and Welsh, H. L., 1965 Can. J. Phys.,
    43:1985.

Stoicheff, B. P., 1957, Can. J. Phys., 35:730.

Treffler, M., Cappel, A. M., and Gush, H. P., 1969, Can. J. Phys.
    47:2115.

Van Kranendonk, J., 1959, Physica 25:1080.

Van Kranendonk, J., 1960, Can. J. Phys., 38:240
    Solid Hydrogen, Plenum Press, New York 1983.

INDUCED LIGHT SCATTERING IN DISORDERED SOLIDS

Vittorio Mazzacurati, Giancarlo Ruocco and
Giovanni Signorelli

Dipartimento di Fisica, Università "La Sapienza," Rome

Michele Nardone

Istituto di Fisica, Università di Camerino

ABSTRACT

The interpretation of light scattering spectra in disordered
solids is from many aspects, an incompletely solved problem, expecially when it is desired to extract from the spectra information
about the dynamics of the particles of the system. In this paper,
we outline a formalism that can be easily applied to disordered
molecular solids, and which can be extensively used in several
other cases, even for some liquid samples when certain conditions
are satisfied. This formalism is then applied to two particular
cases of partially disordered crystals: α-AgI and Ice Ih. In both
cases the relation between Raman scattering lineshapes and the
densities of vibrational states is clarified; acoustic and optic
phonon densities of states are derived and compared with neutron
scattering experiments. The results are encouraging and suggest
further applications of the formalism.

INTRODUCTION

The aim of the present paper is to show how a rather general
formalism can be used to interpret the Raman spectra of a large
variety of systems which we shall briefly indicate as "disordered
solids". This formalism provides a good deal of qualitative information about the spectra, which in some cases may become more
quantitative allowing the determination of precise structural and
dynamical properties of the system. We shall discuss in detail the
results obtained for two particularly different disordered solids,
an orientationally disordered molecular crystal, Ice Ih, and a
superionic conductor, AgI.

DISORDERED SOLIDS

Since we are interested in the vibrational dynamics appearing in light scattering spectra for frequency shifts larger than a given ω^* ($\simeq 1$ cm^{-1}), we can include in the "disordered solids" all systems possessing some degree of disorder, provided that the atoms can oscillate about quasi-equilibrium positions defined at least for $\simeq$ 5 ps ($1/\omega^*$). Therefore, the formalism we will develop should provide a reliable interpretation scheme also for some molecular liquids when the existence of a long lived local structure allows atomic vibrations for frequencies larger than ω^* to be relatively well defined (March, N H., and Tosi, M.P., 1976) and confines the orientational dynamics to the long time domain governed by relaxation equations (Kivelson, D., and Keyes, T., 1972). The formalism should also have some relevance in interpreting the light scattering spectra from dense monoatomic fluids as suggested by the similarity between Raman spectra and the vibrational density of states of a Lennard-Jones glass both obtained by Rahman et al. (1976, 1978).

As defined here, the term "disordered solid" ranges over a widespread class of systems which are not easily classified in a rigorous way. We wish to distinguish, however, between "fully disordered" systems, in which no periodic long range structure is present, and "partially disordered" systems, in which some atomic species (or some combination of them such as the center of mass of a molecule) form a periodic lattice, while the other species are randomly distributed. Partially disordered systems will be of particular interest to us, since in this case the dynamical behaviour of the "regular" part of the sample can be treated using the well established phonon formalism. When the spectral response due to this dynamical motion can be identified, the analysis of the actual spectra can yield information both on the scattering mechanism and on the details of the vibrational dynamics. A further classification based on the nature of the forces responsible for the aggregations occurring in these disordered systems is of some help in identifying the origin of the scattering process. We shall therefore distinguish among the following systems:

a) molecular systems, in which the electronic properties are localized on "units" (rare gas atoms, ions, real molecules) interacting with each other via forces which are weak compared with those responsible for the localization of their electrons.

b) covalent systems in which the electronic clouds responsible for the scattering process actively participate in the binding.

c) intermediate systems, such as hydrogen bonded systems, in which part of the electronic cloud is localized on a single molecule and part is involved in the intermolecular bonds.

Typically class a) includes totally disordered systems such as the amorphous semiconductors, Lennard-Jones glasses and partially disordered systems such as molecular crystals, superionic conductors

and liquid crystals. True glasses (silica, etc.) are fully disordered
systems belonging to class b), while KH_2PO_4 and Ice Ih are particularly interesting members of class c).

LIGHT SCATTERING IN DISORDERED SOLIDS

For simplicity let us assume a 90° scattering geometry in
which the incoming beam and its polarization lie along the laboratory frame axes. The scattered intensity at a frequency shift ω
from the incoming frequency is then given by (Cowley, 1964)

$$I_{ij}(\vec{q},\omega) \cong \iint d\vec{r}_1 d\vec{r}_2 \; e^{-i\vec{q}(\vec{r}_1-\vec{r}_2)} \int dt e^{i\omega t} \langle\langle P_{ij}(\vec{r}_1,t)P_{ij}(\vec{r}_2,0)\rangle\rangle \quad (1)$$

where $P_{ij}(\vec{r},t)$ is the ij cartesian component of the polarizability
density tensor of the sample, $\vec{q} = \vec{k}_i - \vec{k}_s$ the exchanged wavevector
and $\langle\langle \; \rangle\rangle$ indicates both thermal and configurational averages.
When the polarizability is due to optical electrons localized in
volumes with dimensions much smaller then the wavelength of the light,
it is convenient to express $P_{ij}(\vec{r},t)$ in terms of an effective
molecular polarizability α_{ij}^{μ} (Briganti, el al., 1981) or sometimes
an effective bond polarizability α_{ij}^{b} (Galeener, et al., 1978). The
latter will be useful in describing class (b) systems and we may
write (Mazzacurati, et al., 1979)

$$P_{ij}(\vec{r},t) = \sum_b \tilde{\alpha}_{ij}^{b}(\{\vec{R}_\chi(t)\}, \vec{B}_b(t)) \cdot \delta(\vec{r}-\vec{B}_b(t)) \quad (2)$$

where $\vec{B}_b(t)$ is the instantaneous "position" of the bond b, $\vec{R}_\chi(t)$
that of the nucleus χ and the curly brackets indicate the set of
all possible nuclei χ. The effective molecular polarizability used
in describing class (a) system may be cast in the following form

$$P_{ij}(\vec{r},t) = \sum_\mu \tilde{\alpha}_{ij}^{\mu}(\{\vec{R}_{\chi'\mu'}(t)\}, \vec{B}_\mu(t)) \; \delta(\vec{r}-\vec{B}_\mu(t)) \quad (3)$$

$\vec{B}_\mu(t)$ is the center of mass position of the molecule μ and $\vec{R}_{\chi'\mu'}$
is that of the necleus χ' of the molecule μ'. Both expressions relate the fluctuations of the macroscopic polarizability to the
motions of all the nuclei present in the sample through as yet
unspecified mechanisms determing the effective bond or molecular
polarizabilities that are involved. Throughout this work we will
refer only to Eq. (3), although many of the conclusions hold also
for Eq. (2).

It is customary to separate the effective molecular polar-
izability $\tilde{\alpha}_{ij}^{\mu}$ into that of the isolated molecule α_{ij}^{μ} (permanent
polarizability) and into an interaction induced term $\Delta\alpha_{ij}^{\mu}$ due to
the presence of the surrounding medium, namely,

$$\tilde{\alpha}_{ij}^{\mu} = \alpha_{ij}^{\mu} + \Delta\alpha_{ij}^{\mu} \quad (4)$$

In a disordered solid, as defined in the introduction, the time dependence of the first term in the right hand side of Eq. (4) arises only from internal motions and from librations of molecule μ itself. The interaction induced term on the contrary depends also on the dynamics of all the other molecules relative to molecule μ. Cross terms between permanent and induced polarizabilities will be neglected throughout this paper since in molecular solids the time scale characterizing molecular vibrations and rotations is in general much longer than the one characterizing molecular translations.

In this work, we will be concerned only with those induced terms which arise from a Taylor expansion of the induced molecular dipole moment in powers of the local electric field and from a multipole expansion of the local field itself (Buckingham and Pople, 1955; Buckingham, 1967) (i.e., neglecting overlap and exchange contributions). Furthermore, we limit ourselves to pair-wise additive contributions to the induced polarizability. It is easily shown, in this case, that $\Delta\alpha_{ij}(t)$ is always written as an appropriate combination of terms having the following structure

$$\sum_{\mu'} h_{\overline{\alpha}}^{(k)}(\mu) \otimes T_{\overline{\beta}}^{(\ell)}(\mu\mu') \otimes g_{\overline{\gamma}}^{(m)}(\mu') \; \Delta(\overline{\alpha}, \overline{\beta}, \overline{\gamma}; \, ij) \tag{5a}$$

where $h_{\overline{\alpha}}^{(k)}(\mu)$ (as well as $g_{\overline{\alpha}}^{(k)}(\mu)$) is the $\overline{\alpha} = (\alpha_1, \alpha_2 \ldots. \alpha_k)$ component of a k-rank tensor representing an electronic property of the isolated molecule μ and is therefore a function only of the internal nuclear coordinates of the molecule. $T_{\overline{\alpha}}^{(k)}(\mu\mu')$ is the $2^{(k-1)}$-pole propagator; it has the general structure of a multiple derivative of the function $1/R$ calculated at the point $\vec{B}_{\mu\mu'} = \vec{B}_\mu - \vec{B}_{\mu'}$, and therefore it depends only on the relative coordinates. This propagator has a defined parity for the interchange of molecule μ and μ'. Finally, the factor $\Delta(\overline{\alpha}, \overline{\beta}, \overline{\gamma}; \, ij)$ is 0 or 1 according to the self-compatibility of the set of cartesian components $\{\overline{\alpha}, \overline{\beta}, \overline{\gamma}; \, ij\}$.

In what follows the term induction mechanism signifies a simple contribution to $\Delta\alpha_{ij}$ that is a sum over all the compatible cartesian components $\overline{\alpha}, \overline{\beta}, \overline{\gamma}; \, ij$ of terms involving the same g and h molecular properties. This contribution will be called gTh and indicated by

$$\sum_{\mu'} h(\mu) \otimes T(\mu\mu') \otimes g(\mu') \tag{5b}$$

For instance if we consider the well known D.I.D. interaction from point polarizable scatterers (McTague and Birnbaum, 1971) of polarizability α_μ, then

$$h_{\alpha\beta}^{(2)}(\mu) = g_{\alpha\beta}^{(2)}(\mu) = \alpha_\mu \, \delta_{\alpha\beta} \; ; \quad \ell = 2 \tag{6a}$$

and we obtain

$$\Delta\alpha_{ij}^{\mu}\Big|^{DID} = \sum_{\mu'}\alpha_{\mu}\alpha_{\mu'}\, T_{ij}^{(2)}(\mu\mu') \tag{6b}$$

As another example, we can consider the induced polarizability arising from the interference of the local electric field due to permanent dipoles $d(\mu)$ with the laser field via the first hyperpolarizability $\beta_{\alpha\beta\gamma}(\mu)$ (De Santis and Sampoli, 1983). In this case we have

$$h_{\alpha}^{(1)}(\mu)= d_{\alpha}(\mu) \quad ; \quad g_{\alpha\beta\gamma}^{(3)}(\mu) = \beta_{\alpha\beta\gamma}(\mu) \quad ;\ell = 2 \tag{6c}$$

and obtain

$$\Delta\alpha_{ij}^{\mu}\Big|^{"\beta Td"} = \sum_{\mu',\alpha\beta} d_{\alpha}(\mu')\, T_{\alpha\beta}^{(2)}(\mu\mu')\beta_{\beta ij}(\mu) \tag{6d}$$

Introducing the internal nuclear coordinates

$$\vec{\rho}_{\mu\chi} = \vec{R}_{\mu\chi} - \vec{B}_{\mu} \tag{7a}$$

or, equivalently, 3s-3 (s being the number of nuclei in each molecule) appropriate linear combination of their cartesian components $\rho_{\mu\chi}^{\gamma}$

$$q_{\mu}^{\nu} = \sum_{\gamma\chi} c_{\nu,\chi\gamma}^{\mu}\, \rho_{\mu\chi}^{\gamma} \tag{7b}$$

we can expand the effective molecular polarizability about the equilibrium positions of all the nuclei.

The usual expansion of the permanent polarizability leads simply to

$$\alpha_{ij}^{\mu} = \alpha_{ij}^{\mu}(eq.) +\sum_{\nu} \frac{\partial\alpha_{ij}^{\mu}}{\partial q_{\mu}^{\nu}}\Bigg|_{eq.} \cdot q_{\mu}^{\nu} \tag{8}$$

while the expansion of the interaction induced terms of Eq. (5b) becomes

$$\sum_{\mu'}h(\mu)\otimes T(\mu\mu')\otimes g(\mu') \approx \sum_{\mu'}h^{eq}\cdot(\mu)\otimes T^{eq}\cdot(\mu\mu')\otimes g^{eq}\cdot(\mu') +$$

$$+\sum_{\mu'\gamma}h^{eq}(\mu)\otimes\frac{\partial T(\mu\mu')}{\partial B_{\mu\mu'}^{\gamma}}\Bigg|_{eq} \otimes g^{eq}(\mu') \cdot\delta B_{\mu\mu'}^{\gamma}(t) + \tag{9}$$

$$+\sum_{\mu'\nu}\frac{\partial h(\mu)}{\partial q_{\mu}^{\nu}}\Bigg|_{eq} \otimes T^{eq}(\mu\mu')\otimes g^{eq}(\mu')\, q_{\mu}^{\nu}(t) +$$

$$\sum_{\mu'\nu}h^{eq}(\mu)\otimes T^{eq}(\mu\mu')\otimes\frac{\partial g(\mu')}{\partial q_{\mu'}^{\nu}}\Bigg|_{eq} q_{\mu'}^{\nu}(t)$$

The first terms on the right hand side of both Eqs. (8) and (9) represent the effective molecular polarizability when all the atoms are in their equilibrium positions, i.e. $\widetilde{\alpha}^{\mu}_{ij}$ (eq.); they give rise to a scattering contribution which can only be modulated in time by virtue of the delta-functions appearing in Eq. (3). All the remaining terms, representing fluctuations of the effective molecular polarizability due to the motions of the nuclei in the system, will be indicated by $\delta\widetilde{\alpha}^{\mu}_{ij}(t)$.

Let us discuss first the scattering contribution arising from the equilibrium effective polarizability. Even if this contribution is not particularly relevant in describing experimental results, its derivation is nevertheless useful to understand the role played by the disorder properties of the system. If we perform an expansion in the $\vec{B}_\mu(t)$ coordinates about their equilibrium values $\vec{B}_\mu(eq.)$, the leading inelastic term reads

$$\sum_{\mu\mu'} \left\langle \widetilde{\alpha}^{\mu}_{ij}(eq.)\widetilde{\alpha}^{\mu'}_{ij}(eq.) \right\rangle_c e^{-i\vec{q}(\vec{B}_\mu(eq.)-\vec{B}_{\mu'}(eq.))} .$$

(10)

$$\sum_{\gamma\varepsilon} q_\gamma q_\varepsilon \int dt\, e^{i\omega t} \left\langle \delta B^{\gamma}_{\mu}(t) \delta B^{\varepsilon}_{\mu'}(o) \right\rangle$$

in which $\delta B^{\gamma}_\mu(t)$ is the γ cartesian component of the center of mass displacement of molecule μ and configurational and thermal averages have been separated.

In order to introduce the disorder properties of the system we make the following ansatz

$$\left\langle \widetilde{\alpha}^{\mu}_{ij}(eq.)\widetilde{\alpha}^{\mu'}_{ij}(eq.) \right\rangle_c = \left\langle \widetilde{\alpha}^{\mu}_{ij} \right\rangle^2_c + \left\langle \left(\widetilde{\alpha}^{\mu}_{ij} - \langle\widetilde{\alpha}^{\mu}_{ij}\rangle_c\right)^2 \right\rangle_c \cdot f(\vec{B}_{\mu\mu'},\lambda) \quad \text{(11a)}$$

where $f(\vec{r},\lambda)$ is generally a decreasing function of $\vec{r}=\vec{B}_\mu(eq.)-\vec{B}_{\mu'}(eq.)$, parametrized by some correlation length λ. This function describes the correlation of orientation and has the following properties

$$f(\vec{B}_{\mu\mu'},\lambda)\xrightarrow[\lambda\to o]{}\delta\mu\mu' \; ; \; f(\vec{B}_{\mu\mu'},\lambda)\xrightarrow[\lambda\to\infty]{} 1 \; ; \; f(0,\lambda)= 1 \quad \text{(11b)}$$

Since the average of the off-diagonal elements of α_{ij}(eq.) must vanish in an isotropic sample, it follows that

$$\left\langle \widetilde{\alpha}^{\mu}_{ij}(eq.)\widetilde{\alpha}^{\mu'}_{ij}(eq.) \right\rangle_c = \bar{\alpha}^2\delta_{ij} + \left\langle |\delta\widetilde{\alpha}^{\mu}_{ij}(eq.)|^2 \right\rangle_c f(\vec{B}_{\mu\mu'},\lambda) \quad \text{(11c)}$$

where $\bar{\alpha} = 1/3\, \mathrm{Tr}\, \widetilde{\alpha}^{\mu}_{ij}$(eq.) and $\delta\widetilde{\alpha}^{\mu}_{ij}= \widetilde{\alpha}^{\mu}_{ij}- \langle\widetilde{\alpha}^{\mu}_{ij}\rangle_c$. Recalling that (Hansen and McDonald, 1981)

$$G(\vec{r},t) = \frac{1}{N}\sum_{\mu\mu'}\int\left\langle\delta(\vec{r}_2+\vec{r}-\vec{B}_{\mu'}(0))\cdot\delta(\vec{B}_\mu(t)-\vec{r}_2)\right\rangle d^3r_2 \quad \text{(12a)}$$

we may write the well known dynamical structure factor as

$$S(\vec{k},\omega)=1/2\pi\int d^3r\; e^{-i\vec{k}\cdot\vec{r}}\int dt\; e^{i\omega t}\; G(\vec{r},t) =$$

$$= \frac{1}{2\pi N}\sum_{\mu\mu'}\int dt\; e^{i\omega t}\left\langle e^{-i\,\vec{k}\cdot(\vec{B}_\mu(t)-\vec{B}_{\mu'}(0))}\right\rangle$$

(12b)

In the case of a solid

$$S(\vec{k},\omega)\simeq\frac{1}{2\pi N}\sum_{\mu\mu'}e^{-i\vec{k}\cdot(\vec{B}_\mu(eq.)-\vec{B}_{\mu'}(eq.))}\delta(\omega) +$$

(13)

$$+ \frac{1}{2\pi N}\sum_{\mu\mu'}e^{-ik\cdot(\vec{B}_\mu(eq.)-\vec{B}_{\mu'}(eq.))}\sum_{\gamma\varepsilon}k_\gamma k_\varepsilon\left\langle\delta B_\mu^\gamma(t)\delta B_{\mu'}(o)\right\rangle dt\, e^{i\omega t}$$

The inelastic term (Eq. 10) can now be simply rewritten as

$$2\pi N\bar{\alpha}^2 S(\vec{q},\omega)\delta_{ij}+2\pi N\left\langle|\delta\tilde{\alpha}_{ij}^\mu|^2\right\rangle_c\cdot q^2\int d^3k\frac{1}{kq^2}\, f(\vec{q}-\vec{k},\omega)S_q(\vec{k},\omega)$$

(14)

where $S_q(\vec{k},\omega)$ is the first order expansion of the dynamical structure factor of the molecular center of mass and $f(\vec{k},\omega)$ the Fourier transform of $f(\vec{r},\omega)$.

The first term in Eq. (14) which gives rise to only polarized scattering, describes the Rayleigh-Brillouin doublet confined to frequencies smaller than ω^*. It does not depend strongly on the disordered properties of the system. In the second term, where strict polarization selection rules are absent, the degree of disorder plays a crucial role in determing its spectral properties. If the disorder allows one to consider the sample as totally isotropic, any dependence on the directions of the $\vec{k}$ and $\vec{q}$ vectors must be lost and the second term in Eq. (14) becomes

$$\left\langle|\delta\tilde{\alpha}_{ij}^\mu(eq.)|^2\right\rangle_c\sum_j\int d^3k\; f(\vec{q}-\vec{k},\lambda)\;\cdot$$

$$\sum_{\gamma\varepsilon}q_\gamma q_\varepsilon e_j^\gamma(\vec{k})e_j^\varepsilon(\vec{k})\left\langle q_{\vec{k}j}(t)q_{\vec{k}j}(0)\right\rangle$$

(15a)

where $q_{\vec{k}j}(t)$ is the vibrational normal coordinate of the sample and $e_j^\gamma(\vec{k})$ is the γ component of the oscillation induced by mode $\vec{k}$, j in molecule μ (Maradudin et al., 1971) (apart from the phase factor exp $i\vec{k}\cdot\vec{B}_\mu(eq.)$). Using the well known properties (Marshall and Lovesey, 1971)

$$\left\langle|\vec{q}\cdot\vec{e}|^2\right\rangle_c=1/3\; q^2;\quad \left\langle q_{\vec{k}j}(t)\cdot q_{\vec{k}j}(0)\right\rangle=((n(\omega)+1)/\omega)\cdot\delta(\omega-\omega_{\vec{k}j})(15b)$$

we obtain

$$\left\langle \left| \delta\tilde{\alpha}^{\mu}_{ij}(\text{eq.}) \right|^2 \right\rangle_c \frac{n(\omega)+1}{\omega} \frac{q^2}{3} \sum_j \int d^3k \; f(\vec{q}-\vec{k},\lambda) \; \delta(\omega-\omega_{\vec{k}j}) \qquad (15c)$$

Indeed if the value of $\delta\alpha^{\mu}_{ij}(\text{eq.})$ is totally uncorrelated from one molecule to another (total "electrical" disorder), $f(\vec{k},\lambda=0)=1$ and the scattered intensity due to this term becomes

$$4\pi/3 \left\langle \left| \delta\tilde{\alpha}^{\mu}_{ij}(\text{eq.}) \right|^2 \right\rangle_c \; q^2 \; \frac{n(\omega)+1}{\omega} \; \rho(\omega) \qquad (15d)$$

thus yielding a spectrum reproducing $(n(\omega)+1)/\omega$ times the translational density of states of the system, $\rho(\omega)$, much like in incoherent neutron scattering.

In the totally disordered case, the integrated intensity of this contribution (Eq. 15a) is smaller by a factor

$$\left(\left\langle (\delta\tilde{\alpha}^{\mu}_{ij})^2 \right\rangle_c / \bar{\alpha}^2 \right) \cdot 10^{-8}$$

than the integrated intensity of the Rayleigh-Brillouin doublet (first term in Eq. 14) (Briganti et al., 1981). The factor 10^{-8} arises because in Eq. 15d, N normal modes, with eigenfrequencies ranging up to typically 100 cm^{-1}, contribute to the scattering with a $(n(\omega)+1)/\omega$ weighting factor, whole in the Rayleigh-brillouin intensity the $\omega=\omega(q)$ mode contributes to the scattering with a $N\cdot(n(\omega)+1)/\omega(q)$ factor, $\omega(q)$ being normally much smaller than 1 cm^{-1}.

In the opposite limit ($\lambda \to \infty$; totally ordered system)

$$f(\vec{k}-\vec{q},\lambda=\infty)=\delta(\vec{k}-\vec{q})$$

and the order dependent second term in Eq. 14 assumes the same structure as the first one, with comparable integrated intensity $(<|\delta\alpha^{\mu}_{ij}|^2>_c\cdot \bar{\alpha}^{-2})$ and frequency range, the only difference being the polarization properties. As a matter of fact the second term can give rise to depolarized scattering as well. On the other hand, if a finite correlation of the orientation exists, $f(\vec{k},\lambda)$ will always be a decreasing function of the variable $\vec{k}-\vec{k}_o$, where $|\vec{k}_o|$ is either 0 or π/d, where d is nearest neighbour distance) depending on whether the correlation of $\delta\alpha^{\mu}_{ij}(\text{eq.})$ between adjacent molecules is positive or negative. Therefore the effect of $f(\vec{k},\lambda)$ will be to cancel the contributions to the spectrum of the translational density of states related to $\vec{k}$ values very different from $\vec{k}_o$, decreasing in this way also the total integrated intensity of this contribution. In conclusion, whenever the spectral contributions due to the equilibrium values of the effective molecular polarizabilities given by Eq. (14) will appear in the frequency range of interest ($\omega>\omega^*$), they will be too small to be detectable.

Let us now focus our attention on the fluctuations of the effective molecular polarizability $\delta\alpha_{ij}^\mu(t)$ due to the nuclear motions. These are represented by terms other than the first appearing on the right hand side of Eq. (8) and (9). When we include these time dependent quantities in the scattering equation, retaining as usual only the leading inelastic term, we obtain

$$\int dt\, e^{i\omega t} \left\langle\!\!\left\langle \sum_{\mu\mu'} e^{-i\vec{q}\cdot(\vec{B}_\mu(eq.)-\vec{B}_{\mu'}(eq.))} \,\, \delta\widetilde{\alpha}_{ij}^\mu(t)\delta\widetilde{\alpha}_{ij}^{\mu'}(o) \right\rangle\!\!\right\rangle \tag{16}$$

We can now substitute in Eq. (16) the explicit expressions for $\delta\widetilde{\alpha}_{ij}^\mu(t)$ from Eqs. (8) and (9).

The second term on the right hand side of Eq. (9) gives rise to a scattering contribution given by

$$\sum_{\mu\mu'\mu''\mu'''} \sum_{\gamma\varepsilon}\int dt\, e^{i\omega t}\left\langle e^{-i\vec{q}\cdot(\vec{B}_\mu(eq.)-\vec{B}_{\mu'}(eq.))}\right. .$$

$$\left. L_{\mu\mu''}^\gamma(eq.)L_{\mu'\mu'''}^\varepsilon(eq.) \left\langle\!\!\left\langle \delta B_{\mu\mu''}^\gamma(t)\,\, \delta B_{\mu'\mu'''}^\varepsilon(0) \right\rangle\!\!\right\rangle \right. \tag{17}$$

where

$$L_{\mu\mu'}^\gamma(eq.) = h_\mu^{(eq.)} \otimes \left.\frac{\partial T(\mu\mu')}{\partial B_{\mu\mu'}^\gamma}\right|_{eq} \otimes g_{\mu'}^{(eq.)} \tag{18}$$

We can proceed further and show how this equation containing relative displacement correlation functions can be expressed in terms of the more usual absolute displacement correlation functions. In order to do so we define

$$\widetilde{L}^\gamma(\mu) = \sum_{\mu''}(L_{\mu\mu''}^\gamma(eq.) - L_{\mu''\mu}^\gamma(eq.))$$

and note that owing to the short range of any induction mechanism (compared to the wavelength of light)

$$L_{\mu\mu''}^\gamma\, e^{i\vec{q}\cdot\vec{B}_{\mu''}} \simeq L_{\mu\mu''}^\gamma e^{i\vec{q}\cdot\vec{B}_\mu}$$

We may therefore rewrite Eq. (17) in the following form

$$\sum_{\mu\mu'} {}_{\gamma\epsilon}\left\langle e^{-i\vec{q}\cdot(\vec{B}_\mu(eq.)-\vec{B}_{\mu'}(eq.))}\widetilde{L}^\gamma(\mu)\widetilde{L}^\epsilon(\mu')\int dt e^{i\omega t}\left\langle\delta B_\mu^\gamma(t)\delta B_{\mu'}^\epsilon(0)\right\rangle\right\rangle \quad (19)$$

Following a similar procedure the scattering arising from the last term of Eqs. (9) and (8) may be written

$$\sum_{\mu\mu'} {}_{\gamma\epsilon}\left\langle e^{-i\vec{q}(\vec{B}_\mu(eq.)-\vec{B}_{\mu'}(eq.))}M_\mu^\nu M_{\mu'}^{\nu'}\int dt\ e^{i\omega t}\left\langle q_\mu^\nu(t)q_{\mu'}^{\nu'}(0)\right\rangle\right\rangle \quad (20a)$$

with

$$M_\mu^\nu=\frac{\partial\alpha_\mu}{\partial q_\mu^\nu}+\sum_{\mu''}\left\{\frac{\partial h^{(\mu)}}{\partial q_\mu^\nu}\otimes T(\mu\mu'')\otimes g(\mu'')+h(\mu)\otimes T(\mu''\mu)\otimes\frac{\partial g(\mu'')}{\partial q_{\mu''}^\nu}\right\} \quad (20b)$$

Eqs. (19) and (20a) now have a form very similar to that of Eq. (10). We can therefore expect them to exhibit coherent contributions, reflecting the $\vec{k}=\vec{q}$ excitations, as well as incoherent contributions. These contributions reflect the density of states of the excitations involved, namely translational motions, Eq. (19), and internal motions and librations, Eq. (20a). All these terms can in principle contribute when $\omega>\omega^*$. Not much can be said about the frequency ranges involved, although any incoherent term will generally be broader than the corresponding coherent one. As far as the intensity is concerned, the incoherent term is not necessarily negligible, since it does not contain the q intensity factor, and it can even become comparable with that of the coherent term of Eq. (10).

We will now show how this formalism can be applied to two particular systems and how informations about the structure and the dynamics of these two systems can be extracted.

INDUCED LIGHT SCATTERING IN SUPERIONIC CONDUCTORS: α-AgI

In the α-phase (above 150°C) of silver iodide, the I^- ions form a b.c.c. lattice, while the Ag+ may be arranged in a variety of non equivalent sublattice sites, as shown in Fig. 1. The cube represents the unit cell with I^- in the center and at the corners of the cube itself (W. Van Gool, 1973). The silver atom sites are, in order of increasing energy, 24 d-sites (represented by ○), 36 h-sites (△) and 12 b-sites (by ■). Since each site belongs to two adjacent cells, 4 silver ions must on the average be distributed among them. Neglecting the existence of a small covalent bond between Ag+ and I^-, we can describe α-AgI as a partially disordered molecular system, in which the molecular units are the atoms. Therefore no internal rotational-vibrational degrees of freedom will be available for our "units" and we will be left simply with the intermolecular dynamics. This motion has already been investigated with neutron scattering experiments (Bruesch et al., 1980), which have measured

576

the dispersion curves of transverse and longitudinal phonon branches and the phonon lifetimes.

Even if silver atoms are known to migrate from one site to another, it is well established that they stay on a d-site, with an

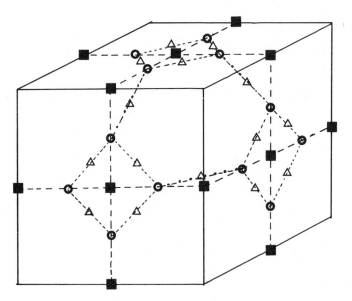

Fig. 1. Unit cell of α-AgI showing the allowed sites for the Ag+ ions (see text). **O** d-sites; $\triangle$ h-sites; ■ b-sites. The I-ions occupy the corners and the center of the cube.

average residence time of 1-2 picoseconds (Pardee and Mahan, 1975). We can therefore classify, for our purpose, silver iodide as a disorder solid.

The spectra obtained from AgI crystals in the α-phase at all temperatures (Fontana et al., 1980) show that the depolarization ratios do not vary with frequency over the whole spectrum. The value of $\rho = I_\perp / I_{//}$ characterizing a given spectrum decreases with increasing T, starting from $\sim 150°C$ up to the melting point (see Fig. 2) (Mariotto et al., 1981). The overall integrated intensity is also a monotonic decreasing function of temperature in the same range, decreasing by more than a factor of ten (Fig. 2). As far as the shape of the reduced spectral intensity

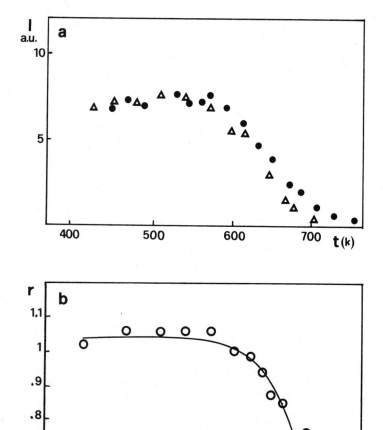

Fig. 2. (a) The experimental values of the integrated Raman intensities as a function of temperature, obtained from two different sets of data;
(b) Circles are the experimental values of the depolarization ratio R=I_{xz}/I_{zz} versus temperature. The solid curve is
the theoretical value of R(T) (see text).

$$J_{ij}(\omega) = I_{ij}(\omega)/(n(\omega)+1)$$

is concerned, we can distinguish at all temperatures two features (corresponding to the energy region of the acoustical and optical modes). These features are only slightly temperature dependent, except for their relative intensity. The picture that emerges from these data is that with increasing temperature the Ag+ distribution becomes more isotropic, reducing the Raman cross section and decreasing the depolarization ratio. The profile of the Raman spectrum is, however, always correlated with the overall density of states of the vibrating I^- ions (Cazzanelli et al., 1983).

In order to explain these results, we have to introduce a model for the local polarizability. The disorder induced terms will then account for acoustic and optic phonon contributions (Mazzacurati et al., 1982).

Representing the ions as spherically symmetric polarizable point particles the first non vanishing terms of the ionic induced dipole moments α cartesian components are

$$\sum_\beta \alpha^\mu_{\alpha\beta} F^\mu_\beta$$

and

$$\frac{1}{6} \sum_{\gamma\beta\delta} \gamma^\mu_{\alpha\beta\gamma\delta} F^\mu_\beta F^\mu_\gamma F^\mu_\delta$$

F^μ_α are the components of the electric field on ion μ, $\alpha^\mu_{\alpha\beta}$ is the usual first order polarizability and $\gamma^\mu_{\alpha\beta\gamma\delta}$ is the first non-vanishing hyperpolarizability of the ion.

The induced polarizabilities arising from these two terms are the well known D.I.D. polarizability

$$\delta\tilde\alpha^\mu_{ij})^{D.I.D.} = \sum_{\gamma\epsilon} \alpha^\mu_{i\gamma} \sum_{\mu'} T^{(2)}_{\gamma\epsilon}(\mu\mu') \alpha^{\mu'}_{\epsilon j} \tag{21a}$$

and what we will call the "charge induced dipole" polarizability (C.I.D.)

$$\delta\tilde\alpha^\mu_{ij})^{C.I.D.} = \frac{1}{2} \sum_{\gamma\epsilon} \gamma^\mu_{ij\gamma\epsilon} E^\mu_\gamma E^\mu_\epsilon \tag{21b}$$

where $T^{(2)}_{\gamma\epsilon}(\mu\mu')$ is the dipole tensor propagator of components

$$\nabla_\gamma\nabla_\epsilon \frac{1}{R} \Big|_{\vec{R}=\vec{\beta}_{\mu\mu'}}$$

and E_ε^μ is the γ component of the local electric field due to the ionic charges surrounding the ion.

The γ hyperpolarizability appears here for the first time as an important source of induced light scattering owing to the intensity of the ionic fields in a system of point polarizable charges.

If we separate the contributions from different ionic species due to other inducing charges, we realize that there can be no D.I.D. or C.I.D. induction on the I^- due to the surrounding iodine ions because of the cubic lattice symmetry nor any C.I.D. or D.I.D. induction on the Ag^+ due to the surrounding iodine ions when the silver atoms are in their equilibrium d-sites. Therefore since the silver-silver ion dynamics are confined to a long time domain and since for times sufficiently long for the iodine lattice vibration to be defined the Ag^+ ions are on their "d" sites with uncorrelated motions with respect to the I^- (Cazzanelli et al., 1983), we are left in the frequency range of interest with only two contributions, namely the D.I.D. and the C.I.D. induction of the silver on the iodine atoms.

We shall deal only with the latter, since the former can be estimated to be sensibly smaller on the basis of the available data for α_I, α_{Ag} and γ_I (Burher et al., 1978).

The scattering in any given polarization configuration will then be given by

$$\sum_{II'} e^{-i\vec{q}(\vec{B}_I - \vec{B}_{I'})} \sum_{\eta\delta} \left\langle A_I^\eta A_{I'}^\delta \right\rangle \int e^{i\omega t} \left\langle \delta B_I^\eta(t) \delta B_{I'}^\delta(0) \right\rangle dt \qquad (22a)$$

where

$$A_I^\eta = \sum_{\gamma\varepsilon} \gamma_{ij\gamma\varepsilon} \left\{ E_\gamma^I \left. \frac{\partial E_\varepsilon^I}{\partial B_I^\eta} \right|_{eq.} + E_\varepsilon^I \left. \frac{\partial E_\gamma^I}{\partial B_I^\eta} \right|_{eq.} \right\} \qquad (22b)$$

Eq. (22a) has the same structure as Eq. (19). In this case the configurational averages must be taken over the Ag^+ configurations around any I^-. We have therefore calculated (Mazzacurati et al., 1982) the energy differences between all possible arrangements of silver atoms in the "d"-site cages, keeping in mind that any cage having 3 Ag ($\mathcal{C}_3$) must have as a counterpart another cage with 5 Ag ($\mathcal{C}_5$) in order to preserve the overall charge neutrality (see Fig. 3). We have also pointed out that the lowest energy configuration is the symmetric $\mathcal{C}_4^o$ followed by the $\mathcal{C}_4^1$. The energy of a $\mathcal{C}_3$ configuration plus that of a $\mathcal{C}_5$ is much higher than that of a $\mathcal{C}_4^o$ plus a $\mathcal{C}_4^1$ (see Table 1). Nevertheless, two neighbouring $\mathcal{C}_3$ and $\mathcal{C}_5^o$ configurations

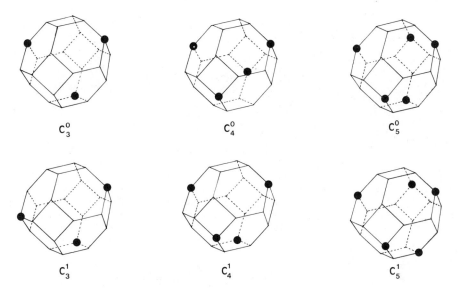

Fig. 3. Lowest energy sets of configurations in a single cage of d-sites $\mathcal{C}_h$ with n=3,4,5 and k=0.1).

may have a total energy which is smaller even than that of the pair $\mathcal{C}_4^o$ and $\mathcal{C}_4^1$.

When the relative populations of these configurations are known, we are able to predict the behaviour versus temperature of the integrated intensities and hence of the polarization ratios. In particular we obtain that both $\mathcal{C}_3^o$ and $\mathcal{C}_5^o$ configurations yield a polarization ratio $\rho=I_{xz}/I_{zz}=1.05$, while $\mathcal{C}_4^1$ yields $\rho=0.68$ and $\mathcal{C}_4^o$ does not contribute to the intensity, giving zero electric field on the I^-. Indeed at low temperatures, where $\mathcal{C}_3^o+\mathcal{C}_5^o$ configurations are predominant, the experimentally measured polarization ratio agrees quite well with the value of 1.05. Furthermore, if we obtain the ratio of $\mathcal{C}_4^o+\mathcal{C}_4^1$ to $\mathcal{C}_3^o+\mathcal{C}_5^o$ configurations from the temperature dependence of the I(T) integrated intensity, we can reproduce quite satisfactorily the complete temperature behaviour of $\rho(T)$.

Returning to Eq. (22a), we can now use the existing neutron scattering data, and modeling the configurational averages in terms of the I-I' ionic distance we can reconstruct the Raman spectral lineshapes (Cazzanelli et al., 1983). Following the same steps used in deriving Eq. (11a), we may transform Eq. (22a) to read

$$\sum_{\gamma\varepsilon}\int d^3k f(\vec{q}-\vec{k},\lambda)\int dt\, e^{i\omega t}\sum_{II'}e^{-i\vec{q}(\vec{B}_I-\vec{B}_{I'})}\left\langle \delta B_I^\gamma(t)\delta B_{I'}^\varepsilon(0)\right\rangle \qquad (23)$$

TABLE I

Configuration	Energy	Electric field	(f_{zz}^2)	(f_{xz}^2)	d_n^k
c_3^o	7.84	1.0	$\frac{2}{9}$	0	72
c_3^1	7.92	1.0	$\frac{2}{9}$	0	144
c_4^o	16.5	0.0			144
c_4^1	16.7	1.41	$\frac{1}{18}$	$\frac{1}{12}$	572
c_5^o	29.2	1.0	$\frac{2}{9}$	0	1440
c_5^1	29.8	1.0	$\frac{2}{9}$	0	2880
c_2^o	2.23	0.0			24
c_6^o	47.2	0.0			5760

We report characteristic quantities for some C_n^k sets. The
repulsive energy values are in eV and the electric field
values are 3.08 x 10^4 in cgs units. d_n^k are the degeneracies
of the configuration for spatial rotation and particle
permutation while $<f_{xx}>$ and $<f_{xz}>$ are the angular average
of Legendre polynomials on the possible Ag+ distribution
belonging to the same configuration

Introducing now the $\omega(\vec{k})$ relations measured by neutron scattering
experiments both for transverse and longitudinal acoustic phonon
branches together with their measured lifetimes and making use of
an inverse correlation length $\bar{k}=2\pi/\lambda$ as the only adjustable parameter
ranging between one and two unitary cells, we can reproduce perfectly
the Raman spectra up to 40 cm^{-1} at any temperature. As expected $\bar{k}$
turns out to be slightly dependent on temperature. The difference
between the experimental and the calculated spectra in the frequency
range above 40 cm^{-1} represents the contribution of the optical
branches and shows (see Fig. 4) a temperature independent shape,
with a maximum in the expected frequency region.

INDUCED LIGHT SCATTERING IN A PARTIALLY COVALENT SYSTEM: HEXAGONAL ICE

Ice (Ih) can be considered an orientationally disordered molecular crystal. The coordination of molecules is tetrahedral and
the disorder arises only from the possible arrangements of the

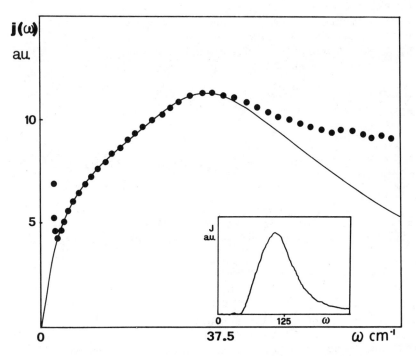

Fig. 4. Full dots denote experimental Raman scattering normalized
by the appropiate Bose-Einstein population factor n(ω)+1.
Solid line plots the calculated acoustic spectral density
as obtained by Eq. (23). The inset shows the optical density
of states obtained as described in the text.

protons around the lattice sites (Hobbs, 1974). The mechanical
regularity of the translational lattice vibrations offers the
opportunity to use both the well established phonon formalism in
treating the translational dynamics of the system and the lattice
dynamics calculations for comparison. The effect of proton disorder
on the lattice dynamics is simply that of modifying the phonon
dispersion curves (as predicted by Bosi et al., 1973). We have therefore accounted for the proton distribution assuming water molecules
to be randomly oriented retaining the harmonic phonon description
of the lattice vibration. Assuming that molecule μ occupies site χ
in the cell 1 we may write (Maradunin et al., 1971):

$$\delta B_\mu^\gamma(t) = \delta B_{1\chi}^\gamma(t) = \sum_{\vec{k}j} e^{i\vec{k}\cdot\vec{x}_1} e\ (\vec{k}j/\chi) Q_{\vec{k}j}(t) \tag{24}$$

where x_1 is the position vector of the 1-th cell and $e^\gamma(\vec{k}j/\chi)$ is the γ cartesian component of the eigenvector of the $Q_{\vec{k}j}(t)$ normal coordinate on molecule χ. Directly substituting in Eq. (17), exploiting the orthonormality of the normal mode and assuming $\exp(i\vec{q}\cdot\vec{B}_{1\chi}) \simeq \exp(i\vec{q}\cdot\vec{x}_1)$ owing to the smallness of the q exchanged wavevector and to the short range of $L^\gamma_{\mu\mu'}$ we find that the scattered intensity becomes

$$\sum_{\vec{k}j} \frac{n(\omega)+1}{\omega} \delta(\omega-\omega_{\vec{k}j}) \cdot$$

$$\cdot \left\langle \Big| \sum_{11'} e^{i(\vec{k}-\vec{q})\cdot\vec{x}_1} \sum_{\gamma,\chi\chi'} L^\gamma_{\substack{11' \\ \chi\chi'}} \left(e^\gamma(\vec{k}j/\chi) - e^{i\vec{k}(\vec{x}_1-\vec{x}_{1'})} e^\gamma(\vec{k}j/\chi') \right) \Big|^2 \right\rangle \quad (25)$$

Furthermore since the configurational average reduces to an average over molecular orientations it can be carried out separately. We will therefore have to deal with quantities such as

$$\left\langle h_\mu^{(eq.)} g_{\mu''}^{(eq.)} h_{\mu'}^{(eq.)} g_{\mu'''}^{(eq.)} \right\rangle_\Omega \quad (26)$$

where the subscript Ω indicates orientational averaging. Recalling that h_μ (as well as g) is an unspecified cartesian component corresponding to an arbitrary rank tensorial property of molecule μ, it can contain an angular independent as well as a zero average angular dependent part. For the former, Eq. (25) becomes

$$\bar{g}^2\bar{h}^2\sum_{\vec{k}j} \frac{n(\omega)+1}{\omega} \delta(\omega-\omega_{\vec{k}j}) \Big| \sum_1 e^{i(\vec{k}-\vec{q})\cdot\vec{x}_1} A(\vec{k}j)\Big|^2 \quad (27)$$

where g and h are the scalar parts of the g and h tensors and the quantity

$$A(\vec{k}j)=\sum_{1',\gamma,\chi\chi'} \frac{\partial T}{\partial R^\gamma}\Big|_{\substack{\vec{R}=\vec{B} \\ 11'\chi\chi'}} e^\gamma(\vec{k}j/\chi) - e^{i\vec{k}(\vec{x}_1-\vec{x}_{1''})} e^\gamma(\vec{k}j/\chi') \quad (28)$$

which does not depend on 1, owing to the regular distribution of the molecular center of mass positions, can be calculated starting from an arbitrary reference cell $\vec{X}_0$. Performing the sum over 1 and remembering the smallness of the $\vec{q}$ wavevector in a light scattering experiment, we are left with

$$\bar{g}^2\bar{h}^2\sum_j \frac{n(\omega)+1}{\omega} \delta(\omega-\omega_{\vec{q}j}) \Big| A(\vec{q},j)\Big|^2 \quad (29)$$

584

This term yields contributions only from $\vec{k}=\vec{q}$ phonons provided $A(\vec{q},j)\neq 0$. Obviously, for acoustic phonons $e^\gamma(qj/\chi)\simeq e^\gamma(qj/\chi'')$ and $A(\vec{q},j)=0$. As far as the angular dependent parts of h and g are concerned, if we assume them to be uncorrelated from one molecule to another, the quantity in Eq. (26) can be written as

$$<h^2>_\Omega<g^2>_\Omega\delta\mu\mu'\,\delta\mu''\mu''' + <hg>_\Omega^2\,\delta\mu\mu'''\,\delta\mu'\mu'' \tag{30}$$

When this is inserted in Eq. (25) we have

$$\sum_{\vec{k}j}(n(\omega)+1)/\omega\cdot\delta(\omega-\omega_{\vec{k}j})\cdot\left[<h^2>_\Omega<g^2>_\Omega\pm<hg>_\Omega^2\right]\cdot$$

$$\cdot\sum_{ll'\chi\chi'}\left|\sum_\gamma\frac{\partial T}{\partial R^\gamma}\right|_{\vec{R}=\vec{B}_{11'\chi\chi'}}\left\{e^\gamma(\vec{k}j/\chi)-e^{i\vec{k}(\vec{x}_1-\vec{x}_{1'})}e^\gamma(\vec{k}j/\chi')\right\} \tag{31}$$

where the $\pm$ sign is determined by the parity of the multipole tensor involved. The curly brackets contain a $\vec{k}$-dependent coefficient $C_{\vec{k}j}$, which weights the different phonons independently from the exchanged $\vec{q}$ vector. It will generally depend on the scattering configuration and affects the overall spectral shape through its $\vec{k}$-dependence. If we could neglect this dependence, which is almost never the case, the spectrum would be simply given by a linear combination of the usual branch density of states $\rho_j(\omega)$. However, in the case of Ice-Ih we can project (Mazzacurati et al., 1981) the eigenvectors set $e(\vec{k},j/\chi)$ onto those for the $\vec{k}=0,j$ mode and define corresponding symmetry projected densities of states $\rho_a(\omega)$, such that

$$\sum_a\rho_a(\omega)=\sum_j\rho_j(\omega)=\rho(\omega)$$

and

$$\int d\omega\,\rho_a(\omega)=\int d\omega\,\rho_j(\omega)=N$$

Since it can be shown in the case of Ice-Ih that the optic normal modes have an appreciable projection only onto one zone center mode at a time, we may write the disorder induced scattering from optic modes as

$$I(\omega)=\frac{n(\omega)+1}{\omega}\sum_a c_a^{ij}\,\rho_a(\omega) \tag{32}$$

where we have explicitly reintroduced the dependence on the polarization indices i, j of the c_a^{ij} coefficients.

Using three independent scattering configurations, we have thus been able to extract, almost without ambiguity, the different $\rho_a(\omega)$ and to reproduce the entire density of states $\rho(\omega)$ simply imposing the normalization condition. The results are in good agreement with

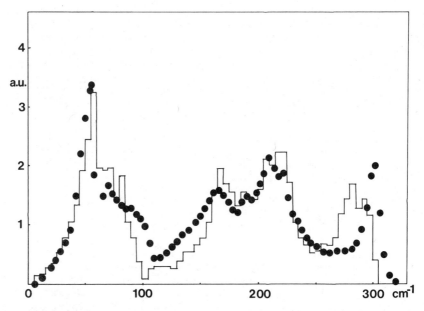

Fig. 5. The total vibrational density of states of ice Ih as extracted from our Raman data (solid dots) compared with that
calculated by Zerbi et al. fitting neutron scattering data.

the lattice dynamics calculation of Zerbi et al., 1973 (see Fig. 5).
A few words must be said however concerning the acoustic phonon
branches, for which a zone center projection would yield vanishing
intensities. As a matter of fact, for small $\vec{k}$ values the coefficient
in Eq. (32) vanishes since $e(\vec{k},j/\chi) \simeq e(\vec{k},j/\chi')$ for a long wavelength
acoustic phonon. It can be shown, however, that in an isotropic
sample it vanishes as k^2, thus yielding for the acoustic phonon
branches

$$\frac{n(\omega)+1}{\omega}\, \rho(\omega)\, k^2 \propto \omega^2 \tag{34}$$

This is in contrast with the low frequency experimental spectra,
which show a substantially flat contribution in this region with a
tendency to increase at very low frequencies. This has been interpreted (Mazzacurati et al., 1981) as due to the partially uncorrelated nature of the hydrogen atoms motions, which very much like in
the case of AgI, can give rise to induced contributions reflecting
$(n(\omega)+1)/\omega$ times the vibrational density of state of the oxygen
atoms.

CONCLUSIONS

We have shown how a simple normal mode expansion of the expressions determining the light scattering spectrum can be applied to interpret satisfactorily the translational spectra of two particular disordered solids. In both cases complementary information, mainly obtained from neutron scattering experiments or from "ab initio" calculations, have been used to reproduce the measured spectra making reasonable assumptions on the scattering mechanism. Unfortunately this can not be done so simply for totally disordered systems nor can it be directly extended for molecular crystals beyond the translational region to include all vibrational modes of the system. In the case of a totally disordered system, the absence of long range order implies that translationaal vibrations cannot be analyzed as plane waves. Specific models must therefore be developed to treat the translational dynamics of the system. Nevertheless, the similarity between the measured intensities and $(n(\omega)+1)/\omega$ times the density of states calculated with these models (Bosi et al., 1973) is surprising. On the other hand, in the case of a disordered molecular crystal, although in the frequency regions of the internal modes a phonon analysis is not directly feasible, the possibility of extracting symmetry projected density of states based on the same criteria which have been demonstrated for the translational region seems plausible. As a matter of fact, the O-H stretching region of ice Ih can be decomposed in four symmetry projected densities of states and the overall density of states, thus reconstructed, appears in good agreement with recent neutron scattering results (Chen et al., 1984).

Work is in progress both in elaborating models for the scattering spectra which are not based on a plane wave analysis of the normal vibrations of the system and in comparing, as far as possible, Raman spectra and neutron scattering results.

REFERENCES

Bosi, P., Tubino, R., and Zerbi, G., 1973, J. Chem. Phys., 59:4578
Briganti, G., Mazzacurati, V., Signorelli, G., Nardone, M., 1981, Mol. Phys., 43:1347
Bruesch, P., Buhrer, W., Smeets, H. J., 1980, Phys. Rev. B22:970
Buckingham, A. D., Pople, J. A., 1955, Proc. Phys. Soc., 68:905
Buckingham, A. D., 1967, Adv. Chem. Phys., 12:107
Buhrer, W., Nicklow, R. M., Bruesch, P., 1978, Phys. Rev. B17:3362
Cazzanelli, E., Fontana, A., Mariotto G., Mazzacurati, V., Ruocco, G., Signorelli, G., 1983, Phys. Rev. B28:7269
Chen, S. H., Toukan, K., Loong, C. K., Price, D. L., Texeira, J., 1984, Phys. Rev. Letters, 53:1360
Cowley, R. A., 1964, Proc. Phys. Soc., 84:281
De Santis, A., Sampoli, M., 1983, Chem. Phys. Lett., 102:425
Fontana, A., Mariotto, G., Fontana, M. P., 1980, Phys. Rev. B21:1102
Galeener, F. L., Sen, P. N., 1978, Phys. Rev. B, 17:1928

Geller, S., ed, 1978, Solid Electrolyte, Springer, Berlin

Hansen, J. P., McDonald, I. R., 1981, Theory of Simple Liquids, Academic Press, London

Hobbs, P. V., 1974, Ice Physics, pg.18, Clarendon Press

Kivelson, D., Keyes, T., 1972, J. Chem. Phys. 57:4599

Mahan, G. D., Roth, L. R., ed., 1976, Superionic Conductors, Plenum, New York

Mahan, G. D., 1976, Phys. Rev. B 14:780

Maradudin, A. A., Montroll, E. W., Weiss, E. W., Ipatova, I., 1971, Theory of Lattice Dynamics in the Harmonic Approximation, Supp.3 of Sol. Stat. Phys., H. Ehrenreich, F., Seitz and D. Turnbull, ed., Academic Press, New York

March, N. H., Tosi, M. P., 1976, Atomic Dynamics in Liquids, Mac Millan Press, LTD, London

Mariotto, G., Fontana, A., Cazzanelli, E., and Fontana, M. P., 1981, Phys. Stat. Solidi, B 101:391

Mariotto, G., Fontana, A., Cazzanelli, E., Rocca, F., Mazzacurati, V., Signorelli, G., 1981, Phys. Rev. B 23:4382

Marshall, W., Lovesey, S. W., 1971, Theory of Thermal Neutron Scattering, Oxford Univ. Press, London

Mazzacurati, V., Nardone, M., Signorelli, G., 1979, Mol. Phys. 38:1379

Mazzacurati, V., Pona, C., Signorelli, G., Briganti, G., Ricci, M. A., Mazzega, E., Nardone, M., De Santis, A., Sampoli, M., 1981, Mol. Phys. 44:1163

Mazzacurati, V., Ruocco, G., Signorelli, G., Cazzanelli, E., Fontana, A., Mariotto, G., 1982, Phys. Rev. B 26:2216

McTague, J. P., Birnbaum, G., 1971, Phys. Rev. A 3:1376

Pardee, W. J., Mahan, G. D., 1975, J. Solid. State Chem., 15:310

Rahman, A., Mandel, M. J., McTague, J. P., 1976, J. Chem. Phys., 64:1564; 1978, 68:1876

Van Gool, W., ed., 1973, Fast Ions Transport in Solids, North Holland, Amsterdam

INFRARED INDUCED ABSORPTION OF NITROGEN AND METHANE ADSORBED IN

NaA SYNTHETIC ZEOLITE

Evelyne Cohen De Lara and Josette Vincent-Geisse

Service de Spectroscopie Moléculaire en Milieu Condensé
Laboratoire de Recherches Physiques associé au CNRS
Université Pierre et Marie Curie, 4 pl. Jussieu, Tour 22
75230 Paris Cedex 05 (France)

ABSTRACT

The infrared spectra of molecules adsorbed in zeolites show important induced effects : forbidden bands and degeneracy splitting due to the intense electric field in the zeolitic cavities. Measurements of the intensity of the induced bands of N_2 and CH_4 give the field value and the splitting of the ν_3 degenerate band of CH_4 is related to the variation of the molecular polarizability.

INTRODUCTION

Synthetic zeolites are porous crystals, made of three-dimensional networks of SiO_4 and AlO_4 tetrahedra linked to each other by the oxygens, containing exchangeable cations for the neutrality of the ensemble. These materials have a high internal surface area available for adsorption due to the channels or the pores which uniformly penetrate the entire volume of the solid.

In the cubic symmetry framework of the NaA zeolite on which the present measurements have been carried out, cavities of 11 Å mean diameter are regularly distributed and connected by windows of 4 Å diameter (Fig.1); the Na cations are located in crystallographic sites in the cavity surface (Breck, 1973). As the structure of these zeolites is well known by X ray scattering, it allows the calculation of the electric field inside the cavities and the potential interaction energy of the adsorbed molecules.

The infrared spectra of some adsorbed molecules show forbidden bands induced by the electric field and from their intensity we can

589

deduce the field strength (Cohen De Lara and Delaval, 1978; Forster et al., 1980).

The integrated intensity of an IR band is given by the following expression

$$A = \frac{N\pi}{3c} \left(\frac{\partial \mu}{\partial Q} \right)^2$$

where N is the number of vibrators and $\partial\mu/\partial Q$ is the transition dipole moment. For a forbidden band, the transition dipole moment is only due to the induced moment, $\bar{\bar{\alpha}}$ being the polarizability tensor,

$$\vec{\mu}_I = \bar{\bar{\alpha}} \, \vec{E}$$

For a spherical top,

$$A = \frac{N\pi}{3c} \, E^2 \left(\frac{\partial \alpha}{\partial Q} \right)^2$$

For a diatomic molecule or a symmetric top and a parallel vibration, if the molecule rotates freely in the field,

$$A = \frac{N\pi}{3c} \, E^2 \left[\left(\frac{\partial \bar{\alpha}}{\partial Q} \right)^2 + \frac{2}{9} \left(\frac{\partial \gamma}{\partial Q} \right)^2 \right]$$

$\bar{\alpha}$ being the mean polarizability and γ the anisotropy of polarizability. $(\partial\bar{\alpha}/\partial Q)^2$ and $(\partial\gamma/\partial Q)^2$ are known from the Raman band intensity, and the measurement of A gives the value of E.

Another important effect of the field is shown in the spectra of the methane molecule adsorbed at very low temperature : the degeneracy splitting of the triply degenerate band ν_3.

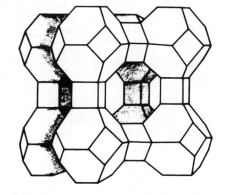

Fig.1   Zeolite A structure

EXPERIMENTAL TECHNIQUES

We shall not describe the IR cells and shall only briefly recall the experimental technique. The NaA zeolite powder is pressed into thin disks (50 to 150 μm); the thickness is measured with a micrometer gauge and simultaneously determined from the area and weight of the pellet. The temperature of the adsorbant is measured by means of a thermocouple adhering to the pellet; the latter is previously dehydrated by heating at 670°K in 10^{-6} torr vacuum in a furnace situated in the upper part of the cell; the sample is lifted up and down by a mechanical device. The number of adsorbed molecules is determined by knowing the temperature and pressure and the adsorption isotherms.

EXPERIMENTAL RESULTS

We present here only the results on the molecules N_2 and CH_4. Homopolar diatomic molecules have no infrared absorption. When adsorbed in the zeolite the stretching vibration of N_2 appears at 2339 cm^{-1} (ν_{gas} = 2330 cm^{-1}). This band is weak (~ 100 cm.mmole^{-1}, $\sim 5 \, 10^{-9}$ cm^2 mol^{-1} s^{-1}) and, for the same number of adsorbed molecules, increases when the temperature decreases. Fig.2 shows the results obtained for three temperatures, n is the number of molecules per cavity and S is the area of the band. The experimental points are somewhat dispersed because of the difficulties of the experiments due to the weakness of the intensity. For n < 1 the intensity is proportional to n and for quantitative interpretation of the results we have always tried to work in this region. In other respects, for a given n, the intensity is temperature dependent. We shall return more precisely to this question later but the explanation is that the mobility of the molecule depends on the temperature. At the highest temperature of adsorption the molecule is relatively free in the cavity and it "feels" a mean field. At very low temperatures it is trapped in a potential well near the surface where the electric field is the highest. At 200 K, the field value obtained with the intensity of the band for one molecule per cavity is 2 10^5 e.s.u. (0.6 10^{10} V/m).

Fig.3 shows the spectrum observed for CH_4 at 200 K. Besides the intense allowed ν_3 and ν_4 bands, one observes the forbidden ν_1 band. The ν_3 band presents large wings, which shows that the CH_4 molecule retains some freedom of rotation in the cavity; the ν_1 band is much more narrow, its width being solely due to vibrational relaxation. At 200 K the field value obtained with the intensity of the ν_1 band is nearly the same as the value obtained with N_2 and the accuracy is higher; indeed the variation of the polarizability is larger for CH_4 than for N_2. We may assume in the temperature range 300-200 K that the contribution to the intensity of the strong ν_3 band arising from the inducing field is small and

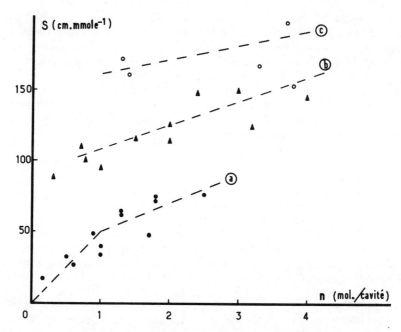

Fig. 2.   Area of the induced band of N_2 adsorbed on NaA
a) T=223 K   b) T=195 K   c) T=180 K.

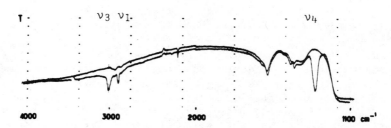

Fig. 3. Infrared spectra of CH_4 adsorbed in NaA zeolite.

can be neglected with respect to the much larger contribution due
to the molecular transition moment. In other words we assume that
the intensity of ν_3 is independent of the position of the molecule
in the cavity while the ν_1 induced band is directly related to the
strength of the field. In this case we measured the ratio of the
integrated intensities of the two bands. It increases rapidly when
T decreases : the intensity of ν_1 increases when T decreases as in
the case of N_2 and for the same reason. In the case of CH_4 we have
some arguments in favour of this interpretation. As a matter of
fact neutron scattering experiments have shown that the methane
molecule adsorbed in a cavity is delocalized at room temperature,
remains close to the surface at lower temperatures and is trapped
in a potential well below 80 K (Cohen De Lara and Kahn, 1981).

Fig.4 shows the change in the spectrum of CH_4 with temperature.
Besides the increasing of the intensity of ν_1, we observe another
interesting phenomenon : from 100 K a splitting of ν_3 appears. The
two components, very well defined below 80 K are 20 cm^{-1} apart.
No such splitting occurs for ν_1. The splitting of ν_3 then cannot be
due to two sites, for example. We propose another explanation : by
neutron scattering experiments the mass centre of CH_4 is seen to be
at rest below 80 K. This site is probably in front of the Na_{III}

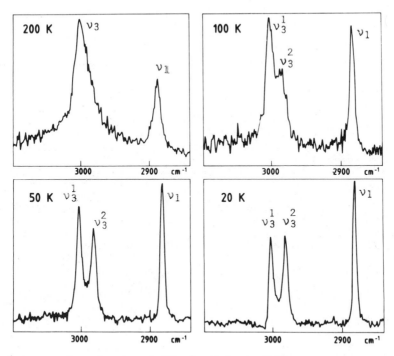

Fig.4. ν_3 and ν_1 bands of CH_4 in NaA at different temperatures.

cation (neutron diffraction (Khan et al., 1982)). In the equilibrium configuration of the couple $Na^+ - CH_4$ found by potential energy calculation (Sauer et al., 1980 ; Mouche et al., 1984) one threefold axis of CH_4 is oriented along the field of the cation with the three hydrogen plane facing Na^+, the octopolar contribution being responsible for the orientation. The large intensity of the field induces a departure of the symmetry of the molecule from Td to C_{3v}. Thus the splitting of ν_3 is due to the splitting of the F band in A and E bands. The relative intensities of these two components vary with temperature, the variation of ν_3^1 being proportional to that of ν_1 ; therefore we attribute ν_3^1 to the A symmetry component and ν_3^2 to the E symmetry (Cohen De Lara and Kahn, 1984).

In conclusion, these systems – molecules physisorbed in zeolites – are particularly interesting regarding the study of induced phenomena. Actually the intensities of the induced bands allows us to measure and analyze them since they correspond to very intense fields. Concerning the splitting of the ν_3 band of methane, it also depends on the value of the field and morever is related to the 2nd derivative of the polarizability of the molecule. The determination of such a molecular quantity, hardly accessible by other techniques, is thus rendered possible.

REFERENCES

Breck, D.W., 1973, "Zeolite Molecular Sieves," Wiley, New York.
Cohen De Lara, E., and Delaval, Y., 1978, J. Chem. Soc., Farad. Trans. II, 74:790.
Cohen De Lara, E., and Kahn, R., 1981, J. Physique, 42:1029.
Cohen De Lara, E., and Kahn, R., 1984, J. Physique Lettres, 45:L-255.
Forster, H., Frede, W., and Schuldt, M., 1980, "Proceedings of the 5th International Conference on Zeolites," Heyden.
Kahn, R., Cohen De Lara, E., Thorel, P., and Ginoux, J.L., 1982, Zeolites, 2:260.
Mouche, E., Cohen De Lara, E., and Kahn, R., 1984, Mol. Phys., 53:749.
Sauer, J., Hobza, P., and Zahradnik, R., 1980, J. Phys. Chem., 84:3318.

CHARGE INDUCED EFFECTS IN SOLID TRITIUM AND DEUTERIUM

J.L. Hunt and J.D. Poll

Guelph-Waterloo Program for Graduate Work in Physics
University of Guelph Campus
Guelph, Ontario, Canada N1G2W1

ABSTRACT

A new type of experiment is described in which spectra induced by electric fields from charges in hydrogen polycrystals are studied. These charges are produced by high energy radiations such as charged particle beams, radioactive decay or γ-irradiation. Experiments involving the first two will be described.

The spectra of the hydrogens irradiated both by protons and β particles at temperatures below 12K show several new absorption features. These features are interpreted as being due to isolated positively or negatively charged damage sites in the crystal which Stark shift the molecular roto-vibrational levels. Specifically, the sites are thought to be occupied by a positive ion (possibly D_3^+) or an electron.

In addition, the proton-beam experiments permit the timing of the growth and decay of these features and they are found to be surprisingly long lived. They grow to saturation on a time scale of minutes and decay on a time scale of hours.

A further experiment to confirm the presence of trapped electrons in the crystal shows a strong absorption in the near infrared which is interpreted as the allowed spectrum of the electron in its trap.

INTRODUCTION

The investigation of the collision induced absorption spectrum (CIA) of the solid hydrogens H_2, HD and D_2 has played an

595

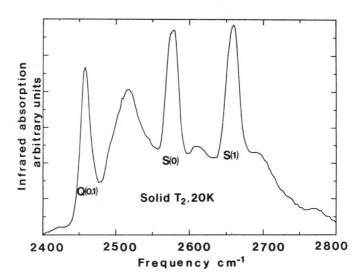

Fig. 1. The fundamental band of solid T_2 at 20 K (courtesy P.C. Souers).

important part in developing both an understanding of CIA phenomena, and in elucidating many subtle properties of the state of this unique molecular solid (see Van Kranendonk (1983)). On the one hand the existence of double transitions was first discovered in the spectrum of solid H_2 by Gush et al. (1957) and on the other, the crystal phase change at 1.1K was discovered by Clouter and Gush (1965) by recording CIA spectra. Until 1979 only the molecules composed of H and D had been studied, but in that year it became possible, at the Lawrence Livermore Laboratories, to observe the CIA spectra of the remaining three molecular species involving tritium, viz. T_2, HT and DT. The group headed by P.C.Souers recorded the liquid and solid fundamental band spectra of these molecules in the pure solid (T_2) and in mixtures (HT and DT); these spectra have been reported in the literature by Souers et al. (1979,1980a).

The spectrum of solid T_2 is shown in Fig. 1 for a sample at a temperature of 20K. The spectrum is in every way similar to that of solid H_2 and can be understood in terms of the many previous studies of solid H_2. The spectrum of solid HT at 14K is shown in Fig. 2. Pure HT has not been prepared but, in this case, occurs as the equilibrium product of the reaction of H_2 and T_2: i.e. 28%T_2, 44%HT and 28%H_2. As a result the spectrum shows not only those lines arising from transitions in HT pairs (lines 1,2,5 and 6 in Fig. 2) but also double transitions from HT-T_2 pairs (lines 3 and 4), and HT-H_2 pairs (line 7). This spectrum shows a further interesting feature previously observed only in HD. This feature is the appearance of a hole in the phonon branches (labeled 2 and 6 in Fig. 2). They occur because of the presence of heteronuclear diatomic molecules. This effect was first discussed by Crane and

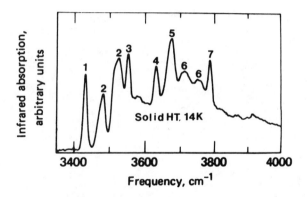

Fig. 2. The fundamental band of solid HT at 14 K in a mixture of $28\%T_2-44\%HT-28\%H_2$.

Gush (1966) for HD and later by Souers et. al. (1980a) in the paper from which Fig. 2 is taken.

In the course of these experiments it was found by Souers et al. (1980b) that new lines appeared in the spectra when the polycrystal was cooled below 12K. The interpretation of these lines has led to the consideration by Souers et al. (1981) of a new effect called "charge induced absorption".

THE TRITIUM EXPERIMENTS

When the spectra of T_2 and mixtures of T_2 with other hydrogens were recorded below 12K two new lines were discovered on the low frequency side of the Q line: the line with greatest red shift is called "A" and the line nearer the Q line is called "B". It was further discovered that, if only a small amount (1%) of T_2 was added to D_2 or HD, the new lines appeared in these spectra as well, although it is well known that such lines do not appear in the spectra of the pure substances. Such a spectrum is shown in Fig. 3 for the case of 10 %T_2 in D_2 at 8K; the spectral region is that of the fundamental band of D_2.* When the solid is in the temperature range from 12K to the melting point the A and B lines are absent.

The observed frequency shifts of the A line from the relevant $Q_1(0,1)$ line are shown as points in Fig. 4; it is seen that the

_____
*A further weak line labeled "C" appears in Fig. 3. As there is, as yet, no convincing interpretation for it, it will not be discussed further.

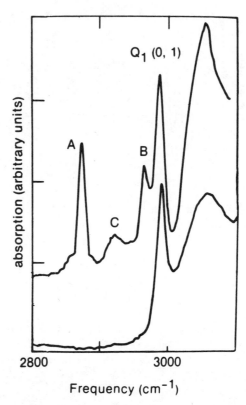

Fig. 3. The spectrum in the region of the $Q_1(0,1)$ line of D_2 for a mixture of 10%T_2 in D_2. The lower curve is the liquid at 19K and the upper is the solid at 8K.

shifts are largest for HD, smallest for T_2 and increase with the rotational constant. (The nature of the spectrometer and light source used in the experiments precluded measurements with H_2.) The frequency shifts of the B lines are much smaller, being in the range 10–20 cm^{-1} and show greater variability with molecular species and mixture ratio.

The experiments showed that the new lines appeared only when tritium was present and strongly suggested that the radioactivity of tritium was the important agent. The high energy β particles (mean energy:5.7 keV) have a range of 0.03 mm in solid H_2 and lose their energy mostly by ionization. The resultant charged fragments may become immobilized in the low temperature lattice and thus act as charge centres around which the host molecules will be polarized in the radial electric field and thus absorb radiation. Further, the field of one elementary charge at a distance of one lattice spacing is sufficiently strong that the molecular levels of the host molecules will be Stark shifted. Thus the A and B lines are

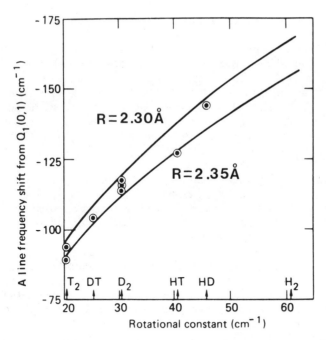

Fig. 4. The frequency shifts of the A line vs. rotational constant from the tritium experiments. The solid curves are calculated values.

interpreted as the vibrational transitions between Stark shifted host molecular levels around positive and negative charge centres.

The interaction between a centre of charge and a neighbouring host molecule is given by

$$H_s = -\alpha q^2/2R^4 + (qQ/R^3 - q\gamma/3R^4)P_2(\cos\theta) \qquad (1)$$

where α, Q and γ are the polarizability, quadrupole moment and anisotropy of the polarizability of the host molecule. The charge in the centre is $q = \pm e$ and $\vec{R}$ is its separation from the centre of mass of the host molecule; θ denotes the orientation of the molecule with respect to $\vec{R}$. The Stark shift calculations were performed by allowing several adjacent rotational states of the same parity to mix under the influence of the perturbation. When the frequency of the transition characterized in its unperturbed state by $\Delta v = +1$ and $J = 0 \to J = 0$ (where v and J are the vibrational and rotational quantum numbers) is calculated, it is found that the A line frequency is reproduced quite accurately for all cases with a positive charge centre and $R = 2.3-2.35$ Å. The result of these calculations and

599

the experimental frequency shifts are given in Fig. 4.

It was thus argued that the A line is a Q type transition in the nearest neighbour molecules of a positive ion in the lattice. The strong polarization forces draw in the nearest neighbours from a lattice spacing of 3.6 Å for D_2 to 2.4 Å. A very rough estimate of the energy of the complex from the intermolecular potentials gives a value for R of 2.65 Å. There are reasons, based on the known reactivities of hydrogen ions, to suggest that this ion may be D_3^+.

The integrated absorption coefficient is proportional to the number density of ions, N, and to the number of nearest neighbours of the ions, z. The observed A line absorption profiles for pure T_2 yield a value of $N \sim 10^{16}$ cm^{-3} for z = 12, or about one part per million.

If the A line is the Stark shifted Q transition due to positive ions, it is reasonable to attribute the B line to negative ions. The shift of the B lines from the unperturbed Q line is, in all cases, considerably less than that for the A line; this implies a value of R larger than that for the A. In fact, for D_2, for example, R is found to be 5.0 Å, a value larger than the lattice spacing. The negative hydrogen ions are indeed larger than the positive ones, nevertheless the arguments advanced above to account for the lattice contracted by polarization still apply, and an ion seems an unlikely candidate to dilate the lattice. For this reason it was assumed that the B line arose from an electron localized in the lattice. The large zero point energy of the electron is thought to account for the lattice dilation in the form of a bubble-like structure, a small polaron, or lattice defect.

THE PROTON-BEAM EXPERIMENTS IN DEUTERIUM

If the interpretation advanced in the preceding section is valid, the new spectral lines should arise from any ion-producing process in the deuterium or hydrogen crystal. In addition, it is clear that a more controllable source of high energy radiation will yield more information about the process of trapping ions and electrons and ultimately de-trapping and annihilating them.

The tritium decay produces a spectrum of electrons with average energy 5.7keV and end-point energy 18.36keV. Protons of 15MeV energy, after penetrating one half cm in solid hydrogen have approximately the same velocity as 5.7keV electrons and should reproduce the ionizing properties of tritium. In addition, the proton beam can be varied easily over many orders of magnitude in intensity and modulated in time. Spectra with D_2 have been obtained by Brooks et al. (1983) using the McMaster University FN

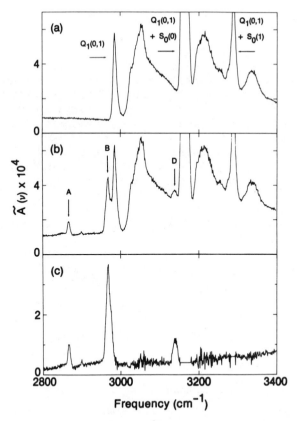

Fig. 5. The spectrum of solid D_2 at 4.2K: a) no irradiation b) with proton beam irradiation c) the difference between a) and b). $\tilde{A}$ is the dimensionless absorption coefficient.

Tandem Accelerator as the proton-beam source.

In general the same type of spectra are observed. Fig. 5a shows the well known spectrum of solid D_2 at 4.2K and in Fig. 5b the spectrum of the same crystal after 2 minutes of irradiation with 15MeV protons at a current density of 15nA/cm^2. Fig. 5c is the difference between the two spectra. The A and B features are again present at the same frequencies as in the tritium experiments and, in addition, a new feature, labelled "D" is observed shifted 21 cm^{-1} to the red of the S$_1$(0) line. This D feature has since been observed in the tritium experiments (P.C. Souers, private communication).

The calculations of the Stark shifted molecular levels which were done to support the interpretation in the tritium experiments were limited in scope. With the unsupported assumption that only the lowest possible states were involved in the $\Delta v = +1$ transition, only the even rotational states for values of $m = 0$ were mixed. The transitions $v = 0 \rightarrow v = 1$, $v = 0 \rightarrow v = 0$, $m = 0 \rightarrow m = 0$ (the analogue of the $Q_1(0)$ transitions) were fitted to the A and B lines to determine the corresponding values of R. In this designation v is the vibrational quantum number, m the magnetic quantum number and v

Table 1. Experimental and Theoretical Frequencies of Q-type Transitions in D_2.

EXPT	Positive Charge, R = 2.3 A				
	$Q_1(0)$	$Q_1(1)$			
	$m = 0 \rightarrow 0$	$0 \rightarrow 0$	$\pm 1 \rightarrow \pm 1$	$0 \rightarrow \pm 1$	$\pm 1 \rightarrow 0$
A 2870±3	2871	2872	2869	2546	3195
	Negative Charge, R = 5.0 A				
B 2977±3	2977	2973	2981	3067	2881

is equal to the value of J in the corresponding unperturbed state. Therefore $v = 0$ denotes the state of lowest energy in the manifold of mixed even rotational states and $v = 1$ is that for the manifold of mixed odd rotational states. The calculations have been extended to the analogue of the $Q_1(1)$ transition ($v = 1 \rightarrow v = 1$); in this case the quantum number m takes on the value 0, ±1. The possible Q-type transitions in D_2 for the cases of: a positive charge with R = 2.3Å, and a negative charge with R = 5.0 Å are given in Table 1. The Stark shifted transitions are calculated using the molecular constants of free molecules (Souers et al. 1979). To compare these with the unshifted Q transitions of the solid we have applied the vibrational frequency shift of -7 cm^{-1} which was observed by Crane and Gush (1966) to all our calculated transition frequencies; it is these values that actually appear in Table 1. Any additional shifts due to the compression of the lattice around either the positive or negative charge have been neglected even though these might be appreciable.

The first line of Table 1 shows three theoretical values corresponding to 2872 ± 3 cm^{-1}, a value well within the experimental uncertainty of the position of the A line. Of the two other values (which involve a change in m) the higher would lie in the strong phonon band of the $S_1(0)$ line and the lower is in a spectral region not yet investigated in these experiments. The second line in Table 1 shows a very similar behaviour for the Q-type transitions with respect to the B line.

While the two experiments have indeed produced substantially the same new spectral lines, there is one significant difference. The ratio of the intensity of the A to B lines is markedly different in the two cases. As can be seen in Fig. 3, for the case of the tritium work, the A line is much more intense than the B: the reverse is true in the proton-beam experiments as seen in Fig. 5. The ratio of the intensities of B and $Q_1(1,0)$ are approximately the same and so it is the A line which is much stronger in the tritium case than in the proton-beam case. While this difference is not understood it should be noted that crystals containing tritium also contain a substantial amount of dissolved He^3 which may be present in the form of positive ions producing extra intensity in the A lines, since only the charge is relevant for the magnitude of the Stark shift.

The proton-beam experiments permit a type of measurement not possible with the tritium experiments: the time rate of growth and decay of any charge induced feature may be measured. Such a measurement for the B line of D_2 at 4.2K is shown in Fig. 6. The time evolution of the B line is complex and can be analyzed in terms of two or (usually) more exponential components. Such an analysis shows that there are two characteristic time scales involved: a short one of the order of 10^1 sec and a long one of the order of 10^1 to 10^2 minutes. Quite clearly, in Fig. 6, the short times are dependent on beam current density. The behaviour of the short times with current is quite well established. If we define $T_{1/2}$ as the time for the short components to reach half intensity, then $T_{1/2}$ varies inversely with the current and therefore with the ionization created by the beam. This fact can be explained if we assume that the unirradiated crystal has a finite number of traps available which are filled by electrons upon ionization. Any further long-time changes are due to damage to the crystal by the beam.

The long time part of the turn-on seems to be approaching a saturation level. It has not been possible to do experiments for a sufficiently long time to verify that the effect indeed saturates.

The most surprising result is the very long times involved in the turn-off of the effect. The data in Fig. 6 give a characteristic time of the order of several hours. The time is obviously very uncertain since it is longer than the data set. The fact remains that the effects are very persistent and spectra may be taken for many minutes after terminating the irradiation. The

603

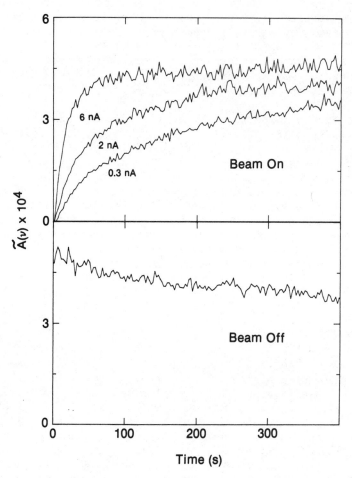

Fig. 6. The growth and decay of the B line in D_2 at 4.2K.

absorption, however, quickly vanishes on raising the temperature of the sample to ~12K for a few seconds.

The timing characteristics of the D line, although much more uncertain due to the small intensity of the line, are similar to those of the B line suggesting that it is of a similar origin.

The timing experiments on the A line are more difficult because of the small intensity of absorption. It is clear however, that it is significantly different from that of the B line. There is a beam-current dependent delay before the feature starts to grow after turning on the beam. This delay is 40 sec at 0.5 nA and decreases to less than a second for currents higher than 4 nA. In addition the turn-on time does not scale in any simple way with the beam current as for the B and D lines. The turn-off characteristic is even more peculiar. On turning off the beam the A line absorption continues to grow for a few minutes and then decays very slowly with a characteristic time of several hours at 4.2K.

A simple model has been proposed by Selen (1983) which accounts for the gross features of the A and B lines. As discussed above, we imagine a fixed number N of electron trapping sites. The proton-beam produces D_2^+ and e^- as its primary ionization fragments, and we must assume a high mobility for the D_2^+, perhaps by charge transfer; the electrons, when first produced are in delocalized states. The trapping of the electrons (perhaps in various types of traps) produces the short-time growth of the B and D lines. The highly mobile D_2^+ produce no regular immobile structures and so produce no spectral features. If, however, the D_2^+ reacts with a D_2 molecule to produce a stable and immobile D_3^+ then the A line appears after a delay which involves the rate of the reaction and the time to reorder the lattice about the D_3^+ ion. Charge neutrality is maintained by a population of N trapped electrons balanced by fN D_3^+ complexes, which produce the A line and (1-f)N D_2^+ mobile ions. There is, in addition, another population of free electrons and positive ions continually being created by the beam and annihilating each other. When the beam is turned off the (1-f)N remaining D_2^+ ions either form D_3^+ and increase the A line or annihilate trapped electrons to start the decay of the B line. When only fN of each type is left the decay of both A and B lines is slow. The experimental results indicate that f~1/2.

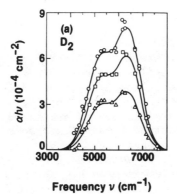

Fig. 7. The electron line in D_2 at 5K with 0.3% T_2. The curves are in ascending order: 15 min., 35 min. and 120 min. after freezing.

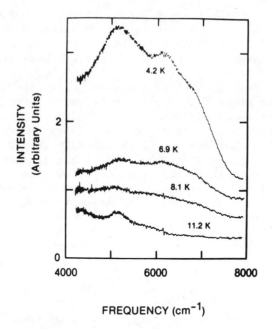

Fig. 8. The electron line in D_2 at four different temperatures induced by proton bombardment at a current density of 6.8 nA/cm².

A CONFIRMING EXPERIMENT

If the model of a stable localized electron in the form of a small polaron or bubble-like structure is valid it should be possible to observe the allowed spectrum of the electron-in-a-box. Calculations indicate that a strong absorption from this process should appear in the visible or near infrared region of the spectrum. Such an absorption was indeed found by Richardson et al. (1981) in the tritium experiments and at first it was so strong as to be saturated. When the concentration of tritium was reduced the electron absorption line was seen by Poll et al. (1983) to consist of a broad two-component feature between 4000 cm⁻¹ and 7500 cm⁻¹. The electron line for the solid at 5K for 0.3% T_2 in D_2 is shown in Fig. 7 for increasing times of irradiation. If solid H_2 is used instead, the line occurs in substantially the same frequency region but it overlaps the fundamental absorption band. In addition the concentration of T_2 must be increased by about 2 orders of magnitude to get the same strength of absorption as for D_2.

The solid lines in Fig. 7 are the result of fitting the spectrum with two Gaussians of identical halfwidth. The two components can be interpreted simply in two ways: They may arise from two spherical traps of slightly different diameters d_1 and d_2 or from a single asymmetrical trap with two characteristic dimensions l_1 and l_2. In the former case $d_1 = 10$ Å and $d_2 = 11$ Å; in the latter, $l_1 = 8.7$ Å and $l_2 = 9.3$ Å. In either case the agreement with $R = 5.0$ Å (i.e. diameter = 10.0 Å) obtained from the Stark shift of the B line is good.

The electron line has also been observed by Selen et al. (1983) in the proton-beam experiments and is shown in Fig. 8. In this case the line shows more structure, being clearly three components on a broader background rising to lower frequencies. The background itself is probably a fourth component with its maximum somewhere between the electron line and the D_2 fundamental band – a region not yet investigated.

The turn-on and turn-off characteristics of the electron line are very similar to those of the B line, further confirming that they have their origin in the same charge species in the lattice.

ACKNOWLEDGEMENTS

The authors would like to thank Dr. P.C.Souers of the Lawrence Livermore Laboratory for the privilege of collaborating with him in his experiments on tritium. We also acknowledge with gratitude our collaborators on the proton-beam experiments: M.Selen, R.Brooks and J.R.MacDonald of the University of Guelph, and J.C.Waddington of McMaster University. The authors and their Canadian collaborators also acknowledge the financial support of the Natural Sciences and Engineering Research Council of Canada.

REFERENCES

Brooks, R. L., Selen, M. A., Hunt, J. L., MacDonald, Jack R., Poll, J. D., Waddington, J. C., 1983, Phys. Rev. Lett., 51:1077.
Clouter, M., Gush, H. P., 1965, Phys. Rev. Lett., 15:200.
Crane, A., and Gush, H. P., 1966, Can. J. Phys., 44:373.
Gush, H. P., Hare, W. F. J., Allin, E. J., and Welsh, H. L., 1957, Phys. Rev. 106:1101.
Poll, J. D., Hunt, J. L., Souers, P. C., Fearon, E. M., Tsugawa, R. T., Richardson, J. H., and Smith, G. H., 1983, Phys. Rev. A, 28:3147.

Richardson, J. H., Deutscher, S. B., Souers, P. C., Tsugawa, R. T., and Fearon, E. M., 1981, Chem. Phys. Lett., 81:26.

Selen, M. A., 1983, M.Sc. Thesis, University of Guelph.

Selen, M. A., Brooks, R. L., Hunt, J. L., Poll, J. D., MacDonald, J. R., and Waddington, J. C., 1983, Nucl. Inst. and Meth., in press.

Souers, P. C., Fearon, D., Garza, R., Kelly, E. M., Roberts, P.E., Sanborn, R. H., Tsugawa, R. T., Hunt, J. L., and Poll, J. D., 1979, J. Chem. Phys., 70:1581.

Souers, P.C., Fuentes, J., Fearon, E. M., Roberts, P. E., Tsugawa, R. T., Hunt, J. L., and Poll, J. D., 1980a, J. Chem. Phys. 72:1679.

Souers, P. C., Fearon, E. M., Roberts, P. E., Tsugawa, R. T., Poll, J. D., and Hunt, J. L., 1980b, Phys. Lett. A, 77:277.

Souers, P.C., Fearon, E. M., Stark, R. L., Tsugawa, R. T., Poll, J. D., and Hunt, J. L., 1981, Can. J. Phys., 59:1408.

Van Kranendonk, J., 1983, "Solid Hydrogen". Plenum, New York.

WORKSHOP REPORTS: SOME CONSIDERATIONS ON SPECTRA INDUCED BY

INTERMOLECULAR INTERACTIONS IN MOLECULAR SOLIDS AND AMORPHOUS SYSTEMS

Salvatore Cunsolo and Giovanni Signorelli

Dipartimento di Fisica
Universita di Roma "La Sapienza"
P. le Aldo Moro, 2 - 00185 Roma, Italy

In many solids we can only observe the absorption or the scattering of radiation induced by intermolecular interactions. This is the case of solid systems composed either of homonuclear diatomic molecules, of monatomic molecules and many other molecular solids. However, in the past 25 years collision induced spectroscopy (CIS) has not been intensively employed to study molecular solids, except for hydrogen and its isotopes. In this field, fundamental information on intermolecular properties has been obtained and this matter has been extensively reviewed (Silvera, 1980; Van Kranendonk, 1983).

The research on CIS in solid hydrogen is still active. A new, interesting phenomenon observed in solid hydrogen isotopes has been reported: the absorption spectra induced by electric charges produced by high energy radiation. The charge carriers are positive ions and electrons localized in bubble-like structures. They give rise to new features in the spectrum of the solid (Hunt and Poll, 1985). Another paper reported in this book is devoted to the investigation of the influence of orthohydrogen impurities on the rotational S(0) line in the orientationally disordered phase of solid hydrogen (Cunsolo et al., 1985). Finally, we mention recent work in solid HD to study the electric multipole contributions to the spectrum (Rao 1984).

Even if in the past years CIS in solids has been mainly employed to investigate the properties of solid hydrogen, nevertheless many interesting results have been obtained in other molecular crystals. Solid CO_2, solid CO and solid nitrogen in the ordered α phase have been studied by far infrared (FIR) absorption measurements (Anderson et al., 1964; Anderson and Walmsley, 1964; Anderson and Leroi, 1966; Walmsley and Anderson, 1964; Ron and Schnepp, 1967) and theoretically (Walmsley and Pople, 1964; Schnepp, 1967). In the following years, further FIR studies have been made on solid nitrogen in the β (Buon-tempo et al., 1979) and γ phases (Marteau, 1985; Thiéry and Fabre, 1976), in solid methane (Marteau, 1985) and ethylene (Brith and Ron, 1969). The measured frequencies and intensities of IR active phonons have been used to test intermolecular potentials and lattice dynamics calculations. Indeed, in the self-consistent phonon approximation, Luty et al. (1980) calculated the frequencies of various phonon modes for solid nitrogen, starting both from an ab initio and an empirical intermolecular potential. Similar calculations have been performed for solid ethylene (Luty et al., 1981).

As far as monatomic solids are concerned, there has been no work since the pioneering effort of Jones and Woodfine (1965) on the spectra induced by heavy impurities (Kr and Xe) in solid argon, and the measurements on CIS in solid argon doped with hydrogen (Kriegler and Welsh, 1968).

A first attempt to treat the collision induced light scattering from a general point of view (Mazzacurati et al., 1985) has been presented in the conference at Bonas. The orientational disorder of the induced contributions in these systems enhances partially the self part of the vibrational and density-density correlation func-tions, allowing a long wavelength probe, such as light scattering, to study the effect of disorder on the dynamical behavior of the particles. In this respect the recent work on amorphous silicon and SiO_2 (Galeener et al., 1978), together with the results of molecular dynamics calculations on monatomic fluids (Rahman et al., 1976 and 1978) can be viewed as particular examples of a more general behavior of amorphous molecular materials.

Many molecular solids possess a phase which exhibits orienta-tional disorder. Sometimes the degree of disorder may be easily varied as, for example, in solid parahydrogen, by varying the quantity of orthohydrogen. In this way it is possible to investigate how disorder affects the collective properties of the system. It is also possible to investigate the decay mechanism of rotational and vibrational excitons, which are not yet well understood even in solid hydrogen.

As far as the study of intermolecular potentials is concerned, much may be learned from the analysis of CIS in molecular crystals (Van Kranendonk, 1983). In particular, the lattice dynamics calcu-lations critically depend on the intermolecular potential. Moreover, by increasing the pressure, it is possible to check the dependence of the potential on the intermolecular distance (Jochemsen et al. 1979).

Finally, as demonstrated by experiments (Jones and Woodfine, 1965; Kriegler and Welsh, 1968), CIS of impurities in monatomic solids can be used to study the acoustical phonons, the in band resonances of heavy impurities and the localized modes with frequen-cies above the unperturbed band for light impurities.

It is evident from the conference at Bonas that, at present, there are very few people involved in research on CIS in solids and amorphous materials, as compared to those involved in CIS in gases and liquids. The reason for this is not apparent, although it is clear from the studies mentioned here that much can be learned from CIS in solids and amorphous systems.

REFERENCES

Anderson, A., Gebbie, H. A., and Walmsley, S. H., 1964, Mol. Phys., 7:401.
Anderson, A., and Walmsley, S. H., 1964, Mol. Phys., 7:583.
Anderson, A., and Leroi, G. E., 1966, J. Chem. Phys., 45:4359.
Brith, M., and Ron, A., 1969, J. Chem. Phys., 50:3053.
Buontempo, U., Cunsolo, S., Dore, P., and Maselli, P., 1979, Phys. Letters, 74A:113.
Cunsolo, S., Dore, P., and Nencini, L., 1985, this volume.
Galeener, F. L., and Sen, P. N., 1978, Phys. Rev. B17:1928, and references quoted therein.
Jones, G. O., and Woodfine, J. M., 1965, Proc. Phys. Soc., 86:101.
Hunt, J. L., and Poll, J. D., 1985, this volume.
Jochemsen, R., Goldman, V. V., and Silvera, I. F., 1979, J. Low Temp. Phys., 36:243.
Kriegler, R. J., and Welsh, H. L., 1968, Can. J. Phys., 46:1181.
Luty, T., van der Avoird, A., and Berns, R. M., 1980, J. Chem. Phys, 73:5305.
Luty, T., van der Avoird, A., Berns, R. M., and Wasintynski, T., 1981, J. Chem. Phys., 75:1451.
Marteau, P., 1985, this volume.
Mazzacurati, V., Nardone, M., Ruocco, G., and Signorelli, G., 1985, this volume.
Rahman, A., Mandell, M. J., and McTague, J. P., 1976, J. Chem. Phys., 64:1564.
Rahmen, A., Mandell, M. J., and McTague, J. P., 1978, J. Chem. Phys., 68:1876.
Rao, K. N., 1984, J. Mol. Structure 113:175.
Ron, A., and Schnepp, O., 1967, J. Chem. Phys., 46:3991.
Schnepp, O., 1967, J. Chem. Phys., 46:3983.
Silvera, I. F., 1980, Rev. Mod. Phys., 52:393.
Thyéry, M. M., and Fabre, D., 1976, Mol. Phys., 32:257.
Van Kranendonk, J., 1983, "Solid Hydrogen", Plenum Press, New York.
Walmsley, S. H., and Anderson, A., 1964, Mol. Phys., 7:411.
Walmsley, S. H., and Pople, J. A., 1964, Mol. Phys., 8:345.

COLLISION-INDUCED EFFECTS IN ALLOWED INFRARED AND RAMAN

SPECTRA OF MOLECULAR FLUIDS

Michel Perrot and Jean Lascombe

Laboratoire de Spectroscopie Infrarouge (L.A.124)
Université de Bordeaux I - 351, cours de la Libération
33405 Talence (France)

ABSTRACT

It has been often assumed that collision-induced effects do not influence the infrared and Raman vibrational spectra. However, recent experimental work and molecular dynamics simulations strongly suggest that, in the liquid state, the intermolecular translational dynamics may play a role in several spectral properties as the molecular intensities and the bandshapes. This paper reports some experimental evidence of induced effects on the spectral profiles and discusses the various methods already proposed to separate the molecular and the collision-induced components from the total observed spectrum.

Infrared absorption and Raman scattering techniques are currently used to study the dynamics of the molecules in a liquid sample. Owing to technological improvements of spectrometers and their coupling with small computers it is possible today to obtain spectra on a broad frequency range with a satisfactory signal to noise ratio.

Numerous experiments allowed for a better knowledge of the orientational dynamics of the molecules (Bailey, 1974; Perrot and Lascombe, 1978) and for the last few years, the vibrational dynamics was also widely studied (Clarke, 1978; Vincent-Geisse, 1980). Nevertheless, for the condensed state, intermolecular induced effects also may influence the spectral profiles.

We have already known for a long time that for liquids composed of atoms or spherical molecules, collisional dynamics

gives rise to purely induced spectra in various spectral regions.
More recently it has been observed that induced profiles of the
same collisional origin are frequently superimposed on the
allowed orientational spectra of anisotropic molecules in the
liquid state. This is observed in depolarized Rayleigh scattering
and in far-infrared absorption (Tabisz, 1979).

For the infrared and Raman vibration-rotation spectra, it has
been traditionally assumed that collision-induced effects were negligible relative to the allowed profiles. But, recent experimental
results (Schroeder et al., 1978) along with molecular dynamics simulations (Frenkel and McTague, 1980; Ladanyi, 1983) seem to indicate
that collision-induced effects do exist on the vibrational infared and
Raman profiles of allowed transitions for some molecular fluids.

So the aim of this paper is to try to present published
experimental results related to vibrational spectra which exibit
evidence of collision-induced effects superimposed on allowed
spectra and to discuss the methods already proposed in order to
separate from these profiles, the allowed and the induced
contributions. We will also try to give some direction for future
experimental work in this field.

DEFINITIONS OF THE SELF, DISTINCT AND INDUCED EFFECTS

Before analysing the experimental results, it is important to
define the various dynamical effects responsible for the spectral
profiles of the molecular liquids.

Let us just recall that a spectral profile $I(\nu)$ is related,
via Fourier transform, to the correlation function of a
macroscopic property A(t) which is governed by all or part of the
dynamics of the ensemble of the molecules of the sample.

For a vibrational infrared transition A(t) reflects the
dynamics of the total transition moment while for Raman spectroscopy
A(t) is associated with the total transition polarizability.

This time-varying quantity A(t) is a very complicated function
of all the intra and inter molecular dynamical variables of all the
absorbing or scattering molecules of the sample.

In order to make possible the analysis of such spectra, various
assumptions are introduced which allow for simpler relationships
between the macroscopic quantity A(t) and the molecular property
a(t).

1) The simpler assumption is to suppose that the macroscopic
quantity is the sum of the molecular properties of the isolated

molecules. In this case the correlation function is

$$\langle A(0)A(t)\rangle = \sum_i \sum_j \langle a_i(o)a_j(t)\rangle \qquad (1)$$

which can be separated in a sum :

$$\langle A(0)A(t)\rangle = N\langle a_i(0)a_i(t)\rangle + N(N-1)\langle a_i(0)a_j(t)\rangle \qquad (2)$$

of a self term (i,i) for the autocorrelation and a distinct term
(j ≠ i) for the pair-correlation.

For mid-infrared and Raman spectroscopy, the molecular
variable a(t) is the derivative of the transition moment or
polarizability with respect to a normal coordinate. So, by using
the tensorial properties of the polarizability, two different
Raman profiles may be obtained: an isotropic profile related to
the trace of the tensor and an anisotropic profile related to
the anisotropic part of the tensor.

If no coupling exist between the vibrators i and j, all the
distinct terms in the correlation function are zero and all these
spectra are only governed by the monomolecular vibrational and
rotational dynamics. Moreover, if it is assumed that vibration and
rotation of the same molecule are uncorrelated, the isotropic Raman
profile is purely vibrational while the anisotropic Raman and the
infrared profiles are the convolution product of a vibrational
component by a tensorial or a vectorial rotational component.

Numerous studies of this kind have been published specially
for linear and symmetric-top molecules (Bailey, 1974; Clarke, 1978).
They allow for the determination of the vectorial $G_1(t)$ and tensorial
$G_2(t)$ orientational correlation functions and for the analysis of
the vibrational relaxation mechanism. Moreover by comparison with
far-infrared and depolarized Rayleigh scattering spectra, one may
also obtain the static angular coupling factors $g_1 = \langle \cos \theta_{ij}\rangle$ and
$g_2 = \langle(3/2 \cos^2\theta_{ij} -1/2)\rangle$ of the molecules in the sample (Perrot
and Lascombe, 1978 ; Vincent-Geisse, 1980).

2) A less restrictive way to study these spectra is to include
into the macroscopic quantity A(t), not only the electrical
properties of the isolated molecules but also their fluctuations
under the variations of the local order originating in the
translational dynamics of the molecules in the liquid state. In this
case, collision-induced effects appear and may modify the spectral
intensity as well as the spectral bandshapes.

A time-varying induced term has to be added to the isolated
molecular quantity, leading to a new correlation function

$$\langle A(0)A(t)\rangle = \sum_{i} \sum_{j} \left< \left[a_i(0) + \Delta a_i(0) \right] \left[a_j(t) + \Delta a_j(t) \right] \right> \quad (3)$$

The induced terms Δa are associated with changes in the dipole moment and the polarizability tensor due to the fluctuations in time of the intermolecular distances. Numerous collisional mechanisms have been proposed to derive the additional term Δa, but whatever their origin be it dipole-induced dipole, multipole-induced dipole, electron clouds overlap, molecular frame distortion or collision induced hyperpolarizabilities, all these induced effects may modify the intensities and the shapes of the vibrational allowed spectra.

Frenkel and McTague (1980) have already proposed to separate this induced term $\Delta a(t)$ into a part that is correlated with the molecular property $a(t)$ and an uncorrelated remainder so that

$$\Delta a(t) = \Delta \overset{P}{a}(t) + \Delta \overset{Q}{a}(t) \tag{4}$$

with $\Delta \overset{P}{a}(t) = \dfrac{\langle a(t) \, \Delta a(t) \rangle}{\langle a(t)^2 \rangle} a(t)$ \hfill (5)

and $\Delta \overset{Q}{a}(t) = \Delta a(t) - \dfrac{\langle a(t) \, \Delta a(t) \rangle}{\langle a(t)^2 \rangle} a(t)$ \hfill (6)

Using these definitions, the total correlation function $\langle A(0) \, A(t) \rangle$ of Eq. (3) can be expressed as the sum of 3 terms

i) a pure "molecular" term $\sum_{i} \sum_{j} (a_i(0) + \Delta \overset{P}{a}_i(0)(a_j(t) + \Delta \overset{P}{a}_j(t)) \rangle$

$$(7)$$

ii) a purely "induced" term $\sum_{i} \sum_{j} \langle \Delta \overset{Q}{a}_i(0) \, \Delta \overset{Q}{a}_j(t) \rangle$ \qquad (8) \quad and

iii) an "interference" term $\sum_{i} \sum_{j} \left[\langle (a_i(0) + \Delta \overset{P}{a}_i(0)) \, \Delta \overset{Q}{a}_j(t) \rangle \; + \right.$

$$\left. \langle \Delta \overset{Q}{a}_1(0) \, (a_j(t) + \Delta \overset{P}{a}_j(t)) \rangle \right]$$

$$(9)$$

giving rise by Fourier transformation to the sum of 3 spectra.

i) a pure "molecular" spectrum whose intensity is modified by the induced effects Δ_a^P generally termed internal field effects,
ii) a "purely induced" spectrum and
iii) an interference spectrum having the possibility to modify the total bandshape even with its zero total intensity.

Now the question is to know if these induced effects are important enough to be experimentaly detected from the infrared and Raman vibrational spectra, and if the answer is yes, is it possible to separate in the entire spectral profile the "molecular" from the "induced" and the "interference" components.

EXPERIMENTAL EVIDENCE FOR INDUCED EFFECTS

Despite the numerous improvements of the spectrometers, quantitative determinations of some spectral parameters are still delicate. The integrated intensities:

$$M(0) \ = \ \int_{band} I(\bar{\nu}) \ d\bar{\nu} \tag{10}$$

are known within 10% to 20%, while the values of the normalized second moments :

$$M(2) \ = \ \int_{band} \bar{\nu}^2 \ I(\bar{\nu}) \ d\bar{\nu}/M(0) \tag{11}$$

may vary hugely according to the authors. For example, published experimental Raman values of $M(2)$ for the ν_3 mode of liquid methyl iodide at 525 cm^{-1} vary from 131 cm^{-2} to 610 cm^{-2} (Wright et al., 1972; Constant, 1978; Bansal et al., 1981).

Nevertheless, even with these large uncertainties, various experimental data strongly suggest that collision-induced effects are present on the vibrational spectra. Among all the published results, the following are the most significant,

1) Molar intensity

There is a large modification of the molar intensity of the bands in passing from the gas to the liquid. Reported values for isotropic Raman bands of several molecules (Table 1) show that the molar intensity in the liquid state is 1.5 to 3 times larger than for the gas phase.

Table 1. Ratio of the molar intensities I liquid/ I gas
for isotropic Raman bands of some liquids
(Sokolovskaya, 1961 ; Hester, 1967).

Molecule	Wavenumber cm^{-1}	I liq. / I gas
C_6H_6	992	2.9
$CHCl_3$	366	2.1
CCl_4	665	1.5
	459	2.6

These changes in the molar intensity may also not be the
same for the isotropic and the anisotropic Raman components giving
rise to a variation of the depolarized ratio according to the type
of the intermolecular interactions (Mierzecki, 1976).

For infrared absorption, the integrated molar intensities have
been measured for the fundamental and the first overtone of hydrogen
chloride in the gas phase and in solutions of halogenated hydrocarbons
(Perrot and Lascombe, 1973). The results (Table 2) show that in
passing from the gas to the solution, while the intensity of the
fundamental increases, the intensity of the first overtone
decreases.

Table 2. Integrated infrared intensity of HCl in the gaseous
state and in solution. ($liter.mole^{-1}.cm^{-2}$).

	Fundamental	1st overtone
HCl gas	3940	90
HCl / $C_2F_3Cl_3$	8300	69
HCl / CCl_4	9400	46

To account for these intensity results, Sokolovskaya (1961) and
Perrot and Lascombe (1973) said that induced effects must be
introduced. From Eq. (3), one may deduce that the molar intensity

depends not only on the molecular term of Eq. (7) often explained by Lorentz internal field correction, but also on the purely induced term of Eq. (8).

2) Far-wing bandshapes

Many times, when the measurements are possible, it is found that far in the wings, the isotropic and anisotropic bandshapes become close to an exponential decay similar to that obtained for purely induced spectra. This is emphasized by using some special representations as

$I(\bar{\nu})$ x $\bar{\nu}^2$ versus $\bar{\nu}$ as used by Schroeder et al. (1978)

$1/I(\bar{\nu})$ versus $\bar{\nu}^2$ as proposed by Zaitsev and Starunov (1965).

In this last case, it has been reported that for liquid carbon tetrachloride the 313 cm^{-1} depolarized Raman band has exactly the same shape as the depolarized Rayleigh profile which is purely induced for this molecule.

Although many similar experimental results seem to indicate that collision-induced effects are present in the vibrational bandshapes, it has to be noted that because of the large experimental uncertainties, the special representations reported here only show that the profiles are not Lorentzian far in the wings, a result which is not absolutely characteristic of induced effects.

3) Normalized second moments

i) Since the work of Gordon (1969), we know that in the absence of induced effects, the orientational second moments of the infrared and Raman bands are, respectively, equal to

$2 kT/I$ (infrared)   and $6 kT/I$ (anisotropic Raman)

for a totally symmetric vibration of a linear or symmetric-top molecule with moment of inertia I. We also know that these values are independent of the density of the sample.

Published results on second moments measurements give evidence for the presence of induced effects. On Table 3, we have reported the theoretical rotational and the experimental second moments measured by anisotropic Raman scattering (Rothschild et al.,1975; Constant, 1978; Schroeder et al., 1978) and infrared absorption (Rosenthal et al., 1976) for various liquids.

These rotational experimental values are obtained after substraction of the vibrational second moment derived from the

isotropic Raman spectrum and assuming no coupling between the
vibrational and the rotational dynamics (Bailey, 1974 ; Clarke,
1978 ; Vincent-Geisse, 1980). It is difficult to evaluate
precisely the errors so introduced because in the liquid state the
vibration-rotation interaction may have two different origins. The
first one, like in the gaseous state, comes from the kinetic part
of the Hamiltonian and seems to have a small influence on the
rotational second moment (Gordon, 1964), especially for molecules
like chloroform and methyl iodide (Van Konynenburg and Steele,
1972 ; Rothschild et al., 1975). The second one is related to
the intermolecular potential which is capable of coupling
rotational and the vibrational variables but has never been
evaluated accurately.

Table 3. Theoretical rotational and experimental second
moments (cm^{-2}) of some liquids.

Author	Molecule	M2 theo.	M2 exp.	
Constant	CH_3I $525\ cm^{-1}$	597	610	
Rothschild et al.	$CHCl_3$ $360\ cm^{-1}$	273	404	R
Schroeder et al.	$CHCl_3$ $3019\ cm^{-1}$	278	510	A M A
	$CDCl_3$ $2256\ cm^{-1}$	268	505	N
Rosenthal et al.	$CHCl_3$ $360\ cm^{-1}$	91	119	I
	$CHCl_3$ $3020\ cm^{-1}$	91	307	R

In all the cases reported here, the experimental second moments are larger than the expected theoretical values.

Another very important result on second moments was given by Schroeder et al. (1978). For chloroform and deuterochloroform, the experimental second moment of the anisotropic Raman spectra may vary by a factor of two when the density of the liquid passes from 1.4 to 1.8 gr/cm³ .

ii) For the second moments of the isotropic Raman profiles, there is no sum rule giving theoretical values of the vibrational second moment. However, for a pure dephasing vibrational relaxation process, the vibrational second moment is the static distribution of the fluctuations of the vibrational frequency (Rothschild, 1976). Then we may expect that M2 vib. become larger for an isothermal pressure increase, and also that for isotopic vibrators, the ratio of the M2 vib. is equal to the inverse ratio of the reduced masses (Bratos and Maréchal, 1971 ; Rothschild, 1976).

The experimental results on chloroform (Schroeder et al., 1978) agree well with the first point as M2 vib. increases with increasing pressure, but the ratio M2 vib. (CH)/M2 vib.(CD) is not equal to the expected value for the reduced mass of the vibrators CH and CD.

This result seems to show that induced effects may also be present in the isotropic Raman bandshapes.

DISCUSSION OF THE BANDSHAPE ANALYSIS

All these experimental results, despite the relatively large uncertainties of the measurements, clearly indicate that collision-induced dynamics may influence the allowed spectra of the vibrational transitions.

These effects strongly complicate the study of the molecular dynamics in the liquid phase from the analysis of the spectral profiles. In order to eliminate such difficulties, several attempts have been made to separate from the experimental bandshapes the molecular contribution. From eq. (3), it is always possible to consider that the bandshapes are the sum of two independent profiles:

i) a molecular component (Eq. (7)) and

ii) an induced component containing both the purely induced effects (Eq. (8)) and the coupling terms between the molecular and the induced effects (Eq. (9)) and to try to extract these two components from the total

However, given the fact that this separation requires the exact knowledge of one of the two components, its validity should be greater if one of the terms is small compared to the other and if there is a large difference between the characteristic times of the two phenomena.

Even though this assumption is currently used, the results of molecular dynamics simulations (Frenkel and McTague, 1980 ; Ladanyi, 1983), show that in many cases, this hypothesis is not valid.

Several decompositions of this kind have been tested assuming that the total collision-induced intensity is small compared to the molecular component (Van Konynenburg et al., 1972 ; Schroeder et al., 1978) and also that the time scale of the collision-induced process is very short compared to the reorientational time (Lallemand, 1971 ; de Santis et al., 1978 ; Hanson and McTague,1980) in order that the pure induced effects essentially occur in the far-wings of the bands (Van Konynenburg and Steele, 1975 ; Amorim da Costa et al., 1975 ; Cox et al., 1979 ; Andreani et al., 1981).

1) For infrared spectroscopy, it is quite difficult to know the real baseline of an absorption spectrum of pure liquid So, in order to extract the pure rotational component, Rothschild (1976) proposed to subtract the induced part of the spectrum by fitting the baseline until the experimental second moment equals the theoretical rotational value.

2) For anisotropic Raman scattering, one generally assumes that the induced component has the same profile as for purely induced spectra. Neglecting the presence of any important cross-terms and by assuming :

$$I (\bar{\nu}) \quad \text{induced} \quad = \quad A \; \bar{\nu}^k \; \exp[- (\bar{\nu} / \Delta)] \qquad (12)$$

The fitting is performed on the decay of the wings for Δ and on the "good" rotational second moment for the relative intensity A (Van Konynenburg and Steele, 1972, 1975 ; Cox et al., 1979 ; Andreani et al., 1981).

Following these hypotheses, one may separately study either the pure orientational dynamics or some collisional properties such the induced second moment.

In their work on chloroform at various densities, Schroeder et al. (1978) showed that the induced second moment decreased while the density increased. By analogy with previous molecular dynamics calculations of Alder et al. (1973) on induced Rayleigh scattering intensity, this experimental result is explained by cancellations between the pair-wise and triplet terms occuring at high density. This result reflects the symmetrisation of the local order around a given molecule as the density increases (Schroder et al., 1978).

By using quantitative results of molecular dynamics calculations, Sampoli et al., (1981) have recently proposed another approach to extract from the spectral profile, the collision-induced plus the cross terms bandshape. To do that, one needs to derive the memory function of the rotational dynamics from a fit of the anisotropic experimental Raman spectrum and to use the ratio of the total intensity over the rotational intensity given by molecular dynamics experiments in order to determine a "difference" profile associated to all the non-rotational components. For nitrogen at various densities, the results agree qualitatively with the spectral shapes calculated by molecular dynamics (Frenkel and McTague, 1980), although the small intensity so detected contains large errors due to the multiple numerical derivations.

A more detailed analysis of this method, for the case of linear molecules, is presented in this book by De Santis and Sampoli (1984).

CONCLUSION

Even if the vibrational infrared and Raman spectra have for long been associated only with the monomolecular vibrational and rotational dynamics, the constant improvements of the spectroscopic techniques allow now for experimental evidence of induced effects in the vibrational spectra of some molecular liquids.

So, the analysis of these spectra becomes very complicated because they reflect the vibrational, the orientational and the translational dynamics of all the molecules of the sample. Even if several methods have been proposed and used to separate these different contributions, in the absence of any tractable theory, such decompositions may be only advanced curve fitting.

In order to get a better insight into this problem, more experimental work is needed:

1) More precise studies of the vibrational profiles for other liquids at various temperatures and pressures to cover a large range of density of the sample, as the density is the pertinent parameter related to the induced effects.

2) The study of the second spectral moments of isotopic vibrators must also give interesting information since in the spectrum, the orientational part has to vary with the moments of inertia, the vibrational part has to vary with the reduced mass

of the oscillators and the induced part must be related to the reduced mass of the colliding pairs.

This method should be specially useful for the analysis of the induced component of the isotropic Raman profiles.

And last, it is obvious that more molecular dynamics simulations using large computers may give useful results about the spectral contributions of rotational and translational dynamics and also on the possible couplings between all those dynamical variables.

REFERENCES

Alder, B. J., Weis, J. J., and Strauss, H. L., 1973, Phys. Rev. A, 7:281.

Amorim Da Costa, A. M., Norman, M. A., and Clarke, J. H. R., 1975, Mol. Phys., 29:191.

Andreani, C., Morales, P., and Rocca, D., 1981, Mol. Phys., 44:445.

Bailey, R. T., 1974, Infrared and Raman Studies of Molecular Motion, "Molecular Spectroscopy," Vol. 2, The Chemical Society, London.

Bansal, M. L., Deb, S. K., and Roy, A. P., 1981, Chem. Phys. Letters, 83:83.

Bratos, S., and Maréchal, E., 1971, Phys. Rev., 56:404.

Clarke, J. H. R., 1978, Bandshapes and Molecular Dynamics in Liquids, "Advances in Infrared and Raman Spectroscopy," Vol. 4, R. J. H. Clark and R. E. Hester, eds., Heyden, London.

Constant, M., 1978, Thesis, University of Lille.

Cox, T. I., Battaglia, M. R., and Madden, P., 1979, Mol. Phys., 38:1539.

De Santis, A., Sampoli, M., Morales, P., and Signorelli, G., 1978, Mol. Phys. 35:1125.

De Santis, A., and Sampoli, M., 1985, this volume.

Frenkel, D., and McTague, J. P., 1980, J. Chem. Phys., 72:2801.

Gordon, R. G., 1964, J. Chem. Phys., 40:1973.

Gordon, R. G., 1969, Error bounds and spectral densities, "Stochastic Processes in Chemical Physics," Advances in Chemical Physics, Vol. 15, K.E. Shuler, ed., Interscience, New York.

Hanson, F. E., and McTague, J. P., 1980, J. Chem. Phys., 73:1733.

Hester, R. E., 1967, Raman intensities and the Nature of the Chemical bond, "Raman Spectroscopy," A. Szymanski, ed., Plenum Press, New York.

Ladanyi, B., 1983, J. Chem. Phys., 78:2189.

Lallemand, P., 1971, C.R. Acad. Sci. Paris, 272:429.

Mierzecki, R., 1976, Proceedings of the Fifth ICORS, H. F. Schulz, ed., Freiburg.

Perrot, M., and Lascombe, J., 1973, J. Chim. Phys., 70:1486.

Perrot, M., and Lascombe, J., 1978, Infrared and Raman bandshapes and Molecular motions, "Organic Liquids," A. D. Buckingham, E. Lippert and S. Bratos, eds., J. Wiley and Sons, Chichester.

Rosenthal, L. C., and Strauss, H. L., 1976, J. Chem. Phys., 64:282.

Rothschild, W. G., Rosasco, G. J., and Livingstone, R. C., 1975, J.Chem. Phys., 62:1253.

Rothschild, W. G., 1976, J. Chem. Phys., 65:455.

Sampoli, M., De Santis, A., and Nardone, M., 1981, Can. J. Phys., 59:1403.

Schroeder, J., and Jonas, J., 1978, Chem. Phys., 34:11.

Schroeder, J., Schiemann, V. H., and Jonas, J., 1978, J. Chem. Phys., 69:5479.

Sokolovskaya, A. I., 1961, Optic and Spectry., 11:259.

Tabisz, G. C., 1979, Collision-induced Rayleigh and Raman Scattering, "Molecular Spectroscopy," Vol. 6, The Chemical Society, London.

Van Konynenburg, P., and Steele, W. A., 1972, J. Chem. Phys., 56:4776.

Van Konynenburg, P., and Steele, W. A., 1975, J. Chem. Phys., 62:2301.

Vincent-Geisse, J., 1980, Experimental Study of Rotational and Vibrational Relaxation in Liquids from Investigation of the Infrared and Raman Vibrational Profiles, "Vibrational Spectroscopy of Molecular Liquids and Solids," S. Bratos and R. M. Pick, eds., Plenum Press, New York.

Wright, R. B., Schartz, M., and Wang, C. H., 1972, J. Chem. Phys., 56:4776.

Zaitsev, G. I., and Starunov, V. S., 1965, Optic and Spectry., 19:497.

RAMAN SCATTERING FROM LINEAR MOLECULES

A. De Santis and M. Sampoli

University of Venice
Dorso Duro 2137, 30123 Venezia (Italy)

ABSTRACT

Induced effects in allowed spectra of light linear molecules are discussed. The behavior of the normalized second moment is carefully analysed in terms of different induced contributions for the fluid N_2, CO and CO_2. In the case of N_2 and CO fluids, it is shown that the DID mechanism of interaction between scatterers, having a point polarizability in their centers, accounts for the observed second moment behavior satisfactorily. The different amount of induced effects in rotational Rayleigh (RAY) and rotovibrational Raman (RAM) bands is also explained.

For the more anisometric CO_2 molecule, the comparison with available computer simulations shows that the center-center model fails.

The distribution of the polarizable matter in atomic sites of the molecule yields computed second moments in better agreement with the experimental ones. In the low density limit, the behavior of the second moment in the center-center model of interaction is also calculated. Induced effects are found to be quite sensitive to the adopted intermolecular potential.

INTRODUCTION

Induced phenomena are widely studied in monatomic fluids where they are responsible for all of depolarized light scattering. The dipole-induced-dipole (DID) mechanism has been found to reproduce quite well the main features (Tabisz, 1979; Madden, 1978; Guillot et al., 1980). That have been reviewed recently by Frommhold (1981).

Other mechanisms can contribute to light scattering in isotropic (Buckingham and Tabisz, 1978; Shelton and Tabisz, 1980; Posch, 1980) and non linear anisotropic polyatomic fluids (De Santis and Sampoli, 1983).

The aim of the present paper is chiefly to discuss how far the DID mechanism takes into account the induced contribution which is present in Rayleigh (RAY) and Raman (RAM) allowed spectra from fluids consisting of light linear molecules. The prime interest in these spectra is to extract orientational dynamic information which is related to the anisotropic part of the intermolecular potential.

The presence of induced effects entangles the orientational information and makes it difficult to derive reliable quantities from light scattering experiments.

From the point of view of induced contributions, a few anisotropic systems have been studied by experiments (Hanson and McTague, 1980; Berrue et al., 1978; De Santis et al., 1982,1984) or by computer simulations as well (Frenkel and McTague, 1980; Ladanyi, 1983). Usually induced contributions are tentatively removed. Empirical "collision induced" lineshapes, with noble-gas-like exponential wings, have been widely used to separate orientational and induced contributions (see for example Vershmold (1981) and references quoted therein). The basis of such a treatment is that the experimental spectrum is the sum of the orientational spectrum and of the "collision induced" one, i.e. that the cross contributions are negligible. However recent results (Frenkel and McTague (1980), Bancewicz (1983)) based on computer simulations (CS) have clearly pointed out that the cross contributions are important and can affect both spectral moments and spectral shapes. Only if "collisions" (i.e. induced phenomena) and reorientations have different time scales, we can take into account the cross contributions by means of an effective polarizability. This is the case of liquid CS_2 which has been widely studied by Madden and Cox (1981). For lighter molecules, such as N_2, it is very hard to separate reliably non rotational contributions from experimental spectra.

To gain some insight into the role of induced contributions, we will analyze the density dependence of the normalized second moment, which must be mainly ascribed to induced contributions.

This analysis is a powerful tool to investigate the role played by these contributions. Direct comparison with CS second moments would be very useful but many CS would be necessary and that would be very expensive and time consuming. Further, such a comparison does not clarify how much of the available information on monatomic fluids can be helpful and how important are the different contributions. Our aim is to construct an interpretative scheme which accounts for the induced effects on the basis of the DID mechanism and some simple approximations. We avoid the use of the projection scheme of the induced interactions (Frenkel and McTague, 1980) since we are not dealing with any actual separation between fast and slow decaying variables. Consequently, induced phenomena will be discussed in terms of isolated molecule polarizabilities. The cases of RAY and RAM spectra of fluid N_2 are discussed in the first two sections whereas the two last ones deal with the RAY spectra from fluid CO and CO_2 respectively.

RAY SECOND MOMENT BEHAVIOUR IN FLUID N_2

In the point molecular polarizability approximation, the DID mechanism in first order gives for the macroscopic polarizability

$$(1) \quad \overset{\leftrightarrow}{A} = \sum_i \overset{\leftrightarrow}{\alpha}_i + \Delta \overset{\leftrightarrow}{\alpha}_i = \overset{\leftrightarrow}{A}_o + \Delta \overset{\leftrightarrow}{A}$$

where

$$\Delta \overset{\leftrightarrow}{\alpha}_i = \sum_{j \neq i} \overset{\leftrightarrow}{\alpha}_i \overset{\leftrightarrow}{T^{(2)}} (r_{ij}) \overset{\leftrightarrow}{\alpha}_j \quad \text{and} \quad \overset{\leftrightarrow}{T^{(2)}} (r) = (3 \vec{r} \vec{r}/r - \overset{\leftrightarrow}{I})/r^3$$

is the static dipole tensor. The summations run over the N particles of a system characterized by volume V and number density $\rho = N/V$. The N_2 molecule has a small value of the anisotropic polarizability, $\beta = \alpha_{//} - \alpha_{\perp}$, with respect to the isotropic polarizability, $\alpha = (\alpha_{//} + 2\alpha_{\perp})/3$ (Bridge and Buckingham, 1966). Therefore we can take into account only the induced contributions due to the isotropic part of the polarizability tensor (IDID approximation). Obviously IDID approximation does not neglect the anisotropic part of intermolecular potential. Indeed cross contributions would vanish if the interaction potential were isotropic. In the IDID approximation the zz component of the total polarizability entering in depolarized RAY bands is given by

$$(2) \quad {}^{\text{IDID}} A_{zz} = \sum_i \frac{2}{3}\beta \, D^{(2)}_{oo}(\Omega_i) + \sum_{i,j \neq i} 2 \alpha^2 \, D^{(2)}_{oo}(\Omega_{ij})/r_{ij}^3 = A_o + \Delta A$$

where $D^{(1)}_{nm}(\Omega)$ stands for the Wigner function and Ω_i and Ω_{ij} for the set of Eulerian angles referring to the axis of the i-th molecule and to the $\vec{r}_{ij}$ vector respectively. The integrated intensity is given by

$$(3) \quad I^{\text{TOT}} \propto \langle A_o A_o \rangle + 2\langle A_o \Delta A \rangle + \langle \Delta A \Delta A \rangle$$

where the three terms appearing in Eq. (3) are referred as rotational (R), cross (X) and collision induced (CI) intensities respectively.

Each term can contribute to the second moment. Of course, the total second moment is given by

$$(4) \quad M_2 = \frac{I^R M_2^R + I^X M_2^X + I^{CI} M_2^{CI}}{I^R + I^X + I^{CI}}$$

where M_2^R, M_2^X and M_2^{CI} are normalized second moments. To compare data at different temperatures, we will also use a reduced second moment defined by

$$(5) \quad M_2^* = (M_2 - 32B^2)/(6kT/I)$$

where 6kT/I is the free rotor classical value and $32B^2$ is the main quantum correction (Gordon, 1964).

At very low densities, only one- and two-body terms can contribute to Eq. (4). All quantities can be evaluated if a good pair intermolecular potential is available by using the low density limit for the classical pair correlation function

(6) $g_{LD}(r_{12}, \Omega_1, \Omega_2) = \exp(-V/kT)$

The two centre Lennard-Jones potential used in computer simulation of fluid N_2 by Frenkel and McTague (1980) has been adopted. At intermediate densities ($\rho < \rho_c$, where ρ_c is the critical density) estimates of the density evolution of the various terms have to be taken into account. The terms of Eq. (3) are given by the following expressions

(7) $I^R = a(4/45)\beta^2\rho(1+\rho f_2) = a(4/45)\beta^2\rho[1+\rho(f_2)_{\rho=0}\eta(\rho,T)]$

(8) $I^{CI} = a4\alpha^4\rho(2S_2+4S_3+S_4) = a8\alpha^4\rho^2(S_2/\rho)_{\rho=0}[\dfrac{2S_2+4S_3+S_4}{2(S_2/\rho)_{\rho=0}}]$

(9) $I^X = a(16/75)\alpha^2\beta\rho^2(\tau_{20}+3\text{-body terms}) = a\dfrac{16}{75}\alpha^2\beta\rho^2(\tau_{20})_{\rho=0}\xi(\rho,T)$

where a is a geometrical factor, f_2 is the second order static orientational correlation parameter, S_n stands for usual n-body CI contributions (Cox and Madden, 1980) and τ_{20} is the parameter introduced by Ladanyi and Keyes (1977). Berrue et al. (1978) have suggested a crude approximation for $\eta(\rho,T)$ and $\xi(\rho,T)$. They write

(10) $\eta(\rho,T) \simeq \xi(\rho,T) \simeq \exp[-\nu(T)\rho]$

where:

(11) $\nu(T) = (8\pi^2)^{-2} \displaystyle\int_0^{r_o} g_{LD} 2\pi r^2 dr\, d\Omega_1 d\Omega_2$

and the cut-off radius r_o is about 1.15 σ. The quantities f_2, τ_{20} and (S_2/ρ) are easily evaluated (De Santis et al., 1982) from

(12) $(f_2)_{\rho=0} = (8\pi^2)^{-2} \displaystyle\int_0^\infty g_{LD} D_{oo}^{(2)}(\Omega_1^{(2)})\, 2\pi r^2 dr\, d\Omega_1 d\Omega_2$

$$(13) \quad (\tau_{20})_{\rho=0} = (8\pi^2)^{-2} \int_0^\infty g_{LD} D_{oo}^{(2)}(\Omega_{12}^{(2)}) \; 2\pi/r \; dr \; d\Omega_1 \; d\Omega_2$$

$$(14) \quad (S_2/\rho)_{\rho=0} = (8\pi^2)^{-2} \int_0^\infty g_{LD} \; 2\pi/r^4 \; dr \; d\Omega_1 \; d\Omega_2$$

The density evolution of the term in brackets of Eq. (8) can be estimated from the CS performed on Argon (Balucani and Vallauri,1979).

Since the N_2 molecule is slightly anisotropic, it can be reasonably argued that cancellation effects in fluid N_2 are very similar to the ones in fluid Argon, where they are mainly responsible for the evolution of the second moment. Therefore we can write:

$$M_2^{CI} = (M_2^{CI})_{\rho=0} [\; M_2^{CI}/(M_2^{CI})_{\rho=0} \;]$$

and estimate the term in square brackets from Argon data (Balucani and Vallauri, 1979). Further M_2^X vanishes in the IDID approximation, while the rotational second moment is given by the well known expression

$$(15) \quad M_2^R = (6kT/I)/(1+\rho f_2)$$

The relevant quantities used for the theoretical estimate of Eq. (4) are reported in table 1. Notwithstanding the various approximations, the experimental results are in good agreement with the predicted ones until about 300 amagat (1 amagat corresponds to 2.687×10^{25} particles/m^3 and for N_2 to about $\rho_c/251$), as shown in Fig. (1). From the analysis of the different terms entering in Eq. (4) we can state the role played by them. At low densities, the decrease of M_2 is due to CI contributions. In fact the CI intensity is non negligible and the CI second moment is lower than the rotational one. The end of the decrease and the following increase after 150 amagat is due to the negative intensity of the cross contribution and to the higher increase of I^X with respect to I^{CI}. At liquid densities the increase of about 25% above the free rotational value must be mostly ascribed to

Table 1. Values for τ_{20}, (S_2/ρ), f_2, M_2^{CI} and ν, at different temperatures, in the low density limit, for 2LJC potential representing N_2. The potential parameters are σ=.331 nm, ε/k=37.7K and l=.110 nm (Frenkel and McTague, 1980).

T (K)	τ_{20}	(S_2/ρ) (nm^{-3})	$f_2 \times 10^5$ (amg^{-1})	M_2^{CI} (cm^{-2})	$\nu \times 10^2$ (amg^{-1})
296	−1.79	24.9	3.48	394	.17
200	−2.18	27.7	5.07	268	.20
150	−2.68	29.4	7.16	200	.23
120	−3.30	32.7	9.94	158	.27

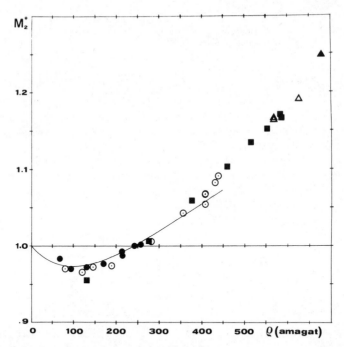

Fig. 1. RAY normalized second moments for fluid N_2 in 6kT/I units. Experimental data points: ● at 296K; ○ at 202K, ■ at 150K, △ at 119K, and ▲ at 89K. The solid line refers to the predicted behaviour at 150K.

the I^X negative intensity. The collisional term contributes only a few percent. More refined calculations in DID instead of IDID approximation give very similar results and validate the neglect of non IDID contributions for bands such as N_2 RAY ones which have a small polarizability anisotropy.

RAM SECOND MOMENT BEHAVIOUR IN FLUID N_2

The density behaviour of the second moment of RAM bands is quite different from that of RAY ones. To explain this behaviour, the IDID approximation is not suitable and we have to adopt the DID one. As a matter of fact the polarizability anisotropy is not very small as for RAY bands. In RAM bands only 2- and 3-body terms contribute to the CI intensity and the cross contribution involves only 2-body terms.

Nevertheless many terms have to be evaluated. The procedure is very similar to that adopted for RAY bands. Explicit calculations are reported by De Santis and Sampoli (1984). Here we point out that the CI terms are evaluated with neglect of all orientational correlations (Kielich, 1982) and that the cross term has a non zero second moment.

632

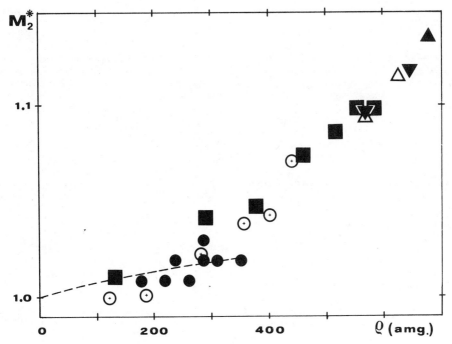

Fig. 2. RAM normalized second moments for fluid N_2 in 6kT/I units.
Symbols for experimental data points as in Fig (1). The
symbols ▼ refer to predicted values using CS results for
cross term (De Santis and Sampoli, 1984). The dashed line
refers to the predicted behaviour from low density calculations at 150K.

The comparison between experimental and "theoretical" results
is shown in Fig. (2). The agreement is good up to 300 amagat. The
disagreement after this density must be mainly attributed to a poor
estimate of the density evolution of the cross term. Indeed, if we
evaluate by CS the parameters which determine the intensity and the
second moment of the cross contribution (De Santis and Sampoli, 1984),
the agreement is also good at 567 and 646 amagat.

Owing to the different permanent polarizabilities involved in RAY
and RAM cases, CI and cross contributions are less important in RAM
bands and more reliable information on rotational dynamics should be
extracted from RAM spectra. Preliminary CS results on different contributions seem to validate these conclusions and support the approximations used (De Santis et. al., 1984). In particular the CI intensity and second moment can be evaluated neglecting all orientational
correlation within a few percent.

Figures (1) and (2) show that RAY and RAM bands yield a different evolution of the second moment. As shown by De Santis and Sampoli (1984), such a difference can be fully explained by the first order DID mechanism, if the differences in permanent polarizabilities and in many-body contributions are taken into account properly. Therefore the DID mechanism seems to explain quite well the density behavior of the second moment for RAY and RAM bands in fluid N_2.

At this point, it is interesting to extend the present analysis to other molecular fluids. In the following section we examine the fluid CO. Since the CO molecule is quite similar to N_2, the DID model should be successful for that fluid too.

RAY SECOND MOMENT IN FLUID CO

The experimental density behaviour of the second moment of fluid CO is shown in Fig. (3). As we can see, the behaviour is similar from a qualitative point of view but the values are quite dissimilar.

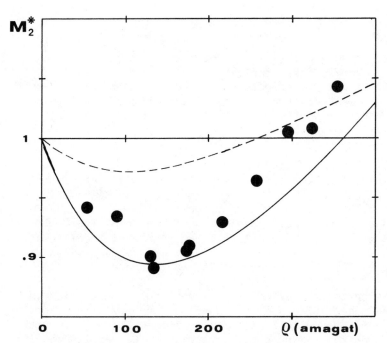

Fig. 3. RAY normalized second moments for fluid CO in 6kT/I units. Experimental data: ●. Full line refers to the predicted behaviour using the 2LJC interaction potential of Frenkel and McTague (1980) modelling N_2. Dashed line depicts the N_2 behaviour for comparison.

This result is surprising. The two molecules are very similar with regard to the critical density, pressure and temperature, and the principle of corresponding states works very well. However, since the polarizabilities are not so similar, we shall try to explain the different behavior on this basis.

The CO polarizability anisotropy β/α is lower than that of N_2 (Bridge and Buckingham, 1966). Therefore, we can adopt the same IDID scheme as for N_2 RAY bands. To calculate the parameters entering in Eqs. (7) to (9), an effective intermolecular pair potential is necessary. Unfortunately, this is not available. However, owing to the similarity of N_2 and CO mentioned previously, we have suggested the use of the $\bar{N}_2$ potential (De Santis and Sampoli, 1984). As in N_2 RAY case, the agreement is good and the small discrepancies above 200 amagat have to be again ascribed to the poor estimate of the density evolution of the cross term. The more pronounced dip is due to the greater contribution of the CI intensity. Indeed due to the different polarizabilities we have

(16) $\quad (I^{CI}/I^R)^{"CO"} = 2.66 \ (I^{CI}/I^R)^{"N2"}$

while:

(17) $\quad (I^X/I^R)^{"CO"} = 1.63 \ (I^X/I^R)^{"N2"}$

The greater value of the cross term determines a steeper increase after 150 amagat.

RAY SECOND MOMENT DENSITY EVOLUTION OF FLUID CO_2

The experimental data are reported in Fig. (4). The high density data can be compared directly with the CS results of Ladanyi (1983), who has used the usual DID scheme as well as an improved one. Indeed the CO_2 molecule is highly anisotropic and a single polarizable point (situated in the molecular center) can represent the molecular polarizability for such a molecule only in a very rough manner. Keyes and Ladanyi (1977) have proposed a DID scheme which takes into account the distribution of polarizable matter by considering the atoms of the molecule as polarizable points, i.e. a DID interaction between atomic sites (s-s) instead of molecular centers (c-c). The s-s scheme adopted by Ladanyi (1983) considers the more polarizable outer atoms only. Our results agree quite well with the CS values obtained in the s-s scheme, while the c-c values are outside any experimental or CS error. This suggests that the s-s scheme should be better for describing the induced terms in fluid CO_2. We must note that the use of an s-s DID interaction involves the rotation in all the CI (and cross) terms, and therefore the analogous 2-, 3- and 4-body contributions are not expected to behave as in monatomic fluids. As emphasized by Ladanyi, the two schemes provide results increasingly different with the density and molecular anisotropy. For low densities,

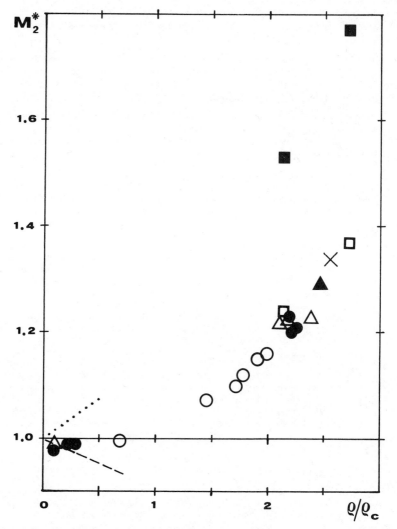

Fig. 4. RAY normalized second moments for fluid CO_2 in 6kT/I units
versus reduced density (ρ_c=236 amagat). Experimental data
points: O at 310K, ● at 296K, △ at 263K, ▲ at 230K and
X at 220K. Computer simulation results of Ladanyi (1983):
■ c-c model, ☐ s-s model. Dotted line is the low density
limit slope obtained from 2LJC potential of Singer et al.
(1977); dashed line slope from 3LJC potential of Murthy et
al. (1981).

the two schemes should provide similar results. Adopting a similar
procedure, as for RAY bands of fluid N_2, we can calculate the low
density slope, i. e.

(18) $\quad (\frac{\partial M_2^*}{\partial \rho})_{\rho=0} = 90 \frac{\alpha^4}{\beta^2} (\frac{S_2}{\rho})_{\rho=0}[(\frac{M_2^{CI}}{M_2^R})_{\rho=0}-1] - f_2 - \frac{4}{5} \frac{\alpha^2}{\beta} \tau_{20}$

from the values of τ_{20}, S_2/ρ, f_2, M_2^{CI} reported in table 2. These are evaluated using Eq. (6) and the 2LJC potential suggested by Singer et al. (1977) and used by Ladanyi (1983). The agreement with experimental values is poor and it suggests that the anisotropy of the interaction potential is not well described. Murthy et al. (1981) have proposed a 3 center LJ potential (3LJC) for fluid CO_2. In table 2 the values obtained from this potential are also reported. The 2LJC provides a large positive slope while the 3LJC a negative one which is in fair agreement with experiment. This seems to indicate that the anisotropic part of the interaction potential is better described by the 3LJC potential.

It is worth remarking that the DID mechanism is able to predict a purely induced isotropic spectrum. Isotropic time correlation functions have been computed in both c-c and s-s models in the case of CO_2 (Ladanyi, 1983) and they are very similar. The isotropic spectrum can be derived experimentally from

(19) $\quad I^{ISO}(\omega) = I_{VV}(\omega) - (4/3) I_{VH}(\omega)$

where VV and VH refer to polarized and depolarized scattering geometries. Measurements have been performed in liquids CS_2 (Cox and Madden 1980) and CO_2 (De Santis and Sampoli, 1983). For liquid CO_2 the weakness of the isotropic intensity with respect to the anisotropic one makes the measurement very difficult. The measured spectrum at $\rho=505$ amagat and T=263K is reported in Fig. (5) and compares fairly well with the CS spectrum obtained using the c-c scheme (Frenkel and McTague, 1980).

Table 2. Low density values of τ_{20}, (S_2/ρ), f_2, M_2^{CI} and slope of the reduced second moment (Eq. (18)), using two different potentials representing CO_2. The first line refers to the 2LJC of Singer et al. (1977) whose parameters are $\sigma=0.299$ nm, $\varepsilon/k=163.6K$ and $l=0.237$ nm. The second one is computed using the 3LJC potential of Murthy et al. (1981) whose parameters are $\sigma_{O-O}=0.301$ nm, $(\varepsilon/k)_{O-O}= 83.1K$, $\sigma_{C-O}= 0.278$ nm, $(\varepsilon/k)_{C-O}= 29K$, $l=0.232$ nm and a quadrupole moment $Q=-1.285\times10^{-39}Cm^2$.

τ_{20}	(S_2/ρ) (nm^{-3})	$f_2\times10^4$ (amg^{-1})	(M_2^{CI}) (cm^{-2})	Slope $\times10^4$ (amg^{-1})	potential
-7.74	40.8	3.43	309	5.7	2LJC
-4.17	38.3	5.66	289	-3.9	3LJC

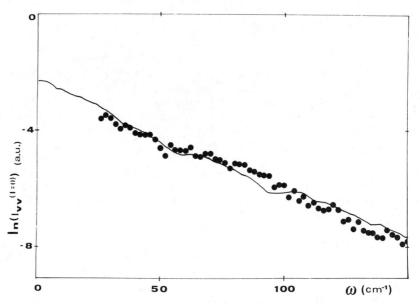

Fig. 5. Induced isotropic RAY spectrum for fluid CO_2 at 263K and 505 amagat. The full line refers to the CS spectrum at about the same thermodynamic state obtained by Frenkel and McTague (1980).

CONCLUDING REMARKS

As shown in previous sections, the DID mechanism is able to explain the main features of the induced phenomena in light scattering spectra from fluids of light linear molecules. However the necessity of using the s-s model for CO_2 suggests that the distribution of polarizable matter within the molecule itself has to be taken into account. In this respect the s-s model is a simple improvement over the point polarizable approximation.

Although the s-s model seems to describe quite well the tested experimental data, we can argue that higher order polarizabilities can affect experimental spectra. Indeed, preliminary results show very high frequency spectral wings in both CO_2 and N_2 (see Figs. (6) and (7)) whose nature is not yet very well understood. In the case of fluid H_2S, it has been suggested that first hyperpolarizability and quadrupole-quadrupole polarizability affect strongly experimental RAY spectral shapes (De Santis and Sampoli, 1983).

The induced effects due to higher order polarizabilities in allowed spectra from simple linear molecule fluids have not been yet considered. In particular the non-negligible first hyperpolarizabil-

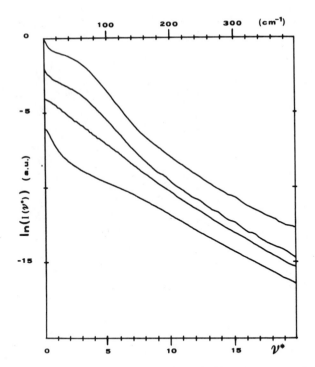

Fig. 6. RAY spectral far wings for fluid CO_2 versus reduced frequency $\nu^* = \nu / \sqrt{(kT/I)}$. The frequency scale at the top of the
figure refers to 263K. Curves are at: 310K and $\rho/\rho_c = .8$,
310K and $\rho/\rho_c = 1.5$, 263K and $\rho/\rho_c = 2$, 230K and $\rho/\rho_c = 2.4$ from
top to bottom, respectively (for CO_2 $\rho_c = 236$ amagat). The
spectra are shifted for clarity.

ity of CO molecule (Ward and Miller, 1979) could explain the differences observed in the far spectral wings between CO and N_2 RAY spectra (De Santis and Sampoli, unpublished results). Our feeling is
that for heavier molecules such Cl_2 or Br_2 the DID induction mechanism could be a rough approximation. In such cases, a careful second
moment analysis could help to understand which induction mechanisms
are involved.

Obviously, direct comparisons of experimental and CS time correlation functions will be very helpful to gain a more detailed knowledge of induced phenomena and to recognize which of them are actually
important in the various cases. However, we think that single state
comparisons are not quite effective, but a wide range of thermodynamic
states needs to be covered by studying the density/temperature evolution at constant temperature/density. Furthermore comparisons have
to be performed with CS results based on interaction potential models
as realistic as possible.

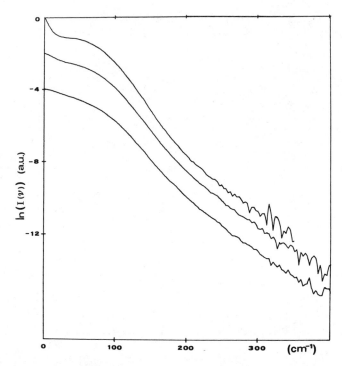

Fig. 7. RAY spectral far wings for fluid N_2 at 150K and 275, 460, and 580 amagat. The density increases from top to bottom. The spectra are shifted for clarity.

REFERENCES

Balucani, V. and Vallauri, R., 1979, Collision induced light scattering at intermediate densities. I. The integrated intensity, Mol. Phys., 38:1099, and 1979, II. The second frequency moment, Mol. Phys., 38:1115.

Bancewicz, T., 1983, Rayleigh light scattering by liquids composed of interacting anisotropic molecules. Spherical tensor approach within the second-order approximation of DID model, Mol. Phys., 50:173.

Berrue, T., Chave, A., Dumon, B. and Thibeau, M., 1978, Mesure du taux de dépolarisation dans l'azote comprimé et évaluation théorique des différents processus qui y contribuent, J.Phys., 39:815.

Bridge, N. J. and Buckingham, A. D., 1966, The polarization of laser light scattered by gases, Proc. R. Soc., A, 295:334.

Buckingham, A. D. and Tabisz, G. C., 1978, Collision induced rotational Raman scattering by tetrahedral and octahedral molecules, Mol. Phys., 36:583.

Cox, T. I. and Madden, P. A., 1980, A comparative study of the interaction induced spectra of liquid CS_2, I. Intensities, Mol. Phys., 39:1487.

De Santis, A., Moretti, E. and Sampoli, M., 1982, Rayleigh spectra of N_2 fluid. Temperature and density behaviour of the second moment, Mol. Phys., 46:1271.

De Santis, A. and Sampoli, M., 1983, Induced contributions in isotropic and anisotropic Rayleigh spectra of fluid H_2S, Chem. Phys. Lett., 102:425.

De Santis, A. and Sampoli, M., 1983, Induced isotropic scattering from liquid carbondioxide, Chem. Phys. Lett., 96:114.

De Santis, A. and Sampoli, M., 1984, Raman spectra of fluid N_2. Temperature and density behaviour of the second moment, Mol. Phys., 51:97.

De Santis, A. and Sampoli, M., 1984, Depolarized Rayleigh bands of fluid CO at room temperature. Induced effects on the second moment, Phys. Lett., 100A:25.

De Santis, A., Sampoli, M. and Vallauri, R., 1984, Raman bands of fluid N_2. A molecular dynamics and experimental study, Mol. Phys., 53:695.

Frenkel, D. and McTague, J. P., 1980, Molecular dynamics studies of orientational and collision-induced light scattering in molecular fluids, J. Chem. Phys., 72:2801.

Frommhold, L., 1981, Collision induced scattering of light and the diatom polarizability, Adv. Chem. Phys., 46:1.

Gordon, R. G., 1964, Molecular motion and the moment analysis of molecular spectra. II. The rotational Raman effect, J. Chem. Phys., 40:1973.

Guillot, B., Bratos, S. and Birnbaum, G., 1980, Theoretical study of spectra of depolarized light scattered from dense rare-gas fluids, Phys. Rev., A, 22:2230.

Hanson, F. E. and McTague, J. P., 1980, Raman studies of the orientational motion of small diatomics dissolved in argon, J. Chem. Phys., 72:1733.

Keyes, T. and Ladanyi, B. M., 1977, The role of local fields and interparticle pair correlations in light scattering by dense fluids. IV. Removal of the point-polarizability approximation, Mol. Phys., 33:1271.

Kielich, S., 1982, Coherent light scattering by interacting anisotropic molecules with variable dipolar polarizability, J. Phys., 43:1749.

Ladanyi, B. M. and Keyes, T., 1977, The role of local fields and interparticle pair correlations in light scattering by dense fluids. I. Depolarized intensities due to orientational fluctuations, Mol. Phys., 33:1063.

Ladanyi, B. M., 1983, Molecular dynamics study of Rayleigh light scattering from molecular fluids, J. Chem. Phys.,78:2189.

Madden, P. A., 1978, The depolarized Rayleigh scattering from fluids of spherical molecules, Mol. Phys., 36:365.

Madden, P. A. and Cox, T. I., 1981, A comparative study of the interaction-induced spectra of liquid CS_2. II. Lineshapes, Mol.

Phys., 43:287, and references therein quoted of previous works on fluid CS_2.

Murthy, C. S., Singer, K. and McDonald, I. R., 1981, Interaction site models for carbon dioxide, Mol. Phys., 44:135.

Posch, H., 1980, Collision induced light scattering from fluids composed of tetrahedral molecules, Mol. Phys., 40:1137.

Shelton, D. P. and Tabisz, G. C., 1980, Binary collision-induced light scattering by isotropic molecular gases. II. Molecular spectra and induced rotational Raman scattering, Mol. Phys., 40: 299.

Singer, K., Taylor, A. and Singer, J. V. L., 1977, Thermodynamic and structural properties of liquids modelled by "2-Lennard-Jones centers' pair potentials, Mol. Phys., 33:1757.

Tabisz, G. C., 1979, Collision induced Rayleigh and Raman scattering, Mol. Spectr., Vol.6, p.136, (Specialist Periodical Reports, the Chemical Society).

Versmold, H., 1981, Depolarized Rayleigh scattering. Molecular reorientation of CO_2 in a wide density range, Mol. Phys.,43:383.

Ward, J. F. and Miller, K., 1979, Measurements of nonlinear optical polarizabilities for twelve small molecules, Phys. Rev. A, 19:826.

THE INTERFERENCE OF MOLECULAR

AND INTERACTION-INDUCED EFFECTS IN LIQUIDS

Paul A. Madden

Physical Chemistry Laboratory
South Parks Road
Oxford   OX1 3QZ
U.K.

INTRODUCTION

The most commonly encountered situation in the spectroscopy of dense fluids is that the sample dipole moment responsible for the spectrum comprises a molecular and an interaction-induced part. For the dielectric and infra-red spectroscopy the appropriate moments are the total dipole moment and its vibrationally modulated part and for Rayleigh and Raman spectra they are the corresponding laser-induced dipoles. This appropriate moment may be written, in general, as

$$\underline{M} = {}^{O}\underline{M} + {}^{I}\underline{M} \tag{1}$$

where the molecular part, ${}^{O}\underline{M}$, is the sum of (gas-phase) molecular moments

$$ {}^{O}\underline{M} = \sum_{i} \underline{m}^{i} \tag{2}$$

and the interaction-induced part, ${}^{I}\underline{M}$, is the sum of the moments induced by the interaction of pairs, triplets, etc, of molecules

$$ {}^{I}\underline{M} = \sum_{ij} \underline{m}^{ij} + \sum_{ijk} \underline{m}^{ijk} + \dots \tag{3}$$

The spectral lineshape $I(\omega)$ is some functional of the correlation function of a component of $\underline{M}$

$$ I(\omega) = I[\int_{O}^{\infty} dt\ e^{i\omega t} \langle \underline{M}(t).\underline{M}(o) \rangle] \tag{4}$$

Thus, whilst the detailed nature of the dipoles and the above functional are specific to the particular spectroscopy being

643

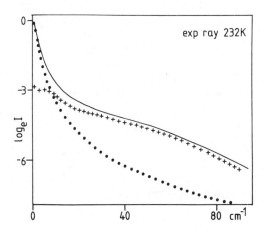

Figure 1. Rayleigh spectrum of CS_2 ____, and its molecular $\cdots$
and collision-induced +++ parts (empirical).(Cox et al,
1979).

considered, there are invariably interference terms between ^OM and
^IM. These complicate the interpretation of the spectrum and limit
the amount of information which can be obtained from it.

The ideal spectrum contains information on the "molecular"
motion (associated with the relaxation of ^OM) and on the intermolecular motion which determines the relaxation of ^IM; furthermore,
the collective Rayleigh and dielectric spectra contain information
on the useful liquid state structural parameters g_1 and g_2 which,
in part, determine $<|^OM(0)|^2>$. The ideal is to obtain as much of
this information as possible by separating the spectrum into a
molecular and intermolecular part. The various approaches to
effecting this separation have been reviewed in this volume (Perrot
and Lascombe 1985). This paper is concerned with the illustration,
by computer simulation studies, of the limitations of the separation
procedure. The studies to be discussed have addressed the issue in
a particular form of spectroscopy (ie, Rayleigh, Raman or dielectric
spectroscopy); it is important to realise that they have a wider
significance through the generality of the interference problem.

The shapes of experimental spectra often suggest the appearance
of distinct low and high frequency features (often of "lorentzian"
and "exponential" shape), see Fig. (1) for example. Historically,
these have been associated with molecular and intermolecular
phenomena by an argument which runs along the following lines:-
The relaxation times associated with the purely induced moments
seen in the depolarised Rayleigh spectrum of an inert gas or the
far i.r. of a non-polar fluid are usually much shorter than reorientation times; furthermore, such spectra are usually much

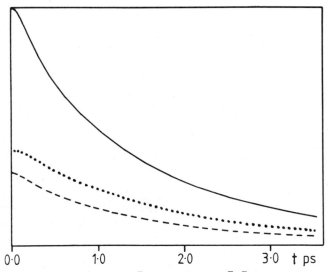

Figure 2. $\langle{}^{O}\underline{M}{}^{O}\underline{M}\rangle$ ___, $\langle{}^{O}\underline{M}{}^{I}\underline{M}\rangle$ ··· and $\langle{}^{I}\underline{M}{}^{I}\underline{M}\rangle$ --- from CS_2 simulation at 244K (Madden and Tildesley, 1984).

weaker than allowed spectra. We might (naively) hope that we can write

$$\langle\underline{M}(t).\underline{M}\rangle = \langle{}^{O}\underline{M}(t).{}^{O}\underline{M}\rangle + \langle{}^{I}\underline{M}(t).{}^{I}\underline{M}\rangle + 2\langle{}^{I}\underline{M}(t).{}^{O}\underline{M}\rangle, \qquad (5)$$

and identify the first term with a low frequency spectral feature, the second with a broad, weak background and neglect the cross-term altogether. However, this argument neglects the fact that in the light scattering of anisotropic molecules or the dielectric spectra of polar ones there are new induced effects not present in the purely induced counterparts. Also, there is no reason to suspect that $^{I}\underline{M}$ is uncorrelated with $^{O}\underline{M}$, so that neglect of the cross-term is without foundation.

The consequences of the fallacy are illustrated in Fig. (2), where the correlation functions of Eq. (5), appropriate to the CS_2 Rayleigh spectrum of Fig. (1), are shown (Madden and Tildesley, 1984). Not only do all three correlation functions relax on the same timescale, but the cross-term between $^{I}\underline{M}$ and $^{O}\underline{M}$ is large. Since the representation of the total dipole correlation function given by Eq. (5) is thereby shown to be inappropriate for a case (CS_2) in which distinctive low and high frequency features appear in the experimental spectrum, the subsequent discussion will be set against a background offered by a different representation. The arguments given below are essentially those of Keyes, Kivelson and McTague (KKM) (Keyes et al, 1971); the simulation work to be described has been undertaken to assess their validity.

We consider the effect of projecting out of $^{I}\underline{M}$ the part which depends upon the configuration of the molecular dipoles. That is, we re-write Eq. (5) as

$$\underline{M}(t) = (1 + G)\,{}^{O}\underline{M}(t) + \underline{\Delta}(t), \tag{6}$$

where

$$G = \langle{}^{O}\underline{M}(o).{}^{I}\underline{M}(o)\rangle/\langle{}^{O}\underline{M}(o).{}^{O}\underline{M}(o)\rangle \tag{7}$$

and

$$\Delta = {}^{I}\underline{M} - G\,{}^{O}\underline{M}. \tag{8}$$

$G\,{}^{O}\underline{M}$ may be interpreted as the mean value of the induced moment when the molecular moments are in a configuration characterised by the value ${}^{O}\underline{M}$ (there are many intermolecular configurations with this same value of ${}^{O}\underline{M}$ but different ${}^{I}\underline{M}$). Δ then results from the fluctuation of the intermolecular variables about their mean and may be expected to relax more rapidly than ${}^{I}\underline{M}$ itself; in particular, unlike ${}^{I}\underline{M}$, $\underline{\Delta}(t)$ does not depend on ${}^{O}\underline{M}(t)$, the two quantities are orthogonal

$$\langle\underline{\Delta}(t).{}^{O}\underline{M}(t)\rangle = 0 \tag{9}$$

In terms of the projected quantities, the total correlation function may be written:

$$\langle\underline{M}(t).\underline{M}\rangle = (1{+}G)^{2}\langle{}^{O}\underline{M}(t).{}^{O}\underline{M}\rangle$$

$$+ [2(1{+}G)\langle\underline{\Delta}(t).{}^{O}\underline{M}\rangle + \langle\underline{\Delta}(t).\underline{\Delta}\rangle] \tag{10}$$

This separates the total correlation function into a part (the first term) which exhibits the relaxation of the molecular dipole and a fluctuation- or 'collision-' induced part (ie, both terms in square brackets). The terms in square brackets depend on the molecular variable ${}^{O}\underline{M}$ only in so far as the fluctuations which give rise to Δ at time t are correlated with ${}^{O}\underline{M}$ at an earlier time, as the equal time correlation vanishes by Eq. (9).

The relaxation of the molecular variable will be determined by molecular reorientation (primarily). If there is an appreciable difference in the timescale of the relaxation of the molecular orientation and of the fluctuations which excite Δ then the first term of Eq. (10) will be slowly relaxing and we might hope that the reorientational character of the square bracketed term is small. If these conditions are realised then the low frequency part of the spectrum should be dominated by a reorientational feature associated with the correlation function

$$C^{O}(t) = (1{+}G)^{2}\langle{}^{O}\underline{M}(t).{}^{P}\underline{M}\rangle \tag{11}$$

and at higher frequencies the spectrum will be dominated by the collision-induced term

$$c^{\Delta}(t) = [2(1+G)<\underline{\Delta}(t).{}^{o}\underline{M}> + <\underline{\Delta}(t).\Delta>] \qquad (12)$$

Under these circumstances it is possible to extract from the experimental spectrum some information on the reorientational and intermolecular dynamics, but the short-time aspects of the former and the long-time aspects of the latter will be masked. The separation of the Rayleigh spectrum of CS_2 suggested by these ideas is illustrated in Fig. 1.

The integrated intensity of the reorientational component is determined by $c^{o}(0)$. Notice that this differs from the mean square molecular dipole $<{}^{o}\underline{M}.{}^{o}\underline{M}>$ by the "local field" factor

$$L = (1+G)^2 \qquad (13)$$

for which we have given a molecular expression in Eq. (7). In order to obtain the orientational correlation parameters g_1 and g_2 from the reorientational intensity, it is necessary to obtain a value for L; the theoretical evaluation of L, in the light scattering case, has been reviewed by Ladanyi (Ladanyi, 1985). The intensity of the collision-induced component of the spectrum is just the mean-square fluctuation of $\underline{\Delta}$, ie,

$$c^{\Delta}(0) = <\underline{\Delta}.\underline{\Delta}> \qquad (14)$$

by virtue of Eq. (9).

The computer simulations may be evaluated through the light they cast on three issues raised above:

i)   How large are the interaction-induced effects in molecular fluids, and how serious are the interpretation problems they pose?
ii) Does the scenario envisaged under the 'existence of a timescale separation' actually occur?
iii) Can the local field (and other intensity factors) be calculated theoretically?

The results of four studies, by Frenkel and McTague (FM, 1980), Ladanyi (Ladanyi, 1983, 1985), Madden and Tildesley (MT, 1984) and Edwards and Madden (EM, 1984) will be reviewed. The first three of these studies were of Rayleigh and Raman spectra and they will be considered first. EM studied the dielectric spectrum of MeCN. The technical aspects of the calculations will not be described, and the common features of the results will be stressed.

STUDIES OF RAYLEIGH AND RAMAN SPECTRA - THE SIMPLE DID MODEL

The essential ingredients of the computer simulation are a potential model and a model for the interaction-induced dipole, a shortcoming of either could be responsible for a failure to reproduce an experimental observable. FM and Ladanyi have carried out extensive simulations of diatomic Lennard-Jones models (Detyna,1980) for N_2, O_2 and CO_2. MT used a triatomic model of CS_2 (Tildesley and Madden, 1981). The N_2 and CS_2 models have been tested against a wide range of structural and dynamic data and are believed to represent those fluids reasonably well; the experimental properties of O_2 and CO_2 are less well characterised and the models are therefore not so well established. (This is particularly true of CO_2; note also that with a diatomic model for this molecule either the mass or moment of inertia is wrong.)   All three groups initially used the first order dipole-induced dipole model for the interaction-induced moment, that is

$$\underline{m}^{ij} = \underline{\alpha}^i.\underline{\underline{T}}^{ij}.\underline{\alpha}^j.\underline{F} \quad , \quad \underline{m}^{ijk} \text{ etc. } = 0 \tag{15}$$

for the Rayleigh interaction-induced dipole, and

$$\underline{m}^{ij} = 2 \, q^i \hat{\underline{\alpha}}^i.\underline{\underline{T}}^{ij}.\underline{\alpha}^j.\underline{F}, \quad \underline{m}^{ijk} \text{ etc. } = 0 \tag{16}$$

in the Raman case. In these equations $\underline{\alpha}^i$ is the molecular polarisability, $\hat{\underline{\alpha}}^i$ is its derivative with respect to the normal coordinate q^i) of the Raman line under study, $\underline{F}$ is an electric field and $\underline{\underline{T}}^{ij}$ is the dipole-dipole interaction tensor

$$\underline{\underline{T}}^{ij} = (3\underline{r}^{ij}\underline{r}^{ij} - (r^{ij})^2 \underline{\underline{I}})(r^{ij})^{-5} \tag{17}$$

where $\underline{r}^{ij}$ is the vector joining the molecular centres. In all three studies the relaxation of the normal coordinate was neglected, ie,

$$<q^i(t)q^j(o)> = \delta_{ij} \tag{18}$$

One finding of all three studies was that, so far as issues i) and ii) of the introduction are concerned, there is no substantive difference between the Rayleigh and Raman cases for the fluids considered; the general results we shall describe below are true of either.

The importance of the interaction-induced contribution to the light-scattering spectra may be expected to increase with the polarisability of the molecule (for molecules of similar shape), the simulations clearly show this effect. Table 1 gives the reduced isotropic polarisability α^* ($= \alpha/\sigma^3$ where σ is the Lennard-Jones parameter for N_2, O_2, Cl_2 and CO_2 and σ_{cc} for CS_2). α^* increases in the series N_2, O_2, CO_2, Cl_2, CS_2. The table also contains

Table 1. Properties of the depolarised Rayleigh spectra in the first order DID model.

	α^*	R_0	R_2	R_4
N_2 (FM)	0.049	0.04	1.24	1.40
O_2 (L)	0.062	0.03	1.26	1.47
CO_2 (L)	0.098	0.14	1.64	2.58
Cl_2 (FM)	0.13	0.34	5.97	–
CS_2 (MT)	0.231	0.68	–	–

several properties which show the importance of the interaction-induced effects for the simulated state point closest to the triple point. Column two gives the ratio

$$R_o = <|{}^I\underline{M}|^2>/<|\underline{M}|^2> \tag{19}$$

for the depolarised Rayleigh spectrum. R_o measures the interaction-induced contribution to the intensity. Columns three and four give the ratio of the second and fourth moments of the total spectrum to the corresponding moment of the reorientational spectrum (denoted R_2 and R_4, respectively). All the ratios are for the centre-centre, first-order DID model. Although for N_2 and O_2 the interaction-induced contributions to the intensity are not large, they have an important effect on the lineshape (as witnessed by R_2 and R_4). For highly polarisable CS_2 the interaction-induced effects predicted by first-order DID give the dominant contribution to the calculated spectrum.

The importance of induced effects in the light scattering spectra of molecular liquids (ie, point i) of the introduction) is thus rapidly established, even for the highly unpolarisable, near spherical N_2 molecule. We turn now to issue ii) and consider the relaxation characteristics of the molecular and interaction-induced components.

The correlation functions appropriate to the Rayleigh spectrum of CS_2 in the KKM representation of Eq. (10) are shown in Fig. 3; these are the counterparts of the unprojected correlation functions of Fig. (2). The fluctuating part of the interaction-induced polarisability (ie, the $<\Delta(t).\Delta>$ correlation function) shows an initial decay which is substantially quicker than the reorientational correlation function; however, at long times it relaxes slowly on the reorientational timescale. The cross-correlation decreases from its initial value (cf, Eq. (9)) on the timescale of the initial decay of $\underline{\Delta}$ but then falls back to zero on what appears to be the rate of molecular reorientation. The shape of the cross-correlation functions found in the N_2, O_2 and CO_2 simulations was the same as shown in Fig. (3); however, in those cases there was no significant difference between the rates of initial decay of the reorientational and $\underline{\Delta}$ correlation functions.

The correlation functions of Fig. (3) are not quite what one would have expected on the timescale separation argument; this would suggest that the cross-term should be small at all times and that $\langle \underline{\Delta}(t).\underline{\Delta}\rangle$ should have no slow decay. The simulations on CS_2 show that as the temperature is lowered the initial rate of decay of $\underline{\Delta}$ becomes appreciably faster than the reorientation decay and the amplitude of the cross-term diminishes; however, it does not become negligible.

This does not mean that the projection scheme is an inappropriate way of resolving the spectrum, since what we need to compare are the reorientational and 'collision-induced' spectra (ie, that which corresponds to the sum of terms in square brackets in Eq.(10). As can be seen from Fig. (3), the slowly decaying parts of the cross-correlation function and the autocorrelation function are of opposite sign and therefore the <u>collision-induced correlation function decays appreciably faster than either</u>. This is illustrated in Fig. (4), where the total Rayleigh spectrum and the reorientation and collision-induced components (from the correlation functions of Fig. (3) are shown. The collision-induced spectrum contains no slowly relaxing components; as witnessed by the small low frequency dip, the negative

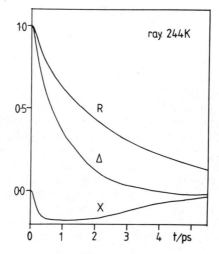

Figure 3.   Normalised acfs of ^OM and $\underline{\Delta}$ (R & Δ respectively) and their cross-correlation function. (Madden and Tildesley, 1984).

650

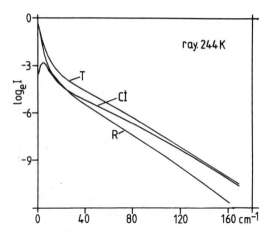

Figure 4. Simulated Rayleigh spectrum (T) and its molecular (R) and collision-induced (CI) components.

tail in the cross function has slightly overcancelled the tail in the Δ autocorrelation function. (Actually, the spectra shown are not quite the simple DID spectra; the magnitude of the $\underline{\underline{T}}$ tensor has been scaled for reasons to be described in the next section.) The spectra of Fig. (4) agree rather well with the experimental ones of Fig. (1); it seems fair to conclude that in the CS_2 case the projection scheme has correctly identified the low and high frequency spectral features. Thus for this case a limited resolution of the experimental spectrum into a reorientational and a collision-induced part is possible, along the lines suggested by the timescale separation argument. Note that the reorientational spectrum becomes non-Lorentzian at frequencies greater than about 25 cm^{-1}; at these frequencies the total spectrum is strongly affected by collision-induced effects so that the non-diffusional aspects of the re-orientational motion are masked.

A further point of practical significance which emerges from Fig. (4) is that the shapes of the collision-induced and reorienta-tional spectra at high frequency are remarkably similar; both appear almost exponential. Thus an exponential lineshape at high frequency cannot be taken to mean that collision-induced effects dominate the spectrum there.

As remarked above, there is no significant difference between the rates of reorientational and intermolecular relaxation in N_2,

651

O_2 and CO_2 (Frenkel and McTague, 1980; Ladanyi, 1983 and 1985) (in simple DID). The total spectra, then, do not show distinctive low and high frequency features, and a practical separation of the experimental spectrum is therefore not possible. Sampoli and de Santis (de Santis and Sampoli, 1985) have carefully compared the experimental and simulated spectral of N_2, with essentially perfect agreement. In a sense, this constitutes the ideal analysis of the spectrum - the total simulated spectrum agrees with experiment and therefore the reorientational and intermolecular spectra are identified as those calculated in the simulation. The only limitation of this kind of analysis (except finite computing resources) is that the model used in the simulation must faithfully represent reality; for N_2 this would seem to have been achieved but, as we shall see below, in other cases it is likely to be more difficult.

It is worthwhile to digress on the question of why CS_2 shows a timescale separation whilst CO_2 and N_2 do not. The two factors which will strongly determine this issue are the elongation of the molecule and the density of the fluid (consider the triple point). The most important aspect in the comparison would appear to be the densities of the two fluids at the triple point. CO_2 crystallizes at a much lower density than CS_2, thus the triple point liquid density is much lower. If CO_2 and CS_2 were conformal (Rowlinson, 1959) liquids, then the ratio of the triple point to critical point temperatures would be equal; for CS_2 the ratio is about 0.35 and for CO_2 about 0.7 - the discrepancy is due to the early crystallization of CO_2. CO_2 is conformal with N_2. From this viewpoint the reduced densities of N_2 and CO_2 do not reach that of CS_2 in its normal liquid range; they are dense gases rather than 'normal' liquids.

The final point to be taken up from the issues raised in the introduction is the extent to which the simulations support theoretical models for the local field factor. This issue has been discussed by Ladanyi (Ladanyi, 1985) with the N_2, O_2 and CO_2 data, and we have only one finding to add to her discussion. As indicated above, the timescale separation argument does not apply to these fluids and so it is not possible to experimentally determine a local field factor for the Raman and depolarised Rayleigh spectra. In light scattering it is normal to discuss the effective polarisability rather than the local field factor; for depolarised Rayleigh scattering, for example, the effective polarisability anisotropy is

$$\gamma_{eff} = \gamma(1 + G) \tag{20}$$

where G is given by Eq. (7) with an appropriate expression $^I\underline{M}$. For CS_2 the experimental value of γ_{eff}/γ is known reasonably well (≈ 0.59 at 295K (Battaglia et al, 1979)) and the ratio of effective Raman polarisabilities is known from the depolarisation ratio of the molecular components of the Raman spectra (Cox et al, 1979).

The simulated effective polarisabilities for CS_2 in the first-order DID model do not agree with these experimental values, the interaction-induced effects are too large (Madden and Tildesley, 1984): γ_{eff}/γ is about 0.43 and the predicted Raman depolarisation ratio is half its experimental value.

This points up a limitation of the first-order DID model; as we have already noted, CS_2 is highly polarisable and the interaction-induced effects are very large, so that truncation of the DID expansion is not justified. This and other limitations of the simple model will be discussed in the next section. For N_2 the polarisability is much smaller and it would appear from the successful comparison of the experimental and simulation data for this fluid that the simple first-order model is adequate (de Santis and Sampoli, 1984).

STUDIES OF RAYLEIGH AND RAMAN SPECTRA - BEYOND SIMPLE DID

The DID model represents the interaction-induced polarisability as a consequence of electrodynamic interactions between the otherwise undistorted charge densities of the molecules; that is, the polarisabilities induced by overlap and dispersion interactions are regarded as small, a viewpoint which is supported by a good deal of gas-phase data (see Madden, 1984, for a general resume). Even within this scheme the simple DID model has two potentially serious limitations in comparison with experimental reality. Firstly, higher-order dipole-induced dipole terms, such as

$$\underline{m}^{123} = \underline{\alpha}^1 . \underline{T}^{12} . \underline{\alpha}^2 . \underline{T}^{23} . \underline{\alpha}^3 . \underline{F} \tag{21}$$

and

$$\underline{m}^{12} = \underline{\alpha}^1 . \underline{T}^{12} . \underline{\alpha}^2 . \underline{T}^{21} . \underline{\alpha}^1 . \underline{F} \tag{22}$$

are ignored. Secondly, the molecular polarisability is treated as if concentrated at a point.

As discussed in the last section, the importance of the higher-order terms in $^1\underline{M}$ is indicated by the size of the first-order ones. In order to examine the importance of the second-order terms, MT calculated their contribution to the effective isotropic and anisotropic Raman polarisabilities ($\hat{\alpha}_{eff}$ and $\hat{\gamma}_{eff}$). The calculation of these factors is no more difficult than the calculation of the first-order collision-induced Raman intensity; however, to obtain the corresponding anisotropic Rayleigh factor or to calculate the time dependence of any of the second-order terms is formidably difficult. MT wrote the first- and second-orders contributions to $\hat{\alpha}_{eff}$ and $\hat{\gamma}_{eff}$ as terms in a series in α^*

$$\hat{\alpha}_{eff}/\hat{\alpha} = 1 - 1.608\alpha^* + 7.38(\alpha^*)^2 + \ldots \tag{23}$$

$$\hat{\gamma}_{eff}/\hat{\gamma} = 1 - 2.788\alpha^* + 7.93(\alpha^*)^2 + \ldots \tag{24}$$

Recalling that $\alpha^* = 0.231$ for CS_2 it can be seen that these series are by no means converging rapidly. To get some idea of how the higher-order terms affect the effective polarisabilities, they constructed Padé approximants, which gave

$$(\hat{\alpha}_{eff}/\hat{\alpha})^{Padé} = 0.89 \tag{25}$$

$$(\hat{\gamma}_{eff}/\hat{\gamma})^{Padé} = 0.61 \tag{26}$$

Thus the higher-order terms are important and they move the simulated effective polarisabilities into better agreement with experiment. Because of the difficulty of calculating the time dependence of the higher-order terms, MT represented the spectrum of CS_2 by scaling the value of the $\underline{T}$ tensor in the simple DID calculation to give effective polarisabilities which agree with the Padé values. It is this scaled spectrum which is shown in Fig. (4). If the higher-order terms are large it is important to ask if they can be quantitatively accounted for by such a scaling procedure (ie, by 'renormalisation' of the dipole-induced dipole interaction (Frenkel and McTague, 1980)). In order for this to be so, then the higher-order terms should be calculable in some simple model of the fluid structure which will allow for an analytic representation of a general higher-order term; such a model has been discussed in this context (Bancewicz, 1983; Kielich, 1982). The simulation results for the second-order projection factors did not appear to support this possibility; they showed substantial contributions from classes of terms which are not included in the renormalisation scheme (Madden and Tildesley, 1984).

It is now well established that the distribution of the polarisable matter in a molecule can have an important influence on interaction-induced phenomena (Buckingham and Tabisz, 1978; Cox and Madden, 1981). Ladanyi (Ladanyi, 1983) has shown how some of the effects of distributing the polarisability may be incorporated in the simulations of O_2 and CO_2. The intermolecular effects are represented by DID interactions between isotropic site polarisabilities located on the interaction sites of the diatomic potential model. The site polarisabilities undergo intramolecular DID interactions to all orders, but the intermolecular DID is truncated at first-order. It was found that this representation of the interaction-induced term led to significantly different results for the spectrum. The amplitude of the interaction-induced effects was smaller than in the simple DID model. Furthermore, the time dependence of the induced terms was appreciably altered; in particular,a better timescale separation was found. Sampoli and de Santis (Sampoli, 1984) have reported that the site polarisability model for CO_2 leads to better agreement with experiment.

Implementation of the site polarisability model is only straightforward when the site polarisabilities are isotropic, all have the same magnitude and are at equivalent sites in the molecule (Ladanyi, 1983). Furthermore, the direct comparison of the centre-centre and site-site models in the diatomic case is somewhat misleading. The objective of the site model is to allow for the polarisation of one molecule by the field gradients caused by the charge distribution of another. A multipole expansion for those terms in a homonuclear diatomic gives (Buckingham, 1967)

$$\underline{m}^{12} = (\underline{\alpha}^1 . \underline{T}^{12} . \underline{\alpha}^2 + \underline{\alpha}^1 . \underline{\nabla\nabla T}^{12} : \underline{E}^2 +$$

$$\underline{E}^1 : \underline{\nabla\nabla T}^{12} . \underline{\alpha}^2 + \underline{E}^1 : \underline{\nabla\nabla\nabla\nabla T}^{12} : \underline{E}^2 + ...).\underline{F} \qquad (27)$$

where $\underline{E}$ is an octopole-dipole polarisability. The simple DID is just the first term in this expansion. The multipole expansion may be slowly convergent, and with the site model one bypasses it by going over to a different representation of the intermolecular interactions. However, the site model should not be viewed as DID corrected for the presence of the extra terms; it is fundamentally different. Consider, for example, the molecular polarisability in the site model. If the magnitude of the site polarisabilities is a and they are separated by a distance x then the molecular polarisability components are (Frommhold, 1981)

$$\alpha = 4a.\hat{a}^2/(1 - \hat{a} - 2\hat{a}^2) \qquad (28)$$

$$\gamma \quad 6a.\hat{a}/(1 - \hat{a} - 2\hat{a}^2) \qquad (29)$$

where $\hat{a}$ is a/x^3. Thus if x is fixed at the intersite distance of the potential model, then only one of α and γ can be indepdnently fixed, and the site model does not reduce to DID even when the molecules are well separated.

We can conclude that the importance of extra-DID terms has been demonstrated in the simulations but that this realisation greatly increases the difficulty of faithfully representing reality.

DIELECTRIC SPECTRA

To date the only simulation in which the interaction-induced contributions to the dielectric spectrum of a polar liquid have been calculated was the study by EM of a model of acetonitrile. The potential model was a three site Lenndard-Jones model (CH_3 was represented by a single site) with point charges on the interaction sites. The charges were chosen to reproduce the dipole and quadrupole given by an ab initio calculation of the electrostatic potential of MeCN. The model gave a liquid structure very similar to that of a more detailed six-site model which itself gave X-ray and neutron scattering patterns in agreement with experiment.

The interaction-induced dipole was represented by the dipole induced by the electrostatic field of the potential model (ie, $\underline{\underline{\alpha}}^1.\underline{F}(\underline{r}^1)$ where $\underline{F}(\underline{r}^1)$ is the field of the charges of all other molecules in the simulation). As well as the (permanent) dipole-induced dipole, it also includes the dipoles induced by the higher-order permanent multipoles, but the molecular polarisability is treated as if concentrated at a point.

Because of the long range of the dipole-dipole interaction, there are a number of technical difficulties associated with the calculation of dielectric properties in a computer simulation (Stell et al, 1981). These led EM to calculate the properties from correlation functions of the transverse and longitudinal fourier components of the dipole density, ie,

$$\underline{M}_T(\underline{k}) = (\underline{\underline{1}} - \hat{k}\hat{k}) \cdot \sum_i (\underline{\mu}^i + \underline{\underline{\alpha}}^i.\underline{F}(\underline{r}^i))e^{i\underline{k}.\underline{r}^i} \tag{30}$$

and

$$\underline{M}_L(\underline{k}) = \hat{k}\hat{k} \sum_i (\underline{\mu}^i + \underline{\underline{\alpha}}^i.\underline{F}(\underline{r}^i))e^{i\underline{k}.\underline{r}^i} \tag{31}$$

where the two terms in square brackets give the molecular and interaction-induced dipoles of molecule i. The correlation functions of the transverse dipole are connected to the permittivity by a Debye-like formula (Madden and Kivelson, 1984; Edwards and Madden, 1984). Apart from this additional complexity, the analysis of the time correlation functions proceeds as in the Rayleigh and Raman cases.

The acetonitrile molecule has a similar elongation to CS_2 and also shows a long liquid range; we might therefore expect that it will exhibit a timescale separation. EM found that this was so, and more surprisingly, that the projection of the induced dipole along the molecular one was remarkably efficient. The mean square molecular dipole of MeCN is about $16D^2$ ($\cong <|^O\underline{M}|^2>$ whereas the mean square total dipole per molecule (ie, from $<|^O\underline{M}|^2> + <|^I\underline{M}|^2> + 2<^I\underline{M}.^O\underline{M}>$) is $25.1D^2$, so that the induced effects account for 35% of the dielectric loss. However, when the projection is taken, the effective molecular dipole (ie, $(1+G)\mu$) is 4.9D, showing that almost all the interaction-induced dipole is projected along the molecular one. The residual collision-induced dipole is very small; $<\underline{\Delta}.\underline{\Delta}>^{\frac{1}{2}}$ is only 0.19D. This may be usefully compared with interaction-induced dipole of CS_2, which accounts for the whole of the dielectric loss in that case;

it is about 0.17D. Thus the interaction-induced dipole is very
large in the polar fluid MeCN; however, for the most part it behaves
as a contribution to the effective molecular dipole and the amplitude of the 'collision-induced' effects is comparable to that
found in a non-polar fluid.

The induced effects were found to exert a significant influence
on the far infra red lineshape: Fig. (5) shows the total and
reorientational (ie, from Eq. (10)) far infra-red spectra calculated
in the simulation. The spectrum of the $\langle\underline{\Delta}(t).\underline{\Delta}\rangle$ correlation function
is also shown. It has a very similar shape to the far infra-red
spectrum of a non-polar fluid.

It is important to be able to make good estimates of the local
field factor in a dielectric experiment in order that the orientational correlation parameter g_1 (the Kirkwood parameter) can be
obtained from measurements of the permittivity. In the analogous
Rayleigh scattering case it is not necessary to calculate the local
field factor, since it can be independently measured from the
Cotton-Mouton constant (Battaglia et al, 1979). Madden and
Kivelson (1984) have investigated a molecular account of the local
field. They have shown how a highly simplified molecular picture
of a polar-polarisable fluid leads to the Frölich result for the
permittivity.

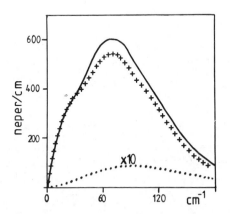

Figure 5. Simulated far i.r. absorption of MeCN and its +++
reorientation component, ···· spectrum of acf of $\underline{\Delta}$
(Edwards and Madden, 1984).

In the simplified molecular model the only orientational correlation which occurs is the long range correlation between permanent dipoles (ie, the part of the pair distribution function which is proportional to the diple-dipole interaction potential). This model permits the analytic calculation of the averages required for the local field factor (ie, the G of Eq. (7)). The long-range dipole-dipole correlation makes different contributions to the averages which occur for the longitudinal and transverse dipole densities; compare, for example, the mean square molecular dipole densities

$$< |{}^O\underline{M}_T|^2 > = 2 < \sum_{ij} \mu_x^i \mu_x^j e^{ikz^{ij}} >$$ (32)

and

$$< |{}^O\underline{M}_L|^2 > = < \sum_{ij} \mu_z^i \mu_z^j e^{ikz^{ij}} >$$ (33)

where we have used a coordinate system in which $\underline{k}$ defines the z direction. If two molecules lie along the x axis, so that the exponential factor is unity, the transverse average receives a positive contribution if the molecular dipoles are parallel and receives a negative contribution if the dipoles are antiparallel and along z (ie, side by side and antiparallel). These are the configurations favoured by the dipole-dipole interaction energy. Consideration of other configurations will show that the long-range dipole-dipole correlation enhances $< |{}^O\underline{M}_T|^2 >$ and diminishes $< |{}^O\underline{M}_L|^2 >$ (Madden and Kivelson, 1984). Similarly, the long range correlation has a different effect on the local-field factors for the longitudinal and transverse dipoles. It can be shown that the transverse local field factor is

$$G_T = \frac{<{}^O\underline{M}_T \cdot {}^I\underline{M}_T>}{<{}^O\underline{M}_T \cdot {}^O\underline{M}_T>} = G^{LR} + \delta$$ (34)

and the longitudinal is

$$G_L = \frac{<{}^O\underline{M}_L \cdot {}^I\underline{M}_L>}{<{}^O\underline{M}_L \cdot {}^O\underline{M}_L>} = -2G^{LR} + \delta$$

where G^{LR} is the contribution from the long-range dipolar correlation and δ is the short-range contribution. G^{LR} is the only contribution to G_T and G_L in the simplified model (and the Frölich formula); furthermore, the G^{LR} may be calculated analytically in the model. The simulation results gave $G_T = 0.173$ and $G_L = -0.412$, whereas the model predicts $G_T = 0.211$ and $G_L = -0.422$.

This finding suggests that the large interaction-induced dipole is largely the result of long-range dipole-dipole correlations;

658

this component is contained within the Frölich formula.

CONCLUSION

The computer simulation studies have shown the tremendous importance of induced effects in the spectra of molecular liquids. The timescale separation condition has been found to hold in some cases, but not in others. The simulations have exposed the difficulties in the way of quantitative theories of local field factors. These (particularly in light scattering) require better models for the liquid structure and more reliable accounts of the effects of the distribution of polarisable matter and of the influence of higher-order DID terms.

REFERENCES

Bancewicz, T., 1983, Mol. Phys., 50:173.

Battaglia, M. R., Cox, T. I., and Madden, P. A., 1979, Mol. Phys., 37:1413.

Buckingham, A. D., 1967, Adv. Chem. Phys., 12:107.

Buckingham, A. D., and Tabisz, G. C., 1978, Mol. Phys., 36:583.

Cox, T. I., Battaglia, M. R., and Madden, P. A., 1979, Mol. Phys., 38:1539.

Cox, T. I., and Madden, P. A., 1981, Mol. Phys., 43:307; 1980, 39:1437.

De Santis, A., and Sampoli, M., 1984, Mol. Phys., 51:97; 1982, 46:1271.

Detyna, E., Singer, K., Singer, J. V. L., and Taylor, A. J., 1980, Mol. Phys., 41:31.

Edwards, D. M. F., and Madden, P. A., 1984, Mol. Phys., 51:1163.

Frenkel, D., and McTague, J. P., 1980, J. Chem. Phys., 72:2801.

Frommhold, L., 1981, Adv. Chem. Phys., 46:1.

Keyes, T., Kivelson, D., and McTague, J. P., 1971, J. Chem. Phys., 55:4096.

Kielich, S., 1982, J. Phys., 43:1749.

Ladanyi, B. M., 1983, J. Chem. Phys., 78:2189.

Ladanyi, B. M., 1985, this volume.

Madden, P. A., and Kivelson, D., 1984, Adv. Chem. Phys., 51:467.

Madden, P. A., 1984, in: "Interaction-Induced Effects in Molecular Liquids," A.J. Barnes, ed., Reidel.

Madden, P. A., and Tildesley, D. J., 1984, Interaction-Induced Contributions to the Rayleigh and Allowed Raman Bands of CS_2, Mol. Phys., to be published.

Perrot, M., and Lascombe, J., 1985, this volume.

Rowlinson, J. S., 1959, in: "Liquids and Liquid Mixtures," Butterworth, London.

Sampoli, M., 1985, this volume.

Stell, G., Patey, G. N., and Hoye, J. S., 1981, Adv. Chem. Phys., 48:183.

Tildesley, D. J., and Madden, P. A., 1981, Mol. Phys., 42:1137.

INTERACTION INDUCED SPECTRA OF "LARGE" MOLECULES

IN LIQUIDS

Thomas Dorfmüller

Fakultät für Chemie
Universität Bielefeld
D-4800 Bielefeld, FRG

ABSTRACT

The induced dipole correlation functions obtained from far
infrared spectra of several liquid alkanes, alkenes, and some of
their chloro-derivatives are discussed in terms of the molecular
mass/moment of inertia, dipole moment, symmetry, and internal
configurations. The experimental integrated absorption and effective
dipole moments are discussed on the basis of molecular structure.

INTRODUCTION

The molecular dynamics of molecules in liquids or liquid like
phases is dominated by the random interactions of the molecules.
This interaction has, to a varying degree, observable consequences
upon the spectral features of the molecule. Low frequency spectra,
i.e. at or below thermal frequencies, are sensitive to perturbations
of thermal origin and are thus more convenient for the study of
liquid dynamics than, for example, electronic spectra. It is
generally accepted that the interaction induced effects can be more
easily studied in liquids consisting of "simple" molecules, which
means that the molecules should be compact, preferably of spherical
or nearly spherical shape, and rigid, i.e. free of internal conformational degrees of freedom. These restrictions are indeed useful in
that they allow us to treat molecules as rigid convex polarizable
bodies interacting with each other by means of electrical forces,
which can be ascribed to well localized charges within the molecules.
The parameters characterizing the various molecular interactions can
thus be reduced to a small number, like center-to-center distances
and angles describing the mutual orientation of the molecules. The

661

problem then reduces to the calculation of molecular correlations in configurational space, where the number of the dimensions of this space is kept sufficiently small.

The study of "large" and hence more complex molecules seems thus, at present, unyielding mainly because of the necessity of a theoretical treatment in a highly multidimensional configurational space. On the other hand, a large number of experimental data on complex liquids have been published, often because the practical interest in learning something about these liquids has dominated the scepticism regarding the feasibility of even a qualitative understanding of the results. Concentrating on the far infrared absorption spectra, one sees that simple as well as complex liquids display at first glance very similar, rather simple spectral features. This similarity between otherwise very different liquids is an indication that complex liquids actually may be in some important respects very similar in their dynamics to the more simple liquids. This seems to be the case for processes taking place in the time scale below 1 psec. This aspect of molecular dynamics is elaborated below and some experimental evidence is provided to indicate that interaction induced far infrared spectra can be used indeed to probe the molecular dynamics of complex liquids.

Generally, intermolecular spectral effects are induced when the surface atoms of two polyatomic molecules approach each other at a distance sufficiently small to produce an observable, time dependent dipole. When dealing with larger molecules, we must consider the effect of frame distortion and, in addition to the intermolecular effects, in some cases intramolecular induction processes. The mechanism of intramolecular interaction induced spectral effects is similar to the mechanism known to be effective in intermolecular spectroscopy. Thus, transient dipoles are likely to be induced in a molecule whenever the intramolecular charge distribution distorts the polarizable electron distribution, this distortion being modulated by the internal motions. If, on the other hand, the internal motion is describable in terms of a conformational transition separated by an energy barrier of the order of kT or less, then the intramolecular induced effect will be, in many respects, similar to an intermolecular spectrum. The conditions for the observation of the latter kind of spectra are often fulfilled by intramolecular torsional modes. It is very probable that, in addition to accidental overlapping between inter- and intramolecular bands, these are physically coupled and hence basically non separable. In order to study this situation, it appears, in the first place, necessary to survey a large number of far infrared spectra of different species, and to attempt to classify them according to the nature of the motions which might be potential candidates for the observed bands.

Interaction induced far infrared spectral lines are present in all kinds of liquids and can, in principle, be studied in polar as well as non-polar liquids. In the former case, however, the presence of a permanent dipole reorientation spectrum may seriously hinder the separate study of the interaction induced component. In spite of

662

this difficulty, a localized dipole in a molecule does not only appear in the spectrum as a dipole reorientation feature, but it will also be a source of an induced spectral component. A separation of these two components is possible if the time scales of the dynamics of the single dipoles on the one hand, and the relative motion of a polarizable structural unit relative to the dipole, on the other, are sufficiently separated. This also may open the way to the study of intermolecular dynamics of non-rigid molecules where the molecular dipole is localized in a different part of the molecule than its most polarizable parts. The possible advantage of studying intramolecular induced spectra comes from the fact that the relative positions of the inducing and the polarizable parts are constrained to move in a narrow range in configurational space, as opposed to the largely random distribution of relative intermolecular positions and motions in a liquid.

EXPERIMENTAL AND DATA ANALYSIS

The spectra upon which the discussion of the following sections is based have all been obtained with a Fourier transform far infrared spectrometer, Polytec IR-30 (Tibulski 1980; Arning 1980 and 1983). The instrument was provided with a high pressure mercury arc light source, a Michelson interferometer, an externally interchangable Mylar beam splitter and Golay detector. The whole instrument was operated under vacuum. The twin cells were machined from an aluminum block with the main cell and the reference cell in good thermal contact. The whole block could be thermostated to $\pm 1^{O}C$. The windows of both cells consisted of high pressure polyethylene or, in some cases, of silicon. By means of spacers, the thickness of the liquid samples could be adjusted from 0.2 to 0.4 mm. Usually, the moving interferometer mirror was displaced so far that the resolution was 1 wavenumber.

The confidence limits for the measured absorption varies strongly with the wavenumber setting, mainly as a consequence of the weak source power of the low frequency region. Thus, below 10 to 15 wavenumbers, the noise was very large. Therefore, the spectra were taken at larger values of $\tilde{\nu}$. On the other hand, at wavenumbers larger than 100 or 200, we generally observe an absorption peak due to internal liberations or combination bands which in many cases overlap with the spectra of interest. In order to minimize the effect of this band on the low-frequency spectra under study, the former was either included in the form of a Lorentzian into the fitting procedure, or the fit was carried out in the range where the overlap was not significant. Both experimental restrictions entail an incertitude as to the precise shape of the spectrum at low and at high wavenumbers.

The data analysis by which the dipole correlation functions are obtained from the experimental absorption spectra involves the following steps (Rothschild 1984; Flygare 1978; Gordon 1960; Mori 1965):

a) Fitting the Mori-type three variable spectral function to the
experimental spectrum given by Eq. 1, thus obtaining the constants E,
K_o, K_1 and γ:

$$\alpha(\tilde{\nu}) = \frac{E \, \gamma \, K_o \, K_1 \, \tilde{\nu}^2}{\gamma^2(K_o-\tilde{\nu}^2)^2+\tilde{\nu}^2(\tilde{\nu}^2-(K_o+K_1))^2} \tag{1}$$

b) Transforming the absorption spectrum in a power spectrum by

$$I(\tilde{\nu}) = \frac{3hcn \, \alpha(\tilde{\nu})}{8\pi^3 c\tilde{\nu}[1-\exp(-hc\tilde{\nu}/kT)]} \tag{2}$$

where c is the speed of light and n the index of refraction of the
sample.
c) Fourier transforming the power spectrum to obtain the dipole correlation function by Eq. 3, either numerically or analytically, the
constants Γ, η, ζ and b being known functions of E, K_o, K_1, γ,

$$c(t) = \frac{\Gamma \exp(-\zeta t) + \left[\frac{\eta + \Gamma\zeta}{b} \sin(bt) + \cos(bt)\right] \exp(-\eta t)}{1 + \Gamma} \tag{3}$$

The normalized experimental dipole correlation functions, on which
the following discussions are based, are defined by means of the following equation:

$$c(t) = \frac{< \vec{M}(0) \cdot \vec{M}(t) >}{< \vec{M}(0) \cdot \vec{M}(0) >} \tag{4}$$

$\vec{M}(t)$ is the value of the macroscopic dipole moment at the time t,
either permanent or induced, resulting from a summation of the molecular dipoles over an equilibrium ensemble.

INTERMOLECULAR SPECTRA AND DIPOLE CORRELATION FUNCTIONS OF
HYDROCARBONS AND SOME OF THEIR CHLORO-DERIVATIVES

The far infrared spectra of liquid hydrocarbons which consist of
non-polar or only weakly polar molecules reflect their interaction
dynamics. However, the question arises as to the nature of the
motions reflected in the spectrum, i.e. whether we have to consider
both translational and rotational motions, and whether the spectra
are shaped mainly by the motions of the molecules as a whole as is
the case with smaller molecules, or whether internal motions must
also be taken into account. The spectra of the first members of the
alkane series along with ethylene and carbon tetrachloride are displayed in Fig. 1. It is immediately obvious that the spectra differ
clearly in many respects. Thus, the peak intensities differ by as
much as a factor of five, the positions of the absorption maxima vary
from 50 to 180 wavenumbers, and the bandshapes are also different.
All of these molecules are non-polar, or only very weakly polar.
More specifically, within the alkane series, with increasing molecular weight, the absorption peaks shift to lower frequencies, and
the widths of the spectra decreases. The ethylene spectrum, although
very similar to the ethane spectrum, is much stronger and is shifted
to lower frequencies. This indicates that the moments of inertia and
the dipole moments, which both are very similar in these molecules,

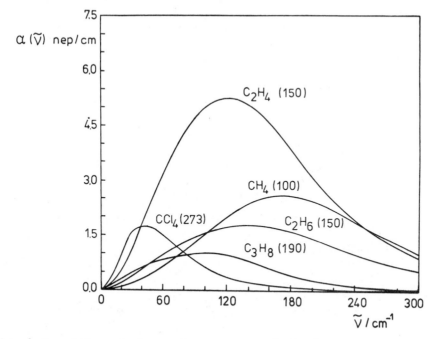

Fig. 1 Far infrared absorption spectra of the lower hydrocarbons
and carbon tetrachloride. The temperatures in K are indicated in parentheses.

are not the only molecular quantities which must be responsible for
the differences of the observed spectral features. At the low
frequency side of the scale lies the spectrum of carbon tetrachloride, as expected from its much larger mass/ moment of inertia as
compared with the hydrocarbons. It should be noted that all of the
spectra in this figure are basically interaction induced and,
consequently, the peak absorption coefficient is relatively small, in
the range from 1.6 to 5.5 neper/cm.

The power spectra of the three alkanes and of ethylene are shown
in Fig. 2. They are calculated from the absorption spectra by means
of Eq. 2 and illustrate even better the progression in the alkane
series, manifested in the half widths at half heights (HWHH) and in
the intensity at zero wavenumber. Here, the spectrum of ethylene
appears also with a much larger amplitude but with a HWHH of 71 cm^{-1},
similar to the ethane value of 77 cm^{-1}. The discussion of the differences between these spectra, and hence between the molecular
dynamics involved, can be made more fruitful on the basis of the
pertinent dipole correlation functions. Figure 3 shows the logarithmic plots of the correlation functions of the three lower alkanes.
In all cases we can distinguish the inertial (short time) and the
diffusive (long time) regimes, the latter being practically absent in
methane. This peculiarity of methane has been described, loosely
speaking, as the dominance of free rotation over the motion deter-

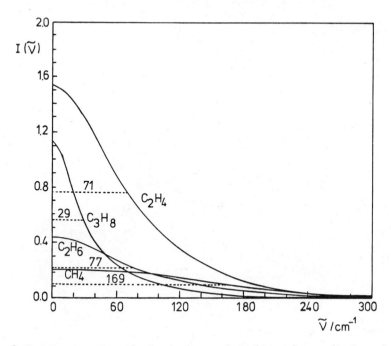

Fig. 2 Power spectra of the hydrocarbon liquids, calculated from
the absorption spectra in Fig. 1.

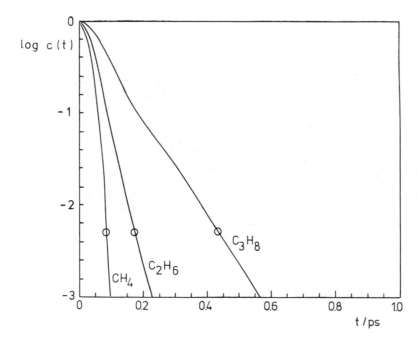

Fig. 3 Correlation functions of the three lower alkane
       liquids. The circles on the curves indicate that the
       molecules are basically non-polar.

mined by the dissipation through intermolecular perturbations. One
can describe the situation more precisely by recalling that molecular
dipoles, either permanent or induced, absorb radiation by rotational
quantum transitions. At sufficiently short times, this will give
rise to a correlation function describing the loss of coherence of an
equilibrium ensemble of independent free rotors. At longer times,
the time dependent intermolecular torques in the liquid will produce
random perturbations of the molecular dipoles dissipating their
angular momentum. This will eventually decrease the decay rate of
the angular correlations at times long enough for the intermolecular
torques to become effective. Additionally, the induced dipoles will
undergo a random modulation by the collective rearrangement, comprising both translational and rotational motions of the molecules of
the cage leading to a change of the local field at the reference
molecule. This process is also dissipative and contributes, together
with the dissipation of the molecular angular momentum, to the long
time exponential section observed in the correlation functions. This
effect by which the local inducing field is modulated by the dynamics
of the cage contains rotational and translational components which,
however, are very difficult to separate. Now, depending on the molecular dynamics and the local structural correlations in each liquid,
the onset of the diffusive regime will become predominant earlier or

later with respect to the inertial regime, thus leading to quite
different, but characteristic, shapes of the correlation functions.
In this frame, one would say that the lifetime of the cage around the
reference molecule in methane is long enough to permit something like
an unperturbed reorientation of the molecule to occur. On the
contrary, the rotation of the larger molecules is slower and the
environment fluctuations randomize the cage in a time which is short
relative to the time required for a full rotation. This is clearly
illustrated in Fig. 3, where both the free rotator and the dissipative correlation times are seen to increase with the size of the
molecule but, contrary to the case of methane, the diffusive regime
for the larger molecules is clearly distinguished from the initial
free rotor decay in the form of a linear section in the logarithmic
plot after a time of approximately 0.1 to 0.2 psec in ethane and
propane, respectively.

    The effect of the molecular mass/ moment of inertia is
demonstrated in Fig. 4 which shows that both the inertial and the
dissipative parts of the correlation functions are strongly affected
by the increase of the molecular mass by a factor of six, between
ethylene and tetrachloroethylene. The two alkene molecules, in which
the quadrupole is the leading multipole responsible for the induced
dipole moment, are directly comparable. On the other hand, the CCl_4

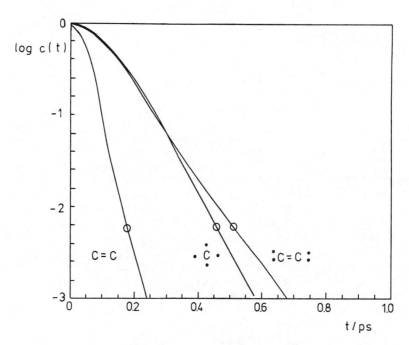

Fig. 4 Correlation functions of ethylene, carbon tetrachloride and
    tetrachloroethylene. The black dots indicate the chlorine
    atoms. The hydrogen atoms are not indicated.

molecule, being a molecule with an octupole as the leading multipole, displays a faster decay of its interaction induced dipole in the dissipation regime. The difference between the two chloro-compounds is presumably not only due to the stronger and more permanent orientational correlation in C_2Cl_4, but also to the shorter range of the inducing electric field of CCl_4. A comparison of the correlation functions of some structurally similar simple molecules is made in Fig. 5. The simple mass/ moment of inertia effect is again visible in the comparison of methane and carbon tetrachloride. However, the correlation functions of methylene chlorid and chloroform are much more long lived, despite the lower molecular mass relative to carbon tetrachloride. One possible reason is obvious since these two molecules have a permanent dipole moment and thus the spectra involve different molecular mechanisms than the spectra of the non-polar molecules. Thus, in principle, the observed spectra may stem from the rotation of permanent molecular dipoles, and/or from the time dependence of dipole induced dipoles.

It should be noted that the general appearance of the correlation functions is quite similar to those of the non-polar molecules, and that the effect of mass/ moment of inertia is also manifested in the differences of the decay rates of the correlation functions of methylene chloride and chloroform. It is important to note that, as can be seen in the Table 1, the integrated absorption of the two polar molecules $CHCl_3$ and CH_2Cl_2 are 24 and 31 nep/cm^2, respectively,

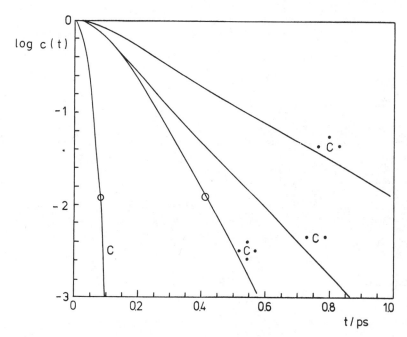

Fig. 5 Correlation functions of tetrahedral molecules. The black dots indicate the chlorine atoms.

Table 1: Static and dynamic properties of some hydrocarbons and their chloroderivatives (Tibulski 1980; Arning 1980 and 1983). A is the integrated absorption coefficient. The square of the effective dipole moment, μ_{eff}, is proportional to the integral $\int \alpha(\tilde{\nu})/\tilde{\nu}^2 \, d\tilde{\nu}$. The dipole moments in column 2 are taken from McClellan (1963). The asterisk (*) indicates a configurational dependent dipole moment. The extremely weak dipole moments observed in saturated hydrocarbons have been neglected (Rothschild et al., 1975). The prefix "t" indicates the trans-isomer.

Substance	μ/D	A $10^{-3}/nep.cm^2$	μ_{eff}/D	τ/ps
CH_4	0	0.32	0	0.03
CH_2Cl_2	1.8	31	4.1	0.27
$CHCl_3$	1.2	24	1.2	0.49
CCl_4	0	0.15	0.1	0.15
$CH_2=CH_2$	0	0.98	0.14	0.07
$t-CHCl=CHCl$	0	0.80	0.38	0.23
$CCl_2=CH_2$	1.3	31	1.3	0.52
$CCl_2=CHCl$	0.8	0.64	0.75	0.47
$CCl_2=CCl_2$	0	0.10	0.08	0.22
CH_3-CH_3	0	0.40	0.38	0.07
CH_2Cl-CH_2Cl	*	16	2.73	0.31
CCl_3-CH_3	1.6	2.3	3.33	2.05
CCl_3-CH_2Cl	1.2	0.90	1.38	0.80
$CHCl_2-CHCl_2$	1.4	0.80	0.90	0.43
CCl_3-CHCl_2	1	0.26	0.81	0.52
$CH_3-CH_2-CH_3$	0	0.15	0.02	0.20

i.e. by one to two orders of magnitude larger than those of the non-polar molecules. With this in mind, the similarity of the correlation functions is no surprise. This can be taken as a clue for a common dynamic basis reflected in the spectra of non-polar molecules. Actually, the former are purely interaction induced, whereas the latter may, in principle, have one component due to the reorientation of the permanent dipole and another one due to the time dependence of the dipole-induced dipole. The molecular dynamics reflected in the interaction induced spectra depend on the anisotropy fluctuations of the local electric fields which are complex functions of the collective translational and rotational motions, and of the ranges of the various inducing multipole fields. Generally, this latter mechanism is more subject to intermolecular perturbations than the single-molecule reorientation mechanism which mainly shapes the spectra of polar molecules. These perturbations tend to destroy the temporal coherence, and as a consequence we observe a faster decay of the corresponding correlation functions.

The single molecule reorientation mechanism, giving rise to the absorption by polar molecules in liquids, often lies in a frequency range too low to be observed, below 20 cm^{-1}. On the other hand, as a consequence of the longer range of the dipole field, the correlation functions of the dipole-induced dipole spectra display larger correlation times than the spectra due to higher multipoles. Thus the difference of the correlation functions of polar molecules as compared to those of the non-polar molecules may be attributed to a large extent to the different ranges of the respective inducing fields. The correlation times listed in column 5 of the Table 1 support this interpretation since they all lie in the range of a few tenths of a picosecond, whereas the overall reorientation times of the same or similar molecules ($CHCl_3$, CH_2Cl_2, CH_3CN) as measured by band contur analysis of vibration-rotation spectral lines are larger by up to one order of magnitude (Rothschild 1984; Grifiths 1973; Maryott and Birnbaum 1956).

The correlation functions illustrated in Fig. 6 can be now rationalized on the basis of what we know from simpler molecules. The molecules of this figure are all rigid, with a common ethylene backbone. The three non-polar molecules have correlation functions ordered according to the increasing ratio of mass and moment of inertia. The correlation functions of the two polar molecules are again much slower, in agreement with what was said above. However, the heavier molecule displays a faster decay than the lighter one. This can be rationalized by considering the structure of these molecules in some more detail. The dipole moment of 1,1-dichloro-ethylene is directed along the main axis, whereas in 1,1,2-trichloro-ethylene the dipole has a component normal to this axis. This means that in the latter molecule intermolecular torques about the parallel as well as about the perpendicular axes will lead to changes of the induced dipole by single-molecule rotation. In contrast, in the former molecule, the torques resulting in a perturbation of the rotation about the parallel axis will not contribute to the decay of

671

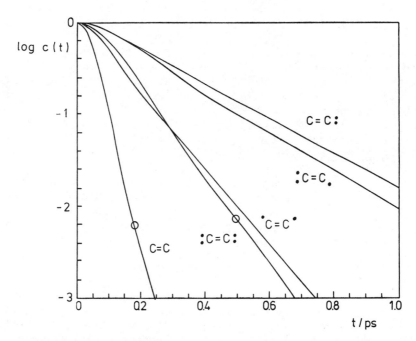

Fig. 6 Dipole correlation functions of the ethylene series. The
circles and parallel lines mark the non-polar molecules,
and the molecules with a permanent dipole parallel to the
symmetry axis, respectively.

the correlation function. Furthermore, due to the asymmetry in the
mass distribution in 1,1-dichloroethylene the dissipative reorientation of this molecule will be more strongly subjected to the environmental friction than in the more balanced molecule. This is also
manifested in the dominance of the linear region over the free
rotator region at shorter times of the correlation function, a
general feature of the non-polar molecules.

A similar observation can be made in ethane and the substituted
ethanes as displayed in Fig. 7. The correlation function of the non-
polar molecule decays more rapidly; the heavier polar molecules,
forming a separate group, are ordered roughly according to their
molecular weights. The exception is again the unbalanced 1,1,1-tri-
chloroethane molecule which is expected to exhibit an abnormally
slowly decaying correlation function, for the same reasons previously
pointed out. The same argument may be invoked for 1,1,1,2-tetra-
chloroethane whose difference to 1,1,1,2,2-pentachloroethane is
inverse to the trend expected from the relation of their respective
molecular mass/ moment of inertia.

In Fig. 8 we see that the correlation function of the single

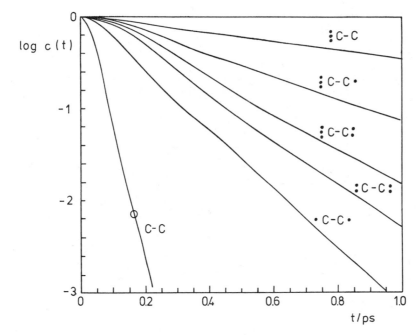

Fig. 7 Dipole correlation functions of the ethane series. The circles and parallel lines have the same meaning as in Fig. 6.

bonded alkane molecule has a slower decay time as compared to the more rigid alkene. The same situation is illustrated in Fig. 9 but, since the two molecules differ also significantly in their molecular mass, the situation is somewhat ambiguous. Both figures, however, provide an argument for the influence of conformational degrees of freedom on the lifetime of correlations. Likewise, the increase in correlation times of propane as compared to ethane shown in the Table 1 is larger than the increase in molecular mass/ moment of inertia of these molecules can rationalize.

A further question which is raised in connection with the con- formational degrees of freedom is the size of the molecular dipole moment which depends upon the molecular conformation, increasing with temperature in some of the liquids, like 1,2-dichloroethane. In this liquid, the more polar gauche configuration is increasingly populated at higher temperatures. Especially in large molecules, given the short range character of the pertinent interactions, we would expect that the DID correlation function rather correlates with the local dipole moment in a given conformation of the interacting molecules than with the total molecular dipole moment.

An argument in favor of using the local dipole instead of the

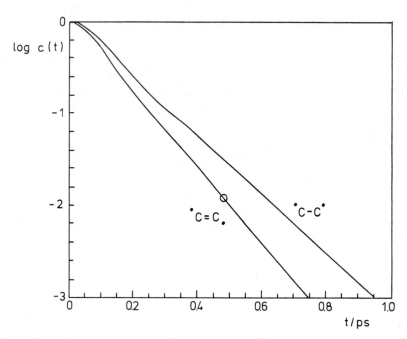

Fig. 8 Dipole correlation functions of the two symmetrically substituted 1,2-dichlorocompounds.

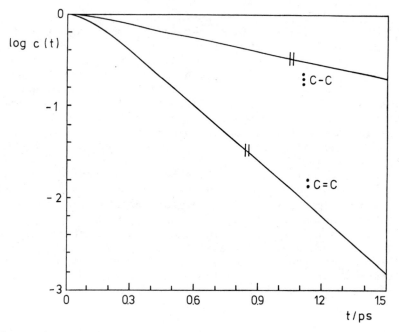

Fig. 9 Dipole correlation functions of the 1-substituted compounds having their dipole moments parallel to the molecular symmetry axes.

overall molecular dipole is furnished by considering the experiemtal effective dipole moments listed in column 4 of the Table 1. The molecular dipole moments of the polar substances in column 2 of the Table 1 lie in the range between 0.8 and 1.8 D. The values of the effective dipole moments correlate with these, the ratio μ/μ_{eff} varying from 0.7 to 1.2, with the notable exception of the two strongest dipoles, CH_2Cl_2 and CCl_3-CH_3. Since the effective dipole moment, as calculated from the spectra, depends upon molecular conformation as well as upon the strength of the induced dipoles, this result is not unexpected.

Another feature of the molecular dynamics of the liquids considered is the appearance, in some cases, of very intense torsional liberation bands in the high frequency range of the absorption spectra, roughly from 100 to 300 wavenumbers. These lines, in many cases symmetry forbidden, appear in the liquid phase spectra as a consequence of the intermolecular perturbation. There is a significant amount of mixing of these lines with the intermolecular lines. Obviously, we are not allowed to neglect the interactions between the overall rotation of the molecule around the parallel C-C axis and the internal rotation of the two groups. Taking this into account would amount to analyzing both motions on a common basis instead of artificially separating the two lines, thus neglecting any cross correlations. The activation energies of these tosional motions vary from approximately 0.7 kJ/mol for ethane to 3.4 kJ/mol for pentachloroethane (Orville-Thomas 1974; Weiss and Leroi 1968; Fateley and Miller 1963; Schwendeman and Jacobs 1962; Brier et al. 1971; Allen et al. 1967). This can, in some cases, lead to the occurence of distinct rotamers in the liquid which may also contribute to some of the differences observed in the interaction induced spectra of the alkane and alkene derivatives.

CONCLUSIONS

This survey of the spectral features and the corresponding dipole correlation functions of seventeen structurally and chemically related substances has shown that a systematic comparison of this kind can be useful in obtaining an estimate for the factors which affect the dynamics of molecules in a liquid. The interaction induced absorption, which is always present in this frequency range, in some cases can be separated from the permanent dipole reorientation; in other cases the borderline is not so clear. It appears promising to use more systematically the inducing effect produced by permanent dipoles of known strengths on highly polarizable molecules. This could be of particular interest for the study of the dynamics of large molecules with internal conformational degrees of freedom.

Acknowledgments: The major part of this work was performed under a project of the "Minister für Wissenschaft und Forschung", Düssel-

675

dorf. The financial aid of the "Fonds der Chemischen Industrie" is also gratefully acknowledged.

REFERENCES

Allen, G., Brier, P. N., and Lane, G., 1967, Trans. Faraday Soc., 63:824.

Arning, H.-J., 1980, Thesis, University of Bielefeld, FRG.

Arning, H.-J., 1983, Dissertation, University of Bielefeld, FRG.

Brier, P. N., Higgins, J. S., and Bradley, R. H., 1971, Mol. Phys., 21:72.

Fateley, W. G., and Miller, F. A., 1963, Spectrochim. Acta, 19:611.

Flygare, W. H., 1978, "Molecular Structure and Dynamics", Prentice Hall Inc., U.S.A.

Gordon, R. G., 1960, J. Chem. Phys., 44:1830.

Grifiths, J. E., 1973, J. Chem. Phys., 59:751.

Maryott, A. A., and Birnbaum, G., 1956, J. Chem. Phys., 24:1022.

McClellan, A. L., 1963, "Tables of Experimental Dipole Moments", Freeman & Co., U.S.A.

Mori, H., 1965, Progr. Theoret. Phys., 33:423.

Orville-Thomas, W. J. (ed.), 1974, "Internal Rotation in Molecules", Wiley, U.S.A.

Rothschild, W. G., Rosacco, G. J., and Livingston, R. C., 1975, J. Chem. Phys., 62:1253.

Rothschild, W. G., 1984, "Dynamics of Molecular Liquids", Wiley and Sons, U.S.A.

Schwendeman, R. H., and Jacobs, J. D., 1962, J. Chem. Phys., 36:1245.

Tibulski, K., 1980, Thesis, University of Bielefeld, FRG.

Weiss, S., and Leroi, G., 1968, J. Chem. Phys., 48:962.

THE INFRARED SPECTRUM OF HD

J.D. Poll

Guelph Waterloo Programme for Graduate Work in Physics
University of Guelph Campus
Guelph, Ontario, Canada N1G 2W1

ABSTRACT

Recent progress in the understanding of the infrared
spectrum of HD is reviewed. Emphasis is given to features
associated with the heteronuclear nature of this molecule. The
properties of the allowed dipole and of dipoles induced in a pair
of molecules are considered in some detail. The appearance of
sharp spectral features, which are characteristic of heteronuclear molecules in general, is discussed both in the approximation of isotropic intermolecular interactions and more
generally. An attempt has been made to review all experimental
and theoretical work prior to January 1985.

INTRODUCTION

The infrared absorption of HD is predominantly due to the
effect of intermolecular interactions. This "interaction
induced" spectrum is caused by dipoles created in pairs of
interacting molecules and resembles that of the homonuclear
hydrogens H_2 and D_2. Because HD is heteronuclear however, it is
also expected to show an allowed absorption spectrum like other
dipolar molecules. In the special case of HD, where the allowed
dipole is due to nonadiabatic effects, the purely allowed
absorption is very much smaller than the induced one. This
unique circumstance, in which the induced dipoles tend to be
larger than the allowed dipole, makes HD an exceptionally
interesting case for studying the influence of interaction
induced effects on allowed spectra. Such effects are, of course,

677

present in the spectra of all molecules, but they are usually overshadowed by an allowed absorption which is much larger than the induced one. A particularly interesting phenomenon, which arises when both the allowed and induced dipoles occur, is the presence of absorption associated with the interference of these two different kinds of dipoles.

In this paper a review will be given of those aspects of the spectra of HD which are due to its heteronuclear nature, i.e. the aspects in which it differs from the homonuclear hydrogens. Although these differences, as pointed out above, are relatively minor they are of considerable interest both in themselves and in the relevance they have to the study of induced effects in spectroscopy in general.

THE ALLOWED AND INDUCED DIPOLE MOMENTS OF HD

The heteronuclear nature of HD suggests that an isolated molecule should have an allowed, or permanent, electric dipole moment. Because the two nuclei in an HD molecule have equal charge however, this dipole moment is very small. In fact, in the adiabatic approximation, in which the electrons are assumed to be able to follow the relatively slow nuclear motion perfectly, the dipole moment is zero. Put more precisely, the dipole moment function, $p(r)$, defined, in the adiabatic approximation, as the expectation value of the electric dipole moment operator in the ground electronic state

$$p(r) = \langle \sum_j e_j z_j \rangle \tag{1}$$

is equal to zero for all values of the internuclear separation r. The coordinate system used in this definition has its origin at the midpoint between the nuclei and its z-axis along the internuclear axis; the sum in (1) is over all particles in the molecule. The adiabatic approximation is a very good one, even for light molecules, and any deviations from it are expected to give rise to small effects only. The matrix elements of the nonadiabatic dipole can therefore be calculated by introducing the nonadiabatic part of the Hamiltonian as a perturbation. Strictly speaking, these matrix elements cannot be written in the form of matrix elements of a function of the internuclear separation defined on a molecule-fixed coordinate system. It turns out however, that to a good approximation this is still possible and we will accordingly introduce a function $p^A(r)$, describing the nonadiabatic allowed dipole moment, in our considerations. Its value at $r = r_e$, $p^A(r_e)$, is often referred to as the "permanent" dipole and is of order 8×10^{-4} D.

The fact that HD has a small allowed dipole was first pointed out by Wick in 1935; his estimate for the $v = 0 \rightarrow 1$ matrix element was within a factor of two of the presently accepted value of approximately 0.5×10^{-4} D. The first experimental observations of the fundamental and overtone bands of the dipole spectrum of HD were by Herzberg (1950) and Durie and Herzberg (1960); the pure rotational spectrum was first observed by Trefler and Gush (1968) and by Trefler, Cappel and Gush (1969). Early theoretical work was reported by Wu (1952), Blinder (1960, 1961), Kolos and Wolniewicz (1966), Karl (1968), Karl and Poll (1970), Poll and Karl (1973), Bunker (1973), and by Wolniewicz and Kowalski (1973). During the last decade considerable progress has been made in the understanding of the infrared spectrum of HD. Accurate theoretical calculations of the matrix elements of the allowed dipole have been made by Wolniewicz (1975, 1976) and by Ford and Browne (1977) for a number of rotational lines in the $v = 0 \rightarrow v = 0,1,2,3,4,5$ bands. The results of these two sets of theoretical calculations agree rather well with each other. The accuracy of the experimental determination of the allowed dipole has also been improved considerably during the last decade. These experimental results will be discussed in more detail in the next section.

We now consider a pair of interacting molecules, either two HD molecules or, an HD molecule together with a collision partner (usually a rare gas atom). Such a pair of molecules has a so-called "interaction-induced" dipole which, in contrast to the dipole on an isolated molecule, is already different from zero in the adiabatic approximation. In this approximation the energy eigenfunctions of a pair of molecules are products of electronic wave functions, $\phi(x_1 x_2)$, where x_1 and x_2 denote the electronic coordinates of the two molecules 1 and 2, and of nuclear wave functions $u(\vec{r}_1 \vec{r}_2 \vec{R})$ describing the nuclear motion in terms of the internuclear separations $\vec{r}_1$ and $\vec{r}_2$ and the distance $\vec{R}$ between the centres of mass of the molecules. The electronic wave function is calculated for fixed positions of the nuclei and therefore depends parametrically on the nuclear coordinates: $\phi(x_1 x_2) \equiv \phi(x_1 x_2; \vec{r}_1 \vec{r}_2 \vec{R})$. Taking the expectation value of the dipole moment operator of the two molecules over the electronic ground state $\phi_0(x_1 x_2; \vec{r}_1 \vec{r}_2 \vec{R})$ yields the induced dipole $\vec{\mu}^I(\vec{r}_1 \vec{r}_2 \vec{R})$ as a function of nuclear coordinates in the adiabatic approximation. As will be discussed in more detail later on, the induced dipole for an HD pair, or for an HD-atom pair, contains contributions that satisfy the same selection rules as the allowed dipole. On the other hand, the allowed dipole itself, being nonadiabatic, is not included in the definition of $\vec{\mu}^I$ given above. There are, of course, also nonadiabatic interaction induced contributions to the dipole of a pair of molecules. These contributions are expected to represent only small corrections to the adiabatic ones however, and will therefore be neglected. Finally, the total dipole moment of a pair of HD molecules will be written as

$$\vec{\mu}(\vec{r}_1\vec{r}_2\vec{R}) = \vec{\mu}^A(\vec{r}_1) + \vec{\mu}^A(\vec{r}_2) + \vec{\mu}^I(\vec{r}_1\vec{r}_2\vec{R}), \tag{2}$$

where $\vec{\mu}^A(\vec{r}_1)$ denotes the allowed dipole of molecule 1 in an arbitrary space-fixed coordinate system. This representation of the dipole is that of Tipping, Poll and McKellar (1978). The dipole matrix elements are calculated by using the adiabatic nuclear wave functions $u(\vec{r}_1\vec{r}_2\vec{R})$ mentioned above. In the approximation in which the intermolecular interaction, U, depends only on the distance between the centres of mass of the molecules, U = U(R), these functions are given by products of internal and translational parts, and the spectrum has a very simple form as discussed in the next section.

It is convenient to expand the total dipole moment function (2) in terms of contributions that each have well defined transformation properties under rotation. In this expansion, first given by Poll and Van Kranendonk (1961), the spherical components of $\vec{\mu}$ in a space-fixed coordinate system are given by

$$\mu_\nu(\vec{r}_1\vec{r}_2\vec{R}) = \frac{(4\pi)^{3/2}}{\sqrt{3}} \sum_{\lambda_1\lambda_2\Lambda L} A_\Lambda(\lambda_1\lambda_2 L; r_1 r_2 R) \Psi_{1\nu}^{\lambda_1\lambda_2 L;\Lambda}(\vec{\omega}_1\vec{\omega}_2\vec{\Omega}) \tag{3}$$

where

$$\Psi_{1\nu}^{\lambda_1\lambda_2 L;\Lambda}(\vec{\omega}_1\vec{\omega}_2\vec{\Omega}) = \sum_{\mu_1,m} C(\Lambda L 1; m, \nu-m)$$

$$C(\lambda_1\lambda_2\Lambda;\mu_1,m-\mu_1) Y_{\lambda_1\mu_1}(\vec{\omega}_1) Y_{\lambda_2,m-\mu_1}(\vec{\omega}_2) Y_{L,\nu-m}(\vec{\Omega}) \tag{4}$$

In these expressions the internuclear separation vectors in the two molecules, $\vec{r}_1$ and $\vec{r}_2$, are represented by the scalar internuclear distances and unit vectors giving the orientation of the molecules in a space-fixed coordinate system where $\vec{r}_1 \equiv r_1$, ω_1, and $\vec{r}_2 \equiv r_2$, ω_2; similarly, $\vec{R} \equiv R$, Ω. The functions Y are spherical harmonics and the coefficients C are Clebsch-Gordan coefficients as defined by Rose (1957). It is evident that the angular functions Ψ in (4) transform like a vector under rotations and that the functions $A_\Lambda(\lambda_1\lambda_2 L; r_1 r_2 R)$ therefore furnish a coordinate-independent classification of the various possible components of the dipole moment. Each of these components is characterized by its symmetry, i.e. by specifying

λ_1, λ_2, L and Λ. For homonuclear diatomic molecules only even λ's can occur and, in addition, L must be odd. For heteronuclear molecules these restrictions do not apply; in all cases we have the parity requirement: $\lambda_1 + \lambda_2 + L$ is odd. Further discussions of this expansion and the alternative forms it can take are given by Poll and Hunt (1976) and by Tipping and Poll (1985). At long range, the A coefficients are, to a good approximation, given by the multipolar induction mechanism in which the dipole on one molecule is due to its polarization by the multipolar fields of the other. For the hydrogens the quadrupolar induction mechanism is the dominant one; it is described by the coefficients

$$A_2(203; r_1 r_2 R) = \sqrt{3}\, Q(r_1)\alpha(r_2)R^{-4}$$

$$A_2(023; r_1 r_2 R) = -\sqrt{3}\, \alpha(r_1)Q(r_2)R^{-4},$$

where α and Q denote the polarizability and quadrupole moment of the molecules respectively. At short range, the A coefficients are associated with the overlap of the electronic wave functions and are usually described by a model involving an exponential dependence on R. For simple molecules a priori calculations can be performed as discussed by Meyer elsewhere in this volume.

Both the allowed and the induced dipole can be expressed in terms of the expansion (3). For example, the part of the dipole with symmetry $\lambda_1 = 1$, $\lambda_2 = 0$ and $L = 0$ is, according to (3) and (4), given by

$$\mu_\nu = A_1(100; r_1 r_2 R) \left(\frac{4\pi}{3}\right)^{1/2} Y_{1\nu}(\vec{\omega}_1). \tag{5}$$

If only the allowed dipole on molecule 1 were present we would have $A_1(100; r_1 r_2 R) = p^A(r_1)$, where p^A is the molecule-fixed dipole moment function introduced earlier. In reality, there will be an induced dipole of this symmetry as well, provided we are dealing with a heteronuclear molecule like HD for which odd values of λ are allowed. The corresponding coefficient, $A_1(100; r_1 r_2 R)$, will therefore be the sum of the allowed part, $p^A(r_1)$, and an induced part, $p^I(r_1 r_2 R)$.

As pointed out above, the induced part of the dipole, $\vec{\mu}^I(\vec{r}_1 \vec{r}_2 \vec{R})$, can be calculated in the adiabatic approximation, i.e. for an electronic charge distribution associated with the nuclei of the two interacting molecules at rest. It follows that, in this approximation, the single dipole moment function $\vec{\mu}^I(\vec{r}_1 \vec{r}_2 \vec{R})$ is appropriate to all possible pairs of hydrogen molecules irrespective of whether we are dealing with H_2, D_2, HD, or with their mixtures. In $\vec{\mu}^I(\vec{r}_1 \vec{r}_2 \vec{R})$ the variable R denotes the separation of the internuclear midpoints of the two molecules.

Because of the symmetry of the adiabatic wave function under the inversion of the nuclei, only terms in which λ_1 and λ_2 are even (and L is odd) will appear in the expansion (3) of $\vec{\mu}^{I2}$. At first sight, the induced components with odd values of λ, that were mentioned above, would therefore appear to be excluded. This is not the case however, because the appropriate coordinates for a dynamical description of a pair of molecules are, apart from the internuclear separations, the displacement between the centres of mass of the molecules. For H_2 and D_2 the centre of mass coincides with the internuclear midpoint but for HD it does not. The complete induced dipole for a pair of HD molecules can therefore be obtained from that for a pair of H_2 molecules by a change of variables as discussed by Tipping et al. (1978) and Tipping and Poll (1985):

$$\vec{\mu}^{HD-HD}(\vec{r}_1\vec{r}_2\vec{R}) = \vec{\mu}^{H_2-H_2}\{\vec{r}_1\vec{r}_2;\ \vec{R} + \frac{1}{6}\ (\vec{r}_1-\vec{r}_2)\}$$

$$= \vec{\mu}^{H_2-H_2}(\vec{r}_1\vec{r}_2\vec{R}) + \frac{1}{6}\ (\vec{r}_1-\vec{r}_2)\cdot\nabla_R\vec{\mu}^{H_2-H_2}(\vec{r}_1\vec{r}_2\vec{R}) + \ldots \qquad (6)$$

A similar result holds for an HD-atom pair. For the purposes of this review we will consider only the first two terms in the Taylor expansion given in (6). The first of these terms is just the "homonuclear induced dipole" with even λ_1 and λ_2 and odd L. The second term refers to a part of the HD dipole for which the coefficients $A_\lambda(\lambda_1\lambda_2L;r_1r_2R)$ are proportional to r_1 or to r_2 and for which either λ_1 or λ_2 is odd and L is even; we will refer to these as "shifted coefficients". Explicit expressions for the shifted coefficients for all possible values of λ_1, λ_2 and L are given by Tipping and Poll (1985). In the following we will be particularly interested in induced dipoles that have the same symmetry as the allowed one, i.e. $\lambda_1 = 1$, $\lambda_2 = 0$ and L = 0. It turns out that the only components of the homonuclear induced dipole that can give rise, using (6), to a dipole of this particular symmetry must have $\lambda_1 = 0$ or 2, $\lambda_2 = 0$, and L = 1. For further details on the definition and properties of both the allowed and induced dipole for the hydrogens we refer to the review by Tipping and Poll (1985).

THE INFRARED SPECTRUM OF HD

The absorption coefficient, $\alpha(\omega)$, is determined by the matrix elements, $\vec{\mu}_{if}$, of the total dipole moment between initial and final energy eigenstates of the system considered, and is given by

$$\alpha(\omega) = (4\pi^2/3\hbar c)\ \omega(1 - e^{-\beta\hbar\omega})\ \phi(\omega), \tag{7}$$

where

$$\phi(\omega) = \frac{1}{V} \sum_{if} P_i |\vec{\mu}_{if}|^2 \delta(\omega-\omega_{if}) \tag{8}$$

is the spectral density. In these expressions V denotes the volume, P_i the Boltzmann factor for state i, and $\omega_{if} = (E_f - E_i)/\hbar$. The effect of stimulated emission is taken into account by the factor exp $(-\beta\hbar\omega)$. The classical analogue of $\vec{\mu}_{if}$ is the Fourier component of the time dependent dipole moment at frequency ω_{if}. It is often convenient to introduce the dipole correlation function $C(t) = V^{-1} < \vec{\mu}(0) \cdot \vec{\mu}(t)>$ instead of $\phi(\omega)$; these quantities are each other's Fourier transform. The dipole moment operator $\vec{\mu}(t)$ occurring in the correlation function is given by

$$\vec{\mu}(t) = \exp(iHt/\hbar)\ \vec{\mu}\ \exp(-iHt/\hbar) \tag{9}$$

where H is the total Hamiltonian and the symbol $<\cdot\cdot>$ denotes a Boltzmann ensemble average. The correlation function satisfies the relation $C(-t) = C(t)^*$. In the case of HD, the dipole moment is represented by a sum of allowed and induced dipoles

$$\vec{\mu}(t) = \sum_j \vec{\mu}_j^A (t) + \sum_{jk} \vec{\mu}_{jk}^I(t) \tag{10}$$

where the summations run over all molecules and pairs of molecules in the system. By a substitution of (10) into the expressions for either the spectral density or the correlation function, it follows that the spectrum can, quite generally, be regarded as a sum of contributions each of a different nature. For the correlation function, for example, we have

$$C(t) = C^{AA}(t) + C^{AI}(t) + C^{IA}(t) + C^{II}(t) \tag{11}$$

where

$$C^{AA}(t) = n\ c_1^{AA} (t) + n^2\ c_2^{AA} (t)$$

$$C^{AI}(t) = n^2\, c_2^{AI}(t) + n^3\, c_3^{AI}(t)$$

$$C^{IA}(t) = n^2\, c_2^{IA}(t) + n^3\, c_3^{IA}(t) \tag{12}$$

$$C^{II}(t) = n^2\, c_2^{II}(t) + n^3\, c_3^{II}(t) + n^4\, c_4^{II}(t)$$

and, in addition

$$c_1^{AA}(t) = \langle\, \vec{\mu}_1^{A}(0) \cdot \vec{\mu}_1^{A}(t)\rangle$$

$$c_2^{AA}(t) = V \langle\, \vec{\mu}_1^{A}(0) \cdot \vec{\mu}_2^{A}(t)\rangle$$

$$c_2^{AI}(t) = V \langle\, \vec{\mu}_1^{A}(0) \cdot \vec{\mu}_{12}^{I}(t)\rangle$$

$$c_3^{AI}(t) = \tfrac{1}{2}\, V^2 \langle\, \vec{\mu}_1^{A}(0) \cdot \vec{\mu}_{23}^{I}(t)\rangle$$

$$c_2^{IA}(t) = V \langle\, \vec{\mu}_{12}^{I}(0) \cdot \vec{\mu}_1^{A}(t)\rangle \tag{13}$$

$$c_3^{IA}(t) = \tfrac{1}{2}\, V^2 \langle\, \vec{\mu}_{23}^{I}(0) \cdot \vec{\mu}_1^{A}(t)\rangle$$

$$C_2^{II}(t) = \tfrac{1}{2}\, V \langle\, \vec{\mu}_{12}^{I}(0) \cdot \vec{\mu}_{12}^{I}(t)\rangle$$

$$C_3^{II}(t) = V^2 \langle\, \vec{\mu}_{12}^{I}(0) \cdot \vec{\mu}_{13}^{I}(t)\rangle$$

$$c_4^{II}(t) = \tfrac{1}{4}\, V^3 \langle\, \vec{\mu}_{12}^{I}(0) \cdot \vec{\mu}_{34}^{I}(t)\rangle$$

A similar decomposition holds for the spectral density. It is clear that $C^{AA}(t)$ is associated with the spectrum that would arise if only allowed dipoles were present; similarly $C^{II}(t)$ describes the contribution from induced dipoles only and finally, $C^{IA}(t)$ and $C^{AI}(t)$ represent the correlation or interference of induced and allowed dipoles. It is straightforward to show that $C^{IA}(t) = C^{AI}(-t)^*$. In (12) each of these correlation functions are decomposed into different contributions which are referred to as one, two, three, or four particle contributions depending on the number of different molecules involved in the dipoles occurring in each. This number is indicated by a subscript in (12);

the number density is denoted by n.

In expression (13) all the different contributions are given explicitly. It should be noted that the ensemble averages in (13) are over the complete system and, therefore, are dependent on the density. At sufficiently low densities and short times each of these correlation functions can be represented by a density expansion; for a discussion of this point see Poll (1980). The terms of lowest order in the density expansion in all of the correlation functions in (13) are independent of density and volume. The physical interpretation of the expressions in (13) is straightforward: The quantity c_1^{AA}, for example, refers to the autocorrelation function of the allowed dipole of a particular molecule, referred to as molecule 1, in the N particle system. The internal degrees of freedom of different molecules are only weakly coupled, and it is therefore expected that the function $c_2^{AA}(t)$ which refers to the correlation between allowed dipoles on different molecules gives only a very small contribution to the spectrum. A similar argument applies to $c_3^{AI}(t)$, $c_3^{IA}(t)$ and $c_4^{II}(t)$; all of these will, therefore, not be further discussed in this review even though they may not be negligible for high density systems. Before turning to a discussion of the remaining contributions, we point out that the analysis given above applies to pure HD. A similar analysis can, of course, be given for mixtures as well.

It is interesting to consider the correlation functions and their corresponding spectra first in the approximation in which the intermolecular interaction between a pair of molecules, which in general is given by $U(\vec{r}_1 \vec{r}_2 \vec{R})$, reduces to the isotropic form $U(R)$. Regarding the total interaction as the sum of pair interactions, we then find that the internal degrees of freedom are not coupled to each other or to the translational degrees of freedom. This implies that the energy eigenfunctions Ψ_i; of the N particle system can be written as products

$$\Psi_i = \phi_{n_1}(\vec{r}_1) \cdots \phi_{n_N}(\vec{r}_N) \chi_t (\vec{R}^N). \qquad (14)$$

The quantum numbers $n_1 \equiv v_1 J_1 M_1$ etc. refer to the internal (vibrational-rotational) degrees of freedom and t to the translational ones. In this approximation very simple and general expressions for the spectral components can be given. The correlation functions in (13) are all of the form $\langle \vec{A}(0) \cdot \vec{B}(t) \rangle$ and for isotropic interactions we have

$$\langle \vec{A}(0) \cdot \vec{B}(t) \rangle = \sum_{nn'} P_n e^{i\omega_{nn'}t} \langle \vec{A}_{nn'}(0) \cdot \vec{B}_{n'n}(t) \rangle_T \quad (15)$$

where $n \equiv n_1, \cdots, n_N$, P_n is the Boltzmann factor for the initial internal state n, $\omega_{nn'} = (E_{n'} - E_n)/\hbar$ a discrete internal transition frequency, and $\vec{A}_{nn'}$ is the matrix element of $\vec{A}$ between initial and final internal states. The symbol $\langle \cdot \cdot \rangle_T$ refers to a correlation function over translational states only. It is seen from (15) that the spectrum consists of components with shapes determined by a translational correlation function only and located at the positions of the possible discrete transition frequecies $\omega_{nn'}$. Writing both $\vec{A}$ and $\vec{B}$ in terms of the expansion (3), it can be shown in a straightforward way that, for isotropic interactions, only components of $\vec{A}$ and $\vec{B}$ with the same symmetry λ_1, λ_2, Λ, L give a finite contribution to the spectrum. Each of the possible combinations of λ_1, λ_2, Λ, L therefore contributes to the spectrum separately and independently of the others. For example, the intensity and shape of the λ_1, λ_2, Λ, L contribution to the pure rotational spectrum, will therefore involve R-dependent matrix elements of the form

$$\langle v_1 = 0, v_2 = 0 | A_\Lambda(\lambda_1 \lambda_2 L; r_1 r_2 R_{12}) | v_1 = 0, v_2 = 0 \rangle \qquad (16)$$

The rotational selection rules are, in all cases, determined by the triangle relations given by Rose (1957), $\Delta(J_1 \lambda_1 J_1')$ and $\Delta(J_2 \lambda_2 J_2')$.

In this review we will focus on the part of the spectrum arising from the $A_1(100; r_1 r_2 R)$ dipole component. As discussed in the previous section, this component includes the allowed dipole, $p^A(r_1)$, and has, in addition, an induced part $p^I(r_1 r_2 R)$. The pure allowed spectrum, determined by the Fourier transform of $c_1^{AA}(t)$, is due to that part of $A_1(100; r_1 r_2 R)$ which is given by $p^A(r_1)$. Because allowed dipole matrix elements, in the approximation of isotropic interactions, are diagonal in the translational states, the corresponding spectrum is given by a series of delta functions at the allowed frequencies. As implied by (8), we have here neglected the small natural and Doppler line widths. The integrated intensity of these lines is given explicitly by Poll, Tipping, Prasad and Reddy (1976). The interference between allowed and induced dipoles, given by $c_2^{IA}(t)$ and $c_2^{AI}(t)$, will also produce sharp features because the presence of the allowed dipole in the correlation function restricts the possible transitions to those that are diagonal in the translational states. According to the theorem that all components λ_1, λ_2, Λ, L contribute independently, the only part of the induced dipole that produces a non-zero interference with the allowed dipole must be the $\lambda_1 = 1$, $\lambda_2 = L = 0$ part. The physical reason for this is that the two interfering dipoles have to satisfy the same selection rules. A $\lambda_1 = 1$ and $\lambda_2 = L = 0$ induced dipole can be obtained by a shift of origin in either the

686

$A_0(001)$ or the $A_2(201)$ component for a pair of homonuclear
hydrogens. Because the expectation value over the ground
vibrational states of $A_0(001;r_1r_2R)$ is zero for reasons of
symmetry (see Poll and Hunt, 1976), it follows that the
$A_1(100;r_1r_2R)$ component of HD which is derived from it is very
small. In the pure rotational spectrum the interference effects
are therefore mainly due to the $A_1(100)$ component of HD which is
derived from the anisotropic L = 1 component $A_2(201)$ for
homonuclear hydrogen even though it is smaller, by about an order
of magnitude, than the isotropic L = 1 component, $A_0(001)$. For
the fundamental band however, the symmetry argument does not
apply and the interference is determined predominantly by the
shifted $A_0(001)$ component (see Tipping et al. 1978). Each of the
sharp lines at the allowed frequencies therefore has a
contribution due to interference and the integrated intensity, or
line strength, S, due to the two effects (at low density) is
roughly given by

$$S^{int}/S^{all} \equiv a\rho \sim 8\pi n\sigma^2 d \ p^I_{nn'}(\sigma)/p^A_{nn'}. \tag{17}$$

where ρ is the density in amagat, σ the diameter of the molecules
and "d" the range over which the induced dipole has an
appreciable value. The quantities $p^I_{nn'}(\sigma)$ and $p^A_{nn'}$ are matrix
elements, of the form (16), of the induced and allowed parts of
$A_1(100;r_1r_2R)$, $p^I(r_1r_2R)$ and $p^A(r_1)$, between the initial and
final internal states in question; $p^I_{nn'}$ is taken at the point
$R = \sigma$. The existence of these interference effects was first
discussed by Tipping et al. (1978), and Poll et al. (1976) where
rigorous expressions for the corresponding line strengths in the
approximation of isotropic interactions are also given. It is
seen from (17) that the effect of interference on the intensity
of the allowed line is proportional to the density (at low
density) and is described by a coefficient "a" which turns out to
be of order of magnitude 10^{-2} amagat^{-1}. In the experimental
determination of allowed dipoles it is therefore important to
extrapolate back to zero density.

We now discuss the purely induced absorption spectrum in the
approximation of isotropic intermolecular interactions. The two
body contribution, $c_2^{II}(t)$, describes the intensity due to the
induced dipole in a given pair of molecules labelled 1 and 2. At
low density this is given by the absorption in isolated binary
collisions. Because induced dipoles are, in general, not
diagonal in the translational states we expect in this case a
broad spectral feature. In fact, for a single binary collision
the correlation between $\vec{\mu}^I_{12}(0)$ and $\vec{\mu}^I_{12}(t)$ extends only over the
duration of one collision, τ_d, and we have a spectral width of
$\Delta\omega \sim \tau_d^{-1}$, i.e. of order 100 cm^{-1} at NTP. For each component $\lambda_1\lambda_2$

ΛL we will have a number of broad features of this type. These broad features are very similar for homonuclear and heteronuclear molecules, the only difference being the occurrence of additional transitions in HD with ΔJ odd which are forbidden for H_2 and D_2. The shape of the two body induced spectrum for isotropic interactions and at low density is, in principle, well understood and can be obtained quite accurately from a numerical calculation as discussed in the review by Frommhold elsewhere in this volume.

The three body contribution to the induced spectrum, associated with $c_3^{II}(t)$, refers to the absorption due to the induced dipoles created by the interaction of a given molecule (labelled 1) with two others. At low density the three body absorption is $\propto n^3$ and under circumstances in which triple collisions can be neglected, $c_3^{II}(t)$ describes the correlation between two subsequent, but not necessarily consecutive, collisions of molecule 1. This process is usually referred to as "intercollisional interference" and was first discussed by Van Kranendonk (1968). The effects due to ternary and higher order collisions was referred to as the "cancellation effect" by Van Kranendonk (1957). Intercollisional interference for the homonuclear hydrogens is discussed in the contribution by Lewis in this volume. In the present review we concentrate on the intercollisional interference of induced dipoles peculiar to the heteronuclear hydrogens and in particular on the induced dipole of $\lambda_1 = 1$, $\lambda_2 = L = 0$ symmetry. The most important difference between this type of dipole and those considered by Lewis and Van Kranendonk (1972) is that we are here dealing with $L = 0$ instead of $L = 1$, i.e. with a scalar in the translational variable $\check{R}$ instead of a vector. This implies that the matrix element occurring in the translational correlation function (15), $\langle vJ|p^I(rR)|v'J' \rangle \equiv M(R)$, is a scalar. For uncorrelated collisions the average value of $M(R)$, in a particular collision of a given molecule, is independent of the value produced in a subsequent collision. The translational correlation function then reduces to a product and is always positive: $\langle M[R_{12}(0)] M[R_{13}(t)]^* \rangle = |\langle M(R)\rangle|^2$. In this case of isotropic interactions there is, therefore, constructive interference between the dipoles induced by molecule 1 in any two subsequent collisions irrespective of their separation in time or by other collisions. The correlation function then extends over arbitrarily long times and the resulting spectral lines are perfectly sharp. This behaviour is in contrast to $L = 1$, or vector, intercollisional interference where the average dipoles in two immediately successive collisions are not independent but point in opposite directions, giving rise to destructive interference. For vector intercollisional interference the correlation between widely separated collisions generally becomes less even for isotropic intermolecular interactions and the resulting spectral feature has a width of the order of the collision frequency ν_c. Scalar intercollisional interference was first discussed by Herman (1979).

We have so far discussed the spectrum of HD in the approximation of isotropic intermolecular interactions. All the observed spectral features are already present in this approximation and in a very simple form. In reality there always exists an anisotropic part to the intermolecular interaction and, in fact, in the case of the heteronuclear hydrogens this part is very much larger than for the homonuclear hydrogens because of the asymmetric position of the centre of mass. The effect of the anisotropic interaction has been discussed by Herman (1979) and by Herman et al. (1979) in the classical path and impact approximation. It is found that the sharp features associated with c_1^{AA}, c_2^{IA}, c_2^{AI} and c_3^{II} discussed above are all broadened into features with a width of order ν_c, i.e. into features that, at not too high density, are still very much sharper than the pure induced features associated with c_2^{II}. The allowed spectrum has the usual Lorentz shape with a width depending on the time taken for the internal degrees of freedom to lose their coherence because of collisions. The intensity due to the inteference between the allowed and the induced dipole of $\lambda_1 = 1$, $\lambda_2 = L = 0$ symmetry and the intensity due to intercollisional interference of this induced dipole both take on a shape which can be represented as the sum of a Lorentzian and of an asymmetrical anomalous dispersion profile. Such a line shape is often referred to as a "Fano" profile; its shape is represented by two parameters Γ and q. Taking the correlation functions c_1^{AA}, c_2^{IA}, c_2^{AI} and c_3^{II} all in their lowest nonvanishing order in the density it is shown by Herman et al. (1979) that the resulting total intensity is given by a Fano profile. The density dependence of this profile is described by a complex parameter $\Delta = \Delta' + i\Delta''$. An expression for Δ in terms of the anisotropic part of the interaction potential has so far only been given in the classical path and impact approximations used by Herman et al. (1979). No theorectical calculations using this expression have been performed so far and the experimental results, which are discussed below, have therefore been interpreted by using Δ' and Δ'' as two real, temperature dependent, phenomenological parameters.

The theorem that the intensity is made up additively of contributions from individual dipole components $\lambda_1 \lambda_2 \Lambda L$ is no longer valid for anisotropic interactions and it is therefore no longer true that the allowed dipole can only interfere with a $\lambda_1 = 1$, $\lambda_2 = L = 0$ component. Effects of this kind may be important but have not been investigated thoroughly so far.

We now review the experimental work that has taken place during the last decade. The first observations of Fano line

shapes in the fundamental band of HD were by McKellar (1973), who
also determined a number of matrix elements of the allowed
dipole. These matrix elements and the ones obtained in further
studies by McKellar (1974) and by Bejar and Gush (1974) were in
reasonable agreement with each other and with the theoretical
values referred to earlier by Wolniewicz (1975, 1976) and Ford
and Browne (1977). More recently, the fundamental band of HD was
investigated again with higher precision by Rich, Johns and
McKellar (1982) and improved values of the dipole moment matrix
elements were obtained. A small discrepancy between experiment
and theory remains in the magnitude of the matrix elements but
there is agreement in their dependence on rotational quantum
number. The Fano line shape of the sharp features in the
fundamental band for the case of pure HD has been thoroughly
investigated by Rich and McKellar (1983) (see Fig. 1) and for HD-
inert gas mixtures by McKellar and Rich (1984). In these
experiments the range of densities used was sufficiently large so
that the effects of interference of allowed and induced dipoles
as well as the scalar intercollisional interference discussed
above were important. It was found that the line shapes as a
function of density could be described quite well in terms of the
parameters Δ' and Δ'' introduced by Herman et al. (1979). These
parameters depend on the transition considered, the temperature,
and on the particular gas mixture invovled. As pointed out
above, theoretical calculations of Δ for realistic intermolecular
interactions have not yet been done. The case of isotropic
intermolecular interactions corresponds to $\Delta' = 1$, $\Delta'' = 0$ and to a
symmetrical line shape; rigorous expressions for the line shape
and the integrated intensity are then easy to write down.

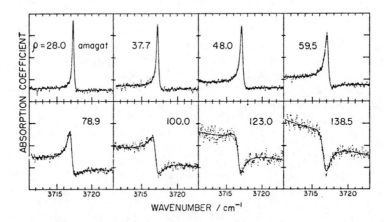

Fig. 1. The absorption profiles of the R (0) transition of HD at
77 K for a range of densities as observed by Rich and
McKellar (1983). The points represent the experimental
spectrum and the solid curves the fitted Fano lineshape
profiles.

For the rotational spectrum of pure HD and of some HD-inert gas mixtures the first detailed experimental investigation of interference effects was performed by Nelson and Tabisz (1982, 1983). They found only small asymmetries in the sharp lines but a significant dependence of the integrated intensity on density. They interpreted their results in terms of the theory valid for isotropic interactions given by Tipping et al. (1978). The matrix elements of the allowed dipole obtained from these experiments agreed well with the theoretical ones. The effect of increased density on the integrated intensity due to interference of allowed and induced dipoles is described by the parameter "a" mentioned previously. The theoretical values for this parameter (for isotropic interactions) and the experimental values found by Nelson and Tabisz appeared to be reasonably close. More recently, however, new observations of the sharp lines in the pure rotational spectrum of HD have been reported by McKellar, Johns, Majewski and Rich (1984) and by Essenwanger and Gush (1984). Whereas the dipole moment matrix elements obtained in these measurements agree well with previous ones and with theory, the interference parameter "a" turned out to be quite different from those found by Nelson and Tabisz. McKellar et al. who investigated the R(0) and R(1) lines at 77K, obtained values for "a" that are an order of magnitude smaller than those of Nelson and Tabisz for the R(1) line at 293°K. It is unlikely that this discrepancy is completely due to the difference in temperature between the experiments. It should be noted that the theoretical value for "a" is proportional to the strength of the $A_2(201;r_1r_2R)$ component of the H_2-H_2 induced dipole, which is not very well known. The theoretical value that was obtained was based on the magnitude of the $A_2(201)$ component given by Poll and Hunt (1976); more recent work by Bachet et al. (1983) suggests a much smaller value however. At the same time, Essenwanger and Gush (1984), who investigated the R(3), R(4), and R(5) lines, obtained values for "a" that are very much larger than those of Nelson and Tabisz for the R(3) line. The magnitude of the interference effect in the rotational spectrum is therefore not yet conclusively established. Tabisz and Nelson (1985) have recently calculated a theoretical value for the parameter "a" including the effect of anisotropic interaction. In this calculation the rotational states of the molecule are mixed at fixed intermolecular separation R and the translational states are kept unaffected; in addition a cut-off is introduced to produce finite answers. The effect of the anisotropic interaction on the parameter "a" obtained in this way is significant. Whether this procedure gives accurate results will have to await more consistent experimental data or a full theoretical treatment.

In this review we have only considered the low to moderate densities for which experimental work is available. At high gas density or at liquid density the interference effects discussed here will be difficult to separate from the much larger two body induced effects because at these densities the duration of a collision and the time between collisions is of the same order of magnitude; both kinds of feature will then have roughly the same width.

REFERENCES

Bachet, G., Cohen, E.R., Dore, P., and Birnbaum, G., 1983, Can. J. Phys., 61:591.
Bejar, J., and Gush, H.P., 1974. Can. J. Phys., 52:1669.
Blinder, S.M., 1960. J. Chem. Phys., 32:105, 582.
Blinder, S.M., 1961. J. Chem. Phys., 35:974.
Bunker, P.R., 1973, J. Mol. Spec., 46:119.
Durie, R.A., and Herzberg, G., 1960, Can. J. Phys., 38:806.
Essenwanger, P., and Gush, H.P., 1984, Can. J. Phys., 62:1680.
Ford, A.L., and Browne, J.C., 1977, Phys. Rev., A16:1992.
Herman, R.M., 1979, Phys. Rev. Lett., 42:1206.
Herman, R.M., Tipping, R.H., and Poll, J.D., 1979, Phys. Rev., A20:1006.
Herzberg, G., 1950, Nature, 166:563.
Karl, G., 1968, Can. J. Phys., 46:1973.
Karl, G., and Poll, J.D., 1970, Lett. Nuovo. Cimento, 3:310.
Kolos, W., and Wolniewicz, L., 1966, J. Chem. Phys., 45:944.
Lewis, J.C., and Van Kranendonk, J., 1972, Can. J. Phys., 50:352, 2881, 2902.
McKellar, A.R.W., 1973, Can. J. Phys., 51:389.
McKellar, A.R.W., 1974, Can. J. Phys., 52:1144.
McKellar, A.R.W., Johns, J.W.C., Majewski, W., and Rich, N.H., 1984, Can. J. Phys., 62:1673.
McKellar, A.R.W., and Rich, N.H., 1984, Can. J. Phys., 62:1665.
Nelson, J.B., and Tabisz, G.C., 1982, Phys. Rev. Lett., 48:1393.
Nelson, J.B., and Tabisz, G.C., 1983, Phys. Rev., A28:2157.
Poll, J.D., 1980, "Intermolecular Spectroscopy and Dynamical Properties of Dense Systems", International School of Physics, "Enrico Fermi"; Course LXXI, J. Van Kranendonk, ed., North Holland, Amsterdam.
Poll, J.D., and Hunt, J.L., 1976, Can. J. Phys, 54:461.
Poll, J.D., and Karl, G., 1973, Can. J. Phys., 51:594.
Poll, J.D., Tipping, R.H., Prasad, R.D.G., and Reddy, S.P., 1976, Phys. Rev. Lett., 36:248.
Poll, J.D., and Van Kranendonk, J., 1961, Can. J. Phys., 39:189.
Rich, N.H., Johns, J.W.C., and McKellar, A.R.W., 1982, J. Mol. Spec., 95:432.
Rich, N.H., and McKellar, A.R.W., 1983, Can. J. Phys., 61:1648.
Rose, M.E., 1957, "Elementary Theory of Angular Momentum", John Wiley, New York.
Tabisz, G.C., and Nelson, J.B., 1985, Phys. Rev. A, 31:1160.

Tipping, R.H., Poll, J.D., and McKellar, A.R.W., 1978, Can. J. Phys., 56:75.

Tipping, R.H., and Poll, J.D., 1985, "Molecular Spectroscopy: Modern Research, Vol III", K.N. Rao ed., Academic Press, New York.

Treffler, M., and Gush, H.P, 1968, Phys. Rev. Lett., 20:703.

Treffler, M., Cappel, A.M., and Gush, H.P., 1969, Can. J. Phys., 47:2115.

Van Kranendonk, J., 1957, Physica, 23:825.

Van Kranendonk, J., 1968, Can. J. Phys., 46:1173.

Wick, G.C., 1935, Atti. Reale Accad. Lincei, 21:708.

Wolniewicz, L., 1975, Can. J. Phys., 53:1207.

Wolniewicz, L., 1976, Can. J. Phys., 54:672.

Wolniewicz, L., and Kowalski, T., 1973, Chem. Phys. Lett., 18:55.

Wu, T.Y., 1952, Can. J. Phys., 30:291.

WORKSHOP REPORT: THE INTERFERENCE OF INDUCED AND

ALLOWED MOLECULAR MOMENTS IN LIQUIDS

P.A. Madden

Physical Chemistry Laboratory
Oxford OX1 3QZ, U.K.

A workshop was held to appraise recent developments in the study of induced contributions to "allowed" light scattering and dielectric spectra and to discuss the direction of future work. It was recognised that perhaps the most important development, over the last few years, has been the greatly enhanced recognition of the importance of induced effects in these spectra, particularly in the field of light scattering. It is now generally realised that these effects limit the reliability of information which can be obtained from the intensity and higher spectral moments of the allowed bands. This realization is stimulating improved experimental work and has led to a more widespread interest in induced phenomena amongst spectroscopists who study liquids.

Several articles in this volume have dealt with recent work in this area. Perrot and Lascombe and Dorfmüller have described the situation as perceived from an experimental viewpoint. Also, Jonas has shown the importance of density as an experimental variable in elucidating the role of induced contributions. Madden has described the computer simulation work which has been done to test the validity of timescale separation concepts and of local field models. Sampoli has shown how simulation and experimental results may be brought together to provide a complete analysis of a spectrum in a case (N_2) where the induction mechanism is sufficiently simple for perfect agreement between simulation and experiment to be achieved. Ladanyi has discussed molecular theories of local field factors, in the light scattering context. This work has shown how the results of a molecular analysis may be reconciled with conventional, continuum models of the local field. The molecular theories go further but applying them quantitatively is very difficult because of the complexity of the fluid structure.

It was generally felt that work of the kind described in these articles had had a significant impact and had contributed to a much improved appreciation of the true nature of allowed spectra. The importance of extending such work was emphasised, particularly with regard to infra-red and dielectric spectroscopy where comparatively little work has been done to date. The objectives of future work should be further examination of the role of timescale separation, understanding and characterising the departure of local field factors from the classical results and improving techniques for separating the induced and molecular components in a spectrum. The reason for the success of the work which has been done was identified as the selection of systems on which experiments whose interpretation was unambiguous could be performed and for which realistic computer simulations could be made. The impact of the work had arisen from the fusion of the two disciplines. The identification of systems with this property for study by dielectric spectroscopy was regarded as an urgent priority. The technology is now available to take dielectric spectra from 0 to 250 cm^{-1} <u>without gaps</u> and to realize simulations of sufficient size and length to obtain dielectric properties of molecules with several atomic sites.

Another aspect of the topic of induced effects in allowed spectra is that the collision-induced contribution to the spectrum arises from fluctuations in the local environment of a molecule which are of different character from the fluctuations which are responsible for the appearance of forbidden spectra. For a centrosymmetric molecule, environmental fluctuations which destroy the inversion centre are needed in the latter case but for allowed spectra, parity preserving fluctuations are sufficient. The collision induced parts of allowed spectra should thus be of interest in the study of intermolecular motion, as a useful adjunct to the study of forbidden processes for this purpose. The most suitable spectra are the collision-induced contributions to isotropic light scattering spectra, despite the experimental problems in obtaining them. For these spectra the timescale separation is likely to hold rather well, the consequences have been examined in computer simulations.

The problem of determining the induced and molecular contributions to allowed light scattering and dielectric spectra may seem a somewhat esoteric concern. The workshop was concerned to emphasise that closely related issues arise in many "relevant" areas of chemistry and physics. From the most general viewpoint the problem is that of accounting for the effect of the environment on a molecular property. In the cases discussed above the property is the dipole moment or polarizability but precisely the same problem is encountered in any attempt to do quantitative spectroscopy in liquids. For example, to describe the n.m.r. relaxation of ^{14}N in MeCN it is necessary to know the nuclear quadrupole coupling constant. In the gas phase this has the value 4.40MHz, in the solid 3.74MHz, which shows an appreciable environmental effect. The value appropriate to the liquid should be somewhere in between, but to decide where involves considerations of timescale separation between reorientational motion and the intermolecular field gradient of precisely the same kind as considered in light scattering and dielectric spectra. Furthermore the spectra contain information about the time evolution of the intermolecular process, in the n.m.r. example the environmental effect is only seen through its effect on a single member. In a similar way the environment alters electronic wavefunctions and energy levels and this affects electronic spectra in a way which depends upon the relative rate of inter- and intramolecular relaxations. The consequences are visible in such phenomena as time dependent red-shifts in fluorescence and in a rapid depolarisation of fluorescence due to relaxation of the intermolecular component of a transition dipole; these effects are now within the temporal resolution of time domain experiments with femtosecond laser pulses. If we stretch this theme a little further, the effects of environment relaxation on the rates of chemical reactions (i.e. environment-induced changes in potential energy surfaces) may be considered as a related topic.

To return to rather less tenuously related topics we may note the tremendous technological interest in the non-linear optical properties of liquids. The property of greatest interest is the non-linear susceptibility $\chi^{(3)}$ which is involved in many aspects of optical signal processing - image processing, phase conjugation, stimulated scattering etc. For molecular liquids $\chi^{(3)}$ is primarily determined by precisely the same correlation functions as determine the Rayleigh scattering lineshape (including the induced effects). An important point is that the primary interest is in the non-linear response induced by very short laser pulses, for which the important processes are the rapidly relaxing ones which contribute to the Rayleigh wing. That is, the importance of induced effects is likely to be enhanced. This point has been explored to a limited extent (see Madden, page 244 in Ultrafast Phenomena IV, eds. D. Auston and K. Eisenthal (Springer 1984)).

697

CONTRIBUTION OF BOUND DIMERS, $(N_2)_2$, TO THE

INTERACTION INDUCED INFRARED SPECTRUM OF NITROGEN

Geert Brocks and Ad van der Avoird

Institute of Theoretical Chemistry
University of Nijmegen
Toernooiveld 6525 Ed Nijmegen, The Netherlands

ABSTRACT

Using the ro-vibrational wave functions from a recent *ab initio* quantum dynamical calculation in combination with an empirical dipole function deduced from the collision induced far infrared spectrum of gaseous nitrogen, we have calculated the intensities of far infrared transitions in $(N_2)_2$ dimers. Employing, moreover, the multipole moment and polarizability derivatives from *ab initio* calculations on N_2 monomers, we have estimated intensities of near infrared transitions. It is demonstrated that the dimer infrared spectra depend sensitively, not only on the intermolecular potential, but also on the different contributions to the N_2-N_2 interaction induced dipole function.

INTRODUCTION

Part of the intensity in collision-induced infrared absorption (CIA) and collision-induced light scattering (CIS) spectra is due to the contributions from bound dimers (Prengel and Gornall, 1976; Birnbaum et al., 1983; Frommhold et al., 1976) or so-called Van der Waals molecules (Blaney and Ewing, 1976). This paper is concerned with the $(N_2)_2$ dimer contributions to the well-known CIA spectra of gaseous nitrogen, both in the far (Bosomworth and Gush, 1965; Dagg et al., 1974; Buontempo et al., 1975) and near (Sheng and Ewing, 1971) infrared regions. Just as is collision induced absorption, dimer absorption is caused by the dipole moment induced via intermolecular interactions. The dimer spectrum should exhibit a more specific and detailed structure, however, since the monomer rotations and (relative) translations causing the rather broad and featureless bands in collision induced spectra are replaced by discrete dimer vibrations (and overall rotations). In most spectra, which were taken at rather high temperatures, this structure is not visible. In the near infrared nitrogen gas spectrum of Long et al. (1973) it has been resolved, however.

In principle, the structure found in such dimer spectra contains detailed information on the intermolecular potential energy surface and the interaction induced dipole function or the interaction induced polarizability changes. In simpler cases, such as rare gas dimers, (Godfried and Silvera, 1982), rare gas-H_2 and H_2-H_2 complexes (Mc Kellar, 1982; Mc Kellar and Welsh, 1971), where the spectra are well resolved and can be more easily interpreted, it has actually been demonstrated (LeRoy and Van Kranendonk, 1974; LeRoy and Carley, 1980; Verberne and Reuss, 1980, 1981; Waaijer et al., 1981; Danby and Flower, 1983) that the positions of the peaks in this spectrum are a most sensitive probe of the potential in the Van der Waals well. Even in these simple systems, it was not possible, though, to deduce the complete intermolecular potential from the infrared spectrum alone, so in a more complex system as N_2-N_2 this will be practically excluded. Information from other sources, such as *ab initio* calculations (Van der Avoird et al., 1980), will have to be used. A beautiful example of the application of such calculations has recently been given by Schäfer and Meyer (1984), who have generated the complete low temperature CIA spectrum of H_2-H_2.

For N_2-N_2 a complete intermolecular potential is available from *ab initio* calculations (Berns and v.d. Avoird, 1980; Mulder et al., 1980). The accuracy of this potential has now been tested for several bulk properties: solid state data (Luty et al., 1980), liquid properties (Allnatt, 1983) and virial coefficients (Van Hemert and Berns, 1982), transport properties, depolarized Rayleigh line widths and rotational relaxation coefficients of gaseous N_2 (Nyeland et al., 1984). Recently, this potential has been used by Tennyson and Van der Avoird (1982) to calculate bound ro-vibrational states of $(N_2)_2$ dimers. In the present paper, we point out how the wave functions resulting from this calculation can be used, together with an empirical dipole function that Poll and Hunt (1981) have extracted from the collision induced far infrared spectrum of gaseous N_2 (Bosomworth and Gush 1965; Dagg et al., 1974; Buontempo et al., 1975), to compute the far infrared absorption intensities for the $(N_2)_2$ dimer. Using, moreover, polarizability and multipole moment derivatives from *ab initio* calculations on N_2 monomers (Svendsen and Oddershede, 1979; Amos, 1980; Langhoff et al., 1983), we can even estimate the intensities in the near infrared spectrum of $(N_2)_2$.

The model which has been employed to calculate the bound ro-vibrational states of $(N_2)_2$ has been described extensively in (Tennyson and v.d. Avoird, 1982). It starts from a hamiltonian which is exact, within the Born-Oppenheimer separation of electronic and nuclear motion, except by assuming that the monomer stretch vibrations can be decoupled from the dimer "Van der Waals" vibrations. Given the large gap between the monomer fundamental stretch frequency of 2330 cm^{-1} and the dimer vibration frequencies lying around 20 cm^{-1} (Tennyson and v.d. Avoird, 1982), this assumption seems to be justified. It is confirmed by the very small shift, 0.1 cm^{-1}, of the monomer fundamental frequency in the $(N_2)_2$ dimer spectrum (Long et al., 1973). Further justification of the decoupling assumption is provided by explicit tests (Tennyson and Sutcliffe, 1983) on the Van der Waals dimer, He-HF. On the other hand, it proved to be necessary (Tennyson and v.d. Avoird, 1982) for such a "floppy" system as $(N_2)_2$, to include the centrifugal distortion and Coriolis terms which couple the dimer vibrations and overall rotations.

It was found convenient, for the calculation of matrix elements, to express the hamiltonian in a body-fixed coordinate system (Brocks et al., 1983) with the z-axis along the dimer axis $\vec{R} = \vec{R}_{AB}$, which connects the monomer centers of mass. The potential has been expanded in terms of coupled spherical harmonics (v.d. Avoird et al. 1980; Steele, 1963; Egelstaff et al., 1975) depending on the polar angles of the monomer axes, (θ_A, ϕ_A) and (θ_B, ϕ_B). The expansion coefficients, depending on the distance R, are available from ab $initio$ calculations (Berns and v.d. Avoird, 1980; Mulder et al., 1980). The hamiltonian is diagonalized in the basis:

$$R^{-1} \chi_n(R) \, Y_{j,k}^{j_A,j_B}(\theta_A,\phi_A,\theta_B,\phi_B) \, D_{M,k}^{(J)*}(\alpha,\beta,0) \tag{1a}$$

with the coupled spherical harmonics:

$$Y_{j,k}^{j_A,j_B} = \sum_m Y_{j_A,m}(\theta_A,\phi_A) Y_{j_B,k-m}(\theta_B,\phi_B) \, (j_A,m; \, j_B,k-m|j,k) \tag{1b}$$

where (β,α) are the end-over-end rotation angles (the polar angles of $\vec{R}$, relative to a space-fixed frame) and $\chi_n(R)$ denotes a set of Morse oscillator type functions suitable for the expansion of bound states in Van der Waals dimers (Tennyson and Sutcliffe, 1982). Although this basis, of which the angular part is also used in close-coupled scattering calculations (Curtiss, 1953; Launey, 1977) is constructed from (normalized) free rotor (Brink and Satchler, 1968) wave functions $Y_{j,m}$ and $D_{M,k}^{(J)}$, it has been found (Tennyson and v.d. Avoird, 1980) that the lowest ro-vibrational states of the $(N_2)_2$ dimer are actually localized around the D_{2d} equilibrium structure dictated by the potential. Characteristic for the "floppyness" of this Van der Waals complex are the large amplitudes of the librational monomer motions, however. Also, the non-negligible probability of tunneling between the two equivalent D_{2d} structures (related by inversion) and the substantial variation of the vibrational spectrum with the nuclear spin species (ortho/para N_2) are typical for non-rigid systems (Bunker, 1979). For the higher bound states the dimer vibrations, especially the librations, become increasingly delocalized. On the other hand, the $(N_2)_2$ dimer, on the whole, is much more rigid than rare gas-H_2 or $(H_2)_2$ complexes, which do not possess a localized structure at all; the H_2 monomers behave almost as free internal rotors.

The solution of the secular problem over the basis of Eq. (1) has been considerably simplified and the resulting ro-vibrational states have been classified (Tennyson and v.d. Avoird, 1982) by using the permutation-inversion symmetry group of the $(N_2)_2$ complex. The symmetry also determines the nuclear-spin statistical weights of the various dimer states, composed of ortho/para N_2 monomers, which will be reflected in the spectral intensities of the (allowed) transitions.

FAR-INFRARED SPECTRUM

The induced dipole function for N_2-N_2 pairs which Poll and Hunt (1981) have deduced from the collision induced far infrared spectrum of gaseous N_2, is expressed in terms of coupled spherical harmonics just as the potential and the wave functions in the dynamical calculations of Tennyson and Van der Avoird (1982). Poll and Hunt have used a space-fixed frame, however, but it is easy to rewrite their dipole function in body-fixed coordinates, in terms of the same angular functions used in the basis of Eq.(1):

$$\mu_\nu(\vec{r}_A,\vec{r}_B,\vec{R}) = 4\pi \sum_{\lambda_A,\lambda_B,\Lambda,K} m_{\lambda_A,\lambda_B,\Lambda,K}(r_A,r_B,R)\ Y_{\Lambda,K}^{\lambda_A,\lambda_B}(\theta_A,\phi_A,\theta_B,\phi_B)$$

$$\times D_{\nu,K}^{(1)*}(\alpha,\beta,0) \tag{2}$$

Our expansion coefficients are related to those of Poll and Hunt as:

$$m_{\lambda_A,\lambda_B,\Lambda,K}(r_A,r_B,R) = \sum_{L=\Lambda-1}^{\Lambda+1} \left(\frac{2L+1}{3}\right)^{\frac{1}{2}} (\Lambda,K;L,0|1,K)$$

$$\times A_\Lambda(\lambda_A,\lambda_B,L;r_A,r_B,R) \tag{3}$$

702

with very simple Clebsch-Gordan coefficients $(\Lambda,K;L,0|1,K)$, and
they satisfy the following symmetry relations:

$$m_{\lambda_A,\lambda_B,\Lambda,K}(r_A,r_B,R) = 0 \text{ if } \lambda_A \text{ and } \lambda_B \text{ are not both even}$$

$$m_{\lambda_A,\lambda_B,\Lambda,K}(r_A,r_B,R) = (-1)^{\Lambda+1} m_{\lambda_B,\lambda_A,\Lambda,K}(r_B,r_A,R)$$

$$m_{\lambda_A,\lambda_B,\Lambda,K}(r_A,r_B,R) = (-1)^{\Lambda} m_{\lambda_A,\lambda_B,\Lambda,-K}(r_A,r_B,R) \tag{4}$$

Since in the far infrared region the (decoupled) monomer
stretch vibrations will not be excited, Poll and Hunt could relate
the collision induced absorption intensity to coefficients B_Λ,
depending on R only, which are defined by averaging A_Λ over the
monomer vibrational ground states, $v_A = v_B = 0$. The $B_\Lambda(R)$ coefficients are then obtained by fitting the experimental spectrum. We
apply the same averaging procedure to our dipole expansion coefficients:

$$M_{\lambda_A,\lambda_B,\Lambda,K}(R) = \langle\phi_0(r_A)\phi_0(r_B)|m_{\lambda_A,\lambda_B,\Lambda,K}(r_A,r_B,R)|\phi_0(r_A)\phi_0(r_B)\rangle$$

$$\tag{5}$$

which are then expressed in the known $B_\Lambda(R)$ via Eq. (3). The resulting coefficients are collected in Table 1. Thus, the dipole
function Eq. (2), is known in terms of the same angular basis Eq.
(1), as the ro-vibrational eigenstates. In order to compute the
far infrared transition strengths for the $(N_2)_2$ dimer, we have to
evaluate angular matrix elements (generalized Gaunt coefficients
(Brink and Satcher, 1968)), which reduce to products of one 9-j
symbol and five 3-j symbols, and radial matrix elements of the
$M_{\lambda_A,\lambda_B,\Lambda,K}(R)$ coefficients given in Table 1 over the basis $\chi_n(R)$,
which can be evaluated by numerical integration. Very similar
matrix elements have been met already in the dynamical calculations (Tennyson and v.d. Avoird, 1982).

The results for a typical series of symmetry allowed vibrational transitions from the ground state in the most abundant
ortho N_2-ortho N_2 species (statistical weight $21/63 = 1/3$) are
displayed in Table 2. Only the $J = 0 \rightarrow 1$ components are given. In
order to produce theoretically a complete far infrared spectrum of
$(N_2)_2$ one has to generate many more of such series, starting from
the higher vibrational states also, if they are sufficiently populated at the considered temperature. Moreover, one has to include
the higher J states in order to simulate the rotational profiles
of the vibrational bands. (The end-over-end rotational constant in
the ground state equals $B_0 = 0.08 \text{ cm}^{-1}$).

Table 1. Contributions to the N_2-N_2 interaction induced dipole function for both monomers in the vibrational ground state.

Mechanism	λ_A	λ_B	Λ	K	$M_{\lambda_A \lambda_B \Lambda K}(R)$
quadrupole induction via isotropic polarizability α	2	0	2	0	$(\frac{9}{5})^{\frac{1}{2}} Q_A \alpha_B R^{-4}$
	2	0	2	1	$-(\frac{3}{5})^{\frac{1}{2}} Q_A \alpha_B R^{-4}$
quadrupole induction via anisotropic polarizability γ	2	2	3	1	$(\frac{14}{105})^{\frac{1}{2}} (Q_A \gamma_B + Q_B \gamma_A) R^{-4}$
hexadecapole induction via isotropic polarizability α	4	0	4	0	$(\frac{25}{9})^{\frac{1}{2}} \Phi_A \alpha_B R^{-6}$
	4	0	4	1	$-(\frac{10}{9})^{\frac{1}{2}} \Phi_A \alpha_B R^{-6}$
overlap	2	0	2	0	$-[(\frac{2}{5})^{\frac{1}{2}} \lambda_1 - (\frac{3}{5})^{\frac{1}{2}} \lambda_3] \exp[-(R-\sigma)/\rho]$
	2	0	2	1	$[-(\frac{3}{10})^{\frac{1}{2}} \lambda_1 - (\frac{2}{10})^{\frac{1}{2}} \lambda_3] \exp[-(R-\sigma)/\rho]$

Empirical parameters		
from best fit (Poll and Hunt, 1981):	quadrupole moment Q	$= -1.09\ ea_0^2$
	hexadecapole moment Φ	$= -10.4\ ea_0^4$
	isotropic polarizability $(\alpha_\| + 2\alpha_\perp)/3 = \alpha =$	$11.92\ a_0^3$
	polarizability anisotropy $\alpha_\| - \alpha_\perp = \gamma =$	$4.76\ a_0^3$
	overlap parameters $\quad \sigma$	$= 3.68\ \text{Å}$
	ρ	$= 0.11\ \sigma$
	λ_1	$= \pm 1. \times 10^{-3}\ ea_0$
	λ_3	$= 1. \times 10^{-3}\ ea_0$

704

Table 2. Transition strengths $|\langle i|\vec{\mu}|f\rangle|^2$ in 10^{-6} $e^2a_0^2$ for A_1^+ (J=0) $\rightarrow$ B_1^-(J=1) transitions[a] from the ground A_1^+ state in ortho N_2 – ortho N_2 dimers.

B_1^- level number	Q^2[b]	Φ^2[b]	$(\lambda_1,\lambda_3)^2$[b],c)	$2Q.\Phi$[b]	$2(\lambda_1\lambda_3).Q$[b],c)	$2(\lambda_1\lambda_3).\Phi$[b],c)	total without overlap	total[c)	Δk	frequency (cm^{-1})
1	32.2	0.8	0.0 /0.7	-10.2	-0.61 /-9.5	-0.1 / 1.5	22.8	23.3 /15.5	1	22.1
2	5.85	0.25	0.13 /0.0	- 2.43	-1.78 / 0.16	0.37 /-0.03	3.67	2.40 /3.80	0	25.1
3	0.567	0.0	0.001/0.039	0.017	0.039/-0.299	0.001/-0.004	0.584	0.624 /0.320	1	33.1
4	8.37	0.94	0.0 /0.38	- 5.61	0.17 /-3.56	-0.06 / 1.19	3.70	3.81 /1.71	1	42.0
5	5.46	1.47	0.16 /0.0	- 5.67	-1.88 /-0.29	0.98 / 0.15	1.26	0.522 /1.13	0	46.5
6	0.0953	0.0619	0.0216/0.0551	- 0.1536	0.0908/-0.1449	-0.0732/ 0.1168	0.00358	0.0428/0.0305	1	47.5
7	0.115	0.0	0.0 /0.009	- 0.004	0.004/-0.063	0.0 / 0.001	0.111	0.115 /0.0579	1	53.9

a) the symmetry labeling of the $(N_2)_2$ dimer states refers to the permutation-inversion group $S_4' \otimes C_i$, see (Tennyson and v.d. Avoird, 1982)

b) contributions from: pure quadrupole induction (Q^2)

   pure hexadecapole induction (Φ^2)

   pure overlap terms $(\lambda_1,\lambda_3)^2$

   quadrupole-hexadecapole interference terms $2Q.\Phi$

   quadrupole-overlap interference terms $2(\lambda_1,\lambda_3).Q$

   hexadecapole-overlap interference terms $2(\lambda_1,\lambda_3).\Phi$

c) results for $\lambda_1 = -1. \times 10^{-3}$ ea_0 and $\lambda_1 = 1. \times 10^{-3}$ ea_0, respectively. (The sign of λ_1 was undetermined (Poll and Hunt, 1981)

Pure end-over-end rotational transitions are forbidden in ortho-ortho and para-para dimers; they occur only in mixed ortho-para dimers (symmetry $E^{\pm}$; statistical weight $18/63 = 2/7$) with transition strengths (for individual $J = 0 \rightarrow 1$ transitions) up to 65×10^{-6} $e^2 a_0^2$. The ground state rotational constant B_0 equals 0.08 cm^{-1} = 2400 MHz, also for ortho-para dimers, the distortion constant $D_0 = 18$ kHz.

Even before finishing the formidable task of generating theoretically a complete far infrared spectrum of $(N_2)_2$ dimers (Brocks and v.d. Avoird, 1984), one can draw some interesting conclusions already from results as those listed in Table 2. The first observation is that several (also higher) transitions from the ground state obtain comparable intensities. This is in contrast with more rigid molecules with nearly harmonic vibrations, where practically all intensity goes into the fundamental bands, and it is another manifestation of the non-rigid nature of the Van der Waals molecule $(N_2)_2$ (cf. the previous section).

The second observation is that the intensities of most transitions are substantially affected by the overlap contributions to the induced dipole moment, particularly via the interference with the long range R^{-4} and R^{-6} contributions. For comparison we quote the conclusion of Poll and Hunt (1981) that the long range terms cause about 90% of the total intensity in the collision induced nitrogen gas spectrum (85% originates from quadrupolar induction and only 5% from hexadecapolar induction), while the remaining 10% is largely due to the interference between the λ_3 overlap term and the quadrupole terms. Such interference terms in general are much more important in the dimer spectrum and they occur also between dipole contributions with different $\lambda_A, \lambda_B, \Lambda, L$ because the N_2 molecules in the dimer are truly interacting via the anisotropic potential. Therefore, it should be possible by looking at the intensities of specific dimer transitions to determine the various induced dipole contributions in more detail, as Dunker and Gordon (1978) have done for some H_2-rare gas complexes. In particular, one can try to establish the sign of λ_1: for positive λ_1 the $\Delta k = 1$ transitions are most affected by the overlap terms, for negative λ_1 the $\Delta k = 0$ transitions are changed mostly (compare the left/right columns of Table 2; the approximate quantum number k denotes the projection of the overall angular momentum $\vec{J}$ on the dimer axis $\vec{R}$). We close this section by concluding that, in spite of the preceding remarks about the overlap terms being relatively more important than in the continuum spectrum, the transition strengths in the $(N_2)_2$ dimer can still be calculated to within a factor of two from the long range contributions alone.

NEAR INFRARED SPECTRUM

The structured part of this spectrum due to the discrete transitions in $(N_2)_2$ dimers has actually been measured (Long et al., 1973) in the region of the monomer stretch frequency, 2330 cm^{-1}. In order to calculate the infrared absorption intensities in this range, in principle one should know the dependence of the induced dipole expansion coefficients, Eq. (2), on the monomer bond lenghts, r_A and r_B. In practice, however, the monomer vibrations can be decoupled from the dimer modes and one can make the assumption that the potential between ground state monomers, $v_A=v_B=0$, practically does not change when one monomer is excited: $v_A=1$, $v_B=0$ or $v_A=0, v_B=1$. The latter assumption is expected to hold well for N_2 molecules as these are very strongly bound and the average bond length hardly changes with (low) vibrational excitations (Herzberg, 1950) $<r>_{v=0} \approx <r>_{v=1}$. For H_2 the changes are more appreciable (LeRoy and v. Kranendonk, 1974; LeRoy and Carley, 1980).

After these assumptions, one can use the same wave functions calculated by Tennyson and Van der Avoird (1982) for the $(N_2)_2$ dimer vibrations and rotations, multiplied by the following monomer vibration functions, adapted to the overall permutation-inversion symmetry:

$$\phi_0(r_A)\phi_0(r_B) \qquad \text{for the ground state, } v_A=v_B=0$$

$$2^{-\frac{1}{2}}[\phi_1(r_A)\phi_0(r_B) \pm \phi_0(r_A)\phi_1(r_B)] \text{ for the excited states lying}$$

around 2330cm^{-1} \hfill (6)

Moreover, the monomer stretch functions $\phi_0(r)$ and $\phi_1(r)$ to a very good approximation may be replaced by harmonic oscillator functions (Svendsen and Oddershede, 1979). Expanding the dipole functions as Taylor series in $\Delta r_A = r_A - r_{A,eq}$ and $\Delta r_B = r_B - r_{B,eq}$, what one needs to know then are the first derivatives of the dipole expansion coefficients $m_{\lambda_A,\lambda_B,\Lambda,K}(r_A,r_B,R)$ with respect to r_A or r_B, taken at the equilibrium bonds lengths, $r_{A,eq}$ and $r_{B,eq}$. In general, these derivatives are not known, but if we invoke the last conclusion of the previous section, that the long range induced dipole contributions alone are sufficient to compute the infrared intensities to within a factor of two, and restrict ourselves to those contributions, then they can be calculated. What is required are the first derivatives of the N_2 quadrupole (Q) and hexadecapole (Φ) moments and the anisotropic polarizability (α,γ) with respect to the bond lenth r. These data are available from accurate *ab initio* calculations (Svendson and Oddershede, 1979; Amos, 1980; Langhoff et al., 1983); the polarizability derivatives have been compared with Raman intensities. The final factors

$$N_{\lambda_A,\lambda_B,\Lambda,K}(R)$$

Table 3. Contributions to the N_2-N_2 interaction induced dipole function for an excited ($v=1$) and a ground state ($v=0$) monomer.

Mechanism	λ_A	λ_B	Λ	K	$N_{\lambda_A \lambda_B \Lambda K}(R)$
quadrupole induction via isotropic	2	0	2	0	$\left(\dfrac{9}{10}\right)^{\frac{1}{2}} \left(Q_A \dfrac{d\alpha_B}{dr_B} \pm \alpha_B \dfrac{dQ_A}{dr_A}\right) R^{-4} \langle\Delta r\rangle_{01}$
polarizability α	2	0	2	1	$-\left(\dfrac{3}{10}\right)^{\frac{1}{2}} \left(Q_A \dfrac{d\alpha_B}{dr_B} \pm \alpha_B \dfrac{dQ_A}{dr_A}\right) R^{-4} \langle\Delta r\rangle_{01}$
quadrupole induction via anisotropic polarizability γ	2	2	3	1	$\left(\dfrac{1}{15}\right)^{\frac{1}{2}} \left(Q_A \dfrac{d\gamma_B}{dr_B} \pm \gamma_B \dfrac{dQ_A}{dr_A}\right.$ $\left. + Q_B \dfrac{d\gamma_A}{dr_A} \pm \gamma_A \dfrac{dQ_B}{dr_B}\right) R^{-4} \langle\Delta r\rangle_{01}$
hexadecapole induction via isotropic	4	0	4	0	$\left(\dfrac{25}{18}\right)^{\frac{1}{2}} \left(\Phi_A \dfrac{d\alpha_B}{dr_B} \pm \alpha_B \dfrac{d\Phi_A}{dr_A}\right) R^{-6} \langle\Delta r\rangle_{01}$
polarizability α	4	0	4	1	$-\left(\dfrac{5}{9}\right)^{\frac{1}{2}} \left(\Phi_A \dfrac{d\alpha_B}{dr_B} \pm \alpha_B \dfrac{d\Phi_A}{dr_A}\right) R^{-6} \langle\Delta r\rangle_{01}$

The N_2 monomer transition moment $\langle\Delta r\rangle_{01} = \langle\phi_0(r)|\Delta r|\phi_1(r)\rangle$ has been replaced by its harmonic oscillator expression $\left(\dfrac{\hbar}{2\mu\nu}\right)^{\frac{1}{2}}$, with reduced mass $\mu=7$ amu and fundamental frequency $\nu=2330$ cm^{-1}

Ab initio parameters (Amos, 1980)

$$\left(\frac{dQ}{dr}\right)_{r_{eq}} = 1.15 \ ea_0 \qquad \left(\frac{d\Phi}{dr}\right)_{r_{eq}} = -2.53 \ ea_0^3$$

$$\left(\frac{d\alpha}{dr}\right)_{r_{eq}} = 5.8 \ a_0^2 \qquad \left(\frac{d\gamma}{dr}\right)_{r_{eq}} = 6.5 \ a_0^2$$

Table 4. Transition strengths in 10^{-9} e^2a^2 for $A_1^+(J=0) \to B_1^-(J=1)$ transitions[a] from the lowest A_1^+ state in ortho N_2 (v=1) - ortho N_2 (v=0) dimers

B_1^- level number	Q^2[b]	Φ^2[b]	$2Q \cdot \Phi$[b]	total	Δk	relative frequency[c] $\nu(cm^{-1})$
1	9.4	0.8	5.4	15.6	1	22.1
2	3.97	0.25	1.99	6.21	0	25.1
3	1.10	0.0	-0.02	1.08	1	33.1
4	2.38	0.92	2.97	6.27	1	42.0
5	3.77	1.45	4.67	9.89	0	46.5
6	0.240	0.061	0.241	0.542	1	47.5
7	0.0526	0.0	0.0026	0.0552	1	53.9

a) symmetry labeling as in Table 2

b) contributions from:

pure quadrupole induction (Q^2)

pure hexadecapole induction (Φ^2)

quadrupole-hexadecapole interference terms $2Q \cdot \Phi$

c) absolute frequency = 2329.7 ± ν

applied in calculating the near infrared intensities in the $(N_2)_2$ dimer, which replace the

$$M_{\lambda_A, \lambda_B, \Lambda, K}^{(R)}$$

factors (Table 1) used for the far infrared transitions, are given in Table 3.

Looking at the same series of dimer transitions $A_1^+(J=0) \to B_1^-(J=1)$ in ortho N_2-ortho N_2 as in Section 3, we find the results presented in Table 4. These transitions now occur as side-bands to the monomer transition at 2330 cm^{-1}, which is practically not shifted (0.1 cm^{-1}) in the dimer. These $A_1^+ \to B_1^-$ transitions are allowed when the excited state monomer wave function (6) has the plus sign; this plus sign reappears in the coefficients of Table 3 which are used to calculate intensities. In addition to these transitions, other dimer transitions from the A_1^+ ground state become allowed: $A_1^+(J=0) \to A_2^+(J=1)$. Such transitions correspond with the minus signs in Eq. (6) and Table 3, and they are forbidden in the far infrared region. Their intensities are listed in Table 5.

Comparing the results of Table 4 and Table 5 with those in Table 2 we can draw the following conclusions. Generally, the near infrared transition strengths are about 1000 times smaller than the far infrared values. This is mainly determined by the size of the monomer transition strength $\frac{1}{2}|<\phi_0|\Delta r|\phi_1>|^2 = 0.00185$ e$^2 a_0^2$. The variations in the individual ratios for corresponding $A_1^+ \to B_1^-$ transitions in the far and near infrared are much smaller, but still significant. This can be understood if one realizes that the first term in Tables 1 and 3 yields the dominant contribution to the far and near infrared line strength, respectively; the contributions from the other long range terms are not negligible, however, and those terms have opposite signs in Tables 1 and 3. The intensities of $A_1^+ \to A_2^-$ transitions which are forbidden in the far infrared, are even larger than those of the $A_1^+ \to B_1^-$ transitions. The first term from Table 3 is clearly dominant here. The first $A_1^+ \to A_2^+$ transitions is a pure end-over-end rotational ($J = 0 \to 1$) transition. This transition is stronger than the vibrational ones, just as we have found for the ground state (previous section); it forms part of the P and R branches observed by Long et al., (1973). In the ground state such rotational transitions are allowed only for mixed ortho-para dimers, however, whereas here they occur also in the homogeneous, ortho-ortho and para-para, complexes.

CONCLUSIONS

The present calculations have shown that the structure in the collision induced far and near infrared spectra which is due to dimer contributions contains detailed information, not only on the inter-

Table 5. Transition strengths in 10^{-9} $e^2 a_0^2$ for $A_1^+(J=0) \to A_2^-(J=1)$ transitions [a] from the lowest A_1^+ state in ortho N_2 (v=1) – ortho N_2 (v=0) dimers

A_2^- level number	Q^2 [b]	ϕ^2 [b]	$2Q \cdot \phi$ [b]	total	Δk	relative frequency [c] $\nu(cm^{-1})$
1	524	0	-20	505	0	0.165
2	227	0	-14	214	1	16.8
3	1.30	0	0.09	1.39	0	17.1
4	18.7	0	- 1.1	17.6	0	22.1
5	4.64	0.02	- 0.55	4.10	1	30.1
6	5.53	0.03	- 0.81	4.75	0	33.3
7	28.5	0.1	- 3.4	25.1	1	35.9

[a] symmetry labeling as in Table 2

[b] contributions as in Table 4

[c] absolute frequency = 2329.7 ± ν

molecular potential, but also on the interaction induced dipole function. In order to extract this information from the spectra and, in particular, to evaluate the importance of different contributions to the induced dipole, one first has to interpret the dimer spectra. This task is very difficult indeed, because Van der Waals complexes such as the $(N_2)_2$ dimer are too "floppy" to apply the more or less standard models for the dynamics of rigid molecules, on the one hand, while, on the other hand, they are substantially more rigid than $(H_2)_2$ dimers, where the infrared spectrum becomes relatively simple again due to the nearly free internal H_2 rotations. Calculations as the present one can be very helpful with this interpretation. Further work in trying to generate a complete infared spectrum of the $(N_2)_2$ dimer including all the bound-to-bound vibrational transitions with their rotational profiles, is in progress (Brocks and v.d. Avoird, 1984). We think that it would be profitable also if one could (re)measure the near and far infrared spectra of $(N_2)_2$, with higher resolution and/or sensitivity (at lower temperatures, possibly in molecular beams), because we expect that actually more transitions should be visible than those found by Long et al. in 1973.

REFERENCES

Allnatt, A.R., 1983, private communication.

Amos, R.D., 1980, Mol. Phys., 39:1.

Avoird, A. van der, Wormer, P.E.S., Mulder. F., and Berns, R.M., 1980, Topics in Current Chem., 93:1.

Berns, R.M., and Avoird, A. van der, 1980, J. Chem. Phys., 72:6107.

Birnbaum, G., Frommhold, L., Nencini, L., and Sutter, H., 1983, Chem. Phys. Lett., 100:292.

Blaney, B.L., and Ewing, G.E., 1976, Ann. Rev. Phys. Chem., 27:553.

Bosomworth, D.R., and Gush, H.P., 1965, Can. J. Phys., 43:751.

Brink, D.M., and Satchler, G.R., 1968, "Angular Momentum", 2nd ed., Clarendon, Oxford.

Brocks, G., Avoird, A. van der, Sutcliffe, B.T., and Tennyson, J., 1983, Mol. Phys., 50:1025.

Brocks, G., and Avoird, A. van der, 1984, to be published.

Bunker, P.R., 1979, "Molecular Symmetry and Spectroscopy", Academic, New York.

Buontempo, U., Cunsolo, S., Jacucci, G., and Weiss, J.J. (1975) J. Chem. Phys., 63:2570.

Curtiss, C.F., 1953, J. Chem. Phys., 21:1199.

Dagg, I.R., Reesor, G.E., and Urbaniak, J.L., 1974, Can. J.Phys., 52:821, 52:1764.

Danby, G., and Flower, D.R., 1983, J. Phys. B, 16:3411.

Dunker, A.M., and Gordon, R.G., 1978, J. Chem. Phys., 68:700.

Egelstaff, P.A., Gray, C.G., and Gubbins, K.E., 1975, in: "Physical Chem. Ser. 2, Vol. 2, Molecular structure and properties, MTP Internat. Rev. Sci.," Buttersworths, London.

Frommhold, L., Hong, K.H., and Profitt, M.H., 1976, Mol. Phys.
     35:691.
Godfried, H.P., and Silvera, I.F., 1982, Phys. Rev. Lett., 48:1337.
Hemert, M.C. van, and Berns, R.M., 1982, J. Chem. Phys.,76:354.
Herzberg, G., 1950, "Molecular spectra and molecular structure,
     I. Spectra of diatomic molecules", 2nd ed., Van Nostrand,
     New York.
Langhoff, S.R., Bauschlicher, C.W., and Chong, D.P., 1983,
     J. Chem. Phys., 78:5287.
Launey, J.M., 1977, J. Phys. B, 10:3665.
LeRoy, R.J., and Kranendonk, J. van, 1974, J. Chem. Phys., 61:4750.
LeRoy, R.J., and Carley, J.S., 1980, Advan. Chem. Phys., 42:353.
Long, C.A., Henderson, G., and Ewing, G.E., 1973, Chem.Phys.,
     2:485.
Luty, T., Avoird, A. van der, and Berns, R.M., 1980, J. Chem. Phys.,
     73:5305.
McKellar, A.R.W., and Welsh, H.L., 1971, J. Chem. Phys., 55:595.
McKellar, A.R.W., 1982, Faraday Disc. Chem. Soc., 73:89.
Mulder, F., Dijk, G. van, and Avoird, A. van der, 1980, Mol.
     Phys., 39:407.
Nyeland, C., Poulsen, L.L., and Billing, G.D., Feb. 1984,
     J.Phys.Chem..
Poll, J.D., and Hunt, J.L., 1981, Can. J. Phys., 59:1448.
Prengel, A.T., and Gornall, W.S., 1976, Phys. Rev., A13:253.
Schäfer, J., and Meyer, W., 1984, this volume.
Sheng, D.T., and Ewing, G.E., 1971, J. Chem. Phys., 55:5424.
Steele, W.A., 1963, J. Chem. Phys., 39:3197.
Svendsen, E.N., and Oddershede, J., 1979, J. Chem. Phys., 71:3000.
Tennyson, J., and Avoird, A. van der, 1982, J. Chem. Phys.,
     77:5664.
Tennyson, J., and Sutcliffe, B.T., 1982, J. Chem. Phys., 77:4061.
Tennyson, J., and Sutcliffe, B.T., 1983, J. Chem. Phys., 79:43.
Verberne, J., and Reuss, J., 1981, Chem Phys., 50:137.
Waaijer, M., Jacobs, M., and Reuss, J., 1981, Chem. Phys., 63:257.

VIBRATIONAL SPECTRAL LINESHAPES OF CHARGE TRANSFER COMPLEXES

David W. Oxtoby

Department of Chemistry and The James Franck Institute
The University of Chicago
Chicago, IL 60637

ABSTRACT

I examine the effect of charge transfer complex formation on
vibrational spectral lineshapes. A simple cell model for the liquid is used, together with a generalized Langevin description of
the dynamics. I show that a simple three-variable theory can encompass both the interaction induced types of spectral lineshapes
found in weak complexes, and the dephasing-broadened lineshapes
characteristic of strong complexes.

INTRODUCTION

Charge transfer complexes in solution have attracted considerable interest both from theoreticians and from experimentalists
in recent years (Mullikan and Person, 1969). Most of the attention
has focussed on the presence of a new electronic transition which
arises when such complexes are formed; its origin lies in the mixing of the ground state wave function of the pair of molecules with
an excited state wave function involving the transfer of an electron
from one molecule in the complex to the other, a state which is then
stabilized by the attractive Coulomb energy of the two parts of the
complex. Because there is generally a large change in dipole moment
for the complex between these two states, the transition dipole moment is large and a new intense electronic absorption is seen in the
visible or ultraviolet region of the spectrum. By varying the concentrations of the components of the complex and the temperature,
one can study the equilibrium constant for complex formation as well
as the enthalpy and entropy changes accompanying the process.

Much less attention has been paid to the effect of complex formation in the vibrational region of the spectrum. Yarwood (1973) has reviewed experimental and theoretical studies of infrared and Raman vibrational spectra of charge transfer complexes. Shifts in band frequencies are seen and attempts have been made to correlate the magnitudes of these shifts with the strength of the complex formed. Intensities of vibrational bands have been investigated and correlated with changes in dipole moment during formation of a complex. Certain vibrational bands which are absent for symmetry reasons in the isolated molecule (such as infrared absorption in a homonuclear diatomic like I_2) are seen when the symmetry is broken through complex formation. In isolated cases (Rosen et al., 1971; Cohen and Weiss, 1980) vibrational spectra for complexed and uncomplexed molecules have been separated.

There has been relatively little attention paid to the spectral lineshapes of vibrational bands in charge transfer complexes, although such lineshape studies could provide a rich source of information about equilibrium and dynamical aspects of complex formation. My goal in this paper is to set up a theoretical framework for describing vibrational spectral lineshapes of such complexes. The theoretical approach I propose is general enough to encompass both very weak (so called contact) charge transfer complexes which are closely connected to interaction induced phenomena, and strong complexes which may usefully be pictured as "super-molecules" showing new vibrational modes beyond those of their separate parts.

CELL MODEL

I begin with a relatively crude but useful model of motion in the liquid state, the cell model (Herzfeld and Litovitz, 1959). In this model, a molecule is pictured as moving in a spherical cell of radius R_c formed by its N_c nearest neighbors. In the cases which interest us for charge transfer complexes, the molecule in the center of the cell will be a simple molecule such as Cl_2 or I_2, while the surrounding molecules will be a second component such as benzene (bz) or pyridine (py). The potential energy between the two components is denoted as $V(r)$ and for simplicity I take this to be an isotropic potential, independent of the orientations of the two molecules, although the latter could be included if desired. $V(r)$ includes energy contributions not only from the charge transfer stabilization of the complex but also from electrostatic, induction, dispersion, and repulsive interactions. While a radial distribution function approach is more fundamental than the cell model, not enough is known about distributions in mixtures of molecular liquids to justify such an approach at the present time.

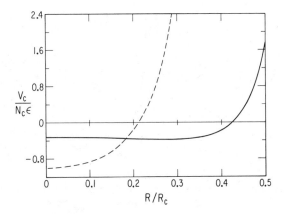

Fig. 1. The cell potential $V_c(R)$ for a Lennard-Jones interatomic potential: $V(R) = 4\varepsilon \left[(\sigma/R)^{12} - (\sigma/R)^{6}\right]$. ———: $R_c/\sigma = 1.5$; — — —: $R_c/\sigma = 2^{1/6} = 1.122$. Note that in the first case there is a maximum near $R = 0$, while in the second there is a minimum.

In the cell model the N_c nearest neighbors that form the shell are spread uniformly over the surface of the sphere on which they lie. I can define a cell potential $V_c(R)$ which is a function of the displacement R of the molecule from the center of the cell. $V_c(R)$ is calculated by averaging the pair potential $V(r)$ over angles θ and ψ that describe the location of the surrounding molecules on the surface of the sphere:

$$V_c(R) = \frac{N_c}{4\pi} \int_0^{2\pi} d\psi \int_0^{\pi} d\theta \, \sin\theta \, V(|\vec{R} - \vec{r}(\theta,\psi)|)$$

$$= \frac{N_c}{2} \int_0^{\pi} d\theta \, \sin\theta \, V(\overline{\sqrt{R^2 + R_c^2 - 2RR_c \cos\theta}})$$

This integral can be evaluated for any choice of pair potential $V(r)$ and cell radius R_c. $V_c(R)$ rises sharply as R approaches R_c because of the repulsive interactions of the central molecule with those that make up the walls of the cell, as shown in Fig. (1).

717

It is instructive to examine the behavior of V_c for values of R small relative to R_c. An expansion gives

$$\frac{V_c(R)}{N_c} = V(R_c) + [\frac{1}{3} R_c V'(R_c) + \frac{1}{6} R_c^2 V''(R_c)] \ R^2$$

$$+ \ [\frac{1}{30} R_c^3 V'''(R_c) + \frac{1}{120} R_c^4 V''''(R_c)] \ R^4$$

The coefficient of the R^2 term can either be positive or negative. For a one-component liquid R_c is close to the minimum in the potential, so that $V' \approx 0$ and $V'' > 0$ and $V_c(R)$ has a minimum at $R = 0$. For a two-component liquid this may no longer be true and the sign of this coefficient can be negative. I anticipate that weak complexes will be characterized by a broad, shallow minimum near $R = 0$, so that the molecule in the center will exchange rapidly between neighbors (the interaction induced limit). In a strong complex, on the other hand, the central molecule will be preferentially bound to one of its neighbors so that the lowest energy position in the cell will be displaced from the origin. The stronger the complex, the larger will be the force constant resisting motion from this displaced minimum.

In this paper I will consider only infrared absorption spectra, although the methods introduced here could be applied as well to Raman spectra. The absorption coefficient $\alpha(\omega)$ is related the Fourier transform of the dipole moment autocorrelation function through

$$\alpha(\omega) \propto \frac{2\omega(1-e^{-\beta\hbar\omega})}{\beta\hbar(1+e^{-\beta\hbar\omega})} \int_{-\infty}^{\infty} dt \ \langle \vec{\mu}(t) \cdot \vec{\mu}(0) \rangle$$

$$\equiv \frac{2\omega(1-e^{-\beta\hbar\omega})}{\beta\hbar(1+e^{-\beta\hbar\omega})} I(\omega)$$

In writing this expression, I have made a simple semi-classical approximation to take account of detailed balance. Following Guillot et al. (1982) I have written the full quantum mechanical $\alpha(\omega)$ in terms of the anticommutator of the dipole moment, and have then taken the classical limit of the anticommutator. This allows a classical treatment of the particle dynamics while satisfying detailed balance for $\alpha(\omega)$. The angular brackets $< >$ refer to an ensemble average over the complexes in the sample. The diple moment of each complex is modulated both by relative motion of the two parts of the complex (through the coordinate R in the cell model) and by vibrations of the two molecules that make up the complex.

718

In other words, both a bz - I_2 stretch and an I-I stretch will mod-
ulate $\vec{\mu}(t)$ and affect the spectrum. In this paper, I will first
consider only the former contribution (ignoring internal modes of
molecules in the complex), and then will turn to a consideration of
the latter contribution at the end.

Just as I introduced the pair potential V(r) so I can also introduce a pair dipole moment function $\vec{\mu}(\vec{r})$ for the dependence of
the dipole moment of the complex on the separation r between the
two molecules that make it up. $\vec{\mu}(\vec{r})$ depends both on charge transfer and on other short and long range interactions. I take the
dipole moment to lie along the internuclear axis r so that

$$\vec{\mu}(\vec{r}) = \vec{r}m(r)$$

The cell model dipole moment now involves an average of the pair
dipole moment $\vec{\mu}(\vec{r})$ over positions on the spherical shell:

$$\vec{\mu}(\vec{R}) = \frac{N_c}{4\pi} \int_0^{2\pi} d\psi \int_0^\pi d\theta \sin\theta \ \vec{\mu}(\vec{R} - \vec{r}(\theta,\psi))$$

$$= \hat{R} \frac{N_c}{2} \int_0^\pi d\theta \sin\theta \ [R - R_c \cos\theta] m(\sqrt{R^2 + R_c^2 - 2RR_c^2 \cos\theta}\ )$$

This can be expanded for small R to give

$$\frac{\vec{\mu}_c(\vec{R})}{N_c} = [m(R_c) + \frac{1}{3} R_c m'(R_c)]\ \vec{R}$$

$$+ [\frac{4}{15} \frac{m'(R_c)}{R_c} + \frac{7}{30} m''(R_c)]\ R^2\vec{R}$$

Through these expressions the dynamics of the dipole moment function
can be related to the ensemble average of correlations in the cell
dynamics R(t). I will restrict myself to simple linear dependence
of $\vec{\mu}$ on $\vec{R}$, although nonlinear terms could be included without difficulty.

The dynamics of R(t) are described here though a projection
operator approach (Mori, 1965) in which the dynamical variable R is
coupled to two other variables, its first and second time derivatives. Specifically, I take as a complete set of slow variables
the set

$$A_1 = \mu_R R(t)$$

719

$$A_2 = \dot{A}_1 = P(t)$$

$$A_3 = \dot{A}_2 = F(t)$$

where for simplicity I have introduced a proportionality constant of the reduced mass (μ_R) in the definition of A_1. A_2 is a momentum and A_3 a force. Other dynamical variables are assumed in the projection operator approach to be rapidly-varying quantities that give rise only to damping of the explicitly included variables.

What is the rationale for this choice of dynamical variables? A single variable theory gives rise to simple exponential decay and is unsatisfactory. The second variable, P, must be included in order to allow for inertial effects that are important for motion in a harmonic well; it allows for a reasonable treatment of damped harmonic motion. Finally, the third variable (a generalized force) is necessary for proper treatment of anharmonicities in the cell potential $V_c(R)$ and of fluctuations in the forces: $V_c(R)$ is not in fact fixed, but fluctuates as the molecules that make up the cell move in and out. A three-variable theory is the minimum satisfactory theory for describing spectra of charge transfer complexes.

The projection operator equations are simplified if the variable A_3 is replaced by one which is orthogonal to A_1:

$$A_3 \rightarrow A_3 - \frac{<A_3 A_1>}{<A_1 A_1>} A_1 = F + \mu_R \omega_0^2 R = F + kR$$

where brackets refer to an equilibrium ensemble average over motion in the fluid and where ω_0 is the average harmonic frequency and k the average force constant in the cell. The new A_3 can be represented as δF, where δF is that part of the force that does __not__ arise from simple harmonic motion in the average cell potential. It is due only to anharmonicities and to fluctuations.

The equations of motion for the set of variables A_i can be written in matrix form. If $\vec{A}(t)$ is vector with components $A_1(t)$, $A_2(t)$, and $A_3(t)$ then the projection operator approach gives

$$\frac{d}{dt} \vec{A}(t) = [i\overleftrightarrow{\Omega} - \overleftrightarrow{K}] \cdot \vec{A}(t) + \vec{f}(t)$$

where $\vec{f}(t)$ is a vector of delta-correlated random forces

$$<f_i(t) f_j(0)> = \delta_{i3} \delta_{j3} \, \delta(t) \, \alpha <A_1 A_1>$$

and where $\overleftrightarrow{\Omega}$ is a frequency matrix and $\overleftrightarrow{K}$ a damping matrix. In the projection operator approach $\overleftrightarrow{\Omega}$ and $\overleftrightarrow{K}$ can be related to equilibrium ensemble averages involving the variables A_1, A_2, and A_3, and to the damping coefficient α.

RESULTS

The result of such a calculation is

$$i\overleftrightarrow{\Omega} - \overleftrightarrow{K} = \begin{bmatrix} 0 & 1 & 0 \\ -\omega_0^2 & 0 & 1 \\ 0 & \dfrac{\omega_1^4}{\omega_0^2} & -\gamma \end{bmatrix}$$

where

$$\omega_0^2 = \frac{<A_2 A_2>}{<A_1 A_1>} = \frac{<P^2>}{\mu_R^2 <R^2>}$$

$$\omega_1^4 = \frac{<A_3 A_3>}{<A_1 A_1>} = \frac{<(\delta F)^2>}{<A_1 A_1>}$$

$$\gamma = \frac{\alpha}{\omega_1^4}$$

ω_0 is the average harmonic frequency and can be calculated from the cell potential. ω_1 depends on the anharmonicities and fluctuations in forces and is more difficult to calculate, while γ (through α) brings in the relaxation time scale for the fluctuating forces. From these equations of motion the correlation function $<R(t)R(0)>$ can be calculated, and its Fourier transform is proportional to the spectral intensity $I(\omega)$ for infrared absorption. The result of the calculation is

$$I(\omega) = \frac{2\omega_1^4/\gamma \; \omega_0^4}{\left[1 - \dfrac{\omega^2}{\omega_0^2}\right]^2 + \dfrac{\omega^2}{\gamma^2}\left[\dfrac{\omega^2}{\omega_0^2} - \dfrac{\omega_1^4}{\omega_0^4} - 1\right]^2}$$

From this the absorption coefficient $\alpha(\omega)$ can be calculated.

How do we expect the parameters to behave for strong and weak

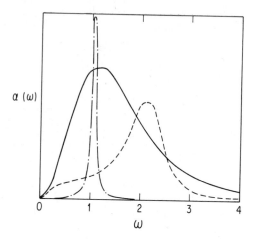

Fig. 2. Absorption intensity $\alpha(\omega)$ plotted against reduced frequency ω (in units of ω_0) for three choices of parameters. ————: $\omega_1/\omega_0 = 1.65$, $\gamma/\omega_0 = 5$; — — — —: $\omega_1/\omega_0 = 1.42$; $\gamma/\omega_0 = 1$; — • — • —: $\omega_1/\omega_0 = 0.68$; $\gamma/\omega_0 = 1$.

complexes? A strong complex will be characterized by a large force constant and relatively weak fluctuations or anharmonicities, so that ω_1 will be much smaller than ω_0. With this in mind, I have done sample calculations for several values of the three parameters in the theory. Three of the results are shown in Fig. (2). In two cases $\omega_1 > \omega_0$ (weak complex) while in the third $\omega_1 < \omega_0$ (strong complex). Small changes in ω_1/ω_0 have a large effect because this ratio appears raised to the fourth power in $I(\omega)$. The weak complex absorption $\alpha(\omega)$ closely resembles that for interaction induced spectra such as arise from Ne atoms dissolved in liquid argon. In fact, a three-variable theory of the same form as the present one has been used successfully by Guillot et al. (1982) to describe absorption by rare gas mixtures. Their calculation could be carried farther because the identification of $\vec{\mu}(\vec{r})$ with the force between the atom pair allowed an explicit evaluation of the parameters ω_0, ω_1, and γ for a real liquid instead of involving the cell model as in the present approach. The strong complex absorption resembles that due to simple vibrational dephasing (Oxtoby, 1979; 1981) in which a vibrational line is damped by weak fluctuating forces with correlation times τ_c. My three-variable theory thus encompases both limits in a unified treatment.

I turn now to the effect on the spectrum of the internal vibrational mode q of the molecule at the center of the cell, which for simplicity I take to be a homonuclear diatomic such as Cl_2. The dipole moment function in the cell model can be expanded in q as well as in R and to lowest non-trivial order is

$$\frac{\vec{\mu}_c(\vec{R})}{N_c} = [m(R_c) + \frac{1}{3} R_c m'(R_c)]\, \vec{R}$$

$$+ [\frac{\partial m(R_c)}{\partial q} + \frac{1}{3} R_c \frac{\partial m'(R_c)}{\partial q}]\, q\vec{R}$$

The first term gives rise to the intermolecular band I have discussed already. In the general case there will be a cross term appearing in the dipole moment correlation function and a contribution from the second term alone.

If the vibrational coordinate q is only weakly coupled dynamically to the cell coordinate $\vec{R}(t)$, the analysis is greatly simplified. The cross term no longer contributes in this case because $<\vec{R}(t)\cdot\vec{R}(0)q(t)q(0)>$ vanishes after an average over the phase of the vibrational coordinate q has been carried out. The additional contribution in the spectrum involves the Fourier transform of

$$<\vec{R}(t) \cdot \vec{R}(0)q(t)q(0)> \approx <\vec{R}(t) \cdot \vec{R}(0)><q(t)q(0)>$$

where the averaging has been decoupled because R and q are considered to be weakly coupled. The resulting spectrum will simply be a convolution of the intramolecular mode spectrum calculated earlier, with the pure vibrational dephasing spectrum for the diatomic molecule.

If q(t) is strongly coupled to $\vec{R}(t)$ the analysis is more complicated. This coupling involves cross terms in the potential energy of the form k'qR and leads to a mixing of the original normal modes to produce new modes containing both q and R character; its effect on line shifts for charge transfer spectra has been discussed earlier (Yarwood, 1973). The most straightforward way to treat it is to expand the set of dynamical variables in the projection operator approach to five by adding q(t) and its time derivative p(t) to the set. The relaxation matrix now involves, in addition to the parameters considered earlier, the coupling strength k', the vibrational frequency of the internal mode q(t), and a second damping constant describing the pure dephasing of q(t). The spectra which result generally show two peaks for reasonable parameter choices, but because of the mixing they cannot be assigned purely to R(t) or to q(t) motion. Further details on the calculational methods and results in this case will be given elsewhere.

What I have sketched out is clearly a "bare-bones" calculational framework. While the forms derived for the spectral lineshapes are useful for fitting to experimental data, I have not shown how the parameters that appear in them may be calculated explicitly for real molecules and complexes. Two types of information are necessary for a full first-principles calculation. The first is some knowledge of the pair interaction energy $V(r)$ and dipole moment $\vec{\mu}(\vec{R})$, a problem on which at least some progress can be made using other types of experimental information on charge transfer complexes (Yarwood, 1973). The second involves estimates of effects of fluctuations and time scales for dynamical processes.

The method of approach outlined here leads naturally to the two limiting cases of a weak complex purely interaction induced spectrum, and a strong complex vibrational dephasing spectrum. This general method may be applicable to the study of a related problem, the low frequency Raman spectrum of molten salts (Begun et al., 1972). Some molten salts, such as $AlCl_3$, show clearly-defined vibrational modes from $AlCl_4^-$ complexes, while other less strongly complexed molten salts like $ZnCl_2$ show less vibrational mode structure and are perhaps better described as interaction induced spectra.

ACKNOWLEDGMENTS

I would like to thank Professor S. Bratos for suggesting this problem to me, as well as for a number of very helpful discussions. This research was supported by the National Science Foundation (grant number CHE81-06068).

REFERENCES

Begun, G., Brynestad, J., Fung, K.W., and Mamantov, G., 1972, Inorg. Nucl. Chem. Letters, 8: 79.
Cohen, B., and Weiss, S., 1980, J. Chem. Phys., 72: 6804.
Guillot, B., Bratos, S., and Birnbaum, G., 1982, Phys. Rev. A, 25:773.
Herzfeld, K.F., and Litovitz, T.A., 1959, "Absorption and Dispersion of Ultrasonic Waves," Academic Press, New York.
Mori, H., 1965, Prog. Theor. Phys., 33: 423.

Mullikan, R.S., and Person, W.B., 1969, "Molecular Complexes,"
        Wiley, New York.
Oxtoby, D.W., 1979, Adv. Chem. Phys., 40: 1.
Oxtoby, D.W., 1981, Ann. Rev. Phys. Chem., 32: 77.
Rosen, H., Shen, Y., and Stenman, F., 1971, Mol. Phys., 22: 33.
Yarwood, J., 1973, "Spectroscopy and Structure of Molecular Com-
        plexes," Plenum, New York.

COLLISION-INDUCED EFFECTS IN PLANETARY ATMOSPHERES

R. H. Tipping

Department of Physics and Astronomy
University of Alabama
University, AL   35486

ABSTRACT

The manifestations of collision-induced effects in planetary
atmospheres will be surveyed from both the experimental and theoretical perspectives. By considering the composition, pressure,
and temperature profiles for the atmospheres of the Earth, Titan,
Venus, and the Giant Planets, one can infer the major sources of
collision-induced opacities. The status of the laboratory-based
studies for the relevant collision-induced absorption are reviewed
and several desirable experiments are proposed. Recent theoretical
refinements (e.g., higher multipolar induction mechanisms, line
shapes, interference effects, etc.) that are important for the
analysis of the laboratory data and for the generation of synthetic
spectra will be discussed. Finally, a few examples of the effects
of collision-induced absorption as calculated through simple atmospheric models will be presented.

INTRODUCTION

Collision-induced absorption (CIA) plays a significant role in
the atmospheres of several planets (or satellites) as revealed by
their spectroscopy and thermal structures. In the present paper,
these collision-induced phenomena will be surveyed both from the
experimental and from the theoretical perspectives.

First, by considering the composition, pressure, and temperature profiles for the atmospheres of the Earth, Titan, Venus, and
the Giant Planets, the main sources of collision-induced opacities
are inferred. The status of the laboratory studies on these gases

and gas mixtures are briefly reviewed, and several additional studies desirable for the interpretation of atmospheric spectra are proposed. In some cases, however, because of the difficulties involved in simulating the physical conditions existing in the actual atmospheres, the interpretation of the measured spectra can be assisted by the computation of synthetic spectra. A number of recent theoretical refinements such as the inclusion of higher-order multipolar induction mechanisms (Cohen, 1976; Moon and Oxtoby, 1981), interference effects between allowed and induced dipole moments (Poll et al., 1976; Tipping et al., 1978), more accurate representation of the wings of spectral lines through the use of spectral moments (Hartye et al., 1975; Poll, 1980; Birnbaum, 1982), or quantum mechanical line shapes (Van Kranendonk and Gass, 1973; Birnbaum, 1979; Birnbaum et al., 1984), etc., that must be incorporated in the synthetic spectra before a quantitative interpretation of the observed spectra is possible, are discussed.

Finally, several explicit examples of the effects of CIA as calculated through simple atmospheric models are presented. It is shown that not only must this absorption be included in the analysis before one can extract important structural features (e.g. isotopic abundances, aerosol concentrations or cloud layers, etc.), but also CIA can itself be used to obtain information not easily accessible by other techniques.

EXPERIMENTAL REVIEW

Earth

The atmosphere of the Earth is composed primarily of nonpolar diatomic molecules; dry air is approximately 78% N_2, 21% O_2 with rare gases and trace polar molecules comprising the remaining 1%. There is also present a variable amount of water vapor (up to 3.5%), the upper limit of which depends sensitively on the ambient temperature. Roughly speaking, the atmospheric temperature ranges from approximately 300 K at the surface to about 200 K in the stratosphere. Consequently, the concentration of water vapor, which can be appreciable near the surface, decreases with increasing altitude unlike most of the other constituents which are uniformly mixed throughout.

In view of the above, one would expect the major contributions to collision-induced absorption to result from binary collisions between N_2-N_2, N_2-O_2 and O_2-O_2 pairs; however, because of the larger induced dipoles resulting from collisions with water molecules, the CIA from N_2-H_2O pairs is not negligible at high humidity conditions in the lower atmosphere (Tipping, 1979).

The CIA of pure nitrogen has been extensively studied in the laboratory (Rich and McKellar, 1976) over the range of temperatures of interest for the Earth's atmosphere. Although most of these studies have been carried out at high densities in order to enhance the weak absorption, the density squared dependence of CIA has been well established and enables one to extrapolate accurately to atmospheric pressures. Data exist for the translation-rotational (Bosomworth and Gush, 1965; Buontempo et al., 1983; Guillot and Birnbaum, 1983), fundamental (Reddy and Cho, 1965), and overtone (Shapiro and Gush, 1966) rotation-vibrational bands.

The far IR N_2 absorption has not been detected in atmospheric spectra because it falls in a region where allowed water lines and the associated "water continuum" (Clough et al., 1980) absorb strongly. One would expect, however, that this absorption could be significant for long paths through the stratosphere where the water molecules have condensed out. By contrast, the high frequency wing of the fundamental band occurs in a "window" region devoid of other strong absorptions (Rinsland et al., 1981); its importance on atmospheric transmission has been reported by several groups (Susskind and Searl, 1977; Bernstein et al., 1979; Camy-Peyret et al., 1981). Because of the weakness of the CIA overtone spectra, one would not expect these to play a major role in the Earth's atmosphere.

Oxygen, like nitrogen, has been studied extensively in the laboratory (Crawford et al., 1949; McKellar et al., 1972) over the range of temperatures of interest; data exist for both the pure gas and for O_2-N_2 mixtures (Moskalenko et al., 1979). Again, for the same reasons as discussed above, the far IR CIA spectrum has not been detected in the atmosphere. (This would be weaker than the corresponding N_2 results both because of the lower concentration of O_2 molecules and the smaller quadrupole moment of O_2.) Again, however, the CIA in the fundamental region around 1600 cm^{-1} has been detected in long-path stratospheric measurements (Rinsland et al., 1982). While most of this absorption arises from O_2-N_2 collisions, the O_2-O_2 pairs will also contribute.

The next strongest source of CIA would result from N_2-H_2O pairs. Since this absorption is many orders of magnitude weaker than the allowed H_2O dipole absorption, the best place to observe this effect would be in the high frequency wing of the N_2 band where it would show up as an increase in absorption that is proportional to the H_2O density. Such an effect has been observed (Clough and Kneizys, 1983) in transmission over long paths (8 km). Since radiation in this frequency window is widely used for many purposes, an experimental study (and theoretical analysis) of CIA in this binary mixture would be very desirable.

Titan

The recent Voyager missions to the outer planets have provided
some invaluable information regarding the atmosphere of Titan
(Samuelson et al., 1981; Hanel, 1981; Lindal et al., 1983). Like
the Earth, Titan has a predominantly nitrogen atmosphere; while the
total atmospheric pressure near each surface is roughly comparable,
there are several important differences arising primarily from the
lower ambient temperatures on Titan. (The temperature decreases
from the surface value of 93 K to a low of approximately 73 K at
the inversion layer, before slowly increasing in the upper atmosphere.) On the one hand, water vapor that is responsible for most
of the allowed dipolar absorption of far IR radiation in the
Earth's atmosphere is not present in detectable amounts on Titan.
There, the main trace gas (excluding Ar) is methane, with a
slightly smaller mixing ratio for H_2 and very much smaller ratios
for heavier hydrocarbons and nitrogen compounds. However, because
of the low vapor pressure and the absence of a permanent dipole
moment in CH_4, this molecule does not absorb strongly in the far IR.
On the other hand, because of the lower temperature, the near-
surface atmospheric density is approximately 4.5 times that of the
Earth, leading to CIA that is 20 times greater. This CIA would
result from N_2-N_2, N_2-CH_4, CH_4-CH_4, and N_2-H_2 collisions, with increasingly smaller amounts from other mixtures. The Voyager
spectra show a broad, continuous absorption, increasing from 600
cm^{-1} down to the instrumental cutoff at 200 cm^{-1} (Hanel, 1981).
Thus, any CIA involved would result from the translation-rotational
bands of the gases and gas mixtures mentioned above.

There exist in the literature accurate CIA data for CH_4,
notably by Birnbaum and coworkers (Birnbaum, 1975; Birnbaum and
Cohen, 1975; Birnbaum et al., 1983); these experimental studies
have been performed at a number of different temperatures down to
195 K. In view of the Titan results, additional studies at lower
temperatures and in N_2-CH_4 mixtures are currently in progress
(Birnbaum, 1983). This additional data will enable one to model
the IR spectrum of Titan more realistically than the simple model
discussed in the final section of this paper (Hunt et al., 1983).

C. Venus

The atmosphere of Venus is unique in the solar system; its
massive atmosphere is composed mainly of CO_2 reaching a pressure at
the surface of approximately 90 atmospheres. In addition, the temperature variation in the atmosphere is also enormous, from 730 K
at the surface down to 240 K at an altitude of 60 km (Mutch, 1980).
Under these conditions there is, no doubt, appreciable CIA arising
from CO_2-CO_2 collisions. This effect is accompanied, however, by
large allowed absorption, such that the disentangling of these two

effects would be a formidable problem. To compound the problem, the laboratory studies of CIA in CO_2 (Birnbaum et al., 1971; Mannik and Stryland, 1972; Dagg et al., 1974) have been carried out at substantially different pressures and temperatures, and the theoretical analysis of these results have presented some unexplained complexities.

The Giant Planets

The IR spectra obtained by the Voyager missions for the atmospheres of Jupiter and Saturn demonstrate most vividly the importance of CIA in planetary spectra: these spectra from about 250 cm^{-1} to 700 cm^{-1} are in fact dominated by the collision-induced absorption features of H_2 (Hanel et al., 1981). The exact ratio of the most abundant gases, H_2 and He, is a topic of current interest to astrophysicists since it is thought to closely approximate the "primordial abundances". Thus an analysis of CIA due to H_2-H_2 and to H_2-He pairs is of fundamental importance. Fortunately these mixtures have been studied theoretically (Poll, 1971; Belton and Spinrad, 1973) and in the laboratory over a wide range of pressures and temperatures (Reddy et al., 1977; Cohen et al., 1982; Birnbaum et al., 1984). (The temperature range where most of the CIA occurs is from approximately 50 K to 170 K.) In addition to the overwhelming strength of the absorption, one anomalous feature, a dip at the frequencies corresponding to the $S_0(0)$ and $S_0(1)$ line centers, has also been observed. As discussed in the paper by Bachet (1983), this feature is not an experimental artifact, and its interpretation will pose a challenge to the theoreticians (Frommhold and Birnbaum, 1984). One final point concerning the atmospheres of the Giant Planets deserves mention. The exact ortho/para ratio of H_2 in these atmospheres has been the subject of some speculation (Trafton, 1967; Smith, 1978; Conrath and Gierasch, 1983). It is possible that the modeling of CIA in H_2 and H_2-He collisions may be instrumental in resolving this question for these atmospheres.

THEORETICAL REVIEW

In order to compare theoretical predictions with actual atmospheric spectra, it is important in many cases to incorporate some recent refinements to the basic CIA theory when computing synthetic spectra. For example, in assessing the effects of N_2-N_2 absorption on Titan, only the high frequency wing of the translation-rotational band will contribute to the observed opacity because of the instrumental cutoff at 200 cm^{-1}. Similarly, in the Earth's atmosphere most of the fundamental band of N_2 lies under the strong allowed ν_3 band of CO_2, and thus CIA is only important in the high frequency wing. In both of these cases, one has to be able to model

731

accurately the absorption far from the band centers. Consequently, the shape assumed for the individual lines when synthesizing the spec trum plays a critical role (Frommhold, 1981; Birnbaum et al., 1981). Recent advances based on the theory of moments provide much more relia-ble temperature-dependent line shapes than earlier efforts that were based on Boltzman modified dispersion shapes (Borysow et al., 1984). Of note are the numerical quantum mechanical calculations of collision induced absorption spectra; CH_4-CH_4 (Birnbaum et al., 1983); H_2-He (Birnbaum et al., 1984); and H_2-H_2 (Borysow and Frommhold, 1985).

Another important contribution in the wings of the N_2 bands arises from higher multipolar induction mechanisms, e.g. hexadecapo-lar induction (Poll and Tipping, 1978; Reddy et al., 1980; Poll and Hunt, 1981); even though these lines are considerably weaker than the quadrupole-induced lines, their different selection rules allows for absorption at higher frequencies. In fact, in the translation-rotational band of N_2, the spectrum above 100 cm^{-1} is dominated by hexadecapolar induction.

Similar comments also apply for H_2. For instance, in investi-gating the role of CIA in the interesting 2000 cm^{-1} region of the atmospheres of the Giant Planets where strong absorptions are ab-sent and one sees the effects of trace molecules such as CH_3D, H_2O, PH_3, GeH_4, etc. (Trafton, 1981), one has to be able to model the CIA background from H_2-H_2 and H_2-He collisions; this background results from the high frequency wing of the translation-rotational band including $S_0(J) + S_0(J') $ and $U_0(J)$ contributions (Goorvitch and Tipping, 1982) and the low frequency wing of the fundamental rotation-vibrational band (centered near 4100 cm^{-1}).

Finally, we would like to mention the possible consequences of interference effects. Two different types of interference have been observed in CIA spectra: the "intercollisional interference" (Lewis and Van Kranendonk, 1970; Lewis, 1972; Lewis, 1984) which is destructive and results in dips at the line center frequencies of overlap lines, and "intracollisional interference" (Herman et al., 1979; Nelson and Tabisz, 1982; Rich and McKellar, 1983) which can be either constructive or destructive and results in modification of both line strengths and shapes. Both of these in-terference effects can play a significant role in the analysis of laboratory data as well as in the extraction of information such as isotopic abundance and H/D ratio from planetary spectra (Beer and Taylor, 1978; Macy and Smith, 1978). The recent work by Bragg and coworkers (1982; 1984) shows that the intercollisional inter-ference must be taken into account in determining allowed quadrupole line strengths, while the intracollisional interference was shown previously (Nelson and Tabisz, 1982; 1983) to be responsible for the apparent discrepancy between theoretical and experimental de-terminations of the dipole moment of HD in the ground state. Since both quadrupole lines of H_2 and allowed dipole lines of HD are important indicators of atmospheric conditions (Trauger et al., 1973; Trafton and Ramsay, 1980; Smith et al., 1980), the CIA effects must be taken into account.

MODEL CALCULATIONS

In order to illustrate some of the comments made above, we include here some examples of the effects of CIA in planetary spectra as calculated through simple atmospheric models. The first example is a calculation of the far IR spectrum of Titan; since the details have been reported elsewhere (Hunt et al., 1983), only the results along with a brief description are given here. In Fig. 1 we show the reduced absorption coefficient $A = \alpha(\nu)/\rho^2$ versus wavenumber for the translation-rotational band of N_2 at two temperatures. Using this absorption as the only source of opacity and a simple atmospheric model (Hunt et al., 1983), one obtains the synthetic spectrum from 0 to 600 cm^{-1} as shown in Fig. 2. The actual Voyager measurements are also shown for comparison. While the N_2 absorbs significantly between 50 and 100 cm^{-1}, this alone cannot account for the experimental results.

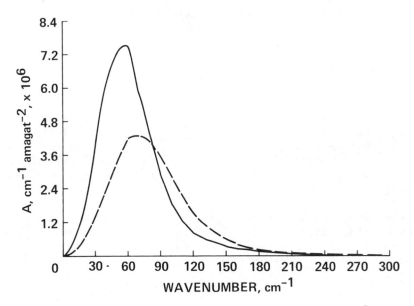

Figure 1.   The reduced absorption coefficient $\alpha(\nu)/\rho^2$ for the translation-rotational band of N_2 at temperatures of 70 K (——) and 120 K (---).

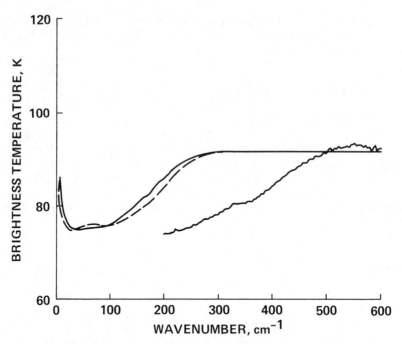

Figure 2. Calculated brightness temperature spectra of Titan with mixing ratios of N_2 and CH_4 equal to 0.882 and 0.0, respectively, for the two emission angles: 7.3° (———) and 52.7° (- - -). The results from Voyager 1 for an average emission angle of 52.7° are also shown.

In Fig. 3 we show the same results except that the estimated CIA of CH_4-CH_4 has also been included. While the results are improved, more opacity in the 200-400 cm^{-1} range is needed. Furthermore, one should obviously include the results of CH_4-N_2, N_2-H_2, etc. opacities in a more sophisticated synthetic spectrum. Whether one can completely account for the Voyager results without invoking aerosol or cloud models (Courtin, 1982) must await these results. In any event, the CIA has to be considered in any quantitative comparison.

The final example illustrates the fact that even a small amount of CIA (small not only in comparison with allowed absorption, but also small in comparison with the peak CIA) may have appreciable consequences. We present in Fig. 4 as synthetic spectrum for Uranus (Goorvitch and Tipping, 1982). The major source of opacity in the spectral region shown is due to CH_3D, and the calculations

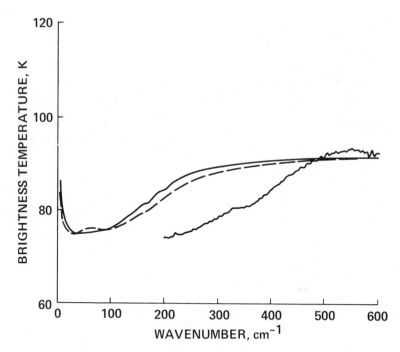

Figure 3. Calculated brightness temperature spectra of Titan with mixing ratios of N_2 and CH_4 equal to 0.882 and 0.06, respectively, for the two emission angles: 7.3° (——) and 52.7° (---). The results from Voyager 1 for an average emission angle of 52.7° are also shown.

were performed with and without the CIA from the double transitions of H_2. As can be seen from the figure, even the small opacity for H_2-H_2 collisions can significantly affect the derived brightness temperature and consequently would alter the line strengths that one would obtain for CH_3D form an analysis of the actual spectrum.

In this example, the CIA that is considered is due to double transitions of the form $S_0(J) + S_0(J')$. While this absorption mechanism is smaller by several orders of magnitude than that of single transitions, it still leads to significant effects. Similar results would also obtain for the other Giant Planets.

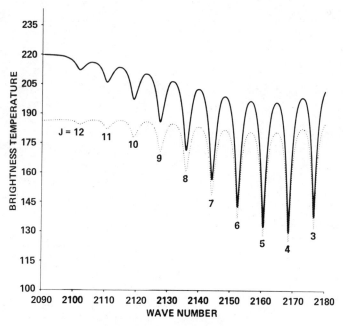

Figure 4. Calculated brightness temperature spectra of
Uranus for the CH_3D opacity (——) and for the
CH_3D plus double-S_0 opacities (...) .

REFERENCES

Bachet, G., 1983, J. Physique Letters, 44:L183.
Beer, R., and Taylor, F. W., 1978, Ap. J., 219:763.
Belton, M. J. S., and Spinrad, H., 1973, Ap. J., 105:363.
Bernstein, L. S., Robertson, D. C., Conant, J. A., and Sandford,
    B. P., 1979, Appl. Opt. 18:2454.
Birnbaum, G., 1975, J. Chem. Phys., 62:59.
Birnbaum, G., 1979 J.Q.S.R.T., 21:597.
Birnbaum, G., 1982, Adv. Chem. Phys., 51:49.
Birnbaum, G., 1983, Private Communication.
Birnbaum, G., Ho, W., and Rosenberg, A., 1971, J. Chem. Phys., 55:
    1039.
Birnbaum, G., and Cohen, E. R., 1975, J. Chem. Phys., 62:3807.
Birnbaum, G., Brown, M. S., and Frommhold, L., 1981, Can. J. Phys.,
    59:1544.
Birnbaum, G., Frommhold, L., Nencini, L., and Sutter, H., 1983,
    Chem. Phys. Lett., 100:292.
Birnbaum, G., Chu, S. I., Dalgarno, A., Frommhold, L., and Wright,
    E. L., 1984, Phys. Rev. A, 29:595.
Borysow, A., Moraldi, M., and Frommhold, L., 1984, J.Q.S.R.T.,
    31:235.
Borysow, J., and Frommhold, L. 1985, this volume.

Bosomworth, D. R., and Gush, H. P., 1965, Can. J. Phys., 43:751.

Bragg, S. L., Brault, J. W., and Smith, W. H., 1982, Ap. J., 263: 999.

Buontempo, U., Maselli, P., and Nencini, L., 1983, Can. J. Phys., 61:1498.

Camy-Peyret, C., Flaud, J. M., Delbouille, L., Roland, G., Brault, J. W., and Testerman, L., 1981, J. Physique Lett., 42:L279.

Clough, S. A., Kneizys, F. X., Davies, R., Gamache, R., and Tipping, R. H., 1980, in: "Atmospheric Water Vapor," A. Deepak, T. D. Wilkerson, and L. H. Ruhnke, eds., Academic Press, New York.

Clough, S. A., and Kneizys, F. X., 1983, Private Communication.

Cohen, E. R., 1976, Can. J. Phys., 54:475.

Cohen, E. R., Frommhold, L., and Birnbaum, G., 1982, J. Chem. Phys., 77:4933.

Conrath, B. J., and Gierasch, P. J., 1983, Nature, 306:571.

Courtin, R., 1982, Icarus, 51:466.

Crawford, M. F., Welsh, H. L., and Locke, J. L., 1949, Phys. Rev., 75:1607.

Dagg, I. R., Reesor, G. E., and Urbaniak, J. L., 1974, Can. J. Phys., 52:973.

Frommhold, L., 1981, Adv. Chem. Phys., 46:1.

Frommhold, L., and Birnbaum, G., 1984, Ap. J., In Press.

Goorvitch, D., and Tipping, R.H., 1982, J.Q.S.R.T., 27:397.

Guillot, B., and Birnbaum, G., 1983, J. Chem. Phys., 79:686.

Hanel, R. A., 1981, SPIE, 289:331.

Hanel, R., Conrath, B., Flasar, F. M., Kunde, V., Maguire, W., Pearl, J., Pirraglia, J., Samuelson, R., Herath, L., Allison, M., Cruikshank, D., Gautier, D., Gierasch, P., Horn, L., Koppany, R., and Ponnamperuma, C., 1981, Science, 212:192.

Hartye, R. W., Gray, C. G., and Poll, J. D., 1975, Mol. Phys., 29: 825.

Herman, R. M., Tipping, R. H., and Poll, J. D., 1979, Phys. Rev. A, 20:2006.

Hunt, J. L., Poll, J. D., Goorvitch, D., and Tipping, R. H., 1983, Icarus, 55:631.

Kelley, J. D., and Bragg, S. L., 1984, Phys. Rev. A., 29:1168.

Lewis, J. C., 1972, Can. J. Phys., 50:2881.

Lewis, J. C., 1984, this volume.

Lewis, J. C., and Van Kranendonk, J., 1970, Phys. Rev. Lett., 24:802.

Lindal, G. F., Wood, G. E., Hotz, H. B., Sweetnam, D. N., Eshleman, V. R., and Tyler, G. L., 1983, Icarus, 53:348.

Macy, W., and Smith, W. H., 1978, Ap. J., 222:L73.

Mannik, L., and Stryland, J. C., 1972, Can. J. Phys., 50:1355.

McKellar, A. R. W., Rich, N. H., and Welsh, H. L., 1972, Can. J. Phys., 50:1.

Moon, M., and Oxtoby, D. W., 1981, J. Chem. Phys., 75:2674.

Moskalenko, N. I., Il'in, Y. A., Parzhin, S. N., and Rodinov, L. V., 1979, Atm. and Oceanic Phys., 15:632.

Mutch, T. A., 1980, J. Geophys. Res., 85:7573.

Nelson, J. B., and Tabisz, G. C., 1982, Phys. Rev. Lett., 48:1393.

Nelson, J. B., and Tabisz, G. C., 1983, Phys. Rev. A, 28:2157.

Poll, J. D., 1971, in: "Planetary Atmospheres,", IAU Symposium 40.

Poll, J. D., 1980, in: "Intermolecular Spectroscopy and Dynamical Properties of Dense Systems," J. Van Kranendonk, ed., North-Holland, Amsterdam.

Poll, J. D., Tipping, R. H., Prasad, R. D. G., and Reddy, S. P., 1976, Phys. Rev. Lett., 36:248.

Poll, J. D., and Tipping, R. H., 1978, Can. J. Phys., 56:1165.

Poll, J. D., and Hunt, J. L., 1981, Can. J. Phys., 59:1448.

Reddy, S. P., and Cho, C. W., 1965, Can. J. Phys., 43:2331.

Reddy, S. P., Varghese, G., and Prasad, R. D. G., 1977, Phys. Rev. A, 15:975.

Reddy, S. P., Sen, A., and Prasad, R. D. G., 1980, J. Chem. Phys., 72:6102.

Rich, N. H., and McKellar, A. R. W., 1976, Can. J. Phys., 54:486.

Rich, N. H., and McKellar, A. R. W., 1983, Can. J. Phys., 61:1648.

Rinsland, C. P., Smith, M. A. H., Russell, J. M., Park, J. H., and Farmer, C. B., 1981, Appl. Opt., 20:4167.

Rinsland, C. P., Smith, M. A. H., Seals, R. K., Goldman, A., Murcray, F. J., Murcray, D. G., Larsen, L. C., and Rarig, P. L., 1982, J. Geophys. Res., 87:3119.

Samuelson, R. E., Hanel, R. A., Kunde, V. G., and Maguire, W. C., 1981, Nature, 292:688.

Shapiro, M. M., and Gush, H. P., 1966, Can. J. Phys., 44:949.

Smith, W. H., 1978, Icarus, 33:210.

Smith, W. H., Macy, W., and Pilcher, C. B., 1980, Icarus, 43:153.

Susskind, J., and Searl, J. E., 1977, J.Q.S.R.T., 18:581.

Tipping, R. H., 1979, USAF-SCREE Report, unpublished.

Tipping, R. H., Poll, J. D., and McKellar, A. R. W., 1978, Can. J. Phys., 56:75.

Trafton, L. M., 1967, Ap. J., 147:S765.

Trafton, L., 1981, Rev. of Geophys. and Space Phys., 19:43.

Trafton, L., and Ramsay, D. A., 1980, Icarus, 41:423.

Trauger, J. T., Roesler, F. L., Carleton, N. P., and Traub, W. A., 1973, Ap. J. Lett., 184:L137.

Van Kranendonk, J., and Gass, D. M., 1973, Can. J. Phys., 51:2428.

TIME-DOMAIN SEPARATION OF COLLISION INDUCED AND ALLOWED RAMAN SPECTRA

G. M. Gale, C. Flytzanis and M. L. Geirnaert

Laboratoire d'Optique Quantique du C. N. R. S.
Ecole Polytechique
91128 Palaiseau cedex, France

ABSTRACT

The subtraction of collision-induced backgrounds from allowed Raman bands can often pose severe problems in conventional Raman spectroscopy as the deconvolution procedures employed frequently rely on theoretical assumptions in respect to the collision-induced line shape. It is shown here that the use of high-dynamic picosecond non-linear optical techniques in the time domain can give direct access to Raman line widths and shapes even when the spectrum is dominated by collision-induced processes.

INTRODUCTION

Vibrational dynamics in molecular liquids and solids have been studied over the last few decades mainly by conventional infrared and Raman spectroscopy (Bratos, 1980). In many cases, even for fundamental modes, these studies are complicated by the presence of neighboring overlapping bands. Contributions from the collision-induced background (which may even dominate the spectrum), from overtone and hot bands - often not precisely known - have to be taken into account and deconvolution procedures (Birnbaum, 1980), which may not always be justified, must be employed.

For vibrational overtones, a subject of current interest (Flytzanis et al., 1984; Graener and Lauberau, 1983; Soussen-Jacob et al., 1982), the problem is even thornier as the direct transition $|0,0\rangle \rightarrow |0,2\rangle$, induced $|0,0\rangle \rightarrow |1,1\rangle$ transition and neighboring hot bands are often intense (see for example Fig. 3). In the solid, analogous problems exist as the localized two-phonon bound state transition, if it exists, is often immersed in the delocalized two-phonon free state band (Flytzanis et al., 1984).

Many of these difficulties may be circumvented by using time-resolved picosecond coherent excitation and probe techniques (Lauberau and Kaiser, 1978). In particular, the observation of a large delay single exponential coherent decay curve, which differs from the system response function, allows one to deduce unambiguously the width of the isotropic Raman band. In the coherent excitation process, one sends into the sample two time-synchronous picosecond pulses of frequency ω_L and ω_S, respectively, with $\omega_L - \omega_S = \omega_V$, the frequency of vibration one wishes to investigate. With the assumption that these pulses are of Gaussian shape of width t_p and t_s, respectively, with $t_s \sim t_p/2$ (Lauberau et al., 1984), one finds that excitation outside $\omega_V \pm \Delta\omega$, with $\Delta\omega \sim 1/t_p$, is negligible and hence frequency discrimination against non-resonant features is obtainable. As the observed signal in coherent excitation and probe experiments is proportional to $[\chi^{(3)}]^2$, where $\chi^{(3)}$ is the third-order non-linear susceptibility of the medium, background features which are weaker than the main line are further suppressed by this technique. However, the most important point for our present concern is the separability of time scales as, in general, collision-induced band widths are much larger than allowed linewidths. Hence, if we assume (Van Konynenburg and Steele, 1972; Kivelson et al., 1971) that the total spectral intensity can be approximated by the sum of two independent contributions, then, in the time domain, the collision-induced contribution will decay much faster than the allowed part, generally in a non-exponential fashion, and large time-delay measurements will yield information on only the time evolution of the (relatively) narrow allowed component. Although the same information could, in principle, be obtained from conventional Raman spectroscopy (at least for isotropic allowed Raman lines) simply by Fourier transforming the spectrum, in practice this does not at present appear to be feasible, except for fairly strong, relatively unperturbed lines, due to limited spectral resolution and sensitivity.

Until recently, coherent picosecond methods have also only been applied to fairly strong Raman lines in pure liquids, and mainly to C-H stretching modes. However, it has been shown (Geirnaert and Gale, 1984) that the dynamic measurement range of coherent techniques may be improved by several orders of magnitude over that conventionally obtained, which allows the investigation of the large delay (and hence small signal) time behavior of coherently excited congested Raman spectra. Note that the equivalent spectral resolution of these techniques is not limited by laser linewidth but is rather determined by the inverse of the maximum delay obtainable.

It should be pointed out here that, although time-resolved coherent methods appear well suited for observation of fairly narrow single-molecule Raman transitions in the fast modulation limit (Kubo, 1962), spectroscopic techniques are still by far superior for the study of the generally broad collision-induced features of the Raman spectrum.

After a brief description of the experimental methods employed,

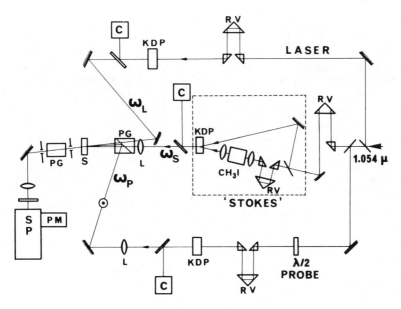

Fig. 1 Experimental system; RV variable delay, C photocell, KDP
doubler, PG Glan polarizer, SP monochromator, S sample
(Raman amplifier).

we present new results on the application of this isotropic linewidth
extraction technique (ILET) to three complex Raman systems:
- the ν_3 mode of CH_3I in solution at very low concentration
  CS_2 liquid;
- the vibrational overtone $2\nu_2$ of CS_2 liquid;
- the two-phonon bound state (bi-phonon) associated with the
  ν_2 internal vibration of CS_2 solid.

EXPERIMENTAL

Our experimental system, shown schematically in Fig. 1, is
driven by single pulses of 5 ps duration and 5 mJ energy at 0.5 Hz,
from a Nd:glass laser system. The vertically polarized, slightly
focussed, infrared laser beam at 1.054 μ passes a first beam splitter
removing 30% of the initial energy, which is then frequency doubled
to serve as a pump beam at 527 nm for vibrational excitation in a
Raman amplifier set-up. Twenty percent of the remaining energy is
subtracted by a second beam splitter, is rotated in polarization by
90° and is frequency doubled as a probing pulse for the coherent excitation. The rest of the infrared beam is directed into a tunable
frequency generator of the required, second, Stokes-shifted excitation pulse. For excitation of vibrational frequencies of less than

741

700 cm^{-1}, a part of the infrared beam is focussed into a cell containing CH3I and produces by self-phase modulation a broad spectrum around 1.054 μ. A small, red-shifted, portion of this spectrum is mixed in an oriented KDP crystal with the rest of the (time coincident) infrared beam to form an intense low-angular divergence tunable "Stokes" beam (illustrated in Fig. 1). When the vibrational frequency to be excited is larger than 700 cm^{-1}, a more efficient process is to amplify a Fabry-Perot selected narrow segment of the self-phase modulated continuum by a dye amplifier pumped at 0.527 μ (Flytzanis et al., 1985). The two horizontally polarized, synchronized pump and "Stokes" pulses are focussed into the 2 mm long sample cell to provide resonant coherent vibrational excitation by transient stimulated Raman scattering. The time evolution of the coherent excitation is followed by coherent anti-Stokes scattering of the vertically polarized, time delayed, green probe pulse which is directed into the sample by a Glan polarizer. The low geometrical divergence of the three input beams allows very precise non-collinear k-matching and the production of a highly collimated anti-Stokes signal beam. Discrimination against anti-Stokes production dusing the excitation process and other sources of noise is provided by a crossed Glan polarizer behind the sample and by severe angular selection. The coherent anti-Stokes signal is detected by a photomultiplier after suitable filters and a monochromator with a 3 Å pass-band.

RESULTS

Weak Solutions: CH3I in CS2

We have investigated the ν3 (C-I stretching mode) of CH3I at 525 cm^{-1} over a wide range of concentration in CS2 using the ILET technique. Note that the the use of this technique requires a very large dynamical measurement range and that with the experimental set-up depicted in Fig. 1 we achieve signal to noise ratios in excess of 2×10^7 in the pure liquid (Geirnaert and Gale, 1984). At concentrations of CH3I in CS2 below 10^{-1} m.f., the Raman spectrum around 525 cm^{-1} is dominated by the background from CS2 which can be mainly attributed to the high-frequency wing of the collision-induced ν2 line (Cox and Madden, 1976). At lower concentrations, the ν3 line of CH3I becomes completely drowned in the collision-induced background.

Figure 2 shows some low concentration results obtained in the time domain where we plot the observed coherent anti-Stokes signal on a logarithmic scale as a function of probe delay for three concentrations of CH3I; 0 m.f. (pure CS2, open circles), 10^{-2} m.f. (triangles) and 3×10^{-3} m.f. (squares). Consider first the results obtained in pure CS2 (open circles). As expected, one observes for this broad

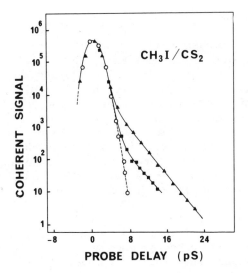

Fig. 2 Coherent signal versus probe delay for weak solutions of methyl iodine in carbon disulphide. Circles, 0 m.f.; squares, 3×10^{-3} m.f.; triangles, 10^{-2} m.f.. Absolute signal levels for the measurements at 3×10^{-3} m.f. are only approximate.

collision-induced band a rapid rise and fall of the coherent signal which is indistinguishable from the cross-correlation function, or the convolution of the intensity envelopes, of the three input pulses which gives the system time response function (dotted line; Lauberau et al., 1984). For the weak solutions one sees initially the same fast rise and fall and subsequently, at signal levels $\sim 10^{-2}$ (10^{-2} m.f.) and $\sim 10^{-3}$ (3×10^{-3} m.f.), respectively, of the peak signal height one observes the time evolution of the drowned coherent vibration of CH_3I. It is noteworthy that even at a concentration as low as 1% one can follow this coherent evolution over a dynamic range of $\sim 10^4$ and hence determine the dephasing time T_2 with precision. For example, from the slope of the line at 1% concentration, we determine directly $T_2/2 = 2.2 \pm 0.1$ ps. The observed large delay exponential decay of the coherent amplitude over four orders of magnitude indicates that the isotropic Raman transition (Lauberau et al., 1984) is predominantly homogeneous.

This technique should be applicable to a wide range of drowned Raman resonances whose linewidths and shapes were previously inaccessible by conventional techniques.

Vibrational Overtones: $2\nu_2$ of CS_2

The study of vibrational overtones (Flytzanis et al., 1984; Graener and Lauberau, 1983; Soussen-Jacob et al., 1982) and the comparison of the dephasing times of different modes of vibration (Flytzanis et al., 1985) can lead to new information on the nature and mechanisms of dephasing processes in liquids. However, it is frequently very difficult (Soussen-Jacob et al., 1982) to extract isotropic Raman linewidths and shapes in classical spectroscopy owing to the weak intensity and cluttered aspect of the overtone spectra. Figure 3 shows the observed Raman spectrum (Ioganen, 1978) in the region of the $2\nu_2$ overtone vibration of CS_2 liquid at 295 K. In addition to the pure overtone line at 795 cm^{-1} which we designate $|0,0\rangle \rightarrow |0,2\rangle$ (or, in spectroscopic notation, $00^0 0 \rightarrow 02^0 0$), there is a prominent hot band at 803 cm^{-1}, $|0,1\rangle \rightarrow |0,3\rangle$ ($01^1 0 \rightarrow 03^1 0$), several other weaker features, and an underlying broad collision-induced background which corresponds to the simultaneous promotion of two neighboring molecules to the v=1 level, $|0,0\rangle \rightarrow |1,1\rangle$ (Delalande and Gale, 1980).

We have studied the temporal behavior of the $|0,0\rangle \rightarrow |0,2\rangle$ transition (Flytzanis et al., 1984 and 1985) by adjusting our experimental apparatus to provide $\omega_L - \omega_S = \Omega_0$, where Ω_0 is the overtone frequency (here $\Omega_0 \sim 795$ cm^{-1}). We note that two-stage population of Ω_0 is not possible in this case, as ν_2 of CS_2 is Raman active. As excitation is produced directly by higher-order Raman scattering, we have named this process time-resolved CAHORS (for Coherent Anti-Stokes Higher Order Raman Scattering). Figure 4 shows the results obtained at room temperature (195 K) and at 165 K (just above the fusion point, $T_f = 162$ K) for the overtone state. In both cases

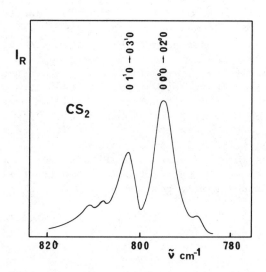

Fig. 3 Raman spectrum of CS_2 liquid at 295 K in the $2\nu_2$ overtone region.

large-delay exponential decay curves are observed which, even for this weak transition, extend over more than three orders of magnitude and are clearly distinguishable from the cross-correlation curve of the three input pulses (system response - dotted line), yielding $T_2/2$= 1.2 ps at 295 K and $T_2/2$= 0.9 ps at 165 K (for more detail see Flytzanis et al., 1985). No significant contribution from off-resonance or broad background features is seen in the experimental plots, and the observed exponential decay indicates that vibrational modulation is rapid for this overtone transition (Kubo, 1962). We are currently engaged in further improvement of our experiemtal set-up which should allow access to even weaker structures and third- or higher-order transitions.

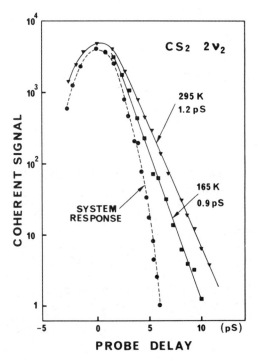

Fig. 4 Coherent signal versus probe delay in CS_2 liquid at 295 K (triangles) and 165 K (squares). Dotted line is system response function.

Two Phonon States: $2\nu_2$ of CS2 Solid

Multiphonon states are related to important processes in crystalline solids (Califano, 1975); until now our main source of information has been conventional infrared and Raman spectroscopy. Non-linear optical techniques can be extended to the selective study of the spectral and dynamical feature properties of multiphonon states and can be used to elucidate (Flytzanis et al., 1984) previously inaccessible features of vibrational motion in crystalls. In contrast to conventional spectroscopy, non-linear techniques and especially coherent excitation allow the creation of multiphonon and large wave vector phonon states in an off-equilibrium configuration.

In the infrared or Raman spectrum of crystals one observes (Califano, 1975) a quasi-continuum of two-phonon states, formed from one phonon branches σ' and σ'' with wave vector k' and k'', respectively, characterized by a total wave vector:

$$q = k' + k'' \simeq 0$$

and an energy $h\Omega$:

$$h\Omega = h\left\{\omega_{\sigma'}(k') + \omega_{\sigma''}(k'')\right\}$$

where $\vec{k}'$ ($\simeq -\vec{k}''$) varies over the entire Brillouin zone. If the intramolecular anharmonic potential is sufficiently large (comparable to or larger than the one phonon branch width which reflects the intermolecular coupling or interaction energy between neighboring molecules), a localized excitation, the bound two-phonon state (Cohen and Ruvalds, 1969; biphonon) may separate out from the quasi continuum, giving rise to a spectral feature with a narrow line width and drstically different dynamical behavior. We show here that these local states can be coherently driven by laser excitation and their subsequent time evolution and decay processes observed.

We have performed the first demonstration of time-resolved picosecond CAHORS in the solid on the bound two-phonon state at 801 cm[-1] in crystalline CS2, associated with the ν_2 internal vibration mode, which in this case is immersed in the two-vibron quasi-continuum. The experimental result in the crystal at 160 K is shown in Fig. 5, yielding an exponential decay with a corresponding relaxation time $T_2 = 14 \pm 3$ ps; a dramatic increase over that observed in the liquid.

It may be shown (Flytzanis et al., 1984; Geirnaert et al., 1984) by the use of Green's function techniques that the loss of coherence of the bound two-phonon state evolves exponentially with a time

746

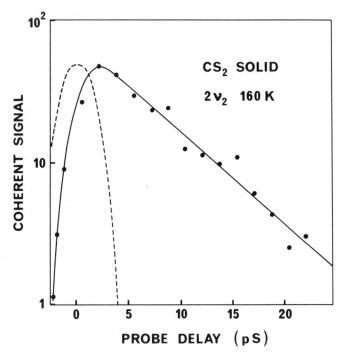

Fig. 5 Coherent signal vs. probe delay in CS$_2$ solid.

constant $T_B \sim 1/\nu_0$, where ν_0 is the density of the free two-phonon states calculated where its overlap with the bound state is maximal. In the liquid, a major complication arises from the interplay of quantum and classical motions and the lack of long range order. Indeed, the stochastic nature of the liquid makes intuitively plausible the observation of shorter overtone lifetimes due to random fluctuations of the oscillator environment (Geirnaert et al., 1984).

As in the crystal $T_2 \sim 1/\nu_0$, we may predict that the coherence lifetime of the bound two-phonon state should be very sensitive to structural phase transitions, since in this situation the joint two - phonon density of states changes dramatically for large wave vector phonons at the edge of the Brillouin zone. Another important feature to notice is that the two-phonon states into which the bound two-phonon state decays and transfers its coherence may, under certain conditions, retain this coherence long enough to engender parametric instabilities.

CONCLUSION

In conclusion, we have shown that improved coherent non-linear optical techniques may be usefully employed in the time domain to allow the unambiguous extraction of Raman linewidths and shapes from collision-induced and other strong perturbations in the liquid, and the analogous separation of the two-phonon bound state and the two-phonon quasi-continuum in the solid.

ACKNOWLEDGMENT

This work was generously supported by the Direction des Recherches, Etudes et Techniques (D.R.E.T. contract n^0 81-239) of the French Ministry of Defense.

REFERENCES

Birnbaum, G., 1980, in "Vibrational Spectroscopy of Molecular Liquids and Solids", Eds. Bratos, S., and Pick, R. M., Plenum Press, p. 143.

Bratos, 1980, S., in "Vibrational Spectroscopy of Molecular Liquids and Solids", Eds. Bratos, S., and Pick, R. M., Plenum Press, p. 43.

Califano, S., 1975, Editor, "Lattice Dynamics and Intermolecular Forces", Academic Press.

Cohen, M. H., and Ruvalds, J., 1969, Phys. Rev. Letters, 23:1378.

Cox, T. I., and Madden, P. A., Chem. Phys. Letters, 41:188.

Delalande, C., and Gale, G. M., 1980, Chem. Phys. Letters 71:264.

Flytzanis, C., Gale, G. M., and Geirnaert, M. L., 1984, in "Picosecond Spectroscopy in Chemistry", Ed. Eisenthal, K. B., D. Reidel Publishing Company, p. 205.

Flytzanis, C., Geirnaert, M. L., and Gale, G. M., 1985, in preparation.

Geirnaert, M. L., Gale, G. M., and Flytzanis, C., 1984, Phys. Rev. Letters, 52:815.

Geirnaert, M. L., and Gale, G. M., 1984, Chem. Phys., 86:205.

Graener, H., and Lauberau, A., 1983, Chem. Phys. Letters, 102:100.

Ioganen, A. V., 1978, Opt. Spectrosc., 45:36.

Kivelson, D., McTagne, J. P., and Keyes, T., 1971, J. Chem. Phys., 55:4096.

Kubo, R., 1962, in "Fluctuations, Relaxation and Resonance in Magnetic Systems", Ed. Ter Haar, D., Plenum Press.

Lauberau, A., and Kaiser, W., 1978, Rev. Mod. Phys., 50:607.

Lauberau, A., Telle, H. R., and Gale, G. M., 1984, Appl. Phys., 34:23.

Soussen-Jacob, J., Breuillard, C., Bessieve, J., Tsakiris, J., and Vincent-Geisse, J., 1982, Mol. Phys., 46:545.

Van Konynenburg, P., and Steele, W. A., 1972, J. Chem. Phys., 56:4776.

COLLISION-INDUCED RADIATIVE TRANSITIONS AT OPTICAL FREQUENCIES

Paul S. Julienne

Molecular Spectroscopy Division
National Bureau of Standards
Gaithersburg, MD 20899

ABSTRACT

A brief overview is given of the field of collision-induced atomic radiative transitions at optical frequencies, including both collision-induced forbidden transitions and light induced collisional energy transfer (LICET). The main focus is on the theory of such processes. The theory of scattering in a radiation field can be used to calculate absorption or emission profiles, and the distribution of final product states. Several simplifying approximations greatly facilitate a qualitative understanding of the profile, but may fail in quantitative studies.

INTRODUCTION

The purpose of this review is to give some indication as to the nature of collision-induced radiative transitions at optical frequencies. It will concentrate primarily on the theoretical description of the phenomena, although brief mention will also be made of various experimental examples. It does not pretend to give an exhaustive review of either theory or experiment, but rather attempts to give an overview of several major aspects of the field, with emphasis on the relation between the scattering and line broadening viewpoints. The reader is also referred to earlier reviews by Yakovlenko (1979) and Mies (1980).

A collision-induced radiative transition is represented by the reaction

$$A + B + n\hbar\omega \rightarrow A' + B' + (n\pm1)\hbar\omega \quad , \tag{1}$$

where two species A and B collide in the presence of a radiation field having n photons of frequency ω and undergo a transition to new states A' and B'. Optical frequency transitions generally require a change of electronic states, whereas infrared or microwave collision-induced transitions involve only a change of vibrational, rotational, or translational states. We assume A' + B' can not be formed from a collision of A + B in the absence of radiation. Furthermore, we shall be concerned with the case where A and B are atoms and will only consider single photon, as opposed to multiphoton, processes. The case n → n-1 describes absorption (photon loss), and the case n → n+1 describes emission (photon gain), either spontaneous (n=0) or stimulated (n >> 1). Fig. (1) gives a schematic description of collision-induced emission.

If atom A undergoes a transition to a new electronic state A' when ω is tuned near a dipole <u>allowed</u> transition frequency ω_A of atom A, but atom B acts only as a perturber which does not change state, B' = B, then the reaction, Eq. (1), represents ordinary atomic line broadening. Such collisions are also called optical collisions (Lisitsa and Yakovlenko, 1974). A good review with attention to theoretical and experimental aspects of atomic line broadening, both historical and current, has recently been given by Allard and Kielkopf (1983).

Optical collisions are not treated in this review, which instead concentrates on those radiatively assisted collisions for which ω is nonresonant with a dipole allowed transition on either atom. For such a collision the radiation does not interact strongly with one of the separated atoms as it does for an optical collision. Rather, the radiation only interacts with A + B during a collision, in which a transition dipole moment is induced in the transient AB quasimolecule due to the interatomic interaction. Since the radiation does not interact strongly with the atoms between collisions, but only during collisions, the theory for the induced spectrum is straightforward, analogous to that for the wings of optical collision spectral profiles. It is only necessary to take into account the effect of one collision at a time, and we do not require the complicated statistical mechanics needed to account for the effect of many successive collisions in the formation of an optical collision line core. Thus, theoretical treatments of optical frequency radiatively assisted collisions have generally not been concerned with calculating the Fourier transform of the dipole autocorrelation function, but have sought with varying degrees of rigor to find the S matrix describing single collisions. As long as the pressure is not too high, the spectral profile may be described solely in terms of the binary collision cross section for reaction (1).

750

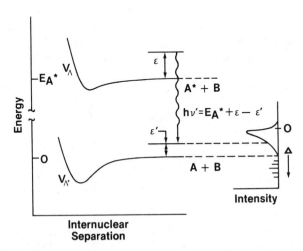

Figure 1: This figure gives a schematic description of a collision-induced emission process. The atoms A* + B collide with
initial relative kinetic energy ε on potential $V_\Lambda(R)$ and produce
final state atoms A + B with final relative kinetic energy ε' in
potential $V_{\Lambda'}(R)$ as a result of photon emission at frequency
$\hbar\omega = h\nu = E_{A^*} + \varepsilon - \varepsilon'$ during the collision. The small figure to the lower
right schematically shows the spectral profile which results from
considering all possible transition frequencies from an initial
state with fixed kinetic energy ε. The spectrum consists of a
continuum due to free-free transitions and a discrete part due to
free-bound transitions. We only concern ourselves with free-free
transitions in this review.

We follow Gallagher and Holstein (1977) in distinguishing between two types of collision-induced transitions. The first class describes the situation where ω is tuned near the frequency ω_A of a dipole <u>forbidden</u> transition of atom A and the perturber B does not change state, $B' = B$. Transitions can occur either in absorption or emission. An example of collision-induced emission is

$$O(^1S_0) + Ar \rightarrow O(^1D_2) + Ar + \hbar\omega \quad . \tag{2}$$

Figures 2 and 3 show the respective potential energy curves for O + Ar and the calculated and measured spectra for this reaction. This reaction has been thoroughly studied, both experimentally (Cunningham and Clark, 1974; Corney and Williams, 1972; Black, et al., 1975; Welge and Atkinson, 1976; Powell, et al., 1975; Hughes, et al., 1976) and theoretically (Julienne, et al., 1976; Julienne, 1978, 1982; Gallagher and Holstein, 1977). Other Group VI - rare gas systems have been studied as well (see Julienne, 1978, and references therein; Black et al., 1975; Powell and Schleicher, 1980). Krauss and Julienne (1977) studied collision-induced emission of $I(^2P_{1/2} \rightarrow {}^2P_{3/2})$ by rare gas perturbers, and Gallagher and Holstein (1977) discuss collision-induced absorption of Cs by rare gas or Cs perturbers.

One possible application of collision-induced emission is as a source of gain in laser media. This was first suggested by the laser group at Lawrence Livermore Laboratory (Murray and Hoff, 1974; Murray and Rhodes, 1976) for Group VI - rare gas mixtures. The hope was to store a large enough inverted population of excited metastable $^1S_0$ atoms, which may be created with high quantum yields by a photodissociation process, and extract their energy in a lasing transition. For this purpose either the atomic $^1S_0 \rightarrow {}^1D_2$ quadrupole transition or the broader quasimolecular collision-induced emission could be used. Lasing on the quasimolecular transition has been demonstrated for ArO (Powell, et al., 1975), KrO (Powell, et al., 1974; Johnson, et al., 1975), XeO (Powell, et al., 1974, Basov, et al., 1976), and KrSe and XeSe (Powell and Schleicher, 1980). The quasimolecular emission is primarily from bound states in XeO, but from free states in the others (Julienne, 1978). A theory for the gain and saturation of collision induced lasing transitions has been developed by Julienne (1977). Unfortunately, problems with the production and storage of metastable $^1S_0$ group VI atoms and the high pressures required for collision-induced gain appears to make such devices impractical. More recently, Rogovin and Avizonis (1981) have discussed collision-induced gain. They suggest that the DF molecule may be a useful perturber for improving the gain characteristics of the $I(^2P_{1/2} \rightarrow {}^2P_{3/2})$ laser.

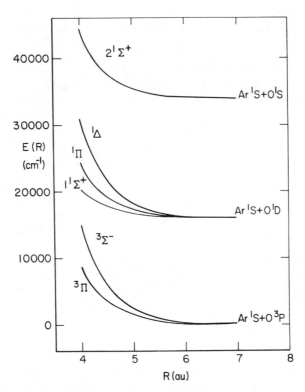

Figure 2: Potential energy diagram for the ArO molecule, taken from Julienne, Krauss, and Stevens (1976). Collision of excited $O(^1S)$ with Ar gives rise to a collision-induced emission continuum in the vicinity of the 558 nm $^1S \rightarrow {}^1D$ forbidden atomic transition. The emission has contributions from the dipole-allowed $2^1\Sigma^+ \rightarrow 1^1\Sigma^+$ and $2^1\Sigma^+ - {}^1\Pi$ molecular transitions.

The second class of transitions listed by Gallagher and Holstein (1977) describes the situation where ω is not tuned near an energy difference of either atom, but near a difference frequency

$$\hbar\omega_\infty = E_A + E_B - E_{A'} - E_{B'} \tag{3}$$

between the two atoms. Both atoms change their state, $A' \neq A$ and $B' \neq B$. Such collisions have been called radiative collisions, laser induced collisional energy transfer (LICET), or radiatively assisted inelastic collisions (RAIC). The possibility of such collisions was first suggested by Gudzenko and Yakovlenko (1972) and Harris and Lidow (1974). The first successful example was demonstrated by Harris, et al. (1976) (see also Falcone et al., 1977),

$$Sr(^1P_1{}^0) + Ca(^1S_0) + n\hbar\omega(498 \text{ nm}) \rightarrow$$

$$Sr(^1S_0) + Ca(4p^2 \, ^1S_0) + (n-1)\hbar\omega , \tag{4}$$

where $\lambda = 2\pi c/\omega = 498$ nm corresponds to the energy difference between $Sr(^1P)$ and $Ca(4p^2 \, ^1S_0)$. A number of other experimental examples are also known (Cahuzak and Toschek, 1978; Green et al., 1979; Green, et al., 1979b; Brechignac, et al., 1980; Zhang, et al., 1982; Debarre, 1983; see also the reviews by Harris, et al., 1979, and Brechignac and Cahuzac, 1983). The phenomenon also includes pair absorption (Gudzenko and Yakovlenko, 1974; White, 1981) and emission (White, 1980), by which two excited states are respectively created or decay by a single photon process. Harris, et al. (1982) suggest that the collision-induced gain from a radiative collision might be a useful way to extract the energy stored in alkali discharges. Radiative collisions are also of interest since they can contribute to the opacity or emissivity of dense gases and because they may permit rapid switching of atomic populations. In the most general case the species A or B can be molecular (Lukasik and Wallace, 1981; Hering and Rabin, 1981), and we even have the possibility of using laser light to influence the course of a chemical reaction (Hering, et al., 1980; Wilcomb and Burnham, 1981; George, 1982).

The present review will consider both classes of collision-induced transitions, that is, (i) a dipole forbidden transition on atom A where the perturber atom does not change state, and (ii) the LICET type collision where both atoms change state. Essentially the same theory is used to treat both classes. We will first describe the quantities needed to characterize the reaction (1). The review will then describe the nature of the induced moments,

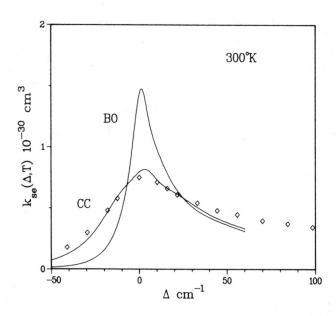

Figure 3: Collision-induced emission spectrum for $O(^1S)$ + Ar at 300°K (Julienne, 1982). The ordinate is the spontaneous emission coefficient of equation (8). The abscissa is detuning $\Delta = \hbar\,(\omega - \omega_\infty)$ from the $^1S \rightarrow {}^1D$ atomic transition frequency. The $\diamond$ symbols show the experimental profile. The solid curve labeled BO gives the profile calculated from Eqs. (8) and (20) by separate numerical two-state calculations of the radiative S_ω matrix (18) for the $\Sigma - \Sigma$ and $\Sigma - \Pi$ transition using the Born-Oppenheimer potentials. The solid curve labeled CC gives the profile calculated from the numerical solution to the full set of coupled equations (16), in which the couplings among the $^1\Sigma$, $^1\Pi$, and $^1\Delta$ final states were included. The numerical calculation is based on ab initio data without adjustable parameters. The figure shows that inelastic couplings (or "nonadiabatic" effects) have a large effect on the profile.

and after that, the types of theories which have been applied to the problem. We will emphasize the unity between the scattering and line broadening approaches to the problem.

DESCRIPTION OF COLLISION-INDUCED RATE COEFFICIENTS AND SPECTRA

Let us assume that the collisions occur in a homogeneous gas for which the pressure is sufficiently low that the time between collisions is much longer than the duration τ_c of a single collision. This is the regime in which theory and experiment for optical frequency, collision-induced radiative transitions have been carried out so far. Since we are justified in neglecting 3-body and higher order effects on the spectrum, all information needed to characterize the binary collision between A and B is contained in the cross sections $\sigma_\omega(\beta{\leftarrow}\alpha,v,\phi,\hat{e}_q)$. The indices α and β designate the collection of quantum numbers needed to characterize the respective initial and final states of the colliding species, A + B and A' + B', and v is the collision velocity. The cross section depends on the frequency ω, intensity ϕ (photons $cm^{-2}sec^{-1}$), and polarization $\hat{e}_q$ of the radiation field. The integral cross section σ_ω, which represents an average over all incoming collision directions and integration over all outgoing scattering angles relative to $\hat{e}_q$, is used to describe experiments in homogeneous cells. The full differential cross section can be used to describe beam experiments.

Since at least one of the species A or B is usually in a degenerate state or has fine structure, the state-to-state cross section $\sigma_\omega(\beta{\leftarrow}\alpha)$ contains more information than is normally available from experimental measurement. Experiments which probe the distribution of final states by measuring polarized fluorescence following absorption of polarized light have been suggested as a useful way to study radiative collisions (Berman, 1980 a,b) and will be described more fully below. For the present let us consider only the total rate of conversion of reactants A + B to products A' + B' through the influence of the radiation field. This rate is given by the second order rate coefficient,

$$k_\omega(\phi) = \langle \sigma_\omega(\beta{\leftarrow}\alpha,v,\phi,\hat{e}_q)\ v \rangle \quad , \tag{5}$$

where the brackets imply an average over the thermal distribution of initial states α and the Maxwellian velocity distribution and a summation over all final states β. The rate coefficient k_ω depends only on the frequency and intensity of the light. Since A + B is converted to A' + B' once for each photon absorbed, the conversion rate is also given by the product of photon flux ϕ times the Beer's law absorption (gain) coefficient γ_ω of the medium. We thus have the relation

$$\gamma_\omega \phi = k_\omega(\phi) N_A N_B \quad , \tag{6}$$

where N_A and N_B are the number densities of reactants A and B. This may be rewritten as

$$\Gamma_\omega = \frac{\gamma_\omega}{N_A N_B} = \frac{k_\omega}{\phi} = \frac{\langle \sigma_\omega v \rangle}{\phi} . \tag{7}$$

The left hand side of Eq. (5) gives the effect of the collision in Eq. (1) on the absorption or emission of photons, namely, the spectrum in a form of a normalized absorption (gain) coefficient Γ_ω having units of $(\text{length})^5$. It represents the line broadening viewpoint. The right hand side gives the effect of the collision on the atoms in terms of the frequency dependent cross section σ_ω for reaction (1). It represents the atomic scattering viewpoint. Note that Γ_ω is independent of density, since our assumption of low pressure insures that γ_ω is proportional to the product of densities $N_A N_B$. Also, Γ_ω is independent of laser intensity ϕ if ϕ is not too large, since σ_ω is proportional to ϕ. The weak-field absorption coefficient Γ_ω depends only on ω and the properties of the colliding species A and B.

The cross section is calculated by formulating and solving the coupled equations which describe scattering in the presence of a radiation field. This is discussed more fully in the theory section below. The magnitude is determined both by the inter-atomic potentials and by the intrinsic magnitude of the radiative coupling, $\vec{E} \cdot \vec{d}$, where $\vec{E}$ is the electric vector of the field and $\vec{d}$ is the induced dipole of AB, which is a function of internuclear separation R. The inherent small magnitude of $\vec{E} \cdot \vec{d}$ for typical laboratory laser intensities insures that the radiative coupling normally acts as a small perturbation. Thus, the field free motion is only weakly perturbed, the probability of scattering in a single collision is much less than unity, and the cross section is linear in $|E|^2$, that is, linear in ϕ since $E \propto \phi^{1/2}$. Typical magnitudes of $\vec{E} \cdot \vec{d}$ as a function of ϕ are illustrated in Table 1 for an assumed value of $d = 1\ ea_o$.

Detailed discussion of the range of validity of the weak field assumption are given by Mies (1980) and Julienne (1977). It is generally safe to assume "weak" fields for power fluxes $\hbar\omega\phi \lesssim 10^9$ watts cm^{-2}. For very strong fields, $\hbar\omega\phi \gg 10^9$ watts cm^{-2}, large cross sections ("gas kinetic" rate coefficients) and saturation effects are possible (Lisitsa and Yakovlenko, 1974; Harris and White, 1977). Experimental measurements support our conclusion that

Table 1

Magnitude of $V^{rad} = \vec{E} \cdot \vec{d}$ for $d = 1\ ea_o$

	Power	$\dfrac{V^{rad}}{hc}$		
	watts cm^{-2}	cm^{-1}		
weak	1	0.0006		
fields	10^3	0.02		
	10^6	0.6		
	10^9	20		Typical Coriolis, spin-orbit, and van der Waals energies
strong	10^{12}	600		
fields	10^{15}	20,000		Chemical Bonding energies

saturation occurs only at very high power levels (Green, et al., 1979). Therefore, we assume henceforth that weak field conditions apply.

Equation (7) applies only to absorption and to stimulated emission. Spontaneous collision-induced emission also is possible, and is described by a two-body rate coefficient. Assume atom A decays to some lower state during collision with atom B. The rate coefficient k_{spon} (ω) for spontaneous emission into frequency interval $d\nu = d\omega/2\pi$ is readily related to the stimulated emission coefficient, Eq. (7) through the relation of Einstein A and B coefficients (Julienne, 1977),

$$k_{spon}(\omega) = \frac{8\pi}{\lambda^2}\, \Gamma_\omega \quad , \tag{8}$$

which has units of (length)^3 (time)$^{-1}$ (frequency)$^{-1}$ = (length).^{3} The total rate coefficient of spontaneous decay integrated over the whole profile is

$$K_{spon} = \int_0^\infty k_{spon}(\omega)\, \frac{d\omega}{2\pi} \quad , \tag{9}$$

which has units of $(length)^3 (time)^{-1}$ for a second order rate coefficient. Thus, atom A has an effective decay rate, $K_{spon} N_B$, and a unit normalized spectral profile

$$g_{spon}(\omega) = \frac{k_{spon}(\omega)}{K_{spon}} . \tag{10}$$

In the discussions in this section, we have assumed that the transitions are free-free transitions that can be described by a cross section. Of course, bound states of the AB molecule will also be populated in a thermal ensemble and will give rise to absorption or emission. A bound state will generally only be important if its dissociation energy is larger than kT, generally not the case for van der Waals molecules at room temperature. The effect of bound states can often be taken into account by using classical or quasistatic methods (Julienne, 1978). We will not consider bound states in this review.

INDUCED MOMENTS

There are two possible approaches to calculating the induced transition dipole moments. The first, which may be called the atomic viewpoint, has been widely used. The collision of two atoms occurs under the simultaneous influence of the interatomic potential $V^{AB}(R)$ and the radiative interactions, $V^{rad}(R) = \vec{E} \cdot \vec{d}$, where R is the internuclear separation. The presence of $V^{AB}(R)$ causes a perturbation of the atomic wavefunctions so that an electronic transition dipole is induced in the system which can interact with the radiation. To first order in the interatomic potential $V^{AB}(R)$, the collisional perturbation to the wavefunction of the atoms in state 1 is

$$|AB\rangle \approx [1 + G_1^{AB} V^{AB}(R)] |A_1\rangle|B_1\rangle , \tag{11}$$

where G is the resolvent operator

$$G_1^{AB} = \frac{1}{\hbar} \sum_{nm} \frac{|A_n\rangle|B_m\rangle\langle B_m|\langle A_n|}{\omega_{n1}^A + \omega_{m1}^B} \tag{12}$$

The components of the electronic transition dipole moment induced in the system between initial state $|A_1\rangle|B_1\rangle$ and the final state $|A_2\rangle|B_2\rangle$ are

$$\vec{d}_{21}(R) = \langle A_2|\langle B_2| V^{AB}(R) G_2^{AB} \vec{d} + \vec{d} G_1^{AB} V^{AB}(R)|A_1\rangle|B_1\rangle, \tag{13}$$

where $\vec{d} = \Sigma_n e_n \vec{r}_n$ is the dipole operator of the AB molecule. The induced electronic transition dipole $\vec{d}_{21}(R)$ represents the effect of the A-B interaction $V^{AB}(R)$ on the electronic wavefunction only. Collision-induced transitions at optical frequencies differ from those at infrared or microwave frequencies in that the transition dipole is off-diagonal in the electronic state for the former but electronically diagonal for the latter. In both cases the R-dependence of $\vec{d}(R)$ comes from the R-dependence of V^{AB}. For example, the asymptotic induced transition dipole for the reaction in Eq. (2) comes from the R^{-4} dipole-quadrupole matrix element on O and the frequency-dependent polarizability of the perturber Ar at the frequency of the $O(^1S \rightarrow {}^1D)$ optical transition (Julienne, 1978). On the other hand, it has generally been assumed for the LICET type of collision, such as Eq. (4), that a single term ("virtual state") dominates the resolvent due to a small energy denominator. A summary of the various types of terms that can contribute is given by Berman (1980b). Geltman (1976) has shown that the dipole-dipole R^{-3} term applies when the product of atomic parities is different in the initial and final states, whereas the dipole-quadrupole R^{-4} term applies when these products are the same. If all four states (initial and final of atoms A and B) are S states, then only terms second order in V^{AB} appear, varying as R^{-7} (Whisnant and Beyers-Brown, 1973). In all of the above cases, we assume the transitions are spin-allowed. Experimental examples are known for both R^{-3} transitions (for example, Falcone, et al., 1977, or Cahuzac and Toschek, 1978) and R^{-4} transitions (for example, reaction (2) or Green, et al., 1979b, and White, 1980, 1981).

The atomic picture based on the long range perturbation expression, Eq. (13), is undoubtedly very helpful in achieving a qualitative understanding of collision-induced radiative transitions. However, it is deficient for quantitative calculations, since it breaks down for hard collisions due to the neglect of exchange-overlap effects on the electronic wavefunctions. Furthermore, it is not at all obvious what measure of accuracy to attach to approximations to Eq. (13) which use only a single virtual state.

An alternative approach, which may be called the molecular viewpoint, views the transition dipole as a property of the AB quasimolecule, just like the transition moments of ordinary bound state molecular spectroscopy. Although the short range $\vec{d}(R)$ generally is very difficult or impossible to extract from experimental data, it may be calculated from ab initio AB molecular wavefunctions. The ab initio approach can properly account for all exchange-overlap effects on $\vec{d}(R)$ and also go properly to the long range perturbation results. However, great care must be taken in the ab initio calculation that the asymptotic variational wavefunction has the flexibility and convergence to represent adequately the typically small long range moments (Julienne, 1978).

Calculations on Group VI $^1S \leftarrow {}^1D$ emission induced by collisions with rare gas atoms have shown that the long range atomic perturbation moments are adequate to give a qualitative account of emission coefficients for light gas collision partners but are inadequate for the heavier rare gases (Julienne, 1978). Essentially quantitative agreement between experimental and theoretical spectra is achieved for $O(^1S\leftarrow{}^1D)$ + Ar when the short range ab initio transition moments with the proper asymptotic behavior are used (Julienne, 1982). This is illustrated by Figs. (3) and (4). Figure (4) shows the far wings on a logarithmic scale and illustrates the importance of having the correct short range transition moment. Use of ab initio moments is especially important for O + Xe and S + Xe, for which factor of 10 or larger errors occur if the perturbation moments alone are used.

THEORIES FOR THE CROSS SECTIONS

In order to calculate the desired cross sections it is first necessary to set up the coupled equations which describe the collisions which occur under the simultaneous influence of the coupling of the atoms to each other through the molecular Hamiltonian, $H^{AB}(R)$, and to the radiation field through the dipole operator, $V^{rad} = \vec{E}\cdot\vec{d}$. In general, one or both of the atoms will be degenerate in its ground or excited state, that is, not in a $^1S_0$ state. Therefore, H^{AB} and V^{rad} are represented by matrices which respectively account for all elastic and inelastic couplings between the atoms and for all radiative couplings. The diagonal elements of H^{AB} give the scattering potentials, and the off-diagonal elements are responsible for inelastic (i.e., state changing) scattering events. As discussed in the previous section, the radiative couplings are expressed in terms of the components of the induced dipole of Eq. (13),

$$V^{rad}(R) = \left(\frac{2\pi\hbar\omega\phi}{c}\right)^{1/2} \hat{e}_q\cdot\vec{d} , \qquad (14)$$

where $\hat{e}_q$ is the polarization vector of the light. If the molecule-field wavefunction is expanded in a basis of product function utilizing the field free states of the colliding atoms (Mies, 1980), that is,

$$\psi_\gamma = \sum_\alpha |\alpha\rangle |n\hbar\omega, \hat{e}_q\rangle \, F_{\alpha\gamma}(R)/R +$$

$$\sum_\beta |\beta\rangle |(n-1)\hbar\omega, \hat{e}_q\rangle \, F_{\beta\gamma}(R)/R, \tag{15}$$

then the coupled equations describing the collision (1) take on the following form (Mies, 1980; Julienne, 1982):

$$\left[\frac{\hbar^2}{2\mu} \frac{d^2}{dR^2} + E - H_{\alpha\alpha}^{AB}(R) - n\hbar\omega \right] F_{\alpha\alpha}(R) = \sum_\beta V_{\alpha\beta}^{rad}(R) \, F_{\beta\alpha}(R)$$

$$+ \sum_{\alpha' \neq \alpha} H_{\alpha\alpha'}^{AB}(R) \, F_{\alpha'\alpha}(R)$$

$$\tag{16}$$

$$\left[\frac{\hbar^2}{2\mu} \frac{d^2}{dR^2} + E - H_{\beta\beta}^{AB}(R) - (n-1)\hbar\omega \right] F_{\beta\beta}(R) = \sum_\alpha V_{\beta\alpha}^{rad}(R) F_{\alpha\beta}(R)$$

$$+ \sum_{\beta' \neq \beta} H_{\beta\beta'}^{AB}(R) \, F_{\beta'\beta}(R)$$

Equations such as (16) are the starting point for all theories of collision-induced radiative transitions. The difference between the various theories is in the degree of approximation that is introduced in order to achieve relatively simple solutions. The highest degree of rigor is achieved by the fully quantum mechanical close coupled formulation of scattering in a radiation field. Such time-independent scattering formulations have been given by T. F. George and coworkers (Zimmerman, et al., 1977; DeVries, et al., 1978a, 1978b, 1978c, 1979) and by Mies (1980). A specific application to collision-induced transitions has been given by Julienne (1982, 1983). The analogous time-dependent semiclassical formulation for radiative collisions has been given by Berman (1980a). These theories account for the role of atomic degeneracies and nonradiative inelastic scattering. If the coupled equations can be solved, we obtain the full matrix of scattering amplitudes required to describe the collision-induced radiative transition. Unfortunately, sufficient information about molecular potentials and radiative and nonradiative couplings is rarely available to solve the coupled equations. Therefore, various approximations have been introduced to simplify the problem and, hopefully, to gain at least a good qualitative description of collision-induced emission.

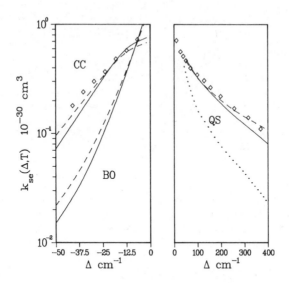

Figure 4: Collision-induced spectrum for $O(^1S)$ + Ar at 300°K
(Julienne, 1982), same as Figure 3, except on a logarithmic scale.
The red wing is the same as for Figure 3. The solid line is for
300K and the dashed line for 400K. Only the quasistatic profile
(Eq. (23) below) and the experimental points are shown for the
blue wing. The lower dotted line for the blue wing shows the
spectrum that is calculated if only the long range R^{-4} induced
moment is used.

The most important of the simplifications is the introduction
of a two-state approximation, that is, the role of inelastic
scattering events (or "nonadiabatic" effects) among the manifold of
initial states or among the manifold of final states is ignored.
Since the only remaining inelastic event is the transition caused
by the radiation, this permits us to isolate the effect of the

radiation. This approximation is equivalent to the adiabatic approximation of ordinary line broadening theory (see, for example, Szudy and Bayliss, 1975). Atomic motion occurs only on single potentials, one for the initial and one for the final state. This approximation has been used nearly universally in theories of radiative collisions.

If a partial wave expansion of the scattering wavefunction is made in states of total angular momentum J, the cross section for the collision-induced radiative transition (1) from initial state 1 to final state 2 for a relative collision velocity v is

$$\sigma_\omega(v) = \frac{\pi}{k^2} \sum_J (2J+1) \left| S_\omega(2{\leftarrow}1,J,v) \right|^2 . \tag{17}$$

where $\mu v = \hbar k$, and the square of the S-matrix element, $\left| S_\omega \right|^2$, gives the probability of a collision-induced transition. This expression applies for any field strength, even for very intense light. The relation of the cross section expression (17) to the usual Franck-Condon type of line broadening theories is readily established in the weak field limit, since the distorted wave approximation can be used for the scattering amplitude (Mies, 1980),

$$S_\omega(2{\leftarrow}1,J,v) = -2\pi i \left(\frac{2\pi\hbar\omega\phi}{3c} \right)^{1/2} \langle v_2 J_2 | d(R) | v_1 J_1 \rangle, \tag{18}$$

where $|v_1 J_1\rangle$ is an energy normalized continuum radial wavefunction for collision with velocity v_1 and angular momentum J_1 and similarly for $|v_2 J_2\rangle$. The final velocity is determined from the initial velocity and the detuning from the asymptotic frequency, Eq. (3),

$$\frac{1}{2} \mu v_2^2 = \frac{1}{2} \mu v_1^2 + \hbar(\omega-\omega_\infty) . \tag{19}$$

The induced dipole d(R) in Eq. (18) is the collision-induced electronic transition dipole moment connecting states 1 and 2. The factor of 3 occurring in Eq.(18) comes from averaging over all orientations of the colliding atoms relative to $\hat{e}_q$. It is also generally assumed $J_1 = J_2 = J$. Therefore, the thermally averaged collision-induced normalized absorption (or gain) coefficient, Eq. (7), may also be written

$$\Gamma_\omega = \frac{4\pi^2\omega}{3cQ_T} \sum_J (2J+1) \int_0^\infty \left| \langle v_2 J | d(R) | v_1 J \rangle \right|^2 e^{-\frac{\varepsilon_1}{kT}} d\varepsilon_1 . \tag{20}$$

where $Q_T = (2\pi\mu kT/h^2)^{1/2}$ is the translational partition function per unit volume.

Gallagher and Holstein (1977) have taken the molecular line broadening viewpoint of collision-induced absorption. Their theory essentially amounts to a time dependent semiclassical evaluation of the free-free dipole Franck-Condon factors in Eq. (20). (They also introduce a summation to account for atomic degeneracies). In semiclassical theories the summation over J in Eq. (20) is replaced by an integration over impact parameter $b = \hbar J/\mu v$. The expression for the cross section analogous to Eq. (17) is

$$\sigma_\omega(v) = 2\pi\int_0^\infty bP_\omega(2\leftarrow 1,b,v)db, \qquad (21)$$

where the semiclassical transition probability P_ω corresponds to the quantum probability $|S_\omega|^2$. Herman and Sando (1978) have shown how introducing the WKB approximation, the classical trajectory, and the random phase approximation into the $\langle v_2|d|v_1\rangle$ Franck-Condon matrix elements leads to time dependent semiclassical expressions which are equivalent to the basic expressions of Gallagher and Holstein (1977). Thus, we have the correspondence

$$|\langle v_2|d|v_1\rangle|^2 \leftrightarrow \frac{2}{h^2}\left|\int_0^\infty d(R(t))e^{-i\omega t + \frac{i}{\hbar}\int_0^t \Delta V(R(t'))dt'}dt\right|^2, \qquad (22)$$

when $R(t)$ is the classical trajectory for impact parameter b and ΔV is the difference potential. The right hand side of Eq. (22) is the basic expression of the time dependent semiclassical theories.

The expression (20) in its quantum or semiclassical form, Eq. (22), applies to the whole profile. Gallagher and Holstein (1977) showed that their profile for $O(^1D\leftarrow^1S)$ + Ar reproduces the fully quantal profile calculated by Julienne, Krauss, and Stevens (1976) when both calculations use the same ab initio potentials. Good agreement was found for both the antistatic and quasistatic wings, as well as the core. Of course, if a stationary phase point R^* exist where $\Delta V(R^*) = \hbar\omega$, considerable simplification is possible since the standard quasistatic expression of line broadening theory can be used for the profile (Gallagher and Holstein, 1977; Herman and Sando, 1978; Julienne, 1978),

$$\Gamma_\omega = \frac{32\pi^4}{3\lambda}\frac{R^{*2}d^{*2}}{\left.\frac{d\Delta V}{dR}\right|_{R^*}}e^{-V_1^*/kT} . \qquad (23)$$

In general we may expect the quasistatic formula to give an excellent representation of the two-state profile as long as a single stationary phase point exists.

Application of the two-state formula, Eq. (20), even using semiclassical or quasistatic approximations, requires a knowledge of the initial and final state potentials, $V_1(R)$ and $V_2(R)$, and of the induced transition dipole moment $d(R)$. The simplest possible theories obtain these quantities in terms of the properties of the colliding atoms by using the lead terms in an R^{-n} expansion based on the point-multipole expansion of V^{AB}: the potentials are R^{-6} van der Waals long range potentials and the dipoles are R^{-3} or R^{-4}, as discussed previously. All of the original theories of collision-induced radiative transitions introduce time-dependent semiclassical evaluation of $P_\omega(b)$ based on such a multipole expansion (Gudzenko & Yakovlenko, 1972; Lisitsa and Yakovlenko, 1974; Harris and Lidow, 1974; Geltman, 1976; Harris and White, 1977; Gallagher and Holstein, 1977; Payne, Anderson, and Turner, 1979). Such theories achieve the greatest simplicity at the expense of making the severest approximations. By and large such theories have been successful in explaining the basic qualitative features of the spectral profile of collision-induced radiative transitions. Such profiles are asymmetric, peak close to the asymptotic atomic difference frequency ω_∞, have widths with an order of magnitude $= 10$ cm^{-1}, and have wings extending up to 100 cm^{-1} or more. Estimates of the cross section using only a single virtual state in the resolvent, Eq. (12), generally give the correct order of magnitude of the cross section for radiative collisions. The cross sections can be quite large at high laser power; for example, Green et al. (1979a) measure a magnitude of about 10^{-13} cm^2 for the reaction in Eq. (4) at 10^9 watts cm^{-2}. At very high power, say $\geq 10^9$ watts cm^{-2} for (4), the cross section begins to saturate and no longer increases linearly with increasing ϕ (Harris and White, 1977). This is due both to the unitarity of S, i.e., $P(b) \leq 1$, and to ac Stark shifts in the atomic levels.

The reason why long range theories work as well as they do in explaining the qualitative features of the cross section is due to the long range nature of the induced transition dipoles, $d(R)$. At large impact parameter, the difference potential is usually small in comparison to $\hbar\tau_c^{-1}$, where τ_c is the collision duration. Therefore, the profile in the core or "impact" region of the profile is determined by the R-dependence of $d(R)$ in Eq.(22) rather than by the difference potential. This is in contrast to optical collisions (pressure broadening), where $d(R)$ is an R-independent constant, and the impact broadening is determined only by the difference potential $\Delta V(R)$ in Eq. (22), which varies as R^{-6}. Therefore, for large b and $|\omega - \omega_\infty| \leq \tau_c^{-1}$, the probability varies respectively as b^{-4}, b^{-6}, and b^{-10} for R^{-3} radiative collisions, R^{-4} radiative collisions, and optical collisions. If we define the Weisskopf radius b_w as the impact parameter for which

$$\frac{1}{\hbar} \int_{-\infty}^{\infty} \Delta V(R(t)) dt = \pi \quad , \tag{24}$$

then Harris and White (1977) found that about 70 percent of their cross section for reaction (4) came from impact parameters $b > b_w$; a similar result was obtained in the close coupled quantal model of Julienne (1983). This is in contrast to optical collisions, for which most of the optical broadening cross section comes from $b \leq b_w$. Thus, we may reasonably expect the two-state core profile to be given by long range theories. On the other hand, the quasistatic wing typically comes from small impact parameters, $b \leq R^*$, where the stationary phase points $R^* < b_w$. In this region overlap-exchange effects on the molecular wavefunctions are important, and we may no longer expect long range theories to be adequate; knowledge of the true molecular potentials is needed.

We perhaps may be led to conclude that the theory of colli-sion-induced radiative transition spectral profiles is well understood and adequately treated by the two-state, or adiabatic, approximation. Although simple theories are appealing and lead to the right qualitative description, they are also quantitatively inadequate in certain respects. They seem not to account for the falloff of intensity in the quasistatic wing of the profile (Brechingnac, et al., 1980; Debarre, 1983). This inadequacy is also exhibited by both sets of close coupled calculations by which the coupled equations (16) were solved numerically using realistic potentials, nonadiabatic couplings, and transition dipoles (Julienne, 1982, 1983). One system is $O(^1S \rightarrow ^1D)$ + Ar with an R^{-4} long range d(R) (Julienne, 1982), and the other is a hypothetical system in which two ^1S initial states go to ^1S and ^1P final states (Julienne, 1983) with an R^{-3} long range d(R). Errors of a factor of 2 or more were found in the profile functions when the exact results were compared with the predictions of adiabatic 2-state models. The reason for these errors is related to the necessity to take the rotation of the molecular axis into proper account. The reader is referred to Julienne (1982, 1983) for further details.

Before concluding this review, we wish to point out a new type of approach to collision-induced transitions. So far the object of concern has been the absorption profile, or equivalently, the total conversion rate of reactants to products. Alternately one may also study, either experimentally or theoretically, the distribution of product states which result from the reaction (1). An example of this is the type of experiment which has been suggested by Berman (1980). The idea is to absorb polarized light in a collision-induced transition and then detect final state coherences, for example, by measuring polarized fluorescence of an excited product atom. Berman suggests that coherence detection provides a more sensitive method of studying radiative collisions than population detection, and also serves as a probe of the interatomic interaction. One such experiment has been reported for the radiative collision (Debarre, 1982)

$$\text{Eu}(^{8}P_{9/2}) + \text{Sr}(^{1}S_{0}) + \hbar\omega \rightarrow \text{Eu}(^{8}S_{7/2}) + \text{Sr}(^{1}D_{2}).$$

Linearly polarized light is incident on a low pressure cell containing the initial state atoms, and the fluorescence intensity from $\text{Sr}(^{1}D_{2})$ was measured with polarization parallel and perpendicular to the incident polarization vector. This determines the polarization ratio (normalized Stokes parameter) $(I_{||} - I_{\perp})/(I_{||} + I_{\perp})$.

Such polarized light experiments are similar to the ones which have recently been carried out for optical collisions (Thomann, et al, 1980; Alford, et al., 1983; Cooper, 1983; Burnett, 1984). In such experiments a ground state Sr or Ba atom is excited to a ^{1}P state during a collision with a rare gas perturber by absorption of a linearly polarized photon in the profile wings, $|\omega-\omega_{\infty}| \tau_{c} \gg 1$. This is followed by measurement of the polarization ratio of the re-emitted light at frequency ω_{∞}. Such experiments in general yield information about the molecular dynamics of electronic angular momentum $\vec{L}$ coupling to the molecules axis. Furthermore, study of the pressure dependence of the polarization ratio yields the rate of collisional depolarization.

A general theory of the distribution of final states in either radiative or optical collisions has been developed by Julienne (1983) and Julienne and Mies (1984). The theory has the same structure as the theory of product distributions in molecular photodissociation (Greene and Zare, 1982). For both collision-induced radiative transitions and photodissociation, linearly polarized light incident on a homogeneous gas cell introduces a preferred direction in space. Absorption produces a product atom alignment characterized by a nonmicrocanonical distribution of Zeeman sublevels. Berman (1980) used the atomic viewpoint to explain the alignment as resulting from the mutual interaction of the polarized radiation dipole field and the two unpolarized correlated multipolar fields due to the interatomic interaction $V^{AB}(R)$. The molecular viewpoint explains the alignment as resulting from absorption to molecular states of definite Λ. The general scattering formulation of Julienne and Mies (1984), based on the coupled equations (16), encompasses both viewpoints and can account for the polarization ratio which results from absorption in any part of the profile.

CONCLUSION

In summary the phenomenon of collision-induced optical frequency radiative transitions has been amply demonstrated experimentally. The theory of how to treat such collisions is basically well understood, and it may be formulated either in a S-matrix form or in a Franck-Condon line broadening form. The equivalence is illustrated by eq. (18), which may readily be extended to include nonadiabatic (inelastic scattering) effects (Julienne, 1982). The use of simple two state long range theories are attractive for their ability to enable us to understand the collision-induced spectrum qualitatively and even semi-quantitatively. However, such theories rely on many assumptions that are overly simplistic and are unlikely to hold for realistic atomic collisions. They do provide a phenomenological framework for characterizing collision-induced radiative transitions, but they should not be overinterpreted, nor should we be surprised if they fail. There are still questions concerning the role of switching between the long range nonrotating and short range rotating molecule descriptions. The possibility of significant effects on the spectral profile exists. Alignment experiments offer the possibility of studying axis rotation dynamics. There is still a need for further work if we wish to obtain a truly quantitative understanding of optical frequency collision-induced radiative transitions.

REFERENCES

Alford, W. J., Burnett, K., and Cooper, J., 1983 Phys. Rev., A27:1310.
Allard, N., and Kielkopf, J., 1982, Rev. Mod. Phys., 54:1103.
Basov, N. G., Babeiko, Yu. A., Zuev, V. S., Mikheev, L. D., Orlov, V.K., Pogorel'skii, I. V., Stavrovskii, Startsev, A. V., and Yalovoi, V. I., 1976, Sov. J. Quantum Electron., 6:505.
Berman, P. R., 1980a, Phys. Rev., A22:1838.
Berman, P. R., 1980b, Phys. Rev., A22:1848.
Black, G., Sharpless, R. L., and Slanger, T. G., 1975, J. Chem. Phys., 63:4546,4551.
Bréchignac, C., Cahuzac, Ph., and Toschek, P. E., 1980, Phys. Rev. A21:1969.
Bréchignac, C., and Cahuzac, Ph., 1983, in "Spectral Line Shapes", Vol.2, edited by K. Burnett, (de Gruyter, Berlin) pp. 721-735.
Burnett, K., 1984, in "Electronic and Atomic Collisions," edited by J. Eichler, I.V. Hertel, and N. Stolterfoht (North Holland, Amsterdam, 1984), pp. 649-660.
Cahuzac, Ph. and Toschek, P. E., 1978, Phys. Rev. Lett., 40:1087.
Cooper, J., 1983, in Spectral Line Shapes, Vol. 2, edited by K. Burnett (de Gruyter, Berlin) pp. 737-753.

Corney, A., and Williams, O.M., 1972, J. Phys., B5:686.
Cunningham, D. L., and Clark, K. C.,1974, J. Chem. Phys., 68:1118.
Débarre, A., 1982, J. Phys., B15:1693.
Débarre. A., 1983, J. Phys., B16:431.
DeVries, P. L., Mahlab, M. S., and George, T. F., 1978a, Phys. Rev.,
    A17:546.
DeVries, P. L., and George, T. F., 1978b, Mol. Phys., 36:151.
DeVries, P. L., and George, T. F., 1978c, Phys. Rev., A18:1751.
DeVries, P. L., and George, T. F., 1979, Mol. Phys., 38:561.
Falcone, R. W., Green, W. R.,. White, J. C., Young, J. F., and
    Harris, S. E., 1977, Phys. Rev., A15:1333.
Gallagher, A., and Holstein, T., 1977, Phys. Rev., A16:2413.
Geltman, S., 1976, J. Phys., B9:L569.
George, T. F., 1982, J. Phys. Chem., 86:10.
Greene, C. H., and Zare, R. N., 1982, Ann. Rev. Phys. Chem., 33:119.
Greene, W. R., Lukasik, J., Willison, J. R., Wright, M. D., J. F.,
    and Harris, S. E.,1979a, Phys. Rev. Lett., 42:970.
Greene, W. R., Wright, M. D., Lukasik, J., Young, J. F., and
    Harris, S.E., 1979b, Opt. Lett., 4:265.
Gudzenko, L. I., and Yakovlenko, S. I., 1972, Zh. Eksp. Theor. Fiz.
    62:1686. [Sov. Phys. JETP, 35:877].
Gudzenko, L. I., and Yakovlenko, S. I., 1974, Phys. Lett. 46A:475.
Harris, S. E. and Lidow, D. B., 1974, Phys. Rev. Lett. 33:674.
Harris, S. E., Falcone, R. W.,. Greene, W. R.,. Lidow, D. B.,
    White, J. C., and Young, J. F., 1976, in "Tunable Lasers and
    Applications," edited by A. Mooradian, T. Jaeger, and P. Stoketh
    (Springer-Verlag, New York), pp. 193-206.
Harris, S. E.,. and White, J. C., 1977, IEEE J. Quantum Electron,
    QE-13: 972.
Harris, S. E., Young, J. F., Greene, W. R., Falcone, R. W.,
    Lukasik, J., White, J. C., Willison, J. R., Wright, M. D., and
    Zdasiuk, G. A., 1979, in "Laser Spectroscopy IV," editors, H.
    Walther and K. W. Rothe (Springer, New York) pp. 349-358.
Harris, S. E., Falcone, R. W., and O'Brien, D. M., 1982, Opt. Lett.
    7:397.
Herman, P. S., and Sando, K. M., 1978, J. Chem. Phys., 68:1163.
Hering, P., Brooks, P. R., Curl, R. F., Judson, R. S., and Lowe, R.
    S., 1980, Phys. Rev. Lett., 44:687.
Hering, P., and Rabin, Y., 1981, Chem. Phys. Lett., 77:506.
Herzberg, G., 1950, "Spectra of Diatomic Molecules," 2nd edition (Van
    Nostrand, Princeton, N.J.).
Hughes, W. M., Olson, N. T., and Hunter, R. T., 1976, Appl. Phys.
    Lett., 28:81.
Johnson, A. W., Bingham, F. W., and Rice, J. K., 1975, IEEE J.
    Quantum Electron. QE-11, 56D.
Julienne, P. S., Krauss, M., and Stevens, W. J., 1976, Chem. Phys.
    Lett., 38:374.
Julienne, P. S., 1977, J. Appl. Phys., 48:4140.

Julienne, P. S., 1978, J. Chem. Phys., 68:32.
Julienne, P. S., 1982, Phys. Rev., A26:3299.
Julienne, P. S., 1983, in "Spectral Line Shapes," Vol. 2, edited by
    K. Burnett (de Gruyter, Berlin) pp. 769-785.
Julienne, P. S., and Mies, F. H., 1984, Phys. Rev. A., (to be
    published).
Krauss, M., and Julienne, P. S., 1977, J. Chem. Phys., 67:669.
Lewis, E. L., Harris, M., Alford, W. J., Cooper, J., and Burnett,
    K., 1983, J. Phys. B 16:553.
Lisitsa, V. S., and Yakovlenko, S. I., 1974, Zhur. Exp. Theor.
    Fiz., 66:1550. [Sov. Phys. JETP 39:759].
Lukasik, J., and Wallace, S. C., 1981, Phys. Rev. Lett., 47:240.
Mies, F. H., 1981, in "Theoretical Chemistry: Advances and Perspec-
    tives," ed. by. D. Henderson (Academic, New York) Vol. 68, pp.
    127-198.
Murray, J. R. and Hoff, P. W., 1974, in "High Energy Lasers and
    Their Applications," edited by S. Jacobs, M. Sargent III, and
    M. O. Scully (Addison-Wesley, Reading, Mass.).
Murray, J. R. and Rhodes, C. K., 1976, J. Appl. Phys. 47:5041.
Payne, M. C., Anderson, V. E., and Turner, J. E., 1979, Phys. Rev.
    A, 20:1032.
Powell, H. T., Murray, J. R., and Rhodes, C. K., 1974, Appl. Phys.
    Lett., 25:730.
Powell, H. T., Murray, J. R., and Rhodes, C. K., 1975, IEEE J.
    Quantum Electron., 11:27D.
Powell, H. T., and Schleicher, B. R., 1980, J. Chem. Phys., 73:5059.
Rogovin, D., and Avizonis, P., 1981, Appl. Phys. Lett., 38:666.
Szudy, J., and Baylis, W. E., 1975, J. Quant. Spectrosc. Radiat.
    Transfer, 15:641.
Thomann, P., Burnett, K., and Cooper, J., 1980, Phys. Rev. Lett.,
    45:1325.
Welge, K. H., and Atkinson, R., 1976, J. Chem. Phys., 64:531.
Whisnant, D. M., and Byers-Brown, W., 1973, Mol. Phys., 26:1105.
White, J. C., 1980, Opt. Lett., 5:239.
White, J. C., Freeman, R. R., and Liao, P. F., 1980, Opt. Lett.,
    5:120.
White, J. C., 1981, Phys. Rev. A, 23:1698.
Wilcomb, B. E., and Burnhan, R., 1981, J. Chem. Phys., 74:6784.
Yakovlenko, S. I., 1978, Kvantovaya Elektron. 5:259. [Sov. J.
    Quant. Electron., 8:151].
Zhang, D. Z., Niklaus, B., and Toschek, P. E., 1982, Appl. Phys. B
    28:195.
Zimmerman, I. H., Yuan, J. M., George, T. F., 1977, J. Chem. Phys.
    66:2638.

COMMENTS ON HYPER-RAYLEIGH SCATTERING

George Birnbaum

National Bureau of Standards
Gaithersburg, MD 20899

We mention briefly a subject, which although germane to this book, was not included in the Workshop because there had been no recent progress in the area.

The nonlinear polarization, P, of a system can be expanded in a power series dependent on the applied electric field, E,

$$P_i = \alpha_{ij}E_j + (1/2)\ \beta_{ijk}E_jE_k + (1/6)\ \gamma_{ijkl}E_jE_kE_l + \cdots$$

where i, j, k, and l denote the Cartesion coordinates and α_{ij}, β_{ijk}, and γ_{ijkl} refer to the polarizability, hyperpolarizability, and second hyperpolarizability, respectively. The β-term describes the interaction of the medium with two light waves to produce second harmonic radiation and the γ-term describes third harmonic generation. Molecules with a center of symmetry do not exhibit second harmonic scattering (SHS) or hyper-Rayleigh scattering. However, if the molecular symmetry is destroyed by the application of an external field (Kielich, 1979) or by the electric field of neighboring molecules such as those due to fluctuating molecular quadrupole and hexadecapole moments, (Kielich, et al., 1973), then hyper-Rayleigh scattering may be observed in molecules which are centro-symmetric when isolated. This theory, developed by Kielich et al., (1973), which is restricted to pair interactions, was used to obtain values for the quadrupole moments of cyclohexane and trans-decahydronapthalene from measurements of the depolarization ratios of hyper-Rayleigh scattering in the liquid (Lalanne et al., 1975). It may be interesting to explore this area further, but the effects of interactions involving three or more particles must be considered.

Since in the isolated atom $\beta = 0$, SHS cannot occur in atomic fluids by considering the scattering from individual atoms. Moreover, cooperative, two-body interactions such as those involved to explain SHS in fluids consisting of centro-symmetric molecules clearly cannot produce SHS. However, three or more atom interactions could produce SHS and if observed could lead directly to three particle correlation functions. The theory of this effect has been developed by several investigators and its magnitude has been estimated (Samson and Pasmanter, 1974; Gelbart, 1973). Although the effect is so small that it is doubtful whether measurements are feasible, the possibility of observing it is nevertheless intriguing, since it would provide a direct method of studying three particle interactions.

Very recently, interaction-induced, subpicosend phenomena in liquids involving the second hyperpolarizability have been discussed (Madden, 1984).

REFERENCES

French, J.M., 1981, Hyper-Rayleight and hyper-Raman spectroscopy, in: "Chemical Applications of Nonlinear Raman Spectroscopy," A. B. Harvey, ed., Academic Press, New York.
Gelbart, W. M., 1973, Chem. Phys. Lett., 23:53.
Kielich, S., Lalanne, J. R., and Martin, F. B., 1973, Cooperative second harmonic laser light scattering in liquid cyclohexane, benzene and carbon disulphide, J. Raman Spectroscop., 1:119.
Kielich, S., 1979, Second harmonic generation of laser beam in electrically polarized atomic and molecular fluid mixtures, in: "Nonlinear Behaviour of Molecules, Atoms and Ions in Electric, Magnetic or Electromagnetic fields," L. Neel, ed., Elsevier Scientific Pub. Co., Amsterdam.
Lalanne, J. R., F. B., and Kielich, S., 1975, Molecular quadrupole moment determinations from measurements of laser wave hyper-Rayleigh scattering by dense fluids, Chem. Phys. Lett., 30:73.
Madden, P. A., 1984, Interaction-induced, subpicosecond phenomena in liquids, in: "Ultrafast Phenomena IV," D. H. Auston and K. B. Eisenthal, eds., Springer-Verlag, Berlin.
Samson, R., and Pasmanter, R. A., 1974, Multi-particle effects in second harmonic generation, Chem. Phys. Lett., 25:405.

COMMENTS ON THE SPECTRA OF HALOGENS AND

HALOGEN COMPLEXES IN SOLUTION

George Birnbaum

National Bureau of Standards
Gaithersburg, MD 20899

The halogen molecules Cl_2, Br_2, and I_2 are non-polar and like N_2 should exhibit collision-induced spectra. In addition, when the halogen molecules are dissolved in certain solvents, molecular complexes with the solvent molecules are formed that may involve charge transfer. Vallauri (1985) has reviewed the results of computer simulation studies of the induced light scattering (superimposed on an allowed spectrum) and induced infrared absorption in liquid Cl_2. Oxtoby (1985) has presented an initial approach to a theory of spectral shape which encompasses induced absorption by the halogen molecules and absorption arising from a charge transfer complex. However, there is a background of experimental work on the spectra of the halogen molecules and their solutions, which while not discussed in these articles, may be of interest to readers of this volume.

Yarwood (1973) and Yarwood and Brownson (1973) have reviewed infared intensity and band shape measurements on molecular complexes of the halogens. In general, a region of absorption is observed at a frequency somewhat lower than that of the allowed vibrational Raman band of the halogen molecule (Put, et al., 1981). This band may be attributed to the perturbed vibrational band of the halogen molecule. Another absorption region (over and above that of the solvent) occurs at lower frequencies from about 50 to 100 cm^{-1} and is presumably due to the translation and vibrational motion of the complex or of the transient dipoles induced in collisions of the halogen molecules with the solvent molecules. [See also, Lake and Thompson (1967)]. The low frequency band has also been observed in pure liquid Br_2, I_2, and the mixture $Br_2 : I_2$ (Wagner, 1969). Acetylene complexes with atomic and molecular iodine have been recently studies by infrared and ultraviolet spectroscopy in argon matrices (Engdahl and Nelander, 1984).

Although no infrared spectrum of Br_2 and I_2 have been obtained in the gaseous state because of their low-vapor pressure, the pressure induced fundamental absorption band of gaseous Cl_2 has been observed in the region around 550 cm^{-1} (Winkel et al., 1969). A computation of the integrated intensity of this band on the basis of quadrupole induced dipole moments only accounted for about one fifth of the observed intensity (Wong and Whalley, 1973).

It appears from this brief survey that much needs to be done before a quantitative understanding of the far infrared spectra of the halogens is attained.

REFERENCES

Lake, R. F., and Thompson, H. W., 1967, Far infrared spectra of charge-transfer complexes between iodine and substituted pyridines, Proc. Roc. Soc., A297:440.

Wagner, W., 1969, Infrared absorption of liquid Br_2, I_2, and $Br_2:I_2$, Z. Physik, 224:353.

Winkel, R. G., Hunt, J. L., and Clouter, M. J., 1969, Pressure-induced fundamental infrared absorption band of gaseous chlorine, J. Chem. Phys., 50:1298.

Wong, P. T. T., and Whalley, E., 1973, Intensity of the pressure-induced fundamental infrared band of gaseous chlorine, Can. J. Phys., 51:696.

Yarwood, J., and Bronson, G. W., 1973, Infrared intensity and band shape measurements on molecular complexes of halogens, Adv. in Molec. Relax. Processes, 5:1.

Yarwood, J., 1973, The Measurement and Interpretation of Vibrational Spectra of Complex Molecules, and Complexes of m and π donors with halogens and related acceptors, in: "The Spectroscopy and Structure of Molecular Complexes," J. Yarwood, ed., Plenum, London.

Put, J., Mass, G., Huyskens, P., and Zeegers-Huyskens, Th., 1981, Study of the solvent effect on the Raman Spectrum of I_2 and IBr Comparison with Br_2, Spectrochimica Acta, 37A:699.

Engdahl, A., and Nelander, B., 1984, Complex between acetylene and atomic iodine, Chem. Phys. Lett., 106:527.

Oxtoby, D. W., 1985, Vibrational spectral lineshapes of charge transfer complexes, this volume.

Vallauri, R., 1985, Molecular dynamics study of interaction induced absorption and light scattering in diatomic systems, this volume.

AUTHOR INDEX

777

CHEMICAL INDEX

This chemical index includes all the atomic and molecular systems for which quantitative information on collision-induced phenomena and related properties is given in this book.

A listing of a molecule (chemical compound), for example, CO_2, signifies that the information which follows refers to single molecule or allowed phenomena, but may also refer to induced phenomena accompanying allowed phenomena. A listing of two molecules, or two atoms, or a molecule and an atom separated by a hyphen, for example, CO_2-CO_2, CO_2-Ar, Ar-Ar, signifies that the information which follows refers only to collision induced phenomena. The symbols (ℓ) and (s) indicate that the system is in the liquid (ℓ) or solid (s) state. With rare exceptions, the gaseous state is not indicated; hence the absence of (ℓ) or (s) means gaseous state. An entry such as HCl/CCl_4 (ℓ) means HCl dissolved in liquid CCl_4. Since there is no hyphen, this entry signifies information related to allowed phenomena and possibly accompanying induced phenomena. Information concerning correlation functions, spectral moments and integrated intensity will be found under --spectrum. Infrared bands may be assumed to be the fundamental unless otherwise noted.

All atoms and molecules are listed under their chemical formulae considered as words; for example, CCl_4 as Ccl, C_2H_2 as Ch, and CH_4-CH_4 as Chch.